Special Edition
USING AMERICA
ONLINE®
SECOND EDITION

Special Edition

USING
AMERICA
ONLINE®

SECOND EDITION

Written by Gene Steinberg

Special Edition Using America Online, Second Edition

Credits

PRESIDENT
Roland Elgey

PUBLISHING DIRECTOR
Brad R. Koch

EDITORIAL SERVICES DIRECTOR
Elizabeth Keaffaber

MANAGING EDITOR
Michael Cunningham

DIRECTOR OF MARKETING
Lynn E. Zingraf

ACQUISITIONS EDITOR
Elizabeth South

PRODUCT DIRECTOR
Lisa D. Wagner

PRODUCTION EDITORS
Lori A. Lyons
Sarah Rudy

EDITORS
Elizabeth Barrett
Kate Givens
Nick Zafran

ASSISTANT PRODUCT MARKETING MANAGER
Christy Miller

TECHNICAL EDITOR
Jim Johnston

TECHNICAL SPECIALIST
Nadeem Muhammed

ACQUISITIONS COORDINATOR
Tracy Williams

OPERATIONS COORDINATOR
Patty Brooks

BOOK DESIGNER
Ruth Harvey

COVER DESIGNER
Dan Armstrong

PRODUCTION TEAM
Marcia Brizendine
Amy Gornik
Heather Howell
Bob LaRoche
Kaylene Riemen
Paul Wilson

INDEXERS
Jennifer Eberhardt
Brad Herriman

Composed in *Century Old Style* and *Franklin Gothic* by Que Corporation.

To Barbara and Grayson with love and appreciation always.

About the Author

Gene Steinberg is an inveterate desktop computer user who first joined America Online in 1989. He quickly became addicted to the new online service and finally earned positions on its computing forum staff. At present, he is forum leader of the service's Macintosh Desktop Video and Multimedia Forum and curator of AOL Portrait Gallery, a library containing photos of America Online members and their families.

In his regular life, Gene has worked at several occupations. He first studied broadcasting in school and then worked for a number of years as a disc jockey and newscaster. Gene is now a full-time writer and computer software and systems consultant. His published work (in addition to the first edition of this book) includes *Using America Online with Your Mac*, *Using America Online with Windows 95*, and *Special Edition Using the Macintosh* for Que Corporation, and feature articles and product reviews for *Macworld*.

Acknowledgments

The book you hold in your hands is almost encyclopedic in size, and although my name is shown as the author, it is not a project a sane or almost sane person can do alone. I am grateful for the assistance of many, working behind the scenes, who made this book possible.

Among America Online's in-house staff, I have special praise for Lyn Cameron, Jeff Crowe, Chris Hamilton, Howard Rosenman, Angela Maben, Pam McGraw, Kathy Ryan, and Deborah Shaw for their ongoing help in making this project a success. I'd also like to thank Daniel Fishbach for his assistance in maintaining an up-to-date list of the service's keyword shortcuts.

I am also grateful to America Online's Tim Barwick and my friend and sometimes co-writer John Stroud (one of AOL's favorite Mac forum leaders) for getting me involved in America Online's forums to begin with.

A number of experts in the computing industry have provided special assistance in researching several chapters of this book. They include Rick Barron of Affinity Microsystems (publishers of Tempo II Plus), Clayton Cowgill of the Supra division of Diamond Multimedia, Brian Combs, John Files, Ric Ralston and Mike Rosenfelt of Power Computing (the first official Macintosh-compatible manufacturer), Joanne Sperans Hartzell and Mary Smaragdis of Insignia Solutions (publishers of SoftWindows 95), and Pieter Paulson, currently a technical wizard at Oregon's Adaptive Solutions.

I want to single out the leaders of America Online's Computing forums for their special assistance in compiling the information for Chapters 19, 20, and 21, covering their respective areas of expertise.

The Macintosh forum leaders: Stuart Gitlow, M.D. (Coordinator), Peter Baum, Richard E. (Rick) Doucette, Sarah Edwards, Craig de Fasselle, Christopher Ferino, Michael Fischer, Keith Jablonski, Gary A. Jacobson, Gayle Keresey, Ellen Lorang, David Stovall, Andy Polk, John Stroud (once again), Carey Tewes, John Thatcher, Marty Wachter, Rod Whitten, Floyd Zink, and Cheryl Zuckerman.

The forum leaders of America Online's PC computing forums: Simon Rich (Coordinator), Audrey Beck, Robin Bush, Kate Chase, Bob Dover, Roger Frazier, Peter L. Hotchkiss, James M. Lambeth, Jonathon Lawrence, Ronald Liechty, David Pacheco, Tracy Martin, Thomas L. Quindry, Debbie Rogers, Chuck Smith, Dave Swarz, Kevin Williams, Norma Williams, and Mike Wiseman.

Somehow, despite the long hours in front of my computer to write this manuscript, my forums on AOL managed to keep rolling anyway. For that I must give heartfelt praise to my staff at the Macintosh Desktop Video and Multimedia Forum (Rob Sonner, Russ

Coffman, Mark Elpers, Marshall Goldberg, Robn Kester, Trish Meyer, and Rodney L'Ongnion) and my staff at the AOL Portrait Gallery (Adam Lasnik, Diana L. Laduke, Michael T. Lester, Michael McDaniel, Alex Podressoff, Paul Valach, and Tom Wiseman).

I must give special praise to the team at Que Corporation for putting up with my many eccentricities and for allowing me a great deal of latitude in outlining and writing this book. They include Elizabeth South, Lisa Wagner, Lori Lyons, and Sarah Rudy. Thanks to Que's production team for putting through hundreds of pages of text. Dedicated, fearless technical editor, Jim Johnston, deserves to be singled out for pouring through every written word and every illustration to verify that they were absolutely correct to the last, minute detail.

And last, I wish to offer a heartfelt, loving thank you to my wonderful, beautiful wife, Barbara, and my extraordinary son, Grayson, for putting up with the long hours I spent chained to my computer so that my work could be done on schedule.

We'd Like to Hear from You!

As part of our continuing effort to produce books of the highest possible quality, Que would like to hear your comments. To stay competitive, we *really* want you, as a computer book reader and user, to let us know what you like or dislike most about this book or other Que products.

You can mail comments, ideas, or suggestions for improving future editions to the address below, or send us a fax at (317) 581-4663. For the on-line inclined, Macmillan Computer Publishing has a forum on CompuServe (type **GO MACMILLAN** at any prompt) through which our staff and authors are available for questions and comments. The address of our Internet site, the Macmillan Information SuperLibrary is **http://www.mcp.com** (World Wide Web). Our Web site has received critical acclaim from many reviewers—be sure to check it out.

In addition to exploring our forums, please feel free to contact me personally to discuss your opinions of this book. My e-mail address is **lwagner@que.mcp.com**.

Thanks in advance—your comments will help us to continue publishing the best books available on computer topics in today's market.

Lisa D. Wagner
Product Director
Que Corporation
201 W. 103rd Street
Indianapolis, Indiana 46290 USA

N O T E Although we cannot provide general technical support, we're happy to help you resolve problems you encounter related to our books, disks, or other products. If you need such assistance, please contact our **Tech Support department** at 317-581-3833.

To order other Que or Macmillan Computer Publishing books or products, please call our **Customer Service department** at 800-428-5331. ▪

Contents at a Glance

Table of Contents

II | Communicating Online

IV Kids and America Online

VII | Personal Finance

26   Online Investment and Tax Information   469

VIII | Entering the Information Superhighway

X | Appendixes

Introduction

The way people live and work has undergone, for all intents and purposes, a revolution. No, not the revolutions of old where governments were overthrown and new leaders took over in the wake of violence and misery. This revolution is peaceful and there are no losers left to suffer, yet it impacts every element of our society.

It is a revolution in communications, and a revolution in the way we live and work. It begins with sending messages to others—not by dropping an envelope in a mail box or picking up the telephone to dial someone, but in sitting down in front of a personal computer, typing a letter to another person anywhere in the world, and having it reach its destination in moments.

It is a revolution in the way people work, where millions of citizens no longer brave the hustle and bustle, traffic jams, and crowded buses and trains. Instead they travel no farther than another room in their home, and again sit in front of a personal computer, perhaps with a fax machine and a modem, to do their regular work.

When millions of viewers watched television coverage of a murder trial involving a famous athlete accused of killing two people, many of them shared their views about the case across a picket fence that consisted not of wood and metal, but of ones and zeros, the binary language of computers—a picket fence found along an Information Superhighway that spanned the entire world. ■

The History of America Online

The dream of an Information Superhighway wasn't even a glimmer in anyone's eye in 1985, when America Online was founded as Quantum Computer Services. In that year, the Apple Macintosh was just a low-powered niche computer, and Microsoft Windows didn't exist. But the Commodore computer was king, and a new, easy-to-use, and affordable telecommunications service was established. It was called Q-Link.

Q-Link might best be compared to a national Bulletin Board Service (BBS), where computer owners could communicate with one another. Members with a specific interest, such as a special type of software, could congregate in a single meeting place called a *forum*. Members could meet for interactive conversations called *chats*.

From this humble beginning, support was added for other computer platforms, such as Apple II and Tandy's DeskMate. The Apple Macintosh and IBM PC and compatibles soon followed.

Today America Online is a publicly owned company that offers an online community for over five million members (with millions more joining each year). The service offers online shopping, information services such as daily newspapers and magazines, and even virtual reference books such as encyclopedias. In addition, America Online lets you reach out beyond the borders of its service, by providing a direct gateway to the Internet, which serves tens of millions of computer users across the world.

But just as important, America Online is like a huge city, with many people hanging out and communicating with one another on a host of subjects, from the time of day and the weather to the state of the nation and the world. The online experience is unlike any you've ever seen. After you have been introduced to America Online, you'll undoubtedly want to stick around.

Some Nuts and Bolts Information About America Online

Our daily press and broadcast news outlets commonly refer to communicating online as being a part of the Information Superhighway, and this is likely an apt expression. But it's an expression designed to represent the entire global information network, not just a single service, and I like to think of that network as more akin to a planet than a highway. So let's consider America Online as one large city (or country) that exists on that planet.

Let's take that description of a city a bit further. Besides all those people, you can find neighborhoods, highways, stores, libraries, and schools. You interact with that community from your own computer and modem, using America Online's unique graphical interface, which transports you from one place to another when you click an icon or type a simple keyboard command.

But behind that easy-to-use technology is a huge network of micro- and minicomputers storing many gigabytes of data, linked to the outside world by advanced fiber-optic telephone cables.

Looking at AOL's Distributed Network

Bear with me for a moment as I give you a few insights into the state-of-the-art equipment that resides at America Online's headquarters in Vienna, Virginia. It is a truly advanced setup.

America Online's computers are built on the client-server model with a peer-to-peer application architecture. The systems consist of Stratus RISC processors running the VOS operating system, Hewlett-Packard RISC processors running the UNIX operating system, and PCs running DOS or OS/2. All these computers are interconnected by high-speed networks. Using a technique called *distributed processing*, they can share information-handling tasks, resulting in extremely fast data processing, enabling thousands of simultaneous transactions. This capability means that thousands of America Online members can log on to the network at the same time without any loss in system performance.

America Online's computer rooms are at a temperature of a constant 70 degrees with low humidity. If a power outage occurs (which has happened occasionally), America Online has a battery backup system that provides full power to the system for a short time, until a diesel generator kicks on and continues to supply juice to keep the computers running. The generator can run up to 72 hours between fill-ups, which is more than enough time to replenish fuel or for power to be restored.

Each day, all the files on America Online's huge rigid drives are backed up. Backups are moved off site, so America Online's huge store of data is always protected in case of an emergency.

Understanding How Your Computer Links with America Online

When you connect to America Online, it seems like such a simple process. For you it involves a single click of the mouse, but behind that simple action is a complex process of data transfers and computer processing.

You generally hook up to America Online with two electronic boxes: your computer and a device called a modem. A modem is a small computer that converts a stream of digital ones and zeros into audible tones that are fed through telephone lines and received by another modem at a remote location.

N O T E There is another way to connect to America Online. If your computer is part of a network with TCP/IP access to the Internet, you can access America Online without ever calling a local telephone number via your modem. ▪

When you first dial up America Online (see fig. I.1), your software dials a local telephone number that connects your computer to a modem on what is called a PAD (packet assembler/disassembler) in the public data network. This PAD, owned and operated by a packet carrier company such as AOLNet, SprintNet, or Tymnet, is called a *node*.

FIG. I.1
Steps 1 and 2 get your modem ready to dial, and then dial the local telephone number; the third step connects to that number.

A *node* can be described as a collection of modems that can handle many connections from computers like yours at one time. These local nodes ensure that users who live far away from America Online's host computers don't have to pay long-distance phone charges for direct access to the America Online network.

Requesting Network Attention

When your modem dials the local access number, the modem negotiates a connection with the node. Those blips, burps, and squeals that emanate from your modem (if the sound is turned on, of course) describe a process called *handshaking*. Your modem is adjusting its speed and method of communication to the remote modem.

After the connection is established, you receive a message on your computer, as shown in figure I.2.

FIG. I.2
The next stage of hooking up to America Online is to request network attention.

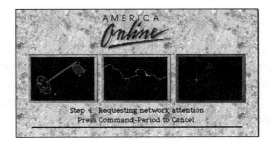

Talking to the Network

The next step is to tell the node who you are and whom you want to call. At this point, your software sends the address to the America Online host computer (see fig. I.3), saying something like, "Hey, I'm an America Online member. Can you connect me?"

FIG. I.3
The next stage of hooking up to America Online is to identify yourself.

Connecting to America Online

After the carrier service knows the host computer to which you want to connect, the service dials up America Online's host computers by the fastest method possible (see fig. I.4). This setup might change periodically depending on line conditions. But it all happens behind the scenes and takes mere seconds to accomplish.

FIG. I.4
"Hey, there, anybody home?"

When connection with America Online's host computers has been made, the next step is to knock on the front door.

Using Your Password

Before AOL admits you, America Online's host computers have to know who you are and whether you have an active account. In seconds, the host computers examine the records of millions of America Online members to confirm who you are and to check whether anybody else inside the online community is presently using the same account (see fig. I.5).

FIG. I.5
"Hey, there, who are you?"

Then the front door is opened, and you're welcomed into the sprawling but friendly online universe.

Who Will Find This Book Helpful?

The main portion of this book has been written with the assumption that you are already a member of America Online, and that you have at least some experience using this service or other online services. With this book as a guide, you'll be able to discover many parts of the service you've never visited before and find resources you probably didn't know were available. This book also provides special coverage of the newest versions of America Online's Macintosh and Windows software, and plans for expanding Internet features.

But if you've never logged on to a service like America Online before, I've provided several appendixes that take you through the first steps of joining the service and learning to use AOL's Macintosh and Windows software. After you've begun to travel the sprawling online city, you can use the rest of this book as a reference for places to visit and things to do.

This book is organized into nine parts and the appendixes, each of which covers a specific area of the America Online network and the most effective and fun-filled ways to use the service.

Part I: Getting Online

The first part of this book concentrates on the AOL software for users of the Apple Macintosh and the Microsoft Windows operating system. While some of you have, no doubt, settled on one computing platform, it is more and more common for users to work in both environments. Toward that end, I offer advice on getting the most effective use of these two versions of America Online's software. Throughout the book, I provide instructions for both platforms and use illustrations representing both versions interchangeably, because they are designed to look and operate in very similar ways. In Part I, "Getting Online," you get power-user tips, information about software add-ons to make your online visits more fun, and valuable advice for mobile computing that you can apply not just to your America Online visits, but to general computing purposes too.

Part II: Communicating Online

Because America Online is so close in concept to a large city, communications skills are very important. In Part II, "Communicating Online," you learn how to meet other America Online members, participate in real-time chats and conferences, and use the service's advanced electronic mail and instant messaging capability (the latter is a feature that lets you communicate with fellow members while they are online—on a one-to-one basis). As you probably know, some of the world's most famous personalities (from the business, literary, political, and entertainment worlds) have appeared at AOL's popular interactive conferences.

You also learn the most effective methods of using America Online's active message boards. The elements of a message board are dissected, piece by piece, and you learn how to locate messages that may interest you and how you can get involved in some of these online discussions. There's also helpful information on the rules of the road, so you can learn the elements of online etiquette and present your messages in the most effective manner.

Part III: A Wealth of Entertainment at Your Fingertips

America Online has a huge amount of entertainment-related resources. In Part III, "A Wealth of Information at Your Fingertips," you read about forums devoted to movies, television, and even radio. There is coverage of areas devoted to lifestyles and interests, ranging from hobbies to special information areas you might want to visit often. You'll discover information about board games, computer games, and video games, and explore forums devoted specifically to the world of sports.

Part IV: Kids and America Online

Because America Online is a family-oriented service, you'll be pleased to know that there are resources designed specifically for kids ages 5 through 14 in Part IV, "Kids and America Online." There are also special features, known as Parental Controls, that allow you to control your children's access to specific online areas and also to direct their ability to connect to the Internet.

Part V: Computing Resources Online

Because you interact with America Online through a personal computer, it's nice to know that there is a tremendous amount of support for computer users on this service. In Part V, "Computing Resources Online," you'll discover where you can learn to use your computer most effectively and how you can contact many of the major hardware and software manufacturers, online, to receive free technical support.

You also learn how to search AOL's huge databases, consisting of tens of thousands of Macintosh and Windows files, to find the software you want. I've included recommendations of some of the most popular files provided by the folks who manage AOL's computing and software forums.

Part VI: News and Reference

America Online can serve as a newspaper, a newsstand, and an encyclopedia. In Part VI, "News and Reference," you'll find resources that cover such topics as the top news stories of the day, updated real estate listings, and assistance to help you cope at tax time.

America Online has a special feature for students where they can literally page an online teacher for help with homework or a special research project. You can also continue your education during your online visits using the facilities offered by a number of educational institutions.

Part VII: Personal Finance

A growing number of online users actually buy popular merchandise at special prices on America Online. In Part VII, "Personal Finance," you'll learn the secrets of online shopping, check the latest stock market prices, and learn more about the firms you want to add to your portfolio.

Because shopping goes hand-in-hand with travel, you'll read about America Online's resources for travel information and you'll discover how you can easily make your own airline, hotel, and car rental reservations during your online visits.

Part VIII: Entering the Information Superhighway

This introduction has provided just a brief overview of the Information Superhighway. Part VIII, "Entering the Information Superhighway," explores the subject in much more detail. You learn how to tap a global resource for information and discussion areas right from America Online.

There's extensive coverage of such features as Internet e-mail, database searches, UseNet discussion groups, and the latest and perhaps the fastest growing Internet resource, the World Wide Web. All of these features, and more, are available to you when you log onto America Online.

In addition, I'll tell you how you can access the World Wide Web on AOL while continuing to use other browser software, such as Microsoft's Internet Explorer or Netscape.

Part IX: Making Your Online Visits More Productive

Not only does this book deal with ways to save money by using America Online's resources the next time you buy a product, but Part IX tells you how you can reduce your online charges as well.

With the growing popularity of low-cost high-speed modems, and the availability of high-speed access to America Online, you'll learn tips and tricks for improved connections and faster throughput. There's also information on how to tweak your modem for best performance and how best to deal with connection problems.

Part X: Appendixes

Appendixes A–D serve as tutorials on joining America Online and using the software. Appendix D is a glossary of terminology and Appendix E lists America Online keywords, organized by subject matter.

Conventions Used in This Book

This book uses various conventions designed to make it easier to use. That way, you can quickly and easily learn the most important features of an America Online department or program feature and how to access them.

With most programs, you can use the mouse or keyboard to perform operations. The keyboard procedures may include shortcut key combinations or mnemonic keys.

In this book, key combinations for the Microsoft Windows environment are joined with plus signs (+). For example, Ctrl+X means hold down the Ctrl key, press the X key, and then release both keys. Some menu and dialog box options have underlined or highlighted characters that indicate mnemonic keys. To choose such an option using the mnemonic key, press the Alt key and then press the indicated mnemonic key. In this book, mnemonic keys are underscored: for example, File.

Key combinations for the Macintosh are separated with a hyphen (-). The ⌘ symbol means to hold down the Apple command key on your keyboard and then press the mnemonic key.

The book uses several other typeface enhancements to indicate special text, as indicated in the following table.

Typeface	Meaning
Italic	Italic is used to indicate variables in commands or addresses, and also terms used for the first time.
Bold	Bold is used for text you type and for Internet addresses. AOL keywords are also in bold.
`Computer type`	This special type is used for on-screen messages and for commands (such as the DOS COPY or UNIX cp command).

Tips suggest easier or alternative methods of executing a procedure.

N O T E Notes provide additional information that may help you avoid problems or offer advice or general information related to the topic at hand. ▪

CAUTION

Cautions warn you of hazardous procedures and situations that can lead to unexpected or unpredictable results, including data loss or system damage.

TROUBLESHOOTING

Troubleshooting sections anticipate common problems—and then provide you with practical suggestions for solving those problems.

Cross-references direct you to related information in other parts of the book.

▶ **See** "Making E-Mail Work for You," **p. 95**

Faster Than a Speeding Screenshot

Since 1994, I have written several books about America Online. Every time I revise one of my books, or write a new one, I've observed vast changes and improvements in the way the service is run and the way it looks.

As with any large city, America Online is growing and changing constantly. You will find that the service's look and feel develops and improves still further over time. Some of the places pictured in this book might look a little different on your screen, too. But the information in these pages will be useful for a long time as a guide to learning about America Online.

As you begin to explore the online community, keep this book at hand. When you have a question or want to learn more about a particular place, you can move directly to that chapter for the information you want.

I began writing books about America Online as an experienced visitor to the service. But as the writing progressed, I explored many of the nooks and crannies in the online city that I had never visited before. The process has been a tremendous, rewarding, learning experience.

The online community has, over the years, become my second home. It's a place where I can meet and interact with my friends and even conduct business. I have made deals and begun work projects with people whom I know only by e-mail.

Indeed, the dream of the Information Superhighway has, to us, become an up-close and personal reality, and I want you to share that dream, too. Let the pages that follow be your starting point on the road to a learning experience that might be unlike any other you've ever had.

Gene Steinberg
Scottsdale, Arizona
America Online address: **aflgenes@aol.com**

Getting Online

Getting Past the Opening Screen

America Online has become the number one online service in the world for good reason. The software is relatively easy to use, and the online interface is friendly and accommodating.

Behind its simple, accessible interface, America Online's software offers a wealth of powerful features that allow you to enjoy a huge array of services and to explore the vast, uncharted waters of the worldwide Internet network.

Throughout this book, I want you to get used to some simple steps that will allow you to easily navigate AOL's vast landscape via keystrokes. I will often describe a particular area's location by its keyword, a keyboard command that you can specify *only* while you're connected to America Online. Keywords will take you just about anywhere on America Online, even if you don't know the exact route.

To use a keyword, press ⌘-K if you're using a Macintosh or Ctrl+K for Windows; then enter the keyword in the entry field of the Keyword dialog box (see fig. 1.1). Press Enter, and in just a few seconds, you'll be transported to the place you want to visit. If the keyword that you enter is wrong, you'll see a message to that effect, and you'll have the option to search some alternate keywords to see which one is correct. ▉

FIG. 1.1
Use a keyword to go to a specific spot on America Online.

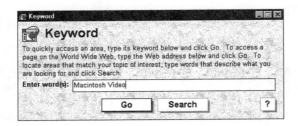

This book is filled with tips and tricks for making your online visits more fun and more productive. In addition, many chapters contain helpful troubleshooting advice, so if you run into a problem, you can find a simple solution. America Online has its own support area, too, conducted in a department that is free of online charges.

If you run into chronic problems in getting and staying online, you'll first want to read Chapter 41, "Secrets of High-Speed Access on AOL," for advice on coping with such difficulties and on configuring your modem for best performance.

If you still have a problem getting connected consistently, use the keyword **Help**. You'll go to AOL's customer service area, where you can get further assistance via an extensive list of text-based information. You'll also have access to an area called Tech Live, where you can have an online conversation with an AOL representative about your problem.

If You Are New to America Online

This book is written with the assumption that you are already an AOL member and that you have your software installed, so that you're ready to go out and enjoy your experiences in cyberspace.

I realize, though, that some of you are still fence-sitters. You've read about America Online in a magazine or your daily newspaper, or you've seen some of the ads on national TV, and you're curious enough to want to know what the service is all about. Perhaps you're using this book as a guidepost to help you decide whether it's worth signing up or not.

If you're in this category, I won't give you a sales pitch and say that you should join America Online, except for this: I became an AOL member in 1989, and I have never looked back. The service has been a regular source of useful information and fun for me and my 10-year-old son (who has become a regular online visitor).

AOL also serves an important business function for me: the service allows me to communicate with my publisher and with my clients without ever leaving my home office. Through AOL's Internet capability, I'm able to send e-mail across the world and to log on to remote sites to obtain files that I need in my work as a writer and consultant.

I hope that this book will whet your appetite to explore the service, taking advantage of one of those 15-free-hour disks to experience America Online firsthand. If you haven't yet received one of those disks (or the disks that you find in a magazine are for a PC and you've got a Mac, for example), you can call America Online directly and ask for a sign-up kit. The number is (800) 827-6364.

See you online!

The First Bold Steps

If you haven't yet established an account and signed on, read the back of this book first. Seriously! The first three appendices are designed to be a full-featured tutorial for America Online. Appendix A, "If You're New to the Online World," takes you through the process of logging on to America Online for the first time, creating your online account, and taking a brief tour of the service.

In Appendix B and Appendix C, I dissect the Apple Macintosh and Windows versions of AOL's software, respectively, covering all the hidden features that you won't see described fully in the help menus.

After reading those sections, you'll soon become adept at using AOL's Mac and Windows software to navigate the service, and you'll be ready for the main event. In the rest of this book, I will take you through every department of America Online and also provide detailed coverage of all the newest Internet access features.

Which Platform Is Best for AOL?

Nope, I will not get involved in a platform war. More and more folks have a Mac at home and a Windows-based PC at work, or vice versa. Having to adapt to both computing platforms is normal, and you should be able to enjoy your online visits fully no matter which version of the software you use. The following section details the differences between the Mac and Windows AOL software versions.

> **N O T E** If you're really interested in engaging in an online discussion about the merits of the Mac versus the Windows operating systems, you'll find ongoing discussions on the topic in the Windows magazine forum on AOL (keyword: **Windows**, then click the magazine's icon), Power Macintosh forum (keyword: **PowerMac**), and the Mac Operating Systems Forum (keyword: **MOS**). Several Internet Newsgroups also contain discussions (and sometimes outright arguments) about this, too. Before you plunge into those discussions, however, you'll want to read Chapters 9, "Using America Online Message Boards" and 32, " Joining and Participating in Internet Newsgroups" of this book. ▪

The Differences Between AOL for Macintosh and AOL for Windows

With a few exceptions here and there, I've included illustrations and instructions for the Macintosh and Windows versions of AOL software interchangeably. That's because the programs are meant to interface with you, the member, in a similar manner. AOL's software development teams have also worked hard to make both the Mac and Windows offer a similar user experience, in much the same way as the Mac and Windows versions of Microsoft Office software look and feel the same on the two computing platforms.

If you routinely switch between computing platforms, however, you'll encounter some differences. To a great extent, these differences are due to ways in which document windows and dialog boxes are displayed.

The following sections show the differences in the features of the Mac and Windows versions of AOL software.

Macintosh-only Features

The following features of Macintosh version 3.0 of the AOL software are not duplicated in the Windows version. Minor differences exist in the graphic formats supported (such as PICT on the Mac and BMP on the PC), but I won't detail them here.

- ▪ *Text-to-speech capability.* This feature uses Apple's PlainTalk and Speech Manager technologies, which allow text windows, chats, and Instant Messages to be spoken in voices that you select.

- ▪ *QuickTime movie support.* This feature allows movies created in Apple's QuickTime format to be played through AOL's software (provided that you have Apple's QuickTime System extension installed).

- ▪ *Spell Checking.* E-mail messages you write in the Mac version of AOL software can be spell-checked before you send them.

■ *Apple Guide Help.* Apple's interactive help feature, Apple Guide, is fully supported on your Mac AOL software.

Windows-only Features

The following features of Windows version 3.0 of the AOL software are not duplicated (or available in a different form) in the Macintosh version. Minor differences exist in the graphic formats supported (such as PICT on the Mac and BMP on the PC), but I won't detail them here.

■ *Graphics editing tools.* When you have a graphic image open in your AOL software, the Show Tools command (Edit menu) displays a toolbar that enables you to rotate, scale, and make minor adjustments in a graphic file.

■ *Windows AVI movies.* This feature allows you to play movies created in AVI format, if you have the proper AVI drivers installed.

■ *Windows help.* Windows online help lets you print help text windows for later review.

N O T E Because AOL's Mac and Windows software is in a constant state of development, you can expect that one platform's feature-set will occasionally leap-frog the other, and vice versa. ▨

Reviewing the AOL Software Changes

This book is written with the assumption that you will want to use the very latest AOL software, which at this writing is version 3.0. A good way to see if an upgrade makes sense to you is to see the list of changes from version to version. I'll summarize the newest AOL features, the ones described in detail throughout this book, in Chapter 2. In the meantime, here's a brief history of the changes and enhancements that AOL software has seen over the last few years.

Macintosh AOL 2.1

This version of AOL's software added the features described in the following sections.

High-Speed Support   The program's telecommunications capabilities are updated to support connection at 9,600 bits per second and 14,400 bps, using AOL's expanded network of AOLNet and SprintNet access numbers. Modem personality files are available to provide optimum performance with most popular modems.

Localities   *Localities* are files that contain connection setups to access AOL. You can create such setups for your home, for your office, and for use while you're on the road. Each Locality contains your connection numbers, any options that you select, and data on the kind of modem that you're using. (You can specify your desktop modem for home or office use and your PowerBook's or Duo's modem for use while you're traveling, for example.)

Multiple File Uploads   This feature allows you to attach more than one file to an e-mail message and then to compress it with Aladdin's StuffIt program (a popular Mac compression program that's built into AOL's software). Support for the PKZip format (a PC compression technique) also is included.

Macintosh AOL 2.5 and 2.5.1

When you install this version of AOL's software, the service gives you a new interface, graphics-viewing options and other features that are described in the following sections.

New AOL Interface   The differences between this version of AOL software and previous versions are obvious as soon as you log on. You'll see the following features:

- A new Main Menu screen, offering 14 departments through which you can access all services on AOL.

- When you log on to AOL, a screen called In the Spotlight appears above the Main Menu and informs you about featured areas and the latest news, and also tells you whether you've got e-mail waiting.

New Multimedia Capabilities   AOL's graphical features are enhanced by an instant-photo feature that displays a picture on your screen while a file is being downloaded. When you check out a graphic file online, you'll find that many files offer miniature (*thumbnail*) views of the graphic.

In addition, you can open and view graphics created in ART, GIF, JPEG, and PICT formats, which means that you no longer have to download a separate viewer program to view many of the files that you download.

CAUTION

Viewing graphics with AOL's Macintosh software requires System 7.0 or later and a color-capable Macintosh (68020 CPU or better). If you don't need to view graphic files, you can use a black-and-white Mac (68000 CPU) and System 6.0.7 or later.

Additional Member Features   In addition to the new interface, you have an assortment of new options that make your online visits more efficient and fun. These features include the following:

- Additional member preferences that confirm your actions when you designate e-mail with the Send Later option and when you add something to the Download Manager.

- You can use the Command key (⌘) to choose multiple, non-consecutive entries from your Address Book.

- You can add color to your e-mail for display on a color Macintosh. This option is available in the Edit menu.

Personal Choices   You can customize four elements of your AOL software setup by accessing a single feature: Personal Choices.

Among the services and features that you can customize are:

- *Parental Controls*. This feature restricts access to certain parts of the service— a useful feature if you have children using your AOL account.

- *Marketing Preferences*. You can use this feature to allow AOL to send you special offers about new products from time to time.

- *Set Preferences*. This feature enables you to set your regular AOL program preferences.

In addition, you can add and delete screen names and also edit your member profile from the Personal Choices dialog box.

Mac AOL 2.6

This version of AOL's software was released in the spring of 1995. The software contains the added features described in the following sections.

Apple Speech Manager Support   If you have Apple's PlainTalk or Speech Manager software installed, you can take advantage of the following new features:

- *Text-to-Speech*. This feature allows your Mac to read selected text, chat-room comments, and instant messages to you.

- *Speak Unknown Users*. This feature activates speech playback for selected text and for items typed in a chat-room window or contained in an instant message without having to preselect a sound for a particular member.

■ *Allow Simultaneous Speech.* This feature allows your Mac to recite two instant messages to you at the same time (which, I suppose, creates a chorus effect, if you like such things).

■ *Set Default Voices.* This feature allows you to attach a particular voice to an AOL member.

Multimedia Support   America Online software now can play System 7 sound and MIDI sound files. You can also open and play QuickTime movies if you have Apple's QuickTime System extension installed.

World Wide Web Browser   This feature was offered as a separate application that is linked to your Mac AOL software.

Background Downloading   You can download files in the background while doing other work on AOL. You can read your newsgroups while you download your files, chat in the lobby, or look for more files during downloading. When you sign off during a background download, you can finish your download at another time, when you log on to AOL again. You cannot upload files in the background, however.

Mac AOL 2.7

This is the version of AOL software that shipped in the spring of 1996. It is the one still provided on floppy disks when you join AOL. You'll be able to upgrade to version 3.0 from AOL's free Upgrade area (keyword: **Upgrade**) or if you install from a CD-ROM.

Online Database Repair Tool   One of the banes of the Mac AOL user's experience was occasional corruption of the Online Database file if your Mac crashed. This file contains your account information and other data AOL's program needs to run. Until now, some users managed to get around this problem by reinstalling the software from scratch, or running the Online Database file through Apple's ResEdit resource manager software. With Mac AOL 2.7, AOL has incorporated a special repair tool that will fix most cases of corruption of this file.

Updated World Wide Web Browser   Mac AOL 2.7 offers an improved World Wide Web browser program, with more accurate translation of WWW pages. The Print command from the File menu provides fully formatted output of the active WWW page. There are also bug fixes, including improved communication with the regular Mac software and support for Macintosh drag-and-drop.

Windows AOL 2.0

Version 2.0 of AOL's Windows software allows members in the Windows environment to share many of the new interface capabilities offered in the Macintosh version. The following sections cover some of the specifics.

New AOL Interface   The differences between this version of AOL software and previous versions are obvious as soon as you log on. You'll see the following features:

- A new Main Menu screen, offering 14 departments through which you can access all services on AOL.

- When you log on to AOL, the top screen, called In the Spotlight, appears above the Main Menu and informs you about featured areas and the latest news, and also tells you whether you have any e-mail waiting.

New Multimedia Capabilities   AOL's graphical features are enhanced by an instant-photo feature that lets you see a picture appear on your screen as it's being downloaded. When you check out a graphic file online, you'll find many offer a miniature (thumbnail) view of what the file actually looks like.

In addition, you can open and view graphics created in the ART, BMP, GIF, and JPEG formats, which means that you no longer have to download a separate viewer program to view many of the files you download.

Personal Choices   You can customize four elements of your AOL software setup by accessing a single feature, Personal Choices. Among the services and features that you can customize are:

- *Parental Controls*. This feature restricts access to certain parts of the service— a useful feature if you have children using your AOL account.

- *Marketing Preferences*. You can use this feature to allow AOL to send you special offers about new products from time to time.

- *Set Preferences*. This feature enables you to set your regular AOL program preferences.

In addition, you can add and delete screen names and also edit your member profile from the Personal Choices dialog box.

FlashSessions   A feature first introduced in the Mac AOL software has been added to the Windows version. FlashSessions allow you to run an automated session to send and receive e-mail and to download attached files or files added to the program's Download Manager. It also helps you reduce your online charges by making your sessions more efficient.

Windows AOL 2.5

This version of Windows AOL software was released in the spring of 1995. The software includes the new features described in the following sections.

New Install Program   The SETUP.EXE program has been redesigned to provide better performance and enhanced upgrading capability from older AOL software versions. The new installer offers the following features:

- Improved capability to detect modems
- Improved progress feedback during installation
- Automatic transfer of all artwork and account information from previous versions during the upgrade process

Favorite Places   This feature allows you to easily mark your favorite AOL and Internet areas so that you can revisit them easily by choosing them from a directory listing.

Personal Filing Cabinet   Personal Filing Cabinet is an organization tool that enables you to assemble your e-mail, downloaded files, list of Favorite Places (described in the following section), and newsgroups in a single location. This feature also supports the following capabilities:

- You can drag and drop items from one folder into another folder.
- You can select multiple items by Shift+clicking consecutive items and Ctrl+clicking non-consecutive items.
- You can create and delete folders for personalized file organization.
- You can search the material in the Personal Filing Cabinet.

World Wide Web Browser   This feature, integrated into your AOL software, enables you to access World Wide Web pages on the Internet.

New Compression Support   AOL's automatic decompression tool now supports ZIP files compressed with PKZip 2.0 and later.

Multimedia Support   America Online's Windows software can now play WAV, MIDI, and AVI files. Simply open the File menu and choose the Open command; then select the file. To take advantage of this feature, you need a sound card for sound support and AVI drivers to play AVI movies. Sounds play automatically after they are downloaded.

Drag-and-Drop Support   You can drag selected text from one open window and drop it into another window by using the Ctrl+click method. You can attach files to e-mail by clicking the file in File Manager and dragging it to the Attach File icon in the mail form. To play a sound, drag the sound icon from File Manager to any empty space in the AOL for Windows application. For the sound feature to work, you need to have a sound card properly installed.

Background Downloading You can download files in the background while doing other work on AOL. You can read your newsgroups while you download your files, chat in the lobby, or browse for more files while downloading. When you sign off during a background download, you can finish your download at another time, when you log on to AOL again. You cannot upload files in the background, however.

From Here...

Consider this chapter an introduction to the rapidly changing online landscape at America Online. Whether you're a new member or you've been active for a while, you can see the way the access software has developed over time, and the full range of features worth exploring further. I want you to consider this book to be a fun book, not a textbook, and I hope that you will keep it on hand for convenient reference as you become more involved with the online community.

AOL's software has undergone big changes over the years, and there's been a more compelling reason over time to upgrade to the newest version. AOL makes it easy, because the latest software is always free online, and available in an area you can reach via the keyword **Upgrade**.

But the preceding is only a taste of what is to come. In Chapter 2, I'll tell you all about version 3.0 of AOL's Mac and Windows software, both of which provide a whole new array of features, including the ability to run third-party Internet software as part of your AOL session without having to set up anything special.

How (and Why) to Upgrade Your AOL Software

It's a sure thing that constant software upgrades can bring many a headache. In addition to having to pay money for the new software, you have to get used to a new interface, new manuals, and perhaps new bugs.

Because the online universe is very competitive and many services are vying for your membership, AOL has been steadily upgrading its software to offer an improved user experience. But, unlike many of those productivity programs, AOL's software upgrades are always available online, free of charge. And there's plenty of helpful information, such as this book, to guide you through all the new features. ■

New AOL Features

In the previous chapter, I detailed the progression of AOL's software, showing you all the changes beginning with version 2.0 of AOL's Mac and Windows software. If you are using any of those versions, no doubt you're wondering just what's so special about version 3.0, and whether it makes sense for you to upgrade.

The descriptions and illustrations shown in this book reflect the newest versions of the software. And when you see them, perhaps you'll see why I strongly recommend your upgrade. Just take a look at the list of new features offered below and you'll see many compelling reasons to get that AOL upgrade.

Mac AOL 3.0

In the fall of 1996, AOL made some major changes to the Macintosh software. These changes not only brought the software in line with the features offered in the Windows version, but surpassed it in some respects. They all combine to take you to a new level of user friendliness when you visit AOL. Here are some of the highlights of the new software.

Updated User Interface   The new Mac AOL software brings with it big changes in the sign-off and sign-on screens. There's an updated Welcome menu, and the Main menu has been replaced with a Channels screen, offering a host of new online areas for you to visit. As you travel around AOL, you'll find that many of your favorite online departments have undergone reorganization that's available only with the new AOL software. Finding your way around is enhanced by a new integrated Find feature (see fig. 2.1) that lets you look for members, places, files, and upcoming online events, all from a simple, friendly interface.

FIG. 2.1
AOL's new Find feature lets you quickly locate people and places online.

Progressive Artwork Downloading   In the past, whenever you visited a new online area in which an artwork download to your computer was necessary, things came to a screeching halt. You had to sit by for seconds and sometimes minutes, observing a procession of progress bars, till the artwork download was done.

Not so with Mac AOL 3.0. Using a feature called Smart Art, whenever you enter a new area that offers updated artwork, you can go about your business and enjoy the area without interruption. You'll see a skeleton window appear on your screen, with generic AOL icons replacing the fancy buttons. As you continue to browse through the area, the artwork will be transferred in the background. You'll see the outlines of the new AOL area change magically before your eyes until the artwork download is done (you'll see the flashing lights on your modem as all this is happening, if you have an external modem).

If you decide to close the new area's document window before the artwork is done, the download stops. It won't resume until or unless you visit that area again. And, of course, when the artwork download is finished, it's not repeated unless the artwork, or part of it, has changed.

Adjustable Artwork Database Sizing   An important feature of AOL's World Wide Web browser has been carried over to the regular software, too. You have a new Art Storage Preferences option that lets you choose the maximum size of the downloaded artwork you receive from AOL. When the size you set is reached, the oldest, least used artwork will be cleared first.

Personal Filing Cabinet   Personal Filing Cabinet (see fig. 2.2) is an organizational tool that enables you to assemble your e-mail, downloaded files, list of Favorite Places (described in the following section), and newsgroups in a single location. This feature also supports the following capabilities:

FIG. 2.2

The Mac version of AOL's Personal Filing Cabinet puts your stored mail and other stuff in a convenient Finder-like window for easy access and editing.

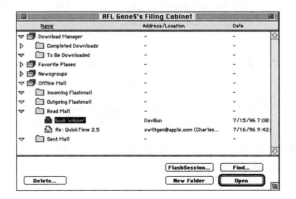

Part

I

Ch

2

- You can drag and drop items from one folder into another folder.

- You can select multiple items by Shift+clicking consecutive items and Command+clicking non-consecutive items.

- You can create and delete folders for personalized file organization.

- You can search the material in the Personal Filing Cabinet.

Favorite Places   This feature allows you to easily mark your favorite AOL and Internet areas (see fig. 2.3) so that you can revisit them easily by choosing them from a directory listing.

FIG. 2.3
Favorite Places is a feature that first started in the Windows AOL version, letting you build a custom list of your favorite online spots.

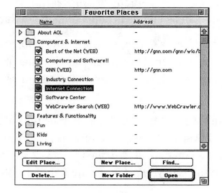

Improved World Wide Web Browser   The Mac WWW browser is based on Microsoft's Internet Explorer and is now fully integrated into the regular AOL program. It's no longer a separate program that launches when you call up a WWW page. The browser appears as a standard AOL document window and offers speedier retrieval of Web pages. The new browser includes support for many of the HTML 3.0 features you find in Netscape. These include Netscape frames, which formats a WWW page as a set of separate panes, each with its own scrollable area.

Enhanced E-Mail Form   The e-mail form has been enhanced to make it easier to use. You'll also find it more convenient to format your e-mail for the best possible appearance.

New Toolbar   AOL's software now has a handy, color toolbar that puts your favorite features just a click away. The toolbar can be moved or hidden if you prefer.

Drag-and-Drop Support   There's now support for Apple's drag-and-drop feature, which allows you to drag elements from one document window and place them in another (or on your Mac's desktop).

Support for Third-Party Internet Software   With Mac AOL 3.0, you can now run a third-party Internet program, such as another WWW browser or Internet Relay Chat client, while you're logged on to AOL. All you have to do is open those programs and continue with your online session.

This feature, however, works with a regular connection to one of AOL's telephone access numbers. It doesn't work if you're logged on to AOL via PPP or SLIP Internet access (in which case you can already run that third-party Internet software).

Part

I

Ch

2

Apple Guide Support   You have full support for Apple Guide's interactive help features, which guide you through the most complex steps in using your AOL software.

E-Mail Spell Checker   You can now spell check your AOL e-mail messages, so you can be sure everything is spelled properly before you send your e-mail.

Buddy Lists   Is your AOL friend online? Whenever he or she logs on, you'll know with AOL's Buddy Lists feature. It takes just minutes to configure with the list screen names you want Buddy Lists to recognize. And if you want privacy, you can also bar your screen name from appearing on other Buddy Lists.

New Address Book   AOL's Address Book has been redesigned to make it easier for you to build a personal listing of your online friends and colleagues.

Downloadable Software Enhancements   The new AOL software is extensible, meaning that new features can be downloaded to your computer to expand the capabilities. As updates become available, you'll be offered either an opportunity to download them from a special software library, or they will be offered to you before you log off the service. You'll find, as a result, that the look and feel of the program will evolve over time as more updates are provided. Minor program bug fixes can also be offered in this way.

Windows AOL 3.0

In the summer of 1996, AOL made some major changes to the Windows client software. They all combine to take you to a new level of user friendliness when you visit AOL. And you'll find general performance is much better, too. Here are some of the highlights of the new software.

Updated User Interface   The new Windows AOL software brings with it big changes in the sign-off and sign-on screens. There's an updated Welcome menu, and the Main menu has been replaced with a Channels screen, offering a host of new online areas for you to visit. As you travel around AOL, you'll find that many of your favorite online departments have undergone reorganization that's available only with the new AOL software. Finding your way around is enhanced by a new integrated Find feature that lets you look for members, places, files, and upcoming online events, all from a simple, friendly interface.

Progressive Artwork Downloading   In the past, whenever you visited a new online area in which an artwork download to your computer was necessary, things came to a halt. You had to sit by for seconds and sometimes minutes, observing a procession of progress bars, till the artwork download was done.

It won't happen anymore with Windows AOL 3.0. Using a feature called Smart Art, whenever you enter a new area that offers updated artwork, you can go about your business and enjoy the area without interruption. You'll see a skeleton window appear on your screen, with generic AOL icons replacing the fancy buttons. As you continue to browse through the area, the artwork will proceed to be transferred in the background. You'll see the outlines of the new AOL area change magically before your eyes until the artwork download is done (you'll see the flashing lights on your modem as all this is happening).

If you decide to close the new area's document window before the artwork is done, the download stops. It won't resume until or unless you visit that area again. And, of course, when the artwork download is finished, it's not repeated unless it's changed.

Adjustable Artwork Database Sizing   An important feature of AOL's World Wide Web browser has been carried over to the regular software, too. You have a new Graphics Viewing Preferences option that lets you choose the maximum size of the downloaded artwork you receive from AOL. When the size you set is reached, the oldest, least-used artwork will be cleared first.

Adjustable Personal Filing Cabinet Size   To keep your Personal Filing Cabinet from overwhelming your hard drive, there's now a feature to set the maximum size of the file. It's part of the Personal Filing Cabinet choices in your AOL program preferences.

Improved World Wide Web Browser   The integrated WWW browser includes support for many of the HTML 3.0 features you find in Netscape. These include Netscape frames, which formats a WWW page as a set of separate panes, each with its own scrollable area.

Enhanced E-Mail Form   There's a new feature on your e-mail and instant message forms, which looks like the formatting toolbar you find on many word processor programs. This toolbar provides a set of basic text-formatting features, such as changing the color of your text or the background of your message. You can change point sizes, and text styling, and add hyperlinks to your favorite online area (including an Internet-based source).

New Flashbar   AOL's handy Flashbar has been updated with new colorful icons, and more logical choices. And, if you somehow forget what a particular Flashbar icon means, just hold the mouse cursor above that icon, and in a few seconds you'll see a handy display showing its purpose.

Support for Third-Party Internet Software In the past, whenever you wanted to use another WWW browser, FTP, or Internet Relay Chat program with your AOL session, you had to go through some convoluted steps in installing a custom Winsock.ddl file in your Windows directory.

With Windows AOL 3.0, there's a feature that auto-loads AOL's own Winsock software whenever the program is launched. To use a third-party Internet program, all you have to do is open it and use it.

This feature, however, works with a regular connection to one of AOL's telephone access numbers. It doesn't work if you're using another Winsock.ddl file, say to allow you PPP or SLIP Internet access.

Right Mouse Button Support At last AOL has recognized that extra button on your mouse. You'll find that when you click the right mouse button while in a text document, it brings up a special shortcut menu in your AOL software. The special menu provides a full range of text-formatting features, which are similar to those offered via the toolbar in your AOL e-mail form.

Buddy Lists Is your AOL friend online? Whenever he or she logs on, you'll know with AOL's Buddy Lists feature. It takes just minutes to configure with the list screen names you want Buddy Lists to recognize. And if you want privacy, you can also bar your screen name from appearing on other Buddy Lists.

Downloadable Software Enhancements The new AOL software is extensible, meaning that new features can be downloaded to your computer to expand the capabilities. As updates become available, you'll be offered either an opportunity to download them from a special software library, or they will be offered to you before you log off the service. You'll find, as a result, that the look and feel of the program will evolve over time as more updates are provided. Minor program bug fixes can also be offered in this way.

Speedy Application Launches When you open your Windows AOL software, you'll find the program launches much faster, shaving many seconds off the time it takes before the program is ready for you to begin your online visit.

Where to Get the Latest AOL Software

The nicest thing about the newest versions of AOL software is the lack of the upgrade notice and the little check boxes for you to add your credit card number. That's because AOL's software upgrades are free, and available online as soon as the product is released.

To get your AOL upgrade, simply use the keyword **Upgrade** (see fig. 2.4). You'll be taken to an area free of online charges, and given the chance to download the latest software.

FIG. 2.4
AOL's Upgrade center provides the latest service software for you to download.

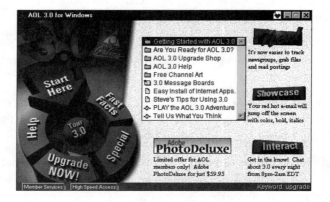

 To keep your AOL software download-free, choose the Download Now option in AOL's Upgrade center. The Download Later option returns you to the paying area, which means the download will be on your time, not AOL's.

During the early phases of an AOL software introduction, you may find the pre-release version offered in a public preview. This is very similar to what Netscape and Microsoft have done with their WWW browser software. A public preview lets you get an early look at a new software package and have the opportunity to try it out and report your reactions (and maybe the bugs you encounter) directly to the development staff, to help make the release version a more reliable product.

Some Quick Installation Tips

Installing the newest AOL software is almost always a double-click away. AOL's software installers, both the Mac and Windows versions, take you through the process quickly, and the software is up and running within a few minutes. Here's some helpful advice to consider when you upgrade.

- **For Mac Users Only:** If you're upgrading from a previous version of the software on a Mac, use the Upgrade option when you open your AOL software for the first time. That will transfer all of the account information, program preferences, and much of the downloaded artwork to the new version.

- **For Windows Users Only:** All of your program settings, account information, and downloaded artwork transfers to the new version during the installation process.

If you don't want the information transferred, just delete the path name when prompted during the install.

- If you have experienced crashes or other problems with your old AOL software, you may prefer to do a clean installation instead. In that way, a new version of the program is installed, and nothing is carried over from the previous installation. You only need to enter your screen name and password where the certificate number information is requested to restore your account information to the new software version.

Part

I

Ch

2

CAUTION

Files you've downloaded from AOL's software libraries will not be transferred to the new version of AOL's client software when you install it. If you intend to delete the older version of AOL's software, be sure you move the downloaded files to a new location—otherwise you'll delete them, too.

Windows 3.1 versus Windows 95—Does It Make Any Difference for AOL?

The version of AOL software described in this book is the 16-bit version, which works in essentially the same way for both versions of Windows. However, by the time you read this book, a true 32-bit Windows 95-compliant version may well be available, also.

The 32-bit version will be offered as a downloadable upgrade, and you can expect the features to be essentially the same as the Windows 3.1 version, with the exception of enhancements to support the newer operating system. One of these is support for the Add/Remove Programs utility. This will allow for fast installation and removal of the AOL program and support files.

From Here...

In the future, you may expect AOL's software to change greatly from the versions described here. As Apple and Microsoft enhance their operating systems with new features, AOL will upgrade its software to take advantage of those features, and provide a wider array of options that will make your online sessions speedier and even more enjoyable.

- To discover the secrets of mastering your AOL Macintosh software, read Chapter 3, "Getting the Most from AOL's Macintosh Software."

■ To discover the secrets of mastering your AOL Windows software, read Chapter 4, "Getting the Most from AOL's Windows Software."

■ You'll find detailed information on AOL's services throughout this book, but your best launching point is Chapter 6, "Where Do We Begin?"

■ If you want to learn the secret of reducing your online bills, read Chapter 39, "How to Save Time and Money."

■ If you want your children to share your online experiences, read the three chapters of Part IV, "Kids and America Online."

■ The mysteries of the global Internet network are explained in the seven chapters of Part VIII, "Entering the Information Superhighway."

■ If you're new to America Online, you'll want to read Appendix A, "If You're New to the OnlineWorld."

■ New Macintosh users of AOL software will want to read Appendix B, "Using Your America Online Macintosh Software."

■ New Windows users of AOL software will want to read Appendix C, "Using Your America Online Windows Software."

Getting the Most from AOL's Macintosh Software

Logging on and visiting your favorite online places is only half the story. It's so easy to take the software for granted. The interface is so comfortable, you tend to forget how sophisticated the underlying software is, a flexible telecommunications program with many hooks into the best the Mac operating system has to offer.

In this chapter, we'll try to stretch the software's boundaries further and see just how far you can go with a few simple add-ons. ■

Planning Your Online Visits

Many of you are motivated by the thrill of discovery and adventure when you begin your online visits. I'm certainly not one to pour cold water on the fun of just hanging out and looking around. But if you take a few moments to plan what you're going to do during your visit, and the places you're going to visit you can definitely make your logins more productive and save a few bucks, too.

The best way to make your online visits more fun is to have a plan of action before you log on. Decide in advance the areas you wish to visit and what you want to do when you get there. Here's a sample plan to govern a typical visit (feel free to adjust this to your special needs):

1. Check e-mail.
2. Send responses to previously composed e-mail.
3. Check messages in your favorite online forum.
4. Respond to messages that interest you.
5. Attend online conferences.
6. Choose software to download, using the Download Later Option.
7. Set FlashSession to receive files.
8. Log off.

Throughout this book, I'll cover the subjects of participating in message boards, using AOL FlashSessions, and the most effective ways to find and download software that interests you. Some of the relevant chapters you might want to read include Chapter 6, "Where Do We Begin?" Chapter 8, "Using America Online E-Mail," Chapter 9, "Using America Online Message Boards," Chapter 10, "Chatting Online," and Chapter 20, "Tips and Tricks on Finding Software."

Making Your AOL Software Work Faster

Your enjoyment of your online visits can be much greater if you can only get your AOL software to work better. Not every step I'm about to describe comes free; some of it involves getting new hardware. But by considering these options, you may be able to fine-tune your AOL software for the maximum possible performance on your Mac. You'll also want to read the section following this one, covering AOL Software Add-Ons, for additional techniques that will get you the best possible speed during your online visits.

You can speed up your AOL software by doing one or more of the following:

■ Get a Faster Modem. America Online supports connection speeds up to 28,800 bps (v.34) in many U.S. cities. If you have a high-speed access number in your city, a faster modem will more than pay for itself in reduced online charges. And it will make your AOL software perform at a much higher level, not only for software downloads and uploads, but for text display, too. The keyword Access will allow you to review the latest telephone connection numbers. You'll learn more about getting the best possible performance from your modem in Chapter 41, "Secrets of High-Speed Access on AOL."

■ *Get a Faster Mac.* If you have more than one Mac at your home or work site, installing AOL software on the fastest computer will offer speedier screen redraws, faster application launching, and other performance enhancements. If you have an older model Mac, the new low-cost Macs and Macintosh clones, and their extraordinary higher-speed capability, can be quite attractive items to consider.

■ *Get the Program More RAM.* Viewing graphic files is RAM-intensive, taking up a large portion of the memory space AOL's software occupies. If you have enough available memory, you can give more to the AOL application. Just do the following:

1. Be sure to quit the AOL application.

2. Click the AOL application icon once.

3. Choose Get Info from the Finder's Special menu.

4. Enter a larger figure in the Preferred Size list box. An additional 500K to 1,000K is enough for starters.

5. Close the Get Info window and launch AOL's program.

■ *Turn off Virtual Memory.* Apple's virtual memory makes your RAM go further by allowing hard drive space to be used as RAM. But because a hard drive runs much slower than real RAM, you may experience lags in some programs. Graphic redraws in AOL's software may slow down with virtual memory. You may get somewhat better performance from Connectix RAM Doubler, which simulates virtual memory, but uses your real RAM instead.

■ *Use Few System Extensions.* Some system extensions, because of minor conflicts with other software, can slow down your Mac's performance. You should be certain that all of the system add-ons you're using have a beneficial effect. The programs I describe in the next section of this book will work reliably in most installations with little or no performance impact.

Part

I

Ch

3

Getting There Faster with the Favorite Places Feature

One of the quickest ways to speed up travel around AOL is to add your favorite AOL spots to the list of Favorite Places (see fig. 3.1). This is done simply by clicking the handy icon at the upper right of an area's title bar, which brings up a request for you to confirm if you want the area added to your list (see fig. 3.2).

FIG. 3.1
Click the heart-shaped icon on the right side of the title bar to add this area to your list of Favorite Sites.

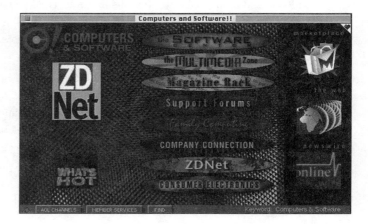

FIG. 3.2
If you do want your Favorite Places selection added, a sound will confirm your selection.

You can bring up your Favorite Places directory at any time while using your AOL software by clicking the icon at the right side of the program's Flashbar. You can also select a general preference to display the Favorite Places window as soon as your AOL program starts. Once you've added an item to your personal Favorite Places listing (see fig. 3.3), you can go to a specific site by double-clicking its entry. And it even works on Internet newsgroups and Web sites.

AOL Software Add-Ons

Most of your online activities can be performed quickly and effectively using AOL software alone. However, there are some convenient tools available that will not only provide some features missing from AOL's software, but they offer additional tools that will add extraordinary power to help automate your online visits. There are other tools that won't make your software run any faster or speed up any processes, but they will make your visits more fun. I'll cover these first.

FIG. 3.3
Your personal Favorite Sites window is truly personal; you can alter its look to your taste.

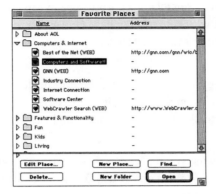

How to Let AOL Talk to You

Beginning with version 2.6, AOL's Mac software supports Apple's Speech Manager technology. Apple's Speech Manager (and PlainTalk speech recognition software) can read text back to you. This provides for some fascinating possibilities during your AOL sessions. At the very least, you don't have to be in front of your computer during a conference, because the text can be read back to you as it appears on your screen.

CAUTION

Sound capabilities are only available in your AOL Mac software if you have a Macintosh with PlainTalk or Speech Manager software installed. Otherwise, this feature, which appears in the Edit menu, won't work.

N O T E Apple's speech technology (and similar features used on other computing platforms) is not advanced enough to provide perfect speech-to-text capability. Some words may not be enunciated properly by your computerized speaker, making those words difficult to understand. In other cases, when the way a word is pronounced varies by its context, you may have difficulty figuring out what the computer is trying to tell you. The talking computer that many of you know from *Star Trek* episodes is something we shouldn't expect to see for quite some time. ■

Using QuicKeys

After you've worked with AOL's software for a while, you begin to think about little things you wish you could do that aren't yet supported; or a means to record frequently used steps so you don't have to do them all manually. One easy way to make your software do more is CE Software's QuicKeys, a commercial program you can buy from your favorite software dealer.

QuicKeys is a macro program, but it also adds handy shortcuts that allow you to extend beyond that capability. In its simplest form, it records the keystrokes and mouse actions you take and allows you to play them back with a single keyboard command that you select.

In addition to recording what you do, it can also support features that are not a part of America Online's software. For example, I use QuicKeys to insert my online signature at the end of all of my e-mail and messages.

Extending the Extended Keyboard   If you have an Apple Extended Keyboard, Apple Design Keyboard, or a similar keyboard that includes Function keys F1 through F4, Undo, Cut, Copy, and Paste, you'll notice quickly enough that America Online's Macintosh software supports none of these keystrokes. While Macintosh drag and drop helps you to move selected blocks of text around, having those simple keystrokes is helpful, but only at the core of what a program like QuicKeys can do.

QuicKeys lets you use those missing keystrokes (and any others you want), working seamlessly in the background, so you don't even notice that it's this program doing the magic rather than the AOL software.

QuicKeys is configured via keysets, which are files containing all of the shortcuts that are dedicated to a specific program. There are also so-called universal shortcuts that will work in the same way in any program.

Using QuicKeys Toolbars   The most effective way to harness the power of QuicKeys is to let the program help you make a custom toolbar for your favorite programs. It's done through the handy QuicKeys editor (see fig. 3.4), a utility that lets you quickly create your shortcuts.

Once you've created your brand-new toolbar for a particular program, you can get on with the process of creating shortcuts for it. You can choose existing shortcuts from the QuicKeys editor, or make new ones. The program's online help and clear-cut manual will show you the way. Once the shortcuts are created, you simply drag them to the new toolbar, and you'll be left with a series of blank icons on the toolbar (see fig. 3.5).

FIG. 3.4
The QuicKeys editing utility allows you to build keystrokes, toolbars, and more to make your Mac (and your AOL sessions) more productive.

FIG. 3.5
The second step in making a custom program toolbar is to drag the shortcuts to a blank toolbar window.

Of course, a blank icon is apt to appear somewhat drab. While the name of the shortcut will appear below the toolbar when you move the mouse cursor above it (just like AOL's own toolbar), you'll want to apply a pretty face to the icons you've selected. For that, QuicKeys gives you a boatload of choices. To create an icon for the toolbar, double-click the appropriate icon to bring up the display (see fig. 3.6).

FIG. 3.6
Just choose the toolbar icon you want from the choices supplied via QuicKeys.

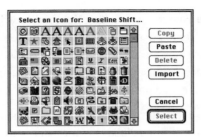

Once you've set up your shortcuts, click the OK button to automatically save the changes you've made. If your shortcuts have become complex, you can even print a QuickReference Card the program creates for you, so that you can see a hard copy of all of the shortcuts you've selected.

Part
I

Ch
3

QuicKeys can automate such a wide range of functions, it is limited only by your imagination. You can change printers on the fly, launch applications, open documents, restart and shut down your Macintosh, even scroll your document screen horizontally, which is useful when you want to view a document that may exceed the width of your Mac's monitor.

If you want to learn more about QuicKeys and download some really flexible keyboard shortcuts that you can use with AOL's software and other programs, visit the publisher's forum on AOL keyword: **CESoftware**.

Using Tempo II Plus

Tempo II Plus from Affinity Microsystems is another highly sophisticated macro utility for the Macintosh. Tempo can record your actions and play them back instantly. Beyond that, you can add intelligence to macros by having them test for conditions. Tempo uses *externals*, which are modules that provide many of the program's advanced functions.

One of the most popular uses for Tempo II Plus is automating the process of reading messages on America Online. With Tempo, you can connect to AOL, copy all new messages from your favorite forums, and then disconnect. Tempo can do this in a fraction of the time it would take you to do it manually, without you having to babysit the process.

Automating the Message Reading Process

Once you've set up your macro (or series of linked macros), you can call it up via a single keystroke. When you activate the macro, Tempo launches the America Online program and clicks the Sign On button. Then, Tempo waits until the Welcome to America Online window appears and checks for your mail. You can use the following examples to create macros that will read messages for you.

Reading all Messages in a Folder   By clicking the Find New icon for a selected folder in an AOL message board, Tempo determines from the response whether there are new messages or not. If there are new messages, Tempo clicks the Read button, copies the first message to another document, sends a keyboard return, and looks for a right arrow with the words Next Message (see fig. 3.7).

If this icon appears, Tempo clicks the right arrow and repeats the same copy routine. When the right arrow is gone, Tempo closes the message window, closes the folder window, and goes on to test the next folder.

Tempo uses its BitMatch external module to look for the arrow. That way it knows which macro to play. You need to enter the commands in the format shown below:

```
BitMatch(image,true macro,false macro)
```

FIG. 3.7

The Next Message arrow on a regular message board screen.

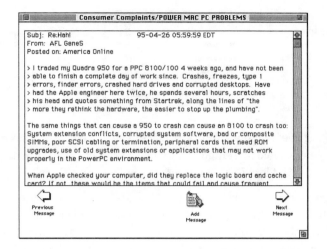

Consumer Complaints/POWER MAC PC PROBLEMS

Subj: Re:Hah!   95-04-26 05:59:59 EDT
From: AFL GeneS
Posted on: America Online

> I traded my Quadra 950 for a PPC 8100/100 4 weeks ago, and have not been
> able to finish a complete day of work since. Crashes, freezes, type 1
> errors, finder errors, crashed hard drives and corrupted desktops. Have
> had the Apple engineer here twice, he spends several hours, scratches
> his head and quotes something from Startrek, along the lines of "the
> more they rethink the hardware, the easier to stop up the plumbing".

The same things that can cause a 950 to crash can cause an 8100 to crash too:
System extension conflicts, corrupted system software, bad or composite
SIMMs, poor SCSI cabling or termination, peripheral cards that need ROM
upgrades, use of old system extensions or applications that may not work
properly in the PowerPC environment.

When Apple checked your computer, did they replace the logic board and cache
card? If not, these would be the items that could fail and cause frequent

Previous Message   Add Message   Next Message

You'll notice how closely this series of commands resembles a programming language. In this case, you can name your Tempo External macro:

```
BitMatch(next msg,Copy next,check next folder)
```

Basically, here's what the macro is doing: If the Next Message arrow icon is there, Tempo plays the macro that copies the next message. If the Next Message arrow is not there, Tempo plays the macro that closes the current window and message folder and then types a down arrow to go to the next folder.

If the message board is threaded and displays responses to individual messages, a similar BitMatch routine can test for an icon such as Next Response, and copy those responses as well, continuing until that icon is no longer present. If you want to know more about the setup of AOL's message boards, read Chapter 9, "Using America Online Message Boards."

To snap a BitMap image (which captures a portion of your screen), you type Tempo's BitMap FKey, ⌘-Shift-8. This attaches a small marquee to the cursor arrow (see fig. 3.8). You can press the plus or minus keys to enlarge or reduce the marquee to fit the image. When you click the mouse button, it takes a snapshot of the area within the marquee and lets you name it, then saves it as either Window-relative or Screen-relative. If it's saved as Window-relative (the same location as the Window is at the time), Tempo always looks at the same spot in the window for the image that matches the one you shot, even if you move the window around.

FIG. 3.8
You can save your screen
image at Tempo's Save
Bitmap dialog box.

Checking Every Folder   After the macro I've just described has copied all of the new messages to a folder, Tempo types a down arrow to select the next folder. Now's the time for a Check Folders For New Messages macro and a Check For Last Folder macro.

The first macro, Check Folders For New Messages, clicks the Find New button that you see when you open a message board window, and once again uses the BitMatch external described above to look at the response. If new messages have been added since the last time you opened this folder, a list of the new messages appears, and Tempo branches to the copy routine outlined above.

If there are no new messages, Tempo sees the dialog box indicating that fact and checks for the name of the message folder. Tempo gets the name of the folder by clicking the Read First Message icon. This opens a window with the folder name as the window name. Tempo copies the name of the window into an internal variable, which is like Apple's own clipboard except that Tempo saves it to its own file. Then Tempo compares that window name to the name of the last window it had opened. If the names are the same, then you've traveled through all the folders and you're done with the current forum. If the window name is new, then Tempo continues testing the folders.

Two Tempo externals make it possible to scan AOL's message boards: GetWindowName and Eval. The first external macro copies the name of the message window to a variable— for example, the window name. When the next window is opened, it copies that name to another variable, such as new window name. The Eval external then compares the two and lets Tempo know if they match or not. If they don't match, Eval copies the name of the new message window into the old window variable to use the next time around.

Copying the Message Contents to a Storage File   Your Copy Messages macro could simply click in the message window, select all the text, copy, switch to a word processor, save, and return. This would give you one long file of all your messages.

If you'd rather store them more usefully, Tempo can select the name portion of the message, store that as a name variable, and perform the same routine with the date or subject portions. Tempo will then copy the text, switch to a database, type out the name and other saved portions into their proper fields, and finally paste in the text of the message.

This way, your messages will be neatly filed by categories that are more meaningful to you. If you'd rather cut online time to a minimum, combine the two: First copy all messages to a single file, then, offline, let Tempo parse the files for you, copying them to your database.

Other Macro Possibilities   Tempo II Plus can also be used to automate complex routines such as these within and between any Macintosh applications. It can even be used with other scripting programs, such as Apple's own AppleScript. And, because Tempo can share variables with AppleScript, it can pass along to unscriptable programs information that is generated by AppleScript or other programs, including FileMaker Pro, HyperCard, Frontier, and others.

If you've never used a macro program, you may find some of the steps described above somewhat complex. Not to worry. Tempo II Plus comes with thorough documentation that will show you how to easily access all these powerful macro creation capabilities.

As for the macros I've just detailed, they were created especially for this book by Affinity, and you'll find this entire macro file and others in the company's support area on AOL (keyword: **Affinity**). You'll also find complete details about this marvelous program there, in case I've whetted your appetite for more.

A Brief Note about DM Assist   Although AOL's Download Manager is a useful way to control your downloading activities, it has some limitations. You cannot, for example, change the order of files shown in the directory, nor can you restrict your download to certain files and hold other entries for later download. It's all or nothing, with only the Finish Later option in your download progress bar enabling you to stop the process.

AOL DM Assist works with the Download Manager to address some of its limitations. It enables you to rearrange the downloading order, put queued files on hold for later FlashSessions, and even rename a partially downloaded file. The program is available in the software libraries of the Macintosh Utilities Forum (keyword: **MUT**).

Using Now Menus

Now Menus (see fig. 3.9) is part of Now Utilities, a popular set of system enhancements from Now Software. It's an enormously flexible utility that creates hierarchical menus on your Apple menu (sub-menus), adds icons on your menu bar to provide pull-down commands to launch applications, and creates pop-up menus that you can access by a keyboard shortcut.

Each of those pop-up menus can be easily configured with a number of options, such as active applications and recently used files, and you can add your installed applications (such as AOL's software) one by one to the list, which makes those menus an application launching dock. But one of the neatest features of Now Menus is the capability to add keyboard shortcuts to menu bar commands on the fly (see fig. 3.10), simply by highlighting a command and typing the keyboard shortcut you want to use.

FIG. 3.9
Now Menus from Now
Software lets you create
keyboard command
shortcuts on the fly.

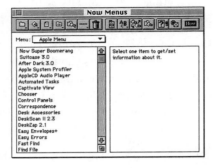

FIG. 3.10
Attach a keystroke to menu
bar commands with Now
Menus, such as the one I've
added to the Go To Menu
(⌘-Shift-C for the Channels
Menu). You can choose any
free keyboard shortcut for a
specific command.

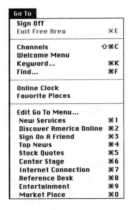

N O T E In Now Utilities 6, the version shipping when this book was being prepared, the option
to add custom keystrokes for menu bar commands was optional. You have to activate
the feature in the Now Menus Control Panel. It's a check box labeled Assign Hot Keys directly in
menus. ■

CAUTION

When you add a keyboard shortcut with Now Menus, you should first check to make sure that
command is not already attached to another function in that program (Now Menus won't put up any
warning about it). Otherwise, you may find the command doesn't work or performs the newly selected
function rather than the original function. Fortunately, if this happens, you can remove a Now Menus
command shortcut simply by highlighting that item and pressing the Delete key.

How Do You Spell it?

Version 3.0 of AOL's Mac software includes a built-in spell checker, just like your word processing program. It lets you check your e-mail, but doesn't support the messages you post in a message board or an Internet newsgroup. If you want to take spell checking to new heights, consider Casady & Greene's Spell Catcher (formerly known as Thunder 7). As you type, Spell Catcher works behind the scenes, monitoring your keystrokes. If you make a mistake, the program sounds a pre-selected warning (or flashes the menu bar—my preferred way of doing it). If you receive this warning, you can fix the mistake, or if you need further advice, type a handy keyboard shortcut to bring up the program's suggestion window (see fig. 3.11).

FIG. 3.11
Spell Catcher checks your keystrokes as you type, and warns you when you've made a mistake.

Spell Catcher also includes a handy thesaurus to help you find the right word for the right purpose, the ability to automatically modify selected words, Internet-style quoting, the ability to change uppercase to lowercase, and much more, including batch spell checking. It also offers a feature called Ghostwriter that backs up your keystrokes in text format, so you can easily retrieve them in the event your Mac crashes.

Another useful spell-checking program is Deneba's Coach Professional, which shares many of the basic features for Spell Checker but doesn't offer the same breadth of options.

Keyboard Power

Even if you haven't enhanced the capability of navigating through AOL's software with Now Menus, QuicKeys, Tempo II Plus, or a similar program, you've still got a good basic set of keyboard commands that you'll want to keep in mind.

Table 3.1 lists many of the keyboard shortcuts available with your America Online Macintosh software. They are based on AOL version 3.0, which became available at the time this book was written. Future versions may offer additional shortcuts.

Part
I

Ch
3

Table 3.1   Macintosh Keyboard Shortcuts

Function	Keyboard Shortcut
AOL guide	⌘-?
Bold	⌘-B
Check spelling	⌘-=
Close window	⌘-W
Compose mail	⌘-M
Copy	⌘-C
Cut	⌘-X
Exit free area	⌘-E
Find a member online	⌘-F
Get member's profile	⌘-G
Insert hyperlink	⌘-H
Locate a member online	⌘-L
Move to next entry field	Tab
New memo	⌘-N
Open an existing file	⌘-O
Open keyword window	⌘-K
Open lobby window	⌘-L
Paste	⌘-V
Plain text	⌘-T
Print	⌘-P
Quit application	⌘-Q
Read new mail	⌘-R

Function	Keyboard Shortcut
Save a file	⌘-S
Send an instant message	⌘-I
Underline text	⌘-Underline
Undo	⌘-Z

From Here...

Beyond the menus and commands, it is easy to configure America Online's Macintosh software to provide greatly enhanced performance and make your online visits more fun and more productive. By working with the tools I've described here and browsing through AOL's software libraries, you'll find many additional techniques to increase your online computing power.

■ If you must cross computing platforms from time to time, you'll want to read Chapter 4, "Getting the Most from AOL's Windows Software."

■ You'll find a detailed overview of AOL's services throughout this book, but your best launching point is Chapter 6, "Where Do We Begin?"

■ If you want your children to share your online experiences with you, read the three chapters in Part IV, "Kids and America Online."

■ The mysteries behind the global Internet network are explained in the chapters that comprise Part VIII, "Entering the Information Superhighway."

■ And if you want to learn secrets about reducing your online bills, read Chapter 39, "How to Save Time and Money."

■ If you're new to America Online, you'll want to read Appendix A, "If You're New to the Online World."

■ New Macintosh users of AOL software will want to read Appendix B, "Using Your America Online Macintosh Software."

Getting the Most from AOL's Windows Software

It's very easy to take your AOL software for granted after a while. The process is so simple: logging on, visiting your favorite parts of the service, then logging off. You may tend to ignore the underlying software you've used, which is a highly sophisticated telecommunications program. And you may not have taken the time to see just how far you can stretch the software's boundaries to provide a superior online experience and make your visits more productive. ■

Planning Your Online Visits

Many of your online visits will no doubt be motivated by the thrill of discovery and adventure. I'm not one to pour cold water on the fun of just hanging out and looking around. But, if you take a few moments to plan what you're going to do during your visit, and the places you're going to visit, you can definitely make your logins more productive and save a few bucks, too.

The best way to make your online visits more fun is to have a plan of action before you log on. Decide in advance the areas you want to visit, and what you want to do when you get there. Here's a sample plan to govern a typical visit (feel free to adjust this to your special needs):

1. Check e-mail.
2. Send responses to previously composed e-mail.
3. Check messages in your favorite online forum(s).
4. Respond to messages that interest you.
5. Attend online conference.
6. Choose software to download, using the Download Later Option.
7. Set FlashSession to receive files.
8. Log off.

Getting There Faster with the Favorite Places Feature

One of the quickest ways to speed up travel around AOL is to add your favorite AOL spots (see fig. 4.1) to the list of Favorite Places. This is done by simply clicking the heart-shaped icon at the upper right of an area's title bar, which brings up a request for you to confirm that you want the area added to your list (see fig. 4.2).

FIG. 4.1
Click the heart-shaped icon on the right side of the title bar to add this area to your list of Favorite Places.

Favorite Places icon

FIG. 4.2
If you do want your Favorite Places selection added to the list, a sound and screen message will confirm your selection.

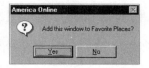

You can bring up your Favorite Places directory at any time while using your AOL software by clicking the heart-shaped folder icon at the right side of the program's Flashbar. You can also select a general preference to display the Favorite Places window as soon as your AOL program starts. Once you've added an item to your personal Favorite Places listing (see fig. 4.3), you can go to a specific site by double-clicking its entry. And it even works on Internet newsgroups and Web sites.

FIG. 4.3
Your personal Favorite Places window displays the online areas you've added. You can move the selections around as you see fit by selecting and dragging an item to its new position.

Part

I

Ch

4

Learning the Ropes

Throughout this book, I'll cover the subjects of participating in message boards, using AOL FlashSessions, and the most effective ways to find and download software that interests you. Some of the chapters about these subjects you might want to read include Chapter 6, "Where Do We Begin?," Chapter 8, "Using America Online E-Mail," Chapter 9, "Using America Online Message Boards," Chapter 10, "Chatting Online," and Chapter 20, "Tips and Tricks on Finding Software."

Making Your AOL Software Work Faster

Your enjoyment of your online visits can be much greater if you can only get your AOL software to work better. Not every step I'm about to describe comes free; some of it involves getting new hardware. But, by considering these options, you may be able to fine-tune your AOL software for the maximum possible performance on your PC. You'll also want to read the section following this one, "AOL Software Add-Ons," for brief descriptions of some very popular software that will make your online visits go faster and more efficiently.

You can speed up your AOL software by doing one or more of the following:

- *Get a Faster Modem*. America Online supports connection speeds of up to 28,800 bps (V.34) in many U.S. cities. If you have a high-speed access number in your city, a faster modem will more than pay for itself in reduced online charges. It will also make your AOL software perform at a much higher level, not only for software downloads and uploads, but for text display, too. Keyword **Access** enables you to review the latest telephone connection numbers. You'll learn more about getting the best possible performance from your modem in Chapter 41, "Secrets of High-Speed Access on AOL."

- *Get a Faster PC*. If you have more than one PC at your home or work site, installing AOL software on the fastest computer offers speedier screen redraws, faster application launching, and other performance enhancements. If you have an older model, the new low-cost Pentium PCs, and their extraordinary higher speed capability, can be quite attractive items to consider.

- *Get More RAM*. Viewing graphics files is RAM-intensive, and using AOL's integrated Web browser with its image caching routine can also eat up additional memory. Computer manufacturers, striving to keep costs down, often supply the bare minimum amount of memory with their models. You may want to consider a RAM upgrade at the earliest opportunity.

- *Operating System Fine-Tuning*. There are a huge number of software products that are designed to add functions to the Windows operating system, or add cute little effects, visual and sound. But, some of these programs can also rob your computer of the best possible performance, or cause incompatibilities with other software. You should always select system enhancements with care, and see if they really do improve the way your computer runs, and not the reverse. Product reviews in your favorite computing magazine (many of which have forums on AOL) are a good resource on this subject.

AOL Software Add-Ons

AOL's own software provides an enormous degree of flexibility, enabling you to automate a number of online functions. The ability to easily include your regular online spots as part of your custom Favorite Sites listing, for example, makes for fast navigation around the network. However, there are some convenient tools available that not only provide some features missing from AOL's software, but will add extraordinary power to help automate your online visits.

N O T E In order to locate any file in the software libraries of AOL's Computing department, including the ones that are described in this chapter, simply choose the Find command from the Go To menu of your Windows AOL software and select the option to search for software. When the search window comes up, enter the name or subject of your file search in the list field. A complete list of the selections that match your search will appear in a few seconds. To get more information about a file, and to download the file, simply double-click the name of a file that interests you from the listings you receive. For more information on finding and downloading software, see Chapter 20, "Tips and Tricks on Finding Software." ▪

CAUTION

The arrival of Windows 95 has created a big question mark about the compatibility of some of the Add-On programs for AOL's software. If you are using Microsoft's new operating system, you'll want to read online file descriptions carefully before downloading the programs you want. You can expect that many of these handy utilities will be upgraded as necessary to be fully compatible with Windows 95 and future versions of AOL's own software.

You'll find these and other handy programs listed in the Windows AOL Add-Ons library of the Windows forum (keyword: **Windows forum**).

N O T E Before downloading any of these handy Windows AOL utilities, be sure to check the file descriptions about hardware and software needs. Some of these programs (such as PowerTools) require that you install Visual Basic Runtime Version 3.0, a free program available in AOL's software libraries, which can be located using the File Search tool. For more information on finding and downloading software, see Chapter 20, "Tips and Tricks on Finding Software." ▪

CAUTION

Although the programs described in this chapter are very popular with users of the Windows version of AOL software, they are not officially supported or endorsed by America Online, Inc. You are therefore using such software at your own risk. Should you have any problems in using this software, your best resources for support are the publishers or authors of these programs.

Part

I

Ch

4

CROOM

Author: **Tartan Software**

CROOM is a program that adds style and color to your chat and conference room visits (see fig. 4.4). Features include the ability to highlight other members' chat text in the color of your choice, choosing another font or type style for chat text, and changing the background color. You can also send macros created in other programs (such as Whale Express, which is described later in this chapter) from your keyboard.

FIG. 4.4
Add style and color to your chat room visits with CROOM, which has enhanced the chat room shown.

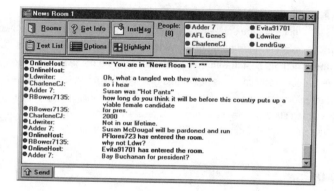

CROOM also offers an expanded people list, so you can see an expanded listing of those present in a chat. You also have an Ignore Members option, which enables you to hide the chat text originating from the members you designate. At the risk of seeming anti-social, it's a way to cope with possible online harassment, or for times when you may not wish to be in touch with a particular member for reasons of your own. Settings you make are saved by the program, so they can be used again for future online visits.

PICPOP

Author: **Compunik Creations**

Here's a shareware program that adds exciting multimedia possibilities to your online visits. It works with your e-mail, instant messages, message board postings, and your chat room postings. After it's installed, in the material you send, you simply type:

```
{p picfile soundfile}
```

(Picfile refers to the name of your picture file, and soundfile refers to the name of your sound file.) When the recipient opens this material, a picture pops up on the recipient's screen, and a sound plays. The program supports BMP and GIF image file formats, and the WAV sound format.

N O T E To see the pictures and hear the sounds, your recipient also has to have a copy of PICPOP installed, along with the corresponding picture and sound files. ▨

You change the default sounds of Windows AOL just like you change any other sound association, through the Control Panel.

SWEETALK

Author: **Compunik Creations**

SWEETALK (see fig. 4.5) attaches fixed sounds and images to your online messages, but this program goes one step further. The authors tell me that this shareware program is dedicated to online romantics. It offers the following features:

FIG. 4.5
SWEETALK puts up a movable button bar that can be used to access its features.

- When SWEETALK is opened (or closed), Windows AOL automatically opens and closes, too.
- SWEETALK lets you send a sound (or a WAV) to "say" sweet stuff to your online friend or sweetheart (male or female equally implied).
- SWEETALK lets you send phrases (sweet nothings), up to 1,000 characters, without typing them.
- SWEETALK saves that special e-mail or posted message to a file with the click of a button.
- When you go online, clicking a button called Who's-On-First very quickly tells you if your friends are online and where. Then a couple of clicks enable you to send Instant Messages to the ones that are online.
- For those times when someone is sending you not-so-sweet Instant Messages (IMs), there is a virtual switch that automatically turns IMs off and on.
- SWEETALK also offers meters that display how long you have been sweet-talking in the pay areas and free areas of AOL.
- SWEETALK gives you a convenient scrollable list of sounds and phrases.

PowerTools for AOL

Author: **BPS SoftWare**

By far the most popular AOL add-on is probably PowerTools. More than 110,000 AOL members had downloaded various versions of this shareware program as of the time this book was being prepared. The program offers a set of very powerful enhancements for AOL's program (see fig. 4.6). The major features include a colorized chat room, a macro "phrase" manager, an instant answering machine, and a wide array of other tools. The product's Control Panel attaches to the bottom of your AOL window and provides buttons and controls for many common and special tasks. A wide variety of add-on modules greatly increases the program's flexibility.

FIG. 4.6

When you install PowerTools, the entire look and feel of your AOL software undergoes many changes, typified by the new, expanded toolbar functions shown here.

Here are some of the major features of this program:

- PowerTools gives you many options to customize your AOL Flashbar, and its own toolbars.

- A Hotlist Manager replaces AOL's Favorite Places feature, and lets you store additional locations to revisit, such as your favorite People Connection rooms, ftp sites, and more.

- An Auto SignOn feature expands upon AOL's FlashSession feature by enabling you to automatically log on whenever you perform a function that requires you to be online.

- PowerTools replaces AOL's chat room window with its own Color Chat window, which enables you to assign colors for member names, extract chat text by member name, and enhance your logging options.

- PowerTools incorporates a Get In button that keeps trying to enter a crowded chat room until someone leaves, enabling you to automatically enter.

- You can establish a library of standard text phrases, organize them by category, and use the program's Phrase Manager to play them as you wish. You can even insert variables within your stored phrases, so phrases can be linked. The phrases can be sent as part of your e-mail, instant messages, or message board postings.

- An IM Manager can be configured to return Instant Messages with preselected phrases, arrange IM windows neatly on your desktop, selectively ignore messages, and log the messages to a file complete with your comments.

■ Additional features let you manage your text messages, send WAV files from a pop-up list, and keep an accurate billing log of your online sessions, covering all screen names, so you can keep precise records of your accumulated online time.

PowerTools has enhancements for just about everything you do online (and perhaps many of the things you only imagined doing more efficiently). Because it is shareware, you can try it before you buy—it may become an indispensable tool for you.

Whale Express

Author: **Bill Pytlovany (Tartan Software)**

Whale Express is a scripting utility that enables you to create scripts to sign-on, sign-off, retrieve and send mail, send and capture text and posts, and more. The version posted on AOL is a trial version that lets you store up to 10 commands. When you download Whale Express, you'll find ordering information in the README file.

Whale Express comes with sample scripts and Windows-based help that assists you in writing powerful online scripts to automate your AOL visit. Even capturing e-mail from multiple screen names is possible with the NewScreenName command.

E-mail can be created while you are offline using the Whale Express integrated editor, and sent via the SendMail script command. Online lectures can be prepared and reused over and over using the SendText command. Entire message boards can now be read and captured in a text file with the intelligent ReadList command.

The scripting language is easy to understand and requires no knowledge of complex programming structures. Error handling and calling other scripts can all be done with simple commands.

Part

I

Ch

4

AOL for OS/2?

If you're a user of OS/2, you might be hoping that a version of America Online's software specifically tailored for this operating system might come some day. But, it isn't something you should hold your breath for. However, as I've explained in Chapter 19, "Visiting the Computing and Software Forums," there is indeed a very active OS/2 forum on AOL, and the forum creators had to get online somehow to write about it.

With a little advice from the folks at the OS/2 forum, I've put together a few tips to get AOL's software up and running with pretty good compatibility in that environment. AOL's programmers have put a special (and largely unrecognized) emphasis on ensuring optimal compatibility with the Windows version of AOL's software OS/2's Win-OS/2, both Seamless and Full Screen Modes.

Here are some suggestions you might consider to get the best possible performance from the Windows AOL-OS/2 combo:

- For proper connections to AOL, you MUST have a serial I/O card that has a 16550a UART (an 8K buffer chip) on it or an internal modem that has a 16550a UART on it. Most older serial cards don't have a 16550a UART, but fortunately a new card with a 16550a UART is fairly inexpensive and readily available at most retail outlets.

- Download and install Ray Gwinn's SIO COM drivers for OS/2. You can get a copy of SIO from the OS/2 Forum library's "Top Picks" area. I'll include some settings a little later in this section.

- Increase EMS_MEMORY_LIMIT to 8M in your Windows AOL software object settings notebook.

- Set IDLE_SENSITIVITY to 100 in the same settings notebook.

- Run your windows AOL software in Standard Mode if possible, as it seems to run better in that mode.

- If you are using Windows for Workgroups v3.11, replace your Windows COM drivers with the Windows v3.1 COM drivers.

- It is reported that on some systems it may be necessary to turn off the AOL Web browser's caching feature, although in other systems the feature seems to work properly.

- As a general rule, you'll want to disable the browser's internal helper applications feature and use external helper applications instead. The OS/2 forum staff reports good success with native OS/2 helper programs.

- Disable your Windows's AOL software's auto-extraction (expansion) feature. For file compression and expanding utilities, you'll want to use InfoZip's ZIP and UNZIP programs for OS/2. You'll find them available for download from the New Files & Free Uploading library of the OS/2 forum. For additional information, you'll want to check out the file descriptions directly.

- In some cases setting SIO_Mode_DTR to Handshake Signal will help provide better connections to AOL.

- Similarly, the OS/2 experts on AOL suggest you set SIO_Screen_Sync_Kludge to ON.

If you're still having problems getting your AOL software to work properly under OS/2, contact the folks at the OS/2 forum for assistance. Keyword: **OS/2**.

> **CAUTION**
>
> There have been some reports of occasional difficulty during the initial installation (but not updating) of Windows AOL software when the SIO drivers are installed. The workaround for this is to do the initial installation of the program under native DOS/Windows. You might also try temporarily disabling the SIO/VSIO drivers and re-enabling the native OS/2 COM/VCOM drivers in your OS/2 config.sys. Then reboot and install your Windows AOL software, disable OS/2's native COM/VCOM drivers and re-enable the SIO/VSIO drivers and reboot again.

Keyboard Power

Even if you haven't enhanced your ability to navigate through AOL's software with some of the handy macro utilities I've discussed in this chapter, there is still a good basic set of keyboard commands available that you should keep in mind.

Table 4.1 is a list of many of the keyboard shortcuts available with your America Online Windows software. They are based on AOL version 3.0, which became available at the time this book was written. Future software versions may offer additional shortcuts.

Part

I

Ch

4

Table 4.1   Keyboard Shortcuts for Windows

Function	Keyboard Shortcut
Access Download Manager	Ctrl+T
Cancel an action	Esc
Cascade windows	Shift+F5
Close a window	Ctrl+F4
Copy	Ctrl+C
Cut	Ctrl+X
Find a member, file, area	Ctrl+F
Get member profile	Ctrl+G
Locate a member online	Ctrl+L
Move to next button	Tab
Move to next window	Ctrl+F6
Move to previous button	Shift+Tab
Open a new text file	Ctrl+N

continues

Table 4.1 Continued

Function	Keyboard Shortcut
Open an existing file	Ctrl+O
Open Channel	Ctrl+D
Open Keyword window	Ctrl+K
Open Mail window	Ctrl+M
Paste	Ctrl+V
Read new mail	Ctrl+R
Save a file	Ctrl+S
Scroll down a page	Page Down
Scroll up a page	Page Up
Send an instant message	Ctrl+I
Tile windows	Shift+F4

From Here...

Beyond the menus and commands, it is easy to configure America Online Windows software to provide greatly enhanced performance and make your online visits more fun and more productive. AOL's software libraries contain dozens of handy utilities in addition to the ones I've described here. By spending a little time browsing through the file descriptions, you'll find many additional techniques to increase your online computing power.

- You'll find a detailed overview of AOL's services throughout this book, but your best launching point is Chapter 6, "Where Do We Begin?"

- If you want your children to share your online experiences with you, read the three chapters in Part IV, "Kids and America Online."

- The mysteries behind the global Internet network are explained in the chapters that comprise Part VIII, "Entering the Information Superhighway."

- If you're new to America Online, you'll want to read Appendix A, "If You're New to the Online World."

- New users of AOL's Windows software will want to read Appendix C, "Using Your America Online Windows Software."

America Online and Mobile Computing

We live in a mobile society. We travel often, and whether it's for business or pleasure, no doubt you'll want your personal computer at hand to stay in touch, or to get some necessary work done. Whether you take a Macintosh PowerBook or PC laptop with you, you probably want to reach out to the world awaiting you on America Online. ■

Getting connected

Quickly find your local access numbers to America Online.

Finding new connection numbers

Change your access numbers in your America Online software.

Connecting to AOL at 28,800 bps

Choose from hundreds of high-speed access numbers worldwide.

Easily connecting in different cities

Save multiple-connection settings that you can switch to with a couple of mouse clicks.

Accessing AOL while traveling

Log on to AOL easily from hotels and offices in cities across the world.

Enjoying mobile computing

Prepare your portable computer for travel.

Finding Local Access Numbers

Online services are quite competitive, and the cost of connecting to America Online, in particular, will come down over time to keep up with industry price trends. Unless you have money to burn, though, you still need to watch your online costs. By finding the closest number to the place from which you are calling, you keep your telephone bills from going through the ceiling.

Although not every location in the United States has a local access number, most do, and those are the ones you want to use. In addition, through AOL's GlobalNet access network, you can also hook up to America Online in other parts of the world.

After you know the number, you also need to tell the America Online software that you know it. Locating those numbers involves just a few quick steps.

Getting Numbers the Easy Way

In the latest releases of America Online's Mac and Windows software, you can find a local access number not only while you're online or when you're first configuring your America Online software (see Appendixes B and C), but anytime you find yourself wanting to call America Online from a location where you are not certain of your local access number.

If you have not already done so, open the America Online program and select New Local# from the pop-up menu (see fig. 5.1). If you need to dial 9 or some other access code to reach an outside line, first enter that code in the connection setup document. The same goes for any codes you have to enter to disable call waiting. Refer to Appendix B, "Using Your America Online Macintosh Software," and Appendix C, "Using Your America Online Windows Software," for information on setting options in the Connection Settings dialog box.

FIG. 5.1
New Local# is America Online's automated process to find your local access number.

With your calling options now set, begin the connection to America Online's toll-free number by clicking the Sign On button, or pressing Enter. In just a few seconds, you are looking at America Online's Access Number Location screen (see fig. 5.2). To find the location of the phone numbers closest to you, simply enter the area code so that the program knows what area of the country to search for your access numbers. Enter the area code from which you're calling, or an area code from somewhere you plan to travel, and click the Continue button.

FIG. 5.2
Type your area code in America Online's Access Number Locator window.

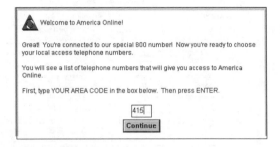

The next step is to select your first connection number from the list of available access numbers (see fig. 5.3).

FIG. 5.3
You can choose your first connection choice from a list of numbers.

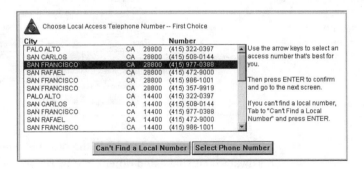

To select a number as your first choice, double-click the number closest to the location from which you are calling (or will be calling). Now, in case you're unable to connect using the first number, the America Online host computers repeat the process by asking you to select a number as your second choice. Double-click the number of your second choice, or optionally click the Same as First Choice button if no other number is acceptable. If you are unable to locate a nearby access number, the Can't Find a Local Number button will offer you the choice of phone numbers in another area code that might be suitable (but you'll want to check long-distance charges to be sure it's practical).

Now the Magic Begins

After you confirm your access number choices, America Online disconnects from the toll-free 800 number and automatically presents you with a new, untitled Connection Settings window with the selected numbers already entered in the proper places (see fig. 5.4 for the Mac version and fig. 5.5 for the Windows variation).

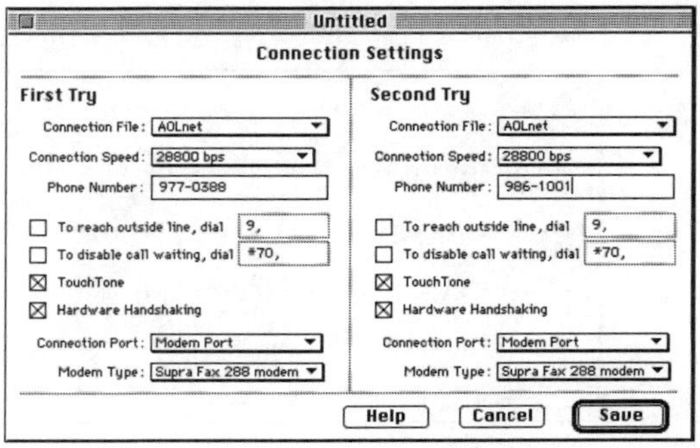

FIG. 5.4

The two access numbers you selected are automatically entered in their respective boxes in the Mac version of AOL software.

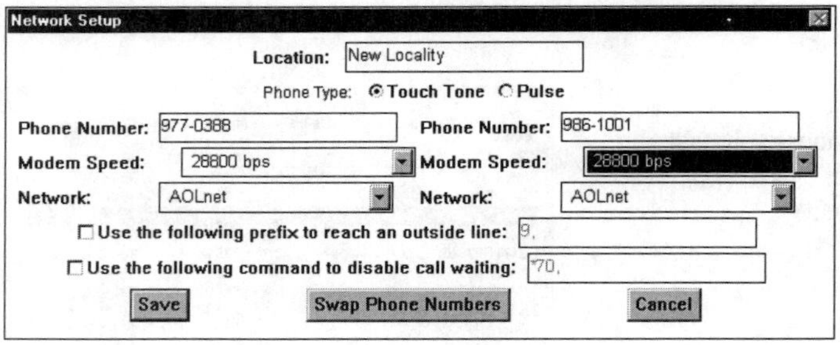

FIG. 5.5

The Windows version of AOL software offers similar settings, but with an option to swap phone numbers.

The new setup window matches your regular Setup box, but without custom-calling settings, such as hardware handshake and other options. Before saving this file, you should add whatever additional options you want.

After you make your corrections or changes, choose Save from the File menu, and enter the name of your new Locality file. When I travel, I generally name the files after the city to which I'm traveling, such as Boston, Paris, San Francisco, and so on.

Wait! I'm Already Signed On!

Great! You like to plan ahead, which is better than a last-minute scramble to take care of forgotten details. If you're already online and want to find local access numbers, enter the keyword **Access**. You are then taken to a free area online that contains a database of all the access phone numbers you could ever need while on your world-wide excursions (see fig. 5.6).

FIG. 5.6
Use America Online's local telephone access number menu to find a local connection.

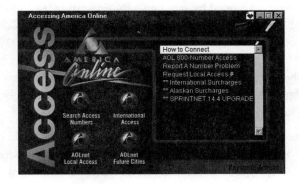

These numbers are generally considered local telephone calls from most cities and do not incur toll charges from most residential telephones. If the nearest access number is not a local call, your local telephone service adds the per-minute charges to your phone bill. These charges are separate from the America Online connect time charges. You might want to call the phone company in the city you're visiting to learn just what toll charges you might incur. This may be important if you're connecting from a hotel, where you may be charged an extra fee for long-distance access.

After you arrive at the Accessing America Online screen in the free area (an area where you don't incur online charges), click the Search Access Numbers item, and press Return or Enter on your keyboard to open the Search Access Numbers screen (see fig. 5.7).

Part
I

Ch
5

FIG. 5.7
The Search Access Numbers screen is the most versatile method of locating the AOL connection number closest to you.

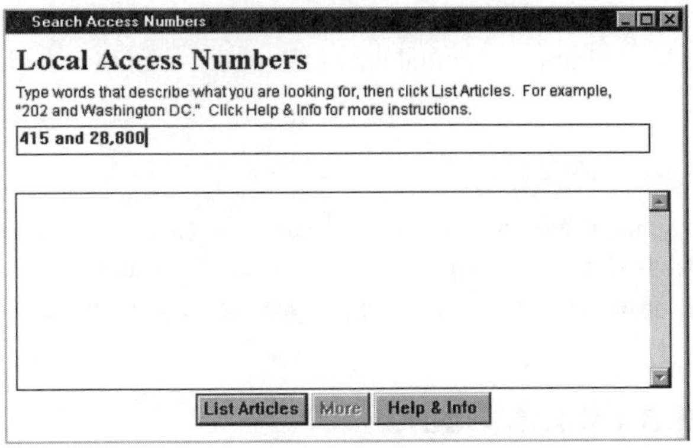

Search Access Numbers

Local Access Numbers

Type words that describe what you are looking for, then click List Articles. For example, "202 and Washington DC." Click Help & Info for more instructions.

415 and 28,800

List Articles   More   Help & Info

A text entry field, which is the smaller of the two panes in the window, is set up for you to enter the location or area code from which you are calling.

America Online has arranged the telephone number database into a collection of searchable documents arranged by area code. Entering the area code from which you're calling is the fastest way to locate a nearby access number. In figure 5.7, 415 has been entered as the area code from which to connect to America Online; 28,800 indicates that the search should be for numbers offering 28,000 bps access for this area code. If no 28,800 bps access numbers are available in the entered area code, the search will result in no matches. If 28,800 bps numbers are found in the area code, then all access numbers are displayed, including lower-speed access numbers.

Because not all areas have 28,800 bps hookups yet, you'll probably want to enter just the area code by itself in the search field. Then click the List Articles button or press Return or Enter to display the matching online document containing the results of the search (see fig. 5.8).

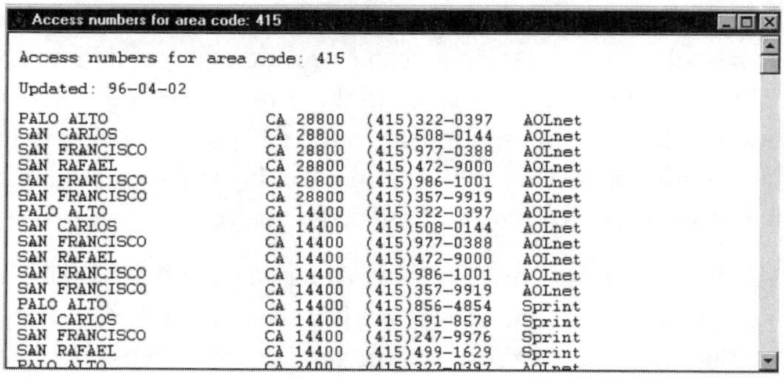

FIG. 5.8
Here are the results from the search for numbers in area code 415.

```
Access numbers for area code: 415

Access numbers for area code: 415

Updated: 96-04-02

PALO ALTO          CA 28800   (415)322-0397   AOLnet
SAN CARLOS         CA 28800   (415)508-0144   AOLnet
SAN FRANCISCO      CA 28800   (415)977-0388   AOLnet
SAN RAFAEL         CA 28800   (415)472-9000   AOLnet
SAN FRANCISCO      CA 28800   (415)986-1001   AOLnet
SAN FRANCISCO      CA 28800   (415)357-9919   AOLnet
PALO ALTO          CA 14400   (415)322-0397   AOLnet
SAN CARLOS         CA 14400   (415)508-0144   AOLnet
SAN FRANCISCO      CA 14400   (415)977-0388   AOLnet
SAN RAFAEL         CA 14400   (415)472-9000   AOLnet
SAN FRANCISCO      CA 14400   (415)986-1001   AOLnet
SAN FRANCISCO      CA 14400   (415)357-9919   AOLnet
PALO ALTO          CA 14400   (415)856-4854   Sprint
SAN CARLOS         CA 14400   (415)591-8578   Sprint
SAN FRANCISCO      CA 14400   (415)247-9976   Sprint
SAN RAFAEL         CA 14400   (415)499-1629   Sprint
PALO ALTO          CA 2400    (415)322-0397   AOLnet
```

If you want to view the numbers contained in the document, double-click the title to open a window containing the actual list of telephone numbers and the cities in which they are located.

> **CAUTION**
> There's an extra charge for using AOL's 800 phone number, some AOL numbers in Canada, and AOL's GlobalNet service in other parts of the world. Check the updated rates shown in the Access area before using any of these numbers, so you won't see any unexpected surprises added to your AOL bill.

Maintaining a Phone Book

I heartily recommend that you save the entire list of numbers for your chosen area code, and not just the number closest to your current location. If you unexpectedly find yourself a city or two away from your usual calling place, looking up the nearest number is as simple as double-clicking the saved list. Choose Save from the America Online File menu to save the list to your hard disk or floppy. Or just choose File, Print to make a hard copy of your list of phone numbers.

Searching by area code is simple; it offers you all the numbers serving the area in which you live, and keeps you prepared when you need to call from anywhere in your area code's coverage (and, in many cases, even nearby area codes).

 You also can search for an access number by typing a city name, the communications carrier (AOLNet, SprintNet, or Tymnet), or even the first three digits of the telephone number.

What to Do When You're Not Near a Phone

If you don't have immediate access to your computer or to America Online, there's another way to get the nearest local access number, and that is to telephone SprintNet, which provides a large portion of AOL's high-speed connection network. Just dial 1-800-473-7983, and tell the operator your location. The operator will suggest the nearest access numbers.

 Before you hit the trail, please be sure to make a note of the local access numbers for your destination. You can find these numbers easily while you're online, as described earlier in this section.

You might want to get more than one number, just in case the primary number you try is busy for some reason. Using the steps described earlier in this chapter, you can create new Location setups to add these new numbers.

CAUTION

Please bear in mind that SprintNet's operators don't usually have a map handy. So it's up to you to determine whether the numbers you get are local or not. Usually a quick call to the local phone company will produce that information.

Part

I

Ch

5

Changing Your Modem Setup

Earlier in this chapter, you learned how to have America Online software locate numbers for you by searching the database of access numbers. You can learn one more trick: creating new connection documents by editing existing connection settings offline.

By creating new connection documents in this fashion, you are able to save various options and access numbers for simple point-and-shoot selection from the Welcome to America Online screen, as shown earlier in figure 5.1. One reason for doing this is to connect to the same access numbers from two locations; one that requires you to dial 9 to reach an outside line (such as an office, perhaps), and the other that doesn't (such as your home).

For more information about setting up your modem, see Appendixes A, "If You're New to the Online World," B, "Using Your America Online Macintosh Software," and C, "Using Your America Online Windows Software."

1. Open America Online.
2. Choose New Location from the Select Location pop-up menu on your sign-on screen.

   This brings up the screen shown in figure 5.9.

FIG. 5.9
You can create a new
location profile by using
America Online's new
location management
feature.

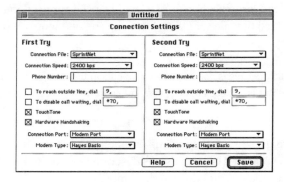

3. Enter the appropriate information and check the options you need. Appendixes B and C describe the options you'll want to consider. Don't forget to select a modem type and communications port, if necessary.
4. Click the Save button to give your new setup a name and write it to your hard drive.

After saving the new setup to your hard drive, you can select it from the Locality pop-up menu that appears when you open America Online.

By this point, you have all the information you need to enter the correct information in your America Online Connection Setup documents, obtain that information from America Online, and add and change new connection documents when your travel plans dictate.

Sending Faxes on America Online

We know the Information Superhighway still needs a few more on- and off-ramps for the rest of the world. When the time comes to send mail to someone who does not yet have access to AOL or other e-mail services, what can you do? Why, send regular U.S. mail or a fax, of course!

Using your America Online software to send information is just as easy as sending e-mail. In fact, the only difference between e-mail and fax/paper mail is how the mail is addressed. The form is exactly the same as the one you use to send e-mail to online members.

You can send paper or fax mail by following these steps:

1. From the Mail menu, select Send Fax/Paper Mail. Alternatively, select Compose Mail.
2. In the To field, type:

    Addressee Name@usmail

    For example, to send paper mail to John Smith, type:

    John Smith@usmail

3. Type in the addressee name exactly as it would appear on an envelope, as many as 33 characters. You will be prompted later for the complete mail address and your own return address.

    You are able to easily send the same message to multiple postal addresses by separating each addressee name with a comma. For example:

    John Smith@usmail, Jane Jones@usmail, Mike Johnson@usmail

N O T E You cannot send a message to paper mail and regular e-mail or paper mail and fax mail addresses at the same time. ■

4. When you are ready to send your mail, select the Send Now icon.
5. You are presented with a window to enter the return address. Enter the address, select Continue, and type the address to which your paper mail should be sent.

Certain formatting rules apply to paper mail. You can learn more about these rules, and other information unique to paper mail, online by choosing Mail, Fax/Paper while connected to the America Online service.

Part

I

Ch

5

Fax mail is even easier. In the Compose Mail window, type the fax address in the To or CC field in this format:

addressee@phone number, such as **John Smith@415-555-1234**

Voila! Your fax is on its way.

The phone number portion of the address must contain the area code of the receiving number and should not contain any other prefixes, such as a 1, before the area code. You can send fax mail to other fax addresses by separating the addresses with a comma, as in paper mail, and you can send fax mail to normal AOL screen name addresses by way of additional recipients listed in the To or CC boxes. As with paper mail, special formatting rules apply. You can learn about these rules using the same path as paper mail.

N O T E When you send e-mail or an instant message, you only pay for your online time. Fax or paper mail is an extra cost service. You'll want to review America Online's current prices before you use this feature. ■

If you have general questions about the fax or paper mail service, or specific questions about fax or paper mail you've sent, send your questions to America Online through the free customer support area online; the keyword is **Help**.

Why Send E-Mail to Yourself?

Nope, it's not just another way to talk to yourself.

It's clearly difficult, if not impossible, to take everything you need for efficient computing with you on a trip. Later in this chapter, in the section titled "Hard-Won Tips for Computing on the Road," I describe some of the essential items you should pack in your bag. The important watchword in personal computing, though, is backup. You should back up all of your critical documents on another disk, if possible. That way, if your computer breaks down or your hard drive fails for some reason, you have another copy of your document to work on.

Having an extra drive or two on the road isn't always practical, but America Online gives you a convenient outlet to back up your most important work—the service's e-mail feature. Simply attach any file that you work on to a piece of America Online e-mail (see Chapter 8, "Using America Online E-Mail"), and send it to yourself. The file will be waiting safely in your America Online mailbox when you arrive home. It will wait up to one month for your arrival (after a month, e-mail is automatically deleted from your online mailbox).

America Online and Cellular Phones

They are found all over the countryside. Cellular telephones are used by millions of people on the road to stay in touch with the office or the home. Almost every part of the country can support cellular connections. There are times when you will travel to places where no telephone line is handy, but you still need to stay in touch. You may want to consider attaching a modem to your cellular telephone so that you can connect to your favorite online service—America Online. Unfortunately, cellular phones, while quite reliable in regular use, present unique problems in maintaining stable connections.

 TIP To avoid getting a `Mail Waiting` notice every time you log on while on vacation, you can create an alternate screen name and have mail you don't want to read right away addressed there.

Connecting to a Cellular Telephone

The important thing to realize is that, while the technology behind them is truly a wonderful achievement, cellular telephone connections aren't nearly as stable as your regular home telephone. As you travel from place to place, the signal from your telephone is passed off from one cellular center to another. The quality of the signal can vary as you drive past tall buildings and hills. To cope with this occurrence, Microcom, a developer of the technology for modem error correction schemes, has an MNP-10 error correction protocol that's supported by some modems. The manual for your modem should indicate whether this compression scheme is supported.

A modem that doesn't have MNP-10 most likely works, but at reduced efficiency. You also need an interface of some sort to hook up directly to a cellular telephone. Global Village, a manufacturer of Macintosh modems, has a product that is designed to provide improved cellular connections. Called the PowerPort Coupler, this product is a base to which you can attach the headset of your cellular phone (or even a pay phone). The other end hooks into your laptop's modem. This acoustic coupler promises reliable transmissions at up to 9600 bps.

Many PC-card modems include support for MNP-10. If you have a PC laptop or a recent Macintosh PowerBook computer (or a similar model), you may want to check into one of these products. Two manufacturers of cellular-compatible, high-speed modems are Apex and Megahertz. Many PC-card modems designed for a PC will work on a Mac that supports this interface, although you may need different software. Check with the manufacturer about compatibility issues.

Part
I

Ch
5

Wireless Modems

One solution to this dilemma is the arrival of devices that incorporate a cellular telephone and a modem (wireless modems). Manufacturers such as Motorola are introducing these units that, although presenting the utmost in convenience while traveling, are higher priced than a separate phone and modem.

There's yet another type of wireless modem, one that operates similarly to your stereo or TV's remote control. This sort of modem includes a transmission/receiving device that attaches to your standard phone line (or even the modem jack on a cellular phone) and to a convenient AC outlet. The modem itself looks similar to a regular PC-card modem, but has a small rectangular module attached to it that exchanges signals with the device that's hooked up to your phone line.

One wireless modem I've used is the AirPlex from VST Power Systems, Inc. (a manufacturer of accessories for Macintosh PowerBooks). The AirPlex has a transmission range of up to 50 feet. It gives you the freedom of total portability—you can telecommunicate free of both your power and phone lines (well, at least until the battery power runs out).

Hard-Won Tips for Computing on the Road

I know that business trips sometimes come on short notice, and there isn't much time to plan in advance. But if you take a few moments to assemble your computing equipment and add a few extras, your mobile personal computing experience and your visits to America Online will be fast, efficient, and relatively trouble-free. A few ideas follow to make computing on the road easier.

When you book your hotel reservation, it is a good idea to ask if the phones in the rooms have a data port—a euphemism for a modem line. Many hotel phones do not have such a connection, although an increasing number do. If the room doesn't have a modem connection, but it has a standard modular (RJ-11) phone plug, you can disconnect that plug from the telephone and attach it directly to your modem (I've done it often).

But here's the important part: Double-check to see if the hotel is using a PBX (digital) telephone system. A PBX system provides state-of-the-art service, but it's also a serious problem for an analog telephone device, such as your computer's modem. Hooking up your modem to a PBX line may damage the modem. If the hotel uses a PBX installation, contact the manufacturer of your modem as to whether they have a special interface card or module for use with such services. Global Village Corporation has such an interface available; the device is designed for use with their modems, but may work with other models too, on both a Mac and a PC. Another product you might consider is the DataDapter from Konexx, which is designed to work with any modem.

A final bit of advice: Some hotels will exact a large surcharge for telephone calls you make from your room (even local calls in many cases). You may find, after your arrival, that another access number for America Online will run up a lower surcharge. At the very least, you may want to be more careful about the amount of time you spend online if the hotel adds a per-minute charge for your call.

Before leaving on a trip, you'll probably want to get some useful accessories that are bound to make your laptop computer work more effectively on the road. The following sections concentrate strictly on items that you can easily pack in a portable computer case or an overnight bag. A visit to your favorite computer dealer will reveal many more treasures from which to choose.

N O T E If you experience sudden disconnections while you're online, it may be because someone is trying to reach you on the hotel phone. Before beginning your AOL session, you may want to ask the hotel operator to hold your calls (if possible) until you're done to avoid this problem. ▉

Modem—Internal or External?

If you're buying a new laptop computer, you may want to consider the convenience of having it equipped with an internal modem. Although it may cost a few bucks extra, you don't need to pack an extra device in your storage case. Because America Online is adding 28,800 bps (V.34) connection numbers throughout the country, consider a high-speed modem. It'll also help you save money because your online sessions will be shorter, and, if you connect with a long-distance call or with a cellular phone, your phone bills also will be reduced.

N O T E External modems will generally work on both a Macintosh or a PC. The only difference is the modem cable and the software. However, internal modems (except for PC-card models) are usually designed to support a specific computing platform or model. Make sure a modem is fully compatible with your laptop before you purchase it. ▉

Part
I

Ch
5

Portable Fixed Hard Drive

The hard drives that come in laptops (except for the most expensive models) generally have limited capacity. They are also expensive to replace. If you're doing a large presentation or heavy-duty graphics work requiring a great deal of storage space, you'll want to consider products such as the APS Technologies Companion II or the Liberty portable drives, both of which offer the extra storage capacity you may need in small, convenient cases. VST Power Systems, Inc. also has a line of high-capacity drives and magneto-optical (MO) devices that fit into the expansion bay of some laptop computers.

For laptops with one or more PC-card slots, you may want to look into adding a small hard drive to fit into a slot (if the slots aren't already occupied). One manufacturer of such products is Kingston Technology, which also manufactures a hard drive that attaches to the parallel port of a PC.

Portable Removable Hard Drive

If you need to transfer files to different locations, a removable drive is a plus. The ever-popular Iomega ZIP drive uses media hardly bigger than a floppy disk. The 3 1/2-inch Iomega Jaz and SyQuest cartridges weigh just three ounces and are also quite suitable for travel.

 If your laptop computer has a PC-card slot, you can plug in an additional drive or other peripheral device, such as a high-speed modem. Check the manual or contact the manufacturer for expansion compatibility.

Other convenient removable devices include the Zip drive and Bernoulli cartridge drives from Iomega, and a portable optical drive (which is available from a number of manufacturers).

If you need high capacity, consider Iomega's Jaz or SyQuest's SyJet, both of which support low-cost media that stores more than 1G of data.

 Some laptops provide the ability to customize settings, such as when the hard drive powers down, to conserve battery life. Check your computer's manual for the particulars.

Laptop Carrying Cases

So many shapes and sizes of carrying cases are now available that you are bound to find one that meets your needs. Some products combine an overnight bag with a compartment for your laptop and some accessories. Other cases are hardly larger than the computer. My suggestion is that you get one with straps to hold your laptop computer securely, and with a sufficient amount of cushioning to protect it from the routine hazards of travel. There should be a pouch that is large enough to contain phone and external drive cables, disks, and whatever accessories you need on your trip.

 Always travel with a set of backup operating system disks, hard disk diagnostic disks, and floppy backups for your most important software packages so that you can quickly get up and running in the event of a disk crash.

SCSI Terminator

If your laptop has a SCSI connection port (which is true of all Macintosh models), and you want to hook up an external device to it, you need a SCSI terminator, which is used, in effect, to end the SCSI circuit. You can buy a standard SCSI terminator for $10 to $20 at your local computer or business equipment store. Alternatively, you may want to consider the $39 APS Technologies SCSI Sentry. This is an active terminator that uses digital circuitry to maintain proper current and impedance across the SCSI chain, and reduce problems that sometimes affect a SCSI setup.

Extra Battery and Recharger

If you need to do a long work session on the road, it is probably a good idea to purchase a second battery and a separate recharger that will keep you running when power is low.

Modular Telephone Cord

You can buy a modular telephone cord at your supermarket, if your modem wasn't shipped with one (although they usually are). Just get a simple cable with the standard RJ-11 modular jacks at each end.

Digital Phone Switch

One of the manufacturers of Macintosh PowerBook modems, Global Village, offers a phone switch that provides an interface between a PBX digital phone system and your laptop's modem. It'll work on any Mac or PC.

NOTE Although computer makers generally suggest caution when running your laptop computer and disks through the X-ray devices at an airport security check-in, the chances are almost nonexistent that you would be at risk of damage to your data. If in doubt, insist on a manual inspection. Some laptops, such as the Macintosh PowerBook, can be placed in an idle or sleep mode, rather than shut off, so that they can be quickly activated for the benefit of skeptical airport security personnel. ▪

Part

I

Ch

5

Portable Printer

Even though your travel bag is apt to get crowded with all the accessories you can buy, if you intend to create many documents, you might want to bring along a portable printer. Apple, GCC, Hewlett-Packard, and other manufacturers offer lines of small printers that you can use to process your mission-critical documents during a trip. Don't expect any of these models to be speed demons compared to your desktop printer, but they more than make up for their slower performance in terms of convenience.

TIP If you don't have a portable printer handy and you want a hard copy printout, fax a document to your hotel's fax machine. But remember, your hotel will usually charge for faxes by the page.

TV/VCR Interface

If you expect to use your laptop to generate a slide show or other presentation, you'll want to have an interface unit, such as the Focus L/TV Portable. These products allow you to attach many portable models directly to a TV or VCR. Before buying such a product, however, make sure your computer can work with such a device.

From Here...

Whether your trip is for business purposes or just to satisfy your wanderlust, you'll want to prepare in advance and make certain your computer has all the tools you need in case trouble arises. You'll also want to be certain you can make your America Online connections quickly and efficiently. Chances are that you want to find other America Online members who are nearby. You can search for other America Online members not only by name, but also by hobby, special interest, occupation, and more. You can travel to just about any major city across the globe and still stay in touch with America Online for the latest news and information to make your trip even more rewarding.

For more background information on some of the topics discussed in this chapter, refer to these chapters:

- In Chapter 7, "America Online's People Connection," you can find tips and tricks about meeting fellow AOL members.
- In Chapter 8, "Using America Online E-Mail," you learn all you ever wanted to know (and maybe more) about how AOL's high-speed e-mail system works.
- In Chapter 9, "Using America Online Message Boards," you receive step-by-step directions on how to navigate through message boards, post messages, and search for responses.
- In Chapter 27, "Secrets of AOL's Travel Department," you can learn tips about planning your trip and getting the best prices for airfare, car rental, and your hotel stay.

Where Do We Begin?

The first five chapters of this book offered hints and tips about getting the most out of AOL, both at home and on the road. Chapters 3 and 4, for example, are filled with tips and tricks about making AOL's software work faster and more efficiently for you. Chapter 5 gives you advice on how to handle your sessions while you're on the road, perhaps with your laptop computer and even a cellular phone at hand.

This chapter assumes that you've established your AOL membership, and you've at least had a chance to log on for an online session or two. You might even be an experienced AOL user. But, I'll tell you one thing: even after several years of membership, I wasn't prepared for the sheer depth of features AOL offered until I sat down to write the Using America Online books. Whether you're a beginner or an experienced online traveler, you'll discover that there's a vast world of entertainment and information just waiting to be discovered on America Online. ■

America Online's channels

AOL's online departments offer convenient gateways to the areas you want to visit.

Contacting other members

Learn simple techniques for sending e-mail and instant messages.

Get the software you want

Learn techniques for transferring files on America Online.

Forum chats

Meet with others and discuss topics online in a forum.

Paper Mail/Faxes

Send paper mail and a fax to someone who doesn't have an online account.

The Internet

Get a brief look at the Internet-related features offered by America Online.

Selecting the Right Channel

Finding the right place to visit on AOL is similar to selecting a channel on your TV set, except you click an icon rather than push a button. Once you've signed on to AOL and learned how to get the most out of its highly flexible software, you'll want to do more than just get your feet wet.

Every time you log on to America Online, you'll see the Welcome screen (see fig. 6.1), also known as In The Spotlight. This screen shows you the major highlights of the service and informs you if you have e-mail waiting.

FIG. 6.1
See the highlights and check your new mail when you first log on to America Online.

TROUBLESHOOTING

Hey, what's wrong with my computer? When I connect to AOL, I see a totally different screen from the one you show in your book. Is it me or is it you? It's both. The screen I'm showing here requires version 3.0 of AOL's Mac or Windows software (or a later version) to display properly. Older versions of AOL software will offer up the basic 14 channels and a different Welcome screen format, because those versions of the software don't support the new artwork styles.

To see exactly what I see when I log on to AOL, you'll want to upgrade to the latest and greatest version of the software. To do that, just use the AOL keyword Upgrade to access the download area. And, so long as you use the Download Now feature to get the file to your computer, you don't have to pay for the update. Such a deal!

This chapter goes a bit deeper, beneath the In The Spotlight window, actually, to the Channels screen and more, where you'll explore the various virtual neighborhoods, known as *departments,* of America Online (see fig. 6.2). The Channels screen is located just beneath the In The Spotlight window when you first log on to America Online. The fastest way to bring it up front is just to click the shaded CHANNELS rectangle at the left side of your Welcome screen.

FIG. 6.2
AOL's virtual city is divided into channels, reflecting different areas of the online experience.

Each of the online channels or departments shown in figure 6.2 is identified by a major topic of interest. A channel contains a number of forums, folders, services, and other areas related (sometimes loosely) to that topic. You'll learn more about those areas in Part II, "Communicating Online." For now, we'll just scratch the surface.

N O T E If you've closed the Channel menu during your online session, you can bring it up again by simply opening the Go To menu and choosing Channels. ■

 T I P Almost every area of America Online can be reached by pressing ⌘-K (or Ctrl+K for Windows users) and typing a simple keyword. A list of many of these keywords is included in Appendix E, "America Online Keywords."

Find...

AOL provides a handy search tool to help you find exactly the kind of information or service you want (see fig. 6.3). You can choose from Places and Things, People, or Events online. Just enter the topic that intrigues you in the search screen and AOL's host computer will dig up a list of likely prospects for you.

FIG. 6.3
What do you want to find on AOL? Here's a helpful tool to do it.

Computers and Software

Keyword: **Computing**

Welcome to my home area on America Online. Because people use their personal computers to connect to America Online, the Computing department is clearly one of the most popular places to visit on America Online (see fig. 6.4). Whether you use an Apple Macintosh or a PC running Windows, DOS, or OS/2, you'll find information, help, and extensive libraries of software for you to download in this area. In addition, many of the major hardware and software manufacturers have fully staffed support areas on America Online, where you can get quick solutions to problems with a specific product, or even advice on how to use that product more effectively. You'll learn more about it in Part V, "Computing Resources Online."

FIG. 6.4
America Online's Computing area is one of the service's most frequently visited online departments.

Digital Cities

Keyword: **Digital City**

This channel is like an online travelogue (see fig. 6.5). Just by clicking the map that identifies a particular region of the U.S., you can bring up a list of the many forums that relate to that area. You'll find, for example, that many of the major cities or their newspapers have set up their own AOL forums to help travelers or even residents learn about the news and lifestyle information. You can even use the search tool to focus on a specific city or state or even a number of the major foreign cities (now that AOL is fast becoming a worldwide online service).

FIG. 6.5
Take an online vacation to many spots in the U.S. and around the world with AOL's Digital Cities channel.

Entertainment

Keyword: **Entertainment**

Movies, television, books, political and humorous cartoons, *Disney Adventures Magazine,* RockLink, the Trivia Forum, and LaPub—these are just a few of the Entertainment department features that draw huge numbers of membership on a regular basis. Almost no other department online has the continuous drawing power of the Entertainment department. Both children and adults frequent Entertainment for its culturally diverse content. Be sure to stop by during your travels across America Online (see fig. 6.6).

Part
I

Ch
6

FIG. 6.6
This screen will give you a quick glimpse of just some of the services offered in AOL's Entertainment channel.

Games

Keyword: **Games**

It may be the latest CD-ROM game, a video game, or one of the thousands of files available for download on AOL. Or, it may be advice on how to solve those clues in your favorite computer game. Whatever the reason, AOL's Games channel (see fig. 6.7) is a place you'll want to visit often for fun and some exciting online adventures.

FIG. 6.7
AOL's Games channel offers information, software, and even the chance to participate in interactive games online.

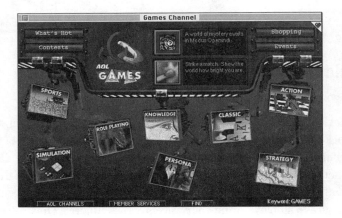

Health & Fitness

Keyword: **Health and Fitness**

Are you concerned with your health, or whether exercise would be of benefit or not? Well, we all are, and AOL's Health & Fitness channel (fig. 6.8) is a place you'll want to visit.

You'll read news of the latest developments in medical research, and get informed advice on how to live better and longer.

FIG. 6.8
The Health & Fitness channel provides advice, news, and a wide range of common sense information.

The Hub

Keyword: **Hub**

I'm always a bit at a loss for words to describe this channel, except to say that The Hub (see fig. 6.9) is at the center of the action online. It's a place for entertainment and information, and the best way to find out more about it is for you to pay a visit.

FIG. 6.9
The action begins at AOL's The Hub. Just check it out to see what I mean.

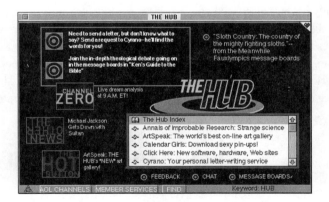

Part
I

Ch

6

The International Channel

Keyword: **International**

The time has long since passed when America Online was restricted to just "America." Through partnerships with a number of international media companies, AOL has expanded into Canada, Europe, Japan, and other major world centers. AOL's International channel (see fig. 6.10) allows you to quickly access some of AOL's worldwide features.

FIG. 6.10
AOL's International channel shows you how AOL has rapidly joined the international community.

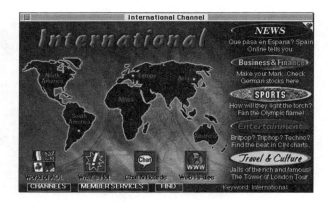

If you're following this in order on your Channels screen, you'll see I'm skipping the Internet Connection for now. I'll get to it later in this chapter, in the section entitled "Traversing the Superhighway."

Kids Only

Keyword: **Kids**

I really haven't discussed special places for kids yet on America Online, but I'll remedy that right now. As shown in figure 6.11, young people have lots of special and very friendly places to visit on America Online. *Disney Adventures Magazine* is on-hand with a special forum. There are Kids Chats (online conferences), and also special Kids Only versions of America Online's most popular clubs, such as the Astronomy Club and the Star Trek club. Three chapters in Part IV, "Kids and America Online," are devoted to the subject.

FIG. 6.11
Kids have a special area to call their own on America Online.

Learning and Culture

Keyword: **Education, Learning**

Do you need help with a homework assignment, or do you want to take some special courses on a particular topic of interest? Well, you can do that and more on America Online's active Learning & Culture channel, shown in figure 6.12. Here, you can pay a virtual visit to the Library of Congress or the Smithsonian, sign up for a correspondence course, or get information about the next round of college board examinations. For more information, refer to Chapter 25, "Learning and Reference."

FIG. 6.12
Sign up for a special course or visit a museum during your visit to America Online's Learning & Culture channel.

Because learning and reference are so intertwined, I'll briefly show you the opening screen from AOL's Reference Desk (see fig. 6.13). It's a place where AOL has grouped together many information resources, including databases you can search across the worldwide Internet, and you'll want to use this channel in concert with your online educational pursuits.

FIG. 6.13
Another learning center on AOL is the Reference Desk. The keyword is **Reference**.

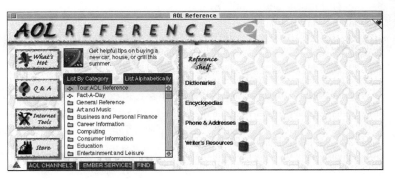

Part

I

Ch

6

Life, Styles & Interests

Keyword: **Lifestyles**

Want to join an online club, access an online health guide, learn tips about home improvement, charitable work, religion and ethics, and more? Well, AOL's Life, Styles & Interests channel will provide a great repertoire of information for you (see fig. 6.14). You can join an astronomy or cooking club, share information about better health and exercise, all this and more in one convenient online department.

FIG. 6.14
A large range of subjects form the forums that make up AOL's Life, Styles & Interests channel.

Marketplace

Keyword: **Marketplace**

The marketplace is your AOL center for shopping galore! Whether you are looking for America Online goodies, such as T-shirts and coffee mugs, wanting to buy or sell a car, or looking for computer training aids, AOL's Marketplace channel offers you these things and more (see fig. 6.15).

MusicSpace

Keyword: **Music, MusicSpace**

Whether you dig rock and roll, classical, country, or easy listening, AOL's MusicSpace channel (see fig. 6.16) can take you to a wide world of entertainment. It's a place where you can learn what your favorite performers are up to, download sound and video files, and share your views with other AOL members.

FIG. 6.15
Time to go shopping and
save some cash right on
America Online.

FIG. 6.16
The word is music and the
place to discover more
about it is AOL's MusicSpace
channel.

The Newsstand

Keyword: **Newsstand**

It's hard to imagine what the world was like only 100 or so years ago, when almost any news of the world, or even the country, took days or weeks to reach the eyes and ears of those who were around then. Even 15 years ago, we still waited for the morning newspapers to get more than just a headline service about current events. In this age of the so-called Information Superhighway, we need not wait even that long (see fig. 6.17).

Part
I

Ch
6

FIG. 6.17
The corner newsstand was never quite like this.

America Online's Newsstand department offers a vast amount of information about the world today that is as current as it gets. In some cases, such as the *Chicago Tribune, New York Times, Arizona Republic, San Jose Mercury News,* and many other daily, weekly, and monthly publications, the information is on America Online before the papers themselves hit the streets.

> **NOTE**   I am not deliberately passing over AOL's People Connection. But because it doesn't have just one main screen to show (other than the Lobby, which I'll describe in the next chapter), I'll just explain that it's AOL's meeting place, where members get together and move on to the next channel. ■

Personal Finance

Keyword: **Finance**

This department can be considered an extension of Today's News (see fig. 6.18). The Personal Finance department lets you delve more deeply into all aspects of handling your personal finances—from reviewing the day's business news (and how it might affect your income and investment strategies) to seeking out the profile of a company you might want to add to your stock portfolio. A surface glance at the main Personal Finance department window shows you lots of information resources, many of which are covered in Chapter 26, "Online Investment and Tax Information."

Sports

Keyword: **Sports**

When America's national pastime, baseball, disappeared in the summer of 1994 due to a players' strike, the importance of sports in our lives didn't diminish one iota. We simply talked about the football season instead. America Online's Sports department, shown in figure 6.19, covers the world of sports. It's a repository of the latest sports news, plus discussion groups and regular conferences on your favorite sports. And sometimes you'll be able to converse, through cyberspace, with some of your favorite sports figures, too.

FIG. 6.18
America Online's Personal Finance department has a vast storehouse of business news and advice.

FIG. 6.19
If you open your newspaper to the sports section first, you'll want to make a regular stop to this online area.

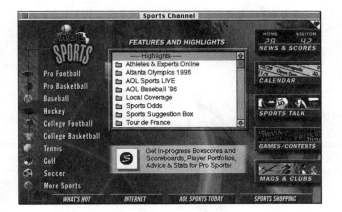

Today's News

Keyword: **News**

Here's your online daily newspaper. Besides providing the top news of the day, the Today's News department has special sections for stories related to the U.S. and World, Business, Entertainment, Sports, and Weather (see fig. 6.20). You also can use the Search feature, at the bottom of the screen, to locate stories about a particular item of interest. This area is described in more detail in Chapter 23, "The News of the Day."

Part
I
Ch
6

FIG. 6.20
AOL's Today's News channel is an easy way to stay on top of the ever-changing events around the world.

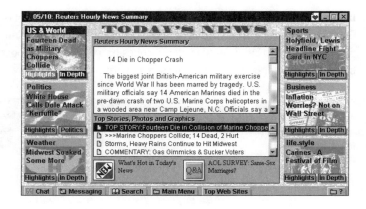

Style

Keyword: **Style**

When you click this screen, you'll hear the reassuring sound of a camera shutter clicking (that is, of course, if the sounds on your computer are turned on). A visit to AOL's Style channel is a quick way to learn the latest from the fashion world (see fig. 6.21). New clothing, hints and tips about makeup—that's just part of the picture. Because the Olympics in Atlanta topped the news when this chapter was written, there was, of course, an emphasis on Olympic style fashion.

FIG. 6.21
Look your best with a little information from AOL's popular Style channel.

Travel

Keyword: **Travel**

As the name implies, travelers gain gratification in the areas that comprise this department (see fig. 6.22). One of the principal services of AOL's Travel channel is travel reservations. You can book flights on any major airline, reserve rental cars and hotel rooms, or just check schedules and prices during your visit to the Travel channel. You'll also learn about the best places to visit, where to eat, and which places to avoid.

FIG. 6.22
Book a flight or learn about your favorite tourist spot in America Online's Travel department.

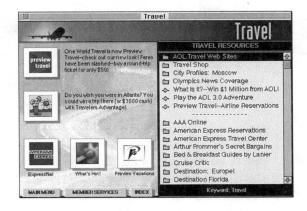

...and More

By now, you realize that America Online's channels contain vast areas to explore, and this chapter has highlighted only a few of them.

The Presenting feature, at the end of the AOL Channels menu, will offer you a selected roster of new and special online areas worth checking further.

All of America Online's channels are described in-depth in the remaining chapters; but for now, look around and become comfortable with their general layout. When the time comes to explore your chosen areas of particular interest, the later chapters will guide you through.

Making E-Mail Work for You

Part
I

Ch
6

We've been hearing for a few years about the Information Superhighway. A major chunk of this roadway has already been paved by such services as America Online and is already being traveled by you and me. One of the ways to travel this road is by using *e-mail*.

America Online's electronic mail (e-mail) system is by far one of the most solid features the service offers and one of the most widely used (see fig. 6.23). AOL's e-mail system is simple and efficient; it can easily be scheduled to pick up mail waiting for you and deliver your outgoing mail without any intervention from you. You don't even have to lick a stamp or address an envelope.

FIG. 6.23
The America Online e-mail form can also be used to format your message in basic text sizes and styles. This is the Windows version; the Mac edition looks different and includes a built-in spell checker.

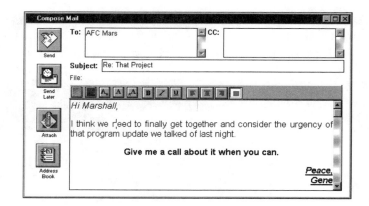

You can send e-mail at any time, day or night, and also include *attachments*—files from your computer's hard disk connected to your outgoing e-mail to be delivered to another AOL member, or even a member of another online service. To send e-mail, simply enter the recipient's screen name in the To box, type a heading in the Subject line, and type or paste your message in the large message box. Your message can be more than 25,000 characters long (about 400 words).

The people to whom you are sending your e-mail can read your message and retrieve any files you might have attached at their leisure. You and your recipient need not be online at the same time, which saves you the aggravation and effort it would take to prearrange a time when both of you would connect your modems to complete a communication session. Using America Online's e-mail is explained fully in Chapter 8 "Using America Online E-Mail."

Sending E-Mail to Other Services

E-mail on America Online doesn't just have to be sent to members of this service. You can also address your e-mail to members of other online services too, and, in fact, to anyone who has access to the vast, global Internet network. Sending mail through the Internet isn't much different from sending it to a fellow AOL member. The main difference is the way you address the letter, which follows a very specific convention. For an example of how a typical Internet e-mail letter is set up, see figure 6.24.

The address format is always the same. First you enter the screen name or number of the recipient, and then use the at symbol (@), followed by the domain or address of the service that the recipient is using. In the example in figure 6.24, I'm actually writing a letter to myself, but it's being sent to me at my account on AT&T's WorldNet service. To learn the ins and outs of Internet e-mail, refer to Chapter 30, "Secrets of Internet E-Mail and Mailing Lists."

FIG. 6.24
Sending Internet e-mail is easy on AOL.

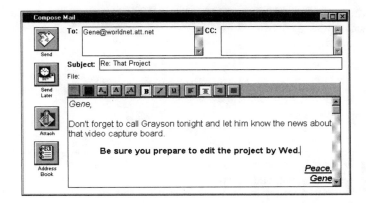

Using Instant Messages for Interactive Meetings

Regular e-mail, as describced in the preceding section, is a sort of formal and structured way of communicating messages of short to moderate length to other members, whether they are currently online or not (even if they're on another service with Internet access). It's the electronic equivalent of a letter you would send through the U.S. Postal Service.

Instant messages, or IMs for short, differ from e-mail in several ways and have distinct advantages and disadvantages. When using regular e-mail, you need know only the screen names of your correspondents to be able to send a message to them, and they need only to click a Reply button to respond to you. The messages you exchange in this fashion do not require any knowledge on your part of the other person's activities or presence online. You can pick up mail sent to you at any time, up to a month after it was issued. Exchanging instant mail, however, requires that both you and the other party be online at the same time (see fig. 6.25).

One big advantage of using instant messages is that both sides of the conversation take place in *real time* (while you and the recipient are online), and the topic is more easily followed without the time delays of e-mail.

Another major difference between the two types of messages is that when using e-mail, you can include as many screen names in the addressing boxes as you desire, hundreds

Part
I

Ch
6

even! On the other hand, using an instant message is just between two people, and no more. IMs are as private as AOL's e-mail and are a good way to carry on an online conversation to get to know someone better.

FIG. 6.25
AOL's Instant Message window shows a two-way mini-chat.

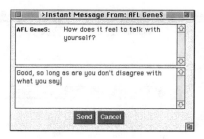

 To find out whether an online friend or colleague has logged on, just refer to AOL's Buddy List screen (keyword: **Buddy List**).

For more information on e-mail and instant messages, see Chapter 7, "America Online's People Connection," and Chapter 8, "Using America Online E-Mail."

Secrets of Transferring Files on America Online

Let's clear the air about a couple of online terms before going on. *Downloading* is the transfer of programs and files from the host computer to your computer's hard drive or floppy disk. *Uploading* is just the opposite; you send files from your own hard drive to AOL.

There is no doubt about it; you are going to find yourself downloading files sooner or later (probably sooner). Most of you joined America Online in the first place to be able to download files. While exploring the AOL departments, you probably ran across some file libraries, and, perhaps, have already dabbled in downloading.

You can download files from two sources on America Online: the first is from department forums, and the other is from e-mail attachments. The way you set up a download session is slightly different between the two, but once begun, both use the same file transfer method.

Starting the process of uploading is distinctly different, though. Using e-mail is the most straightforward of the two; simply click the Attach button on your new e-mail window and select the file or files you want to send to someone else.

In the Computers & Software forums, and other America Online libraries, you need to first complete a form that requests information about the file you plan to send. You'll learn more about uploading in Chapter 20, "Tips and Tricks on Finding Software."

America Online Forums: Where the Action Is

The central meeting points on America Online are called *forums*. A forum, according to Webster, is a place for discussion of public matters or current issues, or an opportunity for open discussion. This could be no truer anywhere else other than America Online. Forums on America Online cover numerous topics, computer-related and otherwise. There are more than a dozen forums, for example, in the Windows side of AOL's Computing & Software department (see Chapter 19, "Visiting the Computing and Software Forums") and a similar complement of Macintosh forums, many dealing with comparable topics.

One example, for Macintosh users, is a Mac AOL Text Map in the Mac Beginners' Software library that you can open, save, and read. Find that area by using the keyword **Mac Help** (see fig. 6.26), which takes you to a forum designed to help beginning users learn more about their computers and AOL.

FIG. 6.26
The America Online Mac Help forum (and the PC equivalent) shows newcomers the ropes.

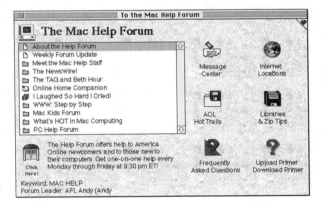

NOTE Macintosh forums are available to users of the Windows version of AOL software, and PC and Windows forums are available to Macintosh users. The special artwork you find in a forum's main window may look different on the opposite platform, sometimes appearing just as a list box. ■

While the basic setup is different from one forum to another, there are certain features that you'll find in just about every AOL forum, and a few that might be specific to certain forums. In the next section, I'll dissect a typical forum in AOL's Computers & Software

Part
I

Ch
6

area. You can use this as a guidepost during your first forum visits. For this little exercise, let's take a look at the Mac Operating Systems forum (see fig. 6.27), which is run by my friend and colleague John Stroud (AFL Bear). John (most of his friends just call him "Bear") worked with me on the first two editions of the original *Using America Online* books.

FIG. 6.27
The Mac OS forum is designed to help you get a handle on dealing with Apple's system software.

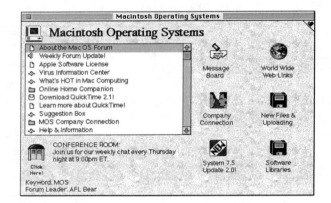

Most of the services offered in an AOL forum are clearly labeled. I'll just detail a few of them here; you'll see them in the list box or represented by an icon of one sort or another (those designs may change from forum to forum). It's important to know that not all of the features you see here will be shown or even labeled precisely as they are here.

- *About the Forum.* This is where the Forum Leader writes a few paragraphs describing the scope and mission of the forum and a few of the features visitors will want to check out.

- *Meet the Staff.* This is where the staff of the forum is introduced. You'll often read a biography of the forum's staff. In some forums (such as mine), this information is integrated into the About the Forum text.

- *New Files & Free Uploading.* This is the software library that you use to upload files to the forum's library. Chapter 20, "Tips and Tricks on Finding Software," describes the techniques of uploading software to America Online, and some of the basic requirements. Some forums call this library New Files & Free Uploading to indicate that the very latest files released by the forum staff are presented here.

The following list covers the features that are revealed when you click the forum window icons. The design of these icons might vary somewhat from forum to forum, and they are slightly different on the Macintosh platform, but the purpose is pretty much the same.

- *Help & Information.* If you are a new member of America Online, and you have questions about what to do when you visit a forum, clicking this icon (it's shown as a question mark in the Macintosh forums) will take you to the computing and software Help Desk, a place where you can get friendly advice and a selection of tips and tricks that you'll want to explore further. Some forums may offer this feature in the list box instead.

- *Software Libraries.* Here's the place where many members go first, because seeking out and downloading software is one of the most exciting activities on America Online. You can choose from tens of thousands of Macintosh and Windows software files, covering everything from commercial updates to spreadsheet templates and games. Chapters 20, 21, and 22 offer basic software tips and a listing of the most popular software now available on AOL.

- *Conference Center (or Room).* One of the most popular activities of any forum is the regular chat. Some forums hold them once a week, others hold them daily. These chats give you a chance to meet the forum staff, fellow members, and, sometimes, special experts on a variety of subjects.

- *Message Boards.* This is the part of a forum that is devoted to self-expression, and so it is one of the most popular areas. You can read what other members have to say, the responses from staff, and even ask your own questions or respond to other messages. For a comprehensive look at how you can use a message board to your best advantage, you'll want to read Chapter 9, "Using America Online Message Boards."

- *Company Connection.* Hundreds of major hardware and software manufacturers are represented on America Online. Each forum includes a gateway to firms that offer products related to the forum's mission. So, in the case of the Mac OS forum, the firms listed will offer products and services designed to support or enhance the Mac operating system. Sometimes a company will get its own icon, such as the one for Apple Computer in this forum.

N O T E If you need assistance with a problem that is not handled within a particular computing and software forum, you'll want to visit the regular Company Connection area instead (Keyword: **Industry**), where you can visit all of the firms on AOL that have products devoted to the computing platform you use.

Part

I

Ch

6

Joining an Online Conference

Conferences are hosted not only by forums, but also by other departments of America Online. Different areas' conferences have different flavors—some conference hosts use a formal protocol to determine who speaks at what time; some hosts hold contests where everyone speaks (all right, they really *type*) at almost the same time. Each area's conference room usually has posted rules of conduct for members to read before entering, and you should do just that so that you will act according to local customs. To use a cliché, when in Rome, do as the Romans do.

More conference room information is located in Chapter 10, "Chatting Online."

Traversing the Superhighway

When you log on to America Online, you are not just accessing a single online service. Through AOL's Internet Connection (see fig. 6.28), you also have access to a huge, sprawling network encompassing other services throughout the world. No doubt you've read about the Internet in your daily newspaper, or you've heard or seen stories about it on the broadcast media.

FIG. 6.28
AOL's Internet Connection is the entranceway to the global Information Superhighway.

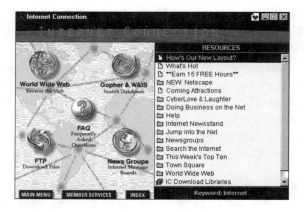

America Online was one of the first major online services to offer a huge set of Internet-related features. Some of them are summarized here. If your curiosity has been piqued, go right to Part VIII, "Entering the Information Superhighway," for a full description of AOL's Internet features. Besides telling you how they work, there are suggestions of popular mailing lists, newsgroups, and World Wide Web sites you should visit during your online sessions.

Among the Internet features AOL offers are:

- *TCP/IP access.* If you have direct network access to the Internet, you can log on to AOL at ultra-high speed from anywhere in the world.

- *Internet E-mail.* You can send e-mail directly to other online services and individual Internet subscribers.

- *Internet mailing lists.* Join any of thousands of popular mailing lists on the Internet. These mailing lists are devoted to just about everything from computers to cooking.

- *Gopher and WAIS.* America Online lets you do a comprehensive database search for information and files on any subject throughout the Internet.

- *Internet Newsgroups.* Join exciting, informative discussion groups on your favorite subjects. You can choose from thousands of active newsgroups.

- *File Transfer Protocol (FTP).* Directly from AOL, you can download software directly from the major software and hardware manufacturers, such as Apple and Microsoft, and access a huge storehouse of shareware and other useful files located on computers and services across the world.

- *World Wide Web.* Much of the content of the Internet is in text form, but it's easy to navigate through America Online's friendly, helpful interface. The World Wide Web is the newest Internet feature that combines text, pictures, and even sound into a single, unified presentation. Using hypertext links, you are able to click a topic and jump right to the material related to that subject. (Macintosh users familiar with HyperCard have already had somewhat of a sample of what the World Wide Web looks like.)

In the coming years, America Online will be exploring other Internet services. You can be assured that these services will be tightly integrated into AOL's friendly, easy-to-use software, so you won't have to learn a complex new interface to take advantage of the newest features. A good indicator of what is to come can be found in the monthly letter from the service's outspoken president, Steve Case, in which he offers you his vision for the service and acquaints you with upcoming new services.

TROUBLESHOOTING

How do I stop a text window from scrolling on my screen? The standard Mac Cancel keystrokes (Command-period) will halt the display of text in a text window or a directory listing in a directory window (including the listing of mail you've read or sent). It takes a few seconds for AOL's host computer to get the message, though, and sometimes, if you have a high speed modem connection to America Online, the text or directory information will finish displaying before the display process can be stopped.

From Here...

In this chapter, you've seen a picture of the way America Online is organized and the sorts of services that are offered. These services will undergo changes with time; the Information Superhighway is never stagnant. New areas will be added and older ones will be changed or removed.

The remainder of this book details each of the services that are briefly introduced here using a task-oriented approach. Set a goal for yourself; perhaps you want to learn more about your computer, plan a trip, or buy some merchandise. Then consult the following chapters to learn how to find the area that caters to that interest and use that area's resources most efficiently:

- Chapter 7, "America Online's People Connection," gives you more information about communicating with others online.
- Part III, "A Wealth of Entertainment at Your Fingertips," tells you more about the entertainment-related features offered by America Online.
- Chapter 20, "Tips and Tricks on Finding Software," shows you how to find software for your computer.
- Chapter 25, "Learning and Reference," describes many of the sources for learning and reference that you'll find in your online travels.
- Chapter 27, "Secrets of AOL's Travel Department," helps you out with your travel plans.
- Part VIII, "Entering the Information Superhighway," tells you how to participate in the world's largest computer network.

Communicating Online

CHAPTER 7

America Online's People Connection

In the hundreds of pages throughout this book, I discuss what you can find in AOL's channels or departments. But AOL is not just about forums and libraries and message boards. For many, the most enjoyable aspect of becoming an America Online member is the ability to meet others with similar interests, whether computer-related or not.

If that's your interest, you'll find that AOL's People Connection is where it's at.

People Connection offers a number of resources to help you meet other online members. You find out about these resources in the following paragraphs. But first, you probably want to learn how to introduce yourself to others. ■

Create a profile

Make yourself known to the rest of the online community.

Learn about other members

You can easily view other members' online profiles.

Find your friends

Learn how to know when your friends are online.

Proper online conduct

Follow proper online etiquette while meeting other members.

Anyone out there?

Learn how to find other members with similar interests.

AOL's most popular hangouts

Find the very best online areas where you can meet people.

Creating and Updating Your Online Profile

Every member of America Online has at least one screen name. You can create as many as five screen names to use when the mood strikes you or for use by other members of your family. Every member also can create an online profile for each of those online names, for other members to view (see fig. 7.1). Your first step toward meeting people is complete when you fill out your own online profile.

FIG. 7.1

This sample online profile shows the kind of information you can provide.

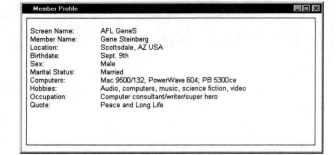

Besides the expected information such as your real name, screen name, and location, you can enter personal information about yourself to indicate your interests to others. Hobbies, favorite quotes, your occupation, and the kind of computers you use are some of the entries you might want to provide for your profile. To create or change your profile, open the Members menu of your America Online software and choose Edit Your Online Profile. Figure 7.2 shows a complete list of the data you can enter.

FIG. 7.2

Here's the data-entry screen for your personal online profile.

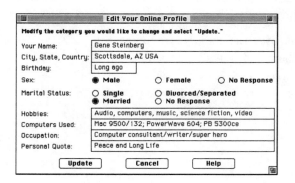

N O T E   The first time you create a profile, it defaults to include your full name. For reasons of privacy, you may prefer to delete this information and identify yourself online under only your screen name.

As you look at the Edit Your Online Profile screen, make a note to yourself about which of the entries you want other people to be able to see when they look up your profile. You might or might not want to reveal certain information, such as your gender, real name, marital status, and so on. Fill in only the information you would not mind telling a stranger. In figure 7.2, for example, my profile states my City, State, Country, but you may prefer to identify a region of the country (say southwest or northeast), rather than provide more specific information about your residence.

If you do not want to reveal your gender, be sure to click on the No Response button on that line. (If your name happens to be Pat, you could sure keep 'em guessing!) Also click on No Response for your marital status if you want that information to remain undisclosed.

TIP After you learn how to look up other people's profiles, take some time to look through a few other members' entries for ideas.

The remaining four fields give you the chance to tell other people about yourself as a person instead of simply listing statistics. You begin by describing the kind of computer or computers you have, then you list the hobbies you have and the line of work you're in, and then you can quote a saying or motto that appeals to you (or use the opportunity to create one of your own).

After completing your online profile, review it for spelling accuracy. This step might seem fairly obvious, but after you look at a few profiles, you'll know why I mention it.

After you've reviewed your completed profile and are satisfied with it, click the Update button to finish off the job, and you can move on to more exciting online activities.

TIP When you create an online profile for yourself, feel free to be humorous, but try to be accurate and truthful, as well. Remember, you can change or update your profile any time you want.

If you are not sure about your entries or have second thoughts about revealing some facts about yourself at this moment in time, you might prefer not to complete your online profile. In this case, click the Cancel button. Your profile is not saved, and the information you typed will vanish into cyberspace. If you want more information about the Edit Your Online Profile screen, click the Help button.

Part

II

Ch

7

> **CAUTION**
>
> Your online profile is subject to America Online's Terms of Service. It is also a reflection of the face you want to put forth to the public. You are expected to refrain from using vulgar language as part of your profile description.

Secrets of Meeting Other America Online Members

Meeting people on America Online has had some interesting outcomes over the years since the online community was launched. The syndicated television program, *The Jerry Springer Show,* even spotlighted a number of AOLers who had met and married. America Online users often inhabit the various People Connection rooms, such as the Flirt's Nook and Romance Connection, in search of friendship, camaraderie, and, yes, even love.

After you've looked around at the dozens of areas where other people congregate, you'll have a hard time tearing yourself away from America Online and the friends you will soon meet! (Of course, you'll want to watch your online time too, because you can easily forget how long you've been logged on, and how much of a bill you're creating for yourself.)

Are you ready to dive in? Saying hello to people you meet on America Online is certainly a lot easier than opening a conversation with a stranger, because on America Online, with millions of members, you'll find that many have things in common with you, so remaining alone is difficult.

Locating Other America Online Members

You probably realize that you're not alone on America Online, right? But you might ask yourself this question in your first few sessions: Where are all the rest of the people? It's a good question. Being online is not exactly like walking into a restaurant and looking around to see whether you know anyone there. It's more akin to entering an office building—you need to know where the people are and go there before you can meet anyone.

On busy evenings in recent weeks, America Online has had literally thousands of members in interactive areas at one time! But as you stare at the Welcome to AOL screen, you aren't able to see any of these people. They are all behind virtual closed doors, and those doors are soundproof. Your first step to finding other people is to open these doors and look around. By far, the easiest place to find other members is in the People Connection area of America Online. The People Connection department houses most of the noncomputing-related chat rooms where members like to congregate and socialize.

To get there, simply choose People Connection from the Channels menu. You are immediately transported to the foyer of America Online's People Connection, as shown in figure 7.3. These windows represent rooms in which as many as 23 people can gather and get to know one another by exchanging chat. If the Lobby is full when you enter, the room expands to additional rooms, and the room name has a number after it, such as Lobby 23.

The mechanics of chatting involve typing what you want others to see in the small box in the lower portion of the Chat window and sending it by clicking the Send button or by pressing Enter on your keyboard.

FIG. 7.3

America Online's Lobby in the People Connection area is one place you can chat with other members.

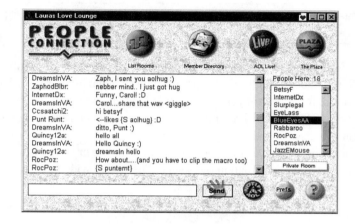

If you're like a lot of folks who are new to the online world, don't worry about starting a conversation right away; just hang around the Lobby (online regulars call it *lurking*) and watch what other members type to each other. While you're lurking, chances are that someone will say hello to you. Don't worry about sending a reply if you aren't comfortable; no one will mind.

 TIP When visiting People Connection rooms for the first few times, you might get a better feel for the rooms' atmospheres by just watching for a few minutes or more.

Look at figure 7.3 again. This window contains some items of interest apart from the text you type and the text other people have typed. For one thing, now that you've located some people online, you can find out a little more about them.

Viewing Other Members' Profiles

If you want to view another member's profile, you need to know the member's screen name or be in the same chat room with that member. The Lobby is as good a place as any to start.

Members' screen names are shown at the start of each line as it is displayed in the Chat window of the Lobby. If you wish to know when a member enters the room or leaves, simply click the Prefs button at the lower right of the Chat room window, and click the check boxes to be notified of a member's arrival and departure (it'll show up as an entry in the Chat room window).

Part

II

Ch

7

To see who is present, just take a gander at the People Here listing at the right side of the window. You may have to use the scroll bars to see the entire list. The list is updated as people enter and leave, so you can watch it to observe their comings and goings.

 T I P You can quickly check AOL's membership roster in the People Connection chat room simply by clicking the Member Directory icon at the top of the screen.

Now, you can find out about someone! Just double click a member's name in the People Here list box, which brings up the window shown in figure 7.4. Then click the Get Info button. If the person you selected filled out an online profile, you see it in just a few seconds. If that member has not filled out a profile, you receive a message indicating that there is no profile available for that name. In that case, try using some of the other names in the list until you find someone who has provided profile information. Depending on how much information the selected person provided, you see one or more lines of information in the Profile window.

FIG. 7.4
You can choose to check a member's profile or send an instant message from this window.

The other option shown in figure 7.4, Message, brings up AOL's Instant Message window. You'll learn more about that feature in Chapter 8, "Using America Online E-Mail."

 TROUBLESHOOTING

Help! I get annoying messages from someone online whenever I enter a chat room. What do I do? You are entitled to enjoy your online visits in comfort and safety, free of annoyance from such people. The fastest way to deal with this problem is to click the Notify AOL button at the bottom of the chat room screen. It will bring up instructions to help you inform AOL's Community Action Team about the problem.

Finding a Member Online

As you become more comfortable using the conference rooms and People Connection rooms of America Online, you will probably begin to recognize some of the regulars. Perhaps you also know someone who uses America Online and want to find out if that person is signed on at the same time as you.

America Online provides a fast, easy method of locating people using the service. Select Locate a Member Online from the Members menu, or press Ctrl+F (Command-F for Mac users), and type the screen name of the person you want to locate (see fig. 7.5).

FIG. 7.5
Enter the member's name in this Locate a Member Online window.

If a person you seek is online when you attempt to find him or her, the America Online host computer tells you one of two things: either that the person you want to find is Online, but not in a chat area, or the name of the chat or conference room where the person is currently. If the person is not online, America Online tells you exactly that.

Using AOL's Buddy List

Wouldn't it be nice if you could be notified when a friend or business acquaintance of yours is online? It would be like an online beeping or paging service.

Well, AOL offers just such a feature. It's called a Buddy List (see fig. 7.6), and it will automatically notify you whenever someone you know is online, and let them know you're online, too.

FIG. 7.6
AOL's Buddy List greets you when you log on with a list of friends who are online.

If you want to send a message to your friend, just click the Send IM button to open up an Instant Message window. Just write up your message and send it on its way. I'll describe Instant Messages in more detail in Chapter 8, "Using America Online E-Mail." For now, just consider this feature your way to have a private, one-on-one online conversation with a friend, virtually in real time, as they're online. It's a feature you will want to use often.

Of course, before AOL's handy paging service does its stuff, you've got to set it up. To do that, simply type the keyword **Buddy** to bring up the setup window (see fig. 7.7).

Part
II

Ch
7

FIG. 7.7
It takes just a few minutes to create or change your own personal Buddy List.

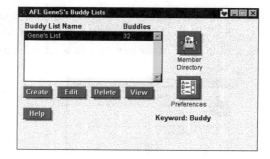

To create your own Buddy List, click the Create button, and enter the screen names of your friends in the setup window (see fig. 7.8).

FIG. 7.8
Enter the names of the online friends, so AOL can notify you of their presence online.

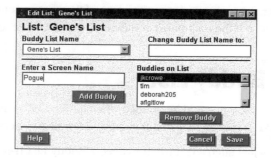

N O T E   You do not, of course, have to allow others to know you're online. If there's someone you'd rather not notify when you're online—or you don't want anyone to add you to their Buddy List, simply click the Preferences icon, and choose whether specific members, or any members can include you on their Buddy List. AOL will respect your privacy. Keep in mind that others may prevent you from knowing they're online in the same way. ■

You can create a separate listing from different groups of AOL members, and establish a different set of Buddy List preferences for each of those groups or individuals. Once your custom Buddy List is set up, it'll appear the next time you log on to AOL. The same buddy list is not available to all screen names on your account, so you need to create a separate Buddy List for each of your AOL screen names.

A Neighborhood in Cyberspace

Of all the areas online where people congregate, the People Connection's Lobby is far and away the place you find most of the people who want to talk. On a busy evening, you can easily find hundreds of people in the various lobbies of the People Connection.

Entering the Lobby

You might be saying to yourself, "Hey, wait a minute—didn't you say earlier that only 23 people can gather in a room at one time?" Well, yes, that's correct, as far as it goes. What happens after the 23rd person enters the Lobby is that a new room is automatically created to hold the 24th person and all the other people soon to follow. That room is called *Lobby 1,* and after it reaches 23 people, other rooms follow it with names like *Lobby 2, Lobby 3,* and so on.

The People Connection lobbies are usually bustling, crowded areas. Think Grand Central Station here; people are constantly coming and going. Often they are leaving for other People Connection rooms with specific themes or going to Computing & Software conference rooms to discuss the latest industry news. Private rooms are also available. This is discussed later in this chapter.

As with most public areas in real life, the People Connection rooms have their own etiquette and rules of conduct. First and foremost is TOS, or Terms Of Service. TOS is America Online's equivalent of real-life laws. You should take some time during your first few sessions to acquaint yourself with TOS. Use the keyword **TOS** to go to AOL's free help area, and look over the Terms Of Service, which is displayed in separate text files according to category. Spend at least a few minutes reviewing the contents of this area. (After all, it's free!) By making this effort now, you can feel more comfortable the first times you visit the public area rooms, and you'll have a greater understanding of how things work in general on America Online. The contents of each Terms Of Service topic can be saved or printed (see Appendix B or C for an explanation as to how to save and print files in the Mac and Windows versions of AOL software).

Briefly, the most important parts of TOS simply state that you are expected to be a good citizen when you visit America Online. You are expected to refrain from using vulgar language and to respect others in the same way you expect them to respect you. For more information about proper online behavior, read Chapter 10, "Chatting Online," and Chapter 16, "Parental Issues and Internet Access."

Entering the LaPub Entertainment Connection Room

Lobbies are the places in which you automatically arrive when you select Lobby from the Go To menu. For this reason, they are busy places. America Online's staff saw the need for regular visitors to have a place online where they could sit back, relax, and enjoy ongoing, pleasant conversation—and have some fun while there. With this idea, LaPub was born (see fig. 7.9). To get to LaPub, type the keyword **LaPub**, or enter through the Online Games Forum or Entertainment Forum.

FIG. 7.9
The LaPub is a pleasant gathering place.

The bar was constructed, the refreshments were ordered and stocked, and the cheerful, highly capable Pub Tenders were rigorously trained. All this preparation was for the sake of creating one of the liveliest of the People Connection areas ever seen online anywhere. The best part is that you don't have to drive anywhere; just sit in your most comfortable chair with the one-eyed monitor of your favorite computer in front of your face. Most likely, you will have at least one free online beverage of your choice offered on your first visit. Accept it, and enjoy!

LaPub offers more than just a place to chat with members and partake of the occasional festivities. Besides the LaPub chat room, you find a special area, the LaPub Cellar, offering files uploaded by other LaPub patrons, including pictures of some of the regulars, sound files, and transcripts of notable LaPub events (see fig. 7.10).

FIG. 7.10
The LaPub Cellar is a collection of marvelous and entertaining files.

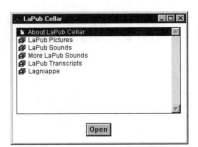

The LaPub Pictures library contains all the pictures of your favorite LaPub patrons, PubTends, and PubSubs—that is, if they are not shy. Ever wonder what somebody looked like offline? Check out this library and see whether your favorite friend's picture is available. And don't forget to upload your own picture! You also might want to check out America Online's portrait library, the Gallery, which is discussed a little later in this chapter.

Check out the LaPub Sounds library for the latest in LaPub chat sounds. Install it with your Online Sounds, and watch the fun as some rowdy PubTend tosses a lemon meringue pie at your LaPub neighbor!

 T I P The files you access from this area will generally come with instructions on how to install them.

Remember that fun party last Friday night? Relive the experience by downloading the transcript of LaPub from that night from the files in LaPub Transcripts. LaPub Notes also has a folder available for the discussion of LaPub Cellar. You can use this folder to announce a neat, new file you have just uploaded or to talk about the latest new file in LaPub Cellar. Archived LaPub Notes are also available within this library.

While visiting the LaPub area, be sure to check for upcoming events and contests in LaPub's schedule. You don't want to miss out on their unique happenings!

Visiting Private Chat Rooms

If you are like many of the People Connection's regular visitors, you'll eventually meet someone online with whom you want to communicate further. You want more privacy than the public People Connection rooms are able to offer, while still maintaining the ability to communicate with more than one person in real time. (Instant messages and e-mail are discussed in more detail in Chapter 8, "Using America Online E-Mail.")

Private rooms look and feel exactly like any public chat room, such as the Lobby or forum conference rooms.

The only difference between a public chat room and a private one is that the name of the room does not appear in any of the People Connection room lists. To join another member already in a private room, you must first know the exact name of that room.

The first step to creating this private area is to go to the Lobby in the People Connection. Then click the Private Room button at the bottom right of the Lobby chat window. To enter the room you want, or to create a new one, simply type it in the window shown in figure 7.11. Remember this room name so that you can send it in an instant message or e-mail to those members you want to join you.

A Few Chat Basics

There are two types of chat rooms on America Online. The first, described above, is a small area where you can have an interactive discussion with a group of fellow AOL members, and all of the things you say are shown in the chat window. The chat rooms in AOL's

Part

II

Ch

7

Computing & Software area and other parts of AOL are structured similarly, but are larger than those in the Peoples Connection area and will hold several dozen members before a new room is created.

FIG. 7.11

You create or enter a private room by using this screen.

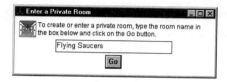

There's yet another kind of chat room on America Online, one that allows hundreds, even thousands of members to gather and attend a meeting that usually involves a special guest, such as a popular show business personality. But it's not a place where a large group exchanges comments with one another. The area is known as Center Stage, and the rooms there are set up as virtual auditoriums, where you sit in a row and can chat only with the others who are sitting in that row. You actually interact with the guests on stage by sending them messages or questions. If you want to know more about online chats and conferences and how to get involved with both, read Chapter 10, "Chatting Online."

Some Additional People Connection Chat Room Features

In addition to the features mentioned above, there are just a few more fancy icons in the Chat Room screen that I'd like to mention here.

- List Rooms: Clicking this icon brings up a list of active rooms, any one of which you can enter simply by double clicking the title.

- AOL Live: Clicking this icon brings up a listing of online conferences you'll want to check out. You'll learn more about these conferences, some of which feature notables from the world of entertainment, politics and sports, in Chapter 10, "Chatting Online."

- Plaza: This is the hub of the People Connection channel (see fig. 7.12). Here you'll see a listing of upcoming special events and be able to enter some of the popular forums for interactive conversations on a host of subjects.

Entering the Gallery

Keyword: **Gallery**

When you meet someone online, do you ever wonder what the other person really looks like? Well, there's a way to find out. Many members of America Online have made disk copies of photos of themselves and their families, and can send them to you via e-mail. There's another resource for photos of AOL members, a forum devoted strictly to the service's own photo album.

FIG. 7.12
The Plaza is the People Connection's central meeting point, where you can explore all of its features.

It's called The Gallery (or sometimes the AOL Portrait Gallery). The Gallery might turn out to be one of your favorite places online, because there you get to place faces with the screen names of people you meet online (see fig. 7.13).

FIG. 7.13
The AOL Portrait Gallery is one of the most popular forums on AOL.

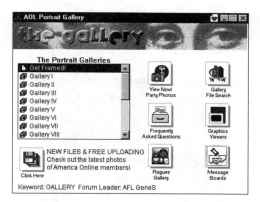

The Gallery is a collection of photos put in computer-readable form and uploaded for all to see. Thousands of America Online members have already uploaded their portraits or sent their photos to the Gallery's staff to digitize for free. As you get to know some of the regulars online, chances are good that you'll be tempted to find out what they look like, and the Gallery is the place where you may find their photos.

Part
II

Ch
7

A separate library is also included in the Gallery for family-album types of pictures. You can gather your own clan's photos and send them to the Gallery. You can upload the files directly to the Gallery's New Files and Free Uploading library or submit your photo to be scanned and uploaded by the Gallery's staff. The address to which you should send your photos for scanning is listed in the library information texts.

To make viewing these photos easy for all America Online users, regardless of the type of computer, the Gallery photos are currently provided in *GIF* and *JPEG* formats. These two formats offer high-quality images with a small file size. The small size keeps your download time short and makes it more convenient if you want to see photos of a number of your fellow members. Of the two formats, JPEG gets you a slightly smaller size and better quality, but the Gallery will accept digitized photos in either format.

The very latest versions of America Online's Macintosh and Windows software allow you to actually see a photo gradually appear on your screen while it's being downloaded to your computer, as shown in figure 7.14. To view the photo files after they are downloaded, simply choose Open from the File menu and then select the file you want to see. After the file is opened (or has appeared on your computer's screen right after the download process is over), you'll be able to print it just the same as any other document.

N O T E   If a photo has been uploaded with the newest version of AOL's software, you'll be able to see a thumbnail (miniature or preview version) of the photo when you view the file description in the Gallery's libraries. Thumbnails are not available for photos sent using older versions of AOL's Mac and Windows software. ■

FIG. 7.14
As you download a file from the Gallery, the photo begins to display on your computer's screen. The complete photo is shown when the download is finished.

The handsome young man shown in figure 7.14 is, by the way, my son Grayson, who was just shy of 10 when the photo was taken. If you want to know more about placing your photos in the Gallery, look at the directory window in the Gallery, and double-click the Get Framed! listing (see fig. 7.15).

FIG. 7.15
Read the text here for instructions on submitting a photo to the Gallery; you'll have to scroll through the text window to read it all.

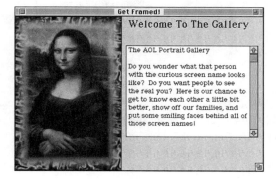

> **CAUTION**
>
> Photos are not accepted in the AOL Portrait Gallery unless they adhere to the Terms Of Service. That means you won't find any nude or explicit photos there that would be against AOL's family character. Remember that this is a member portrait gallery, so it includes both adults and children.

The Get Framed text at the right of the information window can be saved and printed using the appropriate commands from the File menu of your AOL software. It covers the type of photos accepted, the maximum acceptable size of the photo (640x480 pixels), and file-naming conventions. Because photos must be viewable by both Mac and PC users (including many who have yet to upgrade to Windows 95), they should adhere to the standard PC naming convention, consisting of eight letters for the file name, followed by a period and the GIF or JPG extension (depending on which file format the photo is saved in). For example: THEPHOTO.GIF or THEPHOTO.JPG. The information text screen also includes instructions about AOL's free scanning service, which is provided to members who cannot get their own photos scanned.

Besides the regular Gallery libraries, there are some special features of the AOL Portrait Gallery discussed in the following section. These special features are accessed by the icons at the right of the forum window:

■ *View Now!: Party Photos* is a library showing photos of member gatherings. To see a photo, just double-click its name and it will appear on your computer's screen in just a few seconds (see fig. 7.16).

Part
II

Ch
7

FIG. 7.16
A library of AOL party photos is provided in a special instant download format. The picture shown here will be clear when it's fully downloaded.

■ *Gallery File Search* lets you use AOL's database search feature to examine all of the libraries in this forum to locate the photo you want. Just enter the member's screen name in the list field. If the member's photo is in the forum's libraries, it'll show up in a directory listing in just a few seconds (see fig. 7.17).

FIG. 7.17
Use this window to search for a photo in The Gallery.

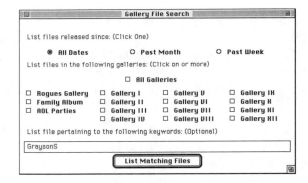

■ *Frequently Asked Questions* provides useful information on techniques for scanning your photo and responds to common questions about viewing the files you've downloaded from the Gallery (see fig. 7.18).

FIG. 7.18
Answers to many of your Gallery-related questions are found here.

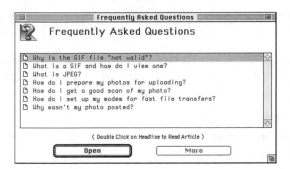

N O T E   Many forums on America Online have a selection of FAQs (Frequently Asked Questions) that provide helpful introductory material for visitors to these areas. Consider them the online equivalent of the ReadMe files that often ship with new computer software. It's a good idea to read these FAQs when you first enter a new forum, as many of your questions about that forum and how to take advantage of its services are described in these helpful information texts. ■

■ *Viewer Resource Center* is a second forum within the AOL Portrait Gallery. It's devoted to information on what the various graphics formats are all about, which computer platforms support those formats, and how you can open files saved in these formats. There are also two libraries for Mac and Windows users that contain software, both free and shareware, that you can use not only to view graphics files, but to convert files from one format to another. You can also go to this forum directly via the keyword **Viewers** (see fig. 7.19).

FIG. 7.19
Download photo-viewing programs and easy-to-use image editing software from this library.

■ *Rogues Gallery* is devoted to folks like me who hold positions of one sort or another with America Online. Examples include those who run online forums and those who actually work in AOL's own offices.

■ *Message Boards* is one of the most exciting parts of AOL Portrait Gallery, other than finding out what a fellow AOL member looks like, of course. Discussions in this forum only begin with Gallery issues and sometimes go far afield, as you'll see when you read the messages.

There is one more library in the Gallery, but you have to scroll through the directory window to find it. It's Family Album, a library devoted strictly to photos of AOL members' families.

Online Abbreviations

When you chat online, the other person cannot, of course, see whether you are smiling, or crying, or frowning. So a nifty shorthand language has been devised in cyberspace so you can communicate your feelings and reactions to what other online visitors say. Some of these letters and symbols are downright obscure; others are fairly obvious when you see the shortcut, such as LOL, which stands for Laughing Out Loud.

In Chapter 10, "Chatting Online," I've gathered a set of these shortcuts for you to keep on hand as you become accustomed to the online universe. Some of them are quite obscure, and seldom-used (though you encounter them occasionally). But many will soon become familiar to you and, I'm sure, second nature as you begin to experience the rewarding experience of meeting fellow travelers of the online universe.

From Here...

This chapter introduces you to what is really one of the most popular online areas, the People Connection. But the best way to understand how it works is to experience it yourself. Just lurk in the Lobby for a while, or attend a conference or two. The People Connection will soon become a regular part of your AOL sessions.

If you have young children in your household who use America Online, be sure also to read Chapter 16, "Parental Issues and Internet Access," for information about parental controls. This feature lets you assert your parental rights and helps you decide whether your children should use certain features of America Online. You may not want them to visit some types of chat rooms or be able to use instant messages.

You can find other related information in these chapters:

- In Chapter 9, "Using America Online Message Boards," you'll learn how to locate messages, the elements of online etiquette, and how to find responses to your message.

- In Chapter 10, "Chatting Online," you'll learn how to participate in chats, conferences, and one-on-one communication with fellow members.

- In Chapter 19, "Visiting the Computing and Software Forums," you'll learn where to seek support and information about all of your computer-related problems and how AOL can help you enhance your computing experience.

- In Appendix B, "Using Your America Online Macintosh Software," you receive a hands-on tutorial that will help you master your software and unlock many of its secrets.

- In Appendix C, "Using Your America Online Windows Software," you receive full instructions about this particular version of AOL's software.

Using America Online E-Mail

When you sit down to make a list of the things you want
to do online, e-mail is often at the very top of the list for
many members. When I wrote about America Online's
People Connection in the last chapter, I described it as
a place where you can meet fellow AOL members—
your online neighbors. On any given evening, it is not
uncommon to find thousands of members in the various chat rooms of People Connection, Computers &
Software conference rooms, and other online gathering
places. As for e-mail, although you don't see it, millions
of pieces of it fly across cyberspace at all hours of the
day and night.

This chapter covers the various areas of America
Online designed to let you communicate with members
who share similar interests or, in the case of the Debate Forum, even opposing views. ■

AOL's e-mail and instant messages

Learn how to take advantage of
AOL's e-mail and instant messaging
features.

The e-mail formatting toolbar

Explore how to use text formatting
options to make your e-mail sparkle.

AOL's auto session feature

Discover how to run a FlashSession
to automate your e-mail, newsgroup
reading, and file transfers.

The Right Way to Use Electronic Mail

Of course, not everyone can be online at the same time as their friends for chats, which makes America Online's e-mail feature a very busy item indeed, because we all want to stay in touch with our online friends. The system is one of the best, if not *the* best, in the industry. It has proven to be extremely reliable, simple to use, and, because it can be automated for the shortest possible connect times, you can save substantial online connection charges. What's more, through AOL's Internet Connection, you can write to members of other online services and computer networks throughout the world. See Chapter 30, "Secrets of Internet E-Mail and Mailing Lists," for more information about AOL's Internet Connection.

E-mail begins with a single, simple step: selecting Compose Mail from the Mail menu bar item. Keyboard enthusiasts may simply press ⌘-M (Ctrl+M for Window users) to begin a new mail message. The resulting form is the jumping off point for all your original e-mail (see fig. 8.1 for the Mac version and fig. 8.2 for the Windows edition). Later in this chapter you learn how to reply to e-mail without using a new mail form.

FIG. 8.1
America Online's Macintosh e-mail form includes a convenient spell checker feature.

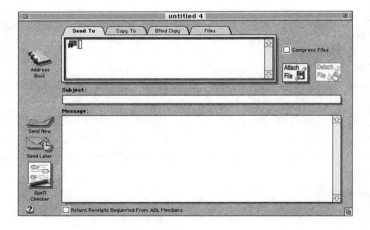

When you first conjure up a new e-mail window, the cursor is automatically positioned within the To field of the form. Most folks begin composing electronic mail by first addressing it. If this does not suit your tastes, simply press the Tab key to move the cursor to any of the other fields contained in the e-mail window, or click the desired field.

America Online is unflaggingly insistent about a few things regarding its e-mail system. You must include at least one address, a subject, and a message. And it does make sense. After all, receiving a blank message is like picking up the telephone and finding no one on the other end.

FIG. 8.2
America Online's Windows e-mail form has a handy formatting toolbar to give your e-mail sparkle.

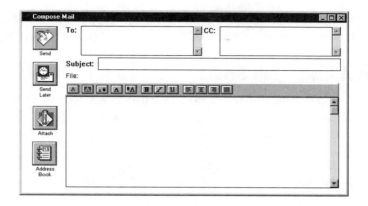

The address fields of the e-mail window can contain literally hundreds of electronic mailing addressees. If you use AOL's Windows software to send a message to more than one person, each person's screen name must be separated by a comma or a return. (On a Mac, be sure to press Return, not Enter; hitting Enter sends the message.) When you use the Return key to separate multiple names, the window list is easier to read than when the names are separated by commas. In the example shown in figure 8.3, which shows the Mac version of AOL's e-mail form, the fields for each e-mail option are separated by tabs. Just click the tab that represents how the recipient is to be handled.

FIG. 8.3
Addressing e-mail to more than one person is simple on AOL. The Mac version of the e-mail form separates e-mail categories with handy tabs.

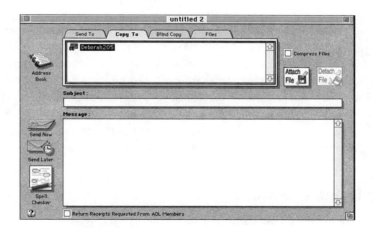

If you've entered any addresses in your AOL Address Book, you can also click the Address Book icon to select names for the e-mail addresses. See the section "How to Use AOL's Address Book," later in this chapter.

Now that you've decided who's getting the message, move to the Subject field and let the recipient know what your message is about without making them read it to find out. This step is both convenient and considered normal e-mail etiquette. After the subject, move the cursor to the message body and compose your message.

Using AOL's E-Mail Styles

A unique feature of America Online e-mail is that you may style your message by using a different type of size, style, and color. The Mac AOL Text Format toolbar displays the attributes you may change within the e-mail message (see fig. 8.4).

FIG. 8.4
Changing e-mail text styles
using the Format menu.

On both the Mac and Windows versions of AOL's e-mail form, using the handy toolbar, you can make your format changes right on the e-mail window (reminiscent of the ones you may see in a word processing program).

You can give your e-mail more impact with these features, but don't overdo it; there's a limit to the number of fonts and styles one document can contain, and overly complex styles look gaudy anyway. If you opt to vary the color of different parts of your e-mail, the recipient must have a color computer and a color monitor to see the results properly; otherwise, the colors just appear as varying shades of gray.

N O T E   A cool AOL e-mail feature is the ability to insert a hyperlink in your message. This embeds a double-clickable path to an AOL forum or Internet source. It's a terrific way to take your friends directly to an online place you want them to see. To insert a hyperlink on your Mac, simply choose Insert Hyperlink from the Format menu and enter the information in the body of your e-mail message. On the Windows version of AOL software, you can insert a hyperlink simply by highlighting the item in your e-mail message, clicking the right mouse button, and choosing Create Hyperlink from the drop down box. Or, just drag the hyperlink reference from your Favorite Places folder and drop it directly in your e-mail message. ■

How to Send E-Mail

After you compose your e-mail, you can send it in a number of ways. When you're logged on to AOL, the fastest way to send your e-mail is to click the Send Now icon on the left side of the e-mail window. The mail is sent immediately, along with any attachments. See "Attaching Files to E-Mail," later in this chapter.

If you compose your outgoing e-mail when you're not connected to AOL, or sign off before composing it, you can choose to use the Send Later feature that saves the outgoing mail on your hard drive. Send your saved mail manually on your next online visit, or automatically during your next automated mail session. Please note, however, that if you attach a file, you can't move or delete that file until after you send your mail.

How to Receive E-Mail

This is the easy part! All you have to do is log on to AOL and, if you have mail, the happy guy that lives inside the AOL program tells you, "You have mail!" (that is, assuming that you have your Mail Sounds turned on in the Member Preference settings; if you're a Windows user you also need a computer with a sound card). A special You Have Mail icon is also displayed on the Welcome screen (see fig. 8.5).

FIG. 8.5
The Welcome screen indicating you have mail waiting to be read.

Click here to see
your incoming mail

You can click the You Have Mail icon on the Welcome screen, or you can press ⌘-R (Ctrl+R for Windows users) to view a list of new mail (see fig. 8.6). You can then double-click to open each piece of mail. You may also click the Next arrow icon on the mail form to advance to the next message (see fig. 8.7). The Previous arrow lets you move backward through the mail. The left and right arrow keys on the keyboard are equivalent to clicking the Next and Previous arrows.

FIG. 8.6
Here's a list of e-mail waiting to be read.

TIP

If you want to send a letter you just received to another online address with your added comments, use the Forward icon.

FIG. 8.7
Here is the Read E-mail form. Note the navigating arrows in the lower corners.

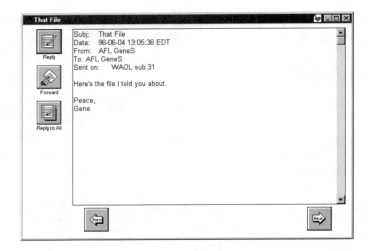

As you read each piece of mail, a check mark is placed in front of the item as it appears in the New Mail window. If you do not read all your mail in one session, the pieces that have the check mark do not show up when you next open the New Mail window. Only those items you have not previously read appear there.

Clicking Ignore is functionally the same as clicking Read, except no Read Mail window opens. Of course, if the person who sent you the e-mail checks the status of the message, he or she will know if you ignored the message. So, you may want to consider the feelings of the person who sent the message before you decide to ignore it.

Clicking the Delete button removes the message from your list of incoming mail, unread. Of course, the person who sends you e-mail will know, in checking the message status, that you have deleted the message.

The Keep As New button allows you to keep the message among your list of waiting mail even after you've read the message. It's useful if you want to use that message as a reminder of an upcoming event or if it contains a specific bit of information you want to review the next time you visit America Online.

Attaching Files to E-Mail

America Online's e-mail system allows you to attach files from your computer (files on your hard drive or from a disk placed in your computer's floppy drive) to a piece of e-mail. When you send your e-mail, you also send the files you attached to it.

To attach a file when composing e-mail, simply click the Attach icon, and use the accompanying dialog box to select the file you want to attach (see figs. 8.8 and 8.9).

N O T E   On the Mac version of AOL's software, you may also choose to compress the file you
attach by selecting the Compress Files option before clicking the Attach File button.
If you elect to attach more than one file, the AOL software automatically compresses them. ■

FIG. 8.8
In the AOL Windows e-mail
form, the Attach icon is
located on the left margin;
it's at the right for the Mac
version.

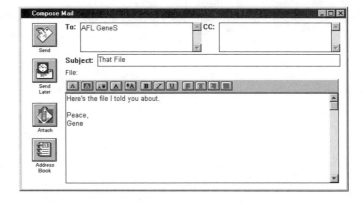

FIG. 8.9
Selecting files to attach
is easy in this dialog box.
Note that long file names
under Windows 95 will be
truncated for the 16-bit
version of AOL's software.

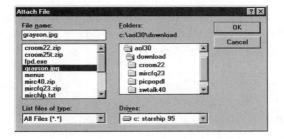

The file you attach must be on a disk drive connected to your computer or a drive you've
mounted from your network, and you must attach the file before you send the e-mail. The
recipient sees two extra buttons at the bottom of the received e-mail window (at the right
on the Mac e-mail window), Download File and Download Later. Clicking the Download
File button transfers the file from America Online's host to the recipient's computer. Clicking Download Later marks the file for the Download Manager for transfer at a later time
(see fig. 8.10). For additional information on the Download Manager, see Chapter 20,
"Tips and Tricks on Finding Software," and Appendixes B and C.

When you send attached files via e-mail, you are charged only for the time needed to send
your message and the attachments to the AOL mail processing area. Similarly, the recipient of the attached file is charged for the time needed to transfer the file from AOL's host
to his or her computer. Because this costs money on both ends, it is not a good idea to
send unnecessarily large files through e-mail.

FIG. 8.10

A Windows e-mail window with the Download File and Download Later icons indicating an attached file.

Use file compression whenever possible and, if you believe other AOL members could make use of the file, consider posting the file to a forum library instead of sending it on e-mail. By posting the file to a forum, you are not charged for the connect time spent sending (uploading) the file to AOL's host. Read Chapter 20 for more information about uploading files to an AOL software library.

 TIP   If you are transferring a GIF or JPEG image file to another AOL member, compression is probably not going to provide much benefit. These formats are already compacted internally and rarely benefit from additional compression. Besides, you probably want both Mac and Windows users to be able to download these files with similar ease, and the compression technique that works on a Mac may not work if the file is downloaded by a Windows computer.

N O T E   The Attach File icon changes to Detach after you attach a file to your e-mail. In the event you decide not to send the attached file, but you still want to send the original e-mail message, you can click Detach to break the link between the unsent e-mail and the file (see fig. 8.11 for the Windows e-mail form). At this point you can still attach a different file to your letter before it's sent. ■

FIG. 8.11
Detaching files is a simple matter of clicking the Detach icon, located where the Attach icon used to be.

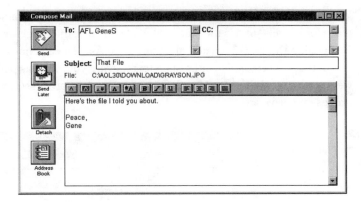

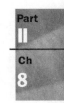

Attaching Files to Internet E-Mail

If the recipient of your e-mail is a member of another service, you can still attach files to your e-mail in most cases. You should not have to do anything special to the file or your e-mail. AOL's e-mail system will convert the files behind-the-scenes to a format that can be read via most Internet-based services. If you are unsure if the process will work or not, send a brief file attachment to the member of the other service as a test—or simply have that person contact the service for information about whether it supports files attached to AOL e-mail.

For the full story about working with AOL's Internet e-mail feature, you'll want to read Chapter 30, "Secrets of Internet E-Mail and Mailing Lists."

Saving for Posterity

After reading each piece of your e-mail, you have a few options. The first is to simply click the close box of the window, which sends the mail into oblivion. (Well, not quite—you can always find and read mail you've previously viewed, in the Check Mail I've Read menu item, found on the Mail menu.)

Mac Option Only: Mac users have the option of copying mail to their Personal Filing Cabinet, a file stored on their hard drive that can hold tons of saved e-mail, newsgroup messages, information about downloaded files, and other online information. To save to the Personal Filing Cabinet, click the labeled icon on the e-mail you've received. You can retrieve this e-mail item at any time, even if you are offline, in which case it can be accessed through your Offline Mail Drawer.

You can also save your e-mail as an individual file. America Online has two special file types for e-mail—one is the standard e-mail format, the other straight text (see fig. 8.12). By opening the File menu and choosing Save As, you can choose to save your e-mail as one of these types of files or as plain text. Saving your mail as plain text enables you to view or change the contents of the e-mail in any text processor, such as your favorite word processing program.

FIG. 8.12
Here are your handy file Save options for your AOL e-mail.

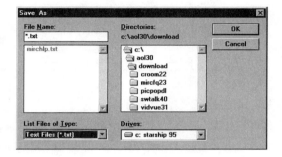

Printing E-Mail

To print a hard copy of your e-mail, open the File menu and choose Print. This works the same way as in almost every other application that supports printing. Remember, however, that if you changed printers since the last time you printed anything from AOL, you first have to choose Page Setup to verify your printing options.

> **CAUTION**
>
> If you are using a Macintosh and do not have a printer selected in the Chooser after you start your AOL program, you will likely not be able to print a text window; you'll just see a little flicker from the File menu when you choose the Print or Page Setup functions. Should this happen to you, log off America Online, selecting the Quit rather than Sign Off option. Select your printer in the Chooser, launch America Online's software, and then log on again. You should now be able to print normally.

▶ **See** "Sending Faxes on America Online," **p. 73**

How to Use AOL's Address Book

Use your America Online Address Book to store mail addresses that you use regularly so that they are available at the click of a mouse. Use this feature to build a file card system to keep track of your online friends.

Suppose that you have an online friend named James Bond, and you exchange mail with him often. His screen name on America Online might be Bond007. You'll probably find it more convenient to store his name in your Address Book rather than to type it manually each time you compose mail. To add the name to the Address Book, do this:

1. Open the Mail menu and choose Address Book.

2. Click the Create button. A new Address Group entry form appears on-screen (see fig. 8.13).

FIG. 8.13
Here is the AOL Address Group screen name entry form.

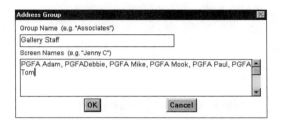

 T I P As you meet new friends and associates online, be sure to add their names to your Address Book. That way, you won't lose track of your online contacts.

3. Type the name of your friend in the Group Name field; for example, **James Bond**.

4. Type the screen name of your friend in the Screen Names field; for example, **Bond007**.

Now, the next time you want to send a piece of mail to James, or any other person, simply open a new mail window, click the Address Book icon on the left side of the e-mail form, then click the name of the person to whom you are sending e-mail.

Mac Users Only: The Mac user's Address Book feature looks different from the one shown here, which comes from the Windows version of AOL software. The options in the Mac Address Book are tabbed, labeled Edit Book to add or change entries, and Address Book, which is what you also see when you select it from the e-mail form.

I mentioned earlier in this chapter that you can enter groups of people in the mail window if you want to send a single e-mail to a number of recipients. Well, you can also include group addresses in your AOL Address Book. As an example, suppose you have a group of online associates with whom you correspond regularly, perhaps your staff at work or your favorite Forum Leaders on America Online. Here's how you can create a group of addresses in your Address Book:

1. Open the Mail menu and choose Edit Address Book.

2. Click the Create button. A new address form appears on-screen.

3. Type a name for your group in the Name field; for example, **My Staff**.

4. Type the screen names of all the people you want in that address group into the Accounts field; for example, **SteveC, TimB, Gene**.

Congratulations! You set up a group address and, when you select My Staff from your Address Book, all the names you entered for that group appear on the e-mail address field on your Mail form.

N O T E The next two sections of this chapter have separate sets of instructions about using the FlashSession feature in both AOL's Macintosh and Windows software. Because the techniques are similar, some of the text is the same. Unless you're using both platforms, there's no reason to read both.

Using FlashSessions with AOL's Macintosh Software

You can set a schedule for your America Online Macintosh software to log on automatically at those times when you're too busy or nowhere near your computer. You can even schedule these sessions for any one or all of the screen names on your account. Here's what you can do in a FlashSession and how to set it up.

First choose Set Up FlashSession from your AOL Mail menu, which brings up the screen shown in figure 8.14.

FIG. 8.14
Your Auto AOL Preferences are used to decide what tasks AOL will perform.

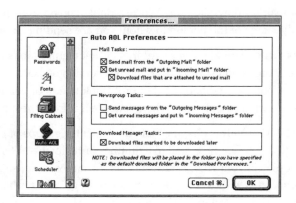

Here are the options you can select. Just click the appropriate check box to activate that task during your FlashSession. The e-mail and files you receive will also be displayed in your Offline Mail Drawer (which is accessed from the Mail menu).

- **Mail Tasks**. Here you choose whether to send and receive your AOL e-mail and whether to receive files attached to your e-mail.

N O T E If you're on a tight budget, you may prefer to uncheck the option to download attached files, because you would have no control over whether a large file is being sent during your FlashSession.

- **Newsgroup Tasks**. You can send and receive messages from your selected Internet newsgroups. To activate this function, though, you must first select newsgroups from which to download messages in AOL's Newsgroups area (Keyword: **Newsgroups**). I explain how to do that in Chapter 32, "Joining and Participating in Internet Newsgroups."
- **Download Manager Tasks**. This feature will result in automatic downloading of any files left in your download queue during your FlashSession. You can see the list of files in the queue at any time by choosing Download Manager from the File menu.

CAUTION

AOL only stores unread e-mail for about five days. This means that if files are attached to that mail, they may become inaccessible. So, you'll want to try to retrieve your e-mail via FlashSessions at shorter intervals, or just tell those who send you e-mail with file attachments when you expect to be available to receive it.

Scheduling FlashSessions

If you want to have your mail automated using America Online's FlashSessions, you are almost there. You've selected the FlashMail options in the previous section, and all that remains is to set up the FlashSession schedule and enter the passwords for the screen names used during these sessions.

The next step involves calling up the Scheduler Preferences (see fig. 8.15), by clicking the Schedule icon at the left of the Preferences window.

Now you need to follow these steps:

1. Click the Perform scheduled Auto AOL sessions check box to activate your FlashSessions.
2. Click the pop-up menu to the right of the Sign On option to determine how often your sessions will be run (it ranges from every half hour to once per day).
3. Under On the Following Days, click the check box to the left of the days of the week you want your sessions to run.

FIG. 8.15
Use the FlashSession scheduling window to decide when your automated logons will occur.

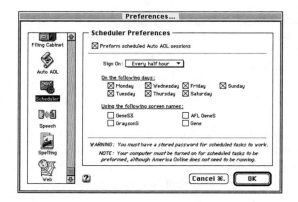

4. Under Using the Following Screen Names, choose the names you want to use for your FlashSessions here.

5. Click OK to close this window and to store the settings you made.

> **CAUTION**
> In order for your Mac AOL FlashSession to run, your computer must be on at the appointed time. However, AOL's clever Scheduler system will automatically launch the software if it isn't running when your FlashSession is due to begin.

Storing Your Passwords

This feature allows you and your family to enter passwords for your screen names. This is necessary so that you do not have to be present for scheduled FlashSessions. Otherwise, you have to enter your password manually each time you log on to AOL.

> **CAUTION**
> When you save a stored password with your America Online software, anyone who has access to your computer can log on to the service with your account, and use online time that is charged to your monthly bill. Before using this option, be certain your computer is not easily accessible to others without your permission. You may want to consider, for example, using a security program to prevent unauthorized access to your computer.

To store your passwords, follow these steps:

1. Click the Passwords icon in AOL's Preferences window.

2. Enter your passwords in the fields next to the screen names shown. Notice as you enter your password that bullets (small round circles) appear rather than the characters you type. This feature prevents others from looking over your shoulder and seeing your password on-screen.

3. Click the Valid only for FlashSessions check box if you want to store the passwords strictly for automated sessions on AOL.

4. Click OK to save your settings.

America Online's internal log-in calendar is now working and connects to the service at the times you scheduled. To turn off automatic connections, select the FlashSessions menu item, click the Schedule FlashSessions icon, deselect the Starting At check box, and click OK.

 Another way to automate your AOL e-mail sessions is with a nifty program from Apple Computer's Claris division, Emailer. You can use this program to run automatic e-mail sessions on all of your AOL screen names and send and receive files from each of them. What's more, if you have accounts on AppleLink, CompuServe, and a number of Internet-based services, you can run your sessions from these services as well, all with Emailer. Because I have a number of online accounts, I have found this program to be an invaluable way to keep tabs on all the e-mail I have to manage.

Scheduling FlashSessions with AOL's Windows Software

FlashSessions are a marvelous way to have AOL do the walking for you, as it were. You can schedule your America Online Windows software to log on automatically at those times when you're too busy or nowhere near your computer. You can use these sessions to send and receive e-mail, and to download attached files and those in your Download Manager queue. And you can use them to handle your Internet newsgroup messages (see Chapter 32, "Joining and Participating in Internet Newsgroups," for more information).

To set your FlashSession preferences, select FlashSessions from the Go To menu. The first time you choose this option, America Online guides you through the process of scheduling your automated session, using a special feature called Walk-Through (see fig. 8.16).

FIG. 8.16

America Online's FlashSessions Walk-Through guides you step-by-step through the process of activating automatic e-mail sessions.

Scheduling FlashSessions Using Walk-Through

The center button at the bottom of your first Walk-Through window gives the option of an Expert Setup. If you are familiar with setting up FlashSessions in the Macintosh version of America Online's software, or you've done it before in the Windows version, you may prefer to use the Expert Setup. You then have the many choices described above in configuring the Mac AOL software for a FlashSession.

If you'd rather go through the process in a more leisurely fashion, click the Continue button to continue your Walk-Through, which brings up the screen shown in figure 8.17. This screen gives you the option of retrieving unread mail during your FlashSessions.

FIG. 8.17

Your first decision in preparing a FlashSession is whether you want to receive your unread mail during these automatic logons.

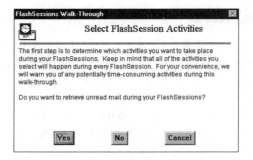

The next screen, shown in figure 8.18, only appears if you decide to retrieve incoming mail. You are then presented with another choice, whether to download files attached to your e-mail. If you don't accept this option, you are instructing the AOL software not to download files that are attached to incoming e-mail. This can be a real money saver if you ever receive a large file attachment while you are in a hotel room paying exorbitant phone charges for even a local call.

FIG. 8.18

Here you decide whether to automatically download files attached to your e-mail during a FlashSession.

If you select No, you have the capability, for five days after you read the e-mail, to download its attached files manually. Even easier, you can select the Forward icon on the e-mail you receive with the attachment and send it to yourself. Turn on the Automatically Download Attached Files option before the next connection, and the file is downloaded at that time.

> **CAUTION**
>
> AOL only stores unread e-mail for about five days. This means that if files are attached to that mail, they may become inaccessible. So, you'll want to try to retrieve your e-mail via FlashSessions at shorter intervals, or just tell those who send you e-mail with file attachments when you expect to be available to receive it.

The next e-mail option, shown in figure 8.19, is whether to automatically send your outgoing mail by a FlashSession. This choice is very useful. It allows you to compose all of your e-mail while offline, so you don't incur online charges to your account. When you complete your e-mail, simply click the Send Later icon, and it is added to your queue of Outgoing Mail. The only disadvantage is that you cannot select which mail to send during a particular FlashSession. It's all or nothing. But, you will probably want to click the Yes button for this option.

Download Manager Preferences

The Download Manager stores a list of files you've selected using the Download Later option. This feature allows you to transfer all the files you want in a single session. The option shown in figure 8.20 allows you to retrieve all your selected files in the Download Manager automatically during a FlashSession. Because you cannot selectively download a single file this way, you may want to think a bit about this option before giving it the okay.

FIG. 8.19
Here you decide whether to automatically send your outgoing e-mail during your FlashSession.

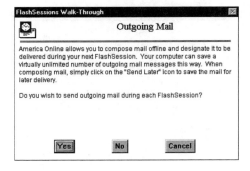

FIG. 8.20
If you choose Yes, you'll be able to retrieve all the files selected via AOL's Download Manager during your scheduled FlashSession.

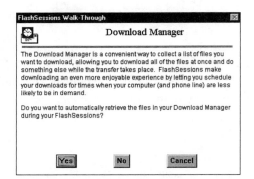

Internet Newsgroup Options

You can also receive and send messages from Internet newsgroups as part of your AOL FlashSession. You have separate options to receive Incoming Newsgroups and to send messages via Outgoing Newsgroups. In order for this feature to work, however, you need to actually specify which newsgroups you want to be included in your FlashSessions. For more information on how to choose those newsgroups, read Chapter 32, "Joining and Participating in Internet Newsgroups."

Saving Passwords

When you get past the Newsgroups option, you'll see another screen, shown in figure 8.21, that allows you and your family members to enter passwords for your screen names. This step is necessary so that you do not have to be present for scheduled FlashSessions. Otherwise, you have to enter your password manually each time you log on to AOL. Remember that if you store your passwords, be sure that no unauthorized persons have access to your machine. As you enter your password, what you type will be entered as asterisks, so someone looking over your shoulder won't see what your password is.

FIG. 8.21
To log on automatically during a FlashSession, you need to enter your password for each account for which you want to schedule your session in this window.

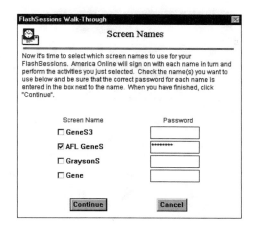

CAUTION

When you save a stored password with your America Online software, anyone who has access to your computer can log on to the service with your account, and use online time that is charged to your monthly bill. Before using this option, be certain your computer is not easily accessible to others without your permission. You may want to consider using a security program to prevent unauthorized access to your computer.

Scheduling FlashSessions

Up until now, you've decided what you want to do when you run a FlashSession on America Online. Now it's time to decide when to run those sessions. There are two ways to have a FlashSession. One is simply to open the Mail menu and choose Activate FlashSession Now, click the check boxes corresponding to the screen names for which you want to run your session, and then click the Go Ahead button. The FlashSession begins on the spot, using the preferences you've selected.

The second choice is to run an unattended FlashSession at regularly scheduled intervals. The next few screens of your FlashSession Walk-Through allow you to plan your FlashSessions in advance. You can change your settings at any time, as your needs change. The first screen, shown in figure 8.22, gives you the option of scheduling your FlashSessions. If you opt to run the sessions manually, click the No button; otherwise, Click the Yes button to continue. You then have three sets of selections to make.

FIG. 8.22
If you want to automate your
FlashSessions, click the Yes
button. If you want to decide
later on, or run the sessions
manually, click No.

1. The first option, shown in figure 8.23, lets you choose the days of the week when you want your FlashSessions to take place. If you use your computer at work, you'll probably check only the weekdays, unless, like your cheerful authors and stressed-out editors, your work knows no such boundaries.

FIG. 8.23
Click the boxes corresponding to the days of the week
you want to schedule
FlashSessions on AOL.

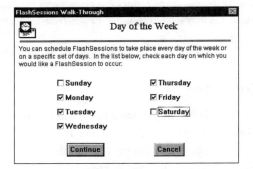

2. Your next choice, shown in figure 8.24, is how often you want to schedule a FlashSession, ranging from every half hour up to just once per day.

3. Finally, you want to decide what time your FlashSession should begin, as I've done in figure 8.25. If your computer is not on during a scheduled FlashSession, you receive no warning message that the session did not run.

America Online's internal log-in calendar is now working and connects to the service at the times you scheduled. To turn off automatic connections, select FlashSessions from the Mail menu, click the Schedule FlashSessions icon, deselect the Starting At check box, and click OK.

FIG. 8.24
Click the boxes corresponding to the frequency of your FlashSessions.

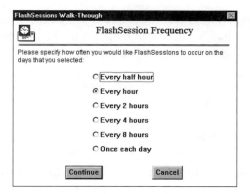

FIG. 8.25
Indicate the starting time for your first FlashSession for each day you've selected.

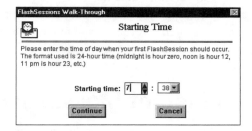

CAUTION

If a FlashSession that includes attached files for downloading is interrupted for any reason, the status of the download process is reflected in the Download Manager. The next time you log on to AOL, either for a regular session or a FlashSession, you'll be able to resume the download precisely where it left off. Do not delete the partial file created during the original download or move it to a different directory or folder; if you do, you won't be able to resume the download where it left off and you'll have to start the process from the beginning. If your file *upload* is interrupted for any reason, however, you'll always have to start from scratch. And remember, your computer must be turned on for a FlashSession to be run.

Incoming and Outgoing Mailboxes (for Both Mac and Windows Users)

Each piece of e-mail you create for a FlashSession is a separate file. The mail you want to send is placed in the Read Outgoing Mail directory (or folder) which you can choose from the Mail menu (it's called Offline Mail Drawer in the Mac version). You can open individual letters to review or edit the contents. You can even delete a message, should you not want to send it. After all of your outgoing letters have been sent, the Read Outgoing Mail item is grayed out (a clear indication that it's empty).

 TIP The best time to schedule FlashSessions to download software is early in the morning or late at night. That's when traffic on AOL is lowest, and download times are speedier.

The Read Incoming Mail directory (or folder), also available from the Mail menu, is your personal mailbox (or the Offline Mail Drawer for the Mac version). Each e-mail letter you receive from a FlashSession (or from using the Save to FlashMail option when you open a new e-mail message online) is stored in this mailbox as a separate file. To read a letter, just double-click its listing in your incoming mailbox. You can save and print these letters when you want, or delete them when the amount of e-mail begins to get a little overwhelming. When the entire contents of your incoming mailbox have been deleted, the Read Incoming Mail selection in the Mail menu is grayed out.

The Lowdown on Instant Messaging

The first part of this chapter described how to use e-mail to communicate with other AOL members. Although e-mail messages are sent almost instantaneously to other AOL members, and with some delay through the Internet, the only way they can be read is for the recipient or recipients to log on to the service and open your message (or to run a FlashSession). This section describes the technique used to communicate with fellow AOL neighbors one-on-one, while both of you are online, using Instant Messages.

NOTE If you send an instant message and don't get a response immediately, it doesn't mean that the other member is being rude or ignoring you. Sometimes a person is online but not present in front of his or her computer, such as during a FlashSession. At other times, the member may be in the middle of uploading a file and cannot respond to you. If you don't receive an answer, try sending another instant message after a few minutes, or just use e-mail instead. ▩

To send an instant message while online, select Send Instant Message from the Members Menu or press ⌘-I (Ctrl+I for Windows users). You see a new window in which to address and compose your message (see fig. 8.26).

If you receive an instant message, respond to it by clicking the Send button, entering your reply in the lower portion of the Instant Message window, and clicking the Send button (see fig. 8.27).

FIG. 8.26
Here's the originator's Instant Message window.

FIG. 8.27
And here's the recipient's Instant Message window.

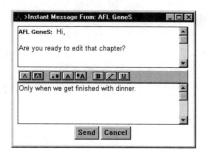

Part

II

Ch

8

> **N O T E** If you are using a Macintosh, you can press the Enter key on the numeric keypad rather than click the Send button to send your instant message. You can't use the Return key to send your message because this key starts a new line in your message text. If your keyboard does not have an Enter key, use ⌘-Return. If you are using America Online for Windows, you can press Ctrl+Enter rather than click the Send button. ▪

You can have a two-way conversation with any AOL member by leaving the Instant Message window open after you send a response. When a new message arrives from your friend, it appears in that window. (If your online sounds are turned on, the arrival of the message follows a pleasant musical tone.) The actual conversation appears in the upper text field, while the responses you type appear in the lower portion of the window. You can hold numerous instant message conversations simultaneously.

> **N O T E** Using instant messages is a simple and unobtrusive process. If you are typing in a different window at the moment an instant message arrives, for example, you can automatically send the incoming instant message behind the top window with your next keystroke, provided you turn off the option to bring instant messages to the front (this option is in your AOL application Preferences, described in Appendixes A and B). ▪

As with other types of text windows in AOL, you can print or save the Instant Message window's contents by opening the File menu and choosing Print or Save.

N O T E   If you send an instant message to someone just when they log off, or they are disconnected from AOL for some reason, the message appears to go through, but you soon see a message in your Network News window (the small information window at the top of the screen) that the message didn't reach its recipient. ▦

TROUBLESHOOTING

Help! My desktop is cluttered with instant message windows. When I hear that little noise about their arrival, I just don't know what to select. Welcome to the club. We've all had that problem. What I try to do is close the instant message windows for conversations I'm no longer involved in. Then I group the rest of the windows in a neat pile at one corner of the screen (on your windows PC you can minimize the windows). All together, this helps keep my desktop relatively free of scattered instant messages (most of the time, anyway).

From Here...

If the '80s were the Information Age, the '90s are the Communication Age. Instant access to people all over the world is a reality, regardless of their location or time zone.

- ▦ For more information about e-mail and instant messages, see Chapter 6, "Where Do We Begin?," Appendix B, "Using Your America Online Macintosh Software," and Appendix C, "Using Your America Online Windows Software."

- ▦ For information on how to seek out and participate in message boards, read Chapter 9, "Using America Online Message Boards."

- ▦ America Online Computing and Software forums and forum conferences are described in-depth in Chapter 19, "Visiting the Computing and Software Forums."

Using America Online Message Boards

How you choose to become active with America Online is entirely up to you. Your online visits can be either passive or active.

The passive technique involves seeking out and reading information on a topic that might interest you, such as the news of the day, or methods to solve common problems with your favorite software. This technique is passive, because you are not actually communicating with anyone else during your online visit.

In Chapters 7 and 8, you learned several ways to actually talk to fellow members, such as sending e-mail, participating in chats, attending conferences (more of which is covered in Chapter 10, "Chatting Online"), and exchanging instant messages with another member. These last items can be considered active. They are especially enjoyable because you get an instant response from your fellow member, and it's surely a terrific way to build a lasting friendship. This chapter deals with a more permanent form of online expression, the use of forum message boards. ■

Finding the Right Message Area

Message boards and e-mail are similar, with one major exception. E-mail contains a message that is designed for a single recipient or a group of recipients. A message board is, pure and simple, a public statement, put on display in an area where any other member of America Online can read and respond to it (sort of the online equivalent of a neighborhood bulletin board). A message board in a particular forum is generally devoted to one subject. For example, in the computing and software forums, messages might be devoted to one aspect of your computing experience, such as handling problems with your computer's operating system, or finding the right multimedia software with which to make a presentation. In a cooking forum, messages might be devoted to the best ways to use a wok for preparing vegetables, or how to make a particular kind of omelet.

One advantage of message boards on America Online is that you don't have to communicate only with members who are online at the same time as you. When you leave a message, you can wait several minutes, hours, or even days before checking back to look for responses. Or you can simply respond to a message posted by someone else.

Chapter 6, "Where Do We Begin?," presents a capsule summary of many of AOL's departments. Throughout the book are chapters that detail the workings of each of those departments and the forums they include. You can use these chapters as a guide to help you choose the forums that seem to match the topics that interest you during your online visits.

Before posting anything in a forum's message boards, you should take some time to learn about a particular forum and its specific topics of interest. To do this, you need to explore and get a feel for the material discussed. You'll want to read older messages (you learn how to limit your search a bit later in this chapter), so you can see if the comment you want to make has already been voiced by another member, or if the question you want to ask has already been answered. Most forums have a weekly update text that you can read to find out what's new and what's happening in that forum.

For an example, take a look at the forum information from the Macintosh Desktop Video Forum (see fig. 9.1); the keyword is **MVD**. (Of course, because this is my book, I figured I may as well show my own forum.)

 The best thing to keep in mind when getting accustomed to AOL's message boards is to look and read before you post. Be sure your message is appropriate to a particular board, and please don't post the same message over and over again.

FIG. 9.1

This is the author's AOL forum, Mac Desktop Video.

Finding Forum Messages

After you find forums that you want to explore further, and after reading the forum update information, look over the message boards to see if there are any discussions in which you want to get involved.

N O T E This section describes the various descriptive icons and labels you find on AOL message boards, and I'm showing a few of them as they'll appear during your AOL visits. Depending on which icon you click, you'll bring up a different range of options to see the messages you want to read. But once you know what the options mean, the sequence in which they appear doesn't make a big difference. ■

 To find messages in a forum that might interest you, click the Message Boards icon, which generally appears on the forum's main screen. This brings up the window shown in figure 9.2, or one very similar to it. The general subject matter of the forum is described briefly in the Message Boards window.

FIG. 9.2

Typically, a brief introduction describes the purpose of a message board.

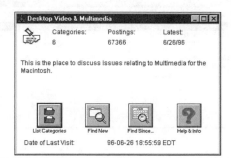

There are four icons at the bottom of this window, three of which take you further along the road to finding messages you want to read:

■ *Browse Folders* (or sometimes *List Categories*). This icon opens a list of discussion topics.

■ *Find New*. This icon brings up a display of posted messages and topics created since the last time you entered that forum (AOL's host computer keeps a record of your previous visit).

If you are visiting a forum for the first time, choosing this icon can literally produce dozens of topic folders and hundreds of messages. You might be better off using the next option, Find Since.

N O T E If you lose your online connection for any reason (such as getting disconnected because of a problem with your telephone line), AOL's host computer will usually still record your visit to a forum message board, even though you never finished reading the contents. You might end up getting a window that indicates that there are no new messages, even though you didn't read them all the first time around. If this happens to you, use the Find Since option and choose the time frame for which you want to find messages. ■

■ *Find Since*. This icon lets you set the duration of time spent searching for new messages. Its default is 1 day, but when you enter a forum for the first time, you might want to read all messages added in the previous 30 to 60 days, so you can get the flavor of the forum and the kind of messages the board contains.

■ *Help & Info*. This icon is your route to the Mac or PC Help Desk; the PC Help Desk is shown by title for Windows users.

For now, click the Find Since icon, enter **14** in the In Last Day(s) box, and click Search. A list of discussion topics posted in the last two weeks will appear, as shown in figure 9.3.

FIG. 9.3
Forum messages are subdivided by topic.

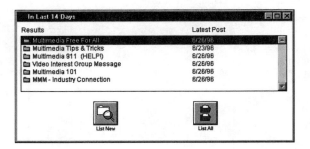

Each forum divides its message boards by titles, which represent a group of general topics that relate to the forum's field of interest. The message board in figure 9.3 has five general topic titles.

To get to the next step in your message-reading process—the actual names of the message boards themselves—click one of these general topics, and then click List New to see the collection of subtopics (see fig. 9.4).

FIG. 9.4

A list of discussion topics in a message board.

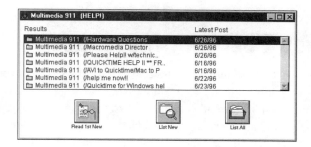

There are three icons at the bottom of the window:

- *Read 1st New.* Select the topic in which you want to read messages, then click here to jump right into the first new message in the folder.

 TIP After you open the first message, use the arrow keys on your keyboard to move to the next or previous message.

- *List New.* This is the fastest way to check for all the recent postings without wading through a sea of months-old messages.

- *List All.* This choice brings up a window that lists all the messages posted under this subtopic. You can review this directory and decide which messages to read. Then double-click the message itself to open that message window.

In most message boards, you have a Create Topic option that allows you to make your own folder, name it, and describe the subject matter.

NOTE You'll only get this option if you accessed the message board using List All.

There are actually three types of message boards on America Online. The most common format is the one I've just described, but there are two other methods of organization for message boards. The second, which I'll describe later in this chapter (in the section titled "A Brief Description of Message Threading"), is a message board in which all responses to a single message are grouped together with the initial posting. The third type of message board is threaded too, but organized somewhat differently and, for now, is confined to AOL's Newsgroups area. The Newsgroup variation of a thread message board is detailed fully in Chapter 32, "Joining and Participating in Internet Newsgroups."

N O T E   Before you respond to a message, read the other responses first. It's possible that the message has already been answered or your question has already been dealt with by another member. ■

Before You Post Your Messages

After you've found a suitable message board in which to post your message, you'll want to prepare your message and then add it to that message board. Before doing so, though, it's a good idea to think carefully about what you're about to say. Although writing a message seems very similar to writing an e-mail letter, there's a very important difference. With e-mail, you are usually creating a personal message, designed for one recipient or a group of recipients, quite often someone you already know. Your language can be conversational and personal in nature. When you get involved in a message board discussion, you have to think about a wider audience.

America Online has millions of members; at the very least, thousands of those members might read your message while it's available. This means you have to consider your comments much more carefully than you might when just communicating among friends. Here are a few thoughts to consider when preparing your message:

■ Check your message carefully for spelling errors and poor grammar. Remember, the message reflects on you, and spelling mistakes detract from what you are trying to say.

 T I P   To ensure that your messages are properly constructed, you might want to prepare them in a word processor program (which affords you spell checking, and sometimes a thesaurus and grammar checker), or use one of the many shareware text editors available from AOL. You then can use the Cut and Paste option to insert the message into an AOL message form.

■ Do not include personal information, such as your address, telephone, or credit card number. Remember, you are revealing this information to a potential audience numbering in the millions. If you are writing a message in an area run by a software publisher, do not include the serial number of your software (which might reveal it to a software pirate). If the publisher wants it, they'll contact you via private e-mail.

■ Be sure the topic your message covers is relevant to a forum's message boards. You wouldn't want to discuss your favorite Windows software in a Macintosh forum, or vice versa, or discuss cooking in a forum devoted to home audio systems.

N O T E After a period of time, America Online forum staff members often remove outdated messages or archive them to software libraries. If your message suddenly disappears, this might be the reason. If the message is not considered appropriate to the forum, though, you'll usually get a message from the forum staff about it. ■

Posting a message after you write it is a one-click process not unlike sending e-mail. Click the Add Message icon, or Respond in some forums (discussed later in this chapter), enter the subject in the first text entry window, and insert your comment in the second text entry window. By default, the subject of the message to which you're responding appears, preceded by the reference (Re:). You can, however, delete this subject and choose one of your own, if you are not responding to a previous message.

After you write your message, click the Post icon, and the message is added to the topic folder you are viewing. When your message is actually posted, your screen name and the time it was sent will automatically appear at the top of the message.

 T I P As with regular e-mail, it's considered good online etiquette to sign the messages you post in a message board.

CAUTION

Posting a message more than once in a single forum is considered bad online etiquette. Some AOL members might even get upset about having to read the same message over and over again on billable time. When you have something to say, take a moment to choose the topic folder or directory that closely matches what you want to write about. In many forums, you can create your own topic to begin a discussion.

A Brief Description of Message Threading

If you are a frequent visitor to a user group bulletin board system or some of the other online services, you might be familiar with a feature called *message threading*. This is a technique that automatically groups all messages devoted to a single subject, one right after another, rather than having them mixed in with other messages about other subjects.

When you post a message in a threaded message board, you get the option to respond or reply to an individual message, rather than just post a new one. There's an important difference between responding and posting. When you respond to a message, your reply is added to the thread, so readers can read the original message and all the responses it brings in one group. If you post a message, it is simply added to the message folder or directory in chronological order without regard to which message you're responding to. Even where message threading is available, you'll want to post a message if you prefer to begin a new topic.

You'll find one form of message threading available in America Online's Newsgroups area (keyword: **Newsgroups**). Because Newsgroups are discussed in much more detail in Chapter 32, "Joining and Participating in Internet Newsgroups," for now it's enough to know that message threading is spreading to different message boards throughout America Online. The ability to keep all of the messages on a single subject together makes browsing through messages much easier, at least when you get used to it.

Here's the setup of a typical threaded message board on America Online (see fig. 9.5). (At first glance, the organization is similar. However, some message board commands have different results when the board is threaded.)

- *Read 1st Response.* This icon brings up the first answer to the message you are reading. If no responses have been made, you see a display window to that effect.

- *List Responses.* This icon provides a list of the responses made to the message you're reading, if any.

- *Read 1st New Response.* This icon takes you to the response added since the last time you checked this message thread.

- *Add Message.* This icon creates a new message on a new topic that doesn't respond to any previous message posted in a particular folder.

- *Post Response.* Click this icon to respond to the message you're reading (see fig. 9.6). The message form is almost the same as the one used in the regular AOL message boards, with one exception, which is described next.

FIG. 9.5

This message is part of a message board where the contents are threaded (by subject), rather than placed simply in the order in which they're posted.

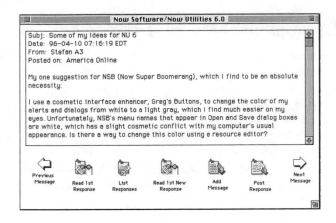

FIG. 9.6
Responding to a message in a threaded board gives you the choice of sending an e-mail copy to the member to whom you're replying.

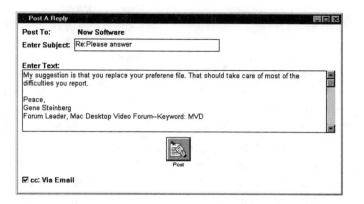

You should consider the threaded message setup described in this chapter to be an interim version. Threaded messaging is available only in some AOL forums. In the future, you can expect to see further updates in the message board area that combine some of the best features of the threading technique with the way it's organized in the Newsgroups area. So take a look at that area at your leisure to get an idea of what the future may bring (perhaps even by the time you read this book).

Common Sense Advice on Online Etiquette

So far this chapter discussed how to locate and use message boards and the mechanics of writing your message. Over the years, a set of unofficial online traditions has been established that cover the organization of messages and good online behavior. Chapter 16, "Parental Issues and Internet Access," describes America Online's Terms of Service, which cover, to some extent, proper use of language in message boards. This section describes some of the rules of the road. They are similar to what is called Internet *netiquette*, which is one of the topics discussed in Chapter 32, "Joining and Participating in Internet Newsgroups." Here are a few tips based on my experiences over the years on America Online and other services:

- Read before you post. Be sure your message is appropriate to a forum, and also review past messages just to be sure your questions or comments haven't already been covered.

- When you respond to a message, consider that you are not just posting a response to a single person, but to an audience that could number in the millions. If you decide you want to restrict your audience to a single person, send that person e-mail instead.

■ Show respect and be polite when you post a message. If you disagree with someone's statement, try to stick to the issues, and refrain from personal attack. Such attacks are regarded as *flaming*, and while they might be entertaining on some television talk shows, they are not considered good taste in an America Online message board. In addition, a personal attack can be considered a violation of AOL's Terms of Service.

■ When responding to someone else's message, quote the relevant portions of that message at the beginning of your response, or before each part of your response that refers to that message. Don't quote the entire message (it wastes a lot of space). The usual convention is to place a forward sign (>), to signify a quotation mark at the beginning of each line, as shown in the following example. Just remember that this message is just meant as a sample; I happen to have enjoyed just about every Tom Hanks movie I've ever seen:

```
> I really don't understand what the big fuss

> over the new Tom Hanks movie is all about.

> I thought Philadelphia was a much better

> flick.
```

■ Be brief. Cover the points you want to bring up, or ask your question in a clear and direct manner. Although you might be tempted to add a literary flourish if you like to write, remember that those who are reading your message are paying for their online time, as you are, and would prefer that you get right to the point.

■ When you click the Post button in a typical America Online message board, the topic of the previous message will automatically be inserted into the subject line, preceded by the abbreviation Re: (see fig. 9.7). If your comments are not intended as a response to the previous message, be sure to change the subject line to one that's appropriate for your own message.

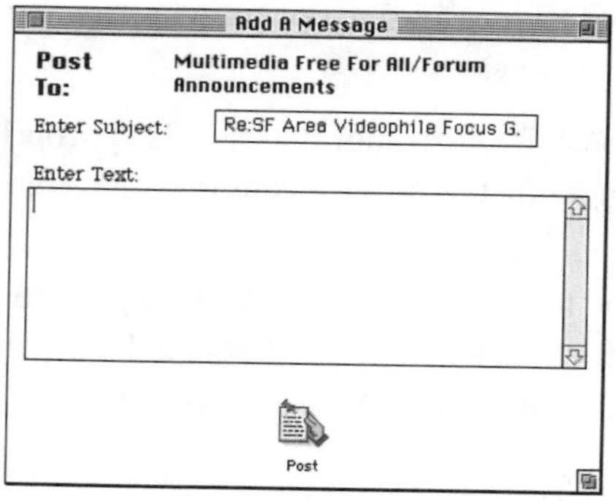

FIG. 9.7

If the subject of your reply doesn't relate to the original message, it's best to clear the Subject: line and start over. (Some forums may not allow the creation of new topics.)

- Express emotions and humor with care. When you speak with someone in person, very often body language and the inflection of your voice reveal whether you are serious or not, or whether you are angry or happy about something. Your words alone must be the mirror of your feelings on America Online. Experienced online users express emotions with smileys :). See Chapter 10, "Chatting Online," for a list of common smileys and emoticons, and a few that aren't so common.

- Watch your language. Four-letter words and other vulgar epithets might be a part of many books and movies (and perhaps the conversational demeanor of many people), but they have no place on America Online, which is a family-oriented service. Also remember that using such language might result in having your message removed by the forum staff, or a Terms of Service complaint being lodged against you by another member.

- Do not post copyrighted material without the permission of the copyright holder. You can, of course, quote portions of a copyrighted work when commenting on that material. That is considered "fair use," but try to limit your quotations to no more than a few sentences at most.

- Do not cross-post. Choose the forum in which you want to post your message, and then select the message topic that seems most appropriate or, if possible, create a topic of your own. But don't post the same message over and over again. Internet surfers call this *spamming*, and I call it bad manners, because it's not polite to expect fellow members to read the same thing over and over again.

Looking for a Response

After you've posted your message, no doubt you will be anxious to read an answer of some sort (if you posted a question), or see if anyone else has commented about your message. But posting a message does not guarantee that someone will respond; this is a hard fact, but one that's generally true. However, a forum with a well-stocked message board tends to get a large number of visitors, so it is very likely other AOL members will, in time, get to read your message. Some might have a response. And if you've asked a question directed to specific people, such as the manufacturer's technical support representatives in a company's support area, it might take a little while to see a reply—especially if you post on a weekend, when support people are not generally online.

The best thing to do is be patient. The next time you visit America Online, return to the forum's message area, and use the Find New feature in the forum's message window to see the messages posted since the last time you logged on.

N O T E If you don't see an immediate response to a question you've posted, you might be tempted to post the same message again, perhaps in a different topic. My advice is don't. Other AOL members who see the latest messages will just end up seeing both messages, and might become annoyed rather than informed, when they read the same thing a second time. ■

If you don't see a response to your message or question after a few days, look over AOL's departments and see if there's another forum that might be related to the subject of your message. For example, if you have a problem with a modem, you might seek out the Mac or PC Telecommunications Forums, or the Mac or PC Hardware Forums. Posting one message in each forum isn't against good online practice; in fact, it might be a good idea, because you can reach an additional audience. Not everyone will necessarily visit both forums.

N O T E Until you get used to posting messages and perhaps have a regular list of forums to visit when you log on, you might want to use AOL's memo feature to create a log of the messages you've posted and where you posted them. That will make it easier for you to return to those message boards again when you are looking for responses. ■

From Here...

America Online's message boards are fun and informative to read. Participating in these message boards gives you an outlet for self-expression and a chance to get involved in discussions about a variety of issues.

- For more information about e-mail and instant messages, see Chapter 6, "Where Do We Begin?" and Chapter 8, "Using America Online E-Mail."

- For more information about using America Online chat rooms and auditoriums, see Chapter 7, "America Online's People Connection," and Chapter 10, "Chatting Online."

- The America Online Computing & Software forums and forum conferences are described in depth in the four chapters that comprise Part V, "Computing Resources Online," which includes Chapter 19, "Visiting the Computing and Software Forums," Chapter 20, "Tips and Tricks on Finding Software," Chapter 21, "The Best Macintosh Software on AOL," and Chapter 22, "The Best Windows Software on AOL."

- For more information on message threading and using America Online's Internet Center, see Chapter 32, "Joining and Participating in Internet Newsgroups."

Chatting Online

All about online meetings

Learn about finding upcoming chats and conferences.

Get the most from an online conference

Master the ground rules for participating in online chats.

How to behave online

Discover what chat protocol is all about.

Finding a conference of interest

Explore how to use AOL's conference rooms.

Secrets of online slang

Learn what smileys are all about.

Over the past couple of years, I've attended conferences featuring such diverse personalities as best-selling author Tom Clancy, comedian Milton Berle, *Tonight Show* host Jay Leno, actress Teri Hatcher, star of ABC's *Lois & Clark,* and a number of famous music stars. The best part is, I didn't have to leave my home or office, brave rush-hour traffic and long lines at a ticket counter, or fight the teeming crowds for a good seat. I was able to attend every one of these meetings while seated in front of my desktop or laptop computer, simply by logging on to America Online.

Every night on America Online, literally dozens of virtual rooms and auditoriums are open and active. In them, you'll find thousands of members engaged in online chats or sitting in the audience of huge online auditoriums. And in those auditoriums, you'll have a chance to meet famous movie stars, TV stars, and authors. ■

The Differences Between Chats and Conferences

You can think of a chat room as the equivalent of a small classroom or meeting room. Capacity is limited to 23 folks in the People Connection before another room is opened automatically. In a forum chat room, the capacity is 48; then, as in People Connection, a new chat room is automatically created.

Because forum conferences are designed to be held in just one room, however, the second room created for an overflow crowd is best suited for hanging out until someone leaves the main room again. It's very much like waiting for an available seat in a restaurant. The setup is quite informal. Many times, you can just make a comment on the proceedings (so long as you don't interrupt the chat) without having to get anyone's attention. When a special guest is present, some forums will invoke something called chat protocol, which is explained shortly.

If you've been an AOL member for a while, you know that some very famous personalities have been invited to participate in online conferences. As you realize, some of these personalities, especially the world-famous rock stars who visit America Online, can draw crowds sometimes numbering in the thousands. A regular chat room just won't cut it for handling that kind of crowd; having hundreds of AOL members vying for the guest's attention by posting questions and comments in a chat window would be chaotic.

All About the Action Center Stage

Keyword: **Center Stage**

There is a special kind of online environment that's designed to handle such highly attended events more sensibly. It's structured in such a way that folks have a chance to interact with the special guest, but not at the expense of having hundreds of questions asked all at once. To solve this dilemma, America Online and People Connection came up with a unique interactive concept: the AOL Auditorium (see fig. 10.1). You can compare this conference area to a regular auditorium, complete with rows for the audience and a stage for the guests. There are several auditoriums available at any one time, all of which you can reach through the keyword **Center Stage**.

N O T E America Online's Computing and Software department has another auditorium for large gatherings, known as The Rotunda (keyword: **Rotunda**). The instructions that follow also apply to your visits to the Rotunda (although it is a separate area). More information about the Rotunda and its special schedule is provided in the next section of this chapter. ▪

FIG. 10.1
The People Connection Auditorium is where hundreds can gather.

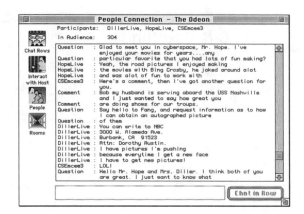

Part
II

Ch
10

Center Stage is America Online's largest gathering place, capable of accommodating thousands of members for fun-filled game shows and special events, spread over several separate auditoriums. You'll learn just how conferences are conducted a little later in this chapter.

 T I P If you're still unsure of the setup in a particular conference room, you'll want to check out the Auditorium Help window that appears at the upper left of your AOL program window when you enter the room.

Entering the Rotunda

Keyword: **Rotunda**

AOL's Rotunda is quite similar to AOL's Center Stage auditoriums, except it's devoted strictly to computing-related topics (see fig. 10.2). Like Center Stage, the Rotunda's virtual auditorium can handle thousands of visitors at any one time. Like other auditoriums, there is a center stage for conference hosts and guests. There are also chat rows, where you can sit during the conference and interact with fellow members.

Before you make your first visit to the Rotunda, you'll want to learn more about it by reading the Welcome to the Rotunda text (see fig. 10.3). A complete schedule of upcoming Rotunda events is shown in the list of Upcoming Rotunda Events, available from the main Rotunda window.

FIG. 10.2
Computer-related topics are discussed in AOL's Rotunda.

FIG. 10.3
Double-click the items in the list box for information on how the Rotunda operates.

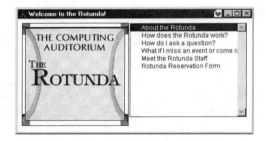

> **NOTE** In case you miss a chat, don't worry. The Rotunda staff logs most every event, and the logs are always posted in the area's software libraries. Because the logs consist of straight, unformatted text (which you can usually open with your AOL software or any word processor), the file sizes are small; you can generally download a log in just a minute or two. ▪

Joining an Online Chat

Before you go to a chat or conference, you'll first want to find out which one you should attend. Forum chats and conferences are sometimes promoted with a special icon in AOL's Welcome window, which you see when you first sign on to the service (see fig. 10.4).

FIG. 10.4
A special icon in the Welcome window announces an active online conference.

In addition, the Computers & Software channel of AOL (see fig. 10.5) has its own custom announcement display, What's Hot (also known as the Computers & Software Spotlight), which is accessed from the main screen of this channel. To return to the regular Computing channel window, simply click the Computers & Software Main button.

Part
II

Ch
10

FIG. 10.5
The Computers & Software Spotlight contains announcements of in-progress chats and conferences.

Another place to locate information on online chats may be labeled What's HOT in Computing and Software (see fig. 10.6)—as opposed to the What's Hot icon in the main Computers & Software channel screen. You can find it after you click the Support Forums button which is available in the main directory of the Computers & Software channel and in many forum areas. You'll find listings in the directory window of upcoming chat events that you'll want to check out regularly.

FIG. 10.6
This variation of the What's HOT theme gets you a list of information about computing and software chats.

In addition to these resources, you can visit a particular forum directly to check its upcoming chat schedule. A main forum window (see fig. 10.7 for an example from the PC Graphic Arts forum) will also display the dates for regularly scheduled chats (such as every Friday, etc.).

FIG. 10.7
Computing and software forums show when their regular chats are held.

Center Stage conferences are advertised in the AOL Live window (see fig. 10.8), which you can access via the keyword **Live**. The day's conferences are listed when you click the Today's Live Events icon. The Coming Attractions icon offers a list of upcoming events.

FIG. 10.8
Check AOL Live for a listing of upcoming conferences.

N O T E In case you've missed a Center Stage chat, you'll be able to download conference transcripts and photos of some of the special guests who have appeared in online conferences. The libraries are accessed by clicking the Events button. You'll have the choice of a listing of available transcripts, or a Search tool you can use to find the log of a particular event. ▪

Participating in Online Chats

Once you know what chat or conference you want to attend, the next step is to enter the conference hall by clicking the appropriate icon in a forum, Center Stage, or Rotunda window (refer to fig. 10.8).

When you first enter Center Stage, the service (euphemistically referred to as Online Host) reminds you that only those in the same row as yours can see the text you type to the screen. You can talk simply by entering text in the conference room window, and then clicking the Send button (or pressing the Return or Enter key). If you find that the conversation of members in the same row is distracting from your concentration on the main event (somewhat like being disturbed by folks around you in a movie theater), you can turn off the chat feature. Just click the Chat Rows icon shown in the conference room window; then click the Turn Chat Off button in the window that appears (see fig. 10.9). When the Chat feature is turned off, you can enjoy the event while seeing only text that appears from the stage—text from your hosts, guests, and contestants.

Part

II

Ch

10

FIG. 10.9

More chat controls for the Center Stage Auditorium are found in the Chat Rows window.

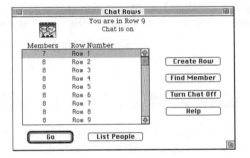

From this window, you also can look for other members who might be online (so you can tell them what a great time you're having on Center Stage), list people in your chat row or any other row, and create a new chat row. If you wish to move to another seat, just select the row you want to enter, and click the Go button. Because chat rows are each limited to eight members, you won't be able to enter a row that's already filled.

You also can highlight selected speakers or contestants. Highlighting causes the conversations of the selected people to appear in bold type in the chat window so that you can follow the conversation more easily. First (if you're a Mac user), click the People icon on the left side of the Center Stage window. Then click the Who's Onstage button. Finally, select the individual on the stage whom you want to highlight, and choose the Hilite button (see fig. 10.10). Windows users will see the same information in the People on Stage directory at the upper right of the conference room window.

FIG. 10.10
Select Hilite to highlight on-stage guests in Center Stage.

Of course, the best part of attending an online conference is to ask a question of the special guest and have it answered. To pose your question, click on the Interact with Host icon in the main conference room window, enter your question, and then indicate, by clicking on the appropriate button, whether it's meant to be a question or a comment.

N O T E Because online conferences might be attended by hundreds or thousands of AOL members, quite often there isn't enough time to answer all of your questions. The conference moderator will try to use a representative sample of the questions submitted, but do not expect that your question, however important it is to you, can always get a response. Sometimes, though, guests will respond to unanswered messages via e-mail. It depends on the conference. Show business personalities, for example, often appear using temporary online accounts and will probably not respond to e-mail after the conference is over. ■

Instant Messages and Online Chatting

Instant messaging on AOL, as described in previous chapters, is a great way to have a one-on-one conversation with a fellow AOL member. During a forum chat, it's also a way to get information about the subjects dealt with in a chat or to elicit further information from a guest or a forum staff.

If you see someone involved in a chat whom you'd like to know better, you can send an instant message to that person. If you have a problem or a question about a subject other than that being discussed, you can send an instant message about it.

But there are a few things you should consider before you send an instant message:

- Try not to send an instant message to a special guest in a chat. Quite often, that guest will be busy answering questions and won't have time to engage in personal chit-chat with you. It might be better to wait until the chat is over or send the person e-mail.

- Participants in an online conference in one of AOL's auditoriums are usually unable to receive instant messages while on stage. So don't be disappointed if you don't get a response. Use e-mail instead.

N O T E When you first enter a chat room, quite often you'll receive an instant message from a member of a forum's staff that offers information about the night's chat, and, sometimes, a message as to whether chat protocol is in effect. (You learn what protocol is all about in the next section.) If you get a message of this sort, try not to engage that staff member in an extended instant message chat, because the staff member is probably busy greeting other visitors.

Some Insights into Proper Online Etiquette

As with other online areas, AOL's chat and conference rooms have their own conventions of online etiquette. Beyond normal considerations of courtesy and good taste, there are a few things you should be aware of when attending an online chat.

The Rules of the Road

Chapter 16, "Parental Issues and Internet Access," describes important parts of America Online's Terms of Service, the list of regulations that you are expected to follow during your online visits. You should apply those standards when you attend a chat room also. Here are a few things to keep in mind:

 T I P If you're unsure about the topic or setup of a particular chat, don't hesitate to send instant mail to the forum staff about it (it generally has an AFL, PC, or a similar designation in front of its screen names).

- *Watch your language.* Sometimes chats can become exciting; no doubt you'll find yourself reacting emotionally at times to what someone is saying. Remember, vulgar language in a chat is just as inappropriate as it is in your e-mail, instant messages, and message board discussions.
- *Don't interrupt.* It's hard to know sometimes when you engage in a regular conversation when to add a remark of your own. It's even more difficult in cyberspace, because you don't always know when others have stopped talking. Here are some things to look out for when reading a chat window or when conversing yourself:

1. Use of ellipses (...) to signify that the statement is not yet finished and more text is to be added.

2. Use of the words "go ahead" or the initials GA to indicate that the member's statement is finished and others can now begin to talk.

- *Avoid irrelevant topics.* Unless the chat is an open session, in which there is no particular subject of discussion, try to confine your conversation to the subject or subjects at hand. If you need to contact the forum staff about another subject, you might wish to send an instant message to see whether e-mail would be a better way to raise a subject.

> **CAUTION**
> Deliberately and repeatedly interfering with the flow of dialog in a chat room, even if meant as a joke, can be considered a violation of AOL's Terms of Service. Take the time to watch the flow of conversation in a chat room to see what topics are being discussed.

A chat is meant to be fun and informative. If you pay attention to the ground rules, you can sit back, relax, and enjoy the session, and even participate at the right time.

Using Chat Protocol

When a forum has a large crowd and a special guest, quite often chat protocol will be put into effect. This is not meant to restrict the flow of conversation, but to give everyone a chance to participate without filling the screen with lots of unconnected comments. The rules of chat protocol are simple:

- Type **?** in the chat window if you have a question.
- Type **!** in the chat window if you have a comment about the topic being discussed.
- Don't ask your question or make your comment until you are called upon by name by the chat host (even if your name shows up at the beginning of a list of waiting questioners that appears in the chat window).

At the tail end of a chat, protocol will often end to give visitors a chance to hang out and talk informally about whatever is on their minds. You'll usually see a message about free chat time or a similar announcement when the formal part of the session is over.

N O T E If you miss a chat or arrive late, don't worry. Most of the time, the forum or conference staff will post a log of the chat in a few days (just as is done with Center Stage and Rotunda events). Just watch the software libraries for it.

Using Abbreviations and Shorthand Symbols

Chatting online is, obviously, quite different from talking to a person whom you can see. For one thing, you have no way to convey emotions in the usual manner, by voice inflection or by body language. All of your conversation is conducted via keyboard, with the words that you write, and sometimes it's not very obvious what emotions might be attached to a specific statement. You might mean for something to be serious, sarcastic, or humorous, but the words themselves can sometimes be subject to several meanings. As a result, a series of keyboard abbreviations has been created over the years to convey emotions online.

They're called *smileys* or *emoticons*. This section offers a listing of many of the abbreviations and shorthand symbols you might see while online in AOL's People Connection, in chat rooms, or on message boards. They are a result of the need to show what cannot be shown when online—facial expressions and body language.

Online Abbreviations

Often when chatting, America Online members will shorten long phrases into a few letters so that they can be typed quickly. Here are some of the more common online abbreviations:

Abbreviation	Stands For...
LOL	Laughing Out Loud
ROFL or ROTFL	Rolling On The Floor Laughing
AFK	Away From Keyboard
BAK	Back At Keyboard
BRB	Be Right Back
OIC	Oh, I See
IMO	In My Opinion
IMHO	In My Humble Opinion or In My Honest Opinion
TTFN	Ta-Ta For Now
TTYL	Talk To You Later
NIFOC	Nude In Front Of Computer
GMTA	Great Minds Think Alike
IHTBHWYG	It's Hard To Be Humble When You're Great
<g>	Grin
GA	Go Ahead

Online Shorthand

Learning online shorthand might take a bit of time, because there are so many possibilities in the list that follows. But you'll find, after you gain online experience, that only a relative few are in common use, and some are encountered infrequently at best (a few I've never encountered in years of online visits). In putting this list together, I've collected a number of sometimes brilliant examples of online shorthand—keyboard symbols that convey human expression. Tilting your head toward the left will help you to see most of the symbols; for example, the characters :) form a sideways smiley face. Here are some common examples:

Shorthand	Symbolizes
[ ]	A hug, repeated as needed for degrees of enthusiasm, such as [[[[[[[ ]]]]]]]
:)	Basic smile
:(	Frown
:/	Ho-hum smile
;)	Winking smile
:D	Smile with a big grin
:*	Kiss
8)	Wide-eyed smile
B-)	Wearing sunglasses
[:l]	Robot
:>)	Big nose
:<l	From an Ivy League school
:%)%	Acne
=:-)	Hosehead
:-)8	Well-dressed
8:-)	Little girl
:-)-}8	Big girl
%-)	Cross-eyed
#-)	Partied all night
:-*	Just ate a sour pickle
:-'l	Has a cold

Shorthand	Symbolizes
:-R	Has the flu
:-)'	Tends to drool
':-)	Accidentally shaved off an eyebrow
0-)	Wearing a scuba mask
P-)	Getting fresh
I-)	Falling asleep
.-)	Has one eye
:=)	Has two noses
:-D	Talks too much
O:-)	Smiley face with halo; very innocent
:-{)	Has mustache
:-)}	Has goatee/beard
Q:-)	New graduate
(-:	Australian
M:-)	Saluting (symbol of respect)
8:]	Gorilla
8)	Frog
B)	Frog wearing sunglasses
8P	Bullfrog during mating season
8b	Same as 8P
I)	Salamander
:8)	Pig
3:-o	Cow
:3-<	Dog
pp#	Cow
pq'#'	Bull
}.\	Elephant
+O:-)	The Pope
C=:-)	Galloping Gourmet
=):-)	Uncle Sam

continues

Part
II

Ch
10

continued

Shorthand	Symbolizes
=l:-)	Abe Lincoln
4:-)	George Washington
5:-)	Elvis Presley
7:-)	Fred Flintstone
:/7)	Cyrano de Bergerac
>:*)	Bozo the Clown
#:o+=	Betty Boop
>>-O->	General Custer
8(:-)	Walt Disney
>:^(	A headhunter
-=#:-)	Has wizard status
(: (=l	Going to be a ghost for Halloween
=:-H	Plays for NFL
(V)=l	A Pac-Man champion
M-):X):-M	See no evil, hear no evil, speak no evil
C):-O	A barbershop quartet
C):-O	
C):-O	
C):-O	
>:-(	Sick and tired of reading this nonsense
;^?	Punched out for submitting a sexist article
l-O	Bored
*-)	Shot for the last posting
~~\8-O	Needs to fix frayed cord on terminal
8-O	Took too many No Doz to work on thesis
L:-)	Just graduated
$-)	Just won the lottery
:-@	Extremely angry

Shorthand	Symbolizes
:-o	Shocked
B-)-[<	Wearing sunglasses and swimming trunks
:-#	Punched in the mouth
R-)	Broken glasses
:-7	Talks out of the side of the mouth
%')	Finished off a fifth for lunch
:-(O)	Yelling
. .	Lying down
l:-)	Heavy eyebrows
{:-)	New hairstyle
{:-{)}	New hairstyle, mustache, and beard
(:-)	No hair
:~)	Ugly nose (needs a nose job)
:-E	Major dental problems
C:-)	Large brain capacity
l:-l	Excessively rigid
:-)))	Very overweight
._)	Suffers from Lorentz contractions
:-G-	Smokes cigarettes
:-p~	Smokes heavily
\:-)	Wears a French hat
]:-)	Devil
8=:-)	Chef
$-)	Yuppie
{{-}}}	Refugee from the '60s
0-)	Cyclops

Part
II

Ch
10

From Here...

Participating in a chat or attending a forum conference can be a fun and sometimes exciting experience, especially when you can meet a famous personality while seated in front of your computer, and even have your questions answered by that personality. You'll want to regularly consult AOL's chat schedules to learn about upcoming events. If you are a regular visitor to online forums, you'll find its chat schedule posted in its weekly update.

- For more information about e-mail and instant messages, see Chapter 6, "Where Do We Begin?" and Chapter 8, "Using America Online E-Mail."

- For more information about using America Online chat rooms and auditoriums, see Chapter 7, "America Online's People Connection."

- The America Online Computing & Software forums and forum conferences are described in depth in Part V, "Computing Resources Online."

A Wealth of Entertainment at Your Fingertips

CHAPTER 11

TV and Movie Information Online

AOL's popular Entertainment channel

Find the latest news from the world of entertainment here.

More online conferences

Meet your favorite celebrities in online conferences

Get photos and movie clips

You can download photos and movie clips from your favorite TV programs and motion pictures

America Online has a large, active channel devoted strictly to entertainment, which is the focus of this chapter and the next four. To get the ball rolling, I'll describe the vast online resources for information about television, radio, and movies. Wherever your interests lie, America Online has a place where you can find the entertainment you seek.

This chapter introduces you to online areas where you can simply relax and have fun. ■

> **N O T E**   A quick shortcut to your favorite area is to use a *keyword*. Just press ⌘-K on the Mac
> or Ctrl+K in Windows and enter the name of the area you want to visit (the keyword),
> then click Go. Then you're on your way. The keywords you need to find the features described in
> this chapter are included. ■

Exploring the Entertainment Channel

Keyword: **Entertainment**

To begin the search for entertainment-related information, look at America Online's Entertainment Forum. To access this area, use the keyword **Entertainment**. The directory window shows just a few of the areas you will visit in this chapter (see fig. 11.1). During your online visits, you'll discover many more locations that provide you not only with information but also with your own opportunity to participate in discussions on a host of related subjects; you can even post your own TV and movie reviews.

FIG. 11.1

The Entertainment channel is America Online's gateway to many information resources for TV, radio, and the movies.

 T I P   As explained in Appendixes B and C, you can save and print any text document you see on America Online.

You'll learn about many features in this channel throughout this chapter. New features are added regularly to America Online's resource roster, so you can expect this directory to change often. Special show business events also have their own online forums while the events are current, so some of the special icons you see in figure 11.1 might not be there when you log on.

You can survey the features of the Entertainment department in two ways. There's an alphabetical directory that lists the areas available in the right half of the screen. On the left and at the bottom, there are various topic listings that will quickly transport you to one of your favorite areas. I'll describe some of these offerings here and later on in this chapter.

Hot Internet Entertainment Sites

Keyword: **Webentertainment**

AOL offers you seamless access to the most popular entertainment sites on the World Wide Web. Just as you see in figure 11.2, most every AOL channel and many individual forums take you a click or two away from the Internet.

FIG. 11.2
AOL offers you a tasty plate of Internet-based entertainment sources.

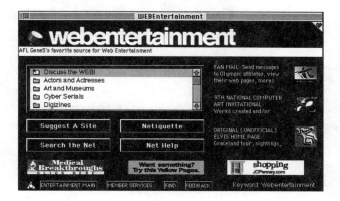

Visiting EXTRA Online

Keyword: **Extra**

EXTRA is a TV entertainment-oriented magazine program that is shown six days a week in syndication around the U.S. The producers of the show have established this online forum (see fig. 11.3) so you can learn about future programs and participate in special events.

Let's tour some of the features shown by icons in figure 11.3. The What's Hot Today icon presents information about upcoming shows. You are also invited to participate in an online poll on issues covered in the program, and write to the program's hosts and staff with your concerns. Click the Meeting Hall and Live Chat icons to interact with the show's staff, fellow AOL members, and visiting celebrities. The Superstar Library offers photos and other files of your favorite stars. Click the Free Newsletter icon and you can add your name to its mailing list for information about upcoming shows and other events that you'll want to know more about.

FIG. 11.3
Here's a forum devoted to a popular TV magazine program.

The buttons at the very bottom of the list, Movie Sites, TV Sites, and Music Sites, will take you to entertainment-related centers on the World Wide Web.

If you are new to an area, you'll want to consult the forum's directory for an item labeled Television Stations & Times for a listing of the local stations that carry the show. And if it hasn't appeared in your area yet, you'll be able to find out when it will be added to a local station's lineup.

A Little Bit about Games Online

Keyword: **Games**

This section serves as a bit of a hint of what is to come. AOL has a number of games-related forums that you can access through the Games channel (see fig. 11.4). Rather than discussing these in detail, the illustration here serves as a brief guide.

▶ **See** "Playing Games Online," **p. 213**

And a Little Bit about Music Resources Online

Keyword: **Music**

The MusicSpace channel is typical of the way many AOL channels are organized; it represents a gateway to other forums, in this case, AOL's music forums (see fig. 11.5).

FIG. 11.4
Many of America Online's popular games-related forums can be accessed via the Games channel.

FIG. 11.5
Many of America Online's music forums can be reached courtesy of MusicSpace.

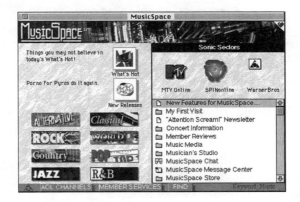

In the next few pages, you'll read about some of the many music-related areas available on America Online. This is only the beginning, as further exploration will reveal many more places to visit during your online travels.

You can also read about music in Chapter 12, "Music, Books, and Art."

Reading Entertainment News and Information

Keywords: **News Sensations**

Gossip makes the entertainment world go around. Getting information about programs, movies, and personalities to the press helps sell tickets, increase ratings, and so on. AOL's

News Sensations forum (see fig. 11.6) groups many of the online entertainment-related resources in one convenient window, with gateways to several forums.

FIG. 11.6
Read the latest entertainment news online.

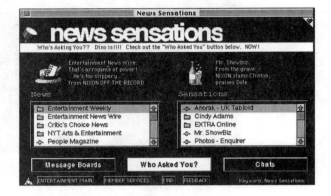

For the latest entertainment news, double-click Entertainment News Wire from the News list box. This option takes you directly to AOL's People & Entertainment news department (keyword: **Entertainment News**) which groups the latest entertainment events of the day into convenient sections (see fig. 11.7), represented by icons; it's sort of the online equivalent of your daily newspaper. (You can also read Chapter 15, "Pursuing Lifestyles and Interests," and Chapter 23, "The News of the Day.")

FIG. 11.7
Here is AOL's People & Entertainment news wire.

The next stop in the News Sensations window, Critic's Choice News, takes you to AOL's popular critic forums. The remaining icons are handy gateways to other AOL entertainment forums that provide related information. Rather than list any of them here—because the lineup often changes—I'll just invite you to revisit this area often. The icon showing Top Internet Sites takes you to databases located on the Internet, a sprawling network consisting of thousands of individual computers and services. For more information about these databases, you'll want to read Part VIII, "Entering the Information Superhighway."

Visiting the Television & Radio Forum Center

Keyword: **TV, Television**

The Television & Radio information area provides a quick link with many of the popular radio TV networks, plus information about upcoming programs (see fig. 11.8). Before you decide what you want to watch or tape, America Online gives you a chance to preview what's coming up on the tube (or on your radio dial).

FIG. 11.8
You'll want to visit AOL's Television & Radio forums often.

Because additional networks are always being added to AOL's roster, the directory window you see in this book is apt to change from time to time, with more and more broadcast entertainment forums being added as months go by. In the bottom of the Television & Radio area is a TV LISTINGS button, where you can check the day's programming schedule. The following sections visit some of the networks.

Visiting ABC Online

Keyword: **ABC**

ABC Online is conveniently divided into separate sections for each programming category (see fig. 11.9). There's an icon at the upper right for ABC Sports, for example, and an icon at the bottom left representing ABC's daytime programming (ABC Soaps). ABC News also gets its own icon. The ABC Kidz icon brings up a roster of the network's popular educational offerings. At the right, ABC TV, you'll bring up areas devoted to all your favorite prime time programs on the network.

FIG. 11.9
ABC Online has separate departments dedicated to all its programming categories.

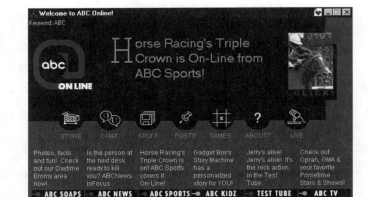

To visit one of ABC Online's departments, just click the appropriate icon. You'll find each area has many things in common. There are full descriptions of the network's programming, a very active message board where fans and forum staff participate, schedules for upcoming shows, and a library of photos of the major stars of various popular shows.

You'll also want to visit ABC's Auditorium to check the conference schedule. Many of the network's popular stars, such as Dean Cain and Terry Hatcher, costars of *Lois and Clark*, have participated in ABC's online meetings, where you have the chance to send questions to your favorite ABC personality. To attend a live event, just click the Live icon for information and a fast entrance to the active conference rooms.

I Want My MTV on AOL

Keyword: **MTV**

MTV is the popular cable TV music network with a rock slant (see fig. 11.10, which you see when you click the illustration in the center of the opening window of this forum). In recent years, its programming has spread far beyond just music videos to include entertainment-related news and interviews.

▶ **See** "Music Resources Online," **p. 198**

Visiting Comedy Central

Keyword: **Comedy Central**

There are a number of cable TV networks that are devoted to just one segment of programming, all of which have forums on AOL. For example, there's Comedy Central where you can watch sketches, sitcoms, funny movies, and delight in the silly walks and other madcap antics of Monty Python's Flying Circus, or view classic episodes of Saturday Night Live (see fig. 11.11).

FIG. 11.10
MTV's Online forum on AOL.

FIG. 11.11
Comedy Central on AOL, where laughter reigns supreme.

You can expect to have a good time on this network's AOL forum too. You can review the network's programming schedule, learn about special shows, or even download multimedia clips from popular shows that you can play on your personal computer. And you can also click Talk To US! (which you find when you scroll through the forum's list box) to interact with the personalities and producers of Comedy Central.

Using E! Entertainment Television

Keyword: **E!**

Here's another specialized TV network, devoted strictly to the world of entertainment, ranging from radio and television to the movies and the literary world. E! Entertainment

Television (see fig. 11.12) has daily programming on entertainment and features classic movies at night.

FIG. 11.12

E! Entertainment Television covers the world of entertainment on cable TV.

Among the most popular E! programs is Howard Stern's controversial half hour shows, which are culled from his popular syndicated radio program.

Looking over the list of top shows in the Now Showing area, you'll learn more about two of the network's top programs, "The Gossip Show" (featuring your very favorite gossip columns from major newspapers) and "Talk Soup." The Hot Off The Press icon provides a listing of special presentations, the sort you'll find when a new movie comes out or when there's a special show business event, such as the Grammys or Oscars. For a full programming schedule, simply click the It's Show Time! icon.

And don't forget a trip to the Message Boards, Talk To & About E!, where you can voice your views about the network's programming, give your own suggestions, or just participate in discussions of programming and personalities.

Visiting the SciFi Channel

Keyword: **SciFi Channel**

Years ago, science-fiction fandom consisted of a small number of readers of magazines, devotees of movies, and the rare television show devoted to the subject. How times have changed. The original Star Trek television program of the 1960s, man's landing on the moon, and the epic Star Wars trilogy (to name just a few examples) have really put science fiction on the map. All this brings us to the online forum run by the SciFi Channel where science fiction reigns supreme from morning until night (see fig. 11.13).

FIG. 11.13
The SciFi Channel's forum, also known to fans of the network as The Dominion.

The SciFi Channel, offered on cable in many parts of the U. S., features science-fiction television series and movies. The network's AOL forum provides news about upcoming shows, and lots of in-depth information about specific programs, new books, television shows, and movies. To check the bill of fare, just click the Table of Contents button to access a full directory of the services offered, which include a bulletin board, program schedules, artwork from your favorite shows, and information about upcoming sci-fi shows and movies.

You'll want to consult the Trader for books, clothing, posters, and other memorabilia dealing with your favorite shows.

Now if my local cable carrier would just offer this channel, I'd be a happy camper.

 You can use your AOL software's Download Manager to queue up files you want to download from various libraries. First, select the files you want, using the Download Later feature. When you log off, you can have the files all download in one continuous operation.

Seeing Your Favorite Shows

Many of your favorite TV shows have forums on AOL (see fig. 11.14), which you find listed when you click Television at the left of the Entertainment channel screen shown in figure 11.1. You can reach that online area directly via the keyword **TV Shows** or

television. Some of the programs represented in this area include *Babylon 5, The Computer Man, EXTRA* (described earlier in this chapter), *The Geraldo Show, Last Call, The McLaughlin Group, The Nightly Business Report, The Ricki Lake Show, Sightings, Washington Week in Review,* and *The X-Files*. As time goes by, more producers will offer online support for their programs on AOL. You're probably already familiar with program segments that include messages and polls conducted in their America Online forums.

FIG. 11.14
Some of the TV shows offering AOL forums are shown when you scroll through the list box.

Radio Online

Keyword: **Radio**

Among the additional features available in AOL's Entertainment area is one devoted strictly to Radio that takes you to a radio forum (see fig. 11.15); you can reach this area using the keyword **Radio** or choosing Radio from the Entertainment channel's list box. Several popular programs and services are represented here. These include the National Public Radio Outreach program, the American Entertainment Network, and an area developed to ham radio enthusiasts.

FIG. 11.15
AOL's Entertainment's Radio Forum offers forums devoted to popular shows.

The icon labeled Computer Radio Shows offers access to a selection of forums run by the producers of several programs devoted to personal computers. The last icon, Soundbites, is just what the name implies, a library consisting of short sound clips, of both comedic and current events, that will add a touch of humor to your collection of sound files.

Accessing the Cartoon Network

Keyword: **Cartoon**

A discussion of America Online's entertainment offerings should definitely include the Cartoon Network forum (see fig. 11.16). Cartoon entertainment appeals to the young-at-heart, from children to adults. America Online has a special library of cartoon art in GIF (Graphic Interchange Format) format. See Chapter 7, "America Online's People Connection," for more information on how to create and view GIF files.

FIG. 11.16
America Online didn't forget cartoons.

A number of special libraries in this forum contain professional cartoon artwork that you can download to your computer, view, and print (at least for your personal use).

The Cartoon forum is also a resource for all you online cartoonists to create and post your own artwork so that others can see it. The Toon Talk section is a message area where you can discuss your favorite cartoon characters.

Reading DC Comics Online

Keyword: **DC Comics Online**

Even though the publisher's name might not always be remembered, I'm sure very few of you are unfamiliar with characters such as Superman or Batman. They all got their start

Part
III

Ch
11

in DC Comics (see fig. 11.17), and even though these characters have migrated to the movies and television, the original color comic books are still published and read across the world. Thus we come to DC Comics Online, where readers of these magazines can discuss and learn more about their favorite characters.

FIG. 11.17
DC Comics has its own support area on AOL, where you can learn more about your favorite fictional characters.

Besides DC Comics, the publisher, Time-Warner, also has established areas devoted to some of their other publications, such as *Mad* magazine, one of the original sources of illustrated satire. The impact of this magazine on American culture has been profound. *Mad* lampoons popular culture, such as movies, television, and commercials each month. This form of satire has gravitated to the broadcast medium too. For example, the radio shows and recordings from Stan Freberg (in the 1950s), the television antics of Steve Allen (in the 1950s and 1960s), and even *Saturday Night Live* (from the 1970s through the 1990s), in some respects, pay homage to the sort of humor pioneered in *Mad* magazine.

Online Celebrity Fan Clubs

While most of the online areas I've described so far are run by the media centers themselves, such as the networks, movie studios, or the producers of an individual program, still others are more or less developed by fans of particular celebrities or programs.

One such example is the Star Trek Club (keyword: **Trek**) as shown in figure 11.18. This forum includes discussions, a regular newsletter, and just as important, regular chats featuring the stars of your favorite Star Trek program or movie. There's even a folder that will tell you about all the episodes of the various programs and when they were first aired.

If you want to meet your favorite stars, you'll want to consult the listings in AOL's Center Stage for news of online conferences. Oldsmobile's Celebrity Circle is also a popular source of online sessions featuring popular figures from all areas of show business.

As you read through the message areas in the various online forums, you'll see many messages from fans of particular shows, with news of the fan clubs they run. Regular viewers of ABC's soap operas are often found in the Backstage Buzz conference room run by ABC Online (who welcomes their participation), and one or more of the stars of the show has been known to make an announced visit.

FIG. 11.18
Where no Star Trek fan has gone before, AOL's Star Trek Club.

Motion Picture Entertainment Resources

The word entertainment, for many people, produces such images as huge dinosaurs roaming the earth, spaceships racing between the stars battling evil-doers of all shapes and sizes, or bold adventurers seeking fame and fortune in untamed, undiscovered lands in exotic portions of the world. And these scenes describe many of the famous action movies that Hollywood has produced throughout the years.

In the next section of this chapter, I'll cover the online services available when you click the Movies icon in the Entertainment department.

Visiting the Movies Forums

Keyword: **Movies**

One of my favorite parts of AOL's Entertainment channel is the Movies section. You can access it via the keyword above, or by choosing Movies at the left side of the Entertainment channel screen. The result is shown in figure 11.19; it will change on occasion as new areas are added to AOL's sprawling online city.

FIG. 11.19
Just some of the forums featured in AOL's Movies department.

You'll find a gateway to America Online's Critics' Choice forum via the Movie area's list box. It's a place where you get your chance to be a critic. In this section, I'll concentrate on some of the other online areas shown and as I've said before, this list will grow in time.

Accessing Hollywood Online

Keyword: **Hollywood**

At any one time, literally dozens of current motion pictures are playing at your local theaters. New flicks are released weekly, and during the summer and Christmas seasons, scores of pictures compete for your attention and your ticket dollars. What to do?

America Online's Hollywood Online area is the resource you can use to learn about these films before they are released (see fig. 11.20). In fact, it's not just a single forum, but a gateway to a number of useful forums.

FIG. 11.20
Hollywood Online is Tinseltown's own forum on America Online.

The following paragraphs describe some of the features you can access from the seven icons included on the Hollywood Online screen:

■ FEATURE PRESENTATIONS! enables you to preview all of the new films before they reach your local screens. When you click this icon, you see the screen shown in figure 11.21.

FIG. 11.21
You can find the latest information about the newest releases from Hollywood's motion picture factory.

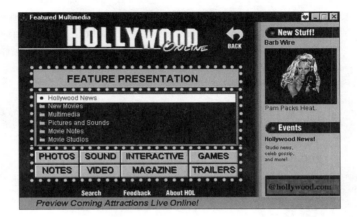

■ Pictures and Sounds is your resource library. Here you can download pictures of your favorite stars, and maybe even a sound bite from your favorite picture. If you've never downloaded files before, you'll want to read Chapter 20, "Tips and Tricks on Finding Software," first.

■ Hollywood News is an information resource where you can learn about what's really happening behind the scenes in Tinseltown. There's even an Ask The Stars feature, which allows you to post questions to your favorite stars and, often, get their personal answers. From time to time, motion picture executives and the stars themselves will have online press conferences that you're invited to attend.

■ Store (back at the main Hollywood Online screen shown in fig. 11.20) gives you a chance to order exclusive promotional gifts from the movie studios and participate in special contests. You may win such prizes as movie posters, complimentary movie passes, and other items. This place is one you will want to visit often.

■ Message Boards (also in fig. 11.20) gives you a chance to express what you like and don't like about a movie and about the actors and actresses in that movie. You can also read and respond to messages on these subjects from other America Online members.

Part
III

Ch
11

■ Multimedia (available when you click the FEATURE PRESENTATION icon) accesses Hollywood Online's software library. Here you find the tools you need to view photos of your favorite stars and to see brief movie clips. Read Chapter 20, "Tips and Tricks on Finding Software," for advice on how to download and use the software you receive from America Online.

■ Movie Notes (also found after clicking the FEATURE PRESENTATION icon) offers you background information about current movie releases. You'll find basic production information that describes the plot of the movie, plus fascinating material about the movie stars themselves. You'll find information, for example, about how a team of special effects artists can create those fantastic and realistic scenes you see in your favorite movie.

■ COMING SOON brings up a listing about upcoming productions. You'll get a gander at some of the promotional newsletters and photos of the newest summer or winter blockbusters, and special behind-the-scenes information direct from the production centers.

From Here...

For more useful material on entertainment-related subjects, refer to the following chapters:

■ In Chapter 12, "Music, Books, and Art," you'll explore additional online entertainment information.

■ In Chapter 13, "Playing Games Online," you'll learn where to find tips about your favorite games, and even participate in some of the online gaming forums.

■ In Chapter 14, "Sports in Cyberspace," you'll read the latest news from the world of sports and learn how to participate in a virtual sporting event of your own.

■ In Chapter 15, "Pursuing Lifestyles and Interests," you'll visit forums dedicated to subjects ranging from cooking to *Star Trek*.

■ In Chapter 17, "Games, Entertainment, Teen Chat, and Netiquette," you'll read about the resources available for those ages 5-14, along with information about proper online behavior.

■ In Chapter 23, "The News of the Day," you'll open the pages of AOL's virtual newspaper and read its many sections.

■ In Chapter 24, "Magazines and Newspapers Online," you'll visit AOL's online newsstand and read the latest issues of many of your favorite magazines. Perhaps you'll discover some that will also soon become your favorites.

CHAPTER 12

Music, Books, and Art

When you look through this chapter and the preceding one, Chapter 11, "TV and Movie Information Online," it's very clear that AOL is fast becoming a culture lover's paradise.

Besides the entertainment resources described in the previous chapter, you can visit areas devoted to such diverse topics as music, games, sports, books, kids' activities, and horoscopes. You find out what America Online has to offer in those areas and how you can find it. Wherever your interests lie, America Online surely has a place where you can find the entertainment information you seek. ■

Visit AOL's MusicSpace

Find the latest music-related news and information.

Express yourself

Become a critic right here on America Online.

Use the online library

Learn about the wonderful world of books.

Entertainment information online

Access a wide range of areas devoted to leisure and the world of show business.

N O T E   Your quick shortcut to your favorite area is a keyword. Just press ⌘-K (or Ctrl+K for Windows), enter the name of the area you want to visit (the keyword), and click OK. Then you're on your way. I've noted the keywords you need to find the features described in this chapter. ■

Music Resources Online

Keyword: **Music, MusicSpace**

They come from all corners of the world, the most famous musical stars of our generation, and they choose America Online for special online conferences. In 1994 and early 1995, for example, such rock 'n' roll stars as Mick Jagger and Eddie and Alex Van Halen held court in America Online's huge conference auditoriums.

If you dig rock 'n' roll music, or prefer country, classical, or jazz, you will appreciate that America Online's music-related forums are your resources for information and online discussion about your favorite performers. The keyword **Music** is just a gateway (see fig. 12.1). Clicking the MusicSpace icon in the Entertainment channel window gets the same result. It's a stopping off point where you can visit the special online areas that cater to music lovers of all persuasions.

FIG. 12.1
MusicSpace is the gateway to the world of music on AOL.

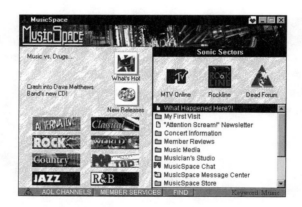

In the next few pages, I'll cover just a few of the vast collections of music information areas available to you in MusicSpace. First, we'll take a brief stopover to the World Wide Web, which is identified by Web in the channel's list box (and you'll want to read Part VIII, "Entering the Information Superhighway," for more Internet-related material).

Top Web Sites

Keyword: **MusicWeb**

Virtually every major music production company, music-related publication, and many artists have found a home in the online world. AOL's WEB TopStops provides a fast-access gateway for music resources beyond the confines of the service. The roster shown in figure 12.2 is but a sample of what you'll find during your online travels. You'll also find reference material and information about special events.

FIG. 12.2
Visit AOL's WEB TopStops for music information from across the globe.

Special MusicSpace Events

Keyword: **Scream**

Many of your favorite music artists and industry executives continue to appear at live events on AOL. To find out about the latest conferences, you'll want to sign up to receive a copy of AOL's "Attention Scream" newsletter (see fig. 12.3 for a look at a typical issue). In addition to the latest schedules, you'll learn news about other media events, and you'll be able to exchange information with other AOL members in the Message Center.

Part
III

Ch

12

FIG. 12.3
Here's a typical issue of AOL's special music events newsletter where you can learn about your favorite artists and other cool stuff.

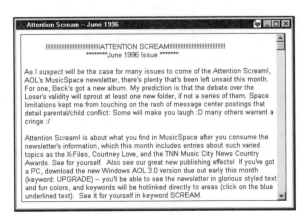

You can view current and recent issues, or just click the Sign Me Up button in the window you access via keyword **Scream** to become a subscriber. Once you order the free newsletter, a copy will show up at regular intervals in your AOL e-mail box.

Checking Out Music Media

Keyword: **Music Media**

You can visit forums run by major networks, top publications, and your favorite artists in the Music Media department of the MusicSpace channel (see fig. 12.4). In the next few pages, I'll touch upon a few of the forums that are a part of this area. You can definitely spend many enjoyable hours here exploring the full roster of information resources.

FIG. 12.4
From print to TV (cable and broadcast), read all about the latest music news from AOL's Music Media information center.

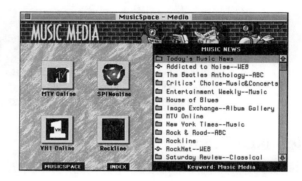

Visiting MTV Online

Keyword: **MTV**

The arrival of MTV fostered a revolution in the way music was programmed on television. Instead of having rock bands lip-sync their popular records on a variety or dance show, they created short movies that either represented the subject matter of their songs, or showed the band in action at a concert. Some of those music videos are major productions that involve elaborate special effects, cost millions to produce, and are directed by major filmmakers.

The MTV forum on AOL mirrors the style and substance of the cable TV network (see fig. 12.5, which you see after you click the MTV globe in the main screen). When you first visit this area, you'll want to look over the News and Hot Spot buttons shown on the main forum directory window at the left. After getting the latest updates, click the Music icon to read reviews and see a list of concert updates. Head Shop isn't quite what its 1960s-type label implies. The area includes a library of photos and brief videos of some of your favorite stars. Before you visit this library, you may want to check out the MTV Multimedia Tools library also, because it contains a selection of Mac and Windows viewing programs that you may need before you download the available graphics files.

FIG. 12.5
If you want your MTV, here it is, but you have to first click an opening screen to get to this one.

There's a full schedule of upcoming MTV programs in the Tube Scan area. The Message Boards area offers that special flavor of chatter that is typical of MTV.

 T I P You can save and print any text document you see on America Online simply by choosing the appropriate command from the File menu.

The Road to Rock & Road

Keyword: **RR**

The Rock & Road forum on AOL (see fig. 12.6) is part of ABC Online. This area is devoted strictly to covering rock bands on the road. The Road Journal (shown in the main directory at the left) offers capsule reports of the activities of popular bands that are giving concerts around the country.

The R&R Newsletter button provides information on how you can subscribe to the forum's newsletter, which will tell you about your favorite acts and upcoming concert dates. The R&R Exchange icon takes you to a very active message board, where you can read concert reviews from fellow AOL members, and offer your own experiences. The Load-In Library offers sights and sounds of popular acts in concert, and you'll want to check out the Chat room and the ever-popular ABC Auditorium for special scheduled conferences (just click the ABC Online icon).

Part
III

Ch
12

FIG. 12.6
Find out what your favorite band is doing on the road, at Rock & Road.

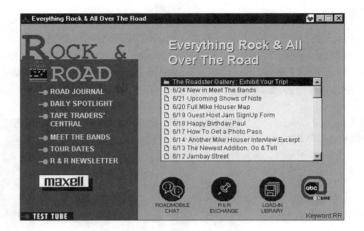

Reading SPIN Online

Keyword: **Spin**

Whether or not you buy the popular rock magazine, *SPIN,* at your local newsstand, you'll want to take a look at its online forum first (see fig. 12.7). You can see the contents of the latest issue before it reaches your city. But, this section is just the first of eight sections that you'll want to check out.

FIG. 12.7
Here you can read *SPIN* magazine online.

For example, the Digital News Data Feast section offers up a huge helping of news about special online events sponsored by the publishers and editors of *SPIN.* The *SPIN*-mart is not just a place where you can order a subscription to the magazine itself; there are also frequent special offers on new rock CDs and collectibles. The Games & Contests area gives you the chance to participate in trivia contests and online treasure hunts, and the opportunity to win a valuable prize. After the preliminaries, you'll want to click the This Month's SPIN button to have a look at the latest issue of the magazine, complete with photographs that display rapidly on your computer's monitor.

Accessing the Grateful Dead Forum

Keyword: **Grateful Dead**

Prior to the death of its leader, Jerry Garcia, the Grateful Dead had the distinction of being one of the longest surviving rock 'n' roll bands still doing regular performances. Interest in the band after Garcia's untimely passing is still strong, and the surviving band members continue to run their own special area on America Online for the Deadheads to visit, read about the band's music legacy, and even share messages with other fans (see fig. 12.8). You'll be especially interested in the GD Chat room, a place where you can have online chats with other members of the online community.

FIG. 12.8
Even the Grateful Dead has its own special place on America Online.

You can discuss your favorite song with fellow Dead fans in the Grateful Dead Messaging area, and learn the latest about what band members are doing in the Announced area.

Exploring Warner/Reprise Records Online

Keyword: **Warner**

Warner/Reprise Records spans generations of music lovers, with musical choices ranging from gospel to alternative. This forum covers the entire Warner/Reprise artist roster (see fig. 12.9).

Part
III

Ch
12

FIG. 12.9

This screen appears when you visit the Warner/Reprise Records Online forum on America Online.

The Warner/Reprise Records Online forum is very popular on America Online for good reason, because it offers a wide range of features. The following paragraphs describe the areas you can visit simply by clicking the icons you find on the Warner/Reprise Records Online screen.

- New Releases describes the latest recordings from Warner/Reprise's vast roster of entertainers.

- You'll also want to visit the forum's Multimedia Library, where you can download sounds and images of some of your favorite artists and sample their newest recordings. There's even a selection of multimedia software that you may need to view and hear these special files.

- No doubt you've read about the Cyber-Talk area in your daily newspaper. Your favorite musical stars will, from time to time, appear online in this huge auditorium for special interactive conferences that you can attend.

- The Warner/Reprise WEB Sites area takes you on a journey to the company's music-related sites on the Information Superhighway. You'll want to check that area out often.

- Contests & Special Events are held from time to time when a recording artist releases a new recording or is beginning a major concert tour.

- Artists on Tour lists the touring plans of your favorite Warner/Reprise Records artists. Is your favorite entertainer coming to your city? Here's where you find out about it.

- As with many other America Online forums, Message Board is the place to read the views of fellow America Online members, and for you to join in on the discussions yourself.

What the Critics Have to Say

Keyword: **Critics**

Like most of you, before I buy a book, see a movie, or even rent a videotape, I want to know what the reviewers have to say about it. America Online's Critics' Choice is a compendium of thousands of reviews and discussions about the entire spectrum of the world of entertainment (see fig. 12.10).

FIG. 12.10
The Critics' Choice area is where you can read what the critics say, and become one yourself if it suits you.

Here you find reviews of your favorite movies, concerts, television shows, books, and even video games. The following paragraphs describe the icons shown on the Critics' Choice screen:

- Contact Critics' Choice enables you to express your own views to the forum staff.

- The Chat Room is another one of AOL's exciting interactive chat rooms, where you'll be able to discuss your favorite books or TV shows, and sometimes even meet your favorite author or movie critic for a fun-filled conference.

- The title, You're The Critic, means what it says. It's your chance to post a message giving your viewpoints about something you've read or seen. In fig. 12.11, an America Online member offers a very personal review about a particular subject.

The icons at the bottom of the Critics' Choice window take you to other entertainment forums on America Online, ranging from movies, video, and TV, to books, music, and games. I covered the areas devoted to AOL's movie and television forums in Chapter 11, "TV and Movie Information Online." By now, you've seen how nearly every forum you visit on America Online provides gateways to other areas that might interest you. It's a journey you will truly enjoy.

Part
III

Ch
12

FIG. 12.11
Here's your chance to become a critic.

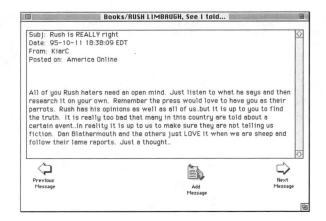

The Wonderful World of Books

Keyword: **Books**

To many of you, the best entertainment is probably sitting down with a good book in hand. But, the selections at your favorite bookstores have become daunting. Literally thousands of new works are on the shelves, ready for you to make your choice. Where do you begin? Well, let's start with AOL's Books & Writing forum (see fig. 12.12).

Whether you prefer fiction or nonfiction, you want to check the Book Nook first to see how your favorite author's works are faring in the marketplace. From there you can find out more about this area of America Online, check out the best-seller lists, and see what's soon to be released. Just Reviews is the place to post your own book reviews and read about the choices of other members of the online community.

FIG. 12.12
AOL's Books & Writing area provides the latest information about best-selling books and upcoming works.

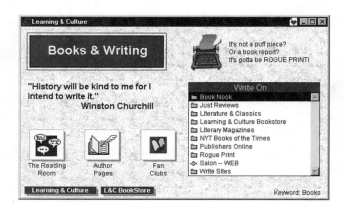

N O T E You'll notice that an option on Just Reviews screen is Critics' Choice. That topic is discussed in more detail previously in this chapter (see "What the Critics Have to Say"). ▪

You can order your favorite books online as well, from America Online's Online Book-store. Chapter 28, "Secrets of Online Shopping," takes you step-by-step through the ordering process (during which I order a certain book some of you are no doubt familiar with).

Graphics and Art Online

America Online is a graphical service, designed to take full advantage of the capabilities of the Macintosh and Windows computing platforms. You can view graphics online, and download photos, sounds, and even short movie clips in many of the online forums. The very latest versions of AOL's Mac and Windows software come complete with graphics viewers that enable you to view photo files in several popular formats. If you're new to America Online, you may want to review Appendixes B and C, which you can consider a brief manual on using this software. You can also refer to Chapter 3, "Getting the Most from AOL's Macintosh Software," and Chapter 4, "Getting the Most from AOL's Windows Software."

Art Workshop

Keyword: **Workshop**

Part
III

Ch
12

The Art Workshop forum (see fig. 12.13) is part of America Online's Family Computing Online department. It's a place where you can learn about the various types of graphics files available online and learn the best techniques for viewing them on your computer's screen.

Whether you want to know more about viewing and preparing your own GIF photos, or need to understand more about what's involved in handling online graphics files, here's the place you can consult for information. Some of the best graphics files are on display in the library available when you click the Member Art Gallery icon. There is also an online dictionary of frequently used terminology, helpful hints and tips, and advice on how to upload your own graphics files.

FIG. 12.13
Learn all about online graphics in Art Workshop.

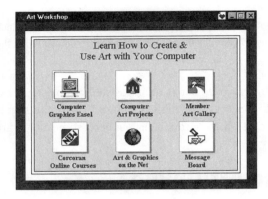

New AOL members can try out their graphics file handling skills in the Computer Graphics Easel area. This particular area, by the way, is free of online charges. So, you can take all the time you need working with files until you are comfortable about doing it for real. And if you need further advice, visit the forum's active message boards. If you are an experienced online traveler, you might just want to provide some advice yourself.

Pictures of the World

Keyword: **Pictures**

Carl and Ann Purcell are experienced travel photographers whose work has appeared in many magazines and newspapers. The Pictures of the World forum is a special library containing some of the best of the Purcells' work (see fig. 12.14).

FIG. 12.14
View photos taken by world travelers from Pictures of the World on AOL.

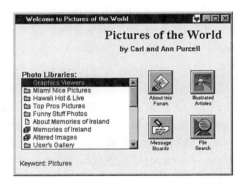

> **CAUTION**
>
> The photos provided in Pictures of the World and many other online areas are copyrighted. You can download these photos for your own personal use, but distribution and resale of these photos is usually prohibited.

The photos are grouped in easy-to-find categories, or you can use the File Search icon to tap the huge database of available material. You can also download illustrated articles about the authors' travels to fascinating spots around the world. By the way, if travel interests you, read Chapter 27, "Secrets of AOL's Travel Department" for full information about AOL's travel resources. But, even if your travel is done vicariously in the comfort of your home, you'll appreciate the artistic merit of this large photographic library.

 TIP If you're using the latest Macintosh and Windows versions of AOL's software, you'll see photos in several graphics formats appear on your screen as they are being downloaded.

Resources for Leisure and Entertainment

This section concentrates mostly on areas of leisure and entertainment other than movies and TV (because I described them in the previous chapter). As always, exploring the resources available to you on America Online is an ever-changing, exciting process. New forums are being added regularly, older ones change and update to reflect new areas.

Leisure Guide

Keyword: **Times Leisure, Times Arts**

The huge daily newspaper, *The New York Times,* has a number of support areas on America Online. The one I'm describing here is the *Times'* Arts & Leisure area, which provides full coverage of popular entertainment and leisure spots in the sprawling New York metropolitan area. This area includes suburban Long Island and Westchester, Connecticut, and New Jersey (see fig. 12.15).

Part
III

Ch
12

FIG. 12.15
The New York Times' Leisure Guide provides news of the hot entertainment spots in the Big Apple and environs.

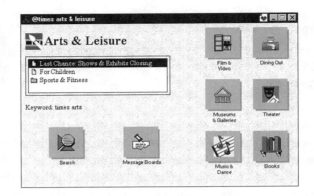

In addition to reviews of top dining spots, movies, and video, you'll find news about special events at many of New York's famous museums, plus information related to other leisure activities, such as sports and fitness.

The Atlantic Monthly Magazine

Keyword: **Atlantic**

Several important magazines regularly appear online at the same time they appear in your favorite bookstore. One of these is *The Atlantic Monthly* (see fig. 12.16).

FIG. 12.16
Here you can read *The Atlantic Monthly* on AOL.

When you first go to *The Atlantic Monthly*'s forum, you'll see the magazine's cover, and a few paragraphs describing the content of the current issue. In order to enter the forum, simply click the button labeled OPEN THE ATLANTIC.

Founded in 1857, *The Atlantic Monthly* is a journal of literature, entertainment, and opinion. Highlights of the latest issue appear online, including features, letters to the editor, and many of the articles that appear in the printed edition.

The Message Board is your chance to communicate with editors, writers, and other online members. As with any magazine of opinion, the discussions can become very active indeed. The Atlantic Auditorium hosts special gatherings involving both editors and writers.

Saturday Review Online

Keyword: **Saturday Review**

Many of you probably remember the *Saturday Review* as a magazine of arts and culture that existed for many years and folded in 1986. During its over half a century of existence, this journal covered such subjects as politics, science, business, literature, and even the world of entertainment.

So, what is a magazine that no longer exists doing on America Online? Well, unlike the other online magazines we've discussed so far in this chapter, *Saturday Review* Online doesn't exist as a printed publication. It's strictly an electronic magazine brought to you by the publishers of *OMNI* and *Compute* (see fig. 12.17).

FIG. 12.17
The *Saturday Review,* reborn as an electronic magazine on America Online.

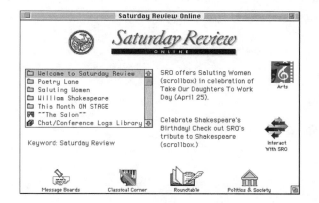

In the tradition of the magazine originally edited by Norman Cousins, this twenty-first century counterpart contains articles of both fact and fiction. It reviews current events in detail from the perspective of many noted writers. As with other online publications, you can participate in its active message boards to share your views with writers and editors. Reading this revived publication is a unique experience indeed.

From Here...

As with other areas on America Online, you don't have to restrict yourself to searching one area for the information you want. For more useful facts on entertainment-related subjects, refer to these chapters:

- In Chapter 11, "TV and Movie Information Online," you can review a full slate of entertainment resources online.

- In Chapter 13, "Playing Games Online," you'll learn where to find tips about your favorite games, and even participate in some of the online gaming forums.

- In Chapter 14, "Sports in Cyberspace," you read the latest news from the world of sports and learn how to participate in a virtual sporting event of your own.

- In Chapter 15, "Pursuing Lifestyles and Interests," you'll visit forums dedicated to subjects ranging from cooking to *Star Trek*.

- In Chapter 24, "Magazines and Newspapers Online," you'll visit AOL's online newsstand and read the latest issues of many of your favorite magazines, and perhaps discover some that will soon become your favorites.

Playing Games Online

You'll find a huge amount of entertainment-related re-sources on America Online. That's why I've devoted several chapters in this book to the subject. Chapter 11, for example, covers movie and television forums, and Chapter 12 covers areas devoted to music, books, and art. This chapter concentrates on gaming, the online kind, and the resources available to help you get better performance from the game software you already have. ■

Visiting the AOL Games Channel

Keyword: **Games**

Just about any visit to entertainment-related areas of America Online essentially begins in the Games Channel, where you will find a huge number of options for fun and frolic online (see fig. 13.1).

FIG. 13.1
AOL's Games Channel, where the action begins.

Games represent, among other things, one of the most popular categories of software sales. They appeal to the young and the young at heart. A computer game enables you to turn your Mac or PC into an outer-space battleground, a deep, dark dungeon, or even a maze. You can pit yourself against evil creatures, machines, or even other human players in a quest to right wrongs, locate a secret castle, or save the world from destruction.

Games Across Cyberspace

Keyword: **Game Sites**

It's no secret that the Internet has become the online place to be, and if games are your bag, AOL offers a selection of resources not just in its own online channels, but across the wild World Wide Web (see fig. 13.2). You'll get direct access to Internet-based games' resources, and you can access them as easily as one of AOL's own forums.

When you click an interesting gaming site, you'll find the information appears within a few seconds in AOL's own World Wide Web browser. The roster changes often, so you'll want to add the ones you like to your list of Favorite Sites, so you can quickly revisit them again and again.

FIG. 13.2
Use AOL to access games information resources across the world.

Visiting the Macintosh and PC Games' Forums

Keywords: **MGM, PC Games**

The Macintosh and PC computing forums are discussed in Chapter 19, "Visiting the Computing and Software Forums," but the games' forums deserve a special place here, because they are a resource that any fan of computer games will want to visit often. Figures 13.3 and 13.4 show the games forum screens.

FIG. 13.3
The Macintosh Games forum is for Mac games enthusiasts.

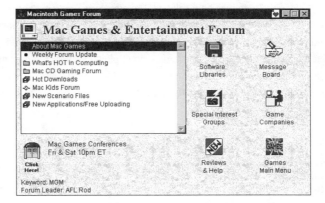

Part
III

Ch
13

As with other computing forums on America Online, these special areas enable you to get advice from other America Online members about their experiences and recommendations on different game software.

The software libraries in these games forums contain demonstration versions of many popular commercial games that you might want to try. You also can find a large number of freeware and shareware games (some award-winning) that can entertain you and your children for hours.

FIG. 13.4
The PC Games Forum is for
DOS and Windows users.

To find out more about all the computing and software forums, read Chapter 19. For now, feel free to explore the software libraries in the Mac and PC games' forums. Check the file descriptions and download the software you want to try. You'll also want to read Chapter 21, "The Best Macintosh Software on AOL," and Chapter 22, "The Best Windows Software on AOL."

N O T E If you happen to find a game only available for a PC, and you're using a Mac, don't despair. There may be a solution. There are now programs and add-on cards that let you run DOS and Windows 95 without having to buy a second computer. Insignia Solutions SoftWindows software products will emulate a Windows 3.1 or Windows 95 environment right on your Mac's screen, as will expansion cards from Apple and other manufacturers. You'll want to check the compatibility information on the product fliers themselves, though, to be sure your Mac can handle one of these PC computing solutions. ▪

Accessing the Online Gaming Forums

Keyword: **Gaming**

Whether you are interested in a casual game of checkers or are involved in a heavy-duty game of strategy, America Online's Online Gaming Forums area is a place you will want to learn about and visit often.

As you can see from the forum's main directory window in figure 13.5, this forum serves as an entrance to a number of areas that deal with gaming. The following sections discuss just a few of them.

FIG. 13.5
The Online Gaming Forums screen is your first stop for information on all sorts of games.

Entering the Gaming Forum Conference Center The Online Gaming Forums area holds regular conferences. Along with online members and forum staff, you can attend conferences, participate in chats, and attend debates and panel discussions that feature experts on the subject. To enter the conference center, click the Conference Center icon in the Online Gaming Forums main window. The screen shown in figure 13.6 appears.

FIG. 13.6
Regular online conferences are held for gaming enthusiasts.

You can also participate in the General Information Board area (shown in the directory listing on the left of the Online Gaming Forums screen) to exchange views with other America Online members. The conference schedule is updated often, so do stop by regularly. If you missed a conference, simply download the log from the Conference Archives library. As with all conference logs, you can view and print them with your America Online software, by choosing Open or Print from the File menu.

Part
III

Ch
13

In addition, there's a separate area for each game category that you'll want to visit regularly, depending on the sort of games you like. You can access an area by double-clicking the appropriate item in the forum directory listing on the left of the forum window. Here's a description, and a few illustrations, of some of the areas:

■ Free-Form Gaming Forum. This forum, shown in figure 13.7, is devoted to games in which the rules are devised by the players on the spot, without resorting to any but the most basic guidelines. You have a chance to let your imagination and those of your fellow players run wild, as long as you stay within AOL's Terms of Service. You'll find a message board where you can exchange ideas with your fellow players before and after your games. This forum can also be accessed via the keyword: **FFGF**.

FIG. 13.7
AOL's Free-Form Gaming Forum let's you explore a wide range of online game activities.

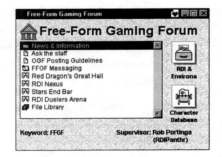

■ Game Designers Forum. This forum is strictly for those who design non-computer games. It's a place that's designed to be a meeting ground for experienced professional designers and those of you who are looking to enter into this industry. Beginners will have a chance to interact with skilled pros, and also to chat with representatives of some of the game manufacturers.

■ Gaming Company Support. Here's a forum in which the major game manufacturers provide direct support for their products. So, if you have a problem with games or strategy, here's a place where you can have your problems solved. Learn professional-caliber secrets that will help improve your play and give you more opportunities to become a winner at your favorite gaming activity.

■ Gaming Information Exchange. This forum has two prime goals. First, it is an active discussion and debate on gaming topics. It's a place for game designers and players. And the real fun part is that this forum is also a place where you can sell and exchange your own games with fellow users. This gives you a chance to trade off the game that you no longer are interested in playing for one you would like to try.

CAUTION

The Gaming Information Exchange is a place where you can learn about product offerings available from other AOL members. As with any such transaction, you should make sure you understand what you are getting and what you are paying or exchanging for it before you send your game or payment. If a monetary transaction is involved, try to use a credit card or ask for COD (Cash On Delivery) service. America Online and the forum staff are not responsible for the transactions you make in this forum, so check everything carefully before you make your deal.

- Play-by-Mail Forum. In days gone by, it was common for folks to play checkers or chess and other games by mail. You'd send a letter containing your play to another player, and then wait a week or two for the other player's response. Well, the method of communication has changed, but the techniques of skill and strategy haven't. This forum lets you use electronic mail and the message boards to communicate with your fellow players. But, as with the games that employed stamps and letters, they may take several months to finish.

- Role Playing Gaming Forum. Here's another forum that allows you to give free play to your own imagination. Here you can become involved in an online play, a game that might involve mighty sword fights, games where you can use your own strength and agility (virtual strength anyway) to defeat evil-doers, and games where you can pilot your starship across the galaxy. Before you decide what role to play, you will want to visit the forum, examine the messages and learn as much as you can about the way the games are run. The forum staff would also be happy to assist you further in creating a viable role for yourself in these fun-filled activities.

- The Simming Forum. This forum, pictured in figure 13.8, is devoted to your favorite science-fiction, fantasy, horror, and mystery themes. The games are in character with the free-form style games described earlier. You have a reasonable amount of freedom to dream up your own characters and work with fellow members on setting up the rules of play.

  Examples of the sort of themes supported in this forum are shown in the forum's directory screen. The Starfleet Online area is based on the same sort of fantasy universe described in such TV programs and movies as *Star Trek* and *Star Wars*. The *X-Files* Sim Forum is devoted to those who are fans of the popular Fox TV program.

- Strategy and Wargaming Forum. A game of strategy covers a host of categories such as, chess, card games, war games, and other activities that depend more on your skills and those of your opponent than on pure luck. This forum provides discussion and activity. You'll also find AOL's Chess Forum here, which has message boards for discussion and for activity.

Part
III

Ch
13

FIG. 13.8
Let your dreams come true in The Simming Forum.

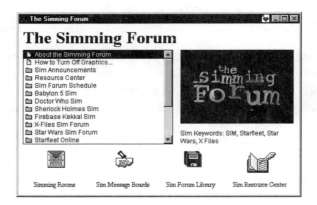

Exploring the GameBase Database   GameBase is a resource for information about the manufacturers of games, new product information, and reviews from both experts and members alike. You can search GameBase for information about your favorite products or a new product you want to know more about. Click the GameBase icon in the Online Gaming Forums main window to access GameBase and display the screen shown in figure 13.9.

FIG. 13.9
The GameBase resource in America Online's Gaming Forum provides you with all kinds of gaming information.

Getting More Gaming Information   Returning to the main Online Gaming Forums window, you can click the Electronomicon Library icon to download an electronic magazine on games.

If you have a problem or question about a specific product, you can click the Gaming Company Support option on the left side of the main Online Gaming Forums window for assistance.

Exploring the Electronomicon Archives

Electronomicon is an electronic newsletter prepared by the staff of the Online Games Forum. Each issue is posted in the Electronomicon Library as soon as it's published. It is an interesting compendium of general gaming news, advice, and forum happenings. The newsletter consists of a text file that you can view and print in almost any text-processing program.

Sources for Computer Game Secrets

Perhaps the most fun of playing a game is the excitement of discovery, of learning tips or tricks that will help you play more effectively, or even defeating that long time opponent after a spirited battle of wits. This section describes a few forums where you can learn some of those previously untold secrets.

Visiting TSR Online

Keyword: **TSR**

TSR is a manufacturer of games, books, and magazines. Its forum on AOL is devoted to the company's vast product line that has been developed over more than a 20-year period (see fig. 13.10). An example is the popular Dungeons and Dragons series.

FIG. 13.10
Here's TSR's support forum on AOL.

Besides getting support for TSR's popular novels, games, and magazines, you can place orders for your favorite products directly from its catalog. TSR has games designed for the popular video game formats, and for your personal computer. Among its popular magazines is *Amazing Stories,* the popular newsstand publication that is renowned as the oldest existing science-fiction magazine.

Part
III

Ch
13

Participating in Unlimited Adventures

Keywords: **Unlimited Adventures**

Unlimited Adventures online comes to AOL courtesy of Strategic Simulations, Inc. (see fig. 13.11). It's a product that lets you actually make your own games, using a suite of artwork and design tools. The forum is designed to help people of all skill levels, from beginners to experts, develop their own fun-filled games.

FIG. 13.11
Build your own games in the Unlimited Adventures forum.

You'll find software libraries with game tools for both Mac and PC users. There is also a library of tutorial information (events, samples, and tutorials) that helps you on the road to building your own games. You'll also want to join in the World-Builders Discussion boards, where you can ask questions and receive helpful answers from the forum staff and fellow members.

Flying Virtual Airlines

Keyword: **Virtual Airlines**

Most of us will never fly, except as a passenger (though AOL's membership does include many commercial and private pilots). But through the Virtual Airlines forum, you can actually have the chance to join an airline that exists solely in cyberspace (see fig. 13.12). This forum, dedicated to users of Microsoft's Flight Simulator software for Mac and Windows, gives you full reign to use your skills to reach many popular destinations in your flights.

Each of the virtual airlines has its own set of rules and regulations as to the number of hours you must spend on the flight simulator before you can sign up and participate. In addition, you actually have the opportunity to start your own virtual airline, but it takes quite a bit of work, and the application must be carefully evaluated before the forum staff decides whether to grant your application. But, it is something to think about if you are very skilled at flight simulation games. In the meantime, while you ponder whether to join an airline or try to begin your own, you can view this forum's message board to learn about the experiences of other members and get a few tips to help make your trips into cyberspace more fun.

FIG. 13.12
This forum will provide information on flying an airline in cyberspace on AOL.

Visiting the Video Games Forum

Keyword: **Video Games**

Video games play a large part in the world of entertainment; this realm includes such home systems as Genesis, SNES, Jaguar, Sony Playstation, and 3DO. This forum, the Video Games Forum, is dedicated to such games (see fig. 13.13). This forum is also devoted to such arcade games as Primal Rage and Cruisin' USA!

FIG. 13.13
AOL's Video Games Forum will offer news, tips, and tricks on the latest games.

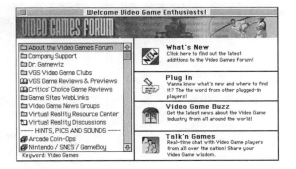

Part
III

Ch
13

One place you'll want to visit is represented by the Plug In icon, which takes you to the message boards, where you can interact with fellow AOL members and forum experts about your favorite game. You'll also want to read messages about games you are thinking about trying, so you can learn some tips and get some ideas about strategy.

If you're in search of helpful hints about your favorite game, you'll want to check out the Hints, Pics, and Sounds libraries (at the bottom of the forum's list box). These are libraries of text files that contain all sorts of advice to help get you over the rough spots and make your games more fun. They also include screen pictures showing the newest games and software, and audio clips that provide some highlights that replay some of your favorite moments in some of these games. You'll also want to participate in the Talk'n Games area, where you can meet fellow game enthusiasts.

AOL's Video Games Forum also includes areas devoted to company support for popular games and a library of game reviews. You can download gaming strategy guides and read the regular online newsletters from the noted game master, Dr. Gamewiz. Because games are prominently discussed in a number of Internet newsgroups, AOL has provided a direct gateway to the service's Internet Connection. For more Internet-related material, see Part VIII, "Entering the Information Superhighway."

Getting Support from the Publishers

Keyword: **CC**

Many of the best known publishers of computer games have support areas on America Online that are accessible through the popular manufacturer support areas in AOL's Company Connection (see fig. 13.14). There is a separate support area for Mac and Windows users, but many of the publishers represented are the same because their products are available in both computing platforms.

FIG. 13.14
Visit AOL's Company Connection area for assistance direct from the publishers of your favorite gaming software.

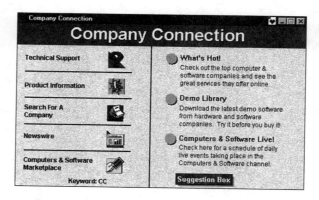

For more information on using AOL's Company Connection support areas, you'll want to read Chapter 19, "Visiting the Computing and Software Forums." But, here's some quick advice now on what to do if you have a problem with your computer game. First, see if the publisher has a list of common questions and answers about possible problems with the program. Then read the messages to see if other AOL members have had problems similar to yours. You might find your questions have already been answered.

If the questions haven't been dealt with yet, try to provide as much detail as possible, including the name of the company's product and revision number. It also helps to provide in your question the kind of computer you have, the version of the operating system you are using, and a short description of other software with which you are working. This helps the publisher's support representatives compare your report to others they've already received.

CAUTION

When you post a message asking for assistance in a company support board on America Online, do not include your address and telephone number. If the publisher needs that information, they'll contact you via regular e-mail. Remember, putting this information in a message board makes it available to millions of AOL members.

Accessing The Trivia Forum

Keyword: **Trivia**

Okay, I admit it. I am far removed from being a chess master (or even from playing a decent game of checkers). My abilities at computer games are laughable, for the most part. But, I do know my trivia. If trivia is one of your favorite pastimes, too, The Trivia Forum might turn out to be one of your favorite online places (see fig. 13.15).

FIG. 13.15
AOL's popular Trivia Forum lets you match wits against fellow members.

Regardless of the subject you are an expert in, whether it's *Star Trek*, radio shows of the 1940s, or famous historical figures, The Trivia Forum is where you can interact with other trivia enthusiasts. (In Chapter 9, "Using America Online Message Boards," you learn how to participate in a message area.) The Trivia Forum has a regular schedule of nightly games in America Online's People Connection (also see Chapter 7, "America Online's People Connection").

Besides the interactive trivia games, you can participate in the forum's message area, post your own trivia questions, or answer those from other users. Click the Trivia Schedule button at the bottom of the forum screen to see a roster of regular games you might want to join as well. Figures 13.16 and 13.17 show a typical question and the response (but, you all knew the answer, right?).

FIG. 13.16
Before you look at the answer, can you guess the name of the classic movie in which the first TV "Superman" appeared?

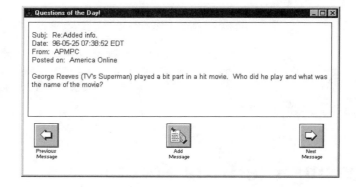

FIG. 13.17
OK, we have the answer, at least part of it. Now what was the name of the character George Reeves played?

You will also want to visit GOTTEM News! (the icon in the top right of the forum window). GOTTEM is the forum's popular newsletter, available for downloading in text file form. It includes all sorts of information about trivia games, photos of forum staff and fellow AOL members, and some really interesting information you'll want to consult to expand your store of trivial information.

From Here...

As with other areas on America Online, you don't have to restrict yourself to a single forum for information related to games. Chapter 17, "Games, Entertainment, Teen Chat, and Netiquette," is a special chapter that describes the game-related features for AOL members ages 5 through 14. You'll also want to look at the following chapters:

- In Chapter 15, "Pursuing Lifestyles and Interests," you'll explore hobbies, special interests, and forums run by charitable organizations.

- In Chapter 19, "Visiting the Computing and Software Forums," you'll find resources where you can learn how to solve problems with your personal computer, use it more effectively, and locate useful software.

- In Chapter 21, "The Best Macintosh Software on AOL," you'll see special recommendations of the best Mac software on AOL, direct from the computing and software forum leaders.

- In Chapter 22, "The Best Windows Software on AOL," you'll read the recommendations provided by the Windows computing and software forum leaders.

Part
III

Ch
13

CHAPTER 14

Sports in Cyberspace

AOL's Sports Channel
Find the latest news from the world of sports.

Behind the scenes information
Review background information and exclusive inside reports about special sporting events.

Play games online
Participate in special sports trivia games and other fun events.

Sporting news isn't always confined to a section in the middle of your daily newspaper. It's not uncommon for news from the world of sports to fill the front pages, too. This was especially true as a result of the baseball strike that abruptly cut the 1994 season short, and lingered on through part of 1995. And, let's not forget the impact of the Super Bowl or world championship boxing match, or when an athlete gets into some kind of legal trouble.

But, for the sake of this chapter, let's consider sports to be less of a serious news item and more of something to be enjoyed, or something you might want to participate in yourself. ■

Visiting AOL's Sports Forums

Keyword: **Sports**

If you played Little League sports when you were a child, have children interested in sporting activities, watch sports events regularly on television, or have been known to attend a game or two, you might want to visit America Online's virtual sports page. To do so, choose the Sports channel icon from AOL's main menu window to display the Sports screen shown in figure 14.1.

N O T E   When you first enter AOL's Sports channel you may see a window labeled Today in Sports, which highlights the latest happenings in this area. ▪

FIG. 14.1
Whatever your favorite sport, you'll find information about it on America Online.

The major sports and highlights of special events are listed in the directory window at the center of the screen. At the left are small icons that represent popular sporting activities (the list may change somewhat from time to time). What follows is a description of some of the features shown in figure 14.1.

Top Web Sites

When you take the giant leap from AOL's own Sports channel to the worldwide Internet, you'll find that AOL reaches out to the Internet behind the scenes, so you only have to concern yourself with the sort of information source you're looking for. And, the roster of Internet-based sporting information resources is huge and growing daily (see fig. 14.2, which appears when you click the Internet button).

FIG. 14.2
Sporting information from
Internet-based resources is
just a click away from
America Online's friendly
interface.

Taking a Seat in The Grandstand

Keyword: **Grandstand**

The Grandstand (see fig. 14.3) is where all you sports lovers can discuss the latest news
about your favorite games, report on how your favorite teams fared the night before, and
participate in online conferences with other fans. It is the entrance to America Online's
sports stadium. But, the biggest attraction of this forum is the participation of sports fans,
a place where you can get involved and post your own messages about the happenings on
or off the field, or the court, or the rink, and so on.

FIG. 14.3
Take your seat in The
Grandstand to enjoy your
favorite sport.

The following paragraphs describe some of the most popular features available through
The Grandstand. And remember, as with other AOL forums, this lineup is apt to change
and grow with time:

■ Sports Flash offers announcements about the long list of regular online conferences on every sport under the sun. As you can see in figure 14.4 (which you'll see when you click any topic shown in the Sports Flash directory), America Online even conducts an online wrestling match (you'll see the bill of fare change regularly)!

FIG. 14.4
Sports Flash announces upcoming meetings for sports lovers.

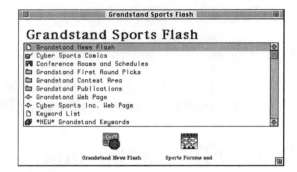

■ The Sports Rooms icon is your admission ticket to The Grandstand's nightly online conferences. After viewing the schedule, you can pop in to the active conference room of your choice.

■ Fantasy Leagues are what the title implies. Participate in your own sports league in cyberspace in the forum shown in figure 14.5. There's a league for your favorite sport. You can have a wrestling match without ever breaking a sweat, and participate in an auto race without ever having to drive a car around a track.

FIG. 14.5
From baseball to auto racing, let your imagination be your guide.

N O T E Participation in The Grandstand's Fantasy Leagues area is an extra cost item. For information on the charges, which are modest, please check the information text in the various Fantasy Leagues forum areas as to how you can join and participate in the various games. ■

- The Sports Libraries icon accesses a huge collection of software, ranging from shareware sports games and utilities to files about your favorite teams. Read Chapter 6, "Where Do We Begin?" for information about finding and downloading files from America Online. Files are available for both Mac and PC users. For all the newest sports-related software, you'll want to visit the Sports Libraries area first.

- Sports Boards are much like the message areas in other America Online forums. You can share your opinions with other online members, forum staff, and occasional experts on the latest information from the world of sports.

At the left side of the main Grandstand screen is a list of special sports-related forums that you might want to explore (see fig. 14.6 for an example). Each forum has its own schedule of conferences, active message boards, and software libraries. Just double-click the forum that interests you.

FIG. 14.6
All the popular sports have their own forums on America Online.

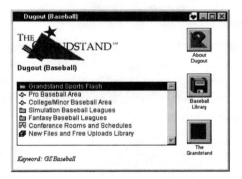

Getting the Latest Sports News

Keyword: **Sports News**

You can conveniently get all the top sports news of the day (see fig. 14.7), from the latest doings of your favorite teams, stories about that new multi-million dollar contract your favorite athlete has signed, and other hot news from the major wire services and top sports journalists.

As with other information text on America Online, just double-click an article to read it. You can also save or print the text for later review, using the appropriate commands from the File menu.

Part

III

Ch

14

FIG. 14.7
AOL's sports pages offer a world of information about the activities of your favorite teams and their prospects for the future.

Checking the Scoreboard

Keyword: **Scoreboard**

After you get past the front pages of your online sports page, you'll want to check out the statistics. The Scoreboard icon takes you to an area that presents the results of the previous day's major sports events, plus selected local games (see fig. 14.8). Remember, when the List More button at the bottom of the screen isn't grayed out, there are many more stories for you to scroll through.

FIG. 14.8
How did your favorite team fare in its last game? Here's where you can read the results.

You can also review the Standings, Results, and Schedules report (which will sometimes be available in the list box or the pop-up menu) for a capsule summary of how well your team is doing in their particular league, and to examine all of the scores in one place. In addition, you'll see a brief schedule of the next day's games.

Now, let's continue our journey across AOL's sports department.

Special Sporting Events

Whenever special sporting events occur, such as a World Series, Super Bowl, or a similar happening, you can be reasonably sure that a forum on America Online will be created to support this activity. When the event is out of season, these forums will no longer be active (at least until the following season). Here's an example of the sport that took over the headlines when I wrote this book.

A Visit to AOL's Baseball Forum

Keyword: **Baseball**

Just click the little baseball icon, and AOL's own Sports department will take over, offering you all the important news you want to read concerning your favorite baseball team (see fig. 14.9), and how it is doing in its division.

FIG. 14.9
From scores, to schedules, to trivia, it's all there in AOL's Baseball center.

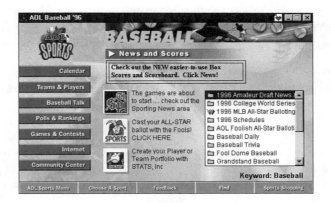

The latest statistics of your home team and your favorite players are just a click away. If you want to pit your sports expertise against that of the experts, or just fellow AOL members, double-click the Baseball Trivia title in the list box. A spirited discussion is always in progress in the Baseball Messages area; you'll probably want to jump in right away and contribute your viewpoints.

The Excitement of Pro Wrestling

Keyword: **Superstars**

Direct from the World Wrestling Federation, you can find news about one of the most controversial sports of all (see fig. 14.10). I won't get into the issue of whether all that

Part
III

Ch
14

mayhem you see on television is real or just an act, but whatever your feelings about it, AOL's Pro Wrestling forum is a way to bring all that action to your computer.

FIG. 14.10
Just what are your favorite wrestling stars up to? AOL's Pro Wrestling area has the story.

One of the highlights of a wrestling match is the posturing and arguing by your favorite stars. You'll be able to meet some of them in regular online conferences in AOL's Center Stage area.

If you want to approach your online interest from a multimedia point of view, click the Bodyslammin' Gallery button, which brings up the screen shown in figure 14.11. Here you'll be able to access a library of photos, videos, transcripts, and sounds covering the top matches from your favorite stars.

FIG. 14.11
Access a huge multimedia library of wrestling photos, videos, and sounds.

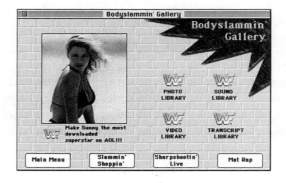

Reviewing Local Coverage

To check out the latest local sports news, simply use the AOL keyword **Sports News**, then click the Local Coverage button to access still another online sports resource (see fig. 14.12).

Three of the online daily newspapers are represented here, so by clicking the appropriate icon, you can read the sports pages of the *Arizona Republic, Chicago Tribune, New York Times, Orlando Sentinel, San Jose Mercury News*, plus a huge array of Internet-based newspapers.

FIG. 14.12
Here's a list of additional sports news forums on AOL.

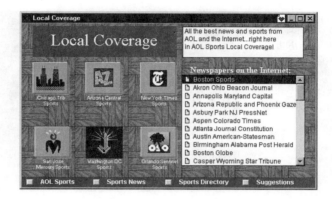

Visiting ABC Sports

Keyword: **ABC Sports**

ABC television has a large online forum, with many interesting features. At times it almost seems as if it's an online service unto itself. The ABC Online area was described briefly in Chapter 11, "TV and Movie Information Online." For now, I'll delve deeper into the ABC Sports area, where you can read and also participate in a number of fascinating activities (see fig. 14.13).

FIG. 14.13
Here's a sports forum run by ABC Sports.

Part
III

Ch
14

There are a number of icons shown here. Stuff offers pictures and sounds from major sporting events that you can download and play on your personal computer. Chat (short for ABC Sports Chat Central!) gives you a chance to join the fun and share your viewpoints of the arcane details of specific games and athletes (see fig. 14.14).

FIG. 14.14
Here's where you can join in the fun; you can talk about your favorite sport events and athletes with other fans.

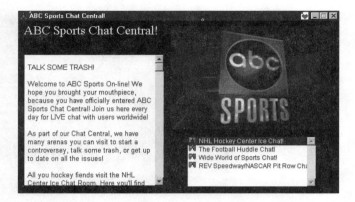

There are more interesting places to go from the ABC Sports forum. These include Inside ABC Sports, offering you schedules and background information about the network's sports programming. As you explore the forum, you'll discover where you can contact ABC Sports personalities and also participate in active sports-related discussions with fellow AOL members. The Store icon takes you to ABC's own specialty shop, where you can learn more about a line of exclusive merchandise. You also have a gateway direct to the ABC Auditorium where you can attend special events featuring network figures and noted personalities. And, if you want to visit the main ABC forums, you can click the icons at the bottom of the screen.

Resources for Sports and Recreation

Now that we've explored some of the news and special event offerings in AOL's various sporting forums, let's tour just one more area, which appears at the right of the main Sports Channel screen shown in fig. 14.1. It's the one labeled Mags & Clubs. America Online has a number of forums run by some of the major publishers or catering to a specific range of interests (see fig. 14.15). You'll want to visit many of the areas shown here during your online visits. As AOL continues to grow, you'll find additional sporting and lifestyle publishers and organizations listed as well.

FIG. 14.15
A list of magazines and
clubs dedicated to various
sporting pursuits.

From Here...

As with other areas on America Online, you don't have to restrict yourself to searching one area for the information you want. For more useful information on sports-related subjects, refer to these chapters:

- In Chapter 11, "TV and Movie Information Online," you'll read about additional entertainment-related resources on AOL.

- In Chapter 13, "Playing Games Online," you'll read about AOL's online gaming resources, and visit areas run by the major game software manufacturers.

- In Chapter 15, "Pursuing Lifestyles and Interests," you'll be able to explore the sporting world even further.

- In Chapter 23, "The News of the Day," you'll discover some of the many resources devoted to the top stories of the day on most any subject under the sun.

- In Chapter 24, "Magazines and Newspapers Online," you'll pay a visit to AOL's virtual newsstand and choose from a wealth of fascinating reading material.

Part
III

Ch
14

CHAPTER 15

Pursuing Lifestyles and Interests

AOL's Life, Styles & Interests area

Find the latest information on health-care issues.

Important happenings in cities around the world

Learn what to see and do in various parts of the world.

Finding members who share your interests

Interact with other members about hobbies ranging from cooking to science fiction.

AOL's discussion areas

Discuss the important issues of the day with other members.

Would you like to explore the stars, upgrade your stereo, look up your family history, or debate with other AOL members about everything from computing platforms to the news of the day? Well, America Online offers all these opportunities and much more in the Life, Styles & Interests channel.

Figure 15.1 shows the Life, Styles & Interests main window, which you can find by typing the keyword **clubs** or **LSI**. As you can see, the features you can call up from this point on are numerous, diverse, and intriguing.

When I sat down to write this chapter, I spent many, many hours exploring all the areas on America Online that cover lifestyles, hobbies, and special interests. Some of these places were discussed in Chapter 11, "TV and Movie Information Online," and Chapter 12, "Music, Books, and Art." You learn even more in this chapter, and you'll finish your little tour of lifestyle information resources in Chapter 24, "Magazines and Newspapers Online." ■

FIG. 15.1

You'll find a diverse array of features in AOL's Life, Styles & Interests channel.

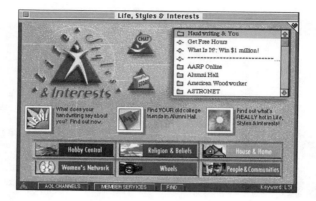

I soon realized that my survey could only scratch the surface. There were hundreds of resources to check, and many more are being added to AOL each week. So, this chapter just touches on the highlights of America Online's Life and Style areas; the rest is left for you to explore at your leisure.

To make it easier to find an area that caters to a specific interest, the forums in this area of America Online are grouped by category. What you see in the channel's screen will change from time to time. Let's explore the highlights.

 TIP If you can't find the specific forum that interests you on America Online, try locating it with a keyword. Most keywords either contain the name of an area or its subject, so if you don't know which keyword is correct, don't hesitate to try a few out. Suppose, for example, that you want to learn more about upgrading your stereo. Type the keyword **Stereo** and guess what? It takes you directly to the Stereo Review magazine forum on America Online.

Looking At Internet Resources

As with other online areas, the Life, Styles & Interests channel can take you to the Internet with just a click or two of the mouse. All you need to do is double-click the item in the list box labeled Top Internet Sites, which I've shown in figure 15.2. You can also reach this area via the keyword **Top Internet.**

The bill of fare will vary as well, but you'll be able to choose the categories that interest you, and the particular group setting that applies to you (Men, Women, and so on). From there you'll see a listing of popular World Wide Web resources that are bound to be worth further exploration.

FIG. 15.2
You can select a listing of easy-access Internet-based resources simply by clicking the appropriate subjects and the group that applies to you.

Visiting People & Communities

Among the various categories of special interest shown in figure 15.1 is the icon labeled People & Communities. Many subjects are listed when you click the People & Communities icon (see fig. 15.3). The purposes of many of these organizations are obvious from their titles (and no doubt some will be changed or added as AOL continues to upgrade its services). The following sections cover just a few of them.

FIG. 15.3
Just a sample of the offerings in AOL's People & Communities forum.

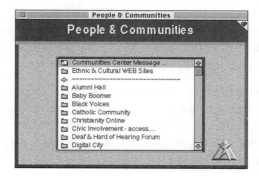

Exploring the Baby Boomers Forum

Keyword: **Baby Boomers**

I suppose it's redundant to explain what a baby boomer is, except to say that those of us who fit into this category share a unique range of experiences ranging from the advent of television to the Korean War, Vietnam, the Kennedy assassination, and more pleasant things such as Elvis Presley and the Beatles.

The focus of AOL's Baby Boomers forum is strictly interaction. You can share your experiences of a host of subjects with others who were born in the same frenetic generation. Figure 15.4 shows the Baby Boomers directory of services.

FIG. 15.4
The baby boomers generation has its own hangout on America Online.

Entering the National Multiple Sclerosis Society Forum

Keyword: **NMSS**

Multiple sclerosis has gotten serious attention in recent years with news that actress Annette Funicello (the original *Mickey Mouse Club* mouseketeer who starred in a string of beach movies in the 1960s) suffered from the disease.

The National Multiple Sclerosis Society has set up this forum on America Online to provide information about the disease, including updates on research for a cure. As you can see in figure 15.5, a host of information is available for you to read. You also can find a Message Center and a Health & Medical Chat room where you can interact with other members, including health-care professionals.

FIG. 15.5
NMSS is another area on America Online that provides health information.

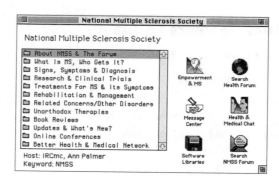

Other areas on America Online are devoted to health interests too, such as the United Cerebral Palsy Association's forum, which is discussed a bit later in this chapter.

Joining the Religion & Ethics Forum

Keyword: **Religions**

It doesn't matter what your religion is, or even if you favor a so-called New Age philosophy. AOL's Religion & Ethics Forum (see fig. 15.6) covers a full range of beliefs and information services. For example, you can debate with other online members in the forum's various message boards.

FIG. 15.6
The Religion & Ethics Forum is a special place to reflect on your religious beliefs.

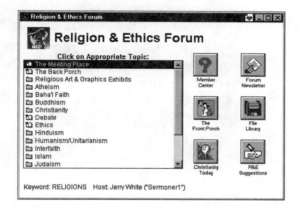

The File Library includes a collection of software that has a religious orientation. Included are educational games, Bible search programs, and more. You also can search the contents of the Bible for specific references and passages in a searchable database.

The Front Porch room is a special locale for impromptu chats or for regularly scheduled meetings on a host of fascinating subjects. The Back Porch takes a different approach to discussions; it's another of this forum's popular message areas.

Still another online resource covering religion is AOL's Religion and Beliefs forum, which offers separate areas devoted to Christianity, Judaism, World Beliefs (such as Buddhism and Islamic/Muslim faiths) and Spiritual Mosaic (covering Alternative Healing, Paganism, and other faiths).

Visiting the Gay and Lesbian Community Forum

Keyword: **GLCF**

AOL has created the Gay and Lesbian Community forum as a forum not only for members of AOL who are gay, lesbian, bisexual, and transgendered, but for family members and others who are friendly to these communities. The forum (shown in fig. 15.7) is one of the largest information centers on AOL. Among the most visited areas is the HIV/AIDS Forum. It's a place to share information about treating and preventing the HIV virus and to learn about new medical discoveries that combat the disease.

FIG. 15.7
AOL's Gay and Lesbian Community Forum has a huge selection of information, plus message boards and conference rooms.

On your first visit to this forum, you'll no doubt want to look at a road map of some of the services. The forum's staff has created a GLCF User Manual (see fig. 15.8) that provides a quick guide to all of the forum's services and related information found throughout AOL and the Internet. The manual can be brought up as a series of text windows that you can save or print.

FIG. 15.8
Read the GLCF user manual to learn all about this forum.

Exploring SeniorNet Online

Keyword: **seniornet**

SeniorNet Online is devoted to the proposition that life truly begins in one's senior years. In a special Computer Learning Center, you can learn how to master your computer. SeniorNet Online also includes active message areas, a Community Center where you can interact with other online members and forum staff, and a wealth of information you can read and download (see fig. 15.9).

FIG. 15.9
SeniorNet Online provides a special meeting place for senior citizens on America Online.

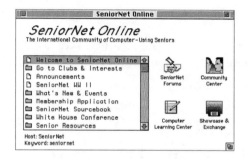

SeniorNet is also a membership organization that offers special benefits and merchandise discounts to its members. You aren't required to join in order to participate in the forum, but a membership application is there in case you want to apply.

Visiting the United Cerebral Palsy Associations, Inc.

Keyword: **UCPA, Cerebral Palsy**

The UCPA is a huge organization, founded in the 1940s, with more than 155 affiliates that work together to help those afflicted with this and other debilitating diseases (see fig. 15.10).

The association's forum on AOL carries regular reports on the progress of science in finding a way to prevent cerebral palsy and to help those who suffer from this disease live a more rewarding, productive life. The forum holds regular online meetings to inform AOL members of their work. You'll find special areas devoted to information about employment possibilities and services available to both individuals and families. In addition to attending the regularly scheduled forum conferences, you can voice concerns and ask questions in the forum's Message Center.

FIG. 15.10
Participate in the important
work performed by the
United Cerebral Palsy
Associations, Inc.

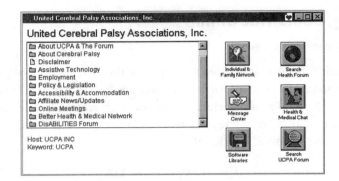

You'll notice, also, that the UCPA forum has gateways to other online health-related areas, such as the Better Health & Medical Network and the DisABILITIES Forum.

For now, though, you'll want to look at more of the features offered in AOL's Life, Styles and Interests channel.

Pursuing Hobbies and Interests

Keyword: **Hobby**

Your interests may be recreational or professional, but it doesn't make a difference on AOL, where you'll definitely find a hobby or club forum to interest you. Type the AOL keyword **Hobby** and see what's available (see fig. 15.11).

FIG. 15.11
Some of AOL's Hobbies and
Interests forums are shown
here.

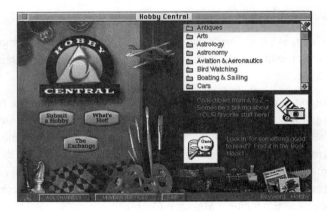

N O T E The directories shown in these forum listings can be scrolled; they generally contain many more features than those shown in the illustrations included in this book. Also, new forums are regularly added to the roster. ▪

Joining the Astronomy Club

Keyword: **Astronomy**

When I was a child, I was absolutely fascinated by the mysteries of the stars and planets and the incredible goings-on in our universe. So, I joined a local astronomy club and even bought myself a little telescope so that I could view the planets in our solar system up close and personal.

A real astronomer, Mr. Astro, better known as Stuart Goldman, has been recruited to host America Online's Astronomy Club (see fig. 15.12). Mr. Goldman works for *Sky & Telescope* magazine as an associate editor.

FIG. 15.12
You can explore the stars with a little help from America Online.

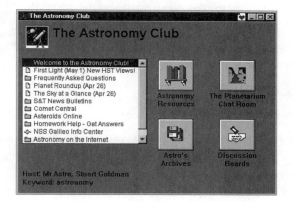

If you want to learn more about the stars and planets, explore the forum's message board. This message board gives you the chance to interact with other America Online members who share an interest in astronomy, or even ask experts, such as Mr. Astro, whatever's on your mind.

Meet fellow astronomers, amateur and professional alike, at their weekly conference in the Planetarium.

Joining the Cooking Club

Keyword: **Cooking Club**

Whether your efforts at cooking are limited to boiling water and warming a TV dinner (which is about the extent of my cooking efforts) or you are a culinary expert, you can find a wealth of useful information in America Online's Cooking Club (see fig. 15.13).

The message boards are places where you can share your favorite recipes or pick up a tip or two from other online gourmets. You can even enter a conference room, The Cooking

Chat room, where regular meetings are held on food preparation or new recipes. And, if your tastes in food are confined to a specific category, such as Vegetarian, you'll want to drop into the Vegetarians Online area.

FIG. 15.13
The Cooking Club is your resource for cooking tips and tricks on America Online.

Exploring the Exchange

Keyword: **Exchange**

The Exchange is a place where you can express yourself on a wide variety of special interests. To make it easier to find discussion groups that interest you, click the icons shown in the main Exchange forum window (see fig. 15.14). There are discussion areas related to men's and women's issues, gardening and other outdoor activities, politics, philosophy, crafts, careers, coin collecting—you name it. You're likely to find something about your interest in The Exchange.

FIG. 15.14
The Exchange is America Online's meeting place for online discussions of all sorts.

As with other areas on America Online, make sure to approach the debate carefully. Don't use vulgar language, don't insult other America Online members (even though the discussions have been known to get hot and heavy), and most importantly, have a good time.

Joining the Genealogy Forum

Keyword: **Roots**

Interested in looking up your family tree? Well, the place to go is AOL's Genealogy Forum, where you find advice and useful information to help you in your search (see fig. 15.15). In active message areas, you can share information and experiences with other online members as you try to find out just who your ancestors are. When I review this forum, I often regret that I never had much opportunity to speak with my grandparents (who passed away many years ago) about their experiences in their home country in eastern Europe.

FIG. 15.15
Get some tips here on researching your family tree.

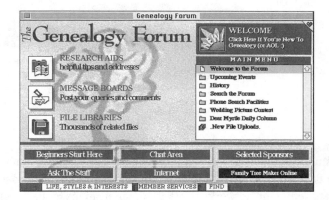

The software library includes programs that help you catalog information about your family history. You can review the findings of many genealogy experts who assist you in your quest. Or you can attend the regular chats in the Ancestral Digs Conference Hall and other conference rooms available in the Chat Area.

Joining the Ham Radio Club

Keyword: **Ham radio**

Ham (or amateur) radio enthusiasts are a breed apart from those of you who sit in front of a CB radio and exchange 10-4s with a friend. A ham radio operator uses a shortwave radio setup to communicate with another radio enthusiast on the other side of the world. In times of disaster, Hams worldwide have used their equipment to get information about the disaster situation to the outside world.

The Ham Radio Club includes a special area devoted to those who like to listen to short-wave radio (see fig. 15.16). With a shortwave radio, which you can buy at many consumer electronics outfits, you can hear actual broadcasts from other parts of the world. Many countries in the farthest corners of the globe have special English-language radio shows and music programs designed to present news about their cultures and politics. These programs are quite different from the capsule summaries you get on network television programs. You'd be surprised, for example, how views of a particular news event are colored by perceptions in a specific country. Also, some of these shortwave radio programs are actually run by the governments of the country from which they originate, so you will often get a very different perspective than you receive from more disinterested news sources.

FIG. 15.16
America Online's special forum for the world of radio communications is the Ham Radio Club.

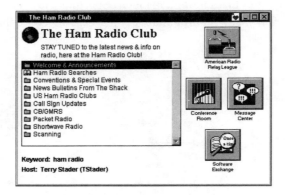

The American Radio Relay League, which is an area of the Ham Radio Club, is an organization devoted strictly to the interests of amateur radio enthusiasts. The group's work also includes setting up networks to offer communications in the event of a local emergency.

Entering the Kodak Photography Forum

Keyword: **Kodak**

As cameras become both cheaper and more sophisticated, high quality photography is not limited to the professional. All you need to produce some very good photos is a camera, a little advice, and your own imagination.

The Kodak Photography Forum, shown in figure 15.17, is conducted by Ron Baird, a photography specialist from Kodak who writes many of their technical manuals. Ron, along with fellow online members, provides you with hints and tips that can make your picture-taking experience more rewarding. If you're looking to sell that old camera and get something better, you can even check out a buy/sell section, available through the forum's Message Center. You can also post your work in The Library Center or have a look at the kind of photographs other AOL members have taken, by downloading the files already in this library.

FIG. 15.17
America Online's Kodak Photography Forum is the place for shutterbugs.

The Chat Room is your place to receive online help and advice when you have a question. You also might want to check the schedule for upcoming conferences. Of course, because the forum is sponsored by Kodak, you'll have direct access to the company's World Wide Web site, where you can learn more about their products.

Reading *Popular Photography* Online

Keyword: **Photos, PopPhoto**

Each month, hundreds of thousands of readers turn to *Popular Photography* for comprehensive photo advice. The magazine's AOL forum offers the entire issue in convenient text form that you can read on-screen, or save and print for later review (see fig. 15.18); just use the File menu in your AOL software. Like the magazine itself, the contents are organized into sections. You can access them from the Department's icon at the right of the forum window. If you're a regular reader, you'll probably rush to the Too Hot Too Handle section first (one of my favorite parts of this magazine). You'll find it in the list box when you click Photo Departments.

The Buying Guide/Test Reports icon offers the same thorough product tests that are in the magazine. The Resource Center section is designed for you to get in touch with product manufacturers. You can write to the magazine's editors in the Communications area.

You can order a subscription and purchase special products at the Pop Photo Store (available when you click the Communications Center button), and the Message Boards are a source for fascinating discussions that you'll want to visit often.

FIG. 15.18
Tips and tricks about photography from *Popular Photography* magazine.

Exploring the Fictional Realm

Keyword: **Fictional Realm**

Fiction is the way to rest our minds and imagine the possibilities of the past, present, and future. For example, science fiction has become a part of our everyday lives. We see the stuff that used to fill novels and movies come to life before our eyes. And yet, our interest in the subject remains insatiable. America Online's Fictional Realm forum is an active pit stop for fans of works covering science fiction, fantasy, horror, romance, mysteries, and interactive fiction. You can share your views about the latest works and learn about upcoming events. Figure 15.19 shows the main Fictional Realm directory window.

FIG. 15.19
Explore the worlds of science fiction, solve the great fictional mysteries, enjoy fantasy and adventure. Visit AOL's Fictional Realm area.

One terrific resource for fans of fiction is *OMNI* Magazine Online, which includes science-fiction tales in addition to its coverage of science fact (see Chapter 24, "Magazines and Newspapers Online").

Resources for Health and Fitness

Keyword: **Health**

A number of AOL forums are devoted to the subjects that are uppermost in the minds of many people—our health. Let's start this section with a look at AOL's Health Channel (see fig. 15.20), which is accessible by clicking the icon in the Life, Styles & Interests department. Some of the online areas listed here were covered earlier in this chapter.

FIG. 15.20
AOL's Health and Fitness forums are a useful source for information and discussion.

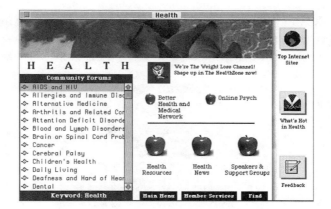

Visiting the Health Resources Channel

Keyword: **Health Resources**

Whether you are a health-care professional or are just seeking the route to better health and a longer, more productive life, the Health channel is a place you might want to visit often.

As you can see in figure 15.21, this channel is a gateway to a huge amount of information on all sorts of health-related issues. It's not intended to replace a regular visit to your family physician; it's designed to give you a better range of knowledge about the issues that are most important to you.

FIG. 15.21
This special area on America Online is for consumers and health professionals.

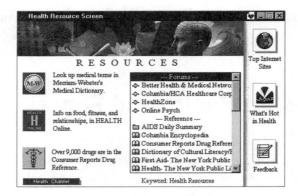

You find many handy health-related resources in this area. There are daily updates on research not only on common illnesses, but on such life-threatening ailments as AIDS (see fig. 15.22). The information you receive when you search this area will help you interact in a more precise manner with your doctor. The forum is also a great resource for information on the latest findings in various health-related fields.

FIG. 15.22
The AIDS daily summary offers updates on current research and results.

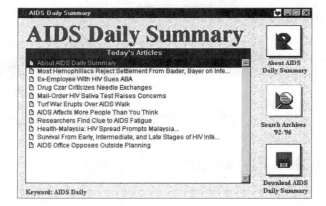

As with other online areas, the Health Resources Channel offers fast gateways to health-related information on the Internet. You'll also find news of important online conferences and many message boards from which you can learn more about your health and share your own information.

Studying Issues in Mental Health

Keyword: **IMH**

The most difficult problems you have to face can stem from relationships. Whether it's your spouse, your children, or just coping with each day's events, the task often can be challenging.

Issues in Mental Health is a place where you can learn about how to deal with everyday problems (see fig. 15.23). Active message boards enable you to interact with other online members and professionals on the problems of daily living.

FIG. 15.23
The complex issues of relationships are discussed on America Online.

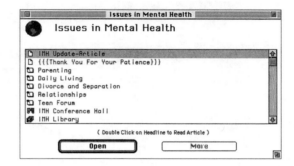

You also might want to explore the forum's vast library of mental health reference materials found in the IMH Library, and attend regular conferences, accessible through the IMH Conference Hall, where you can discuss problems and solutions.

Reading *Longevity* Magazine Online

Keyword: **Longevity**

Longevity magazine exists to inform you of discoveries that may help you live longer (see fig. 15.24). It's brought to you by the publishers of *Omni,* and offers page upon page (or the virtual equivalent) of useful news and opinion.

The primary focus of the magazine is preventive health care; it provides useful articles on how to take control of your own health and how to find ways to help you live longer, healthier, and happier. The magazine's contents—extensive material on what science is learning about the aging process—are available here. There are stories about folks (like my brother) who've found ways to look young and stay healthy. All of the magazine's contents are divided into convenient sections, which you can access by clicking the appropriate icon. You can also get involved in the Health Exchange, which is the forum's spirited message board, and attend regular online conferences in the Longevity Conference and Longevity Chat areas that feature health experts. The online contents of *Longevity* can also be searched using AOL's standard search capability.

FIG. 15.24
Learn how science will help you live longer in *Longevity* magazine.

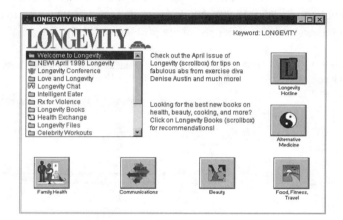

Visiting the Environmental Forum

Keyword: **Eforum**

The news media refer to the 1990s as the "Decade for the Environment." The Environmental Forum is America Online's response to the attention the environment is receiving (see fig. 15.25). This forum has an active message board, the Eco Messaging Center, which covers a host of environmental issues. The discussions can be calm and collected, or hot and heavy, especially when the subject gets intermingled with politics. You'll find that this is an online resource you come back to over and over again.

The Eforum chat room holds regularly scheduled meetings that feature noted scientists and other experts on the environment. Check here often for the guest list and chat schedules.

FIG. 15.25
The Environmental Forum is America Online's center for the "Decade for the Environment."

Visiting the Pet Care Forum

Keyword: **Pet**

Not all pets fit into the cat, dog, or fish category. There are other creatures that some regard as pets. But whatever your choices, the Pet Care Forum on America Online is devoted to helping you find better ways to care for all your animal friends (see fig. 15.26).

FIG. 15.26
Learn more about caring for your pet in America Online's Pet Care Forum.

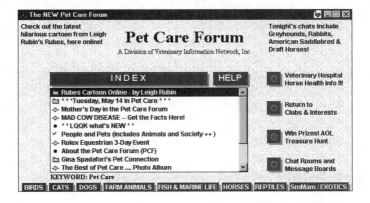

The forum is hosted by veterinarians and is frequented by professional breeders and fellow pet owners. You can participate in active discussions about common problems you might face when bringing a pet into your home. You can use the Animal Talk Chat Room for a spontaneous chat with a fellow animal lover or to attend one of the forum's regular conferences.

Reading *ELLE* Magazine Online

Keyword: **Elle**

Many of you are probably familiar with *ELLE* magazine, an elegant magazine of high fashion that's read regularly by hundreds of thousands of readers (see fig. 15.27). The magazine's online forum has text and photos from the magazine itself, available from the icons shown in the forum window.

FIG. 15.27
ELLE magazine is an online magazine for the fashion-conscious.

The forum is also dedicated to having an active dialogue with its readers (and any AOL member for that matter). One of the icons at the bottom of the forum window, Messages, is the forum's message board that you'll want to visit on a regular basis. You'll also find specific departments devoted to such subjects as fashion, fitness, and health. Each of these departments not only includes material from the magazine itself, but a roster of features that are exclusive to AOL. In addition, there's quick access to *ELLE*'s WWW site, for even more easy-access features.

Visiting *Woman's Day*

Keyword: **Woman's Day**

This forum, run by the publishers of *Woman's Day* magazine, provides an electronic version of the very same magazine you find on your corner newsstand (see fig. 15.28). In addition to the content of the magazine itself, though, there are special features that are exclusive to their AOL forum. These include special message boards, and the *Woman's Day* Odeon, which features frequent conferences from the magazine's writers, editors, and visiting experts. You'll find them all when you click The Gathering Place icon.

FIG. 15.28
A host of women's issues are discussed in *Woman's Day* Online.

The icons on the right of the forum screen group the contents of the magazine into handy sections. If, after browsing through this forum, you decide you want to subscribe to *Woman's Day,* just click the Help icon and you'll get further information. Also, many of the departments get their own special message boards in order to give a tighter focus to messages about specific topics. You can also locate articles on specific topics using the Woman's Day Search Past Articles tool, shown in the directory window on the left of the main forum screen.

Professions and Organizations

A number of professional societies have formed special areas on America Online that cater to members as well as casual visitors who want to learn more about a specific topic. Many of them are conveniently grouped in the Professions & Organizations area shown in the list box of the Life, Styles & Interests channel (see fig. 15.29). A few of these forums are discussed in the pages that follow.

FIG. 15.29
AOL's Professions & Organizations forums.

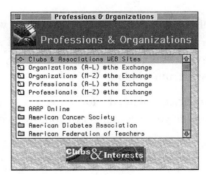

Visiting the Aviation Forum

Keywords: **Aviation, Fly**

Whether your interest in aviation is limited to reading about it in your living room, building a model plane, or piloting a craft yourself, you can find others who share your interest in America Online's Aviation Forum (see fig. 15.30).

FIG. 15.30
The Aviation Club is for armchair and active aviators.

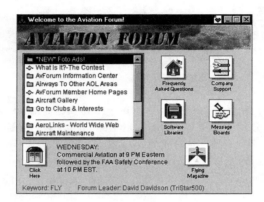

One of the club's most popular spots is its active Message Board. There you can find ongoing discussions about commercial aviation, military aviation, and even model planes.

The Aviation Forum's Software Libraries offer both GIF and text files that you can download and view on your computer. As mentioned in Chapter 7, "America Online's People Connection," a GIF file is a multiplatform format that enables you to view and print photos on your computer.

Visiting the Public Safety Center

Keyword: **PSC**

You don't have to be a professional (fire fighter, police officer, whatever) to be involved in this forum. It's for anyone seeking information on how to deal with common household emergencies that can become disasters if you don't act quickly. Figure 15.31 shows the main Emergency Response Forum window.

As with other forums on America Online, the forum features an active message area and a library containing text files that you can transfer to your own computer for later viewing and printing.

FIG. 15.31
The Public Safety Center is a special forum for online members who work in the emergency services field. •

Joining the Military & Vets Forum

Keyword: **Military**

America Online's Military & Vets Forum is dedicated to those of you who have served the country in the armed forces, whether in war or peace (see fig. 15.32). You can find message areas for both veterans and those still serving in the military.

FIG. 15.32
Armed forces actives and veterans have their interests addressed in the Military & Vets Forum.

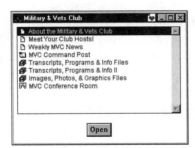

One of the most interesting places to visit is the Images, Photos, & Graphics Files library, which includes image files not only of places where military encounters took place but also of aircraft and ships. I even saw a picture there of an enemy star cruiser from the TV series *Star Trek*.

Joining the National Space Society

Keyword: **Space**

The National Space Society is devoted to promoting research and exploration of space (see fig. 15.33). Its Board of Governors features such luminaries as Hugh Downs, Arthur C. Clarke, Jacques Cousteau, John Glenn, Nichelle Nichols, and Alan Shepard.

If space exploration interests you, you're invited to join the organization. Even as a non-member you can participate in roundtable discussions or regular chats and download photos showing the stars, planets, and our own space probes.

FIG. 15.33
America Online's center for space-related research is the National Space Society.

Leisure & Entertainment Resources Online

Of course, not every part of America Online has quite the serious intent as the places previously discussed in this chapter. There's a very active Leisure & Entertainment area as well. Some of these resources are covered in Chapter 11, "TV and Movie Information Online," and Chapter 12, "Music, Books, and Art." Here are some additional examples of forums that are geared toward providing not just information, but a fun experience too.

Visiting *Car and Driver* Online

Keyword: **Car and Driver**

Okay, just what is next year's model offering that last year's didn't? More horsepower, wider seats, wood inlays on the dashboard? Whenever you are looking for a new car (or you just want to find out what's happening in the automotive field), you'll probably turn to *Car and Driver* magazine at some point in time.

The magazine's AOL online forum, shown in figure 15.34, includes feature articles from the magazine itself, complete test reports of the hot new models, and an active message area where you can learn about the experiences other AOL members have had with these models. Oh, by the way, *Car and Driver's* sister magazine, *Road & Track,* has its own AOL forum too. The keyword is, of course, **Road & Track**.

Both *Car and Driver* and *Road & Track* magazines offer regular online conferences where you can interact with fellow readers and chat with the magazine's editors and visiting experts on a host of issues related to the automotive scene.

FIG. 15.34
Learn how the new cars really perform before you take that test drive.

Visiting Chicago Online

Keyword: **Chicago**

Here's a forum that's huge and sprawling, much like the city for which it's named, and, of course, it has many places you'll want to visit. This section just covers the highlights and leaves you to explore the rest at your leisure.

When first visiting Chicago Online, click the Chicagoland Calendar & Almanac listing found in the main forum directory for the latest news and event information (see fig. 15.35). Whether you're traveling to Chicago for business or pleasure, you'll probably want to read the Chicago Tribune News & Features area for the latest forecasts and important information you'll need to know when you get there. (Also see Chapter 23, "The News of the Day.")

The Ticketmaster icon takes you to the Ticketmaster gateway, a special area where you can learn about concerts and other special events not only in Chicago, but in the state of Illinois too (and it's expanding to other parts of the country as time goes on). When you've found the event you want to attend, you can order your tickets using your keyboard and mouse.

FIG. 15.35
Chicago Online is the gateway to information about happenings in the Windy City.

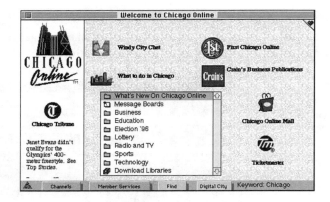

Chicago's Education Guide is a special area in Chicago Online that has information about the city's vast array of educational opportunities. There are previews of special events at different educational institutions, along with detailed enrollment information.

Entering the Gadget Guru Electronics Area

Keyword: **Gadget Guru**

The Gadget Guru, alias Andy Pargh, is a smart fellow who you've no doubt seen on TV from time to time. Whether you're familiar with him or not, you'll want to visit the Gadget Guru Electronics Area forum (see fig. 15.36). You'll learn about the Guru's discoveries of new electronics devices that will eventually end up on the shelves of your favorite stores.

The Gadget Guru Message Board is a forum for America Online members to discuss their likes and dislikes of various gadgetry. I have spent quite some time there reading messages from folks who still remember the good old days; for example, when electronics used tubes, not solid-state devices.

You can also find reviews of upcoming products so that you can learn all about them before they hit the marketplace.

Reading *The New York Times* Online

Keyword: **Times**

Start spreading the news...*The New York Times* is on America Online, with an emphasis on the top features and lifestyle news from each daily edition of the paper (see fig. 15.37). All of the top stories from the newspaper itself are available for you to read online, or save and print for later review.

FIG. 15.36
Consumer electronics gets
its own forum on America
Online.

CAUTION

When you want to find *The New York Times* on America Online, don't forget that the keyword is **Times**. If you want to know how long you've been on AOL since you logged on, the keyword is **Clock**.

If you live in New York, or are planning a visit, click the Arts & Entertainment icon. You'll find news and views about the top dining and entertainment spots in New York City. And don't forget to check out In The Region, a special area devoted to the rest of the tri-state New York metropolitan area.

FIG. 15.37
The New York Times offers
the best of its daily editions
on America Online.

Exploring Wine & Dine Online

Keyword: **Food, Beverages**

This forum caters to all of you who are interested in fine food and drink, whether it involves home cooking or a visit to your favorite restaurant. You can access it by choosing WineBase from the Everything Edible area accessed via the above keyword.

From the right side of the main forum window, you can access a collection of columns from Jerry D. Mead, a syndicated writer in wines, available by double-clicking Wine Columnists & Articles. There is also a Reading Room & Reference area featuring articles that cover everything from wine and food basics to such topics as "How To Buy Wine Futures" (see fig. 15.38).

FIG. 15.38
From wine tasting to fine dining, Wine & Dine Online is your information source.

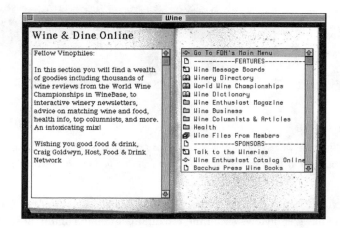

You can find a diverse array of resources that extend from reviews of fine restaurants to a message board where you can exchange news and views with fellow online gourmets. Wine & Dine Online also offers a service to help you locate and purchase wines of rare vintage.

Just scroll through the list box for the full list of features, which includes news about upcoming events, such as wine tastings and other gatherings of interest.

Sports & Recreation

Chapter 14, "Sports in Cyberspace," covered some of America Online's sports-related forums. Here are some more areas you'll want to visit.

Exploring BikeNet: The Bicycle Network

Keyword: **BikeNet**

The Bicycle Network on America Online is sponsored by a number of bicycle organizations in North America. It's a database for publications and text files on bicycle-related information (see fig. 15.39). The network also includes a regular schedule of conferences and an active message board. Even if your bike riding is limited to Sunday afternoons in a local park, you'll be interested in visiting this forum.

FIG. 15.39
BikeNet is the online source of information for bicycle riders.

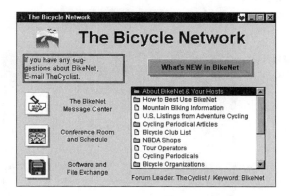

Going Scuba Diving

Keyword: **Scuba**

Like me, I'm sure most of you have become familiar with scuba diving through many of the exciting movies in which characters perform many of their incredible stunts underwater. If you've entertained the idea of trying this sport, pay a visit to AOL Scuba Forum (see fig. 15.40). You'll find a full directory of places where you can learn scuba diving yourself. If you are already a participant in this exciting activity, you'll find helpful tips to really hone your skills.

FIG. 15.40
Underwater sports can be truly exciting, whether you watch or participate yourself.

Information for House & Home

Let's return to those icons shown in the Life, Styles & Interests channel. There's just one more icon, House & Home, that I've yet to present. This icon brings up the directory window shown in figure 15.41.

FIG. 15.41
The House & Home area in the Life, Styles & Interests channel.

A Visit to the Consumer Electronics Forum

Keyword: **Consumer Electronics**

Among the fastest growing retail categories is what has come to be known as Consumer Electronics (see fig. 15.42). Consumer Electronics is a huge area that covers everything from the tape deck you install in your car to the home theater system you add to your home. AOL's CE (Consumer Electronics) Forums are the focal point for all of the areas on AOL devoted to such products. You'll find discussions and information about auto electronics, personal communications products (such as cellular phones), electronic gadgets, and audio and video equipment.

FIG. 15.42
The main screen of AOL's popular Consumer Electronics Forums.

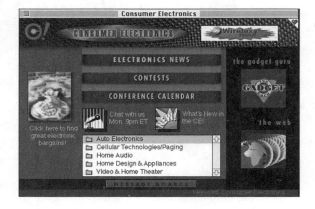

In addition to providing a full-featured forum for these subjects, the Consumer Electronics Forums also offer gateways to other areas dealing with this topic, such as The Gadget Guru, described earlier in this chapter, and *Stereo Review* magazine, discussed in Chapter 24, "Magazines and Newspapers Online." There's also a forum dedicated to video games.

The exciting march of technology is bound to create new segments of the consumer electronics industry. You can expect this forum to be an exciting, rapidly changing place that you'll want to visit on a regular basis.

Visiting the Homeowners Forum

Keyword: **Home, UHA**

Here's a forum that is supported by an activist organization representing the 65 million homeowners in the U.S. It's sponsored by the United Homeowners Association (see fig. 15.43), and it offers a wide array of information that will assist you in dealing with common household-related issues, plus additional material. The Frequently Asked Questions folder, for example, covers common issues you may wonder about, especially when you buy your first home. You can also read online newsletters and study material about the association's activities to protect the rights of homeowners before Congress.

The four icons shown at the bottom of the forum window represent additional features. The Home Improvement area provides a large number of text files offering helpful advice on dealing with common household chores, such as minor repairs and tending your garden. The Message Boards provide a spirited discussion of all sorts of home-related issues. And, the Homeowner Connection is the forum's chat room. Because this is a membership organization, there are special membership offers for AOL members that will get you a regular newsletter and additional services.

FIG. 15.43
The Homeowners Forum on AOL.

From Here...

Brand new Life, Styles & Interests forums are added regularly to America Online, so if you don't find an area that caters to your special interest now, check back often. A number of the special forums mentioned briefly in this chapter, and other information pertinent to your Life, Styles & Interests needs, are also discussed in more detail in the following chapters:

■ In Chapter 11, "TV and Movie Information Online," you'll read more about entertainment-related resources on AOL.

■ In Chapter 12, "Music, Books, and Art," you'll discover forums devoted to additional entertainment-related interests.

■ In Chapter 13, "Playing Games Online," you'll learn how to play games online and receive support for your favorite computer and board games.

■ In Chapter 14, "Sports in Cyberspace," you'll read about resources that cover the latest sporting news and learn how to participate in your favorite sports online.

■ In Chapter 24, "Magazines and Newspapers Online," you'll take a trip to AOL's newsstand and find additional reading resources.

Kids and America Online

CHAPTER 16

Parental Issues and Internet Access

Safe online computing for kids

Review America Online's parental controls.

Be a good online citizen

Learn about America Online's terms of service and what they mean to you.

Responsible parenting

Surveys the special online areas devoted to parents and child care.

AOL is for kids, too

Learn how to introduce your children to the Internet.

As you have seen so far in this book, America Online is basically a warm, friendly place that you might think of as your hometown in cyberspace. But, like your hometown, there are some folks who don't always use common sense and courtesy toward others. And when you, as a parent, allow your kids to enter the online universe, you want to be sure their visits are always friendly, fun, and educational.

The issues in this chapter are of extreme importance to me, as a parent of an intelligent, active youngster who seems to have inherited his father's taste for computers and regular visits to online services. (By the way, he has his own screen name, GraysonS, if you want to drop him some e-mail, and he is a regular visitor to AOL's kids-only forums). ■

Understanding the Risks

The online experience should be friendly and fun, and it is just that for most AOL members. As with other parts of our society, however, there are a very few people who do not have the best interests of you and your child in mind. Throughout this chapter, the methods to help protect your child are outlined. You'll want to read them and discuss them with your children before they begin to explore AOL's online community.

Although problems seldom occur, here are a few things you and your child should watch for during your travels on AOL:

- *Inappropriate material.* As explained later in this chapter, nude or explicit photos and related text material are not allowed on AOL. That does not stop some people from exchanging such files, however. You should instruct your child to bring information about such files directly to your attention, so that the proper authorities at America Online can be alerted.

- *Face-to-face meetings.* You should instruct your child never to give out personal information, such as your home address or telephone number to another AOL member (however friendly that member may seem) without your approval. Any personal meetings between your child and another AOL member should be done under your supervision at a public location.

- *Online harassment.* If your child receives instant messages or e-mail that is threatening, intimidating, or contains objectionable content, have your child bring the material directly to your attention so that you can file a complaint against the member who sends such material.

- *Internet access.* The Internet is largely unregulated and not subject to Parental Controls or America Online's Terms of Service. As a result, you'll want to instruct your child carefully about both the benefits and potential downsides of Internet access before your child begins to explore that area.

In the next few pages, you will learn how to set restrictions on areas your child may visit, and how to deal with problems if they occur.

Setting Parental Controls

Keyword: **Parental Controls**

As with any concerned parent, you may want to restrict your child's access to certain areas of America Online. That's the purpose of Parental Controls. This feature permits the original account holder (the screen name you created when you first established your

AOL account) to block or restrict access by users of other screen names on your AOL account from certain areas and features on America Online (see fig. 16.1). Setting these limits can help protect your child against possible exposure to objectionable material or online harassment in some areas of the service.

FIG. 16.1
The Parental Controls dialog box is used to control your child's access to AOL.

Parental Control can be activated with the keyword **Parental Controls,** or by choosing that command from the Members menu while you're logged on with your master account name (the name that's listed first among your list of available accounts in the main window of your AOL software). It's also available by clicking the icon that appears to the left of most chat room windows. The best way to select Parental Control is to just click the Account Security icon after entering the free Member Services area.

CAUTION

Your account password and billing information are confidential. You will never be asked by an AOL employee online to give out this information. If you ever receive such a request, report it to AOL's Terms of Service area immediately.

You can establish controls for just one or all screen names on your account. After Parental Control is set for a particular screen name, it is enforced every time that screen name logs on. Changes to Parental Control settings can be made by the master account holder at any time.

While you are logged on with your master screen name, you can activate one or more of the following Parental Control features:

- *Block Instant Messages.* Turns off Instant Messages, the immediate, one-to-one communications that can only be viewed by the sender and receiver of the message.

- *Block All Rooms.* Blocks access to the People Connection. The People Connection is the live, interactive chat area of America Online. This doesn't include the chat rooms in the Computing and Software areas.
- *Block Member Rooms.* Only blocks access to the member-created rooms within the People Connection. Other People Connection rooms, such as the Lobby, Romance Connection, and so on, are still accessible when this Parental Control feature is activated.
- *Block Conference Rooms.* Blocks access to the more focused rooms found around various departments on America Online, such as the classrooms in Learning & Reference, the technical forums in the Computing area, and the NeverWinter Nights role-playing game in Games & Entertainment. It does not affect access to rooms in the People Connection.

Or Do It All at Once

There's another option, shown in figure 16.1, that's even more restrictive. It's accessed by clicking the Block All But Kids Only button. That process will block your child's access to all online areas except those available for the Kids Only forums.

NOTE   You can add up to four additional screen names to your AOL account, and it's a good idea to make a separate screen name for your child, or for each of your children. That way you can grant them selective access to AOL services without affecting your own access. If you have a large family, you can always add a second AOL account. In any case, it's a good idea for you to be sure your children give you their passwords, so you can access their accounts in the event of a problem. While giving a child some degree of privacy is a good idea, you are fully responsible for their online conduct. ■

Reviewing America Online's Terms of Service

Keyword: **TOS**

Throughout this book, I've compared America Online to a large, sprawling city, with lots of friendly neighborhoods and lots of friendly neighbors. To take this comparison one step further, let's realize that there are a few who choose not to follow the common sense guidelines of good online conduct, which is to respect your fellow AOL members and treat them with kindness.

When you first sign up with America Online, you agree to accept the Terms of Service, which is the set of rules and regulations under which it operates. Consider these rules somewhat equivalent to the body of laws that govern the conduct of people who live in any community.

The Terms of Service (see fig. 16.2) covers not only your contract with America Online, but a set of rules for online conduct. As in your own hometown, the parents of the children who visit America Online are fully responsible for the way they behave. If your child consistently misbehaves online, you run the risk of losing your AOL membership, so these rules should be taken very seriously.

Part
IV
Ch
16

FIG. 16.2
This is a special information area devoted to AOL's Terms of Service.

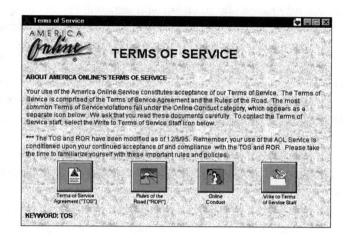

The Terms of Service Summarized

AOL's Terms of Service is available—free of online charge—for you to read at any time. You can also save and print the text material you see there for later review. You may want to make a copy and discuss the contents with your children before they make their online visits.

 You can save and print any text item in an AOL information window for later reference. Just click the text window first.

Many of the important features of the Terms of Service are summarized here for you to review. You can examine the full text during your AOL session via the keyword **TOS**.

- *Offensive Communication.* The AOL Service is a community-oriented service composed of many different communities of people. Our goal is to provide an interesting, stimulating, and fun place for all members. Using vulgar, abusive, or hateful language undermines this goal and is not allowed. Please use your best judgment and be respectful of other members. Remember, there are children online.

If you use vulgar or abusive language online, even if masked by symbols or other characters, you may either receive an on-screen warning by a Guide or Room Host, or, in extreme cases, be terminated immediately.

- *Harassment.* When a member targets another specifically to cause him/her distress, embarrassment, unwanted attention, or other discomfort, this is harassment.

  AOL Inc. does not condone harassment in any form and may suspend or terminate the accounts of any member who harasses others.

  You may have a disagreement with someone's point of view. We encourage lively discussion in our chat rooms and message boards, but personal attacks, or attacks based on a person's race, national origin, ethnicity, religion, gender, sexual orientation, or other such affiliation are prohibited.

- *Graphic Files.* AOL Inc. prohibits the transfer or posting on the AOL Service of sexually explicit images or other content deemed offensive by AOL Inc.

- *Scrolling.* This means repeatedly causing the screen text to move or scroll faster than members are able to type to it. It is caused by a user entering a set of random characters or by repeatedly entering a carriage return or any such action to a similar disruptive effect. Scrolling is an expressly prohibited form of disruption.

- *Impersonation.* This can involve the portrayal of an account in an official capacity, such as AOL Inc. staff, an information provider, or authorized Guide or Host, or communication under a false name or a name that you are not authorized to use.

  Members must avoid the portrayal of AOL personnel or other persons in all forms of online communication, including, but not limited to, screen names, member profiles, chat dialogue, and message postings.

- *Room Disruption.* This includes purposefully interfering with the normal flow of dialogue in a chat room. Room disruption can occur by repeatedly interrupting conversation between members, or by acting in such a way as to antagonize, harass, or create hostility in a chat room.

- *Chain Letters and Pyramid Schemes.* Transmission of chain letters and pyramid schemes of any kind is not allowed on the AOL Service. This material places an unnecessary load on our mail system and is considered a nuisance by many members.

  Certain chain letters and pyramid schemes are illegal.

  Letters or messages that offer a product or service based on the structure of a chain letter are also of questionable legality. At minimum, they are a waste of resources and are not permitted on the AOL Service.

- *Advertising and Solicitation.* You may not use the AOL Service to send unsolicited advertising, promotional material, or other forms of solicitation to members except in those specified areas that are designated for such a purpose (for example, the Classified Area).

■ *What to Do.* If you witness chat in a public chat room that violates AOL's Terms of Service, you can contact an AOL Service Guide by using the keyword **Guide Pager**. You can also contact AOL's Terms of Service Staff about any violation by using the Write to Terms of Service Staff icon located in the Terms of Service area of the Member's Online Support department.

If You See a Violation

If you see anyone misbehaving online, you'll want to be a good online citizen and report the offensive conduct to AOL's online police department, the Terms of Service Staff.

To report a problem, click the Write to Terms of Service Staff icon in the Terms of Service (TOS) area; this brings up the screen shown in figure 16.3.

FIG. 16.3
You can report bad online conduct here.

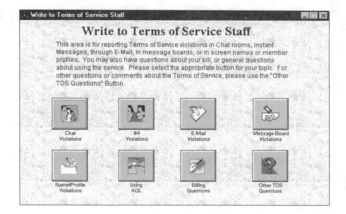

There's a separate form for you to generate for each type of problem. For example, if you see a violation in a chat room area, click the Chat Violations icon; the Chat Area Violations window appears (see fig. 16.4). Enter the information about the problem in the clearly labeled text entry fields.

The kind of violations described in this section don't happen very often. I've been an America Online member since 1989 and a Forum Leader since 1994, and I've only witnessed a handful of violations myself, despite spending thousands and thousands of hours online. The vast majority of online visitors never see these problems either, but it's better to be aware of the possibility and act accordingly.

Part
IV

Ch
16

FIG. 16.4
Use this form to report a
chat room violation.

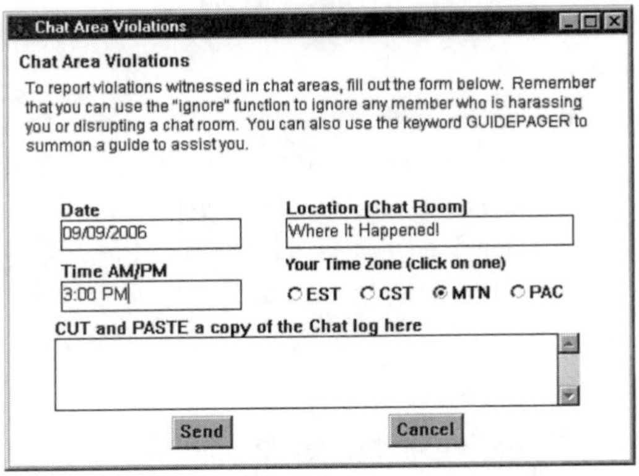

CAUTION

If your child commits repeated violations against AOL's Terms of Service, your account may be closed without notice, and it will require telephone contact with the customer service department to restore the account. So, monitor your child's activities carefully.

Special Forums for Parents

It's a very complex world, which makes the problem of bringing up children more and more difficult. America Online has set up several areas where parents can learn more about coping with the problems of daily living and how to deal with the problems and concerns of their children.

Visiting AOL Families

Keyword: **AOL Families, Parents**

The AOL Families area offers a fully integrated collection of forums dedicated to parental interests and concerns (see fig. 16.5). There are a number of special areas you'll want to consult from time to time in this forum; this section discusses just a few of them.

At the bottom of the AOL Families area are four icons, representing such resources as *Parenting* magazine, the Parental Controls access center, Moms Online, and a What's Hot area that provides up-to-date information you'll want to examine often.

The forum directory lists a number of other useful resources that you'll want to check further. If you have adopted children, or are considering adding a member to the family by adoption, you'll want to check out the Adoption Forum. The Child Abuse Forum is an important center for information to help you protect your children, and for dealing with the sad situation involving children who have been abused.

FIG. 16.5
Pay a visit to the AOL Families center to learn more about dealing with the complex parental issues of the '90s.

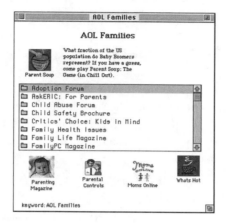

One other listing deserves special mention. Click the Child Safety Brochure icon, and you'll be able to examine a short, informative booklet providing helpful advice for your child's visits along the information highway (see fig. 16.6).

N O T E Most of the photos you see online are in full color. To view them that way, you need a computer that not only supports color, but a color monitor on which to view the photo.

FIG. 16.6
AOL offers a very detailed brochure about child safety online.

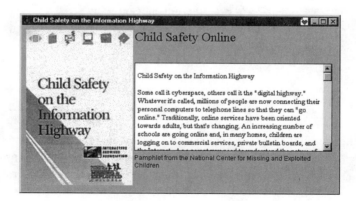

You'll want to review this material carefully; it summarizes many of the concerns parents should have about their child's participation in an online service. The entire text of this booklet can be saved or printed simply by choosing the appropriate commands from the File menu.

The remaining areas of AOL Families are devoted to a whole range of family issues, ranging from family health to interacting with teachers and working with gifted children. Other online areas of this sort are covered in Chapter 15, "Pursuing Lifestyles and Interests."

Using The National Parenting Center

Keyword: **TNPC**

AOL's National Parenting Center forum is designed to provide parents with useful information to make their jobs easier (see fig. 16.7). The center was founded in 1989, and the online area provides a large library of helpful information that deals with common problems and concerns of modern parenting.

The Search The Library icon provides the standard AOL search tool, where you can enter the subjects you want to know more about and see a list of available texts. You'll also want to read the ParentTalk Newsletter and participate in the Parenting Forum message area. The TNPC Store offers a selection of informative literature for purchase. There are also regularly scheduled conferences in the Parenting Conference Center (shown in the forum's main directory window). There's even a special area, labeled Latest Seal of Approval Report, where products are evaluated (also shown in the forum's main directory window).

FIG. 16.7
The National Parenting Center offers comprehensive advice for parents.

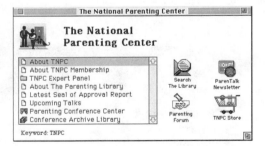

After reading about the activities of The National Parenting Center, you might want to consider becoming a member. Full membership information is provided in this online support area; AOL members are offered a special membership rate.

Kids and the Internet

The Internet is a huge, multifaceted, exciting, but largely unregulated place. A whole section of this book—Part VIII, "Entering the Information Superhighway"—is devoted to Internet issues. This section briefly discusses the things parents should be concerned about when their children make online visits.

The important thing to realize is that the Internet is not a single large online service, but a huge number of smaller networks linked by computers and modems and telephone lines. When you visit America Online's Internet Connection (Keyword: **Internet**), shown in figure 16.8, you are, in effect, leaving the service and visiting places where America Online's Terms of Service simply do not apply. Of course, this doesn't mean that you and your child can behave any differently than when you visit one of America Online's regular areas. Your conduct reflects on the service, and if you violate the Terms of Service during an Internet visit on AOL, it is the same as violating those terms in the regular areas on AOL.

Visiting those Internet areas means that you and your child will encounter areas where the rules and regulations of this service do not necessarily apply, and where others might act in ways you don't approve. One example is the Internet areas that are devoted to sexually explicit material. In addition, it is not uncommon to find material in Internet mailing lists or Newsgroups that contain language that you might consider offensive. What to do?

Here are a few common sense ideas:

■ Before your child enters the Internet area, set limits on the kind of material your child is allowed to see.

FIG. 16.8
America Online's popular Internet Connection.

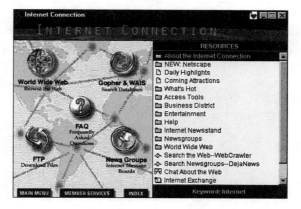

■ Review Internet e-mail Newsgroups, mailing lists, and other information before your child is allowed to participate in them.

■ Although your child is entitled to some measure of privacy, stay in touch with your child's online activities. Take the time to be with your child during online sessions, not just to monitor his or her activities, but to share online experiences with them.

Parental Controls for the Internet

Despite the precautions I've just outlined, you may decide it's better for your child not to have access to certain Internet-based features. So, AOL has established a set of Parental Controls for this area, too, activated in much the same way as the regular Parental Controls described earlier in this chapter.

In order to turn on Parental Controls for the Internet, use the keyword **Newsgroups**, and, at the main Newsgroups screen (refer to fig. 16.8), click the Parental Controls button to get the screen shown in figure 16.9. You can also activate Internet Parental Controls from the regular Parental Controls area.

> **N O T E** As with AOL's regular Parental Controls, you cannot activate the ones in the Newsgroups area unless you have logged on using your master AOL account. ▪

FIG. 16.9

Choose the account name for which you want to edit Parental Controls.

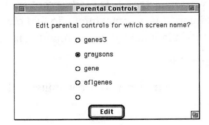

After clicking the button at the left of the screen name for which you want to establish Parental Controls, click the Edit button to get the screen shown in figure 16.10.

FIG. 16.10

Here are the choices available via Internet Parental Controls.

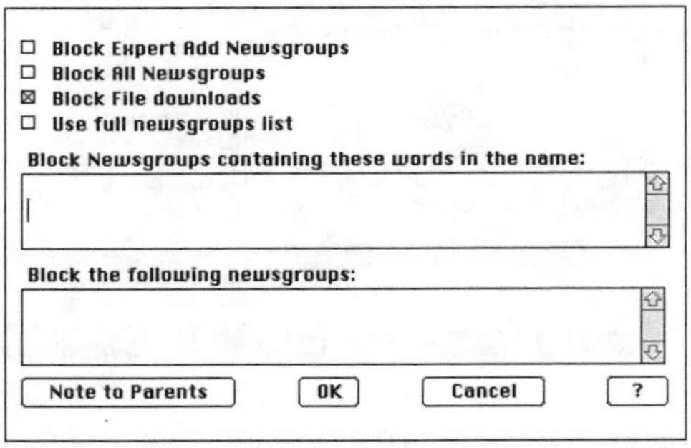

You can click the options shown to control access of other members on your account to specific Internet Newsgroup features. Each option can apply to any screen name you select. Here's the rundown:

- *Block Expert Add Newsgroups.* This feature is used to prevent adding Newsgroups that are not a part of AOL's standard listing.

- *Block All Newsgroups.* For the ultimate level of protection, you may choose this option so that your child has no access to this feature. .

- *Block File Downloads.* This feature is used to prevent a member from downloading encoded files in an Internet Newsgroup. Such files are a possible source of objectionable graphics files.

- *Use Full Newsgroups List.* This feature affords full access to all Newsgroups features, but you can selectively change their availability by selecting one or both of the next two items.

- *Block Newsgroups Containing These Words in the Name.* You can use this feature to specify certain words, such as "sex" or "erotica," that may represent Newsgroups that will offer unsuitable material for your child.

- *Block the Following Newsgroups.* You can use this feature to specify the names of the Newsgroups you want to block for a specific AOL screen name.

- *Note to Parents.* Click this button to get an overview of Internet Newsgroups and the best ways to participate in this exciting Internet feature.

By using one or more of the above Parental Controls, you can allow your child limited access to the Internet within the guidelines you set, and help provide a safe online experience. Remember, though, that these changes can be made only when you've logged on using your master account name (the first screen name shown when you click the pop-up list of names in your AOL Mac or Windows software).

Part
IV

Ch
16

From Here...

The possibilities for danger online might seem intimidating, but there's no reason why your children cannot enjoy themselves online, so long as you, the parent, take a few simple precautions first.

Now that you've learned the ground rules, you and your kids will want to review the next two chapters, which cover the vast resources AOL provides for kids:

- In Chapter 17, "Games, Entertainment, Teen Chat, and Netiquette," I'll describe online entertainment resources available for young people ages 5 through 14.

- In Chapter 18, "Help with Homework and Research," I'll show you how your child can improve performance at school with a little assistance from AOL's educational forums.

Games, Entertainment, Teen Chat, and Netiquette

In the previous chapter, I discussed AOL's rules of the road, commonly called the Terms of Service. These are the terms that you agree to when you join AOL, and you should be as familiar with them as possible. I also discussed the ways AOL offers to protect your child during online visits.

Armed with that information, you'll be able to locate a huge array of services on AOL designed with kids in mind. The areas described in this chapter are places where kids can have fun and learn at the same time. ■

N O T E   Before you introduce your child to the online world, it might be helpful to provide a brief instruction session on creating an America Online screen name, logging on, and maneuvering about the service. It is a good idea to go over basic computer troubleshooting tips as well, in case your computer crashes in your absence, something that's apt to happen with any personal computer. There is a detailed tutorial on using America Online's software in Appendixes B and C. ■

Finding Fun for Kids of All Ages

Keyword: **Kids**

America Online is not just a place for adults. The service offers a variety of online activities for your kids as well; the gateway to that area is AOL's Kids Only area, shown in figure 17.1. Not only can they have fun, they also can learn a few things and become more adept at working with a computer.

FIG. 17.1
Kids Only is a special place for children to participate in activities right on America Online.

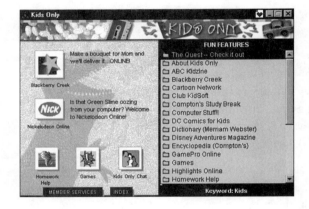

Many of the areas discussed so far in this book have special kids-only departments as well, areas developed strictly for young people. The Kids Only window in figure 17.1 shows just a few of the areas available, all specially designed for kids ages 5 through 14. Some of these places are discussed in this chapter.

As with all America Online sessions, it is suggested that you teach your children how to conduct themselves online. Discuss with them the basics of using America Online software, such as navigating through the network, reading and posting messages, and participating in online conferences. Your child should know how to act responsibly online and refrain from the use of vulgar language. In addition, you should establish limits as to the amount of time your children spend online because you are responsible for any charges they run up during their visits.

For more complete information on proper online conduct, please read Chapter 16, "Parental Issues and Internet Access," which discusses America Online's Terms of Service and special parental advice forums.

N O T E   America Online also gives you the right to exert parental control on your account. As described in Chapter 16, "Parental Issues and Internet Access," you have the right to block access to instant messages, People Connection rooms, member rooms, and many conference rooms. You can give your child a special screen name under your online account and set special restrictions for that screen name. ∎

Here's a highlight of a few of the areas available through Kids Only on AOL:

- ABC Kidzine (keyword: **Kidzine**) is a special service from ABC's AOL forum (see fig. 17.2). Among the special features are a wacky fortune teller and an area devoted to the cartoon character Inspector Gadget. Kids can also chat with other kids in the Kidzine cafe.

FIG. 17.2
ABC's Kidzine area is a place for fun and information.

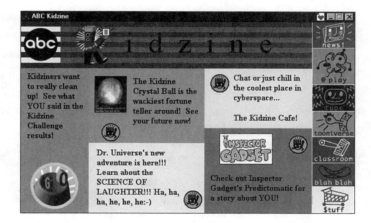

- Homework Help. This is an area that I'll discuss in more detail in Chapter 19, "Visiting the Computing and Software Forums." For now, consider it a place for a youngster to get quick assistance in dealing with a difficult homework assignment. It's possible to contact a teacher on AOL, or even have a brief chat with that teacher, to get assistance with a really vexing problem.

- Club KidSoft (keyword: **KidSoft**) is a forum devoted to software for kids, from games to educational titles (see fig. 17.3). You can sign up for a free newsletter and learn all about new software titles and special contests where you can win valuable prizes. The forum also offers online chats, regularly scheduled games, and fast

Part
IV

Ch
17

access to a select variety of Internet-based sites devoted to popular software. You also have the chance to try out demonstration versions of the latest software titles to see if you want to buy the regular version from the KidSoft Super Store at a special online price.

FIG. 17.3
Club KidSoft lets you get the early word about new software titles and even try out a few game demos.

- Many of the popular children's TV shows are represented on AOL. In addition to the programs featured on the ABC TV network, you'll find a forum devoted to the shows on Nickelodeon, the WB Network, and other popular programming sources.

- The Kids Only Games area (see fig. 17.4) provides quick access to a number of entertaining online resources, such as Game Pro Magazine and the Nintendo Power Source. In addition, you can drop by the Game Grabber area to find the latest software for both Mac and Windows users.

FIG. 17.4
Here's AOL's ever-popular Kids Only Games department.

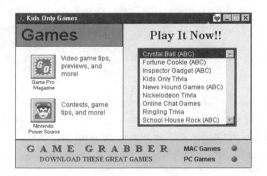

- And then there's the Kids Connection, a variation of America Online's People Connection area that was discussed in Chapter 7, "America Online's People Connection." This area is described in more detail later in this chapter.

The next section covers some of the forums on America Online that are just for kids.

Top Internet Sites

The Kids Only channel on AOL, like other AOL departments, provides easy access to the Internet. AOL has assembled a large listing of the most popular youth-oriented sites on the Internet (see fig. 17.5). Each of these sites can provide a fun-filled and educationally rewarding experience.

FIG. 17.5
The Top Internet Sites selection in AOL's Kids Only area provides many opportunities for online fun.

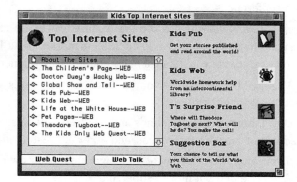

Exploring *Disney Adventures* Magazine

Keyword: **Disney Adventures**

Every month, *Disney Adventures* contains exciting adventures and stories for your children, with emphasis on Disney's own popular movie characters (see fig. 17.6). America Online is the place for your child to read about those many adventures and learn more about the world. The magazine even offers online conferences such as D.A. Live, which takes place in the forum's Odeon Auditorium, where your child can meet other kids with similar interests and enjoy an online chat.

FIG. 17.6
Disney Adventures magazine is a special resource for your child on America Online.

The *Disney Adventures* Magazine forum is structured much like any other online forum, and your online visit to this area involves many of the same steps as visiting any other online forum.

Here's an example of some of the areas available in this forum:

- D.A. Live, as mentioned previously, is your entranceway to the *Disney Adventures* online conferences.

- Search D.A. Articles enables you to use America Online's Search function to look for articles in previous issues. In addition to stories about Disney's own popular cartoon characters, you'll find articles about travel, science, and other topics.

- The Message Board enables your child to post messages and to read messages from other online members.

- The D.A. Library contains sounds and pictures of popular Disney characters, transcripts of special conferences, and other interesting files.

- And if you want to see a copy of the magazine in your own home, click the Subscribe to D.A. icon to find out how to subscribe.

Accessing the Cartoon Network

Keyword: **Cartoon Network**

One of the exciting aspects of cable television is the availability of programs devoted to just one subject or one category of entertainment. Chapter 11, "TV and Movie Information Online," and Chapter 12, "Music, Books, and Art," describe a number of the popular networks of this type that are represented on AOL. This section is devoted to the Cartoon Network forum (see fig. 17.7). Cartoon entertainment appeals to people of all ages, from children to adults. America Online has a special library of cartoon art in GIF (Graphic Interchange Format) files. See Chapter 7, "America Online's People Connection," and Appendix B or C for more information on how to create and view GIF files.

A number of special libraries in this forum contain professional cartoon artwork that you can download to your computer, view, and print (for your personal use).

The Cartoon Network forum is also a resource for all you online cartoonists to create and post your own artwork so that others can see it. Many famous cartoonists started working toward their careers while still very young. In fact, the creators of Superman were barely out of their teens when they developed this famous comic strip character decades ago. You'll also want to look over the Toon Talk BBS section, a message area where you can discuss your favorite cartoon characters.

FIG. 17.7
America Online didn't forget cartoons.

Participating in the Hatrack River Town Meeting

Part IV
Ch 17

Keyword: **Hatrack**

The Hatrack River community online exists to showcase the works of the noted science-fiction author Orson Scott Card, but it covers a much wider range of subjects than the works of just one person (see fig. 17.8). This is a unique forum that you really have to visit before you get a full picture of what it's all about.

FIG. 17.8
AOL's Hatrack River Town Meeting is a popular online gathering place.

As for Card, his novel, *Ender's Game,* described many of the future possibilities of the current online universe; it was actually published online as an electronic document before it appeared in printed form. Written in 1985, the work received both Nebula and Hugo awards, which are the science-fiction world's equivalents of the Emmys and Oscars. In addition to information about his past works, you'll find previews of Card's latest books in this forum.

Regular participants in this forum consider it an online community where young and old can feel at home. There's an active Message Center, an icon representing a large number of newspapers and publications, and the special Hatrack Libraries section, which includes a special library for users under age 18 to upload their own stories and read the writings of other online members.

Online Games

Chapter 13, "Playing Games Online," describes the various online gaming forums, and how to search for secrets of your favorite computer games. This chapter concentrates on games designed strictly for online visitors in the 5 to 14 age group. To reach this resource, choose Games from the Kids Only window, and then click the Online Chat Games from the Play It Now list of games.

To get started, this section gives you the ground rules of some of the popular games offered here. Not all of these games are held regularly, and the lineup changes often, as new games are added and other games are temporarily removed from the list. Here are the games that were being held when this book was written:

- DANGERS. This game requires you to think fast. The host presents the first words of a sentence. You have 15 seconds to type your answer. Now here's the fun part: you'll see a Hit Enter Now prompt, at which time you have to send your answer to the screen. If another AOL member can match your answer, you receive one point.

- TRIVIA. No special rules here. When the host asks a question, you try to answer it. My son usually outscores me on this one.

- ACRONYMS. You read a set of letters from the host. You have to write a sentence using those very same letters as the first letters of the words in your sentence. And the letters have to appear in the exact order presented on-screen. This is a terrific way to exercise your creativity.

- NAMEIT. Here's another area where you have to work fast to get points. The host lists a category. Players enter one item that matches that category, such as apple for fruits. If you're the first player to enter that response, you get two points; others who enter the very same response get one point.

- QUICK NAMEIT. This game is very much like the previous one described but with a new twist. It moves so fast that winning points aren't announced on-screen. You have to keep your own running count because the final points aren't announced until the game ends.

- BRAINBUSTERS. You'll have to think hard to win this contest. The host thinks of a word that describes an object, person, or place. Your assignment is to guess, based on the clues shown on-screen, just what word the host is thinking about. If you guess right on the first round of clues, you get five points; it's four points for the second set of clues, and one less point for each subsequent clue.

- THE FUN PART. The online host offers prizes for the three members who have the highest scores. I won't tell you what the prizes are, except to say that they are designed to make the games more challenging and rewarding.

> **CAUTION**
>
> These games run very fast and they're exciting for young people to play, but that doesn't mean the rules of good online conduct are forsaken. If too many online participants disrupt the contest, the host may decide not to award any prizes. So, please urge your child to behave properly during the contest.

The rules covering online conduct are covered in the next section about Kids Connection. You'll also want to read Chapter 16, "Parental Issues and Internet Access," for a full description of America Online's Terms of Service and advice for showing your child how to become a good online citizen.

Part IV
Ch 17

Conferences for Young People

Among the most popular online activities are *chatting*, interacting with other AOL members, or attending an online conference, where you can sometimes meet a famous person and ask questions. AOL's Kids Only Chat (see fig. 17.9) is the youthful equivalent of the popular People's Connection area, and is designed strictly for members ages 5 to 14. It is carefully monitored by an enthusiastic band of online staffers, whom you'll recognize by the KO in front of their screen names.

FIG. 17.9
Young people ages 5 to 14 will enjoy participating in special youth-oriented chats on AOL.

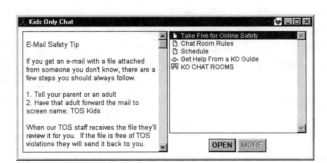

Chat Room Rules

Before your youngster attends a Kids Only Chat event, it's a good idea to discuss the guidelines with your child. And, it would be helpful if you attended a chat or two yourself, to get a feeling of how they're conducted. As with any chat room or auditorium on AOL, the Terms of Service apply, so you'll want to review Chapter 16, "Parental Issues and Internet Access," which covers the guidelines for online conduct. The Chat Room Rules listing in the directory window of the Kids Only Chat area also summarizes some of these simple requirements.

The most important thing to remember, of course, is respect for other online members. Everyone should be treated equally and given equal opportunity to participate in an online session, free of interruptions. If someone else is misbehaving, it is not an invitation for others to disturb the chat as well. Each conference is monitored by a staff of online hosts who try to make sure that the rules of proper online conduct are observed.

> **CAUTION**
>
> Be careful: No AOL employee will ever ask you online or via e-mail for your password or credit card number. If someone asks for this information, ignore them, and report it to AOL's Terms of Service staff immediately. You'll find out how in the TOS information center (keyword: **TOS**). It's also a good idea to change your password regularly—use the keyword **Password** to access the area where your password can be changed.

 TIP If your online session is interrupted for any reason, just log on again. Usually you'll be able to reconnect the second time without further trouble.

Ready to Chat?

At the time this book was being edited, there were six conference halls in the Kids Connection area: The Playground, The Chat Shack, The Barnyard, The Woods, The Club House, and the Fire Escape. Each posts a schedule of regular chats, so you'll want to consult the calendar listings before you enter the chat room of your choice. And, if you miss a really important chat, don't despair. There's a Past Special Chats library where you can download logs of previous chats. You'll find those logs really useful when two or more interesting chats are being held at the very same time.

TIP You can make your own chat log. Simply choose Logs (for Mac users) or Logging (for Windows users) from the File menu and select the appropriate option to start recording your log.

From Here...

As with other areas on America Online, you don't have to restrict yourself to searching one area for the information you want. For more useful information on children's resources on AOL, check the following chapters:

- In Chapter 11, "TV and Movie Information Online," you'll read more about entertainment-related resources on AOL.
- In Chapter 16, "Parental Issues and Internet Access," you'll learn helpful ways to protect your child during online visits.
- In Chapter 18, "Help with Homework and Research," you'll read about online resources that help a child with education.

Part
IV

Ch
17

Help with Homework and Research

Chapters 16 and 17 covered the subject of kids and AOL, proper online behavior (AOL's "rules of the road"), and the many forums where young people can have fun on AOL. This chapter concentrates on more serious subjects—education and research.

While America Online isn't designed to replace the public library and the hands-on experience of reading books, it can supplement that experience in many valuable ways. One is immediacy; you can find the material you want quickly and easily, sitting right in front of your own computer. Another is AOL's tremendous multimedia capabilities, which allow you to review not only text material, but pictures and sounds as well. In addition, there's variety because you can choose from AOL's own extensive educational resources and the information available via the Internet.

Because of the extent and scope of the educational resources available on America Online, this discussion is divided into two parts. This chapter confines your review to areas of interest to young people ages 5 through 14. The remaining educational resources are profiled in Chapter 25, "Learning and Reference." ■

Discover AOL's Reference channel

Learn all about upcoming educational programming on radio and TV.

Do your research on AOL

Tap the resources of huge online libraries.

Locate Internet sites

Seek out reference information from Internet-based sources.

Use AOL's Teacher Pager

Get interactive help with your child's homework.

Reviewing Online Education Resources

As mentioned from time to time throughout this book, AOL's services are all neatly grouped into channels or categories, which you see on the main menu every time you sign on to the service. Some services overlap, so you'll find them in two or more departments. The huge array of learning and reference resources online fall into this category. First, you'll revisit the same department that was described in the previous two chapters, the Kids Only forum.

Entering Kids Only Online

Keyword: **Kids**

Many of the areas available through this forum are covered in Chapter 17, "Games, Entertainment, Teen Chat, and Netiquette." First, look at the items shown in the Fun Features directory on the right of the Kids Only window (see fig. 18.1). To see what the items offer, just double-click the directory name.

FIG. 18.1
Your first gateway to educational resources for kids.

Internet Sites for Reference

There is a huge store of educational information available to you on the Internet, with an emphasis on the World Wide Web. By clicking the Web Reference Tools icon in AOL's Reference channel (keyword: **Reference**), you'll see a large list of specially selected World Wide Web and other Internet-based resources (see fig. 18.2).

T I P If you want to access even more online information centers, use the keyword **Gopher** to call up one of AOL's most important data searching tools. You'll find out more about it in Chapter 31, "Searching for Information on the Internet."

FIG. 18.2
AOL's Web Reference Tools open the door to museums, reference works, and other fascinating information resources.

Watching The Learning Channel

Keyword: **TLC**

The Learning Channel provides special educational programming every day of the week (see fig. 18.3). You'll want to look over the Prime Time Listings in the main forum directory window to get an idea of the scope of the network's programming. If you want to have the full schedule at your fingertips, along with other useful information, in a colorful compact form, read about the *Discovery Channel Monthly Magazine*, which is available by subscription.

Part
IV

Ch
18

FIG. 18.3
Cable TV's popular educational network.

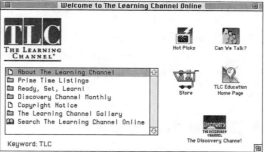

N O T E The Learning Channel is a cable television network that is available in many parts of the country. If it has not been offered in your area, you can contact your cable television provider. ■

The Learning Channel Gallery is a library of photos of the network's most popular broadcasters. The final listing in the directory is AOL's standard search tool that you use to find information.

One of the icons on the right of the forum's window, Hot Picks, enables you to read special information about programming. Can We Talk? offers both a message board and a conference room for the network's regular schedule of online chats. You can order CD-ROMs, videos, and publications in the forum's Store. The TLC Home Page icon takes you to the Discovery Channel's education center. The final icon takes you to the main screen of the forum devoted to The Discovery Channel, which is covered in more detail in Chapter 25, "Learning and Reference."

Discovering Scholastic Kids World

Scholastic Kids World (shown as both an icon and a directory entry in the Kids Only department) is a part of the Scholastic Network, a huge online resource of information for both students and educators (see fig. 18.4). This is discussed further in Chapter 25. For now, this section concentrates on the area devoted strictly to youthful discussions and information.

FIG. 18.4
Kids World is an area for information and discussions on a host of subjects.

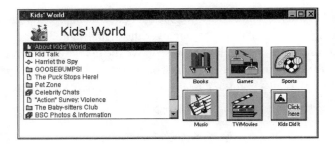

The Kids World forum provides information grouped by topic. It also has an active message board, where young AOL members can discuss a number of subjects and interact with fellow AOL members and Kids World staff.

How to Do Online Research

Another department to check for online educational resources is AOL's Learning & Culture channel (see fig. 18.5), available via the keyword **Learning**. This section is confined to just a few of the features available in this area; a number of additional items are covered in Chapter 25.

As you can see from checking the main Learning & Culture channel window, there's a huge array of resources available for students, parents, and educators. They range from monthly magazines to sections sponsored by the major television networks and educational publishers.

FIG. 18.5
America Online's popular
Learning & Culture
department.

Attending the ABC Classroom

Keyword: **ABC Classroom**

One of the key features of the ABC Classroom (see fig. 18.6), which is sponsored by the ABC Network Online, is a regularly scheduled slate of online conferences. These conferences feature experts on a variety of professions, ranging from astronaut to zoologist, and most anything in between. A recent session, for example, featured a TV cartoon animator.

Part
IV

Ch
18

FIG. 18.6
The educational forum
sponsored by the ABC
Network Online.

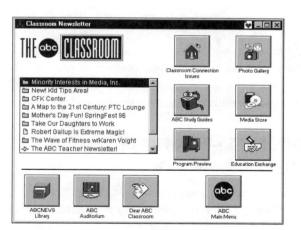

Another popular feature of the ABC Classroom is "Smart Watching Worksheets," which you can reach by clicking the ABC Study Guides icon. The area features Smart Watching worksheets for elementary and secondary students that relate to programs on the ABC network with educational and social impact. The Program Preview icon lists future shows, and the Media Store provides a range of educational products that consist of videos and text. The Education Exchange is the forum's message area. The remaining areas consist of the network's conference auditorium, a place to write letters to forum staff, and a library containing text and graphics files from ABC News.

Reading Barron's Booknotes

Keyword: **Barron's**

As you might already know, Barron's guides are useful abstracts about great literary works and are quite helpful in doing a homework assignment or preparing for that special test. You can search the vast library of Barron's Booknotes on America Online (see fig. 18.7).

FIG. 18.7
Barron's Booknotes is your source for abstracts on great literature.

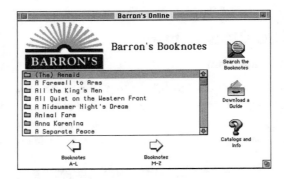

The abstracts are grouped by title, and each title contains useful text files describing the highlights of great works ranging from Shakespearean plays to classic best-sellers. As you read these books, you can use these text files as a guide to better understand what makes great literature so memorable that it survives decades and sometimes centuries.

Accessing Compton's Encyclopedia

Keyword: **Comptons Encyclopedia**

Not so long ago, looking up something in an encyclopedia meant a trip to the public library or purchasing a huge set of books for your home. Although you might not want to replace those voluminous, color-filled works on your bookshelves, consider America Online your second reference resource.

Compton's Encyclopedia has placed its huge database of information on America Online (see fig. 18.8). All you have to do to tap that database is click the Search All Text button, and choose Open (or press Return or Enter).

FIG. 18.8
The resources of a huge encyclopedia are at your fingertips.

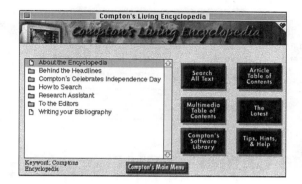

Follow these steps to continue your search for information:

1. Enter the topic or a description of the information you want in the text entry field near the top of the screen.

2. Within seconds, if articles are available on the subject, you see a list of matching entries (see fig. 18.9). If the entry has a folder icon, it means that the entry contains a number of text reports on the subject.

FIG. 18.9
Searching your virtual encyclopedia is an easy task.

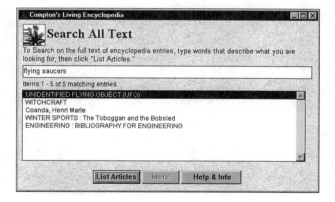

3. In the directory listing, double-click the entry you want to explore (or highlight it and choose the List Articles button), and you see the names of all the articles related to the subject. You can view each article online (see fig. 18.10), or you can save or print the article to read at your leisure.

FIG. 18.10
These are just a few of the articles you can find on a single topic: flying saucers.

Visiting the Career Center

Keyword: **Career**

One of the hardest tasks many young adults have to face is deciding what line of work to enter. Although some of you might have chosen your career during your early childhood, others work long and hard to find the line of work for which they are suited.

America Online's Career Center is an electronic career and employment guidance forum (see fig. 18.11). The forum features an extensive lineup of services that can help the user find the right career or even tap a huge database of available jobs.

FIG. 18.11
America Online offers a center for career counseling and employment opportunities.

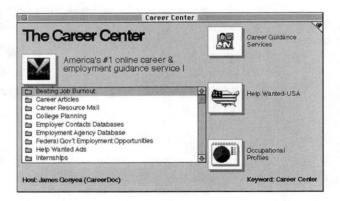

The Career Center also offers you personal career counseling services, where you can exchange e-mail with an experienced counselor or schedule an interactive one-on-one session on America Online. To access these services, click the Career Guidance Services icon.

The Occupational Profiles Database enables you to view the requirements and opportunities offered by a particular line of work. If you are job hunting, a library of resume templates is available for you to tailor to your personal needs.

N O T E Many of the graphics files in the forums discussed in this chapter are available in GIF format. GIF files are discussed in more detail in Chapter 7, "America Online's People Connection." To recap briefly, the current versions of America Online's Macintosh and Windows software can open and view GIF files. ■

Using Teacher Pager

Keyword: **Teacher Pager**

Suppose your child has to write a term paper or do an assignment that is due the very next day. Your child has worked for hours trying to pull it into shape, and there are still questions that need to be answered. Don't despair. AOL offers a way to get interactive help from a staff of online teachers. It's called Teacher Pager (see fig. 18.12).

FIG. 18.12
Choose to page a teacher and review some study materials in the Teacher Pager area.

Part
IV

Ch
18

Now you have three choices. In addition to calling up the Teacher Pager for Kids or the Teacher Pager for Teens, you can click the third icon, AAC Teacher Pager. Here you can consult the Mini-Lesson Libraries, which provide short, helpful texts on a variety of subjects, provided by AOL's Academic Assistance Center. If the information offered isn't enough to answer your questions, you'll want to ask the question directly. To do that, double-click an item in the list box that matches the subject of your question, which brings up a special message window similar to the one shown in figure 18.13. Then enter your question, list the grade level, and send it.

To cite another example, suppose that your child, a grade school student, asks a very common question, "How do you add and subtract numbers with more than a single column?" You or your child enters the question, and then enters the grade level and the topic in which the question fits (in this case, mathematics). After you or your child asks the question, stay online for at least five minutes, because more often than not, your answer will be in your mailbox quickly. If your child needs further assistance, indicate that in the message form and specify when your child can have an online chat with a teacher. Your child will have the chance to meet with the instructor at the appointed time in the Homework Help conference room for a one-on-one tutorial session.

FIG. 18.13
Immediate help for students of all educational levels is provided via AOL's Teacher Pager, where you can ask the tough questions.

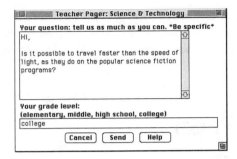

Exploring the Reference Desk

Keyword: **Reference**

Let's look at one more online resource, The Reference Desk. Many of the services listed in figure 18.14 are probably familiar to you. The list box of this channel appears in two forms. First, by category, and if you click the second option, alphabetically, which brings up the entire roster of information sources all in one place. Among the listings, you'll find huge databases of information that you'll want to explore in careful detail. The Internet Gopher and WAIS databases are described in Chapter 31, "Searching for Information on the Internet."

FIG. 18.14
The Reference Desk on America Online offers you a variety of information resources.

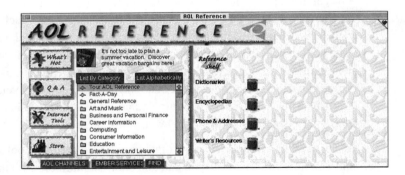

From Here...

This chapter and the previous two chapters cover online resources for young people, but that's not all the information available for kids on America Online. You'll want to encourage your child to take a little extra time to thoroughly explore America Online in search of other entertaining and educational material.

During the course of these online sessions, your child will learn a lot about your computer, which is the subject of the next part of this book, "Computing Resources Online." For further information, explore the following chapters:

- In Chapter 16, "Parental Issues and Internet Access," you'll learn the steps to take to make sure your kids enjoy a friendly and safe visit on AOL.

- In Chapter 17, "Games, Entertainment, Teen Chat, and Netiquette," you'll read about games and entertainment resources for kids ages 5–14.

- In Chapter 25, "Learning and Reference," you'll discover additional educational forums on AOL.

Part
IV

Ch
18

Visiting the Computing and Software Forums

If you didn't join America Online after getting one of those ubiquitous disks in the mail, you no doubt found a sign-up kit in a computer magazine. Surely, the fact that we all connect to the service with personal computers makes forums catering to computers ideal places to visit.

Whether you want to download a fancy new shareware program, a software update, or you're looking for expert advice on any computer-related matter, America Online can help you find the answers.

Suppose that you try to run a new program and your computer crashes every time. It's Friday evening, and the manufacturer's technical support people have gone home for the weekend. You need that new software to finish a special project. What do you do?

Log on to America Online, where you can find both members and manufacturer support people ready and willing to help you out of your jam.

Or suppose that you're looking for a program that can help remind you of special events. Relief is just a download away, in America Online's vast software library containing tens of thousands of software selections (and more are being added daily).

Having worked in the trenches myself for a number of years, I definitely feel the hardworking folks who run AOL's computer and software forums are the unsung heroes of the service. They are available day and night, and often on weekends. They are indeed the backbone of our favorite online service.

It's true that the computing forums don't necessarily offer the razzle-dazzle graphics of some of the other areas of the service, nor does their content make the front pages of the newspapers as other online areas do. But, they provide the help you need when your computer isn't working properly, and they offer huge resources of information to help make your computer run better. Plus, there's always that cool new software posted in their software libraries, with tens of thousands of files to choose from.

There's an AOL computing forum covering every facet of personal computing, from games to the latest hints and tips about using the Mac operating system or Windows 95. You'll find active message boards, huge listings of helpful information, and ready answers to the questions you have. In addition, these forums hold regular conferences, featuring the people who run the forums, as well as industry experts who often come by to tell you about a new product, or simply to hang out and chat with you about a variety of computing subjects.

For this chapter, I invited many of the forum leaders of AOL's Computing department to contribute descriptions of their own online areas, so that you can get the flavor of the way these areas are organized. ■

Exploring the Computing Forums

Keyword: **Computing**

If you want to learn to use your computer more effectively or just want to talk computers with fellow AOL members, visit America Online's Computing forums often. You can access this area either by clicking the Computing icon on the Channels menu, or just using the keyword **Computing**. You see the screen shown in figure 19.1.

The following sections highlight many of the forums. Because a picture truly is worth a thousand words, look closely at the figures throughout this chapter to see many of the services that the forums offer.

As you can see in figure 19.1, the Computers and Software channel screen provides an entranceway to America Online's Computing forums and to other valuable information resources. You can find special areas devoted to specific aspects of computing, computing news, company support forums, and schedules of upcoming chats.

FIG. 19.1
The Computing screen is your gateway to the popular computing forums on America Online.

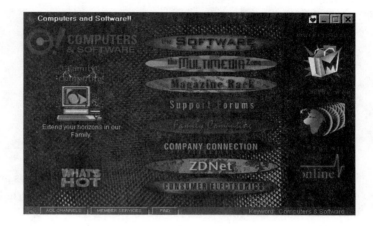

> **N O T E** To get a list of important events and announcements in the Computing channel, simply click the What's Hot icon at the bottom left of the Computers and Software screen (see fig. 19.2). ■

FIG. 19.2
The What's Hot screen spotlights different events, depending on whether you're looking at the Mac or the Windows version.

Part
V

Ch
19

Visiting the Macintosh Help Forum

Keyword: **Mac Help**

From Andy Polk (AFL Andy)

Are you new to AOL? Need help with your Mac? Or, are you looking for answers to basic computing problems? The Mac Help Forum (see fig. 19.3) is your first stop for getting answers to problems with AOL and/or your computer.

FIG. 19.3

When you need a helping hand, the Mac Help Forum on America Online is there for you.

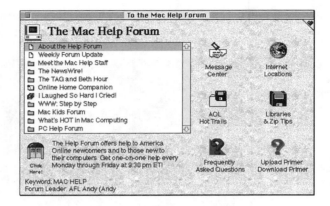

In addition to a convenient Message Center, online conferences are held evenings, Monday through Friday. You'll want to check the forum for the current schedule. Mac Help also maintains a current list of Frequently Asked Questions, where common computing and AOL questions are answered.

In the Mac Help Tool Chests, one can find advanced help for more difficult problems. AOL Hot Trails provides the user with an easy-access road map to popular AOL locations.

TIP Before you post a question, read older messages in the same message folder or in other message areas that deal with a similar topic. You may find a response and a solution to a question much like yours.

Visiting the PC Help Forum

Keyword: **PC Help**

From Kevin Williams (PC Kevin)

The PC Help Forum (see fig. 19.4) was created to make learning to use AOL easy and fun for you. The forum staff knows that you have questions about AOL's offerings and features, and this is *the* place to ask them. The forum's goal is to make the learning curve as pleasant and exciting for you as possible.

There are many areas of the PC Help Forum where you can find the answers you need. Some of the forum highlights include a New Member Guide that covers the questions most often asked, an interactive message board where you're guaranteed a fast staff response to every question, Software Libraries with files for both work and play, and a conference room that's open seven nights a week at 9 p.m. eastern time.

FIG. 19.4
The PC Help Forum (also known as the Beginners' Help Desk) is there to help you get going when the going gets rough.

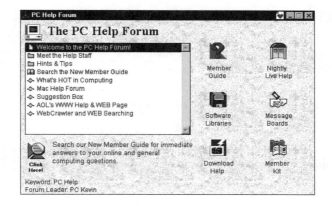

Like the Macintosh Help Forum, the PC Help Forum is a rich information resource. You'll find the answers you are looking for on using your computer to explore the highways and byways of America Online. Armed with that resource (and a copy of this book), you'll have a safe and pleasant trip on the Information Superhighway.

Visiting the Family Computing Forum

Keyword: **FC**

Family computing has become an incredibly popular subject because so many homes have personal computers these days. Whether you have a Mac or a PC, you'll want to visit AOL's Family Computing Forum (see fig. 19.5). The forum is designed to be a fun-filled learning experience for newcomers and an informative resource for those of you who are used to working with computers.

Part
V

Ch
19

FIG. 19.5
AOL's Family Computing Forum provides support with a personal touch.

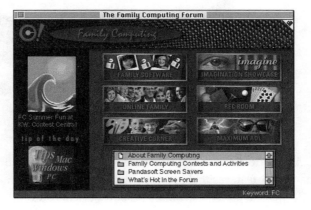

Click the Maximum AOL icon for valuable information on enhancing your AOL experience. You'll find several active message boards where you can put in your two cents about common computing topics. Each icon on the Family Computing forum screen represents a different area of computing experience. A particular highlight you'll want to discover is the Online Family area (which you can also reach by the keyword **Online Family**), to learn more about shared computing experiences.

If you want to have a good time with game software and trivia questions, pay a visit to the Rec Room. The Family Room (available from the Online Family area) provides informative chats that feature knowledgeable guests. Click the icon to get the current schedule or to join a meeting that is already in progress.

Exploring the PC Applications Forum

Keyword: **PC Applications**

From Robin Bush (PC Robin)

In the PC Applications Forum (see fig. 19.6), you'll find support for all word processors, desktop and Web publishing programs, HTML and electronic publishing programs, spreadsheets, databases, business and finance programs, and home and hobby programs for DOS, Windows, and Windows 95/NT.

FIG. 19.6
The PC Applications Forum is your own virtual software store.

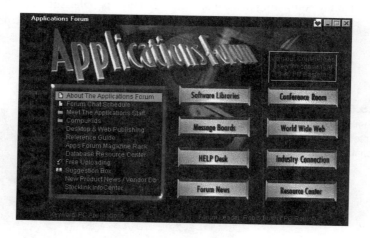

The PC Applications Forum is a dynamic resource. You'll discover messages, software, chats, and other features that provide solutions to problems and new perspectives on using PC applications. The forum's staff of experienced PC users is always happy to assist; however, you are the most important feature of the Applications Forum. The experiences, anecdotes, questions, and answers that AOL members bring to the forum can enlighten thousands of other members who have similar questions and experiences.

On your first visit, check Forum News for information about the forum, the chat schedule, the best industry news and gossip around, and its cool Computer Trivia Contest. Many people are looking for the best files to download, and the PC Applications Forum has some all-time favorites.

If you want to find fun for the younger members of your family, browse the Just for Kids applications library. Looking for the latest in 32-bit shareware? Check our featured Windows 95 and NT libraries. And for the Web-surfing fans, we've included the best libraries we could find on the WWW. To find the forum's libraries, click the Software Libraries icon in the main forum screen.

Finally, you won't want to miss the forum's Database Resource Center, the Stocklink InfoCenter, Apps forum Magazine Rack, and a popular CompuKids area that brings computing fun to the whole family (keyword **compukids**). These items are all shown in the forum's list box.

Visiting the Mac Business and Home Office Forum

Keyword: **MBS**

From Rick Doucette (AFL Rick)

One of AOL's most popular computing forums (see fig. 19.7) supports the use of the Macintosh in business and in the home office. The software categories include accounting, database applications, integrated software, spreadsheets, vertical markets, forms, project management, scheduling, statistics, and tax preparation. You'll find special-interest groups for personal information managers, accounting, 4th Dimension, FileMaker, Helix, spreadsheets, and business presentations.

There's also a huge selection of business-related (including database) shareware and freeware. For the newest files, check the Database and Business New Files and Free Uploading libraries. Our message boards enable you to ask questions, seek help, and network with other business users and consultants, database users, and software developers. The Business Companies area links you to the business software companies that have an Industry Connection support area on AOL. The forum's World Wide Web Sites area gives you a direct connection (through AOL's Web Browser) to many useful business-related Web sites on the Internet.

Part

V

Ch

19

FIG. 19.7
Learn tips and tricks about using your business-related applications in the Mac Business and Home Office Forum.

The Mac Business and Home Office Forum also supports several special organizations, including the Apple Business Consortium (keyword **AppleBiz**), and MacSciTech (keyword **MacSciTech**).

Live forum conferences are held several times a week featuring forum staff and visiting industry experts.

Exploring the Telecommunications and Networking Forums

Keyword: **MCM (Macintosh), PC Telecom (Windows)**

If you're thinking about buying one of those new high-speed modems, or if you're looking for a better way to network your computer, pay a visit to the telecommunications forums on America Online. Figure 19.8 shows the Communications and Networking Forum screen for Macintosh users; figure 19.9 shows its PC counterpart, the Telecommunications and Networking Forum screen.

FIG. 19.8
The Communications and Networking forum is your America Online headquarters for Macintosh modem and networking issues.

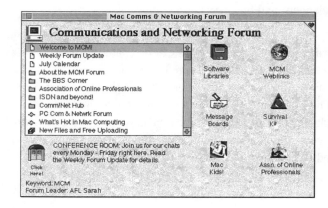

FIG. 19.9
This forum is the telecommunications and networking
headquarters for DOS and
Windows users.

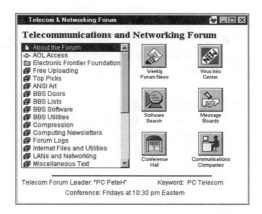

Using a modem isn't always a cut-and-dried process. A modem may take just a few seconds to plug in, but then you have to deal with such issues as communications software (if
you're not logging on to America Online) and with such arcane subjects as configuration
and initialization strings. America Online telecommunications forums are your sources for
helpful advice and useful information of all sorts to get you on your way to confident telecommunications.

When you hook your computer to even a single printer or to another computer for exchanging files, you have established a network. Offices these days commonly have Macs
and PCs working side by side, and the networking issues often get complex. You need a
place where you can get some helpful advice to get you over the rough spots. Like other
forums, the telecommunications forums schedule regular conferences and frequent special events that you probably will want to attend.

Visit the Mac and PC telecommunications forums, and check out the message boards,
software libraries, real-time chats, and other features that help you learn more about the
world of electronic communications.

Visiting the Macintosh Desktop and Web Publishing Forum

Keyword: **MWP**

Desktop publishing is descended from traditional typesetting. Instead of producing text
on machines that melt down hot sticks of lead or on expensive minicomputers that generate characters on photosensitive paper with flashing lights and lenses, you can create
professional publications—this book, for example—on a desktop computer. In addition,
many folks have expanded their desktop publishing to include the creation of documents
for the World Wide Web.

Part
V

Ch
19

The Macintosh Desktop and Web Publishing Forum (see fig. 19.10) caters to beginners and professionals alike. You can find helpful advice on how to select publishing and word processing programs, what fonts you need, and even the best printer to buy. You'll also learn how to build those WWW pages from scratch and make them look good.

FIG. 19.10
Desktop publishing is the descendant of traditional typesetting, and a forum addresses it on America Online.

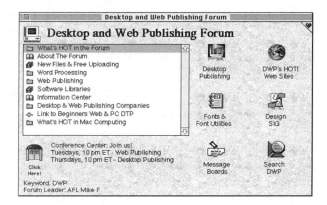

Every week, the forum holds a conference in which you can ask questions of the forum's expert staff members and special guests. The message boards are among the most popular in the computing areas of America Online; you'll want to participate in those areas as well.

Visiting the Developers' Forums

Keyword: **MDV (Macintosh), PC Development (Windows)**

From Marty Wachter (AFL Moof)

The Macintosh Developers Forum (see fig. 19.11) is designed to help people who are interested in programming the Macintosh. All questions about Macintosh programming are welcome. Let's learn from one another.

The forum is there for you to share questions and answers, comments, insights, and "pearls of wisdom." Topics include lively discussions on the art and craft of programming, debugging, development tips, System 7, Mac OS 8, object-oriented programming, Apple/ developer relations, and so on.

The forum's software libraries contain source code in a variety of languages, useful developer utilities, demos of commercial products, technical notes and other information from Apple, archives of past conferences and message-board discussions, and many other things that are of value to Macintosh programmers.

FIG. 19.11
The Developers Forum is a great place to learn about writing your own Mac software.

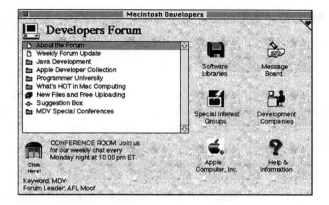

The Mac Developers Forum also hosts weekly conferences that cover a wide range of topics related to Macintosh programming.

From Bob Dover (PC BobD)

Whether you're a programming hobbyist, professional or guru, a Windows or DOS programmer, or just interested in programming topics, the PC Development Forum (see fig. 19.12) has something for you.

FIG. 19.12
Whether your software is earmarked for DOS or Windows, you can seek advice from the experts.

Part
V

Ch
19

Are you new to Windows programming? You've definitely come to the right place. BASIC programmers will find the forum's software library filled with sample BASIC programs to download, no matter which BASIC you use. (Yes, real developers do use BASIC.)

Come meet other developers screen-to-screen in one of the many late-night chats held in the Development Meeting Room. It doesn't matter whether you have a question or just enjoy sharing experiences; everyone is welcome. Click the Weekly Forum News icon to see the monthly chat schedule and news about special events.

Visiting the DOS Forum

Keyword: **DOS**

From David Pacheco (PC Pach)

AOL's DOS Forum (see fig. 19.13) is hosted by a staff of caring computer professionals to help you with your DOS questions and problems. The forum's software library will be your source for all the utilities that DOS forgot, as well as tools to help you with your productivity. The software libraries in DOS are split into separate categories, making it a little easier to find what you are looking for.

FIG. 19.13
Advice and updates are available in America Online's DOS Forum.

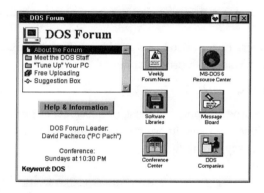

The message area is your source of questions and answers about DOS and related subjects. These questions, problems, and suggestions are answered by the DOS Forum Staff, and the members of this online service. This information service is a place where members can give advice, help and support each other, and spread the knowledge we all have. Additionally, there is a message board (and attached software library) targeted for users of DR DOS, Digital Research/Novell Desktop System Group's DOS version.

Exploring the Macintosh Education & Technology Forum

Keyword: **MED**

From Cheryl Zuckerman (AFL Cheryl)

The Macintosh Education & Technology Forum (see fig. 19.14) is an invaluable resource for educators. The forum is a place where you can meet with other educators from around the country. The regularly scheduled chats typically discuss a broad range of education issues. Because the chats particularly emphasize using Macintosh computers to enhance instruction, the forum sometimes focuses on new software or strategies for using technology in the classroom. Even if you are unable to attend the chats, browsing the boards is a tremendous way to brainstorm and discuss issues that are relevant to education.

FIG. 19.14
When you use your computers in the classroom, you'll want to visit the Macintosh Education & Technology Forum.

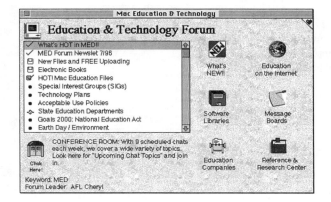

Finally, the files available in Mac Education & Technology Forum libraries cover a broad range of topics, including lesson ideas, software demos, logs of previous chats, and classroom-management tools.

The Mac Education & Technology Forum does not limit its services to educators, however; students find it to be motivating and helpful as well. Students meet online every week to discuss issues that pertain to them; they are encouraged to request help in areas that they are studying, discuss scheduled topics, or simply pay us a visit.

Today, fully educating our young people involves a wide variety of people: educators, students, parents, research scientists, advocates of school reform, and interested community members. All of them will find something relevant and significant in the Mac Education Forum.

Part
V

Ch

19

Exploring the Games' Forums

Keyword: **MGM (Macintosh), PC Games (Windows)**

In Chapter 13, "Playing Games," you learned many ways to have pure, simple fun on America Online. The Games' forums contain shareware games, add-ons, and demos of many popular commercial games. Just as important, the forums offer helpful advice on making play time (for adults and children) more rewarding.

From Rod Whitten (AFL Rod)

The Macintosh Games & Entertainment Forum (see fig. 19.15) has one of the largest available online collections of shareware and freeware games, as well as the easiest to find and download. For games that are hot off the press, check the New Files area. For demos of commercial games that you can try before you buy, check out the Commercial Demos library (which you find among the forum's software libraries).

FIG. 19.15
You have time for a little fun with a game downloaded from the Macintosh Games & Entertainment Forum.

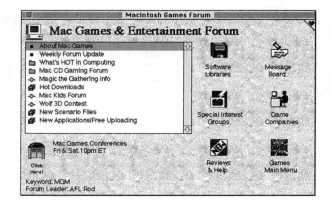

The Mac Games message boards give you hints and help on the most-played commercial and shareware games. The authors of many of the games provide answers to help you through the rough spots. Also, when you read a file description, you can click the Ask the Staff button (which appears in the file description window) to get answers from the friendly Mac Games staff. For short reviews and screen shots of games that are the pick of the staff from our libraries, check out the "Reviews & Help" button on the Main Mac Games Forum screen.

From Debbie Rogers (PC Sylva)

The PC Games Forum (see fig. 19.16) is your center for information about the wide world of games for your PC. Whether the game in question is a "hack-and-slash" adventure game, a joystick-bending arcade game, or a mind-bending simulation, you'll find help, hints, and lively interchange about it here.

If you feel like talking about the latest and greatest in computer gaming, the PC Games chat room is the place to be. Our extensive software libraries offer you the opportunity to download the finest public-domain and shareware games for the PC. Libraries are broken down by file type and include Adventure, Arcade, Board & Parlor, and Commercial Add-ons, as well as six Doom-related libraries.

FIG. 19.16
You can make your PC more fun to use with a game from America Online's PC Games Forum.

Using the Graphics Forums

Keyword: **MGR (Macintosh), PC Graphics (Windows)**

From David Stovall (AFL MacArt)

The Macintosh Graphic Arts & CAD Forum (see fig. 19.17) has more than 70 topical libraries containing more than 11,000 pictures. Experts representing nearly all facets of computer graphics are part of the staff team. The forum has several discussion boards for Macintosh graphics artists, designers, and professionals, subdivided into several special-interest groups: CAD Software, Adobe Illustrator, Adobe Photoshop, PowerDraw, 3-D, and Advertising.

FIG. 19.17
The Macintosh Graphic Arts & CAD Forum is America Online's resource for Macintosh graphics professionals.

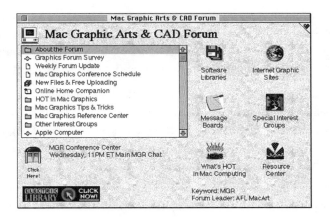

Part

V

Ch

19

Even if your drawing or image-editing skills are limited to a few simple shapes or to scanning artwork with your desktop scanner, you can find useful advice and information in the graphics forums. You'll also want to attend the regular weekly conferences run by the forum and its Special Interest Groups (SIGs).

From Mike Wiseman (PC Mike)

The PC Graphic Arts Forum (see fig. 19.18) is a hub of graphic activity for users and aficionados of computing fine art on the PC platform. The forum is a gallery, exhibition, library, and learning center featuring one of the largest software collections for graphics enthusiasts in the online world.

FIG. 19.18
PC computer artists should check out the Graphic Arts Forum.

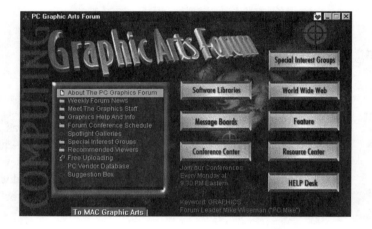

The forum's libraries house more than 22,000 graphics-related files, images, animation, applications, and utilities in over 120 topical libraries. You can leisurely browse individual libraries by selecting the Software Libraries icon or use the intuitive Software Search under the same icon to narrow your search to specific subjects.

Message boards are broken down into 20 different topics ranging from a general art discussion board to specific boards for commercial software discussion. There are also 13 Special Interest Groups (SIGs) devoted to specific aspects of graphics arts production, and each of those groups is like a separate forum with libraries, message boards, and a wealth of information to examine.

You'll also find conferences six nights weekly for friendly and fun discussions on different aspects of computer art. All conferences start at 9:30 eastern time.

Visiting the Hardware Forums

Keyword: **MHW (Macintosh), PC Hardware (Windows)**

From Chris Ferino (AFL Ferino)

The Macintosh Hardware Forum (see fig. 19.19) is a hotbed of hardware information online. We have several resource centers that are dedicated to areas of specific interest, such as the popular PowerBook line of portables and Apple's Power Macintosh and the Mac clones from such companies as DayStar, Power Computing, Umax, and others.

FIG. 19.19

If you're buying a new Macintosh computer, you need to visit the Mac Hardware Forum first.

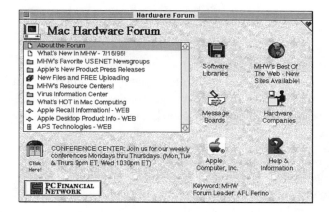

The forum's message boards are full of information from our online experts and thousands of members who have the same interests as you. Are you having a problem deciding which model to buy? Can't get your new peripheral to work properly? Chances are that one of the forum's regulars has experienced the same problem and found the answer online. Don't miss Mac Hardware's regular conferences, in which we tackle all kinds of subjects, ranging from the most basic to the most technical.

Also, don't forget about our software libraries. From various online magazines to the premiere shareware viral utility Disinfectant, you'll discover thousands of files, one of which is sure to interest you.

From Chuck Smith (PC Chuck)

The PC Hardware Forum (see fig. 19.20) is not only a place to find helpful hardware-related information, it also provides members with a place to share their questions, suggestions, and experiences with others who visit the forum's message areas and weekly conferences.

Part

V

Ch

19

FIG. 19.20
In the PC Hardware Forum, you can find out which PC runs Windows the fastest.

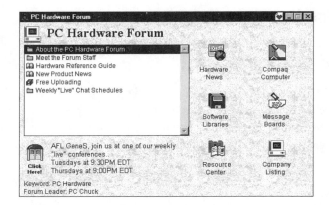

Message boards offer visiting members a place to look for help with a question, seek some advice in upgrading, or offer some help to others who may need it. It's a great place not only to make contact with the PC Hardware Forum's staff and other knowledgeable members who help out, but also to get opinions from others who have similar hardware items that you may be interested in adding to your system before you make your investment.

Within the constantly expanding Hardware Resource Center, you will find technical information such as pinouts, error codes, component information, Frequently Asked Questions (FAQs) and trouble-shooting tips, as well as contact points around America Online and across the Internet's World Wide Web, to locate product information from the various hardware manufacturers, and to keep up-to-date with the latest industry news and happenings.

The forum's libraries contain a wide range of hardware-related files, as well as drivers for the most current MS-DOS, Windows, and OS/2 operating systems.

Visiting the Macintosh HyperCard and Scripting Forum

Keyword: **MHC**

From Peter Baum (AFL HypCrd)

Have you ever wanted to create the great electronic novel? Not just text, but with pictures, sound, and animation? Or create a software tool that lets you do exactly what you want? Well, that's why the Mac HyperCard and Scripting Forum (see fig. 19.21) exists—to provide users with tools, support, and examples, so that they can design, create, and publish interactive projects such as these.

FIG. 19.21
The HyperCard & Scripting Forum gives you help with HyperCard, your personal programming language, and other scripting tools.

The forum focuses on information, techniques, and samples to help scripters, without requiring them to learn the Mac Toolbox or the C language. And there are over 10,000 such files already on AOL. While our roots are in HyperCard, the forum has grown to include new creativity tools, such as AppleScript, JavaScript, and Supercard.

You'll want to come to the forum conferences for scripting tutorials, tips, and techniques. Regular visitors can find answers to their questions in the forum's reference area. You'll also want to grab a few of the latest programming tools from the forum's huge software libraries.

Using the Multimedia Forums

Keyword: **Mac Video (Macintosh), PC Multimedia (Windows)**

The word *multimedia* has been bandied about the computer world for quite a few years. *Multimedia* refers to the marriage of audio and video (still or moving) on your desktop computer. As computers have become more powerful, the tools that manipulate the sometimes huge audio and video files have become cheaper and easier to use.

Major movie production houses have been using desktop computers for their work. The newest models from Apple Computer, such as Power Macintoshes with digital input and output capabilities, offer special tools for multimedia use. Users of these Power Macs can capture video images without having to buy extra hardware (other than a video display, of course). In addition, there are low-cost capture boards you can purchase for models that don't have these built-in features.

America Online's Macintosh Desktop Video & Multimedia Forum (see fig. 19.22) is a meeting ground where amateurs and professionals can share experiences and learn more about this growing art.

Part
V

Ch
19

FIG. 19.22

This forum is where you can keep up-to-date with the emerging sound and video technologies.

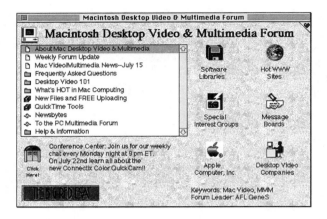

Weekly chats feature desktop video and multimedia professionals and representatives of the major hardware and software manufacturers, who appear regularly to help users solve common problems and fine-tune the finished product to a highly professional level.

From Jonathon Lawrence (PC JonL)

There's the menu up ahead. You have entered another dimension, a dimension not only of sight and sound, but of the mind; a journey into a wondrous land whose boundaries are that of the imagination. You have entered…the PC Multimedia Forum (see fig. 19.23). This forum is designed to offer something for everyone interested in the multi-sensual art form. You will find support from the Multimedia Products Councils as well as developers and manufacturers.

FIG. 19.23

America Online's resource for PC multimedia users is the PC Multimedia Forum.

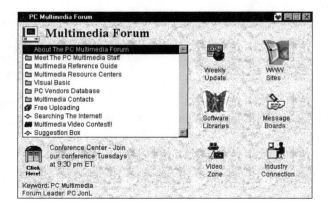

The Multimedia Forum is something new to America Online in more ways than the obvious. Just as Multimedia combines different forms of computer technology, this one forum takes staff from different forums already existing online to give you the best help available. If you have a question, you should post in the appropriate message board in the Multimedia Forum; however, you should also feel free to send e-mail to the staff person that matches your informational need.

Exploring the Music & Sound Forums

Keyword: **MMS (Macintosh), PC Music (Windows)**

From Keith Jablonski (AFL Keith)

The Macintosh Music & Sound Forum on America Online (see fig. 19.24) is the place to go to learn about music, sound, digital audio, MIDI, MOD, samplers, synthesizers, and anything else that causes noise to come from your Macintosh.

FIG. 19.24

The Macintosh Music & Sound Forum is for professional musicians and amateurs alike.

In the Macintosh Music & Sound Forum, you can take part in weekly chats. Every Sunday night, the forum's staff gets together to discuss music education, how to make your Macintosh make sound, MIDI for beginners, and more. From time to time, the forum also presents special guests who discuss topics such as how to make a record in your bedroom, what it takes to be a musician, and pushing the Macintosh to its limits. You can chat live with all the people who frequent the forum and with these special guests.

The forum also has active message boards where you can have your questions answered by other users. If you want to download files, you'll find that the Mac Music & Sound Forum has sound and music files in a variety of formats for all tastes, including SND, AIFF, MIDI, and MOD. (If you can't find it online, you probably won't be able to find it.)

Not enough for you yet? The forum also has Special Interest Groups online. Check out the Composers Coffeehouse, where members discuss composition techniques; Creative Musicians Coalition, which helps independent musicians sell their music; TAXI, which

Part
V

Ch
19

connects with artists who are looking for new songs; and MERLIN (the Music Education Reference Library and Information Network). If you're a programmer, you can link into the Music Programmers SIG to chat with other people who are writing cool music software.

From Norma Williams (PC Norma)

In the PC Music and Sound Forum (see fig. 19.25), we can help with all of your musical needs. Whether you're a music lover or musician, this forum has something for you.

FIG. 19.25

The PC Music and Sound Forum on America Online gives PC music buffs a chance to explore musical tools.

For music lovers, the forum has hundreds of ready-to-play music and sound-effects files for almost any sound board, such as the SoundBlaster 16 ASP, Advanced Gravis UltraSound and UltraSound MAX, Turtle Beach MultiSound, AWE32, and Pro AudioSpectrum-16 cards. They support a multitude of software packages, including Sequencer Gold, Music Studio, and CakeWalk for Windows. Along with the MIDI sequencers, you'll find a large number of useful utilities. There's also a vast assortment of music and sound programs for most Tandy systems and even for PCs.

As you begin to explore the forum, you'll discover an array of message boards that cater to people with all levels of PC audio and multimedia interests. You are invited to post messages frequently. Also, the extensive libraries offer you the opportunity to download the finest public-domain and shareware music files, sound files, and utilities for your PC.

The forum's meeting room hosts regular conferences, where you can join the staff and your fellow members for the best information and conversation about PC music and sounds.

Visiting the Macintosh Operating Systems Forum

Keyword: **MOS**

The operating system usually is the most invisible part of your computer's software. But every function, from turning on and booting your computer to moving and copying files, is managed by the operating system. The software that you use to do your work uses tools provided by the operating system for many of its functions.

The Macintosh Operating Systems Forum (see fig. 19.26) is your information center for System 6; all flavors of System 7; and Apple's UNIX front end, A/UX and discussions about the newest operating system being developed when this book went to press, Mac OS 8. The forum's expert staff advises you on computer problems (such as frequent crashes and other strange behavior) and helps you make your computer work better and faster.

FIG. 19.26
Your computer can't even start without its operating system, which is the subject of this forum on America Online.

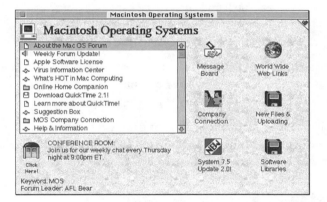

The forum's Apple software libraries contain the latest updates from Apple, including printer drivers, system updates, and special programs to enhance performance. Weekly chats cover all sorts of operating-system-related issues.

Visiting the OS/2 Forum

Keyword: **OS 2**

From Dave Swartz (PC DaveS)

The OS/2 Forum (see fig. 19.27) is by OS/2 users, for OS/2 users. This forum is the place for your questions, problems, tips, and tricks on OS/2. Whether you are a novice or a veteran, you'll find help, support, discussion, and general information on OS/2.

Part
V

Ch
19

FIG. 19.27
The ins and outs of OS/2 are explained in this America Online forum.

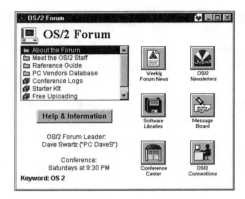

The forum's software library contains a wealth of files and is split into categories to help you find exactly what you want. The forum's staff is here to help with general OS/2 questions and issues. You'll find conferences, message boards, file libraries, and reference areas to help you use OS/2 better. The OS/2 forum is also on IBM's official distribution list for updates, patches, and fixes for OS/2.

If you already run OS/2, this forum can serve you as a helpful information center where you can interact with fellow America Online members, forum staff, and industry experts on how to make your computer run more efficiently.

If you're running into difficulty setting up AOL's software to run under OS/2, you'll want to check out the handy instructions in Chapter 4, "Getting the Most from AOL's Windows Software," which were supplied and tested with the help of PC DaveS.

Exploring the PDA/Palmtop Forum

Keyword: **PDA**

From Craig de Fasselle (PDA Craig)

PDA is the acronym for personal digital assistant, which is a small, hand-held computer. These palmtop marvels are designed to provide all the tools an individual needs for day-to-day organization, and in some cases, communications and other features normally expected on a desktop computer. Whether you already own one of these electronic wonders, or wish to see if they are more than high-priced toys, you can visit the PDA Forum to learn more.

The PDA/Palmtop Forum (see fig. 19.28) is designed to cover every aspect of PDA and palmtop computing, from novice-level support to program development. You'll find this forum is a complete resource for information, discussion, and software for all hand-held devices including the Newton PDAs, Hewlett Packard palmtop computers and OmniGo PDAs, the Palm Pilot, Sony Magic Link, Psion S3 and S3a, Motorola Envoy, and many other PDAs and palmtops. Resource centers for particular PDA categories such as the Newton are included. It's also a multi-platform forum, where you'll be able to get cross-platform translation assistance.

FIG. 19.28
Learn about hand-held computers in this America Online forum.

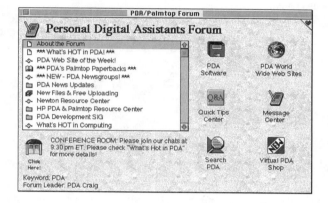

The PDA Forum has more than 70 libraries featuring the best software for hand-held devices. They also feature Palmtop Paperbacks, home to hundreds of public-domain books, electronic magazines, newsletters, and foreign-language texts. Utilities programs are offered that allow these texts to be read on anything from a PDA to a desktop computer.

Some industry analysts are stating that the PDA represents the future of personal computing and that in years to come, even your desktop computer will fit in the palm of your hand. Does that prospect sound intriguing? Visit the PDA forum to learn more.

Using the Macintosh Utilities Forum

Keyword: **MUT**

From Floyd Zink (AFL Floyd)

The Mac Utilities Forum (see fig. 19.29) is devoted to the tools that will help you get the most out of your Macintosh. Every week the forum hosts an interactive conference about a hot topic regarding Macintosh Utilities. They also sponsor visits from numerous luminaries in the Macintosh world, so you may ask your questions directly of the experts. The MUT (this is their nickname, too) libraries contain Control Panels, INITs, Extensions, System and Finder enhancements, hard disk backup programs, installers, text processors, desk accessories, and thousands of other programs that you'll wonder how you ever got along without. You'll also find answers to your questions about the use of

Part
V

Ch
19

these programs in the Message Board. In fact, anything you can think to say or ask about utilities is open for discussion in the forum's message boards.

FIG. 19.29
One of America Online's most popular Mac computing forums is the utilities forum.

A major area in the MUT Forum is the Virus Information Center, which has been redesigned and expanded to help meet the needs of America Online's growing membership. Here you can find a helping hand, download free anti-virus software to prevent virus problems, and find current updates for SAM, Virex, VirusScan, and other commercial programs. The forum also offers AOL Community Updates, the latest news on viruses and threats to online safety, and the best in anti-virus Frequently Asked Questions (FAQs) written both by MUT staff and by experts who have graciously contributed from all over the world.

Visiting the User Group Forum

Keyword: **UGF**

When you buy a personal computer, no doubt you're eager to meet other computer owners, to receive advice, and to share tips and tricks that make your computer run more effectively. A user group is a club, pure and simple; it's an organization that consists of computer owners and is usually devoted to one specific platform, such as Macintosh or PC.

America Online's User Group Forum is a special resource for user-group members (see fig. 19.30). You can have your organization listed so that other users in your area can learn about it. The forum also features a database of news articles containing helpful material that you may want to include in your newsletters. Also, the software library offers useful files that you can download and incorporate into your organization's monthly software disks.

FIG. 19.30
Meet with fellow computer owners right here on America Online.

You can attend the weekly chats to talk with members of groups around the country. If you aren't a user-group member yet, you can consult the forum's User Group Listing for a group in your area.

Visiting the Windows Forum

Keyword: **Windows Forum**

From Kate Chase (PC Kat)

Since the first edition of this book was published, the Windows Forum (see fig. 19.31) has undergone a reorganization of focus, moving away from covering "everything" Windows related to zeroing in on helping members address problems with Windows as an operating system. The emphasis is now on utilities and tips that help Windows to run more effectively.

Part
V

Ch
19

FIG. 19.31
You can make Windows work better by consulting the Windows Forum.

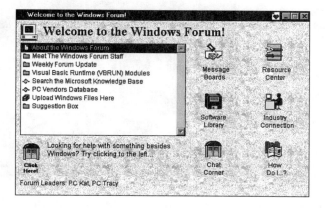

All major releases of Windows are covered in the forum's message boards, libraries, and live help sessions, including 3.1, Windows 95, and Windows NT. Features such as a GPF Reference Guide and a How Do I... guide help to take some of the mystery out of Windows desktop management while the Windows Forum Top Picks library offers top-notch utilities for getting rid of duplicates, monitoring your system performance, and alternative desktop arrangements.

Reading Computer Books and Magazines Online

Keyword: **Magazine Rack**

When you want to learn more about how your computer works, find out how to use a specific piece of software, or just sneak a preview of upcoming products, you are likely to venture into your local bookstore and purchase a book such as this one.

America Online gives you a chance to preview some of those publications before you buy them. You can even search through back issues of many of your favorite computing magazines for a specific article during your online session. Additionally, you can participate in online forums run by the producers of several popular computing-related radio and TV programs.

For your convenience, all these resources have been gathered together and are accessible in AOL's Magazine Rack area (see fig. 19.32).

FIG. 19.32
AOL's Magazine Rack area is an online media center for computer-related information.

Before you visit the individual computer media centers listed in the area's directory, you'll want to check out the regular highlights. (The highlights' icons won't necessarily reflect the same publications that are shown in this book.)

Listening to "Computer America"

Craig Crossman's "Computer America" (see fig. 19.33) is a popular syndicated radio program that provides news and advice for both Mac and PC users. During the program, the host interacts with dozens of callers (who use the show's toll-free lines) and also awards valuable prizes.

FIG. 19.33
A forum is devoted to Craig Crossman's "Computer America" program.

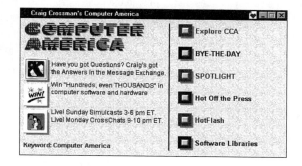

The program's forum on AOL has an active message exchange and contest information. The forum also features regular online conferences in which Craig Crossman holds court, taking on the most difficult questions and offering quick, informative responses.

Visiting *FamilyPC* Magazine Online

Keyword: **FamilyPC**

Personal computers are nearly as ubiquitous as VCRs in our homes these days. And *FamilyPC* magazine (see fig. 19.34) is designed to make the sometimes-confusing world of computers simple. Each monthly issue contains helpful articles and reviews of popular products that will make your computer easier to use and much more productive.

FIG. 19.34
FamilyPC helps you find better ways to work with your home computer.

Part
V

Ch
19

The FamilyPC forum on AOL is not just limited to the contents of the magazine itself. Through active discussion boards, software libraries, and regular conferences, you can gain helpful insights that will enhance your computing experience. You'll also want to click the PC & Mac News icon for the latest news from the world of personal computing.

N O T E   The content of online magazines is not necessarily the same as the newsstand edition. In some cases, features that appear in the print version may not show up in the online version. In other situations, the online edition provides more up-to-date news, because of continuing deadlines. In addition, the online magazine will usually offer other features you won't find in the regular edition, such as active message boards and special areas devoted to online conferences. ▪

Looking at *Home Office Computing*

Keyword: **Home Office**

If you, like many people, work from an office located in your home, you may want to read *Home Office Computing*. This magazine caters to small-business people, offers advice on buying new hardware and software, and provides helpful tips on making your office run more productively (see fig. 19.35).

You are invited to participate in the magazine's active message board, where readers and editors discuss how to get the most mileage out of your computer purchase.

FIG. 19.35
The *Home Office Computing* forum on America Online is a valuable resource for small businesses.

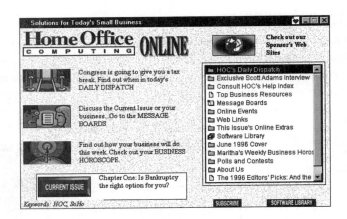

Reading *HomePC* Magazine

Keyword: **HomePC**

The personal computer has taken over almost every area of our lives. Our children work with computers at school, millions of us have computers of one sort or another in our homes. Low-priced computers now are available not only at specialty stores, but also from discount stores and consumer-electronics chains. *HomePC* magazine (see fig. 19.36) is for users of Apple Macintoshes and IBM PCs and compatibles, with an emphasis on home use.

The Ask Dr. PC section provides answers for common problems one faces in learning more about a computer. The HomePC forum provides a special section that covers the latest and greatest children's software products, as well as helpful advice that you'll want to read before you make your next (or first) home computer purchase.

FIG. 19.36
HomePC magazine takes a personal approach to the world of computing.

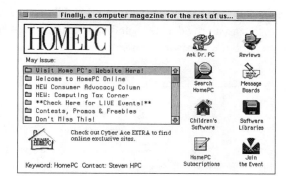

Exploring Reports from "Industry Insider"

Keyword: **Insider**

We've read all the puff pieces put out by computer manufacturers to promote their new products. But, what's really going on behind the scenes at Apple, Compaq, IBM, Intel, Microsoft, and other industry-leader companies? You can find out when you read Tim Bajarin's "Industry Insider" columns on AOL (see fig. 19.37).

FIG. 19.37
Learn all the behind-the-scenes information about the computing industry from "Industry Insider."

Part
V

Ch
19

In addition to reading the latest information from "Industry Insider," you can join the forum's active discussion board and discuss the latest events; you can add your own messages, too.

Introducing *I-Wire* Magazine

Keyword: **I-Wire**

Not all the magazines that run forums on America Online have counterparts on your corner newsstand. *I-Wire* (formerly *COMPUTE*; see fig. 19.38) is brought to you by the publisher of *Longevity, OMNI*, and *Saturday Review*. Like your favorite newsstand computer magazine, this area provides news and information about computers, as well as reviews of the hottest new hardware and software.

FIG. 19.38
A magazine that exists solely in cyberspace: *I-Wire*.

Because it is strictly an online magazine, *I-Wire* emphasizes interaction with AOL members. You'll want to check out the regular conferences (featuring editors and computer experts) and the active message boards, where you can learn valuable tips from other members on the most effective way to use your computer. Windows users also will want to click the Windows Workshop icon to explore new options that can make Windows work better for you.

Reading *MacHome Journal*

Keyword: **MacHome Journal**

If you are new to the world of desktop computers and find such jargon as *CPU, RAM*, and *hard drive access speed* to be a foreign language, you need to read *MacHome Journal* (see fig. 19.39). This publication is designed for those of you who want to learn how to use your computer more effectively without wading through confusing technical material.

FIG. 19.39
You don't have to be a technological wizard to find valuable information in *MacHome Journal*.

As with other online magazines, you can preview the latest issue, exchange messages with fellow America Online members and editors, and download useful software. If you like the magazine well enough to want a copy in your home, you'll find a convenient way to order a subscription.

Exploring *MacTech* Magazine

Keyword: **MacTech**

If you want to write software for the Macintosh, you'll want to check out *MacTech* magazine, which caters strictly to developers and programmers. Each issue is filled with information that helps you learn programming, advice on debugging your software, and even suggestions on finding a solution to a sticky coding problem.

MacTech also regularly distributes CD-ROMs filled with advice for programmers and sample source code that you can use in developing your own software.

Exploring *Macworld*

Keyword: **Macworld**

When you buy a new Apple Macintosh, you get a free trial subscription to *Macworld* (see fig. 19.40). But, even if you haven't made a computer purchase lately, you may want to keep up-to-date on all the new hardware and software products. *Macworld* contains news, features, and columns in which you can learn just what Apple has up its corporate sleeve for the newest generation of Macintosh computers, and in-depth reports on new products.

Online Discussions is a message board that offers breezy and sometimes heated discussions on all sorts of computer-related subjects, involving America Online members and *Macworld* writers and editors.

Part
V

Ch
19

FIG. 19.40
Macworld magazine is available on America Online.

Macworld's software library is a repository of unique shareware reviewed by the magazine and other special files that may interest you. One file puts grammar-checking software through a genuine torture test—something to think about if you want to buy a program that helps you improve your writing skills. You'll also want to attend the weekly conferences in the Macworld Live auditorium, which features many of your favorite *Macworld* writers and visiting experts.

Exploring Mobile Office Online

Keyword: **Mobile, Portable**

The proliferation of Macintosh and PC laptop computers has made it possible for you to do your work almost anywhere in the world, even in the middle of a desert, so long as you have a spare set of batteries or a source of AC power. Mobile Office Online, shown in figure 19.41, is the AOL counterpart of the popular newsstand magazine that caters to this new generation of traveling workers.

FIG. 19.41
Mobile Office magazine keeps tabs on the growing world of laptop computing.

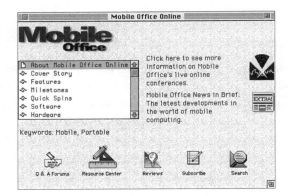

In addition to reading features from the magazine itself, you can investigate Mobile Office Daily, which contains hot news that just can't wait for the next issue. The Q&A forums give you a chance to offer advice, ask questions, and share information with fellow AOL members and the magazine's friendly editorial staff.

Reading *Multimedia World* Online

Keyword: **Multimedia World**

Multimedia World magazine (see fig. 19.42) is published by the same people who bring you *Macworld.* You'll find news and features from the regular version of the magazine by clicking the icon for The Newsstand.

FIG. 19.42
Learn about CD-ROMs, desktop video, and more from *Multimedia World* magazine.

But that's just the beginning. The publisher of *Multimedia World* offers some exclusive features in this AOL forum—features that are not duplicated in the magazine. The Test Track, for example, is a software library from which you can download demonstration versions of some multimedia software products. In the Cafe, you can participate in conferences involving editors and visiting experts; click the icon to see the full schedule or to enter a meeting that is already in progress.

Click the icon for the Office to submit articles and letters to the editor or to subscribe to *Multimedia World.* If you have a problem with your multimedia computer that needs a fast solution, click the icon for the Clinic to find helpful hints.

Part
V

Ch
19

Visiting *PC World* Online

Keyword: **PC World**

PC World magazine, which is a sister publication of *Macworld* and *Multimedia World*, provides its own slant on information about new PC hardware and software products. In a typical visit to the forum (see fig. 19.43), you may find news about a contest, a new family of chips from Intel, or the latest operating-system upgrade from Microsoft.

Virtually the entire text of the current issue of *PC World* is at your fingertips for review. A large software library of PC utilities is also available. You are invited to attend special conferences featuring fellow America Online members, magazine editors and writers, and visiting experts.

The Online Exclusive area offers computer news and information before it appears in the magazine. Because a magazine must be prepared a month or two in advance, America Online members get a jump on newsstand buyers by being the first to learn about new developments in computing.

FIG. 19.43
PC World Online is an information resource for users of IBM PCs and compatibles.

Visiting Redgate New Product Showcase

Keyword: **Redgate**, **NPS**

If you're looking for a particular hardware or software product, but you don't know whether it exists or how to contact the manufacturer, Redgate's popular Product Registry probably will have the information you want. Redgate's New Product Showcase, shown in figure 19.44, has a huge database that contains information on virtually every existing Macintosh product, as well as a directory of PC multimedia products.

The Redgate New Product Registry forum schedules regular conferences with leaders of the computing industry, so that you can learn about products and gain insights into future developments. A special library contains press releases describing new computing products that you may want to check out.

FIG. 19.44
The Redgate Registry is a database of information about thousands of computing products.

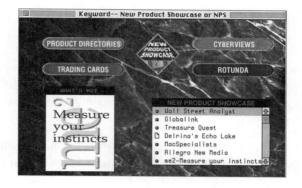

Visiting *WordPerfect* Magazine Online

Keyword: **WPMag**

If you are a user of WordPerfect, the popular cross-platform word processing program published by Corel, the monthly *WordPerfect* magazine (see fig. 19.45) is your source for advice and information about the program. The forum comes in two flavors: the regular version (covering all platforms on which its software is available) and a special Windows-oriented edition.

Text-based copies of the magazine are available for you to read at your leisure. The software library features special files, such as handy macros, that help make your experience with WordPerfect software more productive. The Message Exchange is a gathering place for readers and editors to offer advice and to provide timesaving tips and tricks.

Part
V

Ch
19

FIG. 19.45
Online Access features *WordPerfect* Magazine.

Accessing Ziff-Net on AOL

Keyword: **ZDNet**

No doubt you're familiar with many of the Ziff-Davis computing magazines. Examples include *Computer Life*, *MacUser*, *MacWeek*, *PCUser*, and *PC Week*. ZDNet on AOL (see fig. 19.46) is a gateway not only to the publisher's online resources on AOL, but to the World Wide Web as well.

To read some of your favorite computing magazines online, simply click the explore icon (see fig. 19.47). In addition to selecting the magazine you want to read from the convenient icon, you can also get special deals if you decide to subscribe.

FIG. 19.46
ZDNet offers online magazines, files, conferences, and more on AOL.

FIG. 19.47
Ziff-Davis offers convenient Web access to its popular computing magazines.

Secrets of Using America Online's Company Connection

Keyword: **Company Connection, Industry Connection**

If you've ever spent long minutes listening to voice mail when you try to reach a hardware or software manufacturer for some help, you'll appreciate America Online's solution. Hundreds of firms, ranging from small utility-software publishers to major manufacturers of computer hardware, are represented in America Online's Company Connection area (see fig. 19.48).

FIG. 19.48
Get help right from the source in America Online's Company Connection.

Part

V

Ch

19

These support forums are places where you can get advice on using a company's product more effectively and solving problems when they arise. The companies' own support personnel usually staff the forums; they are often ably assisted by knowledgeable America Online members.

Software publishers often provide free maintenance updates for their products in their support areas, so you don't have to wait for a product update to be mailed to you. You also should check the software libraries often, in case the libraries contain an update that you need.

Finding a Company

Not every firm is represented on America Online yet, but more are being added regularly. You can find computing-industry support areas in the computing and software forums, catering to the kinds of product that the companies support. Suppose that you want to access a modem manufacturer in the hardware and communications forums. You'll see an icon or a list box representing companies with products in that category in the appropriate forum. Just click that icon or double-click the list box to bring up the roster of companies.

If you can't find the company that you're looking for in a computing forum's directory, type the keyword **Industry**, which takes you to America Online's Company Connection section. Then click the Search for a Company icon. If the firm is represented on America Online, it will be listed in the search window.

The fastest method, however, may be using a keyword to go directly to the firm that you want. If you want to find Claris (Apple Computer's cross-platform software subsidiary), for example, type the keyword **Claris**. In just a few seconds, you are transported directly to the front door of the company's America Online support forum (see fig. 19.49).

FIG. 19.49
Apple's Claris software division publishes software for both the Mac and Windows platforms.

Using Company Connection Help

A technical support person can't solve your problem if you don't provide enough information about your setup and the difficulties that you're having with the product. The following letter is typical of the letters that often appear on the message boards in the regular forums and the company support areas:

> Help! My computer is crashing all the time. I can't get any work done when I use your software. I need help.
>
> Harried Harry

This sort of letter is only going to delay the process of getting help, because the letter lacks any information that would help a technical support person to diagnose and, if necessary, try to reproduce the problem. Remember that the only information that a manufacturer has to go on is what you provide in your letter, because the support people aren't present at your work site to see what exactly is going wrong.

NOTE Don't *cross-post*—that is, don't post your message in more than one message folder in a single forum. America Online members don't always take kindly to reading the same message over and over again (because they're paying to read the messages again and again). Before you issue your plea for help, take a few moments to find the right place to post it. Look for an appropriate computing forum or a company support area (the Hardware forum, for example, for a malfunctioning printer), and leave your message there. ■

The following list provides some helpful hints on how to ask a company support person for help:

■ Describe the kind of computer that you have, including the model number.

■ Briefly describe your setup, including the operating system version and the amount of installed RAM. Also list the accessories attached to your system, such as a video card or an additional hard drive.

■ Identify the manufacturer's product by model or version number. Often, a problem affects only a single version of a program or piece of hardware.

■ Describe, completely and concisely, the problem that you're having. If your computer is crashing, report whether an error message appears on your computer's screen. That kind of message may be crucial to figuring out what went wrong.

■ If the problem can be reproduced, describe the steps that you took to reproduce it. That way, if the problem is unique to your setup, the steps can help the support person reproduce the problem.

■ If the problem started after you made a change in your setup (such as a hardware addition or a software installation), mention that, too. The new installation may have caused your troubles.

■ Finally, don't expect miracles. These products are manufactured by human beings who have the same shortcomings as the rest of us. No hardware or software product is perfect; you just want to get it to work as efficiently as possible in your home or office.

Sometimes, a problem is too complex to deal with via e-mail or message board. In such cases, companies invite you to contact their technical support people directly, by telephone.

Part

V

Ch

19

From Here...

In this chapter, we visited America Online's vast sources for computing and software information. You discovered resources for online magazines and the various Mac and PC computing forums.

If you want to learn more about your computer and how to use it more effectively, America Online is your best resource for interacting not only with hardware and software manufacturers, but also with many savvy computer users. For more information on setting up America Online on your computer, finding the software files you want, and getting help, refer to the following chapters:

- Chapter 3, "Getting the Most from AOL's Macintosh Software," where you learn to harness the power of your software during your online visits.

- Chapter 4, "Getting the Most from AOL's Windows Software," where you discover special Windows AOL Add-Ons and other cool stuff that'll make your online visits more productive.

- Chapter 20, "Tips and Tricks on Finding Software," where you'll put AOL's handy File Search feature through its paces.

- For descriptions of some of the most popular software online, read Chapter 21, "The Best Macintosh Software on AOL," and Chapter 22, "The Best Windows Software on AOL."

Tips and Tricks on Finding Software

Where's that file

Learn to quickly and easily find software in America Online's libraries.

Shareware? Whatware?

Learn all about the kinds of software you can find on America Online.

Downloading software

Transfer that software directly to your computer.

Uploading software

Send your own files to America Online's huge software libraries.

What's wrong with that file?

What to do if the software you've downloaded causes your computer to freeze or crash.

The first step many AOL visitors make when they log on is to check out the software libraries. It's one of AOL's most popular features. And there are literally tens of thousands of Macintosh and Windows files from which you can choose. Whether it's an arcade game, a program that lets you create a to-do list, or an update to commercial software you own, America Online is the place to find it.

After you've read about the kinds of software available, you'll want to read the next two chapters, which describe some of the most popular programs to be found in AOL's Macintosh and Windows software libraries. These chapters also include special recommendations direct from some of the forum leaders themselves. ■

Visiting AOL's Software Libraries

When I first joined America Online in 1989, I was the owner of a brand new computer, and I wanted to stock up on software. As an inveterate software junkie, I was a frequent visitor to the service's vast software libraries. It took me a while to discover the rich array of information services available elsewhere online.

Before you go on, here are a couple of computer terms you'll see often in this chapter:

■ *Downloading* a file is simply the act of transferring a file from America Online's host computer, through the telephone lines, to your computer by way of your modem.

■ *Uploading* a file is the process of sending a file from your computer directly to America Online.

Virus Protection

Because there is always the danger that a file can be contaminated by a computer virus, America Online's forum staff checks all uploaded files with an up-to-date virus detection program before posting them online. However, you still should always install and use the latest virus detection software so that all your files are safe.

N O T E   If you want more information about computer viruses, and how to protect your computer against them, visit AOL's Virus Information Center. The keyword is *Virus*. ■

CAUTION

Files downloaded from FTP or World Wide Web sources are not checked by America Online for the presence of viruses. Please use virus detection software to check files you've downloaded from Internet sources to be sure they are in good shape before you attempt to use those files.

Using File Search

The fastest way to locate software you want is to let America Online's host computer do the search for you. To bring up America Online's File Search window, follow these steps:

1. Press Ctrl+K (⌘-K for Macintosh) and type the keyword **File Search** to bring up the search window (see fig. 20.1), or choose Find from the Go To menu and double-click the option to search the software libraries.

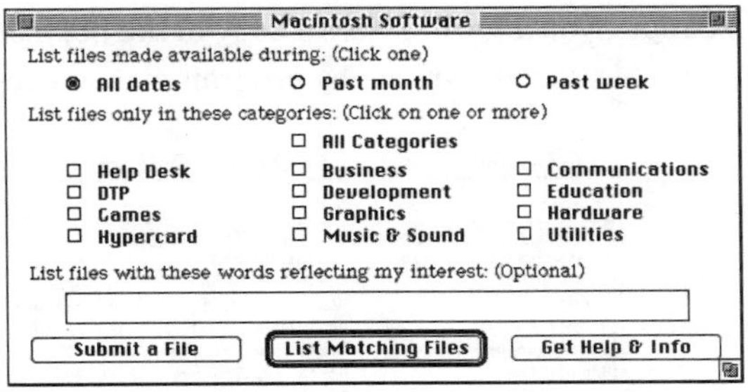

FIG. 20.1

Here is your gateway to America Online's convenient software database as seen from the Mac version of AOL's software.

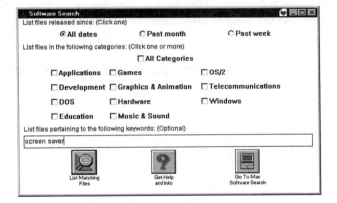

In seconds, you see a large window on your computer that gives you a number of search options (see fig. 20.2). The categories shown will be different, depending on whether you're using the Macintosh or Windows version of AOL's software (the Windows version is illustrated here).

FIG. 20.2

Find the software you want by category or file name.

You can search for software in many ways. You can limit your search to a specific category, such as Games or Graphics. You can even restrict the search to a specific time frame; perhaps you only want to find a file that was posted in the past month.

2. If you want to locate a file by name or subject, enter the information in the List files field. If you want to find a screen saver, for example, enter **screen saver** as the subject of your search.

If files matching your description cannot be found, a window notifies you.

If files meeting your description are found, you see a File List window on-screen (see fig. 20.3). A file might be listed more than once if it is in more than one library on America Online. Because only 20 files are loaded to the File List at one time, you may need to click the List More Files button to see additional entries.

In this example, you'll try to locate a copy of the popular Macintosh shareware arcade game *Maelstrom,* written by programmer Andrew Welch.

FIG. 20.3

Success! The files you are looking for are listed here.

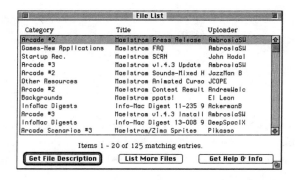

3. To learn more about the file that interests you, either double-click the file name, or choose the Get File Description button, either by clicking it or by pressing Return or Enter. You see a window similar to the one shown in figure 20.4.

FIG. 20.4

Review the file description first.

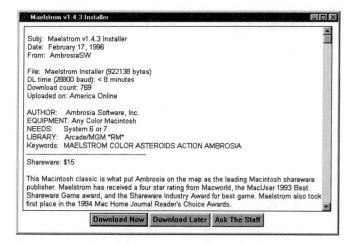

Download Your Files Fast

Now that you've found a file you'd like to download, the next step is to start the download process. The option labeled Download Later will create a file *queue*, which is a list of files to download. That list or directory will be stored in America Online's Download Manager (which is described in more detail a bit later in this chapter). If you want to download the file immediately, choose Download Now.

Here are the steps that cover the typical downloading process. The illustrations shown will be slightly different in the Macintosh and Windows versions of AOL's software (and will probably be altered a bit as software is updated), but the steps you follow will be the same.

 TIP Before downloading a file, check the File Description. This description not only tells you more about the file, but contains information about what kind of computer it works on.

1. The default selection in the software list, at the bottom of the window, is Download Now. Choose this to bring up a window that allows you to indicate where you want to store the file that's being transferred to your computer (see fig. 20.5). You can select the download location in either the Macintosh or Windows version of America Online's software.

FIG. 20.5
Select the place where you want the file sent.

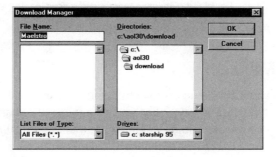

2. Rename the file, if you want to.

3. Click the Save button on your Mac (or OK for the Windows version of AOL software) or press the Return or Enter key to begin the download process.

 TIP To speed up file transfer times, you might want to log on to America Online at a non-peak hour, perhaps early in the morning, when network traffic is less busy.

Part
V

Ch
20

When your file download begins, you see a progress bar showing approximately how much of the file has been sent, and an estimate of how long it will take to transfer that file to your computer (see fig. 20.6).

FIG. 20.6
Here's the file download in process.

> **NOTE**   Macintosh users of System 7, or MultiFinder under System 6, can click the desktop and resume other work while the download is in progress. (Windows users can press Alt+Tab to switch from one application to another.) However, you should avoid CPU-intensive tasks, such as calculating a spreadsheet, while downloading. Doing so can slow down or even interrupt the download process. ■

When the file has been transferred, America Online's friendly narrator will announce (if the sounds are enabled), "File's done!"

> **NOTE**   If you decide you don't want to download the file after all, click the Finish Later button. In a minute or two, the download will stop. If you decide you actually want to resume the download at a later time, *don't* delete the partial file that has been transferred to your computer; if you do, the Download Manager cannot resume downloading at the point where it left off. ■

The Download Manager

You can build a download queue or list by using the Download Manager. You can start the download any time during your online session or when the session ends. When you add a file to the list, you see the acknowledgment shown in figure 20.7.

FIG. 20.7
Another file is added to the listing of files to be downloaded.

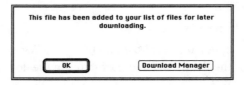

To use the Download Manager, choose the second option available to you when downloading a file—Download Later.

Check the Download Manager any time after adding files to the queue to see whether you want to make changes in the lineup before downloading begins.

CAUTION

If you log on to America Online as a guest, using another member's software, the Download Later function will not work, nor will you be able to use AOL's FlashSession feature.

America Online's Download Manager lets you manage the entire download process from a single window. You can open the Download Manager window when notified that a file has been added to the download queue by selecting the Download Manager button, or you can use America Online's File menu. The Download Manager displays all of the files you've selected for downloading (see fig. 20.8).

FIG. 20.8
The Download Manager lists the files that will be transferred to your computer.

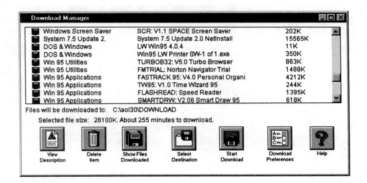

The following options are available to you in the Download Manager window:

- *View Description*, the first option in the lower-left corner of the window, gives you the chance to check whether you really want to download the file. If the file transfer process will take a long time, you probably should review the file descriptions before beginning a download.
- *Delete List Item (or Delete Item for Windows users)* allows you to remove a selected item from the Download Manager's queue if you decide you don't want to download the file after all.
- *Show Completed Downloads (or Show Files Downloaded for Windows users)* allows you to view a list of recent files that you've downloaded. You can check the file description again or remove the file from the list.
- *Select Destination* allows you to select a new default location (folder or directory) on your computer's drive in which to store the downloaded files. All files selected for downloading by the Download Manager will always be sent to this location.
- *Start Download* allows you to begin the entire download process immediately.

Part
V

Ch
20

■ *Download Preferences* allows you to set your download preferences for the best performance.

■ *Help* produces America Online's comprehensive Help menu, which includes instructions and quick tips to help you get the most efficient use of your online visit (see fig. 20.9).

FIG. 20.9
Getting online Help about a download-related problem.

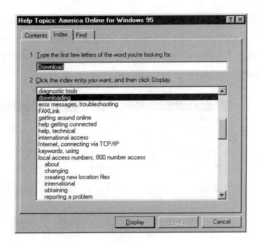

> **TIP** Any text window on America Online, even a file description, can be printed or saved to your computer's drive. If you're new to America Online, you'll want to read Appendixes A, B, and C.

The Download Manager window lists the total size of the files you've selected for transfer to your computer and gives an estimated transfer time at your modem connection speed. Downloads can take a little longer than the estimate during the evening prime-time period or when there is noise on your phone line. At other times, you may find your downloads moving more swiftly than estimated.

How Do You Use the Files You've Downloaded?

Most larger files in America Online's software libraries are compressed to save disk space and to reduce transfer time, thereby reducing online charges.

> **NOTE** If you get a message on your Macintosh that the application that created your downloaded file can't be found, log on and check the file description, or view it offline in the Download Manager's list of Completed Downloads. You might need other software to use the downloaded file, either to decompress it or to run it after it's decompressed. ■

Both Macintosh and Windows America Online software can be set to automatically expand (decompress) files that you've downloaded as soon as you log off. Because some files might be compressed in a format that isn't supported by the software, those files will have to be expanded before you use them.

Before you pick a file to download, read the file description carefully to make sure that your computer, operating system, and software setup are compatible with those of the file.

 TIP If you make a mistake and download a file you can't use, use the keyword *Credit* to request a rebate to your account for the time you wasted online.

If you get a message that the file has been damaged after downloading, you need to remove the file from your computer and download the file again. Although files are not damaged often, sometimes a file might not arrive in perfect condition due to noise on the telephone lines or to a network-related problem.

 TROUBLESHOOTING

Help! My download has been interrupted. What do I do now? If your download is interrupted for any reason (perhaps your connection was terminated because of poor phone-line conditions), a fragment or partial file is left on your computer's drive. If you want to resume the download when you log on again, don't delete or move the partial file. Otherwise, you won't be able to resume your download where it left off.

I can't find the file I just downloaded. Where is it? When you first install your AOL software, the program designates a folder or directory for downloaded files. In the Mac version, it's in the Online Downloads folder. In the Windows version, it's in the WAOL/Downloads directory. You can change the destination to another location, if you prefer, using the Download Manager. You can click the Select Destination icon in the Download Manager window, but most users just leave the setting where it is.

What Types of Software Are Available?

Before you begin to fill your software library, let's discuss the types of software that are available and what software you can find on America Online.

Commercial Software

Commercial software is a retail product. You can find it at your local computer store, user group, or by mail order. You can even order commercial software on America Online through a publisher's company support area or through forums devoted to shopping (see Chapters 19 and 28).

You will not find commercial software in America Online's software libraries, but you can, from time to time, locate a free update program. The author or publisher of a software product can make an update program available so that you can revise your copy of the software to a newer version, usually to fix some bugs.

Like most software, commercial software is covered by a license agreement. Although licenses vary from product to product, in most cases, the license states that you are not buying the software itself, but the right to use it. The agreement spells out what those rights are. For most of you, those rights include being allowed to use the software on a single computer at a time and to make backup copies in case the master disks are damaged.

Because many of us use laptop computers for travel, some software licenses allow you to install the software on both your home or office computer and a portable, assuming that not more than one person will use the software at the same time. If you're going to install the software on multiple computers, you need to buy a site license from the author or publisher.

For more information on obtaining commercial software, see Chapter 19, "Visiting the Computing and Software Forums."

Demoware

Demonstration software is designed to let you try out all or most of the features of a software product before you buy it. *Demoware*, as it's also known, can be either a commercial or a shareware program. In most cases, you can use the software for a limited period of time, ranging from a few days to a week or two. It then expires and you cannot use it again until you buy a copy. Some demoware might simply lock out some program features (such as the capability to save and print a document), which become available in the version you buy or by typing in a password on the demo application.

Shareware

Shareware is a modern-day equivalent of the original try-before-you-buy concept. The author or publisher of a software product gives you a fully functional version (although a feature or two might be restricted). You can try it out on your computer for a period of up to a month. When that period expires, you are asked to pay the author or publisher a small fee for a license to continue to run the program.

Shareware is one of the last vestiges in our society of an honor system. The publisher has no way of knowing whether you are continuing to use the software. If you decide to continue to run it, consider the time and energy the author put into writing and testing that software. Also consider how you would feel if you were not paid for your work.

Shareware is often less expensive than commercial software because it lacks fancy packaging, manuals, and a fully staffed technical support department. Some shareware, however, has become commercial, such as the compression software America Online uses for its Macintosh version, StuffIt. StuffIt was first written by a 15-year-old high school student. It's now published in shareware form, as StuffIt Lite, and as a more fully featured commercial product, StuffIt Deluxe (published by Aladdin Systems).

Freeware

This category covers a wide range of products. *Freeware* is available to you without cost, but the author retains all rights to the program, including how it is to be distributed. Freeware can include a fully functioning program or an update to an existing product. Don't attribute cost to value. You can often find many very useful programs in this category.

Public Domain Software

Public domain software can be used and distributed freely. The author has given up all rights to this program.

Uploading Files to AOL

America Online's computing forums have a special department labeled New Files and Free Uploading. This department allows you to upload software to America Online's software libraries without being charged.

Part
V

Ch
20

CAUTION

Demoware and shareware can contain restrictions on whether they can be uploaded by anyone other than the author, so read the instructions that come with the software before you decide to upload it to America Online. In general, commercial updates, such as system-related software from Apple Computer and Microsoft, may be uploaded to America Online only by the publisher.

Where to Upload

You must do a little research to find out where the appropriate place to upload the file is and to verify that you have the right to send a file. Each computing forum has an information file that tells you its purpose and the kind of software it requires. Rather than waste your time and the forum's by uploading to an inappropriate location, read the description files to be sure that you are uploading your software to the most suitable forum. A screen saver, for example, will likely go in an application or utilities forum.

Before uploading the file—especially if you are not the author—use America Online's File Search feature (described in the section "Using File Search," earlier in this chapter) to make sure that the file you want to send isn't already posted somewhere on America Online.

How to Upload

When you visit a computing software library (see Chapter 19), you'll see a button at the bottom of the software directory labeled Upload File. When you want to send your file, click the button, which opens the window shown in figure 20.10.

FIG. 20.10
Enter information about the file you're sending.

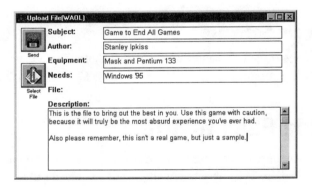

 TIP Before filling out the Upload File information window, review the descriptions of other software to become familiar with the way descriptions are written and the kind of information required.

The Upload File information window has several fields that you need to fill out. Enter the subject of the file, the author of the file, and the kind of equipment needed to use it. Next, give a brief description of the file you're sending. You can enter a list of suggested keywords so that others can locate the file easily.

When you upload the file, you'll see a File Transfer window that's very much like the one displayed when you download a file (refer to fig. 20.6). After the file is received, it is reviewed by forum staff who decide whether it's suitable for their forum. The file description you give may be edited.

Because many of the staff members who review these files are volunteers, expect several days to pass before you hear of the forum's decision. If posted, your file will turn up in their New Files and Free Uploading library.

N O T E In order to reduce download time and your online billing time, many of the files on America Online are compressed, a technique used to make a file smaller. The latest version of America Online's Macintosh and Windows software contains tools to expand compressed files in many formats, such as ZIP and StuffIt. Files saved in other formats are provided in self-extracting form, which means that executing the file (choosing Run under Windows or double-clicking a file icon on a Macintosh) will start the expansion process. Before you download a file, examine the file description carefully to see the form in which the file is provided. You can also find instructions in that description on how to run or install the file before you can use it. ■

TROUBLESHOOTING

The software I just downloaded won't run on my computer. What's wrong? Before you download a file, please check the file description carefully. Usually, the description will list the kind of computer the software will run on, along with the version of the operating system and any additional software you might need. You won't, for example, be able to run a Windows program on a Macintosh, unless you're using an add-on DOS expansion card or a program such as SoftWindows from Insignia Solutions. Although Mac and Windows programs may look and work very much the same, the programming requirements are quite different.

Whenever I try to run the software I downloaded, my computer freezes or I get a system error message. Why? It's the nature of personal computers to crash from time to time. Although the authors or publishers of software may rigorously test their products before release, there's always the possibility of a conflict with someone's setup at one time or another.

I'm lost. I can't get the software I downloaded to run, and there's no help text. What do I do next? If the publisher or author of the program cannot be contacted, you can try the Mac or PC Help Desk (keyword Help Desk). These forums are set up to help members who can't get online assistance anywhere else. The forums also provide a number of information texts that you can review to enable you to better deal with problems of this sort. Between these help resources, and the information in the forums that make the files available, you should be able to find quick advice to handle most problems.

continues

continued

If you encounter any difficulties using the software you download, consider the following:

- Read the documentation that comes with the program. In many cases, there's a trouble shooting section that may detail exactly the problem you're having and suggest a solution.

- If the problem cannot be solved by reading the documentation, contact the author or publisher of the software using the screen name, mailing address, or phone number shown in the documentation or online file description.

- If you cannot get help with the above options, contact the staff who runs the forum you downloaded the software from. Maybe they can help you get in touch with the author or publisher.

From Here...

You now have the basics on how to get software and other files from America Online, and how to post your own files, as well. For more information, see the following chapters:

- In Chapter 19, "Visiting the Computing and Software Forums," you get a picture of the huge range of computer-related resources available to you on America Online.

- For further assistance in using your America Online software, see Appendixes A, B, and C, which cover installation and use of America Online's Macintosh and Windows software.

The Best Macintosh Software on AOL

There are quite literally tens of thousands of software titles available on AOL. And you'll find nearly as many opinions as to which ones are best. So, in compiling this chapter, I went to the best online sources I could find. I asked those who run the computer and software forums to let us know about the most popular and useful software in their forums.

The software covered in this chapter generally falls into three categories: freeware (meaning that you don't pay for it), shareware (meaning that you pay for it if you like it), and public domain (meaning that you don't pay for it and the author retains no rights to it). You'll find more information about these types of software in Chapter 20, "Tips and Tricks on Finding Software."

N O T E   Because the locations of files may change, the easiest way to find them is to use AOL's
File Search feature. Simply enter the AOL keyword **File Search**, enter the name of the
file you want, and then click the List Matching Files button. You'll soon see a listing of files that
match your search string. Double-click the file name to get a description or click Download Now
or Download Later, as appropriate.   ▧

CAUTION

Before downloading any of the files described in this chapter, be sure to carefully read the file
descriptions about system and hardware requirements. Make certain that your computer can run the
software before you actually try to use it. If you have any questions about these files or other files that
you receive from these forums, contact the author or publisher of the software. If neither the author's
nor publisher's name or phone number is available, contact the forum from which you downloaded the
file for further assistance. And one more thing: for one reason or another, it's very possible some of the
titles shown in this book are no longer available (a newer version is out or the program has been
withdrawn from circulation).

Special Software Libraries

Keyword: **Software**

In addition to the software libraries run by the computing and software forums on AOL,
several specialty software libraries are available that contain files which cater to a special
interest or that have been extremely useful or popular. The quickest way to seek out these
sources is to go to the Macintosh Software Center (see fig. 21.1).

FIG. 21.1
The Macintosh Software
Center gets you a direct link
on thousands of software
titles.

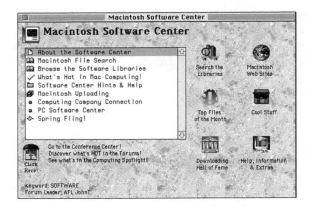

From the main Software Center window, you can access the software libraries of each forum. On the right side of the window are the search icon and icons for special libraries, which are described in the following sections.

Macintosh Top Downloads   The software included in the Monthly Top Files library (see fig. 21.2) represents the most popular titles from various computing forums. The titles displayed in the library window are based on the interest that the programs attract (such as member comments and the number of times they're downloaded) when they are posted in the forums; the library is upgraded monthly.

FIG. 21.2
The most popular Mac software downloads are available here.

Specialty Libraries   Each Mac computing forum has set up a special software library containing files that you ought to check when you visit those forums. The specialty libraries (see fig. 21.3) offer such selections as humorous text files, top Internet surfing tools, shareware fonts, QuickTime viewing and conversion software, arcade games, System-software enhancements, and other material that will find a useful place on your Mac's hard drive.

FIG. 21.3
AOL's specialty software libraries provide useful system enhancements and fun utilities.

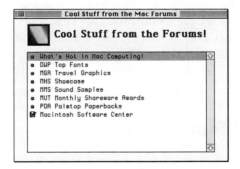

Part
V

Ch
21

Downloading Hall of Fame   Over the years, certain Macintosh files have become classics, either because they have stood the test of time as useful enhancements to the computing environment or because they are just plain fun to use. The Downloading Hall of Fame (see fig. 21.4) was originally established by several AOL forum people, including your humble author. Files are grouped in five convenient categories, ranging from low-cost shareware to fun-filled games.

FIG. 21.4
Some of AOL's most popular software gathered in an easy-to-access software library.

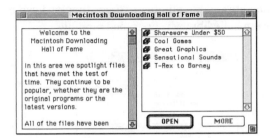

One More Thing   In case you have any questions about the special software libraries, check out Software Center Hints & Help in the Macintosh Software Center. Many questions about downloading and using this software are answered in that area.

AOL Forum Leaders' Software Recommendations

Having worked as a forum leader on AOL for several years, I can tell you that it's sometimes a complicated job. Sometimes you have to be somewhat of a traffic cop and at other times you have to be a moderator who directs the flow of online discussions. During the course of each week, AOL forum leaders receive hundreds of messages about the software available in their libraries. When I began to write this book, I asked my online colleagues to take a little time to compile lists of the software titles that they feel are most useful to AOL members and that best represent the offerings in their libraries.

Macintosh Business Forum

Keyword: **MBS**

Rick Doucette (AFL Rick) recommended the files that are covered in the following sections. Business users will want to check out their FileMaker Resource Center, which is a rich resource for help, general information, and useful FileMaker templates that you'll want to adapt to your own needs. And, because FileMaker is a cross-platform program, Windows users will find some meat and potatoes in this forum as well.

TimeTracker 2.8 *Author: Maui Software*

Do you work or charge by the hour? If so, you'll love TimeTracker (see fig. 21.5). TimeTracker is a simple, $25 time-tracking shareware application that records time tasks on the Macintosh. TimeTracker is useful for consultants, programmers, attorneys, printers, and anyone else who bills on the basis of time (or just wants a simple tool for keeping track of time).

FIG. 21.5
TimeTracker shows you how much time you spent on an important project.

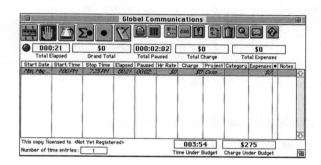

Some of TimeTracker's features include multiple time session capability, the capability to enlarge or minimize windows, categories and hourly rates, the ability to sort time entries, search time entries, and export time entries.

The program includes an extensive FileMaker Pro template for exported TimeTracker data. A free runtime version of FileMaker Pro for use with this template is also available separately.

You'll also find extensive time entry editing controls in one easy-to-use window; marked and unmarked time entries; start, stop, pause, resume, and restart time entries; record time in increments of 1, 6, 15, or 100ths of a minute, and much more.

Address Book 3.7.0p10 *Author: Jim Leitch*

Jim Leitch's Address Book was one of the very first shareware programs I discovered when I was first learning a Mac. It combines an interactive Rolodex, desktop dialing and logging utility, envelope and label printing program, and a lot more in a simple, integrated interface. Before you go out and look at one of the commercial programs, you might want to take this one for a spin and see how it fits your working style.

Daily Planner 3.0 *Author: Steve Murray*

This program works with Claris FileMaker Pro (which is required) to provide extensive power and flexibility for database development. The file structure of this Planner is designed to take advantage of FileMaker Pro's new relational capabilities.

Part
V

Ch
21

Here is a brief look at some of this shareware program's highlights:

- Daily Planner is based on a perpetual calendar, meaning that entries can be made for any date, past, present, or future. You need to update or reset the calendar for each year.
- Daily Planner offers daily, weekly, and monthly views. The daily screen layout is much like many of the popular desktop organizers, but easier to use.
- Daily Planner includes a calendar maker feature that can generate a monthly grid for any month in any year!
- Daily Planner offers a schedule of appointments, a "to do" list, and daily notes. You can make an unlimited number of entries in your daily schedule, and your appointments are sorted by time.

Mac Communications and Networking Forum

Keyword: **MCM**

Sarah Edwards (AFL Edwards) runs a forum devoted to a subject that is at the heart of the computing experience: telecommunications and networking. She has selected some of her forum's software favorites and, I must admit, they are some of mine as well (especially the first on the list).

FreePPP 2.5rf *Author: Steve Dagley*

FreePPP is the freeware successor to MacPPP, a control panel for dial-in PPP (Point to Point Protocol) network/Internet access. It is based on Merit's MacPPP 2.0.1, but adds several new features and fixes a variety of bugs. It is compatible with Apple's new Open Transport protocols.

The program has a clever installer called the Setup Monkey that makes a backup of your existing MacPPP, PPP, and TCP/IP preference files and software so that you can use them again if you decide that FreePPP isn't your cup of tea (something you are not likely to do, but it's nice to know the option is there).

In addition to an easy to use, scriptable setup application (see fig. 21.6), FreePPP includes a Control Strip module and a Control Panel that puts a handy access icon on your Mac's menu bar. It also has a database of popular modem setups, so you don't have to worry very much about configuring your new modem to work with this program.

FIG. 21.6
The FreePPP Setup program allows you to store separate connection profiles for each Internet service to which you connect.

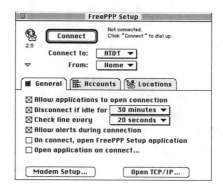

ZTerm 1.0.1   *Author: Dave Alverson*

If you want an easy-to-use, no-frills telecommunications program for general communications purposes, such as logging on to a user-group BBS, ZTerm (see fig. 21.7) will be your mainstay. The program performs most tasks well and has speedy file-transfer capabilities. The interface is relatively uncluttered and free of features that you probably don't need. In addition, the price is much less than similar commercial products because it's shareware. The author, Dave Alverson, continues to update the software.

FIG. 21.7
ZTerm simplifies the process of visiting your favorite BBS.

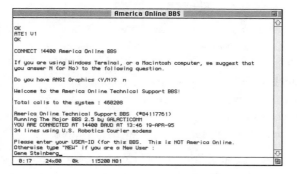

ZTerm also runs "native" (accelerated for PowerPC) on the Power Macintosh, and supports the most popular terminal emulation and file transfer techniques. You can also create simple macro routines to help you automatically log on to your favorite BBS.

Macintosh Desktop and Web Publishing Forum

Keyword: **MDP**

Courtesy of Michael Fischer (AFL MikeF), the following sections describe some files that appeal not only to desktop publishing professionals, but also to people who want to enhance their desktop publishing skills.

Part

V

Ch

21

MacTypingTutor 3.4.1   *Author: W. Rogers*

MacTypingTutor is a popular program designed to help improve your typing (see fig. 21.8). Because it's easy to operate, it lets you get started right away. Because it's modular, you can use only what you need (five separate work areas, each teaching different typing skills, each reinforcing the others). It's flexible, so you can add or delete your own typing materials. Because it's smart, you can work on your typing errors; it remembers words you mistype (or forgets them if you ask). The program also shows error reports, lets you set speed goals, and suggests, in a supportive way, when you should raise or lower goals. MacTypingTutor also keeps records so that you see progress over time.

FIG. 21.8
The shareware program TypingTutor displays a typewriter keyboard on your Mac as you work to improve your typing skills.

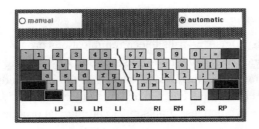

Fonts Manager™ 3.5   *Author: Ed Hopkins*

If you're involved in a lot of document creation work, for desktop or Web publishing, no doubt you have many fonts around that are cluttering up your System Folder. Fonts Manager™ 3.5 is functionally similar to the System 7.5.x Extensions Manager, but it is NOT a control panel and it is not a system extension; hence, it doesn't patch the Mac operating system in any way (which is where you find possible extension-related conflicts). It is more like a Desk Accessory. It lets you enable and disable font suitcases in sets. It supports balloon help and has its own handy help system.

Unlike the commercial utilities that perform the same function, such as Suitcase™ and Master Juggler™, it works on all Macs with System 7.1 or later, including 7.5.3, without modifying the normal startup and operation of your computer. The program is shareware and it's updated often, so you can expect a later version with more features will be available when you check out AOL's software libraries.

DOCMaker 4.6.1   *Author: Mark Wall, Green Mountain Software*

Have you ever wanted to send a letter to someone on a disk, but you weren't sure what word processor the other person had? Do you want to put your own documentation on a disk for other people to read and print without worrying about word processor compatibility? Well, now you have DOCMaker.

DOCMaker is a Macintosh application that creates stand-alone, self-running document files, which means the person you send the document to can open it fully formatted, without having to have the program that created it. The program features scrollable and sizable windows, graphics, varied text styles and fonts, and full printing capability. The stand-alone files are self-executing applications (just double-click the file) that you may distribute to other people to read and print. No other application is required. DOCMaker enables you to distribute documents and information widely with no knowledge of the end users' Mac configurations or software. The current version also supports a number of the latest Apple technologies, such as QuickTime.

Macintosh Graphics Forum

Keyword: **MGR**

The Macintosh Graphics Forum contains thousands of graphics images, ranging from photos to clip art. The variety is extensive, and the libraries are worth exploring. The forum's libraries also contain many other useful files. Forum leader David Stovall (AFL MacArt) listed some items that you'll want to examine.

GIFConverter   *Author: Kevin Mitchell*

The most-requested file in the Mac Graphics Forum is GIFConverter. This program allows members to view the thousands of GIF, TIFF, PICT, JPEG, Startupscreen, and MacPaint pictures uploaded to America Online. More important, the program allows members to convert file formats from one type to another. The most popular conversion is to the Startupscreen file format.

Miscellaneous Files   The following items don't represent specific files for you to download, but they cover a body of work by two very talented Macintosh artists. (You'll learn more about them when you visit the Mac Graphics Forum.)

David Palermo was one of the earliest uploaders of original art to America Online. His first works were surrealistic photo-montage retouched images, usually of beautiful women in extraterrestrial settings; his recent works include fantastic landscape images created in HSC Software's image creation product KPT Bryce. Palermo claims not to be an artist in the traditional sense, but he has proven to be an original artist in the mastery of computer imaging.

Kai Krause came on America Online with a serious Germanic tutorial attitude. The staff of the Mac Graphics forum set him up with a "serious" topic folder to offer hints and tips for Photoshop users. Within a matter of weeks, he underwent a metamorphosis, becoming one of the friendliest dispensers of tips that the online community had ever witnessed.

Part
V

Ch
21

Krause's tips were so good, and demand for them was so high, that he formalized them in a series of files called Kai's Power Tips (KPTs, for short) in a special library. The rest is history. Eventually, his work evolved into a commercial product called Kai's Power Tools (HSC Software).

Macintosh Hardware Forum

Keyword: **MHW**

Chris Ferino (AFL Ferino) listed some useful files that will be of interest to almost anyone who uses a Macintosh computer. The files also can help PC users who want to learn about the other computing platform.

MacHistory   *Author: Harry Phillipo*

MacHistory (see fig. 21.9) presents a chronological history of all Macintosh models released from the Mac's inception. The program lists useful information (such as a model's release and discontinuance date, memory capacity, processor, and speed) neatly and efficiently. If you're looking for a one-stop history of the Macintosh, this program is it.

FIG. 21.9
Learn the history of your favorite Macintosh computer with MacHistory.

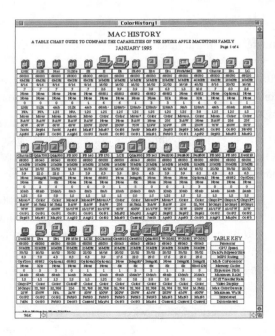

TidBITS   *Editors: Adam and Tonya Engst*

You can find the latest version of this online periodical, by book author and Internet guru Adam Engst, in Mac Hardware's New Files library. From hardware to software and the latest goings-on at Apple, Engst and his colleagues keep you in the know. Back issues are available in a special *TidBITS* library. I should mention that Engst and his wife, Tonya, are the authors of the popular *Internet Starter Kit* books from Hayden.

The Information Alley   *Publisher: Apple Computer, Inc.*

The Mac Hardware Forum also carries *The Information Alley*, a regular publication of Apple Computer's support department in Austin, Texas. Available in stand-alone (self-running), text, Adobe Acrobat, and Common Ground formats so that any user can read it, the publication offers a wealth of information culled from Apple. The publication includes tips about dealing with common Mac software problems and detailed descriptions of all the oddly labeled files that you find in your System Folder after you install the latest Macintosh operating system.

Macintosh Help Desk

Keyword: **Help Desk**

When new Mac AOL members need a helping hand, Andrew Polk (AFL Andy) and the crew at the Mac Help desk are there to provide assistance. Here's some of the interesting files you'll find in that forum.

I Laughed So Hard I Cried   This collection of funny, friendly text files is the work of Sandy Brockmann, who gathered the funniest files that friends have sent her over the years and put them together for you to enjoy.

Beginnings Utilities and Texts   This is not so much a single file as a collection of files. You'll find text and programs that allow you to become more accomplished on your Mac. You'll find information on how to use specific software, such as Adobe Photoshop. You'll also find a number of files containing tips and tricks about getting the most out of your Mac. And even experienced travelers in personal computing are apt to find some interesting advice there.

Beginner's Sounds   This library is a collection of fun sounds for you to use on AOL. Hear AFL Andy's car start, and enjoy dozens of other sound effects that you can play in chat rooms or whenever you have a few minutes to spare for a little fun on your Mac.

Location! Location!   This is a collection of handy information texts that describe some of the most popular spots on AOL and the Internet. You'll learn a little about the area itself, plus see simple instructions on how to get there.

Part
V

Ch
21

Macintosh HyperCard and Scripting Forum

Keyword: **HyperCard**

The following material is courtesy of forum leader Peter Baum (AFL Hypcrd).

MHC HyperCard Player 2.35   *Authors: MHC Forum Staff*

Need a HyperCard Player? We've got you covered! The America Online Macintosh HyperCard Forum has created a custom version of the HyperCard Player, which is compatible with the latest version of HyperCard (v2.3.5). You can use the MHC Player to run any of the 10,000+ stacks available on AOL. Even if you have a previous version of Apple's Player, you will want to upgrade to ours because it not only runs the latest stacks but also contains several features which Apple's Player doesn't.

This program comes in three flavors: Power Macintosh native, "fat" (which works on both PowerMacs and regular 680x0 Macs), and in 680x0 form.

Here are some MHC Player features:

- Opens and runs any stack created with HyperCard 2.3.5 or earlier.
- Lists your favorite stacks for easy, one-click access. The list is fully editable.
- Prints out an entire stack.
- Prints out the contents of any individual field.
- Uses built-in HyperCard virus protection and self-check virus scanning to prevent the spread of all HyperCard viruses known to date.

Subj: SpeakEasy

Author: Bill Westfield

A growing number of people are eagerly using the latest tools to create WWW pages. SpeakEasy is the first HTML editor that allows you to literally "speak a Web page into existence." It also has a complete palette toolbox for those who have Macs without speech recognition capabilities. It is savvy to most WWW specs and many Netscape enhancements, and is (according to its author) quite possibly the fastest HTML editor in the world.

SpeakEasy is a demo program that will expire 15 days after it is first used. The program comes with documentation and information about ordering the full-featured version of the program.

URL Gleaner 1.2   *Author: Peter M. Brigham*

Need a way to extract and store URLs? Here it is! URL Gleaner allows you to extract URLs from any Web page saved "as HTML" and then archive them in an easily searchable index that can be used as an extension of your home page. A mouse click puts any saved URL on the Clipboard so that it can be pasted into an "open location…" dialog box. This version comes with over 200 Web sites already listed, but you can edit the list and add your own favorite sites.

By the way, the program is freeware, meaning you don't have to pay for it if you decide you want to continue to use it.

Macintosh Games Forum

Keyword: **MGM**

 Because game software is likely to be large, be sure to check the file size before downloading the file. Also, for the fastest possible download speed, log on to AOL during off-peak hours (not during evening prime time, when heavy network traffic is likely to slow performance somewhat).

According to Mac Games forum leader, Rod K. Whitten (AFL Rod), the Mac Games Forum Assistants, AFA Alice and AFA Daniel, have assembled a large collection of Macintosh Games, which are organized by game type, in their libraries for your downloading pleasure. These are a small sample of the files that are available.

Barracks 1.0   *Author: Ambrosia Software & Greg Lovette*

The latest shareware game from Ambrosia is a balance between strategy and Arcade. Hard to describe, easy to learn to play, impossible to master and extremely addictive, Barracks will provide hours of playing pleasure. Simply dividing a playing field to capture moving balls into their own area is the premise behind the game, but it does have a few complications, like Bosco, the land shark.

Catacombs 2.0   *Author: Glenn Seemann*

Catacombs is a top down view roleplaying/arcade game similar to the classic arcade game, Gauntlet. The object in Catacombs is to guide one of four available characters through a multi-level dungeon. The dungeon is full of nasty monsters, treasures, potions, magical scrolls, keys, and food. You can also build your own dungeons with Dungeon Builder.

Part

V

Ch

21

Dirt Bike 3.1   *Author: Brad Quick*

Dirt Bike is a sidescrolling motorcycle racing Sports simulation game. You set up your bike and race against up to five opponents. You can design your own bikes or tracks, or download those made by others. You'll have hours of fun with the jumps and straightaway action of this game.

Wolfenstein 3D 1.01   *Author: MacPlay*

The shareware version of the commercial game Wolfenstein 3D (see fig. 21.10) is an exciting 3-D action/adventure game that will play on most all color Macs. When you play Wolfenstein 3D, you can escape from your prison cell, battle your way through seemingly never-ending rooms, corridors and increasingly stronger Nazi opponents, collecting treasure, food, ammunition, and better weapons in the process. There are more than 1,000 scenario files you can download from the Wolf 3D libraries or you can design your own with WolfEdit (a companion program that lets you customize the game). Either way, you'll never run out of opponents. Besides Wolf add-ons, the library has whole sections for other 3D Arcade/Adventure games like Marathon, Dark Forces, or Doom II.

FIG. 21.10
Enjoy excitement and adventure when you play Wolfenstein 3D.

Macintosh Desktop Video and Multimedia Forum

Keyword: **Mac Video**

Because I'm the forum leader, I asked a member of my staff, Rob Sonner (AFA Rob), who manages the Macintosh multimedia software libraries, to provide a list of some of his favorites.

QuickMooV 1.5.3 *Author: Paul C.H. Ho and Pink Elephant Technologies*

QuickMooV is a MIDI-aware QuickTime movie editor and player that allows you to do the following things:

- Rearrange MIDI instruments in a QuickTime movie
- Load files into RAM for maximum speed
- Play movies at double speed or in slow motion
- Play movies at maximum, double, or half-screen size
- Turn off the video, text, sound, or MIDI track

QT <-> AVI Conversion Tools

QT <-> AVI Conversion Tools is a set of instructions and utilities for translating QuickTime movie files to and from the Windows video format.

The file includes the following features:

- A QuickTime-to-AVI conversion program
- A utility for moving AVI files to the Macintosh
- Windows Compressors System extension, which contains compressors and decompressors (CODECs) for Microsoft RLE, Microsoft Video 1, and Microsoft Full Frame formats

Sparkle 2.3.1 MPEG Viewer *Author: Maynard Handley*

Sparkle is an easy-to-use program that plays MPEG and QuickTime movies, and also converts files between these formats. The program is MultiFinder-friendly and, with enough memory, can open multiple documents at the same time.

The Sparkle file also includes the following programs:

- MPEGSplit, for running MUXed MPEG movies in conjunction with MAPlay
- MPEG2 Decoder, for viewing MPEG2 movies (which Sparkle doesn't yet support)

Part
V

Ch
21

Macintosh Music & Sound Forum

Keyword: **MMS**

Here are some of the most popular files from that Keith Jablonski (AFL Keith) and his staff have assembled in their AOL forum.

SoundMaster   *Author: Bruce Tomlin*

SoundMaster (see fig. 21.11) is a Mac classic, and it is updated regularly as Apple releases new hardware and operating systems. SoundMaster is a control panel that allows your computer to make all sorts of interesting sounds whenever it starts, restarts, or shuts down, when a disk is inserted or ejected, when a bad disk is inserted, when a key is pressed; when the Trash is emptied, and much more.

FIG. 21.11
SoundMaster can have your Mac give off sounds when various functions occur, such as ejecting a disk or emptying the trash.

CD Grab Audio   *Author: Theo Vosse*

This program is an easy way to grab audio CD tracks (or portions of tracks) and save them as sound files. Pull the clips into your favorite sound-utility program, and edit to your heart's content. Remember to observe the copyright laws, however.

Sound-Trecker   *Author: Frank Seide*

This program is perhaps the most popular Macintosh MOD player available today. The program allows you to play almost any MOD file that you can find online.

MOD files are a combination of MIDI files and SND files. These files are small, but can play fully orchestrated music for hours. Check out the online MOD libraries as well.

Macintosh Operating Systems Forum

Keyword: **MOS**

The Mac OS forum leader, John Stroud (AFL Bear), says that the most popular files in his forum are the Apple software updates, which cover everything from enhancements to the

Mac operating system to new versions of QuickDraw GX. Because these files are updated frequently (and a listing here may be outdated by the time that you read this book), I devote the following sections to classic files from this forum.

ShrinkWrap   *Author: Chad Magendanz*

ShrinkWrap is a freeware utility made to manage disk images on the Macintosh (Apple generally offers its software updates as disk image form). The program incorporates the functionality of DiskCopy and MountImage in one easy-to-use application, adding on-the-fly compression and decompression with the Stuff It engine, implementing drag-and-drop and AppleScript support, and supporting almost all known image-file formats.

Simply stated, ShrinkWrap mounts disk-image files on your Mac's desktop, allowing you to install software without making floppy-disk copies of those images. The utility is a real time-saver.

MacErrors 1.2.1   *Author: Marty Wachter*

MacErrors (see fig. 21.12) is a small application that shows the result code and description for all the Macintosh System errors (Type 1, Type 11, and so on). The author of this program got tired of looking up the definitions of system errors in a DA consisting of a scrolling list or found in a book, so he wrote the program.

To use MacErrors, launch the application, type a valid error ID, and press Return. The program displays the result code and description. If you enter an invalid ID, MacErrors beeps.

FIG. 21.12
What do those weird system errors mean? MacErrors shows you.

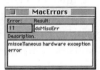

Disk Charmer 2.3   *Author: Fabrizio Oddone*

Disk Charmer is a neat utility that enables you to initialize (or verify) floppy disks conveniently; and if Thread Manager (System 7.5 or later) is installed, Disk Charmer does its floppy formatting chores in the background. You don't have to wait while you are formatting a floppy; you can go back to work while the formatting process is taking place. Help balloons are everywhere.

Part
V

Ch
21

Macintosh Utilities Forum

Keyword: **MUT**

Utilities is a catch-all word that covers a wide selection of software. Forum leader Floyd Zink (AFL Floyd) assembled a representative sample.

Disinfectant 3.6   *Author: John Norstad*

As this book was written, Disinfectant 3.6 was the latest version of the popular freeware virus detection utility. The program offers the best in no-frills virus protection. You can use the application itself to check your Mac for the presence of computer viruses whenever you want, or you can install the handy protection extension, which will monitor your Mac behind the scenes for the presence of viruses. If you try to launch an infected file, the Disinfectant extension will warn you by playing a sound, and then will prevent the file from launching.

Disinfectant checks itself every time you run the program to see if it has been modified, damaged, or infected by a virus. This self-check has been enhanced in version 3.6 to permit changes to the memory partition size and icon information.

StuffIt Expander 4.0.1   *Author: Aladdin Systems, Inc.*

StuffIt Expander 4.0.1 is the latest version of Aladdin's award-winning freeware product. The program can be used to expand StuffIt, Compact Pro, BinHex, MacBinary files, and more.

StuffIt Expander is designed to be the simplest, most efficient way to expand compressed files and encoded files that you may have received from the Internet, an online information service, bulletin board system, over a network, or from a co-worker. Stuff It Expander handles the four most common compression and encoding formats, which are Stuff It and Compact Pro archives (.sit, .sea, and .cpt), BinHex (.hqx), and MacBinary (.bin). Using Stuff It Expander will let you access the millions of compressed and encoded files you will find on the Internet and online services, or even those sent to you by a friend.

It should come as no surprise that both Apple's Cyberdog and Netscape use StuffIt Expander as a helper application to translate files you've retrieved from FTP sites and the World Wide Web.

TechTool 1.0.9   *Author: MicroMat Computer Systems*

TechTool is the acclaimed utility that solves those incurable problems which elude other utilities. With TechTool you can do the following:

- Analyze your system file for damage.
- Zap the entire PRAM chip (even more thoroughly than Apple's Command-Option-P-R shortcut to zap the PRAM).

- Delete the desktop files—the better alternative to desktop rebuilding.
- View, print, and save a multitude of information about your Mac.

TechTool has always been a useful arsenal in my PowerBook's "utility kit." I take it with me when I have to troubleshoot problems while visiting clients and friends, so it gets my personal recommendation, too.

Aaron 1.3.2 *Authors: Edward Voas/Gregory Landweber*

Aaron 1.3.2 is the latest version of a shareware program that provides a Copland look for system 7.5. You'll see a very accurate depiction of what the default theme of the next major release of the Apple operating system, Mac OS 8 (or Copland), is going to look like (see fig. 21.13). Just drop Aaron in your extensions folder and restart for a mind-blowing and very fresh, new look on your system.

FIG. 21.13
Here's a preview of the look of the next version of the Mac Operating system, courtesy of Aaron.

Here are a few of the changes you'll see after you install this program:

- Windows, alerts, dialogs. Windows have a window-shade icon for one-click shading.
- Standard push buttons, check boxes, and radio buttons are modified.
- Menus and the menu bar get a new look.
- Substitutes Espi Sans Bold 10 for Chicago 12 as the system font.
- The menu bar and menus get a light gray background, and selected items are highlighted in the window color specified in the "Color" control panel. In addition, the menu bar and menus use light and dark tinges for a subtle 3-D effect.
- Spinning zoom rectangles are added to the Finder.

From Here...

The programs described in this chapter can make your Mac computing experience more fun, more efficient, and more productive. You can choose among tens of thousands of additional files from America Online's Mac computing and software libraries, which are among the largest available from any online resource.

Part
V

Ch
21

For more information on finding and using this software, read the following chapters:

- Chapter 3, "Getting the Most from AOL's Macintosh Software," where you discover some handy utility software that will make your software do more for you.

- Chapter 20, "Tips and Tricks on Finding Software," where you'll put AOL's handy File Search feature through its paces.

- If you sometimes must cross computing platforms, read Chapter 22, "The Best Windows Software on AOL."

The Best Windows Software on AOL

This chapter covers software for three PC operating systems: DOS, OS/2, and Windows (both 3.1 and Windows 95). America Online offers one of the largest software libraries in the world, with tens of thousands of titles to choose from. To compile this chapter, I went to the best sources that I could find online: the leaders and staff members of the computing and software forums.

Like the software described in the preceding chapter, the files described in this chapter fit into the three standard software categories: freeware (you don't pay for it), shareware (you pay for it if you like it), and public domain (you don't pay for it and the author retains no rights to it). You'll find more information about these types of software in Chapter 20, "Tips and Tricks on Finding Software."

The forum leaders who helped me compile this chapter offer a great deal of useful computing information in their forums. This information will help you solve problems with your PC, as well as make your computing experience more fun and more productive. ■

The best from AOL's software libraries

You discover some of the most popular Windows and Windows 95 programs available on America Online.

AOL is not just for Windows users

You learn about some of the most popular DOS and OS/2 programs on America Online.

More online help resources

You learn where to go for help if you have problems with the software that you've downloaded.

N O T E   Because the locations of files may change, the easiest way to find them is to use AOL's File Search feature. Simply enter the AOL keyword **File Search,** click the Go button, and then enter the name of the file you want in the File Search screen that will then appear. Soon, you'll see a listing of available files that match your request. Double-click the file name to get a description or click Download Now or Download Later, as appropriate. ▪

CAUTION

Before downloading any of the files described in this chapter, be sure to check the file descriptions for information about updated versions, system requirements, and hardware requirements. Make certain that your computer can run the software before you actually try to use it. If you have any questions about these files or other files that you receive from these forums, contact the author or publisher of the software. If neither the author's nor publisher's name or phone number is available, contact the forum from which you downloaded the file for further assistance.

Special Software Libraries

Keyword: **Software**

In addition to the software libraries run by the computing and software forums on AOL, several special software libraries are available, containing software that has been extremely useful or popular, or that caters to a special interest. The quickest way to seek out these sources is to go to the PC Software Center (see fig. 22.1).

The Software Center enables you to access the software libraries of the PC computing forums by clicking the Forum Libraries icon in the lower-right corner of the forum's main screen. The forum's list box contains the entry Best of Computing & Software, which is updated regularly to offer the finest software from the various PC forums. The most popular files are listed in Top Software Downloads. The following sections cover additional software libraries that you can access simply by clicking the appropriate listing in the forum's list box.

Library of the Month

Each month, one software library gets special attention, either because of its importance to your PC computing experience or because its files provide enjoyment. The library shown in figure 22.2, run by the PC Multimedia forum, contains popular multimedia-related software and information files.

FIG. 22.1
Access thousands of files
directly from the PC Software
Center.

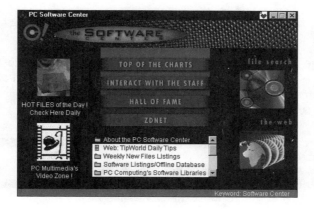

FIG. 22.2
Each month, a software
library gets special attention
in the PC Software Center.

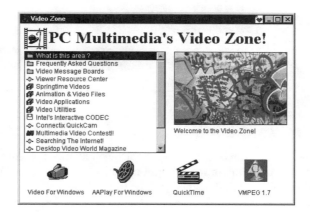

Weekly New Files

When I first log on to AOL, one of the first places that I visit is the list of new files (I've
always been a utility software junkie). The Weekly New Files Listings (see fig. 22.3), compiled by all the forum leaders in the PC computing and software area, focuses on the newest software. You will generally find this compilation in the list box or in the file database.

FIG. 22.3
Lists of the newest comput-
ing and software files on
AOL.

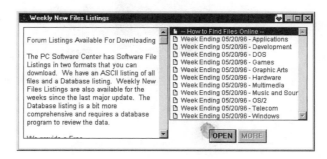

Downloading Hall of Fame

Keyword: **HOF**

Over the years, certain files have become classics, either because they have stood the test of time as useful enhancements to the computing environment or because they are just plain fun to use. The Downloading Hall of Fame (see fig. 22.4) is updated from time to time; it covers many areas of PC computing.

FIG. 22.4
Access your favorite software online from the Downloading Hall of Fame.

Additional Software Libraries

From time to time, the Software Center also will feature one software library or another for a special promotion, or to highlight a feature in a particular forum (see fig. 22.5). The library shown here was designed just for the arrival of spring, part of a regular seasonal emphasis.

FIG. 22.5
Additional specialty libraries are available from the PC Software Center on AOL.

Because the Software Center is meant to emphasize other libraries, I have not described special files, but I'll make an exception for the library discussed in the following section. The information was provided by Thomas Quindry (PC Tom).

SCAN

Author: John McAfee

SCAN is a highly flexible program that you can use to check your computer for viruses—those nasty bits of code that can wreak havoc with your software and hard drive. The program only detects viruses; to rid yourself of the viruses, you also need a program such as John McAfee's CLEAN.

McAfee's programs don't have all the features of commercial programs, such as Norton's Anti-Virus (NAV) and Central Point Anti-Virus (CPAV), but McAfee offers fast customer support by providing updated versions when new viruses are found. His newest generation of SCAN programs includes the functions of CLEAN. Both programs are available online in the PC Computing and Software libraries.

When you choose virus-protection software, your main consideration should be availability of updates as new viruses are discovered. Each of the popular virus programs provides checking for known viruses, but the best way to guard your PC is to check the AOL software libraries for updates of these programs.

AOL Forum Leaders' Software Recommendations

I won't even try to define the job of a forum leader in a single paragraph. Basically, these people generally work online as a hobby; they work full time in other fields (and quite often as professionals in the computer industry). Being a forum leader involves answering hundreds of messages each week, as well as directing the activities of a half dozen or more online staffers in message boards and software libraries. In compiling this chapter, I asked these very busy people to take a little time to compile lists of the software titles that they feel are most useful to AOL members and that best represent the offerings in their libraries.

DOS Forum

Keyword: **DOS**

Here's a list of some of the most popular and productive DOS software available on AOL. As with other online areas, you'll want to use these offerings simply as a guide to further exploration and downloading.

SHEZ 10.6 Compression Companion *Author: Jim Derr*

The latest version of this program offers the capability to configure menu hot-key colors. In 4DOS/NDOS, the capability to copy, move, and delete tagged files has been greatly improved. Menu hot keys now begin with alphabetic characters, and the program offers better capability to recognize self-extracting files.

SHEZ is a premiere full-featured compression shell for managing compressed files. The program supports the ZIP, LHA, ZOO, ARC, ARJ, SQZ, PAK, UC2, and HAP file formats.

HYPER 4.70 HyperWare SpeedKit *Author: HyperWare*

HyperDisk SpeedKit version 4.70 contains the shareware versions of the world-famous HyperDisk, HyperKey, and HyperScreen utilities. Two new utilities are included: HyperRAM (for CPU speedup) and IDE Booster (for increased performance on IDE hard drives). The package includes a new Windows control panel for monitoring cache setup and performance from within Windows.

DISKQWIK: 1.1 Speedup IDE Drive

DiskQwik is a block device driver for newer IDE hard drives that activates these drives' little-known multiple-sector block transfer mode. Many newer IDE drives have this built-in capability, which increases their data-transfer rates significantly. Typically, the transfer rate can be increased by up to 45 percent over the rate offered by the motherboard BIOS. Some of the newest motherboards and high-end host adapters are beginning to offer this special mode, but this great feature of IDE drives has essentially remained untapped until now, thanks to software such as DiskQwik.

This shareware release of DiskQwik is designed to help you determine whether your IDE drive supports multiple-sector block Transfer Mode. Although a large percentage of IDE drives can use this mode, some cannot; therefore, shareware provides a perfect opportunity for a try-before-you-buy evaluation of DiskQwik.

OS/2 Forum

Keyword: **OS2**

The following sections cover a selection of useful OS/2 files provided by the forum staff. You'll also want to check Chapter 4, "Getting the Most from AOL's Windows Software," where I will describe a reliable technique for using AOL's Windows software with OS/2.

INFOZIP Zip and UnZip *Author: Info-ZIP Project*

The INFOZIP Zip and UnZip utilities are must-haves for OS/2 users. These utilities are freely distributed and are available in OS/2 archives around the world, as well as in the OS/2 Forum. UnZip can decompress PKZIP archives as well as Zip archives. INFOZIP supports long file names and extended attributes. These utilities are the OS/2 counterparts of the PKWare PK utilities for DOS.

Stupid OS/2 Tricks   *Author: Melissa Woo*

This is another popular and fun archive for OS/2 users, providing hundreds of tips for using OS/2 and tricks that you can do with OS/2. The tricks included cover features of OS/2 that people often ask about, as well as short REXX scripts that do interesting things. Categories include System, Desktop, Presentation Manager, Command Line, Win-OS/2, and Warp. And did you ever wonder how to get to the "Easter egg" in OS/2? You'll learn about it when you read these tips. The tips shown in figure 22.6 and figure 22.7 show you how to create an application bar and how to manage your desktop icons.

FIG. 22.6

How to create an application bar in OS/2.

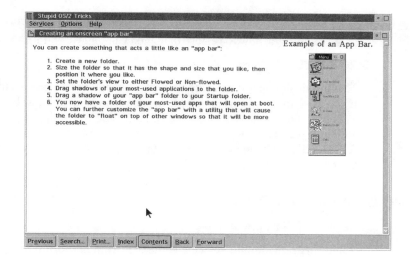

FIG. 22.7

Ideas on managing your desktop icons in OS/2.

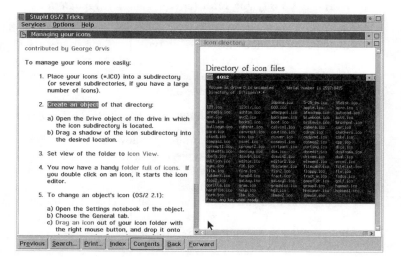

Config.sys Analysis   *Author: Rick Meigs*

This is another must-have collection. If you have ever wondered what everything in the OS/2 Config.sys file is for, this text archive provides a good description of each setting, enabling you to get the most out of OS/2. The archive contains information, tips, warnings, and optimization data.

In addition to explaining the lines and associated parameters of Config.sys, the author includes tips for improving performance, fine-tuning features, and minimizing memory requirements in smaller systems. Topics covered include the following:

- Config.sys described line by line, Netware drivers, Obscure settings, etc.
- Config.sys, how to restore damaged Config.sys, and REXX support from Config.sys.

ROBOSAVE   *Authors: R.R. Kurtz and J.G. Knauth (IBM)*

This is a desktop archive utility that goes beyond the archive feature built into OS/2 Warp. If you need to archive from one file system type to another, Robosave can do it for you. This tool allows you to back up the OS/2 (2.x or Warp) desktop quickly and easily. In addition, you can save a limited number of user-specified files, such as CONFIG.SYS, AUTOEXEC.BAT, and the INI files. If problems occur later, you can restore the saved information to recover these files.

PC Applications Forum

Keyword: **PC Applications**

Robin Bush (PC Robin) selected some files from her forum that you won't want to miss.

FASTYPE: V5.0 Typing Tutor for Win   *Author: Trendtech Corporation (William Letendre)*

FasType (see fig. 22.8) is for computer users who want to become more productive with their PC by learning how to touch type. FasType shows a 3D keyboard image and uses animation plus TrueType fonts to prompt the typist to type correct keys. The author has been a member of the Association of Shareware Professionals since 1987. DOS versions of the program are also available online.

TCHAOS: V4.07a Time & Chaos   *Author: iSBiSTER International, Inc.*

This is iSBiSTER's award-winning Windows shareware PIM. Time & Chaos brings order to the three most common types of time-dependent information: things you need to do (to-do's); appointments you need to keep; and contacts you want to make on a regular basis. On a single screen, you can see at a glance what you need to do today, who you will be seeing, and who you might want to call or write. The program is fully networkable. Powerful features include categories, search, standard, and custom reports. It is available in both regular and Windows 95/NT versions.

FIG. 22.8
FasType helps you get your
keyboarding speed up to par.

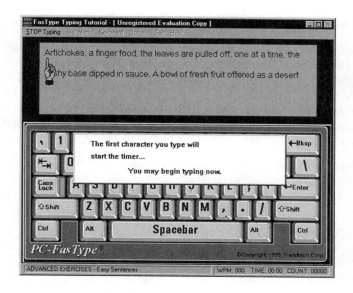

HOTDOGPRO: HTML Authoring *Author: Sausage Software*

HotDogPro is an HTML editor for Windows. It helps you create HTML documents that
are used to make home pages for the World Wide Web. HotDog provides quick access to
tags, attributes, and dialogs to help you create complex elements. This program provides
excellent documentation for those who are new to HTML. A standard version is also available online.

IVIEW: V1.07g Offline HTML Browser *Author: Frank Wu*

I-View allows you to view HTML files offline. You can view an HTML file that you are
creating or one that you copied from the Web without the necessity of being online. You
can also do some editing of an HTML file. No WINSOCK.DLL is required to view your
HTML file with this program.

VCDP: V2.0 Computer Dictionary *Author: BlueStar Software*

The Visual Computer Dictionary Plus 2.0 program was designed to portray computer
definitions in a graphic, attractive, and comprehensive way. This program will appeal to
anybody who owns a computer and would like to be informed about computer definitions,
computer-related terms, DOS commands, symbols, and acronyms. Developed for IBM PC
and compatible personal computers, Visual Computer Dictionary Plus runs in a DOS
environment. This product defines terms on a wide variety of topics with more than 1,100
definitions.

PSP: V3.11 Paint Shop Pro   *Author: JASC, Inc*

Paint Shop Pro is a shareware program that may be the only photo retouching, painting, image format conversion, and screen capturing program you will need. Formats supported by the program include: BMP, CDR, CGM, CLP, CUT, DIB, DRW, DXF, EPS, GEM, GIF, HPGL, IFF, IMG, JIF, JPG, LBM, MAC, MSP, PCD, PCX, PIC, PBM, PGM, PNG, PPM, PSD, RAW, RAS, RLE, TIFF, TGA, WMF, WPG. The version of the program shipping when this book was being written also supported transparent backgrounds in GIF images.

Additional features include painting, photo retouching, image enhancement and editing, color enhancement, image browser, batch conversion, and support for TWAIN compliant scanners. A 32-bit version for Windows 95/NT is also available online.

PC Developer's Forum

Keyword: **PC Development**

Whether you are new to DOS and Windows programming or experienced at the craft, you'll be interested in the following PC developer's utilities as compiled by the forum's expert staff.

YAKICONS Game Developers Library   Yakicons is a shareware graphics library that encompasses many aspects of game design and mechanics. The library, which provides a series of object-oriented modules for Borland C++ version 3.1, covers mouse and joystick support, sampled sound, fast icon drawing, restorable screen areas, editable fonts, tiled maps, and other topics. Although written with Borland C++, this graphics library is useful for all compiler vendors.

START Beginner's Guide to C and C++   If you are interested in moving from one programming language to C/C++ or in learning C/C++ as your first language, this useful guide is written to help you.

Start C/C++ is an introduction to C/C++ for people who are interested in programming as a hobby or as a career. The guide contains information on what you need to write software and where to get it; it also provides answers to questions that beginners do not always ask when trying to learn the ropes about programming. The file explains the difference between C and C++ and the differences among the various compilers. The file includes a list of books and other tools for learning C/C++ at home.

WIDGET Windows Animation Library   The Widget Works is a simple graphic-object library. The philosophy of the Widget library is to provide a means of creating simple animation under Windows with little fuss. This humble library doesn't try to do everything, but what it does, it does simply and well. If your animation ambitions don't extend to putting the Hollywood special-effects studios out of business, this library is for you.

PC Games Forum

Keyword: **PC Games**

This forum gives you a choice of hundreds of files. To help you get started, Debbie Rogers (PC Sylva) selected the most popular game files for you to download at your leisure.

Epic Pinball   *Author: Epic MegaGames*

Epic Pinball captures the look and feel of true pinball machines. The graphics are so good that you'll feel as though you're looking at the real thing. Watch the screen scroll as it keeps pace with the ball moving through the machine. Sound card users will want to play the game just to listen to it.

The Android board is included, but many more are available when you register with Epic MegaGames. The program requires a 386 or better, VGA graphics; SoundBlaster or Gravis UltraSound card supported.

DOOM   *Author: id Software*

This is the shareware version of this popular program. Things have gone terribly wrong on a remote military outpost in space; fiendish monsters straight from the depths have taken it over. Your co-workers have been killed or turned into zombie-like creatures, each eagerly trying to help finish you off. Use a variety of weapons to meet the challenge and survive the levels. VGA graphics and stereo sound highlight this action-packed thriller. This program contains graphic violence. System requirements: 486/33 recommended, 4M of RAM.

Descent   *Author: Parallax Software & Interplay Productions*

This is the shareware version of a popular program—a futuristic underground adventure. Your mission is to enter the mines and destroy the mining robots that have suddenly embarked on revolt. Using a mining ship equipped with lasers and rockets, you descend to face the robots head-on. Blast your way through the tunnels, encountering deadlier, stronger robots as you go. Enjoy high-quality VGA graphics and stereo sound. System requirements: 486/33, 4M of RAM required; 486/66, 8M of RAM or better, recommended.

PC Graphics and Animation Forum

Keyword: **PC Graphics**

The following recommendations come from Mike Wiseman (PC Mike); they represent some of the favorite files from his multifaceted online forum.

POV Trace   *Authors: Various*

This is a suite of files and utilities used to create photo-realistic images without a camera or scanner. Whatever you can imagine, you can create with practice and a bit of effort.

Files and support for this program are directly available via keyword **POV** or in the resource centers in the PC Graphics & Animation Forum.

VUEPRINT *Author: Ed Hamrick*

VUEPRINT is a viewer extraordinaire. The program views and converts GIF, BMP, PCX, TGA, JPG, and TIF formats; it reads and writes Internet graphics files in uuencode format. Included is a screen saver and a slide show feature with more than a dozen options. This program is available in the Recommended Utilities library in the PC Graphics & Animation Forum. Direct support in the forum is available direct from the author.

PC Hardware Forum

Keyword: **PC Hardware**

Chuck Smith (PC Chuck) put together a list of some of his forum's most interesting files.

SYSCHK *Author: Paul Griffith (Advanced Personal Systems)*

This file provides excellent information about your computer's hardware, including the type of processor, drive, and memory. The file can identify the video card and chipset to help you select the correct video driver. SYSCHK is a must-have utility for anyone who needs fast and reliable information without opening the computer's case.

CMOS_RAM *Author: Thomas Mosteller*

This program is designed to back up your CMOS setup to a file called CMOS.RAM, as well as to check it periodically. (The author recommends putting the check file in your AUTOEXEC.BAT file.) CMOS_RAM copies the BIOS RAM to a floppy disk or a file called CMOS.RAM. If and when the battery dies, the battery can be replaced and the BIOS contents restored from the disk. CHEKCMOS, another program by the same author, verifies the battery condition and makes sure that the file created by CMOS_RAM matches the BIOS; if not, the BIOS has been changed, but CMOS_RAM has not updated its file.

SNOOPER *Author: John Vias*

This handy system-information utility reports many operating characteristics of your computer. Snooper tells you all about your computer's CPU, NDP, bus, memory, ports, IRQs, DMA, mouse, disks, network, and much more. The program can run unattended (for batch files); print its screens to a file or printer; and configure itself automatically for Desqview, color, or monochrome video cards.

The Modem Doctor *Author: Hank Volpe*

This excellent utility (see fig. 22.9) checks every serial-port chip (UART) register, checks cables and modems for proper handshaking signals, and informs you if it runs across something that isn't set properly. The program tests modems rigorously, performing handshaking tests and modem self-connect tests that simulate an online connection.

The program also checks IRQ assignment errors, base port addressing errors, and a host of other settings. The Modem Doctor informs you what type of UART and modem you have installed, including what class your fax/modem is, helps with fax-software installations, and even prints a copy of the test results to a printer or a file.

FIG. 22.9
Learn whether your modem is working properly with a little help from the Modem Doctor.

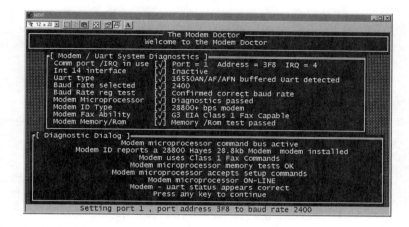

After it is registered, the program offers support for some of the latest high-speed fax/modems and COM ports used in today's high-performance computer systems.

PC Multimedia Forum

Keyword: **PC Multimedia**

The PC Multimedia forum leader, Jonathon Lawrence (PC JonL) oversees the rapidly growing facet of personal computing that combines video, sound, and animation. You'll find some useful files in this forum.

NETTOOB: Net Toob v2.5 *Author: Duplexx Software*

The NETTOOB Multimedia Player plays all of the digital video formats found on the Internet (MPEG-1, AVI, MOV & FLC/FLI), as well as real-time audio and video. It automatically installs itself as the Web browser video helper application for America Online, Netscape, and many other browsers. Users can also save their favorite video clips and run them as screen savers. It has been rated the Number 1 Multimedia Player on the Internet by Stroud's Consummate Winsock App List. This player does work with Windows 95.

C95DEMO2: Elec. Greeting Card Starter Kit *Author: R. Shuler*

E-Card/Card-95 Starter Kit is a shareware program that lets you make multimedia greetings that are short enough to attach to your e-mail or send via floppy disk. You can combine art and MIDI sound files.

The online version includes two sample cards that you can customize with simple instructions; or, you can provide your own art and sounds. It's described as easy to use, and you'll be able to download other samples from the AOL software libraries.

CDSAT32: V3.0 Windows 95 CD Satellite   *Author: Jared DuBois*

CDSAT32 is a 32-bit Windows 95 version of the popular shareware CD player. This program can be used to replace CDPLAYER.EXE, which comes with Windows 95. Like the standard Windows 95 program, CDSAT32 autoloads with new CDs, and you can even uninstall and restore the original Windows 95 CD player.

Here are some of the exclusive CDSAT32 features you won't find on the Windows 95 CD player:

- Auto-remember the songs you like and reload them again automatically.
- Random play songs in any order, any number of times.
- Play extra-large CDs with more than 50 songs on them.
- Has a unique combination status graph that doubles as a status bar. You can click anywhere on the status bar to resume a song at that point.
- A TimeTracks feature will compute the total time for the songs you want to record (plus the song's title information), and subtract them from the total available time for tape or CD. The list can be printed or saved for later review.

PC Music & Sound Forum

A wide variety of music and sound files are available in this forum. Norma Williams (PC Norma) listed the programs covered in the following sections for you to consider.

DEMO: 3.00 Cakewalk Professional for Windows   *Author: Greg Hendershott (Twelve-Tone Systems)*

This demo version of Cakewalk Professional for Windows 3 is mostly functional, except that the Save and Export functions are disabled. Version 3 adds, among other features, a new lyric view feature with lyric events and context-sensitive track editing.

Cakewalk Professional for Windows is a full-featured MIDI sequencer that includes the following features:

- *Multiple views*. Individual windows give you a more comprehensive view of your work.
- *Staff view*. Traditional notation, a track at a time (no printer support).
- *Piano Roll view*. Pitch/time grid.
- *Track/Measure view*. Multiple tracks/measures.
- *Event List view*. Contains color-coded listing of all MIDI events in a track.
- *Controllers view*. Use your mouse to draw controller data.

■ *Faders view*. Records MIDI volume data or reprograms for any MIDI controller.

■ *Tempo view*. Draws tempo changes with your mouse.

■ *System Exclusive view*. Generic MIDI Librarian supports most synthesizers.

■ *Synchronization*. Chases to MIDI sync and supports SMPTE time code.

BANDDEMO: 4.04 Band-in-a-Box Demo   *Author: Peter Gannon (P.G. Music)*

The demo version of Band-in-a-Box 4.04 is for SoundBlaster, AdLib, Covox, and compatible sound boards. Band-in-a-Box is an automatic musical-accompaniment program that provides a three-instrument arrangement (bass, drums, and piano). In this program, you can type any chords for any song, pick a style, and press play.

During playback, you can do the following things:

■ Play along, using the last bottom rows of your computer's keyboard.

■ Change tempo.

■ Change style.

■ Change volume.

■ Change instruments.

TDPRO: 1.10 Windows Drum Machine Sequencer   *Author: Fabio Marzocca*

Drums Professional 1.10 (see fig. 22.10) allows you to create drum patterns easily. The program works with any PC sound card or MIDI instrument through a PC MIDI interface.

FIG. 22.10

Make your computer a professional-grade, drum-sequencing machine.

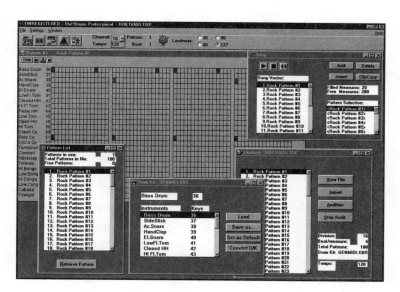

Major features of the Drums Professional include:

- 100 patterns
- Up to 300 song measures
- Real-time-mode recording
- Fully configurable drum kit
- Drum-kit conversion capability
- Librarian function that collects preferred rhythms
- Capability to save and import standard MIDI files
- Support for Windows multimedia extensions
- Up to 300 sample patterns in 3 libraries

CD-BOX: 3.06 Music Player/Shell   *Author: Jeffrey Belt*

CD-Box is a shell/player program that plays back music files on SoundBlaster, AdLib, and compatible sound cards. CD-Box features a slick graphical interface and fun animations—CDs pop up and down and spin, pages scroll, and other random events occur.

CD-Box supports CMF, MOD, MUS, ROL, and VOC music/sound files. (CMF, MOD, and VOC files work only with SoundBlaster.) These files can be stored in ZIP or other archive-format files to save disk space; CD-Box can find and play them from the archives.

PC Telecommunications and Networking Forum

Keyword: **PC Telecom**

The staff of the PC Telecommunications Forum selected two of its most popular files to include in this book. The first file provides a helpful tutorial on the world of the Internet; the second provides highly sophisticated telecommunications capabilities on any Windows-based PC.

INTERNET: 2.0 Beginner's Guide   *Author: Patrick Suarez*

Release 2 of this program is a major overhaul, with more than 30 sections and 16 PCX color images that discuss networks, e-mail, mailing lists, newsgroups, tin, nn, Gopher, Veronica, Telnet, FTP, Archie, WAIS, finding people, IRC, the World Wide Web, Mosaic, Netscape, access via PPP, SLIP, UNIX shell accounts, commercial online companies, freenets, BBSes, Windows, finding a provider, hardware and software needed for access, neat sites to visit, keystroke-by-keystroke sample sessions, and much more.

Written for DOS, the Beginner's Guide now includes a Windows PIF so that you can refer to it while you are online. The text, which is in plain English, describes Internet-related terms and jargon. If you're new to the Internet or just curious about it, this computer-based program is the one to have for a comprehensive education about the Internet. Beginner's Guide is in full color and is easy to load and use.

MICROLINK: 1.05A Win Terminal *Author: MicroWerks*

MicroLink for Windows is a communications application for Microsoft Windows version 3.0 or later. You can use MicroLink to connect your computer to other computers and to a BBS or text-based online service.

The nucleus of MicroLink is the dialing directory, an easy-to-use database in which you can store names, phone numbers, logon scripts, terminal settings, and port settings. Select an entry and click the Dial button; MicroLink instructs the modem to dial for you and to redial if the line is busy. When it is connected, your computer acts like a terminal, giving you access to the remote computer's resources. Eight built-in transfer protocols provide compatibility with nearly any other system for sending and receiving files.

With its simple but powerful script language (in addition to manual programming), MicroLink for Windows can create a script simply by watching the steps you take during a communications session.

PDA Forum

Keyword: **PDA**

Technically, the PDA Forum is neither a Mac nor a Windows-based forum because it covers personal digital assistants, which generally run on operating systems of their own. The forum leader, Craig de Fasselle (PDA Craig), assembled some of the forum's most popular files for you to check out during your online visits. I've grouped them by PDA format so you'll be able to focus quickly on the files you can use.

> **CAUTION**
>
> The files described in the following sections support specific makes and models of personal digital assistants. Do not try to use them on products for which they are not intended.

Newton Software

The products listed in the following sections represent software for Newton PDA models.

Aloha *Author: Hardy Macia*

Aloha allows you to send and receive AOL e-mail with your Newton via FlashSessions. The program works with any Newton package that supports text mail messages.

DateMan *Author: Stand Alone Software*

DateMan is an agenda management that displays all of your appointments, calls, to do items, and daily events over any range of time in a coherent and customizable list. It also allows the creation of links between any two or more items, allowing you to jump back and forth between them.

HP100LX & HP200LX

The products listed in the following sections represent software for these models.

Buddy *Author: Jeffrey Mattox*

Buddy is the "must have" utility for HP100LX and HP200LX palmtops, featuring many keyboard shortcuts and "smart" functions.

Vertical Reader *Author: Gilles Kohl*

Vertical Reader allows you to hold your palmtop like you would hold a book, upright, in one hand.

HP OmniGo

The products listed in the following sections represent software for these models.

OmniGo File Manager *Author: Blue Marsh Software*

OmniGo File Manager enables you to rename and delete files and folders, and rename disks. It also supports file move and copy, as well as creating new folders and displaying the contents of any drive and directory.

OmniGo Installer *Author: Geoworks*

The OmniGo Installer helps you install the package (GPK) files that contain content or applications onto your OmniGo 100.

Psion S3a

The products listed in the following sections represent software for these models.

JAM Monthly Agenda *Author: Martin Sturgess*

JAM Monthly Agenda provides a graphical, scrollable, monthly view for Psion S3a Agenda files. It makes it easy to find open time slots for scheduling appointments.

ViewGIF Viewer/Converter & More *Author: David Lee Yoo-Foo*

This program allows you to view GIFs on your Psion and convert them to storable PIC files.

Magic Link & Envoy

The products listed in the following sections represent software for these models.

WebMail *Author: Pierre Omidyar*

WebMail gives your Magic Cap communicator text-only, non-browsing access to the World Wide Web, FTP, and Gopher. If you know the URL to an Internet resource, you can get it on your PDA—it's not a Web browser, but it's the next best thing.

UUdecode   *Author: Greg Satz*

Uudecode is a handy utility that decodes uuencoded Internet messages and installs the results as a package in the storeroom. This allows others to mail you packages over the Internet!

Windows Forum

Keyword: **Windows**

If you're looking for programs that will make your life at the computer a little easier (or at least more fun), you may want to check out the following four files from the Windows Forum software library, selected by Kat (PC Kat).

WINZIP   *Author: Niko Mak*

WINZIP in both Windows 3.1 and Windows 95/NT versions seems to be the ZIP manager of choice for AOL members not wanting to depend solely on the AOL software's auto decompression feature.

WOLR   *Author: Frank J. Mahaffey*

WOLR is Windows Online Review, a regular covering everything Windows—from popular applications to utilities to Internet offerings.

ODDJOB   *Author: Steve Pugliese*

ODDJOB is not the name of that evil character from a 1960s James Bond film. Actually, it's a PIM and utilities collection allowing you to find and remove duplicates, enhance clipboard abilities, and add nice extras like a trash can. The program also offers superior file search and replace options.

TURBO BROWSER   *Author: Pacific Gold Coast*

TURBO BROWSER is a 16- and 32-bit complete Windows file-viewing package. With this program, you can replace Microsoft Internet Explorer and a raft of utilities with one compact integrated program. From autoviewing (icon, cursor, spreadsheet, database, document, text, graphics, clip art, sound, video, animation), fuzzy search, file filters, compression, conversion, zipping, unzipping, encryption, decryption, printing without native applications, to power-processing with the Qbar, there are so many everyday features not available in Windows 95.

From Here...

I have to thank the friendly PC forum leaders for helping me prepare this chapter. The files you see here represent just the tip of the iceberg. You can spend many fun-filled hours discovering intriguing software during your online visits.

For more information on setting up America Online on your computer, finding the software files you want, and getting help, refer to these chapters:

- Chapter 4, "Getting the Most from AOL's Windows Software," gives you information about some handy programs that will take your software farther than you have imagined.

- In Chapter 20, "Tips and Tricks on Finding Software," you'll put AOL's handy File Search feature through its paces.

- If you sometimes must cross computing platforms, read Chapter 21, "The Best Macintosh Software on AOL."

News and Reference

CHAPTER 23

The News of the Day

Faster than your daily newspaper is AOL's online news department, a place that's updated hourly, or as soon as important news events occur.

When you first log on to America Online, one of the selections offered to you at the bottom of the In The Spotlight menu is the Top News Story, which is the equivalent of the lead headline in your daily newspaper. If you click that icon, you'll open the pages of America Online's own online daily newspaper, a publication consisting of many pages and many sections. ■

AOL's online news department

Read the major news stories of the day.

Exclusive online news sections

Explore up-to-date reports from the worlds of business, entertainment, and sports.

AOL's weather maps

Check out local and worldwide weather information.

Talk about the news

Visit AOL's news-related discussion boards.

Reading Today's News

Keyword: **News**

The Top News Story of the day is always featured at the bottom of the opening screen when you log on (and it may change from hour to hour, depending on new developments, but you won't see the change unless you log off and log on again). You can see the major headlines by clicking the Top News icon, which opens a window called Today's News (see fig. 23.1). What you have here is organized very much like the sections of your daily newspaper. This chapter pages through each section and gives you an idea of what information you can find.

FIG. 23.1
America Online's Today's News department is organized in much the same way as a daily newspaper.

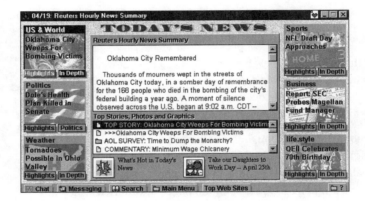

When you bring up the Today's News screen, you'll see the major stories of the day in a directory window, which you can scroll through for additional information. By double-clicking a story listing, you'll be able to read the text of that news item. As with other America Online text windows, you can save the story or print it for later reference. The stories come from the major wire services and are updated regularly as new details arrive. Figure 23.2 shows a typical news story; the text is the same as the reports you find in your daily newspaper, only you get it immediately.

What a Picture Is Worth

Not all of the news you see is limited to just text. Some, like those in your daily newspaper, have an accompanying photograph that illustrates a key element of the story. You'll find many of those stories in the directory labeled Top Stories, Photos and Graphics (see fig. 23.3)

FIG. 23.2
A news story shown in America Online's Top News area.

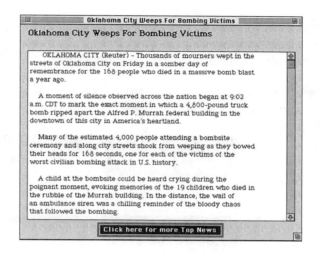

FIG. 23.3
News stories from AOL are sometimes accompanied by photos and a listing of related items.

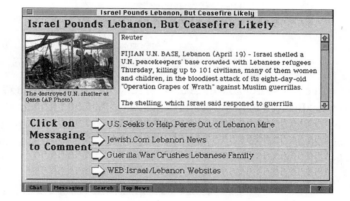

Part
VI

Ch
23

N O T E In order to see photos online, your Mac and Windows AOL software must be up-to-date, and you must have a computer that supports the graphical viewing features. ■

U.S. & World News

Keyword: **US News**

Now that you've read the front page, let's examine the table of contents of your daily newspaper and check out some of the other features (see fig. 23.4). During your online travels, you can set aside pages to read later. The news of the world, for example, is organized by category. There are separate folders for National news, Washington news, Europe, and other topics. If you are seeking information about a particular topic, you'll want to click the Search button at the bottom of the Top News screen.

N O T E   Users of international versions of America Online software will see a selection of news customized for other parts of the world. ■

FIG. 23.4
Here's your online newspaper's national and international section.

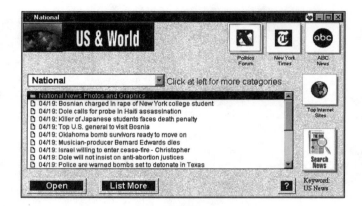

As with other searchable databases on America Online, looking for a news item is a simple process. Just bring up the search window by clicking the icon with the appropriate title, enter the topic of your search (notice it isn't case-sensitive), and you'll see a display of the available articles on that subject (see fig. 23.5)—if there are articles available about your selected topic, of course.

FIG. 23.5
America Online is always making news, and here's what I found when I used America Online as the search string. In order to search a phrase, put single quotes at the beginning and end.

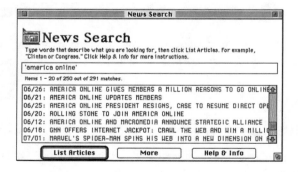

Note that many of the news-related forums on America Online are linked. So, if you open one screen, there are icons that enable you to switch to another area with related information. An example is the Politics Forum icon on the right side of the U.S. & World News screen, as previously shown in figure 23.4.

Business News

Part

VI

Ch

23

Keyword: **Business News**

Let's turn now to the business section (see fig. 23.6). All of the information is divided into convenient categories, so you can easily locate material on a particular topic. The Search News icon in the bottom right enables you to quickly access all of the articles on a single topic. The Market News icon is useful for checking the world's various stock markets. Quotes & Portfolios allows you to review current stock prices. Icons representing some of the business-related online publications appear here; they will change from time to time. You can read more information about personal finance offerings online in Chapter 26, "Online Investment and Tax Information."

FIG. 23.6

Here's your online financial section.

As an example of the sort of information you can find in the Top Business box, select Industry News from the pop-up menu, then choose the Technology pages, where headlines reflect current business developments (see fig. 23.7). You can select an article, double-click the title, or click the Open button. The entire article can be saved as a text file for printing later or for offline reading.

FIG. 23.7
News with a technological
focus can be found in AOL's
Business pages.

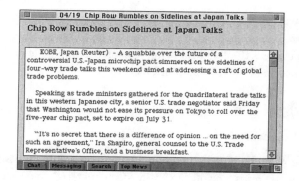

Weather News

Keyword: **Weather**

Because you already read about the sports and entertainment pages in Chapters 11, 12, and 14, this section skips the Entertainment and Sports icons in the Today's News screen and moves on to the final category, Weather.

Although you can't do much to change the weather, you can at least be informed about it. By turning to the weather section in your virtual newspaper, you can review both articles and special forecasts not only country-wide (see fig. 23.8), but from around the world.

FIG. 23.8
When severe weather has a
major impact, AOL has the
latest information.

You can also see maps of weather trends right on your own computer, simply by selecting and downloading them. The forum updates the weather maps daily. You can see them in full color if you have a color monitor. Choose from a satellite view, radar displays, and charts of maximum and minimum temperatures not only for today, but for tomorrow and the next day, as well. If you choose, for example, to view the day's weather map, you get the display shown in figure 23.9.

FIG. 23.9
See the weather displayed on your computer.

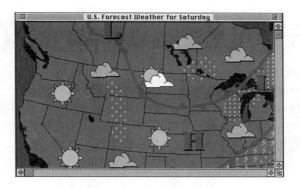

Part
VI
Ch
23

N O T E If you have a color monitor, you'll see your weather maps in full color, in a size sufficient to fill a small computer screen. ■

The forum also offers these maps in the cross-platform GIF format (short for Graphic Interchange Format). After you download the map file to your computer, you can use the latest versions of AOL's Macintosh and Windows software to open and view the file. Just use the File, Open command to bring up the file to your screen.

During the summer and fall seasons, there is a special area devoted to tropical storms and hurricanes. You can check this section to see if any severe weather is expected in your area, and what the trends are for the very near future (within the limits of the science of weather forecasting, of course).

U.S. Cities Forecasts

Whether you are a regular traveler or a vicarious sojourner, you're undoubtedly curious as to the weather in other parts of the world. No problem. America Online's weather page has information about that too, grouped by country or continent and updated regularly. If you're planning a trip abroad, consult this area before you pack your bags (see fig. 23.10).

FIG. 23.10
If you are traveling, review the forecasts in the city of your choice.

Visiting AOL's Politics Forum

Keyword: **Capital, Politics**

After you've reviewed the news of the day, undoubtedly you have some strong ideas about some of the subjects you've read about, especially the goings on in the nation's capital. If you want to examine the issues further, you'll want to visit AOL's Politics forum (see fig. 23.11), where you can immerse yourself in politics and intrigue and get a thorough perspective of the progression of events.

FIG. 23.11

Read and debate the issues in AOL's Politics area.

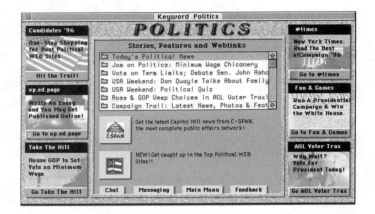

This area is configured very much like AOL's Today's News area. You'll find stories, photos, and WWW links in the main directory screen (see fig. 23.12 for an example).

FIG. 23.12

One example of the sort of news you find in this area—news of the 1996 presidential campaign.

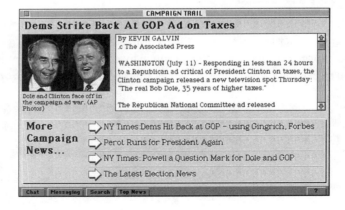

Among the highlights of this forum are the regular polls run by ABC News and AOL, which report public reactions to the issues of the day. You can double-click right to the American Civil Liberty Union's (ACLU) Gopher site on the Internet, where you can review many of the public affairs magazines that are available on AOL, such as *The Atlantic Monthly* and *The New Republic*. You also can check out forums run by National Public Radio, and many other resources.

Part

VI

Ch

23

When election time is near, you can count on America Online to provide the latest political news, opinion polls, and comprehensive analyses of the situation by some of the top political writers. You'll even find some of your favorite candidates holding court in one of AOL's busy conference rooms.

The White House

Keyword: **White House**

The White House runs its own online area (see fig. 23.13), where you can receive an unfiltered view of the activities of the President and his staff. You can examine full-text reports on the President's daily activities, download photos illustrating the President in action, and, if you wish, send e-mail direct to the President. There is no guarantee, however, the President will actually see the e-mail you've sent. These messages are first reviewed by the White House staff, and only summaries of the trend of messages usually reach the President's eyes (though some messages do get all the way to the Oval Office).

FIG. 23.13
The White House also manages an AOL forum.

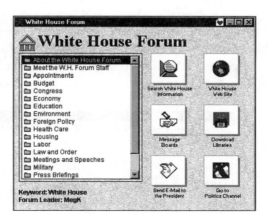

Because there are always many points of view about what a sitting president should do, there's an active message board where you and fellow AOL members can discuss your feelings about the White House staff's activities.

AOL's Daily News Home Delivery Service

Keyword: **News Profiles**

There's yet another way to get the latest news on AOL, and the technique used is somewhat similar to subscribing to a daily newspaper and having it delivered direct to your home. It's called News Profiles (see fig. 23.14), which is an AOL feature that delivers e-mail containing the latest news on the subjects that interest you directly to your mailbox on a daily basis.

FIG. 23.14

Have the latest news sent to your AOL mailbox.

In order to take advantage of the News Profiles feature, you need to create a custom profile, in which you select the subjects of the news stories you want sent, and the sources from which they originate. Let's cover the steps involved in setting up this service. First, click the Create Your Profile icon to get the screen shown in figure 23.15.

FIG. 23.15

Choose the subjects that interest you here.

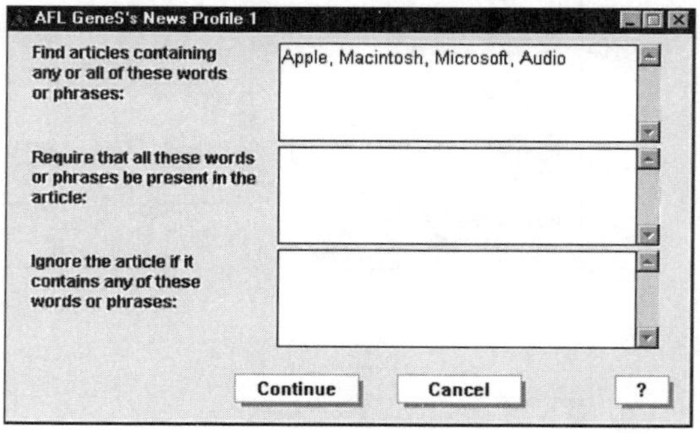

1. Find articles containing any or all of these words or phrases. Enter the words or subjects you want AOL's News Agent to search for you.

   You can refine your News Agent search strings still further with a few handy wild-card characters (not unlike the ones you may use in a word processing program). Here's a listing:

   A. Asterisk (*)

   This letter represents one or more characters and can be used in place of any character to extend the accuracy of your search, such as "computer*," which will include not only the word "computer," but also "computers," "computing," and so forth.

   B. At Sign (@)

   This character can be used to represent a single character. For example, if you type **a@e** in the Ignore box, News Profiles ignores articles containing the words "ape" and "ate."

   C. Plus Sign (+)

   This character can be used to represent a single number. For example, if you type **852+0** in the Find Articles box, News Profiles finds all articles containing the zip code "85260."

   D. Question Mark (?)

   This character may represent a single character or a single number in your search string. It has the functions of both + and @ and can be inserted anywhere in a search string.

   E. Pound Sign (#)

   This character can represent any single word. For example, if you type the phrase **apple #** in the Find Articles box, News Profiles can find such phrases as Apple Computer, Apple orchard, etc.

2. Require that all these words or phrases be present in the article. This is a way to restrict the news report search. You don't have to enter anything in this text field if the subjects you specified are sufficient to identify the topics you want.

3. Ignore the article if it contains any of these words or phrases. If there are items you absolutely don't want to read about, enter that information here. Again this text field is optional—it's not necessary to enter anything. For example, if you don't want to read anything more about a particular public figure, put that person's name in this list.

4. Click the Continue button to continue to create your news profile (see fig. 23.16). Click Cancel to stop the process without making a profile.

FIG. 23.16
Name your profile and
choose the sources to search
for news reports here.

5. Create a title for your news profile. You can enter any title you want here, to help you identify the profile in case you want to change it later.

6. Available Sources. This is a listing of the wire services America Online uses to search for the news items you want. Click the Add arrow icon to move these sources to your Selected Sources listing.

7. If you want to remove a source, click the Remove arrow icon, and the item will return to the list of Available Sources.

8. Number of articles to receive via e-mail each day. You may prefer not to clutter your e-mail box with news, so you have a chance here to restrict the number of items sent to your mailbox (the default is 10).

9. If you want to recheck the search words you included in your profile, click the Previous button.

10. If you decide not to make a profile at this time, click the Cancel button, and all the information you entered will be deleted.

11. If you're ready to create your profile, click the Create Your Profile icon in the News Profiles screen, which will bring up an acknowledgment message (see fig. 23.17) that your profile has been activated.

FIG. 23.17
Get ready to automatically
receive the latest news on
the subjects that interest
you.

Up to five profiles can be maintained for each screen name. As I'll describe in a moment, it's easy to turn them on or off, day by day, so that a different range of articles can be checked for you by AOL's News Profiles feature.

Within a day or so, you'll begin to receive mailings containing news on the subjects that you've selected in your News Agent profile. If you've picked the maximum of 50 items, as I've done, you'll find your mailbox will have a daily avalanche of news items, and you may decide it's just too much to read at any one time. Should this occur (or you just want to select a different range of subject matter), you can always update your profile by clicking the Manage Your Profile icon on the News Profiles window. You get the screen shown in figure 23.18.

Part
VI

Ch
23

> **CAUTION**
>
> AOL's News Profiles feature does its job whether you log on to AOL daily or not. If you want to avoid having your mailbox overflow with outdated news items when you're not going to be connecting to AOL for a while, be sure to modify your profile.

FIG. 23.18
Make your changes here whenever you need to change your news profile.

The buttons at the bottom of the Edit window shown in figure 23.18 let you configure your existing profiles. First highlight the profile you want to change, then click the appropriate button:

- *Edit.* Click this button to bring up the same two profile screens described above, so you can alter your settings as you desire.
- *On/Off.* Click this button to activate or disable the selected profile.
- *Delete.* Click this button to remove the selected profile.
- *Close.* Click this button to close the edit window.
- *?.* If you need additional online help, click this button.

Now you're ready to enjoy America Online's automated news delivery service. You'll find it can save you money too, because it reduces the amount of time you spend online seeking out news stories on the items that interest you.

TIP   If you use both AOL's News Profiles and FlashSessions features, you'll be able to totally automate the process of retrieving online news stories.

From Here...

In this chapter, you read about America Online's own daily newspaper, where you can check out the news of the day divided into handy, easy-to-read sections. The big difference between this newspaper and the one you buy at your local newsstand is the fact that AOL's paper can be updated at any time to reflect important new developments in local, national, and world news. Also, what you've read about here represents just a small part of the vast news resources available on AOL. For related information, you'll want to review the following chapters:

- In Chapter 11, "TV and Movie Information Online," you'll learn all about the entertainment-related resources available on America Online.

- In Chapter 12, "Music, Books, and Art," you'll explore additional entertainment and culture resources online.

- In Chapter 14, "Sports in Cyberspace," you'll learn more about locating sports information on AOL.

- In Chapter 24, "Magazines and Newspapers Online," you'll visit AOL's online newsstand and explore the racks of publications (some of which exist only in online form).

- In Chapter 25, "Learning and Reference," you'll explore online educational resources available to you.

- In Chapter 26, "Online Investment and Tax Information," you'll discover sources for tips and tricks on how to make your dollars go farther, and where to seek further assistance at tax time.

Magazines and Newspapers Online

Growing up in the big city, I used to enjoy the visit to the local newsstand to see my favorite magazines and newspapers. But, now I don't have to leave my home office to visit a newsstand. All I have to do is log on to AOL and click AOL's newsstand channel from the Main Menu (or just use the keyword **Newsstand**).

In previous chapters, I introduced America Online as a friendly community where you can meet and talk with your friends. I showed you where to find information from the world of entertainment, and about your hobbies and special interests. Previous chapters also explained how to use your computer more effectively.

In the last chapter, I presented a description of AOL's resources for up-to-date news and weather information. I've also described some magazines available from AOL's Newsstand in other parts of this book.

As you know, America Online is growing at a breathtaking pace, so the roster of online magazines is bound to increase as time goes on. The highlights are covered in this chapter. ■

Visiting the Newsstand

Keyword: **Newsstand**

I described the popular forums run by two of the major daily newspapers, the *Chicago Tribune* and the *New York Times* in Chapter 15, "Pursuing Lifestyles and Interests." That chapter focused on the feature of lifestyle pages. In this chapter, I cover the news-related sections offered by these papers. When you first visit AOL's Newsstand department, you'll see publications highlighted with special icons at the left and bottom of the department screen (see fig. 24.1). Because these icons change regularly to highlight different online sources, let's choose stop-off points mostly from the Publications list box.

FIG. 24.1
The list of available magazines on AOL's newsstand is increasing rapidly.

Your Daily Newspaper Online

The first online publications we're going to check on our visit to America Online's virtual newsstand are the daily newspapers. Some of the U.S.'s major papers are represented in this area. What makes these publications different from their print counterparts is the fact that additional online features are available. They include special information areas to help tourists who visit the cities, a regular schedule of online conferences, and message boards. Let's begin our tour.

 TIP   A quick way to get right to the front pages of some of your favorite newspapers is the keyword **local news**.

The New York Times

Keyword: **times**

N O T E The keyword **time** takes you to *Time* magazine's forum; the keyword **times** takes you to the forum run by *The New York Times*. So much confusion for just one letter. And if you type the keyword **clock**, you'll bring up a display of the amount of time you've spent online. Now as for the keyword **watch**, I wasn't able to find any area reflecting that word, but one never knows what the future might bring.

The New York Times is a newspaper of record, which means it offers extremely detailed reports of the news of the day, including transcripts of presidential press conferences and extensive background articles about key news events. Besides the huge daily edition available in New York and surrounding states, there's a somewhat smaller national edition you can purchase at bookstores and newsstands just about anywhere in the world.

To read highlights from the latest edition, you've got to go through a two-step process. First, go to *The New York Times* On Line forum (see fig. 24.2).

Part
VI

Ch
24

FIG. 24.2
The New York Times On Line forum on AOL is popular to members from around the world.

The second step is just to click the Today's News icon to bring up the screen shown in figure 24.3.

One more thing: Don't expect to find the entire paper online. Only the major stories from various sections are provided, but it's enough to whet you appetite in case you want to visit your corner newsstand for a copy of the actual paper.

FIG. 24.3

The major stories direct from *The New York Times,* just as featured in the daily editions of the paper.

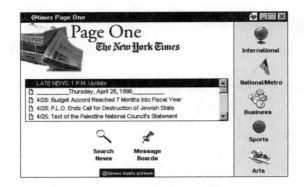

Arizona Central

Keyword: **Arizona**

Arizona's largest daily newspaper, the *Arizona Republic*, is the centerpiece of a large, multilayered forum devoted to residents and visitors to the state (see fig. 24.4). You'll be able to read the major contents of the newspaper, or refer to an extensive library of information. There's even a direct link to the forum's site on the World Wide Web for additional resources.

FIG. 24.4

Whether a resident or just a visitor, you'll learn a lot about the state of Arizona from Arizona Central.

One popular feature is the highly regarded restaurant reviews from writer Penelope Corcoran, who was recently judged one of the nation's top food critics. You'll be able to view a full library of her reviews of the top dining spots in Phoenix and environs.

Chicago Tribune

Keyword: **Chicago Tribune**

In Chapter 15, "Pursuing Lifestyles and Interests," I described the Windy City's special online forum, Chicago Online, which offers information for residents and sightseers alike (see fig. 24.5).

FIG. 24.5
Chicago Online offers a gateway to a full-featured metropolitan daily newspaper.

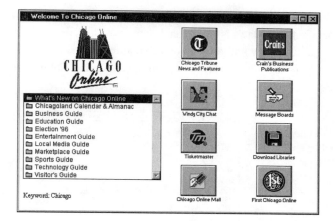

This process is much faster than any trip to a newsstand. To read the contents of the *Chicago Tribune,* simply click the Chicago Tribune News and Features icon (or use the keyword **Chicago Tribune**), which brings up the window shown in figure 24.6. The top stories of that day's edition are featured in the directory list box. If you want to probe more deeply into individual sections of the paper, simply double-click one of the sections listed there.

FIG. 24.6
The news, features, and editorials from the *Chicago Tribune.*

Reader services are shown in the icons on the bottom of the Chicago Tribune window, along with a Message Boards and Classified Ads listing. This is a newspaper you can't quite spill coffee on (but be careful with your computer's keyboard).

Columnists & Features Online

Keyword: **Columnists**

In Chapter 23, "The News of the Day," you were exposed to the latest news and business reports in the Today's News department. Now let's pause for a few moments to review some commentary and opinion on the feature pages. Rather than poring over a pile of newspapers to find your favorite columnists, look in Columnists & Features Online (see fig. 24.7).

FIG. 24.7
Your online features page on AOL is offered by the Newspaper Enterprise Association.

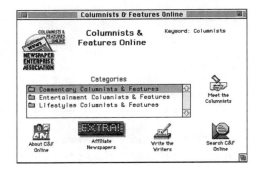

The Newspaper Enterprise Association (NEA) sponsors this forum where you can read the regular features from many of your favorite writers. Read commentaries from such luminaries as Hodding Carter, William Rusher, and Nat Hentoff. You can read reports on the latest happenings from the world of show business and your daily horoscope (it's called *Astrograph,* from writer Bernice Bede Osol). If you have a question about personal finance, radio talk show personality Bruce Williams will answer it for you.

You also have the opportunity to interact with many of your favorite writers, review past columns, and consult from the list of affiliate newspapers to find out which paper carries your favorite writers.

Magazines Online

Now that you've read the contents of your favorite daily newspapers, you're probably ready to browse the stands for some magazines. The major publishers are represented on America Online, and, as a unique twist, some of these online periodicals no longer have a printed counterpart.

Atlantic Monthly Magazine

Keyword: **Atlantic**

Several important magazines regularly appear online at the same time they appear in your favorite bookstore. One of these is the *Atlantic Monthly* (see fig. 24.8).

FIG. 24.8
Read the contents of the *Atlantic Monthly* on AOL.

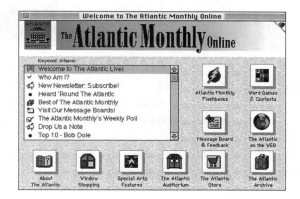

Part

VI

Ch

24

Founded in 1857, the *Atlantic Monthly* is a journal of literature, entertainment, and opinion. Highlights of the latest issue appear online, including features, letters to the editor, and many of the articles that appear in the printed edition.

The message board is your chance to communicate with editors, writers, and other online members. As with any magazine of opinion, the discussions can become very vigorous indeed. The Atlantic Auditorium hosts special gatherings involving both editors and writers.

Reading the *Christian Reader* Online

Keyword: **Christian Reader, CR**

The *Christian Reader* is a popular digest of articles collected from more than 100 magazines with a Christian slant (see fig. 24.9). The magazine has been published for more than 30 years, and was founded by Kenneth N. Taylor, paraphraser of *The Living Bible*.

FIG. 24.9
Browse the pages of the
Christian Reader on AOL.

The contents of the current issue are listed in the directory at the main screen of the
forum. As with other online areas, you can save or print anything you read in the text
windows, using the appropriate commands from the File menu, for later review. The icons
at the left of the window enable you to contact the publishers, subscribe to the magazine,
or send a story of your own to be considered for publication. The CR Message icon at the
left takes you to the Readers Roundtable, a stimulating message board, and also enables
you to review articles from previous issues.

Visiting AOL's Remodeling and Decorating Resource

Keyword: **Home Design, Home Magazine**

Here's a magazine that'll interest you if you're actively planning your dream house, planning a home theater setup, or looking for the best home accessories, carpeting and so
forth. *Home Magazine* Online offers the full table of contents of each issue in the main
directory window, along with a huge library of useful information (see fig. 24.10).

FIG. 24.10
A forum run by a magazine
dedicated to those seeking
to improve their homes,
Home Online.

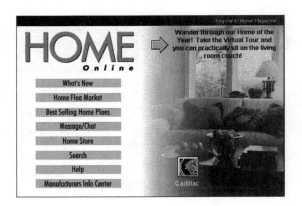

The icons at the left side of the window take you to special support areas for different departments of the magazine. Check out the Home Flea Market and the Home Store for special offers. You'll get some really spectacular ideas about designing your home when you click the Best Selling Home Plans icon. The Manufacturers Info Center offers product literature, and the Message/Chat area is a place where you can read about the home remodeling experiences of other members and post messages about your own projects.

Welcome to Military City Online

Keyword: **MCO**

Military City Online is an online service for those in the armed services, former members of the military, and their families (see fig. 24.11). It's a service from the Army Times Publishing Company and supplements the *Army Times, Navy Times,* and *Air Force Times.*

FIG. 24.11
Military City Online offers an information center for those who have served or are serving in the military.

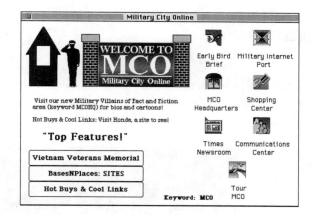

Besides finding top stories from the current issues of these publications, you'll find special reports that are of particular importance to the military family, and answers to questions about often confusing policy issues. The Communications Center, at the right side of the main forum window, gives you the opportunity to share your experiences with other AOL members.

The New Republic

Keyword: **New Republic**

The New Republic is a magazine of opinion that takes an unabashedly liberal viewpoint of the nation and the world. It covers politics, literature, and the arts, with its own unique slant. The magazine is interesting, controversial, and always entertaining, whatever your political leanings (see fig. 24.12).

FIG. 24.12
Whether you agree or disagree with the views offered, *The New Republic* is a magazine many opinion makers read.

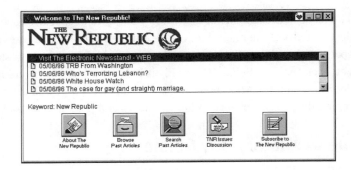

The online forum for *The New Republic* contains a selection of articles from the latest issue, plus a built-in search feature, which you can use to browse and read past articles. The magazine's active TNR Issues Discussion message board hosts lively discussion and debate.

OMNI Magazine Online

Keyword: **OMNI**

Whether interested in learning about advances in space exploration or in reports about UFOs, you can explore the frontiers of science by visiting the *OMNI* Magazine Forum on AOL (see fig. 24.13).

FIG. 24.13
Science fact and science fiction are combined in *OMNI* magazine.

Besides reading many of the features from the latest issue of *OMNI,* you can attend a number of regular chats. The forum always posts the schedules, and the chats feature not only the magazine's editorial staff, but visiting experts of all sorts. One exciting and controversial section of *OMNI* is the Antimatter department, which explores subjects that are often thought of as being beyond the realm of science, such as reports about psychic phenomena and strange things seen in the skies (generally referred to as UFOs).

As many of you have no doubt heard, the printed version of *OMNI* is being gradually reduced in publication frequency, and the online version will get greater emphasis. Just another reason to continue to visit this area for the latest news from the frontiers of science and beyond.

Stereo Review Online

Keyword: **Stereo Review**

It started out years ago as *Hi-Fi Review,* and then it was *Hi-Fi/Stereo Review* when stereophonic audio became popular in the early 1960s. Now it's just *Stereo Review,* and it remains one of the most popular consumer audio magazines in the U.S. (see fig. 24.14). If you want to buy a new stereo system, explore the frontiers of home theater (surround sound), or you just want to read reviews about the latest recordings, visit *Stereo Review* Online.

FIG. 24.14
Learn all about home audio in *Stereo Review* magazine on AOL.

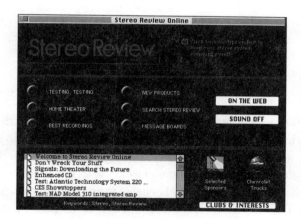

You'll find all of the content of the newsstand issues online, including thoroughly researched product test reports from the magazine's staff of audio professionals. Sometimes audio fans can get sharply opinionated about their favorite hardware, and *Stereo Review*'s active message board is a place where you'll find animated discussions about such diverse subjects as tube amplifiers, whether the sound of your audio system can be improved by buying more expensive cables (the consensus is that it can't, but it's a controversial subject), and the best priced loudspeaker systems.

Visiting *Travel & Leisure* Magazine Online

Keyword: **Travel & Leisure**

If you're an American Express cardholder, you're no doubt familiar with *Travel & Leisure*, a magazine that transports you to the far-flung corners of the world (see fig. 24.15). Whether you are an experienced traveler, or just want a taste of what a trip to a remote port of call would be like, you'll want to visit this forum.

FIG. 24.15
Take a journey around the world with *Travel & Leisure* magazine.

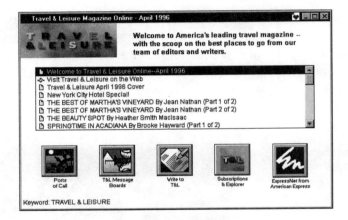

The directory window in the main window of this forum lists articles for the latest issue. The Ports of Call icon at the bottom of the screen represents an area where you can send e-mail to the magazine's staff, browse through past issues, search for material on topics of your choosing, and download material from the forum's library. The next two icons, T&L Message Boards and Write to T&L, enable you to share messages with staff and AOL members. You can also order a subscription to the magazine and, with the last icon, visit ExpressNet, a special forum for users of American Express credit cards.

Getting *Wired* Online

Keyword: **Wired**

The growth of the Information Superhighway means that we are all truly connected by telephone line, by satellite, or by computers. *Wired* magazine is the voice of what it calls the "Digital Generation,"—the people who have grown up and experienced the joining of computers, telecommunications, and the media (see fig. 24.16).

FIG. 24.16
The offbeat *Wired* magazine
is the voice of the Digital
Generation on AOL.

Wired is not necessarily for the casual reader. Its articles are strong, blunt, and often controversial. One of the magazine's editors once summed up the demands of its writers: "Amaze us."

Rather than try to explain what this magazine is all about, I suggest you spend a few moments reading the latest issue online; or search through articles from past issues. The magazine's very individual approach is best exemplified in its message areas or in its regular chats. This forum will not bore you in the least.

Worth Magazine

Keyword: **Worth**

Here's a different approach to presenting financial information. Rather than deal with business news in a cold, dry, analytical fashion, *Worth* magazine considers one's personal needs in providing financial information (see fig. 24.17).

FIG. 24.17
A different, very personal
slant on your finances is
offered by *Worth* magazine.

Each issue contains advice on dealing with all phases of your financial picture, from taxes and real estate to stocks and bonds. *Worth's* online forum offers feature articles and key reports from past issues that you can search by topic or content.

The forum has software libraries (which you'll discover when you access its contents) that include files with advice on investing, plus huge numbers of articles that you can download and read at your leisure.

Saturday Review Online

Keyword: **Saturday Review**

Many of you probably remember the *Saturday Review* as a magazine of arts and culture that existed for many years and folded in 1986. During its over half a century of existence, this journal covered such subjects as politics, science, business, literature, and even the world of entertainment.

So, what is a magazine that no longer exists doing on America Online? Well, unlike the other online magazines we've discussed so far in this chapter, the *Saturday Review* doesn't exist as a printed publication. It's strictly an electronic magazine brought to you by the publishers of *OMNI* (see fig. 24.18).

FIG. 24.18
The *Saturday Review* reborn as an electronic magazine on America Online.

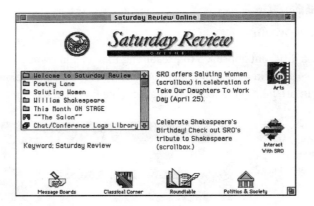

In the tradition of the magazine originally edited by Norman Cousins, this twenty-first century counterpart contains articles of both fact and fiction. It reviews current events in detail from the perspective of many noted writers. As with other online publications, you can participate in its active message boards to share your views with writers and editors. Reading this revived publication is a unique experience indeed.

Cowles/SIMBA Media Information Network

Keyword: **CowlesSIMBA**

The word *media* connotes a variety of industries, from advertising agencies to broadcasting and publishing businesses. The Cowles/SIMBA Media Information Network is a major resource for information about this challenging and ever-changing field (see fig. 24.19).

FIG. 24.19
If you're a media watcher (and a lot of us are), Cowles/SIMBA is your source for the latest information.

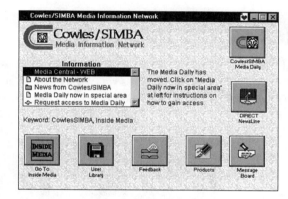

Part
VI

Ch
24

Whether you want to know about the latest deal to acquire a big entertainment conglomerate, or about how your favorite magazine is faring, consult Cowles/SIMBA for current information in an easy-to-read form.

In addition to reviewing the news online, you can order Cowles/SIMBA's business publications, review its vast libraries of information, or interact with other members and industry observers on active message boards.

Another Cowles/SIMBA service you'll want to check on is *Inside Media* Online (see fig. 24.20). *Inside Media* is a popular business magazine that focuses on the print and broadcasting industries; it is definitely tailored toward the media professional.

In addition to examining the current issue online, you can search for specific articles in past issues, contact the magazine's editorial staff, participate in a very active message area, and, if you like what you see, order a subscription.

FIG. 24.20
Inside Media magazine is a major source of news about the media and information industry.

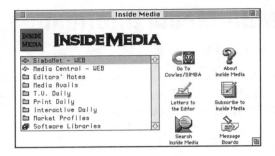

Magazines on the Internet

Not all of the publications you'll find on AOL are provided as part of the service. There are many others that you can easily access via AOL's handy World Wide Web browser (see fig. 24.21). I won't cover all of the contents here, as the roster of popular WWW sites offered by AOL changes often. But, you'll want to examine the Top Internet Sites' offerings during your regular online visits.

FIG. 24.21
Still more online magazines, which you can find on the global Internet.

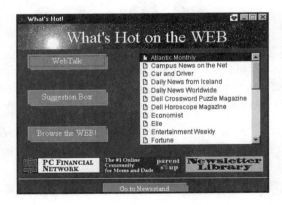

The list in figure 24.21 is designed just to whet your appetite about AOL's Internet resources. I'll list many more for you to check out in Part VIII, "Entering the Information Superhighway."

From Here...

This chapter described America Online as your own personal newsstand, with magazines and newspapers available online for you to browse and read at your leisure. A variety of subjects are covered in these magazines, but they aren't the only magazines you find on

AOL. If you want to find additional publications, the keyword **Newsstand** always provides the latest bill of fare. In addition, you'll want to read the following chapters:

- In Chapter 11, "TV and Movie Information Online," you'll read all about the huge resources for entertainment-related information online.

- In Chapter 12, "Music, Books, and Art," you'll read about additional entertainment-related and cultural resources.

- In Chapter 15, "Pursing Lifestyles and Interests," you'll find valuable information about forums devoted to your favorite hobbies and special organizational interests.

- In Chapter 19, "Visiting the Computing and Software Forums," you'll explore forums devoted to enhancing your computing experience.

- In Chapter 23, "The News of the Day," you'll find additional ways to stay abreast of the top events almost as they occur.

- In Chapter 25, "Learning and Reference," you'll explore many of the educational resources available to you on America Online.

Part

VI

Ch

24

Learning and Reference

Visit online libraries

Tap the resources of huge libraries without a library card.

Advance your education

Take degree-granting courses without ever entering a classroom.

Check reference sources

Find the latest online issues of such magazines as *Scientific American*.

Think of America Online as the largest school in the world; where you can learn something about most anything. You have, at your beck and call, the vast resources of major encyclopedias, home study schools, libraries, museums, and dozens of other information centers, including many that are Internet-based.

In the previous century, your resources for learning were confined to written material (such as books, newspapers, and magazines), or verbal descriptions. The twentieth century brought audio and visual media into play, as well. But interactive learning capabilities have come into their own with the advent of online services such as America Online.

Because of the extent and scope of the educational resources available on America Online, a separate chapter would be needed to fully describe the services of each learning and reference forum. So, just consider this chapter a get-acquainted visit. The Learning and Culture area and the Reference channel are separate on America Online (although their interests often converge), so they'll be described separately. ■

Exploring the AOL Reference Desk

Keyword: **Reference**

The Reference Desk is your gateway to many of the areas that provide information on America Online. Many of the services available are, no doubt, familiar to you. Some of the magazines included in this channel, such as *Consumer Reports* and *Disney Adventures*, are discussed in more detail in other chapters. Other services offer huge databases of information that you'll want to explore in careful detail. The contents of AOL's Computing and Software forums (Chapters 19–22) can also be searched.

The Internet Tools databases identified by an icon in the Reference channel's opening screen (see fig. 25.1) are described in Chapter 31, "Searching for Information on the Internet." But, I'd like to mention just one point now—AOL's Internet resources are generally transparent. This means that the listings shown in various AOL channels may access a local resource or one on the Internet, but either resource is just a click or two away.

FIG. 25.1
The Reference Desk on America Online is a valuable reference tool.

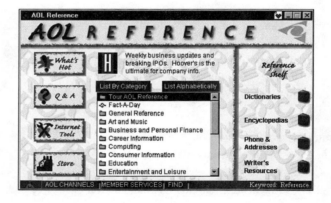

AskERIC

Keyword: **Eric, AskERIC**

ERIC is not a person; it is an Internet-based information center. ERIC is an electronic library containing thousands of information resources for educators, and for parents interested in the best possible education for their children (see fig. 25.2). Eric also provides a place where you can have your education-oriented questions researched and answered by the ERIC staff.

One particular item of special interest is the For Parents folder, an information repository containing common questions and answers on how parents can better involve themselves in their children's education. Recently, I read an article in that folder describing how parents can help prevent drug abuse in our schools.

FIG. 25.2
AskERIC is a question-answering service and information library for parents and educators.

Visiting the Bulletin Board Systems Corner

Keyword: **BBS**

As you know, there is a huge online world outside of America Online. For example, there are thousands of Bulletin Board Systems (BBS), which are, basically, small online services that cater to a single special interest, such as a particular hobby or a particular manufacturer's product line. The Bulletin Board Systems Corner provides a large database that you can search to seek out a local BBS or a BBS catering to an interest of yours (see fig. 25.3).

FIG. 25.3
If you're interested in setting up your own BBS, or you just have some questions about the one you are working with now, you'll want to visit AOL's Bulletin Board Systems Corner.

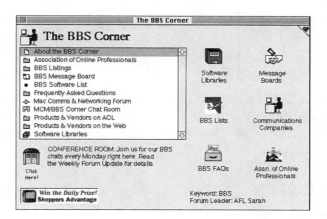

In addition, this forum serves as a meeting point for those of you who run a BBS or who might want to start a BBS. You'll want to review the Frequently Asked Questions folder, and then browse through the Products & Vendors folder, which has a listing of popular BBS software and recommended modems. If you are a system operator (SYSOP) of a

BBS, you'll want to consider membership in the Association of Online Professionals. You can also visit the forum's active Message Boards area, browse through the messages, or maybe post a few of your own.

Accessing Court TV

Keyword: **Court TV**

For most of us, knowledge about the workings of the court system is limited to such TV programs as *Matlock* or *Perry Mason*. In real life, trials are not resolved in 55 minutes. The legal process is complex and convoluted, and often difficult for the layman to understand.

The intense national attention on the O.J. Simpson murder case has placed such cable TV sources as Court TV (see fig. 25.4) in the spotlight. Court TV is a 24-hour network devoted solely to the legal process and how it works. While the Simpson matter was at its highest prominence, a special area was established (shown in the list box at the left) containing the latest information about the case.

FIG. 25.4
Court TV is the popular cable TV network devoted to the legal system.

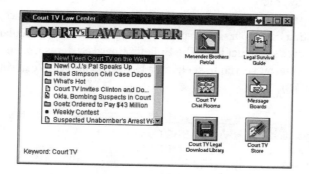

Double-click the Lawyer Locator database listing (you'll have to scroll through the forum's list box to find it), and you'll be able to search for attorneys that specialize in different branches of law. There's also a download library that contains court transcripts and other documents.

Accessing C-SPAN

Keyword: **CSPAN**

Whenever an important hearing is held in Congress, or the President or another important government figure gives a speech, C-SPAN (short for Cable-Satellite Public Affairs Network) is often there with coverage for the entire event.

C-SPAN is available through most cable TV networks (you might want to check to see if it's offered in your area). Not only do you see hearings and press conferences, but you can also find a huge schedule of public affairs programming. The C-SPAN online area gives you the daily schedule, some background information on the service, and a guide to help make your viewing (at home or in the classroom) more informative. Figure 25.5 shows the C-SPAN Online welcome screen.

FIG. 25.5

You can find out all about C-SPAN through America Online.

T I P Remember, all text you see in an online document window can be saved or printed using the appropriate File menu commands.

In the active message area, you can contact other America Online members about the issues being presented on C-SPAN, and you can even interact with C-SPAN's own staff. You'll also want to attend the regular online conferences in the C-SPAN auditorium.

Looking for Searchable Periodicals

Almost all of the online publications, both magazines and newspapers, provide some sort of search tool. This capability allows you to search for specific articles or text in both the latest issue and in back issues. As you can see from the Searchable Periodicals area (see fig. 25.6), the range of resources is extensive. You can access this area from the AOL Reference channel's list box (refer to fig. 25.1).

Three of the online publications are shown by special icons (and these listings change from time to time), which take you directly to that publication's support area. The remaining publications are shown in the directory listing; you can scroll through an extensive list, which will grow as other publishers establish online forums.

FIG. 25.6
You can search AOL's online publications in one convenient location.

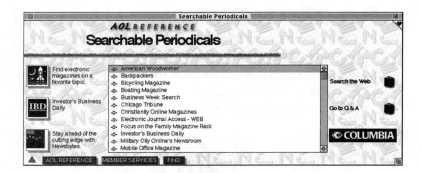

Accessing Smithsonian Online

Keyword: **Smithsonian**

Most of you probably never hear much about the Smithsonian Institution except when reading news about a particular exhibit. If visiting the Smithsonian Museums in person isn't possible, a visit to the Smithsonian Online forum on America Online is a useful substitute (see fig. 25.7).

Here you can read about many of the Smithsonian's exhibits, order one of the Institution's publications, or even see photos of these exhibits. The photos are all available as graphics interchange format (GIF) files, a cross-platform format that enables you to view and print the photo from your computer.

FIG. 25.7
You can visit the world's largest museum on America Online.

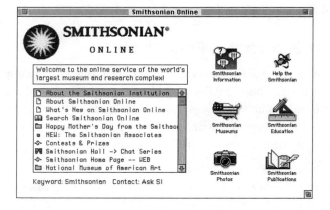

N O T E GIF files are discussed in more detail in Chapter 7, "America Online's People Connection." The current versions of America Online's Macintosh and Windows software can open and view GIF files. ■

Finding the Right Word

Keyword: **Merriam-Webster**

When you need to be certain you're spelling a word correctly, you want to locate another word with a similar meaning, or just want to refresh your skills in the proper use of the English language, you'll want to consult AOL's online dictionary from Merriam-Webster (see fig. 25.8).

FIG. 25.8
Merriam-Webster offers an online dictionary and a lot more in this forum.

Your online experience with the Merriam-Webster forum involves much more than simply looking up words in a dictionary. You'll also find an extensive selection of helpful text information about the history of the English language, good grammar, and proper usage. In addition, there's a message board (shown in the list box at the left) where you can ask questions and discuss the more obscure aspects of language use. There's also a chat room where you can meet the dictionary's editors and other members for assistance, or just to exchange ideas.

Of course, the main reason you visit a forum such as this is to look up a word, so let me show you how it's done. The entire contents of the Tenth Edition of Merriam-Webster's Collegiate Dictionary is online. All you have to do to consult this book is click the Search the Collegiate Dictionary icon or, even better, type the keyword **dictionary**. Either step will present the search screen shown in figure 25.9.

Simply enter the word you'd like to look up in the text field, and click the Look Up button to bring up the result. In order to actually see the word's definition (see fig. 25.10), just double-click the word that appears in the list of matching entries.

FIG. 25.9
Merriam-Webster's handy search tool lets you look up that word in the blink of an eye.

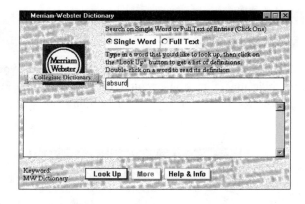

FIG. 25.10
Here's the definition of the word you've looked up.

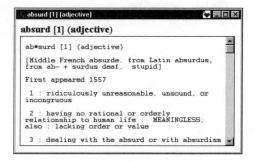

Another useful option available is labeled Full Text, and provides a full listing of related words, along with their definitions, precisely as you'd find it in the print versions of your dictionary. Should you want an actual copy of Merriam-Webster's Collegiate Dictionary on hand, click the Shop the M-W Bookstore icon at the forum's main window, and you'll be able to take advantage of the lowest prices for this and other Merriam-Webster books.

Exploring the Learning & Culture Channel

Keyword: **Education, Learning**

America Online's Learning & Culture channel, shown in figure 25.11, complements the Reference Desk and provides a wide range of information and tools to help you advance your education. The sections that follow describe just a few of the resources available. The contents of this area are grouped into categories, and you can access a particular category by clicking its title once.

FIG. 25.11
You can consider the Learning & Culture channel an online educational institution.

You'll notice that some of the facilities offered are shared with the Reference Desk because they cover both areas. I'll cover some of the highlights of the Learning & Culture channel over the next few pages.

Education on the Internet

Wherever you go on America Online, the Internet is somewhere to be found, and the Learning & Culture channel is no exception. Virtually every category you choose will bring up a list of resources not just on AOL, but on the Internet. For example, the Science & Nature area (see fig. 25.12) offers a list of selected Internet-based resources that are just a click or two away.

Part VI
Ch
25

FIG. 25.12
Many Learning & Culture channel resources, such as the Science & Nature area shown here, are a click or two away from an Internet site.

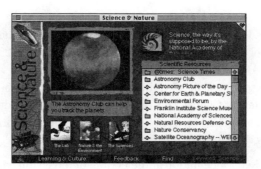

Visiting the Academic Assistance Center

Keyword: **AAC**

Whether you are pursuing higher education, preparing for the College Board exams, or just trying to figure out how to do a homework assignment, consider the Academic Assistance Center a resource for help (see fig. 25.13).

FIG. 25.13
America Online can give help
to the harried student.

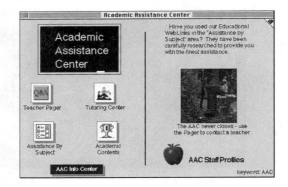

One of the special features of the center is the Tutoring Center. This is a place where you can post messages in order to receive help with a particular problem that you might run across when researching a term paper or writing a book report. You also can access a library of text files on common subjects that you can download.

Teachers' Associations Online

America Online offers a number of educator-oriented forums that are run by organizations.

Visiting the American Federation of Teachers

Keyword: **AFT**

The American Federation of Teachers is a labor organization that represents a large portion of U.S. school teachers. The AFT's online forum (see fig. 25.14), provides information not only for AFT members, but for other AOL members to review. As you can see from the forum's graphical display, there's a gateway to a number of related online areas, such as AOL's Internet Center, The Teachers' Info Network, Education Software Search, AskERIC Online, and The Electronic Schoolhouse. The Search The News feature allows you to quickly locate education-related news items.

The Learning & Reference button at the bottom of the forum window takes you to AOL's Learning and Reference area, which offers a combined listing of many of the forums available in these two departments.

FIG. 25.14
The American Federation of Teachers forum on AOL not only helps advise educators, but gives parents a better insight into the teaching process.

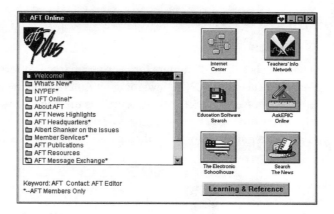

Visiting the NEA Public Forum

Keyword: **NEA Public**

The NEA, National Education Association, is another online resource for professional educators who want to hone their teaching skills and interact with their peers.

The NEA's online organization offers a message area, Talk About Education, where teachers can discuss the major issues affecting curriculums and other important topics. And you can use the Professional Library to download useful material for later reference. Access the wealth of information from the NEA Public Forum screen shown in figure 25.15.

FIG. 25.15
The NEA Public Forum is a resource for the 2.2 million teachers who are members of the organization.

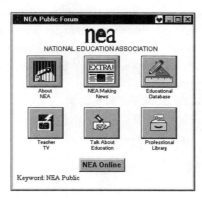

Part
VI

Ch
25

Visiting the CNN Newsroom

Keyword: **CNN**

CNN Newsroom is a daily, 15-minute news program that is offered to schools by Cable News Network. The online CNN Newsroom on America Online focuses on that program and related issues (see fig. 25.16). The forum has message areas where you can communicate with other America Online members or with CNN staff. You can also participate in the regularly scheduled conferences that feature CNN representatives.

FIG. 25.16
The CNN Newsroom online works in cooperation with its valuable classroom information service.

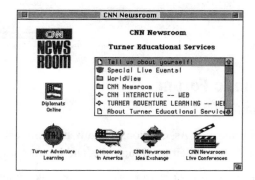

Using College Board Online

Keyword: **College Board**

The College Board is a national organization devoted to the interests of secondary and higher education. You can use the online forum to order books and other materials to help prepare yourself or your child for college entrance exams and to better deal with some of the tougher academic subjects. Figure 25.17 shows the College Board online screen.

FIG. 25.17
College Board online is a source of advice and assistance to students.

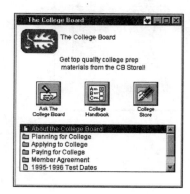

The College Handbook is a database providing informative profiles of many colleges and universities. The Ask The College Board area is a regular America Online message board where you can post questions and receive responses from College Board staff. You also might want to check the Conference Hall for information on the regular schedule of online conferences.

Visiting Simon & Schuster's College Online

Keyword: **College Online**

Simon and Schuster's College Online service (see fig. 25.18) provides both teachers and students with what can be thought of as several forums rolled into one. You can reach each of the related forums by clicking one of the icons shown at the right of the main window.

FIG. 25.18
College Online offers several information centers for students and teachers.

Here are some of these special areas:

- *College Talk.* This is a very active set of message boards on a variety of topics of interest to students and teachers. There are also regularly scheduled chats, with several auditoriums to accommodate concurrent sessions.

- *Faculty/Staff Resources.* This is an area dedicated to the interests of university-level teachers. It offers teaching tips, special information libraries, and regularly scheduled conferences.

- *Student Success.* This forum offers helpful advice for students, software libraries, a directory of information resources, and other useful information.

If you're in search of a specific piece of information, just click the Search College Online button at the bottom of the College Online screen and you can look up texts on a variety of subjects. I found more than two dozen Internet-related articles there when I was researching several chapters for this book.

Teaming Up with the Electronic Schoolhouse

Keyword: **ESH**

Here's a novel idea: A classroom of students in Minnesota exchanges weather information with a classroom in Florida; or articles in one school newspaper are exchanged with another school on the other side of the country. All of these projects can be arranged and run through the Electronic Schoolhouse on AOL (see fig. 25.19).

FIG. 25.19
The Electronic Schoolhouse, where classrooms work together.

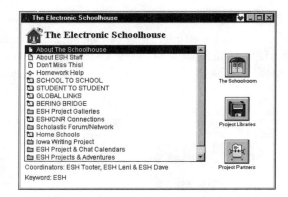

The Schoolroom icon, shown at the right of the forum's window, can be set up as a meeting place, where students and teachers from one class meet with their counterparts on a joint project. The Project Libraries contain a lot of the information you'll need to set up these projects. You'll want to check the Project Partners directory for a listing of classrooms that are looking for project partners. There's also plenty of advice offered that students and teachers will want to examine before linking up.

Getting Help with Home Study Courses

When it wasn't possible to travel to a school for advanced or vocational education, one would take a correspondence course instead. Textbooks and examinations were sent back and forth courtesy of the U.S. Postal Service. With the popularity of online services and electronic mail, it is not surprising to discover that you can get assistance with your home study courses on America Online, too.

Exploring the Electronic University Network

Keyword: **EUN**

Although attending college is often viewed as an exciting time for most students, sometimes traveling to classes just isn't possible. Work and family commitments might prevent you from attending class for an advanced degree, new career studies, or a much-needed remedial course. If so, the Electronic University Network might be able to help you. It's a group of educational institutions that offer interactive learning programs on a variety of subjects (see fig. 25.20).

FIG. 25.20
You can go to college and stay at home at the same time via AOL's Electronic University Network.

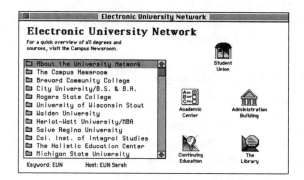

You can consult the Electronic University Network's huge library of educational materials, check on available courses, and even enroll online, from the convenience of your home.

Attending the Komputer Klinic

Keyword: **Komando**

Kim Komando is a newspaper columnist and radio talk show host who has developed a line of tutorial videos designed to make the sometimes obscure world of personal computing understandable. Rather than use complex "technospeak," Kim employs simple words to teach you how to master your computer. You might have even seen the TV commercials about these "Komputer Tutor" tapes. The Komando forum is a source of tips and secrets to help you use your computer more effectively (see fig. 25.21).

FIG. 25.21
The Komputer Klinic is a place to get help with your computer-related troubles.

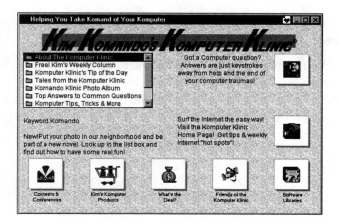

If you need help with a computer-related problem, you can leave a message for Kim and her assistants, who respond in the forum or by e-mail. I can tell you from personal experience that Kim is always a helpful resource, and will frequently go out of her way to answer a question or solve a specific member's problem. You can also order from her line of tutorial videotapes, books, and other merchandise through her mail order sales division (click the Kim's Komputer Products icon).

Exploring the Library of Congress Online

Keyword: **Library**

One of the largest information centers in the world is owned by the U.S. government; it's the Library of Congress. If you are ever in Washington, D.C., you can visit its teeming information archives in person. You also can explore this huge resource on America Online, right from your own computer (see fig. 25.22).

FIG. 25.22
You can tap the huge information resources of the Library of Congress online.

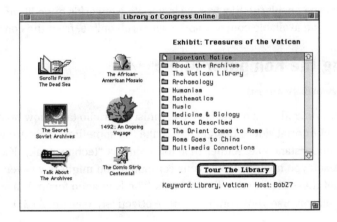

The Tour The Library icon in the forum's main window gives you a brief overview of the Library of Congress' resources.

After you become familiar with the resources available, you might want to click the icons that identify the exhibits that are being highlighted. Besides being able to view, save, and print text reports on the subjects that interest you, you'll find a Voices message board (within the Talk About The Archives icon), where you can read the text of debates on various subjects by noted scholars.

Since the Dead Sea Scrolls were discovered in the Judean Desert in 1947, scholars have spent countless hours researching their scope and meaning. Access this area of the Library of Congress forum by clicking the Scrolls From The Dead Sea icon on the main forum window. Here you can review the scholars' findings and learn the exciting background of this extraordinary archaeological find (see fig. 25.23).

FIG. 25.23
The secrets of the Dead Sea Scrolls are available for you to explore on America Online.

Exploring Princeton Review/Student Access Online

Keyword: **Princeton Review, Student Access**

If you're attending college or seeking career-related information, Student Access is a special center meant for you. Sponsored by *Princeton Review* magazine, it offers special resources for all visitors to the forum.

The forum also features a number of members-only departments, which you can access only if you join the organization (see fig. 25.24). But even if you don't sign up, you can exchange messages with other students, download useful material from the forum's software libraries, and even leave classified ads that are of interest to other students.

Part VI

Ch

25

FIG. 25.24
Student Access is a special online area for those seeking higher education.

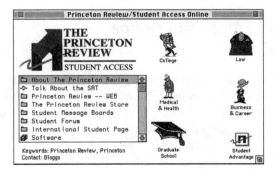

Visiting the Scholastic Forum

Keyword: **Scholastic**

The Scholastic Network Sampler is an online resource for teachers and students (see fig. 25.25). Professional educators can interact with their peers, and if you are a teacher, you can even join the network online.

FIG. 25.25
From your child's classroom to America Online, the Scholastic Forum is the place for educators.

The forum is a center in which to discuss curriculum planning, purchase professional literature, and participate in live conferences on a host of subjects related to educating our youth.

One of the most popular areas in the Scholastic Online forum is Kids' World, a part of the Scholastic Network. It's a place where children can have fun and learn at the same time. Chapter 17, "Games, Entertainment, Teen Chat, and Netiquette," offers a more detailed description of AOL's educational resources for those ages 5 to 14.

Reading *Scientific American* Online

Keyword: **SciAm**

Although it's the oldest magazine still being published in the U.S., *Scientific American* has embraced the latest technologies and established an active, friendly, comprehensive forum on AOL (see fig. 25.26). The major article of the current issue is featured with its own icon at the bottom of the forum window.

FIG. 25.26

Read *Scientific American* on AOL.

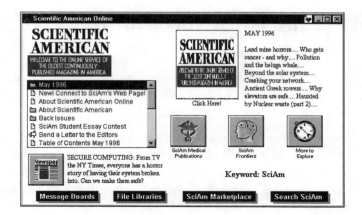

If you want to go directly to the latest issue, click the icon in the upper right of the forum's screen and you'll see the stories in that issue grouped by topic or story title (see fig. 25.27). As with other text material on America Online, you can save or print the text (using the appropriate commands from the File menu) so you can read it at your leisure.

Part

VI

Ch

25

FIG. 25.27

You can read the current issue of *Scientific American* right on America Online.

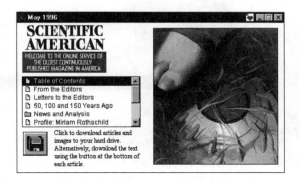

Let's return to the main forum screen for a moment, and look at the other features offered. The public television program, *Scientific American Frontiers,* gets its own icon (SciAm Frontiers), where you can read about upcoming presentations. Articles and graphics images can be downloaded from the File Libraries. The Message Boards will give you a clear indication of the sort of reaction new scientific developments often bring. The other areas of this forum allow you to search for material in the current and previous issues, order subscriptions to *Scientific American,* and explore other information resources on AOL, including the Internet Center.

Visiting the Afterwards Cafe

Keyword: **Afterwards**

Having spent these many hours deeply immersed in your studies on one subject or another, the time might come when you want to relax and perhaps meet with other students for a chat.

America Online's Afterwards Cafe is a pleasant, relaxing environment for serious discussions about all sorts of topics, from current events to literature and the arts. After you're there for a few moments, you will actually be able to imagine its decorative surroundings and comfortable seating. It's a place to get a virtual cup of coffee or a soft drink after completing a hard day's work. Figure 25.28 shows the Afterwards Cafe directory screen.

FIG. 25.28
When your studies are done, you can relax at the Afterwards Cafe.

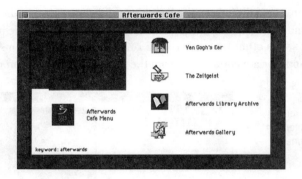

From Here...

America Online's resources for education and reference aren't confined to just the forums mentioned so far in this chapter. The repositories are so huge that the surface has barely been scratched. You need to dig in and explore further on your own to find out what gems of knowledge you can find.

Both newspapers and magazines are valuable learning tools, too, and online resources for both were described in Chapter 23, "The News of the Day," and Chapter 24, "Magazines and Newspapers Online." In addition, you'll want to check out the following chapters for related information:

■ In Chapter 11, "TV and Movie Information Online," you'll discover a wealth of entertainment-related information resources on America Online.

- In Chapter 12, "Music, Books, and Art," you'll explore additional online entertainment information.

- In Chapter 26, "Online Investment and Tax Information," you'll find information to help you spend your money more wisely, seek out ways to invest your income, and get assistance when it comes time to pay your taxes.

Part
VI

Ch
25

Personal Finance

Online Investment and Tax Information

Computers and personal finance go hand in hand. We prepare checks on our computers, do our tax returns, and manage an investment portfolio. If you own a business, the computer is an indispensable tool.

If you use your computer for any sort of financial purpose, you'll want to visit the Personal Finance channel on America Online. There you'll find a wealth of useful financial information.

This chapter covers AOL's Personal Finance department and its many-layered gateways that extend from business news to an online real estate office. ■

AOL's financial forums

Learn where to seek advice and information about business, stocks, and bonds.

World Wide Web financial resources

Explore Internet-based financial information (including the site run by the IRS).

Finding a new home online

Check out the country-wide real estate listings on AOL.

AOL's Tax forum

Helpful hints are available at tax time and throughout the year.

Personal Finance

Keyword: **Personal Finance**

In Chapters 23 and 24, you read the latest news and browsed through the magazine racks. Now you'll delve more deeply into the world of business. America Online's Personal Finance department, shown in figure 26.1, isn't just for your business activities, however. You'll find resources here that will help you take charge of your personal finances, too. Some of them will be covered in the final section of this chapter.

FIG. 26.1
America Online's Personal Finance department emphasizes money management.

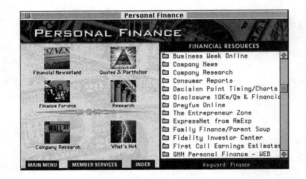

> **N O T E**   Please take note of the disclaimer that you'll find posted in various forums in AOL's Personal Finance channel. The purpose of these areas is to give you information about various aspects of financial management. The forum staff and contributors to those areas are not responsible in any way for the way you use that information to conduct your personal finances.

Using the Online Stock Forums

America Online offers you helpful investment information that guides you toward managing a stock portfolio. You can also check the latest stock prices within 15 minutes after they are posted, so you can see how your favorite stocks are doing.

A little later in this chapter, I'll even show you a sample investment portfolio that I assembled.

Using the Decision Point

Keyword: **DP**

AOL's Decision Point Timing & Charts is a highly specialized forum that is devoted to helping you examine stock market trends (see fig. 26.2). The forum is run by the publisher of Decision Point Alert, a stock market advisory newsletter. Each area in this forum is designed to provide helpful market information.

FIG. 26.2
Learn techniques to evaluate stock market trends in the Decision Point forum on AOL.

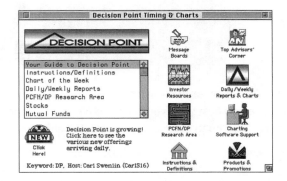

This section covers a few of the forum's highlights that you'll want to check further during your online visits. All of these information resources have a central goal in mind: to help you, as an investor, learn how to use stock market information to arrive at the best possible decisions when managing your own portfolio. Before continuing, notice the forum's disclaimer, which is similar to that shown in other personal finance areas online. Basically, it states that America Online and the forum aren't responsible for the way you use the information provided.

If you're new to the stock market, you'll want to click the New icon, which offers a short and simple course on doing stock market analysis. The remainder of the forum offers charts, advice in the message board area, and the opportunity to buy books and tapes to help enhance your abilities to handle your own investments.

Part
VII

Ch
26

Hoover's Business Resources

Keyword: **Hoover**

Before you decide to invest in a company's stock, you should know something about that company and the related industries. AOL's Hoover's Business Resources forum is an important resource (see fig. 26.3).

FIG. 26.3
Your online resource when
you want a company profile.

The forum lists company profiles alphabetically, by industry, or by location. Choose the search technique that best suits your needs. To give you an idea of the kind of information you can find, I looked up the profile for one major company (see fig. 26.4).

CAUTION

The company profiles offered are, of course, not guaranteed 100 percent. The firms that provide these reports post online terms and conditions that you can read before reviewing the profiles themselves. If you want to learn more about a specific company before investing, you might also want to secure the company's annual report and do additional research before making a financial decision.

FIG. 26.4
AOL's company profiles offer
detailed but concise
summaries of major
companies.

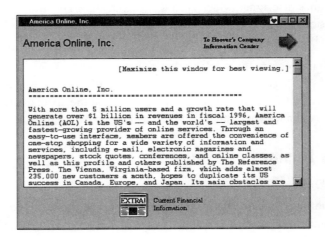

Company profiles are brief but sharply focused to give you the information you need to make important decisions concerning the future prospects of a company.

Reading the *Investor's Business Daily*

Keyword: **IBD**

The *Investor's Business Daily* forum on AOL (see fig. 26.5) provides text copies of the contents of the paper's regular national editions. The forum also offers a full Information Center where you can search for material from past issues and other information resources that supplement the material you read in the paper.

FIG. 26.5
Read each informative edition of the *Investor's Business Daily* during your visit to AOL.

The contents of the issue are grouped by topic, shown by icons along the bottom of the forum window. After reading these sections, you might want to get a Free Trial Subscription by filling out the coupon offered when you click the icon with that label. After reading the issue, click The Week Ahead icon to learn about expected developments from the business world. You can access the forum's active message board from this icon to share your views with other readers and the newspaper's editors and writers.

Investors' Network

Keyword: **Investors, IN**

Some people liken the process of making the correct financial investment to fortune telling. Because you cannot easily predict the outcome of an investment, you need as much information as possible before you make a decision (see fig. 26.6).

The Investors' Network is a resource that you can visit for information before you make a decision. The Main Message Board hosts brisk debates on the state of the financial markets and offers helpful advice.

During this forum's regular chats, you can consult with fellow AOL members and financial experts about the best investment prospects.

FIG. 26.6
This network provides help when you want to know what the best investments might be.

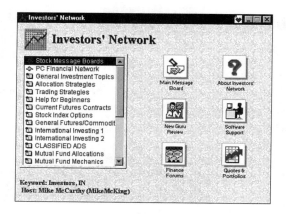

What Is The Motley Fool?

Keyword: **Fool**

Despite what it sounds like, The Motley Fool forum is not simply a play on words derived from the name of a rock band (see fig. 26.7). It is a forum that offers a very unique slant toward financial information, designed not just to inform, but to amuse as well.

Although *The Motley Fool* began life as a printed publication, the introduction to the online world showed the editors a better way to do things. Now this publication exists solely online. It is very difficult to describe this resource in just a few short paragraphs, so let me just suggest you read the regular online issues, check out the message boards, and if your curiosity is really piqued, even attend one of its highly informative online conferences.

FIG. 26.7
Business information doesn't have to be overly serious, according to The Motley Fool.

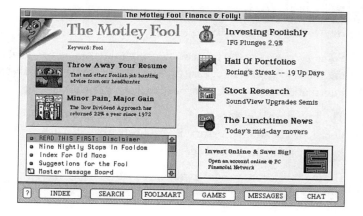

Morningstar Mutual Funds

Keyword: **Morningstar**

A mutual fund is a way to reduce the risk in your investments, by investing in a portfolio of a large number of stocks, rather than two or three. Morningstar Mutual Funds is an independent company that tracks the progress of some 3,400 different mutual funds (see fig. 26.8).

FIG. 26.8
For information on how your favorite mutual fund is doing, check out the Morningstar Mutual Funds forum on AOL.

To learn how the service works, click the Morningstar Marketplace button. It'll take a few minutes of your time, but it offers valuable advice you'll want to consider if you plan to get involved in this sort of investment or just track the progress of mutual funds you already invest in. A handy text-based Mutual Fund User's Guide is available in this forum, which you can use to learn how best to track the progress and history of a mutual fund.

Part
VII

Ch
26

Quotes and Portfolios

Keyword: **Quotes**

How well is your stock portfolio doing? Is your stockbroker's phone busy, or do you just want to see how your favorite stocks are doing before you decide whether to invest? Check out AOL's Quotes & Portfolios forum (see fig. 26.9).

Because America Online's stock is quite popular, I decided to check its present value. Figure 26.9 shows its price and related statistics. Checking the value of stock is easy. First you have to enter the stock's symbol because market entries are usually identified in abbreviated form. The Lookup Symbol feature lets you quickly find the correct symbol. The Add to Portfolio feature is simply a convenience measure, so you can easily track your favorite stocks, whether your interest in the market is from an armchair or as an active investor.

FIG. 26.9
AOL's Quotes & Portfolios area helps you keep your stock portfolio current.

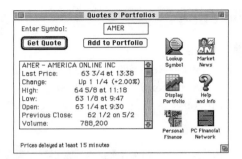

Once you've built your stock portfolio, real or imaginary, you can click the Display Portfolio icon (which brings up the screen in fig. 26.10) to see just how your investments are doing, and how much money you've made or (perish the thought) lost in these transactions. As you can see from my choices, I would have made a small profit had these investments actually been made.

If you want to learn more about a company, look at the Hoover's Business Resources section (described earlier). The Market News icon shown in figure 26.9 takes you to AOL's business news area, the online equivalent of a newspaper's financial pages.

FIG. 26.10
A sample investment portfolio of popular and not-so-popular stocks. Remember, this is just a sample, and doesn't represent my actual profile.

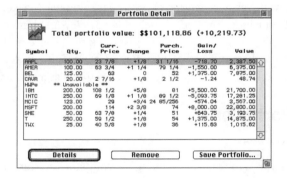

Using the Wall Street SOS Forum

Keyword: **SOS**

SOS is an apt acronym indeed, because the financial world is so complex that many folks venturing into the Wall Street arena for the first time do wish they had some active assistance. That's one of the reasons for the Wall Street SOS Forum (see fig. 26.11). The forum is run by Security Objective Services (hence the SOS), an investment advisory firm since 1970.

FIG. 26.11
You'll get helpful advice on the stock market from the experts at SOS.

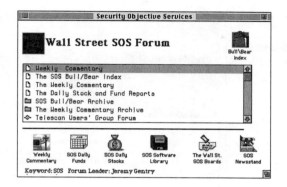

When you enter the SOS forum for the first time (or on your regular visits), you'll want to read the Weekly Commentary, which reports on current trading information on stocks, options, futures, and mutual funds. The Bull/Bear Index is Security Objective Services' own daily summary of market activity. The SOS Daily Funds and SOS Daily Stocks icons provide daily information on mutual funds and stocks. There are also some very spirited message boards, The Wall St. SOS Boards, where you can interact with fellow investors and forum staff on a variety of issues. The SOS Software Library offers archives of material from the forum, and the SOS Newsstand lets you review and subscribe to the firm's own publications.

Before you finish your visit to the SOS forum, you'll want to look over the directory listing for the Telescan Users' Group Forum. This is a forum run by SOS that offers an independent information service dedicated to serious investors.

Internet-Based Personal Finance Resources

There are so many useful financial resources on AOL, you may think that represents the entire picture. Actually, there are many global Internet-based sources that provide still more valuable information for you (see fig. 26.12). AOL has assembled a select portion of those resources, but you can use AOL's handy World Wide Web browser (described in more detail in Chapters 35 and 36) to locate many more.

The U.S. government is quite aware of how valuable the Internet is. Many government agencies have set up World Wide Web pages, including the IRS (see fig. 26.13). You'll be able to check out current tax regulations and even download the latest tax forms from this site. The forms themselves are usually provided in Adobe's Acrobat format, so you can print them out on most printers with excellent quality.

FIG. 26.12

A sample of Internet financial information centers you can access from AOL.

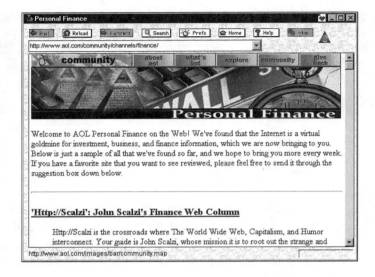

FIG. 26.13

Get current forms and tax information direct from the IRS, via AOL's World Wide Web browser software.

TIP   You can get a copy of Adobe Acrobat direct from its support forum on AOL (keyword: **Adobe**).

Reading *BusinessWeek* Online

Keyword: **BW**

How often do you hear a news item about an important development from the business world, and find the magic words, "according to a report published in *BusinessWeek?*" McGraw-Hill's *BusinessWeek* Online offers the entire contents of the weekly editions of its world-renowned magazine on AOL, with colorful artwork (although you can only see a hint of it in black and white) from the issues as well (see fig. 26.14).

FIG. 26.14
Read the weekly editions of *BusinessWeek* on AOL.

Besides the text and illustrations from the magazine, you'll have the chance to attend live special events, featuring the magazine's editors and noted business figures. You can interact with editors and fellow AOL members in the forum's Talk message board. The remaining icons shown in the forum window represent the contents of the magazine, special offers for new subscribers, and an offering of business-related books from McGraw-Hill.

Part
VII

Ch
26

Reading Financial News Online

Some of this material is covered in Chapter 23, "The News of the Day." But the Financial Newsstand area (accessible by clicking the named icon in the Personal Finance department) offers not only the highlights from the regular news area, such as Market News and Business News, but a direct gateway to other information sources, too (see fig. 26.15).

▶ **See** "Business News," **p. 417**

You can open the business pages of such newspapers as the *New York Times, Arizona Republic, San Jose Mercury News, Chicago Tribune,* and read the regular editions of *Investor's Business Daily.* You also have a direct link with Internet Gophers that are devoted to financial and economic information. For more details on AOL's Internet-based links, read the chapters in Part VIII, "Entering the Information Superhighway."

FIG. 26.15
All of the latest financial news can be accessed from one convenient location.

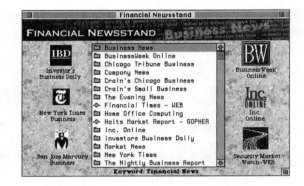

Microsoft Knowledge Base

Keyword: **Microsoft**

Besides providing popular software for the Macintosh and Windows platforms, Microsoft has a huge World Wide Web-based library of information on all aspects of computing. Whether you have a hardware-related problem or difficulty using your Microsoft software, you'll probably find the information you need in its online database (see fig. 26.16).

FIG. 26.16
A vast storehouse of Internet-based, business-related information from Microsoft.

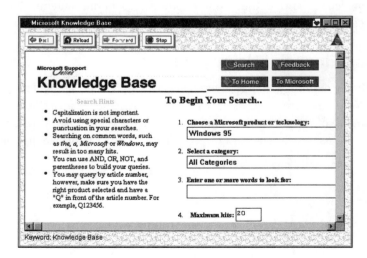

The information you want is conveniently catalogued by topic, or you can search for particular articles that might interest you. As with any text file on America Online, you can read it online, or save or print the file for offline review.

Visiting the Nightly Business Report

Keyword: **NBR**

Each night hundreds of public television stations present the Nightly Business Report, a highly respected program that reports the most important business news of the day (see fig. 26.17). The show's online forum offers a full schedule of upcoming shows, along with a list of the stations that currently carry the broadcast.

FIG. 26.17
Review the highlights of the Nightly Business Report on AOL.

If you miss a show, or want to review the contents again, you can check the transcript library available by clicking NBR Transcripts. This useful feature also allows you to seek out text on special topics from earlier shows. You can also visit the Chat & Boards message area to read and participate in the forum's active message areas. If you're a teacher, you can find advice on how to use the program's content in your classrooms. There's a listing showing current national opinion survey results, and a shopping area called The Best of Good Buys, where you can order helpful videos with a business slant.

Downloading Files from the Personal Finance Software Center

Keyword: **PF Software**

Not every piece of software out there is a commercial product that you would buy at a store or from a mail order catalog. There are a huge number of shareware and freeware offerings that enhance your existing finance software or provide special features you might not find in the regular commercial marketplace. Your resource for these special software gems is AOL's Personal Finance Software Center (see fig. 26.18).

FIG. 26.18
Tap a huge resource of financial software on AOL.

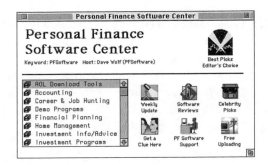

The really nice thing about shareware is that you can try it before you buy it and not have to pay any money to the publisher or author unless you like the software and want to continue using it. This gives you a chance to experiment with different approaches to a specific financial information problem before you settle on the right one.

The Personal Financial Software Center is there to guide you every step of the way. There's an icon labeled Best Picks Editor's Choice, where the top software is described. You'll find reviews of many of the online offerings; you can learn the positive and negative aspects of software before you download the files. And everything is grouped into clearly labeled categories, with detailed file descriptions, so you can get an idea of what the software will do for you before you try it out.

This forum also provides a quick gateway to other finance forums on AOL, and a Software Support icon that transports you directly to the forums run by a number of publishers of financial software.

Real Estate Online

Keyword: **Real Estate**

Are you selling your home or looking for a new residence in your hometown or another state? Whatever your interest in real estate, pay a visit to AOL's Real Estate Center (see fig. 26.19). Here you can find an interactive Multiple Listing Service (MLS), which you can check to find available homes nationwide.

FIG. 26.19
If you're looking for a new home, or you just want to learn more about real estate, here's a forum you'll want to visit.

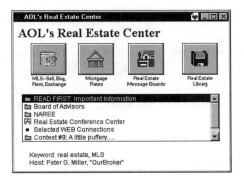

If you are looking to finance or refinance your home, consult the listing of current mortgage rates. The Real Estate Message Boards provide a resource where you get expert advice from a real estate professional and share information with other AOL members.

Consult the forum's Real Estate Library for lots of useful information; there are folders full of advice and tips on all sorts of real estate-related issues.

For more assistance, attend this forum's regular conferences.

Online Tax Assistance

Earlier in this chapter, I presented an illustration of the IRS site on the World Wide Web, where you can get tax information direct from the horse's mouth, as it were.

The final part of this chapter briefly covers some of the tax forums available on America Online. Just remember, before you read this section, that AOL and forum staff can't actually fill out your tax returns for you. Only you or your tax preparer can do that. But, the forums are designed to provide information that will help you over some of the hurdles and ease the process of accurately filling out your tax return. I should also add that, while forums such as the one run by Intuit are available year-round, other tax-related forums only appear during the tax season.

Reading the *Ernst & Young Tax Guide*

Keyword: **Tax Guide**

If you do your own tax returns, you no doubt face the same problem as everyone else, wading through tons and tons of IRS documents to figure out what applies to your own tax return. Undoubtedly, you've seen the *Ernst & Young Tax Guide* at your local bookstore (see fig. 26.20). Now you can read the contents of this guide on AOL. And, using the Save and Print commands from the File menu of AOL's software, you can review the documents at your leisure after your online visits have concluded.

FIG. 26.20
Learn the ins and outs of IRS regulations using the Ernst & Young Tax Guide on AOL.

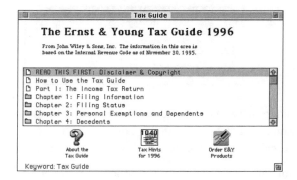

The Ernst & Young forum groups the contents of its guide in convenient chapters, each available in a separate folder. There's also an icon labeled Tax Hints (the year displayed will change, of course), where you can get capsule summaries of information that will help speed up your tax-preparation chores. There's also a quick gateway to AOL's Tax Forum, which is discussed later in this chapter.

 You can easily review long text documents in sequence and save them on your computer's hard drive in one operation. Just open a system log, using the steps described in Appendix B (for Mac users) or Appendix C (for Windows users).

Visiting Intuit Online

Keyword: **Intuit**

Intuit is a publisher specializing in financial software, such as the best-selling Quicken, MacInTax, and TurboTax (see fig. 26.21). These programs, available for both Macintosh and PC users, allow you to use your computer to run most of your financial transactions, from your checkbook to tax preparation.

The company's support forum offers helpful advice on how to use its software in the form of frequently asked questions grouped by topic in the forum's list box. There's also an active Message Center where you can get assistance from the publisher or advice from savvy users. The Software Libraries icon offers product updates and helpful files that will make your financial planning go faster. Double-click Product Information in the forum's list box to locate additional information about specific Intuit software products and techniques for electronic tax filing.

FIG. 26.21

Intuit provides support for its personal finance software on AOL.

Using Kiplinger TaxCut

Keyword: **Kiplinger**

Block Financial (part of the H&R Block Company) is a well-known resource for financial planning information. Among the company's popular products is TaxCut, a full-featured tax preparation package that simplifies preparation of your tax returns. If you want more information about Kiplinger TaxCut and other Kiplinger products, you'll want to visit its forum on AOL (see fig. 26.22).

FIG. 26.22

You can receive online support for Kiplinger's TaxCut in this forum.

Part

VII

Ch

26

The Block Financial Software Support forum offers a large amount of help text documents that contain tax-planning information and the best ways to use the software. There are also active message boards, where you can get assistance from the publisher and experienced users on the most efficient ways to set up and use TaxCut. You can also place your order for TaxCut and other products during your online visits.

A Visit to AOL's Tax Forum

Keyword: **Tax, Tax Forum**

AOL's Tax Forum tends to be seasonal in nature, when preparing your taxes is most often on your mind. The forum provides many current tax forms in disk form, so you can use your personal computer and printer to make copies (see fig. 26.23).

FIG. 26.23
All of AOL's tax assistance resources are available from one convenient forum.

Just click the Tax Shareware icon and you'll find software libraries where you can download useful utilities that simplify the task of calculating the financial information on your tax return. You'll find additional files that help you with general accounting and financial planning. The four icons at the right of the Tax Forum screen take you to areas that provide additional help. Two examples, TAXLOGIC ONLINE and NAEA TAX CHANNEL, are valuable sources of support from tax professionals who provide common sense answers to tough questions. And the icon at the top takes you to an area where you can download the IRS tax forms you need.

From Here...

This chapter describes the many business resources online that help you manage your stock portfolio, navigate through your tax returns, and even check out the real estate market. You'll also want to review the following chapters:

- In Chapter 23, "The News of the Day," you'll discover resources for AOL's online newspapers.

- In Chapter 24, "Magazines and Newspapers Online," you'll visit AOL's newsstand and scan the racks for your favorite publications.

CHAPTER 27

Secrets of AOL's Travel Department

Learn more about other places

Find out about attractions in your destination city.

Book a trip

Prepare your travel itinerary right on your computer.

Use AOL's reservation services

Visit AOL's One World Travel and American Airlines' EAASY SABRE services.

Check flight schedules and fares

Learn how to make your airline, car, and hotel reservations.

Having covered investments and saving money on your taxes in Chapter 26, let's devote this chapter to one way of doing something with some of the money you may save. This chapter and the next are devoted to shopping of one sort or another; this chapter covers shopping for a vacation. Instead of visiting the neighborhood travel agency, you're going to an agency located in cyberspace, available through the friendly interface of America Online.

Using AOL's Travel department, you can pick a spot for a family vacation and gather information about the place you're going to visit without ever leaving your own home or office. You can select a hotel, make reservations, and even rent a car.

Suppose, for example, that you've never taken your children on a trip to California, and have wanted to go there for a long time. This chapter uses Los Angeles as the site for a sample vacation plan. Of course, you can travel virtually anywhere in the world by using the same techniques discussed in this chapter. ■

Visiting the Travel Channel

Keyword: **Travel**

Your first step in preparing for this vacation is to pay a visit to AOL's Travel channel. To access this area, click the Travel icon in the Channel menu or use the keyword **Travel**. You then see the screen shown in figure 27.1 (or the latest version, because it's updated often). Some of the online areas available in this department are described in the next few pages.

> **N O T E** Some of the areas shown in the Travel department are also available as part of AOL's Marketplace department, which is discussed in more detail in Chapter 28, "Secrets of Online Shopping." ■

FIG. 27.1
The Travel department on AOL provides the resources you need before making a business or vacation trip.

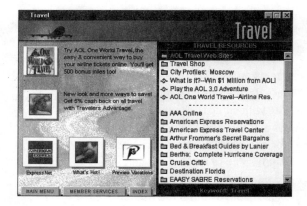

A Look at AOL's Travel Web Sites

Because you are planning a trip to different parts of the world, you'll be pleased to know that you can also travel to different parts of the Internet to access travel-related information (see fig. 27.2). To access this area, just double-click AOL Travel Web Sites in the Travel channel list box.

I'll cover the specifics of AOL's Internet access in the chapters that make up Part VIII, "Entering the Information Superhighway." But for now, just check out AOL's WebCrawler searching tool, accessed from the Top Internet Sites screen using the icon at the bottom left of the screen. You can use that search tool just as you use any regular search tool on AOL, to locate information on specific subjects within seconds. Another useful resource is the GNN Travel Center. I'll cover GNN's services in more detail in Chapters 37 and 38.

FIG. 27.2
AOL offers a useful selection of travel-related sites on the Internet.

Using the EAASY SABRE System

Keyword: **EAASY SABRE**

To get from the Travel window to the EAASY SABRE main menu, first click EAASY SABRE Reservations from the Travel channel list box. Then, in the EAASY SABRE window that appears, select Enter EAASY SABRE. If this is your first visit to this area, select Visitor in the window that follows. In the next window, you can read the terms and conditions of EAASY SABRE, or you can continue to the EAASY SABRE main menu.

Visiting American Airlines' EAASY SABRE forum is much like visiting your local travel agency (see fig. 27.3). You can look up the current weather in the cities to which you are traveling. You can check on the availability of airline flights, hotel rooms, and rental cars. Not only can you find out flight schedules, but you also can check for the lowest available fares and even examine the fine print that lets you know whether you're eligible for a discount.

FIG. 27.3
America Online's EAASY SABRE gateway is your entrance to full-featured reservation service.

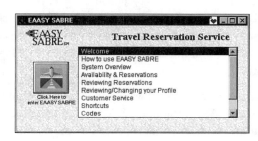

When you've located all the information you want, you can make your reservations, confirm those reservations, and bill the charges directly to your credit card. Your plane tickets and confirmation information will be mailed to your home or office.

TIP   If you have a special preference for seating, such as a window seat, or you're on a special diet, you need to list those preferences in your application. Getting correct reservations is much easier that way.

N O T E   Macintosh users on America Online can use EAASY SABRE's unique graphics menu to navigate the service. If you've used EAASY SABRE on other services, you can opt for the standard text menu instead.

Applying for Membership

Feel free to browse through the EAASY SABRE forum to see what kinds of features it offers. Because membership is free and without any obligation, however, you probably want to become a member so that you can make your reservations whenever you want. When you click the Apply button in the EAASY SABRE main menu, you are taken through a brief questionnaire that asks for your name, address, telephone number, and information about the credit card you want to use for billing (you don't have to include all this information, of course, and you aren't even obligated to use the same credit card to bill your trip).

For security reasons, you are given a personal membership identification number. You can select your own password, too, so that nobody else can make reservations and bill charges in your name. It's a good idea to write down this information, or record it in a notepad program, so you can refer to this number the next time you visit EAASY SABRE. After a few weeks, you will receive a membership kit with further information on how to use the service.

Finding the Best Fares or Flights

The ongoing airline price wars have made just about everyone (your cheerful author included) confused about airline fares. Each airline has its own schedule, with specific rules to obtain those highly touted discount fares. And the prices seem to change almost daily, in response to another airline's announcement about still lower and sometimes more confusing price schedules.

Before making your reservation, you'll want to find out just what the prices really are. You can also use the EAASY SABRE Bargain Finder to find the cheapest fares, and more important, learn about the conditions that apply to those fares. Most times, you have to book your flight a number of days in advance and stay at your destination a specific number of days. It's common, for example, to have to stay over on a Saturday night to get the lowest possible price.

Different Interfaces

Because the face that EAASY SABRE puts forward is different for Mac and PC users, and updates often, let me say in general that you'll see a complete list of menu commands or easy access buttons to guide you along the way. And in addition to making your plane reservations, you can also schedule your hotel and car rentals. In every case, you'll see a list of prices and terms, so you can decide which option is best for you.

You have the choice of letting EAASY SABRE handle your travel reservations for you, or you can use the information to make your own travel reservations by contacting the airlines, rental agencies, and hotels directly. Or, you can have your favorite travel agent handle the chores for you. In any case, you'll find it much easier to make an informed decision about the best travel arrangements by taking a tour through EAASY SABRE.

NOTE To ensure which hotels offer the best accommodations, have their reservations department send you a brochure. The larger hotel chains and tourist spots offer elaborate color booklets describing all of the features that are available and the various room options. ▉

Book Your Trip with AOL's One World Travel Agency

Keyword: **OneWorldTravel**

Another popular travel agency on AOL is One World (see fig. 27.4). In addition to making travel plans at the best available price, you will want to check this area regularly for special deals on car rentals and special tours. There's even a message board where you can learn about the experiences of your fellow AOL members when visiting a specific city, and contribute your own remembrances and advice, too.

To get started, you'll want to make your own custom travel profile, by clicking the One World Travel icon in this forum's main window. In addition to your name and address, you can add such information as the kind of cuisine you prefer on your flight, a listing of your favorite airlines, and whether you qualify for frequent flier mileage on any of them.

Part
VII

Ch
27

FIG. 27.4
AOL's One World Travel agency provides travel advice and an easy method to make your reservations at the lowest possible price.

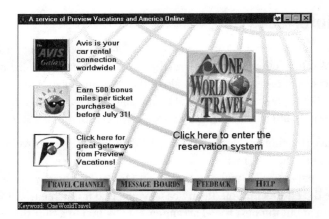

Using ExpressNet from American Express

Keyword: **ExpressNet**

You've heard the commercials: "Don't leave home without it." Well, American Express has teamed up with the folks at America Online to provide a fully equipped interactive customer service center for you (see fig. 27.5). If you're already an American Express cardholder, you can use this forum to check your account status and take advantage of some of the special features, such as travel reservations and special offers.

FIG. 27.5
Before you leave home, be sure you have your credit card ready.

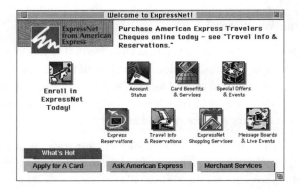

If you are not already a cardholder, you can easily apply for the American Express card by clicking the Apply for A Card button. If you have questions about your account, choose Ask American Express, and you'll be able to send a message directly to the customer support department for a prompt response.

The Message Boards & Live Events area is a place where you can interact with other cardholders, exchange hot travel tips, and get advice on the best hotels and dining establishments in the place to which you're traveling. You'll also want to review the Special Offers & Events area for up-to-date information on exclusive promotions that are available only to cardholders.

Visiting Travelers Corner

Keyword: **Travelers Corner**

The next stopping point on this tour is the Travelers Corner. In addition to using the keyword **Travelers Corner** (see fig. 27.6) to get there, you can double-click the Travelers Corner listing in the Travel channel's list box to reach this area. This forum is hosted by the editors of *Weissman Travel Reports*. The Corner's main focus is the comprehensive profiles about major U.S. and international destinations. You get a brief overview about the high points of a specific city and a list of its main attractions. The report not only describes these attractions, but also suggests the kinds of people who would most like to visit them. This information is especially important if you're taking your children with you.

FIG. 27.6
The Travelers Corner profiles your favorite travel spots.

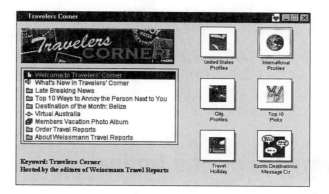

The profiles contain lists of do's and don'ts so that you can learn more about the local culture and etiquette of your destination. This kind of help is especially useful if you're traveling to a foreign country where local customs might be different from the ones to which you're accustomed.

The Travelers Corner screen includes separate icons for the kinds of profiles you want to review—domestic or international. There's even a message center that describes exotic destinations you might want to visit. You can stop over in this area to learn about the experiences of other online travelers, both America Online members and *Weissman Travel*

Part
VII

Ch
27

Reports editors. You also can use this message board to post your own personal reports of your travels, so you can share the information you've discovered with other AOL members.

Because our sample travel plan is taking you to Los Angeles, you can choose the United States Profiles icon to bring up the list of U.S. City Profiles (see fig. 27.7). The window gives you two ways to search: by city name (the Search icon) or by the letters of the alphabet. Profiles contain five or more pages of valuable information about your favorite destination.

FIG. 27.7

You have two ways to search for a profile of your destination.

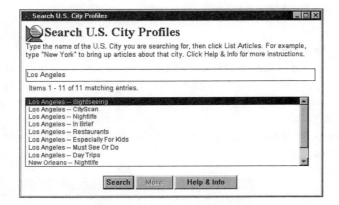

If you want to read more travel-related material at your leisure, choose Order Travel Reports from the Travelers Corner list box. You'll read about a special offer to purchase comprehensive professional profiles of the places you want to visit. These profiles are the same ones that are available through your local travel agency.

Previewing Vacations Online

Keyword: **Vacations**

They say a picture is worth a thousand words, and while it's really nice to read text documents about travel locations online, wouldn't it be great to actually see what these far-off locales look like before you plan your trip?

That's what Preview Vacations Online is all about (refer to fig. 27.8). This forum, sponsored by Preview Media of San Francisco, lets you view full-color photos of popular travel spots, and even participate in a real auction where you can bid on the vacation of your choice. In addition to accessing the forum via a keyword, you will usually find it identified by an icon on the main screen of the Travel channel (refer to fig. 27.1) or from AOL's One World Travel agency (refer to fig. 27.4).

FIG. 27.8
Preview Vacations on AOL is a lot more than just a collection of travel photos.

When I was a child, I used to collect stamps. At times, I'd participate in stamp auctions, where I had to mail my bid to the auction house and it would be judged against other bids. I even got the high bid in a few cases, as I recall. Of course, there weren't online services in those days (let alone low-cost personal computers), but it is only natural that auctions have become a part of the world of cyberspace too. This brings us to the Auction House, where you can place your bid with an online auctioneer on the vacation of your choice. There is no minimum bid. If you've been dreaming about a fantasy vacation for a long time now, this might be a way to get it for an amazingly low price. You also have a chance to win a vacation freebie by taking a Win-A-Trip Travel Survey. Lucky winners are announced on a regular basis.

If your bid on that special trip isn't the highest offer, don't despair. Click the Vacation Offers area and you'll see a large selection of special vacation package offers that you might fancy instead. The offers change periodically; if you double-click the What's Hot icon instead, you'll find some special limited-time offers.

If you need some more advice before you plan your journey, drop in to the Talk! message board, where you can leave a message for the Preview Vacations staff and receive further advice. If you still haven't decided which destination to choose, select the Join—it's free! list to receive a special Preview Vacation package that's tailored to your own requirements.

Taking Advantage of Travelers Advantage

Keyword: **Travelers Advantage, TA**

Chapter 28 describes a way for you to receive discounted meals at the top dining spots around the U.S. Travelers Advantage provides the same sort of service when you make your travel plans (see fig. 27.9). Consider it a discount travel agency, where you can check for the lowest prices and make your travel plans from the comfort of your personal computer.

Part
VII

Ch
27

FIG. 27.9

A visit to the Travelers Advantage forum on AOL.

One of the most attractive features of the Travelers Advantage forum is a list of more than 4,000 hotels in which you can stay at half the regular price. Just click the 50% Off Hotel Rates button to consult the listing. There's also a Hotel Direct package where you can get a 70 percent discount on an additional 7,000 hotels. That's something I'm definitely going to check out the next time I plan one of my twice yearly trips to a computer expo.

N O T E Travelers Express is a membership organization. To take advantage of the special deals that are being offered, you have to sign up for membership first. To sample the service, click the Get a FREE Hotel Night by Joining Now! icon, and sign up. ■

As mentioned earlier in this chapter, the travel business is quite competitive, and prices are apt to change frequently. Travelers Advantage offers a low price guarantee (which reminds me of some of those discount stores you see at your local shopping mall). If you find a lower price after you've booked your airline, car, and hotel arrangements, Travelers Advantage will send you a check for the difference.

After you become a Travelers Advantage member, you can call a special hotline number, shown on your membership card, to take advantage of special travel deals on short notice. The forum also offers special prices on rentals from the major car rental agencies. If you opt to pay with cash rather than credit card, there's an additional five-percent discount on the total price.

If you have further questions, or want advice before you plan your trip, you find the forums' message boards available when you click one of the icons at either side of the screen (such as Cruises). If you're an experienced traveler, you might even want to participate in some of the discussions and share tales of your own travels.

Visiting the Travel Forum

Keyword: **Travel Forum**

The Travel Forum consists of a wealth of resources that contains much of the information you need to know before planning your trip (see fig. 27.10). The main window of this forum contains useful articles on many travel-related subjects. If you're going to travel by air, you receive up-to-date information on the lowest fares. When you travel abroad, you need to know specific things about the country you are going to visit, and you'll find them here.

FIG. 27.10
America Online's Travel Forum is your first resource for information about the places you want to visit.

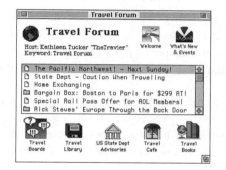

 TIP As with all America Online text windows, you can save the window by using the Save command, or you can print the text window by using the Print command.

Because you're in a traveling mood, here's a brief tour of the Travel Forum:

- The Welcome icon (at the upper right) gives you a brief overview of the Travel Forum and the features it offers.

- The What's New & Events department is similar, in many ways, to your daily or weekly travel newspaper; it contains the latest tips and information useful to all travelers.

- The main directory (center window) consists of articles that have useful information on many travel-related subjects.

- If you want to meet other online travelers, stop over for a while in the Travel Cafe (in the lower right of the forum window). The Travel Cafe is the Travel Forum's online chat room, where you visit with fellow travelers and discuss your experiences and share information. From time to time, regular conferences feature guest experts in the travel industry, so stop by and check the conference schedules.

Part
VII

Ch
27

- The Travel Boards department is your own set of message resources. It's divided into three sections: World Traveler, U.S. Traveler, and Caribbean Traveler. Here, you can exchange travel advice with other America Online members. One more message area, Travel Tips, gives you helpful up-to-the-minute advice from online members and experts alike.

- The Travel Library is a special resource of files that you can download to your computer. There are hundreds of files here that cover every aspect of travel lore. Feel free to browse through the file descriptions before downloading the files of your choice. (See Chapter 20, "Tips and Tricks on Finding Software," for advice on how to download files from America Online.)

- The last department, Travel Books, contains concise news and reviews of the latest books on travel. If a visit to your local bookstore or public library has left you overwhelmed about which book you need, America Online's Travel Books section is where you can find suggestions about the one that's right for you.

N O T E   If you are traveling with America Online and plan to stay at a hotel, be sure to ask in advance for a computer-ready room. Many hotels are happy to offer you a room with an extra phone jack for your modem. If your hotel does not have special rooms for computer users, in most cases, you can simply remove the cable for the phone from the phone jack and insert your modem cable.

Taking a Hike Online

Not all travel plans involve cars, boats, or planes. Some involve traveling the old-fashioned way, on foot. That takes us to *Backpacker* magazine on America Online (see fig. 27.11). This magazine caters to those who enjoy walking through the forests, trails, and deserts around the world in search of adventure.

Let's do our own little walking tour of the *Backpacker* magazine forum. First, there's the National Trails Day icon, which tells you about the activities of the American Hiking Society. The Trailhead Register icon helps you get in touch with fellow outdoorsmen (and women, naturally); you'll find a Buy/Sell Gear message board there too, where you might be able to find the product you want at a real bargain price.

And if you don't find that special product, consider looking over the Contests & Promotions listing, where you can enter a trivia contest and become eligible to win a special prize. There's also Trailside TV, which describes the award-winning public television show, *Trailside: Make Your Own Adventure,* the Backcountry TV area, a popular message board, and the Backpacker Store, where you receive a special discount offer on a subscription to the magazine and other special products.

FIG. 27.11
Backpacker magazine is a popular hiker's resource.

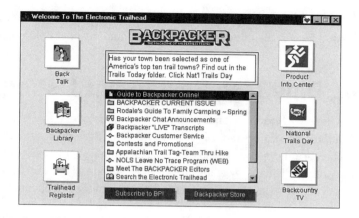

Using Bed & Breakfast U.S.A.

Keyword: **Bed & Breakfast**

If all of those hotels and motels have begun to look the same to you during your trips around the U.S., perhaps you want to consider a very attractive alternative. Bed and breakfast refers to a special kind of lodging that consists of private homes that rent out rooms to travelers, or inns that provide extra-special personal service. Sometimes they're referred to as guest houses or tourist homes. The Bed & Breakfast U.S.A. forum provides an up-to-date listing, from across the country, of this unique kind of accommodation (see fig. 27.12).

FIG. 27.12
Bed & Breakfast U.S.A. offers an alternative to conventional hotel/motel lodging.

Part
VII

Ch
27

AOL's Bed & Breakfast U.S.A. forum contains the regularly updated text of the same guidebook that you can find at your local bookstore. You can examine listings by state, review information on how to seek out the best accommodation for you, and share experiences with other AOL members about your favorite lodgings. If you intend to travel to Canada, there's a special listing showing bed and breakfast lodgings divided by province.

And, one more thing, if you ever dreamed about making your own home into a bed and breakfast establishment, you'll find information about doing that in this forum too.

Using DineBase Restaurant Listings

Whenever I travel to a new, unfamiliar part of the country, the first thing I seek out is a list of the best local restaurants. Goldwyn's DineBase makes the task easy (see fig. 27.13). This forum is a huge database that lists thousands of highly rated restaurants. You can search the listings by state, city, or even cuisine. You can access this area by double-clicking the DineBase Restaurant listing in the Travel channel's list box.

FIG. 27.13
DineBase is an easy way to find the best restaurants.

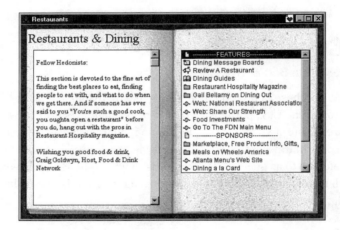

All of the restaurants shown in the listing have been highly recommended by one of the popular rating services, such as AAA, Mobil Travel Guide, Zagat Restaurant Surveys, or other sources. The listing offers a capsule summary of the ratings a particular restaurant received, the average entree price, a list of credit cards accepted, and other useful information. To begin checking out these reviews, just double-click the various items in the list box. At the listing Dining Message Boards, you can contribute your own restaurant reviews or read the ratings of fellow AOL members on these message boards.

In Search of an Outdoor Adventure Online

Keyword: **Adventure, OAO, Outdoor**

Some travelers are content to spend a vacation in a hotel, or visiting popular restaurants and shows. But, if you want to take your travels to the great outdoors, you'll want to visit

Outdoor Adventure Online (see fig. 27.14). It doesn't matter whether you're interested in hiking, skiing, scuba diving, or a host of other outdoor-related pursuits. This is a forum that helps you tap a huge database of exciting outdoor excursions of all types.

FIG. 27.14
Satisfy your quest for adventure with Outdoor Adventure Online.

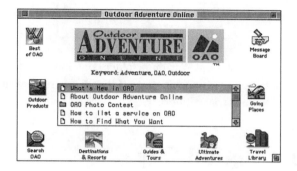

While planning your trip, you'll want to make sure you have just the right wardrobe and gear; for example, you might need a pair of waterproof binoculars, or a set of skis. The Outdoor Products area offers hundreds of product reviews on field-tested equipment, and an active message board where you can read about the hands-on experience of other members who've tried these products.

Click the Search OAO icon to directly link to the forum's huge database of information. The Destinations & Resorts and Guides & Tours areas provide information on many of the best travel spots. If your wanderlust can only be satisfied by some exciting adventures, such as Grand Canyon rafting or an African safari, look over the Ultimate Adventures area.

After you've selected some promising vacation spots, you'll want to consult Outdoor Adventure Online's Travel Library and the Going Places area; the latter offers hot tips and money-saving advice you'll want to consult before you make your reservations.

Part
VII

Ch
27

Consulting the State Travel Advisories

Keyword: **Travel Advisories**

Because the world situation is apt to change at any moment, you'll want to view the official U.S. State Department travel advisories, shown in figure 27.15. You can tap into a huge database of information that covers the entire world, and learn if there are any special considerations for traveling to a specific country.

FIG. 27.15
The State Department's travel advisories can be searched on AOL.

The U.S. State Department Warnings folder contains the latest alerts about problems and limitations of traveling to specific parts of the world. You'll want to review these text files before you plan your travel itinerary.

A Visit to a Digital City

Keyword: **Digital City**

When it comes to visiting another city, there's nothing like being there, but when you make your travel arrangements, it's quite helpful to be able to preview that city and learn more about it before you leave on that trip. AOL's Digital City allows you to search for information on your own hometown and hundreds of cities around the world (see fig. 27.16).

FIG. 27.16
AOL's Digital City channel is a fast and convenient way to tune in any city you wish to visit.

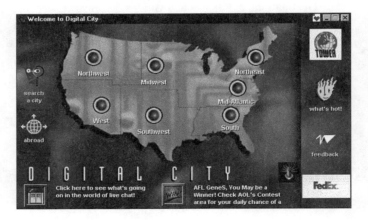

The best way to see how the Digital City feature works is simply to try it on for size. You can choose a general geographic region from the U.S. map display on the channel's opening screen, or you can use the Search Digital Cities feature (see fig. 27.17) to zero in on the significant information in a particular locale. To begin your search, click the Search a City icon in figure 27.16, and enter the location you wish to examine.

FIG. 27.17
The Search a City feature from AOL's Digital City channel is a fast way to learn more about the city you wish to visit.

Because I began this chapter with a discussion about a possible trip to California, I'm using that as an example. The search for information on Los Angeles brought a positive result, an entry in a list box. Just double-click that entry to enter your selected Digital City (see fig. 27.18).

FIG. 27.18
AOL's Digital City feature lets you learn more about the City of Angels.

From Here...

Exploring America Online's resources for travelers is fun, not just for the vicarious voyagers among you, but also for those of you who are planning a vacation or business trip. Because travel brings out most people's desire to shop as well, you might want to read these chapters:

- In Chapter 24, "Magazines and Newspapers Online," you'll visit AOL's virtual newsstand and look over the racks for your favorite publications.

- In Chapter 28, "Secrets of Online Shopping," you'll visit AOL's shopping malls and get tips and tricks on making online purchases.

- Chapter 39, "How to Save Time and Money," gives you a few tips on how to find more money to make a purchase, and how to reduce your online bill.

Part
VII

Ch
27

CHAPTER 28

Secrets of Online Shopping

Consider the average shopping trip. You have to fight traffic and search for parking places at your local shopping mall, or endure long waits at the checkout lines. You waste time going from place to place to find the best prices. Yes, shopping should be fun, but more often these days it's not all that enjoyable. But there is a better way to get your shopping done, with the help of your computer and America Online (of course).

Do you want to save a few dollars on your next purchase? Perhaps you just want to get the most up-to-date information about a particular product or service before you decide whether or not to buy. America Online is the place to do both.

You have already learned how to locate information resources on America Online. In this chapter, you'll go on an enjoyable shopping tour by way of the Information Superhighway. You'll make several brief stops at different shops in an online mall, and you'll even buy a few items along the way. ■

Find the merchandise you want

Search for particular products from a variety of online databases on AOL and the Internet.

Place your order

Buy the items you want while logged on to America Online.

Save bucks

Join a service that will help you save money on your next car.

Advertise on AOL

Place your own classified ad, free of charge.

Find a job

Tap a huge online database of employment opportunities.

A Tour of AOL's Marketplace

Keyword: **Marketplace, Shopping**

America Online's Marketplace, shown in figure 28.1, is a gateway to AOL's huge shopping mall. Because Chapter 26 was devoted to using America Online for your travel plans, this little excursion is limited to the items that strictly concern shopping. Of course, the merchandise you buy during this trip may well be suited for that trip you're planning to take.

FIG. 28.1
The Marketplace department is your gateway to America Online's online mall.

Before you go on, you should realize that the Marketplace, as with other online areas, is definitely a work in progress. Artwork is always being updated, and new shopping features are regularly being added to the mix. So, the Marketplace you visit when you take your own online shopping tour might look a little different from the one shown here.

N O T E The quality of the image you see on your computer screen depends on the size and quality of the monitor, and the capabilities of your computer to display an image at a specific resolution. The image is sent in full color, but whether it appears in black-and-white or clear, crisp, full color varies from installation to installation. ▪

Placing an Order with the America Online Store

Keyword: **AOL Store**

America Online has its own custom line of merchandise, which you can wear, send as gifts, or just keep as souvenirs. Because I collect fancy T-shirts myself, let's order one.

First you access the AOL Online Store from the list box on the right side of the screen, or type the keyword **Marketplace**. The steps you're going to take from here are similar to those you'll follow for most ordering online.

First, double-click the Shop by Product Category folder to get the window shown in figure 28.2.

FIG. 28.2
Choose the product that interests you from the directory listing.

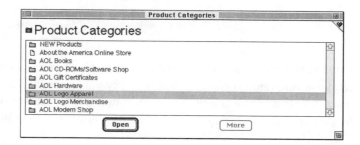

From the list of products, choose AOL Logo Apparel. To see a product description and a full-color photo of the product (see fig. 28.3), just double-click the product's name in the directory.

FIG. 28.3
AOL's graphical interface lets you see the product before you buy.

The descriptive window gives you the very same sort of information you'd find in a mail-order catalog. The description is enticing enough to give you a pretty fair picture of what the shirt really looks like. I think I'm going to order one, so let's select the Click Here To Order button to bring up the screen shown in figure 28.4. Choose the shirt size you want by double-clicking the entry in the directory window.

Part
VII

Ch
28

FIG. 28.4
Ready to order? Select the
size you want here.

In the next screen, you'll choose the number of shirts you want. After you select the merchandise you want to order, you will probably want to double-check your shopping cart to
make sure that you've selected the correct item. AOL's software does this automatically
for you by displaying a confirmation that the product you want has been added to your
shopping cart (see fig. 28.5).

FIG. 28.5
Your selection is confirmed
as you add items to your
shopping cart.

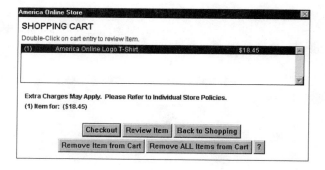

Click the Checkout icon once to bring up a window that allows you to enter billing and
shipping information, and then place your order (see fig. 28.6).

FIG. 28.6
Enter your billing
information.

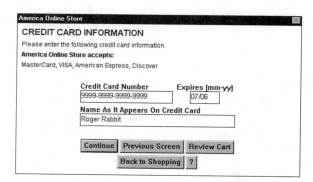

T I P Before visiting your online shopping center, have your credit card handy so that you can enter your billing information without delay.

After you've entered your billing information, enter your correct shipping address. By default, the address recorded for your online account is listed as the billing address (see fig. 28.7). You can have the same address automatically entered for shipping or enter a different shipping location. Click the Continue button to add your shipping information.

FIG. 28.7
Complete the order.
The second Street line is designed to accommodate a longer street address.

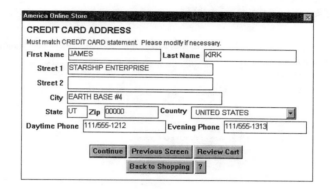

 T I P As with all online information, feel free to save and print the text window whenever you want. Just choose Save or Print from the File menu (as appropriate).

Getting an AOL Software Upgrade

From time to time, America Online upgrades its software to add new features and offer better performance. Whether you use a Mac or Windows-equipped PC, you can choose the software version you want and download either (or both, if you have computers of both platforms) from this download center.

Chapter 1, "Getting Past the Opening Screen," summarizes the differences among the various AOL software versions. Before you download the new version, you might want to refer to that chapter and look over the file description of the new version to see what's being offered.

 T I P You can download the newest AOL software releases for free by using the keyword **Upgrade**, selecting the upgrade you want, and choosing the Download Now option. If you choose Download Later, you will leave the free area and end up paying for the download time.

Now that you've ordered a new T-shirt and downloaded the latest version of AOL's software, how about looking for a brand new car?

Buying a Car

Keyword: **AutoVantage**

AutoVantage is both an online database of new and used car information and a center where you can arrange to service your car, buy accessories, and even order a new vehicle at a discount price (see fig. 28.8).

FIG. 28.8
AutoVantage is your online resource for automobile information.

AutoVantage provides an interface that's very different from other areas on America Online; therefore, this section discusses it in detail. If you are using the Windows version of America Online software, you are, no doubt, familiar with the command-line (text) interface in DOS. This interface probably seems a bit strange to Macintosh users, but AutoVantage makes it really easy to navigate. You are prompted every step of the way, and your answers govern the information that's presented.

To take advantage of AutoVantage's services, you have to join; but, there's almost always a low-cost introductory membership available. To join, follow these steps:

1. Double-click the Access for Non-Members icon (refer to fig. 28.8).

2. In the first window, specify how long your row of text should be. A good size is 60 or 80 characters, which will work effectively on the average 13 and 14-inch computer screen. The narrower the screen, the longer it takes to scroll through the section. If you don't make the correct selection, just close the window, open it again, and start over.

3. The Main Directory lists the services available to non-members (see fig. 28.9). Because this is a text-based interface, you cannot just double-click the item you want to select. You have to let the descriptions in the text window guide you on what to do next. In this case, you have 13 items from which to choose. Simply enter the number of the item you want to learn more about, and either click the Send button or press the Enter or Return key.

FIG. 28.9
The AutoVantage main directory window is used to take you to different areas of the service.

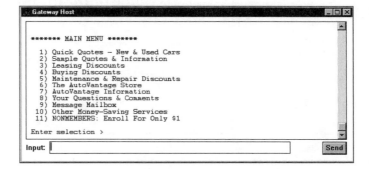

4. For each selection, you are asked to enter a number or further information. If you want to join, you'll be presented with a brief questionnaire that asks for your name, mailing address, and billing information. Pressing Enter or Return when you finish entering the requested data sends it direct to AutoVantage's host computer, and you will then be prompted for further information.

5. After you complete your visit to AutoVantage, you can close the window to leave the text-based service behind and return to your familiar America Online icons and windows.

If you opt to join AutoVantage, you'll receive a letter and other material in a few weeks to confirm your membership and provide helpful hints on how to use the service.

Shopping on the Internet

You'll find that AOL's own shopping areas are only a part of the picture. AOL's easy Internet access provides you with a wealth of shopping opportunities, ranging from direct access to large shopping malls (such as La Jolla, California's University Town Center), to major mail-order houses that are happy to take your direct order. To see the huge listing of Internet-based shopping areas, just double-click the listing labeled Downtown AOL in the Marketplace list box shown earlier in figure 28.1, and then double-click Go To Ads—WEB to get the screen shown in figure 28.10.

Part
VII
Ch
28

FIG. 28.10
Taking a global shopping tour using your own computer and AOL's fast entry onto the Information Superhighway.

Before you start your shopping spree, though, you'll want to check the section entitled "Tips for Online Shopping" at the end of this chapter. With a few precautions to consider, your online shopping can be quite safe and secure, and you'll feel really excited when your package finally arrives, containing the exact merchandise you ordered.

Sending Flowers

Keyword: **Flowers**

Your next stop along the Information Superhighway shopping mall is the cute little flower shop shown in figure 28.11. Maybe a friend or relative is celebrating a special occasion, or you want to give a bouquet of roses to your significant other. You can place your order at 800-FLOWERS. That order is then transmitted to a local florist near the home of the person who will be receiving the flowers. That florist will then deliver your order.

If you want to know more about the product being displayed, simply click the Featured Product info button. You'll see a capsule description of the product, and have a chance to place your order through a technique similar to that described earlier, in the section entitled "Placing an Order with the AOL Product Center." You'll have an opportunity to select your billing option, and review your order before it's sent.

The 800-FLOWERS online store is not limited to flowers. Besides high-quality candy, 800-FLOWERS has other gift items available. This service also has established a full-featured forum on America Online to offer customer service, special offers, and even a Flower Talk message board, in case you want advice from other AOL members or 800-FLOWERS staff before you make your gift purchase.

FIG. 28.11
Say it with flowers or other choice gifts, such as the item shown here.

Buying Books Online

Keyword: **Bookstore**

America Online's Bookstore is stocked with shelves and shelves of the latest titles, both fiction and nonfiction, in all of the major categories. There's a special database that allows you to search for a specific title. To get there, click the Shop Our Catalog button from the bookstore's main screen. Then click the Search button. The Online Bookstore will also take special requests for a book that might not be in stock, and they will be happy to supply additional information about available volumes.

The main directory window displays the latest releases, plus listings of all the major publishing categories. After you bring up a directory of available books, double-click the title for a brief description of what the work is about and its price (see fig. 28.12).

FIG. 28.12
Looking for that best-seller? Does the title sound familiar?

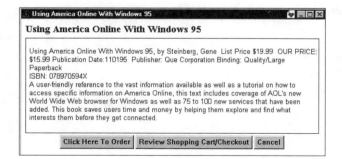

Part
VII

Ch
28

The ordering window for the Online Bookstore is a bit different from those available in other America Online stores (see fig. 28.13). The window allows you to select up to three titles at a time and to enter your shipping and billing information. If you want to order additional titles, bring up the order window again. And, yes, last time I checked, the latest edition of a certain book on how to use America Online was available there.

Online Bookstore
Using Amer Online W/Windows 95
SHIP TO
If you are purchasing more than one item, you may send items to DIFFERENT addresses.
When you finish shopping, you will be asked to provide the address of each recipient.
If you choose MYSELF, please click on Continue.
If you choose SOMEONE ELSE, please specify the Name of the person to receive this item.
Ship To MYSELF (No Name Required)
Ship to SOMEONE ELSE (Please Specify)
First Name
Last Name
Continue
Previous Screen
Cancel
?

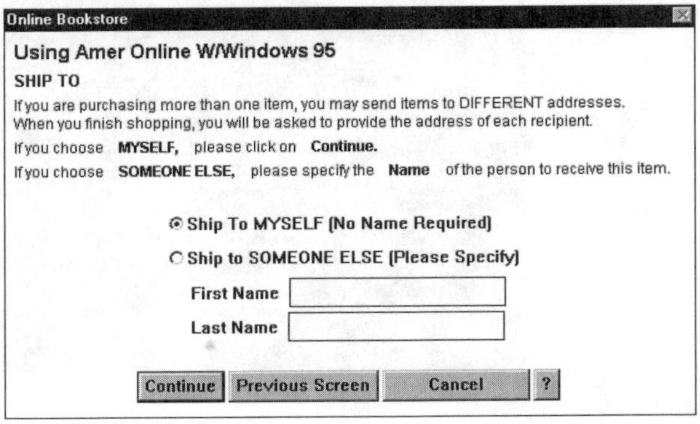

FIG. 28.13
It's time to tally up your order.

Buying Computer Products

Keyword: **Computer Express**

Whether you use a Mac or Windows-equipped PC, you can get large discounts on many computer products on AOL. You can even order a brand-new system and benefit from a big selection and good prices. Here are some of the online resources for these products.

Maybe you want to buy a neat new computer game, you need some hard drive utility software, or it's time to replace that old modem with one of those new high-speed models (and take advantage of America Online's 14,400 and 28,800 bps service). Computer Express is your resource for discount prices on all sorts of computer-related merchandise.

Computer Express lets you search for a specific product or check out the newest software titles and special hot deals (see fig. 28.14).

The Computer Express Store
Computer Express
COMPUTER EXPRESS, your source for Multimedia, Software, Hardware, Video Games, Books & More!
Expand your horizons with the Flight Simulator 5.1 Scenery Pack. Includes scenery for Japan, Hawaii
Keyword: Computer Express
Browse Our Warehouse
Weekly Specials
Other Connections
Review Shopping Cart\Checkout
Customer Feedback
Customer Service
Product Search
Specialty Shops

FIG. 28.14
A complete source for computer software and accessories.

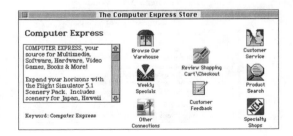

For example, suppose that you decide to look for a new modem. First, bring up the Search Products window by double-clicking Product Search. Next, enter **modems** in the Information field. Click the List Articles button, and you'll soon see a list of related products (see fig. 28.15). In this case, there are dozens and dozens of choices; you need to click the More button a few times to scroll through the entire list of available products.

FIG. 28.15
The Computer Express merchandise database offers some choices for you.

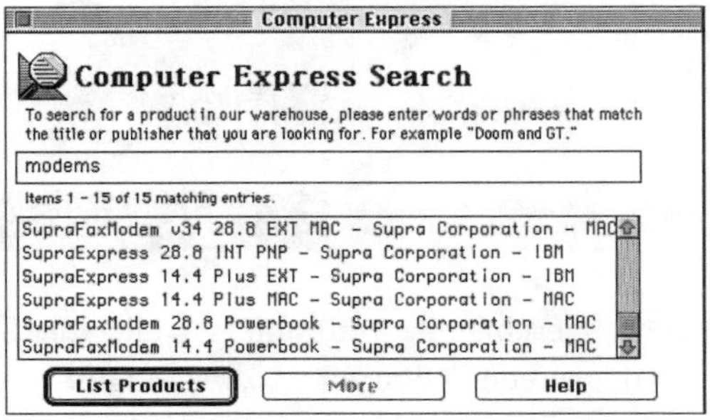

SupraFaxModem v34 28.8 EXT MAC – Supra Corporation – MAC
SupraExpress 28.8 INT PNP – Supra Corporation – IBM
SupraExpress 14.4 Plus EXT – Supra Corporation – IBM
SupraExpress 14.4 Plus MAC – Supra Corporation – MAC
SupraFaxModem 28.8 Powerbook – Supra Corporation – MAC
SupraFaxModem 14.4 Powerbook – Supra Corporation – MAC

Double-click the item that interests you to get detailed descriptions, product specifications, and the latest prices. If you decide you want to buy the product, simply click the Click Here To Order button to add it to your shopping cart (see fig. 28.16).

FIG. 28.16
After you've selected the products you want to buy, you get ready for the checkout counter.

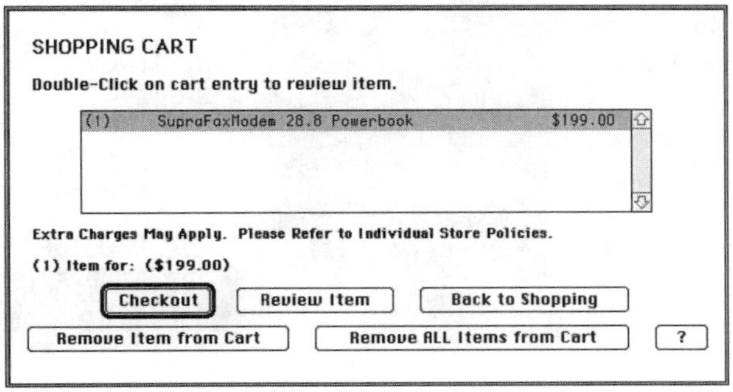

Ordering Office Products

Keyword: **OfficeMax**

The next stop on this shopping trip is a visit to your neighborhood OfficeMax discount store, where you can pick up a new toner cartridge for your laser printer, and maybe get a box of envelopes and some copy paper (see fig. 28.17).

Just like the OfficeMax store in many cities, you can order direct from their retail catalog. If you don't have one, you can request a copy from their Customer Service department, where you can also ask specific questions about a product or inquire about the progress of an order.

Part
VII

Ch

28

FIG. 28.17
America Online's source for discount office products may also be your favorite neighborhood source as well.

A quick way to find the merchandise you want is to click the SHOP OUR STORE icon, which brings you to the screen in figure 28.18. From here you'll have the choice of clicking the icon that represents the product category that interests you; or you can click the Product Search button to bring up one of AOL's standard search screens, and see if they have the office product that you need. More than likely, they do.

FIG. 28.18
Browse through a specific merchandise category, or search for the exact item you want.

The ordering process is similar to other America Online shopping areas. You place your order and review each step of the purchase process as it progresses. If you want to order additional merchandise or change your order, it can be done at any point while you're entering the order. When your order is complete, simply use the Checkout feature, and your order will soon be shipped directly to your home or office.

Office Supplies from Price/Costco Online

In addition to these online shopping resources, you'll find a big selection of computing and office supplies and a big variety of general-interest merchandise from Price/Costco, the popular membership superstore. If you've ever visited one of these huge establishments, you'll find not only a selection of the latest Macintosh and PC hardware, but software, books, stereos, TVs, food products, furniture, and much more.

The Online Gift Shop

Keyword: **2Market**

When the compact disc was first introduced in the early 1980s, it was used as a storage medium to carry musical performances. It also proved to be an excellent medium for storing data. Today, both Macs and PCs come in multimedia dress, equipped with CD-ROMs (which play audio CDs too) and often a set of high-quality loudspeakers. Because CDs can display text, pictures, and sound, they are also well-suited for use as an interactive catalog. Not only do you see a colorful listing of the available products, you can watch a short commercial message or view a demonstration of the features of the products you're considering purchasing.

America Online's 2Market department is quite literally an online gift shop. You can order special gifts for any occasion. Figure 28.19 shows the promotions in effect just before Mother's Day, for example. You can also take advantage of special deals on a variety of products.

FIG. 28.19
2Market is also available in CD-ROM form, so you can view colorful, interactive demonstrations on new products.

In addition, there are special promotions and events where you can get extra discounts and even win a prize or two. If you have a problem or question about the products you're considering, the Shop Talk message board is a place where you can post messages and have discussions with AOL members and 2Market staff.

The most attractive way to order, though, is with the help of 2Market's CD. You can place your order for the CD during your online visit. It'll arrive in just a short time, and it provides entertaining, interactive demonstrations from many of the major manufacturers of the products offered through 2Market.

Part
VII

Ch
28

Even if you don't have the CD handy, you can still see a full-color picture of the product and a complete description showing the important features. Just double-click the product name you want to know more about (see fig. 28.20).

FIG. 28.20
AOL's 2Market service offers a high-quality photo and full product description.

If you want to place your order, just choose the Click Here To Order button. If you don't want to order at this time, just close the display window and continue with your online browsing.

2Market also offers a special Gift Services area (refer to fig. 28.19), where you can have your gift marked with special cards or labels.

N O T E In the coming months, you'll begin to see more CD-ROM-based offerings on America Online. Some of the art content for the service itself might also be offered on a CD. The advantage of this is that it allows the service to provide more detailed artwork and sound in a form that contains too much data to download to your computer efficiently. ▪

Using Shoppers Advantage Online

Keyword: **Shoppers Advantage**

Shoppers Advantage is a discount buying service that lets you purchase up to 250,000 different items right from the comfort of your personal computer (see fig. 28.21). Like AutoVantage (described earlier in this chapter), the interface for Shoppers Advantage is text-based. That is, you navigate through the service by entering simple commands in the text field. By choosing numbers or typing simple words, you are able to view the vast catalog, read product descriptions, and place your order for prompt shipment to your home or office.

When you look over a product's description, you'll see two prices. One is for members; the other somewhat higher price is for non-members. When you find a product you want to order, you'll discover quickly enough whether the low membership fee covers the purchase of a single item (and quite often it does). Members also get a two-year warranty on the products they buy. A typical online shopping trip for a new computer can bring a huge list of choice products from Apple Computer, IBM, and other manufacturers.

FIG. 28.21
Shoppers Advantage Online is your interactive discount mail order catalog.

Exploring the Dinner On Us Club

Keyword: **Dinner On Us**

Eating out can get costly sometimes, especially if you want to try out that new four-star restaurant you read about in your local newspaper, city magazine, or, for that matter, AOL's Travel department (see Chapter 27, "Secrets of AOL's Travel Department"). But if you join the Dinner On Us Club on AOL, you can take advantage of two-for-one prices at thousands of restaurants across the country (see fig. 28.22).

FIG. 28.22
Get two meals for the price of one via Dinner On Us on AOL.

Part
VII

Ch
28

The offers shown in figure 28.22 can change from time to time, but the basic function of the Dinner On Us Club doesn't. If you become a member, you'll be able to take advantage of their special pricing deals at a huge number of quality restaurants. Before joining, you'll want to click the Find 2 For 1 Dining Near You icon to see a list of the restaurants that honor your Premier Dining membership card.

There are many interesting activities, in addition to the discount dining. You can win free prizes, participate in special surveys, and get discounts on new merchandise and on your next vacation. In fact, while I was writing this chapter, the Dinner On Us Club was offering free movie tickets just for accepting a trial membership. You'll want to visit the area for the latest offer next time you are online.

Using the Classifieds Online

Keyword: **Classifieds**

The Classifieds Online forum is the place to post your own ads or check out advertisements from fellow members and commercial outfits (see fig. 28.23). You aren't limited to just computer-related merchandise; you can also place ads for home appliances, electronics, and other types of merchandise.

FIG. 28.23
America Online's buy/sell/ trade center, where you can place your own ads.

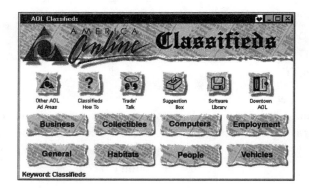

 TIP If you plan to buy merchandise from an AOL classified ad, don't be hesitant about asking the seller for some references. Remember, it's your money and you have a right to spend it carefully.

The guidelines for this area are few and very simple. When you post an ad, describe the merchandise you are selling as accurately as possible, including the warts (like that little scratch on the side of the case). Review other ads of the same sort of merchandise to set a fair price, or do as I have done in the past when I've offered merchandise for sale—let your fellow members make their best offer.

There are thousands of ads in the Classifieds message area. Most of them are placed by well-meaning firms and individuals; in most cases, you will receive the exact merchandise you order. But as with all mail-order transactions, approach the deal with some healthy skepticism. It's a good idea, for example, to use a credit card when you make your purchase. That way, if you are not satisfied with the product or service, the credit card issuer will usually investigate the transaction on your behalf and even credit your account, if necessary.

Other Services

Whenever you want to buy something new, you are faced with a bewildering array of choices. This section discusses one resource where you might find a little help in sorting through these choices so that you can make the one that's right for you. You'll also find coverage about a nationwide buying service, a bill paying service, and an online resource for another kind of shopping—job hunting.

Review *Consumer Reports*

Keyword: **Consumer Reports**

Consumers Union is a nonprofit product test and research center that publishes *Consumer Reports* magazine. The magazine, and a number of special publications released from time to time by Consumers Union, have earned a reputation for comprehensive, accurate reviews of new products in categories ranging from canned soup to home stereos. Millions of readers consult *Consumer Reports* magazine each month for up-to-date product information before they make any purchase.

You'll find selected product reports and special columns in the magazine's America Online support area (see fig. 28.24).

FIG. 28.24
Consumer Reports reviews new products and tells you which ones are best buys.

Part
VII

Ch
28

You'll want to review the magazine's reports online before you make a final decision about purchasing a product. Each April, *Consumer Reports* publishes its annual automobile issue, which contains capsule reviews of all the popular cars, plus the frequency of repair records, so you can see at a glance just how often your vehicle might have to take a trip to the repair shop. You'll find these features and other reports in the magazine's online area.

Job Listings Database

Keyword: **Jobs**

America Online features job listings from two large help-wanted databases: E-Span and Help Wanted-USA. If you are seeking employment in your present field or are seeking a new occupation, you can examine this database for possible job openings. The listings are updated weekly, so you can expect to find jobs that are still available.

The Search Help Wanted USA Database window is typical of most database resources on America Online. Just enter the field in which you seek a job, and if there are any opportunities in the database, you'll see a listing within a few seconds (see fig. 28.25). Simply double-click the listed item, or highlight the item and press Enter or Return to get more information about the employment opportunity.

FIG. 28.25
Looking for a new job is made easier with AOL's huge database of available opportunities.

Tips for Online Shopping

Consider your online shopping tour a modern day equivalent of browsing through a mail-order catalog. Although you can learn a lot about a product or service from the descriptions, there are occasions when the product you buy just won't meet your requirements or the merchandise you've received just doesn't work as it should. Before placing your order, you should keep the following in mind:

■ Before placing your order, read the product description thoroughly. If you have further questions, contact the staff of that particular shopping area.

- Read any posted terms and conditions carefully, in case you need to return the product for an exchange or refund for any reason.

- Merchandise sent via mail will usually include a shipping charge of some sort. If you're comparison shopping, be sure to include the shipping charge as part of the total price.

- Check the product description for estimated shipping times. Remember that shipments can be delayed as a result of conditions beyond the vendor's control, such as late delivery of merchandise from the manufacturer or delays on the part of the shipping agency.

- If you're ordering a product for a special occasion or as a gift, allow extra time for it to reach its destination.

- Make a copy of your order, so you can refer to it later in case you have a further question about the merchandise you've ordered.

N O T E Some online order forms consist of multiple text fields, and choosing the Save option in the File menu might not save the complete text of your order. If this is the case, enter the full details of your order in a text document using AOL's memo feature, or use a screen image capture program to record the actual order screen itself.

- When you receive your package, examine the box and contents for signs of damage. If the box seems ruined beyond repair, contact the online vendor immediately about getting a replacement.

- If you have a problem with the merchandise you've received, follow the instructions posted in the vendor area about whom to contact for customer service.

- If the product you ordered needs to be repaired, review the warranty information that came with the package. Quite often, service must be done through a manufacturer's own authorized service center and not the vendor.

- Bear in mind that you are ordering the merchandise directly from the vendor, not from America Online, who simply makes the vendor's service available. Complaints about products or services are best addressed directly to the vendor, and not to the online service.

- If you use a credit card to make your purchase (and, in most cases, you will), you might also contact the card issuer to assist you if you run into problems dealing with a particular vendor. Remember, too, that some credit cards provide extended warranties and other benefits when you use them to purchase big-ticket items.

> **CAUTION**
> Although online shopping is safe, you should nevertheless carefully guard your credit card and
> AOL password. Remember that *no AOL employee* will ever ask you online or by e-mail for any of
> this information. If you get a request for this sort of information, be sure to report it directly to
> AOL's Community Action Team for action. Use the keyword **TOS** for information on how to report
> this sort of conduct.

From Here...

Sometimes shopping is a headache, especially when you have to fight heavy traffic and
search for parking spaces at a crowded suburban shopping mall. On America Online,
however, there are no crowds and no lines. Simply browse through the virtual shopping
aisles at your leisure, take the time you need to decide what you want to buy, and place
your order. You can even get valuable information about selecting your next car.

- You'll find some helpful shopping advice in AOL's online newsstand. You learn how
  to get there in Chapter 24, "Magazines and Newspapers Online."

- Chapter 27, "Secrets of AOL's Travel Department," helps you prepare for a vacation
  or business trip, without ever leaving the computer screen, simply by logging on to
  America Online.

- Chapter 39, "How to Save Time and Money," gives you a few tips on how to find
  more money to make a purchase and some advice on how to reduce your online bill.

Entering the Information Superhighway

Using AOL's Internet Connection

You read about it almost daily in your newspaper, or you hear about it on television and radio. You even see a reference about it on someone's business card.

Everyone is talking about the Internet—that huge, amorphous, global computer network that is the centerpiece of the Information Superhighway. The reports are filled with such buzzwords as *World Wide Web, UseNet, Gopher, Archie, Veronica,* and a host of other expressions that seem obscure and mysterious (when they don't mean furry animals or comic book characters, of course).

The Internet has even become fodder for political debate in the halls of Congress—for example, the controversy over a measure to ban smut on the Internet. Because the major online services, such as America Online, provide a growing stable of resources to the worldwide Internet community, such debates have provided a source for much discussion on message boards and talk shows.

By providing Internet access, America Online has brought you into an exciting new universe. You are already a member of not only America Online, but also of the exciting Internet, your gateway to communicate with millions of fellow computer users from across the globe. America Online's Internet Connection provides information and access into what have been described as the Internet's most popular features. These include e-mail, database searching, mailing lists, Newsgroups, File Transfer Protocol (FTP), and the colorful World Wide Web.

Over time, America Online will be providing you with instant access to even more features of the Internet. The best news is that the new features won't require you to learn about a whole new environment. America Online has designed the new areas to look and feel very similar to the forums and message boards already on the service—the very same message boards described throughout this book.

Indeed, the Internet can seem like a magical, mystical place—one that is almost a separate world unto itself. In the next few chapters, I'm going to begin to take some of the mystery out of the Internet, and, more importantly, tell you how many of the same techniques you've used so far to travel across America Online's own friendly neighborhood can be used to access a whole world of fascinating information and services. ■

What Is the Internet?

Imagine accessing a worldwide computer network with more than 20 million members, with a software library consisting of hundreds of thousands of files, an information repository consisting of millions of messages, and daily global transfers of electronic mail numbering in the millions of transactions.

And imagine being able to reach that worldwide repository of information and discussion groups and software libraries right from your personal computer, regardless of whether it's a Mac or a PC, no matter which operating system you're using, and no matter where in the world you might be at any given moment. All you need is your America Online account, your modem, and a telephone line (or other network connection), and you can join the true center of the Information Superhighway universe—the Internet.

The History of the Internet

At the very minimum, the word *Internet* describes the interconnection between two networks. But when you look back to the origins of what is called the Internet, you see in it the very beginnings of computer networking in general. Even your local BBS user group or your favorite online service (AOL naturally) owes much in the way it's run to the shape and form that the Internet has taken.

At first, like so many endeavors that ended up in the hands of civilians, the Internet began in the late 1960s as a government project, under the aegis of the U.S. Advanced Research Projects Agency. It was known then as ARPANET, and it was an experiment to learn the best methods to exchange data among remote computers. At first, the new computer network was installed at four educational institutions located in California and Utah.

As it was designed and developed over the years, the Internet has had the unique distinction of having no hubs or central control point, and was designed with the assumption that the rest of the network was totally unreliable. In the 1970s, methods were established to build a networking protocol to enable computers of all shapes, sizes, and operating systems to communicate with each other seamlessly.

The Internet and E-Mail

Because it began as a government-supported project, network traffic in the early stages of the Internet consisted of civilian and military information. The burgeoning network became popular with scientists and other researchers who used it to engage in correspondence, known as electronic mail (*e-mail*), with their colleagues, and to send information files. Central computers or sites were established in which to store files, using File Transfer Protocol (FTP), which I'll discuss later on in this chapter and in more detail in Chapter 34, "Using File Transfer Protocol."

Individual e-mail exchanges also blossomed into mailing lists, in which information was sent to a large number of users, in the form of collections of correspondence, articles, and reports. You'll find more coverage of that subject in Chapter 30," Secrets of Internet E-Mail and Mailing Lists." Internet users with special interests created UseNet (users' network) discussion groups in which messages were posted about their favorite topics and responded to by other users (see Chapter 32, "Joining and Participating in Internet Newsgroups").

Preparing for the Future

By 1983, the rapidly growing network was split into two parts—one was dedicated to military use and the other was dedicated to civilian use. The method used to transfer data along the network was called Transmission Control Protocol/Internet Protocol (or TCP/IP for short).

Today, a growing number of America Online members, in fact, use TCP/IP capabilities to access the service at extremely high speeds. You learn how to do that later on in this chapter.

The Internet stretches beyond the borders of any single country. It has no central authority or governing body. It knows no limitations in terms of the type of computer or the operating system it uses. So the user of a Power Macintosh running System 7.5 can easily communicate with another user who has a mainframe computer or even a Compaq Pentium running Windows 95, to name just a few examples. Ancient boundaries of gender and race are also less relevant on the Internet, which has become truly a global community.

N O T E   Those who first established the Internet probably never realized how much it would impact our present-day society. One of the major uses for the network originally was to enable scientists at widely separate institutions to share their research with each other, which meant only a small number of people were involved originally.

Accessing the Internet

At one time, getting Internet access was difficult. You had to work at a place where access was available, or be able to log on to a network at a local educational institution, or even set your own computer up as an Internet server. It wasn't always a terribly cost-effective proposition either. But times have changed. Beginning several years ago, the powers that be at America Online realized the incredible potential of the Internet and began to introduce access to the global network to its membership. As described later in this chapter, AOL has created an entire department, the Internet Connection (keyword **Internet**), to offer advice to help newcomers and even experienced Net surfers learn the best, most efficient ways to use Internet services.

N O T E   AOL has established a separate Internet-only online service, GNN. You learn more about that service in Chapters 37 and 38.

In this chapter, I want to introduce you to the Internet and help you get started with your Internet access on America Online. It would take a large book to cover the length and breadth of the information and services the Internet offers. At the end of this chapter, I'll recommend an excellent source for further reading.

For now, get ready to travel across the Internet from the comfort of your own home or work area, and your own personal computer.

CAUTION

Because the Internet is still very much an open, largely unregulated frontier, you are apt to encounter files and discussions that contain subject matter and language that is against America Online's Terms of Service. Therefore, it's a good idea for you to carefully monitor the access of children to AOL's Internet Connection. Also, although many of the old hands on the Internet are friendly, helpful people who are only too glad to help newcomers (*newbies*, as they are known on the Net), a small number of folks would prefer to jealously guard their status on the Net, and are not quite as nice to folks who are unfamiliar with its procedures and traditions. My suggestion is that you read this chapter and the next nine chapters, and possibly review the help texts in AOL's Internet Connection before you begin to explore the Net.

▶ **See** "Parental Controls for the Internet," **p. 286**

AOL's Internet Services

Keyword: **Internet**

America Online's Internet Connection is the solution you need to overcome the confusing interfaces and other obstacles presented by the Internet network (see fig. 29.1). Every America Online member is already a member of the Internet. You are able to travel the length and breadth of the Internet just like you use any other part of America Online.

FIG. 29.1
America Online has a special department devoted strictly to Internet access.

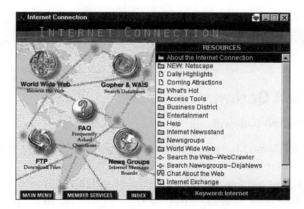

Before you take that trip to the global Information Superhighway, I want to briefly outline the present range of AOL Internet services, and offer you some suggestions for further reading. I'll take it icon by icon, but first, let me suggest you take a look at the Resources directory, which provides a lot of helpful Internet-related information that will ease the burden of your first visits. You have a direct line to the *Wired* magazine forum (see fig. 29.2), a publication dedicated to providing a unique insight into the growing generation of connected people.

FIG. 29.2
Here's some news for the
wired generation.

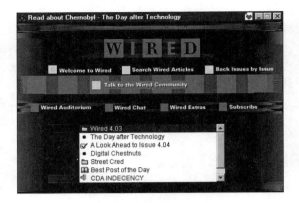

You'll also want to visit the Mac and PC Telecommunications Forums for advice on how to
set up your modem and networks for the best possible service. For additional advice on
getting the most mileage out of your modem, you'll also want to read Chapter 41, "Secrets
of High-Speed Access to AOL."

▶ **See** "A Brief Guide on Installing Your New Modem," **p. 766**

The sections that follow cover some of those Internet access features currently offered
on AOL.

Using the Mail Gateway

Keyword: **Mail Gateway**

Your e-mail doesn't have to stop at the frontiers of the AOL service network. Through
AOL's Internet mail capability (see fig. 29.3), you can send e-mail to your friends and businesses on other online services, and on local BBSs with Internet access. You can also
send e-mail to universities, businesses, and government agencies with direct FTP connections. The process is not much more complicated than sending e-mail on AOL. For more
information, see Chapter 30, "Secrets of Internet E-Mail and Mailing Lists."

FIG. 29.3
AOL's Internet e-mail center
is a repository of advice
on how to send e-mail to
members of other services.

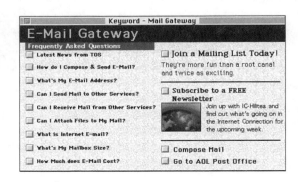

N O T E You do not have to be in AOL's Mail Gateway or Internet Connection to compose Internet-destined e-mail. All you have to do is open a blank mail form, address it accordingly, compose the message, and send it. You can even write your message while offline and send it via a FlashSession. ■

Joining Internet Newsgroups

Keyword: **Newsgroups**

The closest thing to a message board on the Internet is UseNet (see fig. 29.4), offering thousands of discussion boards where you can discuss most anything under the sun, and in some cases (the ones devoted to such subjects as psychic phenomena and UFOs), even beyond the sun. Before you get involved in a Newsgroup discussion, see Chapter 32, "Joining and Participating in Internet Newsgroups."

FIG. 29.4
You can Participate in thousands of Newsgroup discussions on AOL.

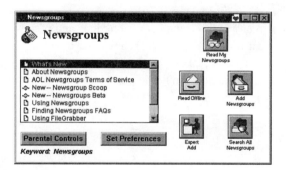

Seeking Information Resources on the Internet

Keyword: **Gopher**

Placing hundreds of encyclopedias end upon end still wouldn't add up to the amount of information you can get from the Internet. The only trick is to find it all. Using AOL's Gopher and WAIS capability (see fig. 29.5), you can seek out many of these information resources, without ever leaving your home. See Chapter 31, "Searching for Information on the Internet," for more information. I'll even describe how to locate Internet files, using Archie (and once again, that's not the comic book character).

FIG. 29.5
AOL's database search tools let you tap a wide range of information resources.

Joining Mailing Lists

Keyword: **Mailing Lists**

AOL lets you join any of thousands of mailing lists and receive information on anything from recipes to car racing. You can search for lists to subscribe to through AOL's Internet Mailing Lists area (see fig. 29.6), and soon your mailbox will be filled with exciting information (but don't overdo it). You'll find more information, along with a directory of popular mailing lists, in Chapter 30, "Secrets of Internet E-Mail and Mailing Lists."

CAUTION

You should exercise some care in subscribing to an Internet mailing list, since any single list can result in filling your mailbox with dozens of new messages each day. If you find your mailbox is becoming overwhelmed with new messages, you may want to consider canceling your subscription to lists that produce messages you don't intend to read right away. I can tell you a few stories about the time a computer hacker put my name and that of others (including the President and Vice President) on over 2,000 mailing lists; that story even earned coverage in *Time* magazine's science column.

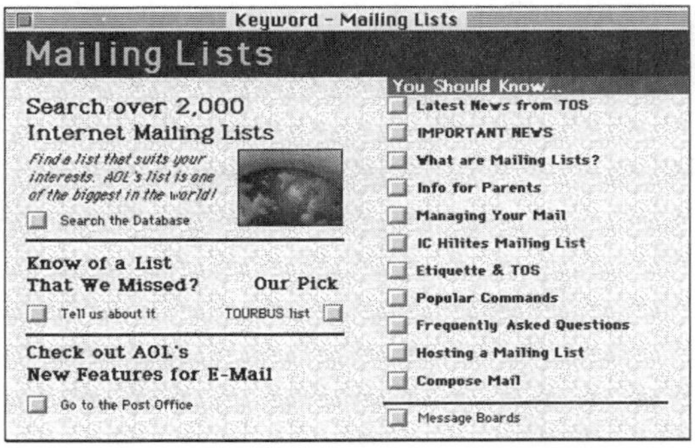

FIG. 29.6
You can easily join an Internet mailing list from AOL.

Internet File Transfer

Keyword: **FTP**

There are thousands of files available through the Internet. They come from such commercial sources as Apple, Microsoft, and Novell, and from many private repositories of freeware and shareware. Internet files are sent via file transfer protocol (FTP), and AOL offers a special area where you can access these huge libraries (see fig. 29.7). Getting these files is not altogether different from downloading files in AOL's own libraries, but you'll want to know a few extra ground rules first (and take some additional precautions), which are describe in Chapter 34, "Using File Transfer Protocol."

FIG. 29.7
Huge software libraries can be tapped on the Internet via FTP.

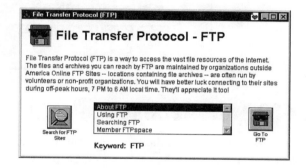

Accessing the World Wide Web

Keyword: **WWW**

Most Internet services up until now have been text-based. So you end up seeing countless directories and text windows during your Net journey (or surfing, as it's generally known). But the World Wide Web is a different animal. Although the technique of creating this information is text-based (using a special text-entry format called hypertext markup language, or HTML), the interface you'll see is decidedly graphical, filled with colorful pictures and text. The sample I'm providing in figure 29.8 is from my publisher's home page (this is the main directory screen). You'll find equally fancy Web facilities from all of the major computer manufacturers, plus many commercial concerns and private institutions. Read all about Web sites in Chapter 35, "Using the World Wide Web" and Chapter 36, "Popular Web Sites."

FIG. 29.8
Direct from AOL's Web browser, here's the home page for Macmillan Computer Publishing.

Secrets of TCP/IP Access

Computers that hook up directly to the Internet speak a language called *TCP/IP*, short for Transmission Control Protocol/Internet Protocol. A number of computer networks (perhaps at your office) have direct Internet connections via this protocol (they don't come cheap, but they are capable of really fast performance).

If your computer network is hooked up to the Internet, here's an ultra-fast way to experience America Online without going through the usual local access phone numbers. Both the Macintosh and Windows versions of America Online's software offer a TCP/IP connection tool. To use it, you need to change your modem setup (the little information window is described more fully in Appendix B, "Using Your America Online Macintosh Software," and Appendix C, "Using Your America Online Windows Software"). Instead of choosing AOLNet, SprintNet, or Tymnet from the connection files offered, choose TCP/IP (TCPack for Mac users), as done in figure 29.9.

When you log onto AOL using the TCP/IP connection, performance is limited only by the speed of your network. It can be several times faster than your present telephone connection. If you have direct TCP/IP access, give it a try and see.

FIG. 29.9
It's easy to set up your AOL
software to connect directly
through TCP/IP via the
Internet.

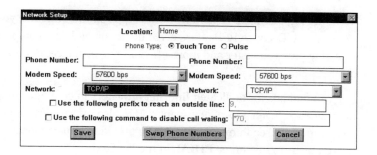

N O T E Macintosh users need Apple's MacTCP software to take advantage of AOL's TCP/IP
capability. MacTCP is available as part of System 7.5, separately from your software
dealer, or by calling Apple Customer Assistance at 800-SOS-APPL. If you're using System 7.5.2 or
later and have Apple's Open Transport networking software installed, you'll make your Internet
settings in the TCP/IP Control Panel. ▪

A Brief TCP/IP How-To Guide

To access America Online through TCP/IP, you need version 1.5 or later of the Windows
AOL software, and version 2.5 or later of the Mac AOL software. Both software packages
install the proper TCP/IP tools on your personal computer. If you're using other TCP/IP
tools to browse the Internet, such as Netscape or Mosaic, your access to AOL through
TCP/IP won't affect the use of these programs. In fact, you can also access them through
your AOL account, as explained in Chapter 35, "Using the World Wide Web." Of course,
with AOL's own integrated Web browser available, you may find yourself using those tools
less and less.

N O T E If you have an older version of AOL software that doesn't support TCP/IP access, use
the keyword **Upgrade** to visit an area where you can download the latest versions of
both the Mac and Windows AOL software. As long as you choose the Download Now rather than
Download Later options in this area, it is free of online charges. ▪

If your computer is attached to a Local Area Network (LAN), you'll want to contact your
system administrator as to whether TCP/IP capabilities are supported by your network
software. You can also get a TCP/IP connection through a dedicated Internet service.
You'll need either a SLIP (Serial Line Internet Protocol) or PPP (Point to Point Protocol)

account to get TCP/IP capability. Both setups allow you to use your modem at its maximum speed. Because PPP offers error detection and data compression capability, it will probably give you faster and more efficient performance, but not all Internet providers offer it.

You can find ads for dedicated Internet providers in computer magazines, local user group magazines, or even a local newspaper. AOL also offers a list of these services, but, of course, doesn't recommend any specific provider. You can locate this list using AOL's File Search feature. Just enter **PDIAL** in the list field.

Using AOL Windows with TCP/IP

After you've secured your TCP/IP capability, logging on through AOL is extremely easy.

Here's what you need to access AOL's TCP/IP capability:

- Windows version 3.1 or Windows 95.
- TCP/IP Winsock version 1.5 or later.
- America Online for Windows version 1.5 or later.

After you've met the minimum requirements, here's what to do next:

1. Open your AOL Windows software.
2. Make your SLIP or PPP connection.
3. Click Setup on the Sign On Screen.
4. Click the Setup Modem button.
5. Choose the TCP/IP (Winsock) release that matches the version number of the America Online for Windows software you are using, such as Winsock version 2.0 for America Online for Windows 2.0.
6. Click OK to save your settings.
7. Click OK to return to the Sign On Screen.
8. Sign on to America Online using TCP/IP.

N O T E   If you cannot get a satisfactory connection to AOL, check to make sure you don't have multiple copies of WINSOCK.DLL on your hard drive. The best way to test for this is to open the Windows File manager and then do a search on your hard drive(s) for the WINSOCK.DLL file. If you find more than one copy on your hard drive(s), you should remove all copies except for the one located in your C:\Windows\System directory.

Using AOL Macintosh with TCP/IP

After you've secured your TCP/IP capability, logging on through AOL on your Macintosh is hardly more complex than making a regular AOL hookup. Just remember that you need the MacTCP or TCP/IP Control Panels properly installed in your System Folder.

Here are the requirements to access AOL's TCP/IP capability on a Mac:

- System 7, or System 6.0.5 with Communications Toolbox installed
- MacTCP version 2.0.6 or later or TCP/IP (when using Apple's Open Transport)
- America Online for Macintosh version 2.5 or later

N O T E Users of Macintosh System 7.5 have received MacTCP version 2.0.4 with their software. If you haven't installed this utility, it can be done by launching your System 7.5 installer, choosing a Custom Install, and then checking MacTCP from the list of Networking options. Free updates are available from Apple for MacTCP version 2.0.6. In addition, the 2.0.6 update is included as part of Apple's System 7.5 Update 2.0, which is available for download from America Online's Macintosh Operating Systems Forum (use the keyword **MOS** for access). If your system software is 7.5.2 or later, you will be using Apple's TCP/IP Control Panel to select these options. ▓

After you've met the minimum requirements, here's what to do next:

1. Open your AOL Macintosh software.
2. Make your SLIP or PPP connection as designated by your network administrator or Internet provider.
3. Select TCP Connection from the Locality pop-up menu on the Sign On Screen.
4. Sign on to America Online using TCP/IP.

N O T E If you cannot find TCP Connection in your Locality pop-up menu, check your Mac's System Folder to make sure that TCPack for AOL is installed in System 7's Extensions Folder. Also check the Online Files folder, which is inside the folder set aside for your AOL Mac software, for two files: TCPack and TCP Connection. If these files are missing (perhaps you removed them by mistake), you'll want to reinstall your AOL software, using the instructions provided in Appendix A, "If You're New to the Online World." Don't trash your older AOL software just yet. When you first open your newly installed AOL software, just choose the Upgrade option to record preference settings, incoming and outgoing FlashMail, and the address book from the older copy of AOL (you can dispose of the old version after you know everything is working properly). ▓

Diagnosing Some Common TCP/IP Connection Programs

If you find that you're having trouble connecting to AOL via TCP/IP, there are several steps that you can follow when attempting to troubleshoot the connection:

- To test whether you have a working TCP/IP connection, it is best to try *pinging* (contacting) a local computer whose TCP/IP address or name is known to you (perhaps on your local network). You can do this by selecting the Ping utility that comes with your TCP/IP software package. If you did not get a copy of Ping with your TCP/IP package, you can always connect to AOL via modem and download a Ping utility from the Communications Forum libraries. Use that software to enter the name or address of the computer that you want to ping. Ping then attempts to contact that computer and get a response from it. If you get a response from the target computer, then you know that your computer is properly connected and talking to the network. If you get no response, then you will need to check the TCP/IP connection.

- Another common problem that can occur is having your TCP/IP driver set to the wrong IP address, broadcast address, or subnet mask. Having an incorrect entry in any of these settings can cause the TCP/IP connection to fail. If you dial in to the Internet with either a SLIP or PPP connection, it is also important to make sure that your login ID and password are set correctly, along with all of your modem and communications port settings. If you check all the settings and the connections still fail, you should consider attempting to deinstall and then reinstall your TCP/IP package.

- If you are able to ping another computer, but are unable to connect to AOL via TCP/IP, try this:

  1. Ping or connect via FTP to a computer on the Internet.
  2. If the above step fails, you should contact either your network administrator or your Internet provider to make sure that your connection to the Internet is currently functioning.
  3. If you are able to connect to another computer on the Internet, but still cannot connect to AOL, contact AOL customer support for further assistance. One effective way to get support is through AOL's free Tech Live area, where you can chat with a support representative and get help with your TCP/IP connection problem.

> **CAUTION**
>
> Because the Internet, unlike your connection to AOL via modem, is not secure, all the information that passes back and forth between AOL and your computer can be intercepted and read. Because this includes your account name and password, it is best to change your password on a regular basis to minimize the potential of someone intercepting and using your account.

For Further Reading

The Internet is a huge, complex, and exciting place to visit. America Online has purchased Internet access companies and has created an entire division with which to provide Internet services for various businesses. After you get your feet wet, maybe you'll want to review some background information about the Internet. At the very least, the information will provide a greater understanding of the whys and wherefores of this global network, and will make your visits all the more enjoyable.

During the preparation of this section, I consulted *Special Edition Using the Internet*, published by Que, for historic information about the Internet, and I recommend it to you highly. The second edition of this massive work (over 1,200 pages) includes a CD-ROM that provides over 100 Internet tools for Microsoft Windows. Even if you have a Macintosh and cannot use those tools (although they probably will work with Soft Window or a DOS card on your Mac), you'll find the material in the book works with both computing platforms. It's well written and highly recommended.

In addition, Que's *Windows 95 Communications Handbook* will help guide you through the hurdles of setting up your PC and Windows 95 for the most efficient telecommunications possible. Some additional titles you'll want to check out at your bookstore include Que's *Using Your Modem* and *Special Edition Using the Internet with the Mac*.

Making Sense of Those Arcane UNIX-style Commands

To better understand the inner workings of the Internet, you'll want to know a few of the text commands sometimes used to navigate through its highways and byways.

The Internet in its raw form presents a decidedly un-Mac- or Windows-like appearance, but the basic commands are not so hard to learn, once you get the hang of it. Although America Online has put a simple, graphical interface on the Internet that largely shields you from these commands, you will probably find it useful to know at least some of them, especially if you intend to join some of the computer-related UseNet Newsgroups.

Many Internet travelers, though, still cannot access the Internet by pointing and clicking; they have to type the names of the commands they want to activate, although there are a number of software programs (many of which are available in AOL's software libraries) that also provide them with a more graphical interface.

There's always a chance you will have to spend a brief tour on a computer with a text-based interface, and be forced to navigate the Internet without the benefit of your AOL account and software. Although most such programs are menu driven, and have clearly labeled commands, it would be a good idea to master a few basic UNIX commands to help you navigate easily through many Internet services. If the command you need to know isn't shown here (and I'm just covering the basics), a simple help or **?** (question mark) entered at the prompt will usually display the information you need. To activate the following commands, always type a return at the end of a text line:

- **passwd.** Changes your password. When you enter a new password, what you type won't be visible (so do it carefully).
- **ls.** Requests a directory or list of file names. The ls function has a few options you can add to bring you additional information in the file list.

  ls -A. Lists all files, except those having . or .. names.

  ls -l. Provides a long listing of files, including the size and when they were last modified.

  ls -R. Allows you to see a list of files in the current directory and in all of the directories below the current one.
- **cd.** Changes the directory you've accessed, equivalent to navigating through directories or folders on your Macintosh or Windows computer. You can move down one directory level by entering the cd command all by itself. Typing **cd ..** takes you up one directory level. The command **cd $HOME** takes you to the main or root level of a directory.
- **mkdir.** Creates a new directory, the equivalent of the New Folder command on a Macintosh.
- **rmdir.** Removes a directory that you've created, as long as you have write privileges for it.

- **chmod.** Allows you to change the level of protection for a file (its mode) so that you can modify or delete the file.

- **rm.** Allows you to delete a file when followed by the name of a file, as long as the mode or protection status of the file (described previously) allows you to remove it. This selection is a one-way trip—there's no way back once the file is gone.

- **cp.** Allows you to copy files.

- **finger.** Allows you to get a list of other users on your system, along with their names, if they are logged on, or the last time they logged onto the system. The resemblance to the term used by movie detectives doesn't seem coincidental.

- **binary.** Places you in the mode to receive files on a Macintosh from an FTP site. You may also use the abbreviation **bin**.

- **get.** Followed by the name of the file allows you to retrieve that file and transfer it to your Internet service provider's computer or directly to your personal computer.

- **write.** Sends messages directly to another user's computer. You have to use `write` on each line of text you send in your message. To close a message, it's traditional to use either `o` or `-o-` to signify the message's conclusion.

- **talk.** Sets up your computer to engage in a one-on-one or interactive conversation with another user. What you type will be visible to the other user, provided that user has also engaged the talk command.

- **logout.** Ends your session and disconnects your modem from the other line. If you see the message `Not login shell`, you may be logged onto another service by way of your service provider. If you see this message, before you can engage logout you must first use `exit`.

N O T E If you log on to a remote system that doesn't recognize the standard `logout` command, try the commands as `exit`, `quit`, or `bye`. The characters `^]` will let you log off from a Telnet connection. ■

From Here...

Yes, those command line instructions just listed may seem somewhat intimidating, unless you are well versed in DOS (and if you are, you'll see some similarities). Fortunately, participating in the Internet via America Online helps you avoid text-based commands and complexities. You can spend more time enjoying your Internet access, rather than worrying about how to use it. Look in the next few chapters for details about the services mentioned in this chapter.

- Chapter 30, "Secrets of Internet E-Mail and Mailing Lists"
- Chapter 31, "Searching for Information on the Net"
- Chapter 32, "Joining and Participating in Internet Newsgroups"
- Chapter 33, "Internet Chats"
- Chapter 34, "Using File Transfer Protocol"
- Chapter 35, "Using the World Wide Web"
- Chapter 36, "Popular Web Sites"

In addition, you'll want to review the following chapters to hone your basic skills in navigating and using America Online.

- For information on locating files on America Online, see Chapter 20, "Tips and Tricks on Finding Software."
- For more information on tapping America Online's huge resources of educational and reference information, read Chapter 25, "Learning and Reference."
- For more information on using America Online's e-mail features, read Appendixes A, B, C, and Chapter 8, "Using America Online E-Mail."
- And to keep up to date on America Online's fast-growing Internet connection, simply type the keyword **Internet** and explore the Internet Connection.

CHAPTER 30

Secrets of Internet E-Mail and Mailing Lists

Sending your e-mail across the world

You learn how to send and receive Internet e-mail.

Sending files

You can also attach files to your Internet e-mail.

A world of information in your mailbox

Learn how to use Internet mailing lists.

When the information gets too overwhelming

Of course, you'll want to know how to get off some of those mailing lists.

When you use America Online's highly flexible and speedy electronic mail features, you're not restricted to sending your messages to other AOL members. Through AOL's Internet Connection, you can send e-mail to members of other online services and, in fact, to anyone with Internet access, all across the world. In addition, you can subscribe to any of thousands of mailing lists and place discussions and information on all sorts of topics in your AOL mailbox. ■

Using Internet E-Mail

One of the most exciting and rewarding announcements you hear during your online session (if you have sounds turned on, of course) is AOL's friendly mailman proclaiming, "You've got mail." That statement might bring with it a message from a friend, confirmation of a business deal from an associate, or an invitation to an upcoming social gathering (online or at a relative's home).

It's no surprise that e-mail is one of the most popular services offered not only by America Online, but through the Internet as well. Right now, you can send electronic mail to, and receive it from, *anyone* connected to the Internet. It makes no difference whether they use America Online. If you have friends who use one of the other online networks, such as CompuServe, Prodigy, AT&T WorldNet, Netcom, MCI Mail, and others, you can send them e-mail from America Online. America Online handles millions of Internet-based transactions each day.

America Online's E-Mail Gateway is a full center that provides information and support for using Internet e-mail (see fig. 30.1). There you'll see updated listings covering addressing and receiving e-mail, plus you'll have access to AOL's Internet search tools (such as Gopher and WAIS). The techniques for finding the information you want are covered in Chapter 31, "Searching for Information on the Internet."

FIG. 30.1
AOL's Mail Gateway provides information to help you send e-mail to other services.

You can begin the Internet e-mail process simply enough by opening a blank e-mail form (see fig. 30.2). Yes, it's the same e-mail form described in Chapter 8, "Using America Online E-Mail." The ground rules regarding content are the same, except for one: Don't bother using special typefaces, styles, or colors in your document. Everything will be converted to raw, unformatted (ASCII) text when your mail travels through the mail gateway. The use of ASCII text allows for total compatibility with millions of computers, using many operating systems and many kinds of telecommunications software.

FIG. 30.2
Only the address differentiates your Internet e-mail from regular AOL e-mail.

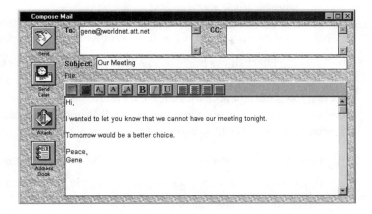

Part
VIII

Ch
30

TIP The best way to learn the address of an Internet correspondent is to simply ask the person for it. You can also access e-mail addresses from a World Wide Web site, **www.four11.com**.

In every other aspect, the process of preparing your Internet e-mail is the same as for letters sent to other AOL members. You include a subject line and your message, and you can write these items in the same way you write any other e-mail. You can even attach files to your Internet-based e-mail, with a few considerations that I'll explain later in this chapter.

Sending E-Mail

Sending e-mail over the Internet works the same as sending normal America Online e-mail to other members. You just type the Internet address of your intended recipient rather than the America Online screen name you normally use to send mail to other AOL members.

Addressing Internet mail is that simple. There are a couple of rules to follow, however. After you've read about those rules, you'll be sending worldwide e-mail with ease.

An Internet address never contains blank spaces. If someone's mail system does allow spaces at the receiving end, the spaces are automatically replaced by underscores (_) in the Internet Address. For example, you might see john_smith@veryhugecorp.com, in which the space between the user's first and last name is replaced with an underscore character.

Also, every Internet address must have the user name and domain (location) specified. For our purposes, the user name is everything before the @ symbol, and the domain is everything after the @ symbol. In the domain, a company name is followed by a suffix that describes what type of organization it is. A business, for instance, uses the suffix *com,* educational institutions use *edu,* military sites use *mil,* a non-profit organization, such as a computer user group will use *org*, and government offices use *gov.*

The following chart shows how you can address Internet e-mail to your friends on other online services. Some additional information about each service has been added, when necessary, to help you prepare your e-mail for that service. If you follow the format provided here, you can easily address other services in much the same manner. The italicized entry labeled *name* is where you need to insert your own AOL screen name:

Location	Long Address	Shortcut	Example
AppleLink	applelink.apple.com	apple	*name*@apple
AT&TMail	attmail.com	att	*name*@att
America Online	aol.com	none	*name*@aol
BITNET	<institution>.bitnet		*name*@<institution>.bitnet
BIX	bix.com	BIX	*name*@bix.com
CompuServe	compuserve.com	cis	12345.678@cis

TIP Some organizations have a private area that uses CompuServe e-mail in their address. You can reach these locations using the format *name*@*organization*.compuserve.com.

Connect	connectinc.com	none	*name*@connectinc.com
Delphi	delphi.com		*name*@delphi.com
EasyLink	eln.attmail.com	none	62<*name*>@eln.attmail.com
Fidonet	p<point>.f<node>.n<network>.z<zone>	none	*name*@p<point>.f<node>.n.fidonet.org<network>.z<zone>.fidonet.org
GEnie	genie.geis.com	genie	*name*@genie
MCI Mail	mcimail.com	mci	*name*@mci
Prodigy	prodigy.com	none	userid@Prodigy.com
Well	well.com	none	*name*@well.com
Rush Limbaugh		none	70277.2502@compuserve.com

N O T E Rush Limbaugh is the popular and often controversial conservative radio and TV personality. The preceding address is listed because of how popular his show has become in many parts of the country. The address is offered for information purposes only, not to represent anyone's political stand. ▨

U.S. Congress	hr.house.gov	none	*name*@hr.house.gov

N O T E Contact your representative for the exact e-mail address. Not all Congressmen are accessible this way, but a growing number have taken advantage of the Internet to receive mail from constituents and other citizens. Some members of the Senate have a different format; you should contact the individual senator's office to find out how to make contact via e-mail. ▨

White House	whitehouse.gov	none	**president@whitehouse.gov vice-president@whitehouse.gov**

The White House also has a forum on America Online that is accessible through the keyword **White House** (see fig. 30.3). You can write directly to the White House using the Send E-Mail to the President button. The mail you send will be reviewed by the White House staff. There's no guarantee that the president or vice president will actually see the original message, except to represent a sampling of public reaction to specific issues and policies.

FIG. 30.3
The White House Forum on AOL.

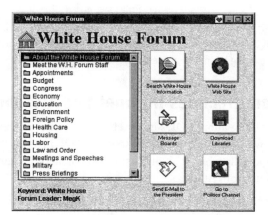

> **N O T E** Each online service has its own requirements and limitations as to how the offered Internet services work. AOL's Internet Connection contains help texts that will help you address your e-mail to other services. As other services change their Internet offerings, these help texts will also be revised. ▦

> **N O T E** To learn someone's e-mail address without asking for it, I suggest you read *Que's Special Edition Using Internet E-Mail*, by Will Sadler, et al., available in most bookstores. Business addresses can also be found in *New Riders' Internet Official Yellow Pages*, by Christine Maxwell and Czeslaw Jan Grycz. ▦

> **N O T E** If you do not address your Internet mail in the correct format, the mail will be returned marked unknown. If this happens to you, verify the original recipient's correct e-mail address (even an error involving one letter or number is enough to bounce the letter). Internet e-mail can travel through a long, circuitous path on its way from AOL's mail server to its destination. Sometimes errors can occur during transmission, and sometimes correctly addressed mail is returned. The best solution (after verifying that the address is correct) is to send the letter again. ▦

Receiving E-Mail

To receive mail from the Internet, you need to know your own Internet address, just as you need to know a recipient's. Your address is simply your America Online screen name, with any spaces removed, plus @aol.com. If your screen name is John User, for example, your Internet address is **johnuser@aol.com**.

> **N O T E** Internet addresses are almost always expressed in lowercase letters. Although this is not an absolute requirement, you should follow this convention for clarity and consistency with existing Internet practices. ▦

How AOL Software Decodes Internet File Attachments

The really neat thing about AOL's Internet e-mail is that you can send and receive files in the very same way you send those files to other AOL members. But there are a few things to consider, especially when it involves someone on another service who may be getting the files you send from AOL:

- ▦ Files attached to your Internet e-mail are automatically converted to MIME format. In order to read those files, the recipient may need a separate program, but that's something that the recipient may have to check with the other service. One example of a good decoder utility is UUCODE by Sabasoft. A quick check of a shareware software library will yield many treasures of this sort.

By the way, MIME isn't something that refers to an actor performing without speaking. It stands for *Multipurpose Internet Mail Extensions*. It's a technique used to convert the file to text form so that it can be read on different kinds of computers.

- If someone sends you a long text message (containing more than 27,000 characters), it will be converted to an attached file. You'll see the first 2,000 characters in the body of the e-mail message, and the full, original message will be attached as a file.

Part

VIII

Ch

30

N O T E America Online's e-mail form can contain up to 27,000 characters, or a few hundred words, of text. If your message is larger than that, you'll want to save your message as a separate file and attach it to your e-mail, and then send it on its way. ■

- Tell the person who is sending you files by the Internet not to attach more than one file to the message. Otherwise, you'll have to use another software program (a MIME converter) to change it back to its normal form. Instead, suggest to that person that they make the files into a single compressed archive, using one of the standard Mac or PC compression programs (we recommend StuffIt or ZIP because AOL's software will automatically decode files in either format). You can find a MIME converter in AOL's software libraries using the File Search feature (click Search Software Libraries from the Go To menu).

 T I P If you ever need a program that will convert MIME files, check AOL's software libraries (using the File Search technique I described in Chapter 20, "Tips and Tricks on Finding Software").

CAUTION

Graphic files on the Internet do not have to follow America Online's Terms of Service regarding nude or sexually explicit content. Be sure to examine the article's header or look at the title and purpose of a Newsgroup before transferring material from that area to your computer.

Finding Internet Mailing Lists

Keyword: **Mailing Lists**

Internet mailing lists (see fig. 30.4) are ongoing e-mail discussions sent via the Internet to groups of people who share similar interests. Using regular Internet e-mail, information is exchanged in a continuing, interactive fashion with people all around the world. The entire text of these discussions will appear regularly in your AOL mailbox (but don't get carried away with subscribing to mailing lists, for reasons that will be discussed later).

FIG. 30.4
AOL's Internet Mailing Lists center.

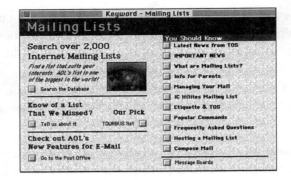

Thousands of Internet Mailing Lists exist today, encompassing almost every topic imaginable: computer technology, American literature, philosophy, cooking, chess, motorcycling, sports, the environment, rock music, UFOs, alternative lifestyles—take your pick.

The Internet Mailing Lists area has various helpful text articles containing background and instructions on using the Mailing Lists features of the Internet Connection.

To locate specific mailing lists that might appeal to your interests, click the Search Over 2,000 Internet Mailing Lists button (or whatever number it's increased to by the time you read this book). You'll discover a database of mailing lists you can search by entering descriptive words (see fig. 30.5).

FIG. 30.5
The Mailing Lists database search window.

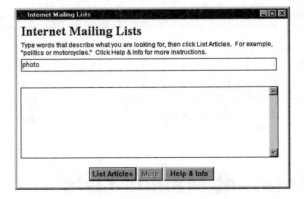

After a list of entries that match your search description appears, click the List Articles button or press Enter. The items that appear after a successful search from this window contain the descriptions of Internet Mailing Lists available from the matches of your search words entered in the search window (see fig. 30.6).

FIG. 30.6
The results of a search on the word "photo."

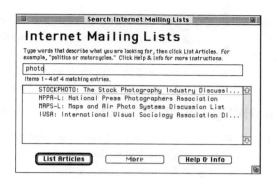

Joining an Internet Mailing List

The descriptions of a mailing list contain instructions on how you can subscribe to other interesting mailing lists by using your America Online Internet e-mail address. Follow the instructions carefully; they tend to differ slightly from list to list. Remember also to note how you can leave (or *unsubscribe*) any lists you join, in case you change your mind later. Most of these lists generate a large amount of mail and can quickly fill your online mailbox if you don't check in regularly.

Remember, also, that these mailing lists are sometimes run not by an individual reading your request, but by a software program. The software program automates the process of establishing and maintaining these mailing lists, and sending the regular mailings to subscribers. Because you are communicating with another computer and not an individual, it's important that you make your requests follow the exact directions in the mailing list subscription.

Here are a few things to keep in mind when joining a mailing list:

- Use the exact commands specified in the information about joining a mailing list to subscribe and unsubscribe.

- Remember that Internet e-mail might take a couple of days to reach its destination, so be patient about getting a response. Also remember that mailings to subscribers might be sent only at infrequent intervals.

N O T E It is common these days for mailing list servers to automatically generate a confirmation letter when you ask to join a specific list. You won't actually get any mailings till you return this request. This step is being taken more and more because of occasional attempts by computer hackers to sign folks up to mailing lists they never really wanted to join. Having faced tons of unwanted e-mail myself as a result of such annoying pranks, I can tell you I'd rather have the confirmation to my subscription request. ■

■ If a mailing list is also available as a UseNet newsgroup, you might prefer to use that option. With a UseNet newsgroup, you don't have to handle unsolicited e-mail. You can easily limit reading messages to the ones that interest you within a given time frame, and ignore messages dealing with topics you do not want to see.

Responding to Mailing List Messages

The material you receive from a mailing list looks the same as any standard e-mail message (see fig. 30.7). And you respond to those messages in exactly the same fashion. Generally you use the Reply to All feature on your mailing list e-mail to include your comments about a particular article in a subsequent group of messages. Just using the Reply option will send your response to the individual whose message you're answering rather than to the list itself.

If you want to post an article to a mailing list, you first want to consult the original instructions for that mailing list to see if any special steps are involved.

FIG. 30.7
Typical e-mail from a mailing list.

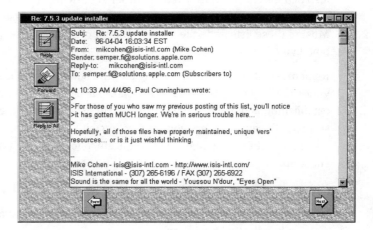

Leaving a Mailing List

The instructions you receive when you first join a mailing list generally include online information on how to cancel the mailing list, or unsubscribe. If the mailing list is run by an automated list server (usually identified by the word "listserv" as part of the address), you must make your request using the exact format contained in those instructions. If the list is run by a person, you can just send a regular e-mail request.

CAUTION

If you change your screen name or cancel your AOL account, be sure to unsubscribe all of your mailing lists (the mail won't be forwarded). If the list is maintained by a person, you can send whatever mail-forwarding information is appropriate. Otherwise, you'll have to resubscribe to the mailing lists from which you want to continue getting e-mail.

What to Do if Your Mailbox Is Filled

There are so many fascinating mailing lists that you will no doubt be tempted to join a number of them. It's not uncommon to overdo it a bit, and you might find your mailbox clogged with messages still unread. FlashSessions can produce huge incoming mailboxes. The best advice is to be judicious about managing your mail so that you aren't overwhelmed.

Presently, your AOL mailbox is limited to 550 items. This number includes not only the mail you have read, but also the mail you have not yet seen. The list of mail you've sent remains in your mailbox for 30 days; mail you've read is deleted after 5 days (at least as of the time this book was being written).

CAUTION

If the amount of read and unread mail exceeds 550 pieces, new e-mail will simply be returned to the sender with a `mailbox is full` message. Consistent returned messages may result in being dropped by your favorite mailing lists. By managing your mailbox carefully, you'll avoid losing messages you might want to read.

Here are some common-sense tips to help you keep your mailbox down to usable proportions:

- Be sure you subscribe only to mailing lists you really want to read.
- Take note of directions on how to unsubscribe to a mailing list when you join, in case the mailing list doesn't meet your expectations or you find your mailbox getting a little too crowded.
- Check your e-mail regularly to keep your mailbox as small as possible.

TIP If you've lost directions on how to subscribe or unsubscribe to a mailing list, simply search for it again using the search feature in the Internet Mailing Lists area. The results of your search can be saved and printed for later review.

A Favorite Mailing List Directory

Mailing lists can change at any time, and the list you want to join today might be discontinued at some time in the future. You'll want to examine the following directory of some popular mailing lists. The list is divided by topic. Each selection has the subject and title of the list, and the address for subscribing. If you want to learn more about a particular mailing list, use the search feature in AOL's Internet Mailing Lists area to locate further information.

Before proceeding, bear in mind that this listing, as with others throughout the Internet section of this book, is meant to represent just a sampling of the areas available on the Internet. As you become experienced with your Internet surfing, you will find thousands of other areas of equal or greater interest.

TIP If a mailing list address includes the listserv entry, the list is maintained by an automated system.

Aviation

Mailing List	Address
Aircraft	listserv@grearn.bitnet
Airline	listserv@cunyvm.cuny.edu
Aviation	listserv@mc.lcs.mit.edu
Flight Simulator	flight-sim-request@grove.iup.edu
Space	listserv@andrew.cmu.edu

Archaeology

Mailing List	Address
American Institute of Archaeology	
aia-1	listserv@brynmawr.edu
ancient-1	listserv@ulkyvm.louisville.edu
anthro-1	listserv@ubvm.bitnet

Mailing List	Address

American Institute of Archaeology

arch-1	listserv@dgogwdg1.bitnet
classics	listserv@uwavm.u.washington.edu
ethnohis	listserv@dgogwdg1.bitnet

Ethnology and History

ethnohis	listserv@nic.surfnet.nl

Human Biology

humbio-1	humbio-request@acc.fau.edu

Ethnology and history

ethnohis	listserv@nic.surfnet.nl

Indigenous Knowledge

indknow	listserv@uwavm.u.washington.edu
marine-1	listserv@uoguelph.ca
museum-1	listserv@unmvm.bitnet

Automotive

Mailing List	Address
autox	autox-request@auox.team.bnet

Electric Vehicles

ev	listserv@sjsuvm1.sjsu.edu
Honda	listserv@mscrc.sunysb.edu

Biology and Environment

Mailing List	Address

Environmental Behavior

envbeh-1	listserv@graf.poly.edu

Environmental Studies Programs

envst-1	listserv@brownvm.bitnet

Forensics Studies

forens-1	listserv@acc.fau.edu

Part **VIII**

Ch **30**

Human Biology

humbio-1   humbio-request@acc.fau.edu

Business, Economics, and Jobs

Mailing List	Address

Economy and Economic Problems for Less-Developed Countries

economy   listserv@tecmtyvm.mty.itesm.mx

fedjobs   listserv@dartcms1.dartmouth.edu

fedtax-1   listserv@sjsi/botmet

Information on the Training and Development of Human Resources

trdev-1   listserv@psuvm.psu.edu

Cultures, Social Groups, and Lifestyles

Mailing List	Address

Electronic Hebrew User's Newspaper:

e-hug   listserv@dartcms1.bitnet

Beatles-Era Popular Culture:

inmylife   listserv@wkuvx1.bitnet

Japanese Food and Culture

j-food-1   listserv@jpnknu10.bitnet

Men's Issues

mail-   mail-menu-x.att.men@usl.request@com.attuncom

Peace Corps

pcorps-1   listserv@cmuvm-csv.cmich.edu

Women's Studies, Issues

wmst-1   listserv@umdd.umd.edu

Games

Mailing List	Address

Advanced Dungeons & Dragons

adnd-1	listserv@utarlvm1.bitnet
dark-sun	listserv@le.ac.uk
chess-1	listserv@grearn.bitnet

Wargames

consim-1	listserv@vm.ucs.ualberta.ca

Super Nintendo Entertainment System

snes	listserv@spcvxa.spc.edu

Government and Politics

Mailing List	Address

Economy and Economic Problems for Less-Developed Countries

amnesty	listserv@vms.cis.pitt.edu
animal-rights	listserv@cs.odu.edu

European Community

ec	listserv@vm.cc.metu.edu.tr

Human Rights Issues

hr-1-1	listserv@vms.cis.pitt.edu

For Libertarians

libernet	listserv@dartmouth.edu

Political Discussions

politics	listserv@ucf1vm.cc.ucf.edu

Health Issues

Mailing List	Address
addict-1	listserv@kentvm.kent.edu
aidsnews	listserv@rutvm1.bitnet
alcohol	listserv@lmuacad.bitnet

Part
VIII

Ch
30

Computers and Health

c+health	listserv@iubvm.ucs.indiana.edu
deafblind	listserv@ukcc.uky.edu
diabetic	listserv@pccvm.bitnet
drugabus	listserv@umab.bitnet

Fitness and Exercise

fit-1	listserv@etsuadmn.bitnet

U.S. Health Reform

healthre	listserv@ukcc.uky.edu

Environmental Health and Safety

safety	listserv@uvmvm.bitnet

Smoking Addiction

smoke-free	listserv@ra.msstate.edu

Hobbies and Home

Mailing List	Address
aquarium	listserv@emuvm1.cc.emory.edu
bicycles	bicycles-request@bbn.com
canine-1	listserv@psuvm.bitnet
comics-1	listserv@unlvm.unl.edu
hunting	listserv@tamvm1.tamu.edu
martial-arts	martial-arts-request@dragon.cso.uiuc.edu
photo-1	listserv@buacca.bitnet
scuba-1	listserv@browvm.bitnet
stamps	listserv@cunyvm.cuny.edu

Genealogical Research

roots-1	listserv@vm1.nodak.edu

Humanities and History

Mailing List	Address
18th Century	
c18-1	listserv@psuvm.bitnet
Ancient Texts	
contex-1	listserv@uottawa.bitnet
History of the Law	
hislaw-1	listserv@ulkyvm.louisville.edu
Classical India	
indology	listserv@liverpool.ac.uk
Middle Ages	
mediev-1	listserv@ukanvm.cc.ukans.edu
Presidential History Forum	
prezhist	listserv@kasey.umkc.edu

Part
VIII

Ch
30

Literature, Fiction, and Writing

Mailing List	Address
American Literature	
amlit-1	listserv@umcvmb.missouri.edu
Creative Writing	
crewrt-1	listserv@umcvmb.missouri.edu
Mystery Genre	
dorothy1	listserv@kentvm.kent.edu
Literature and Related Topics	
litera-1	listserv@tecmtyvm.mty.itesm.mx
Screen Writing for Film and TV	
scrnwrit	listserv@tamvm1.bitnet
sf-lovers	listserv@rutgers.edu
Superheros and Related Fiction	
superguy	listserv@ucf1vm.bitnet

Languages and Linguistics

Mailing List	Address
classics	listserv@uwavm.u.washington.edu

Esperanto

esper-1	listserv@trearn.bitnet

Yiddish Literature and Language

mendele	listserv@yalevm.ycc.yale.edu

Japanese Language

nihongo	listserv@mitvma.mit.edu

Macintosh Computers

Mailing List	Address
hypercrd	listserv@purccvm.bitnet
info-mac	listserv@sumex-aim.stanford.edu

Computer Newsletter

tidbits	listserv@ricevm1.rice.edu

Desktop Publishing

dtp-1	listserv@antigone.uu.holonet.net

Macintosh Systems Advice

macsystm	listserv@dartcms1.bitnet

Music and Dance

Mailing List	Address

Pre-LP Music and Recordings

78-1	listserv@cornell.edu
bgrass-1	listserv@brownvm.bitnet

Folk Dancing

dance-1	listserv@hearn.bitnet

Electronic Music

emusic-1	listserv@auvm.bitnet

Rolling Stones

undercover	listserv@snowhite.cis.uoguelph.ca

PC Computing

Mailing List	Address

Computer Help Questions

tipsheet	listserv@wsuvm1.csc.wsu.edu

MS-DOS Sound Card Forum and Discussions

ibmsnd-l	listserv@brownvm.brown.edu

PC Hardware Discussions

pcbuild	listserv@tscvm.trenton.edu

Small Computing Systems Software Reviews and Issues

softrevu	listserv@brownvm.brown.edu

Publications

Mailing List	Address

Progressive and Alternative Publications and Other Media

prog-pubs	prog-pubs-request@fuggles.acc.virginia.edu

Society for the History of Authorship, Reading, and Publishing

sharp-1	listserv@iubvm.ucs.indiana.edu

Video Production and Operations

vidpro-1	listserv@uxa.ecn.bgu.edu

Religion and Philosophy

Mailing List	Address
baptist	listserv@ukcc.uky.edu
belief-1	listserv@brownvm.bitnet
buddha-1	listserv@ulkyvm.louisville.edu
christia	listserv@finhutc.bitnet

Religion and the Nature of the Universe

obj-rel	listserv@emuvm1.cc.emory.edu
theology	u16841@uicvm.bitnet

Part
VIII

Ch
30

Sciences, Math, and Engineering

Mailing List	Address
chminf-1	listserv@iubvm.bitnet
circuits-1	listserv@uwplatt.edu
fusion	listserv@zorch.sf.bay.org

Holography

opt-proc	listserv@taunivm.bitnet
optics	listserv@toe.towson.edu
physics	listserv@marist.bitnet

Sports and Exercise

Mailing List	Address
cricket	listserv@vm1.nodak.edu

Gymnastics

gymn	owner-gymn@athena.mit.edu

College Hockey

hockey-1	listserv@maine.maine.edu

Play-by-play Sportscasters

pbp-1	listserv@etsuadmn.etsu.edu

Baseball Statistics

statlg-1	listserv@sbcccvm.bitnet
swim-1	listserv@uafsysb.uark.edu
weights	weights-request@mickey.disney.com

Travel

Mailing List	Address

Hosting Foreign Visitors

hospex	listserv@plearn.bitnet

Discussion of Tourism

trvel-1	listserv@trearn.bitnet

Television, Movies, and Theater

Mailing List	Address
90210	90210-request@ferkel.ucsb.edu

Discovery Channel

disc-1	listserv@sendit.nodak.edu
film-1	listserv@vmtecmex.bitnet
melrose-place	melrose-place-request@ferkel.ucsb.edu
sf-lovers	listserv@rutgers.edu
strek-1	listserv@pccvm.bitnet
trek-review-1	listserv@cornell.edu

Part

VIII

Ch

30

From Here...

As you can see, sending and receiving e-mail on the Internet is hardly more complicated than sending e-mail to another America Online member. Subscribing to a mailing list follows basically the same steps. And, from the comfort of America Online's graphical interface, participating in all the Internet's exciting features is just as easy.

- For more information on using America Online's e-mail features, read Chapters 3, "Getting the Most from AOL's Macintosh Software," 4, "Getting the Most from AOL's Windows Software," and 8, "Using America Online E-Mail."

- For information on locating files on America Online, see Chapter 20, "Tips and Tricks on Finding Software."

- For information on how to join and participate in Internet newsgroups, see Chapter 32, "Joining and Participating in Internet Newsgroups."

- To keep up to date on America Online's fast-growing Internet connection, simply type the keyword **Internet** and explore the Internet Connection.

CHAPTER 31

Searching for Information on the Internet

If you've come this far, you've read the descriptions of the Internet as a sprawling, largely unregulated mass of information, both useful and otherwise. You can think of it as the equivalent of thousands and thousands of libraries of books, magazines, photographs, and software, and all of it is there for you to access if you can acquire the catalog file.

Fortunately, America Online offers helpful database search tools that enable you to tap this huge resource of information and get exactly the material you want. ∎

Internet searches

Discover the tools offered by AOL to allow you to quickly search the Internet.

Which tool to use

Learn how to locate the Internet-based material you want.

Search problems

Explore how to deal with common problems in locating information.

Gopher Treasures

Check out AOL's special list of the most popular databases you'll want to access.

What Are Gopher and WAIS?

Before covering the sort of information you can find through database searching, this chapter looks at the tools provided to perform those searches. The names sometimes invoke images other than computers that seek data from far-off points. The name Archie, for example, brings to mind that popular comic book character, as does Veronica, although the origins of these terms are not always as they seem. But Gopher does, as you'll read next, have an animal-related connection, or at least it did when it was first created.

Although some Internet services might require you to perform a separate database search using each of these tools (and others), America Online is structured so that the mechanism used to locate information is transparent to you. You don't have to worry about which database system is finding what information (except, as you'll see later in this chapter, in the case of using an Archie server for searching FTP files). In most cases, you can just concentrate on what is being located. Therefore, this material about the tools you are activating behind the scenes is kept relatively brief.

What Is Gopher?

The Gopher system for searching Internet-based information was originally developed at the University of Minnesota. The name was based on the university's mascot. Consider the Gopher mechanism as being akin to a book's table of contents. It enables you to search for information by category. You use it to browse through information on the Internet. By double-clicking menu entries and icons, you are, in effect, accessing one Gopher server computer after another, located across the world. The system is known as Gopherspace.

What Is WAIS?

As you know, not all the information you want can necessarily be found in a book's table of contents. Often you need to search through the book's index as well. That's where WAIS, or *Wide Area Information Server*, comes into play.

WAIS was originally designed by Brewster Kahle to work with supercomputers. Fortunately for those who worked on personal computers, the system was effective enough to work on computers with normal capabilities too. Moreover, many of the brand-new Pentiums and Power Macs offer performance that seems very much in the supercomputer ballpark.

So, whereas Gopher might find the title of an item, WAIS gets you a more comprehensive response about the kind of information you want.

What Is Veronica?

Aside from being that lusty lady that Archie is always chasing in the comic books, Veronica is a technique used to search through Gopher databases. Whenever you use the Search All Gophers button in AOL's Gopher & WAIS area (and how this is done will be explained later in this chapter), you are using the Veronica system to conduct a global search. Veronica is a very useful tool. It can be a time-saver in many cases, because you don't have to pore over hundreds of directory listings to find specific information.

Veronica has its limitations, however. It accumulates a database of the contents of Gopher servers once every week or so, and consequently might not be up-to-date in the information it finds. So, if your search comes up dry, or the search result seems out-of-date, you might want to do a manual search of specific directories to locate what you want.

Oh, yes, in case you're wondering, Veronica has nothing to do with the comic book character. *Veronica* stands for Very Easy Rodent Oriented Internet-wide Computer Archive.

N O T E When one thinks of all of those sophisticated, interacting, computer-driven database searches, it's sometimes surprising to realize that many of the computer servers providing these capabilities are run by volunteers at colleges and universities throughout the world. So, the quality and content of the material you search might not always be the highest, although usually the volunteers are quite dedicated to their work. ■

Part
VIII

Ch
31

Having Many Tools at Your Disposal

To make your information searches more efficient, AOL combines the best features of Gopher and WAIS, so you can easily find the information resources you want with as little fuss and delay as possible. Most important, the skills required to search through these databases are already known to you. To make Internet database searching as easy as possible, AOL has included it as part of its World Wide Web browser (with a single exception that will be described later).

Next you can look for some information and see how the search is done.

Using an Internet Database

Keyword: **Gopher, WAIS**

The Internet contains hundreds of free databases on topics as diverse as home brewing, NASA news, recipes, Congressional contact information, and the works of Shakespeare. These databases are indexed, meaning that you can search them for information by using key words and phrases, just as you would search for files on America Online by using the File Search feature, described in Chapter 20, "Tips and Tricks on Finding Software." If you've been following current Internet news, you might have heard these databases called *WAIS databases* (see fig. 31.1), which is one tool available on the Internet for searching databases.

FIG. 31.1
AOL offers Gopher and WAIS database search capabilities.

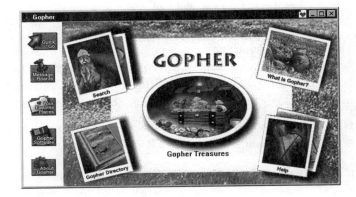

Using AOL's Gopher Database Searching

The best way to demonstrate how an Internet database search works is to conduct one for yourself. America Online's Gopher center offers a list of common topics you might want to search, through its Gopher Treasures feature. We'll describe some of those treasures in more detail later in this chapter. If the topic you want information about isn't shown in the listing, click the Search icon, and enter the subject you want to learn more about in the term box (see fig. 31.2).

FIG. 31.2
You can begin a Gopher search of the Internet by entering the topic in the term box.

It's easy to refine your search request to provide a greater range of information or a more precise description of what you want. Here's how:

1. To find a resource that contains information on two or more topics, separate the topics with the word AND.

2. To get information on either one topic or another topic, use the word OR.

3. To specify certain items you don't want, use the word NOT.

By using any of these words in combination, you can greatly increase the flexibility and accuracy of your search requests and be assured that you will get precisely the material you need.

Using AOL's WAIS Database Searching

The best way to describe the difference between Gopher and WAIS is to say that Gopher is similar to a book's table of contents, whereas WAIS is somewhat like the book's index, much more detailed, capable of providing a more sharply defined range of information.

The beauty of America Online's Internet search interface is that it makes the underlying process transparent to the user. You just check the topics shown in the directories or enter the topic you want to know more about in the search screen. AOL and its Internet gateway do the rest for you behind the scenes, without your having to use any additional software or learn arcane UNIX-based text commands. You don't need to know your WAIS from your Gopher for AOL's host computers to get the job done for you.

Near the end of this chapter, you'll read about some of the most popular Internet databases that are shown when you enter AOL's Gopher & WAIS area.

TROUBLESHOOTING

Help! Why is it taking so long for me to open a Gopher/WAIS database? Is there something wrong with my modem? Unlike accessing other parts of America Online, when you access an Internet database, you are literally logging on to another service. It might take a while for the request to reach that computer and for AOL's host computer network to retrieve the information. This is perfectly normal.

Using Archie to Search for Internet Files

Up until now, this search has been conducted within the comfortable confines of AOL's point-and-click interface. With these instructions on hand, and a cursory glance of menu labels, it is easy to get the hang of seeking out the material you want. But, when it comes to the database search tool that's described next—Archie—you have to write a letter to request the information you want, and you have to watch your language very carefully.

Another database searching technique incorporates the Archie tool, which also seems to be named after a comic book character. Archie (having little to do with Veronica, other than the fact that it also does searching) provides a means to locate files on FTP servers.

FTP, *file transfer protocol,* is the way files are sent via the Internet. Chapter 34, "Using File Transfer Protocol," explains how to use AOL's FTP feature, both by accessing the regular area devoted to that service and by using a Web browser.

Addressing Your Letter   As with other Internet-based resources, when you venture outside of America Online's host computer, you have to pay particular attention to the syntax you use in accessing certain functions.

To begin the task of locating a file, please follow along with this little exercise in which we'll write a letter to an Archie server asking how to make a request. To do that, follow these steps:

1. Open a regular blank AOL e-mail form (see fig. 31.3).

FIG. 31.3
Before you do an Archie search, you'll want to write a letter to an Archie server to request further assistance.

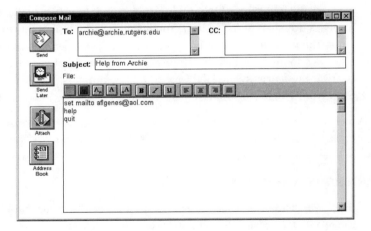

2. Although there are various Archie servers, choose two that are close to AOL's host computer network (in Vienna, Virginia): archie@archie.rutgers.edu and archie@archie.sura.net. (If you want to know, the first server is in New Jersey, and the second is in Maryland.)

3. Enter either address in the To field of your blank e-mail form.

4. Because e-mail cannot be sent without a subject, enter something (anything you want) in the Subject field. You can choose a title that will help you identify the message later, such as Help from Archie. The Archie server doesn't require a subject, but AOL's mail-handling computers do; otherwise, your letter cannot be sent on its way.

5. Type the following text in the body of the letter:

> **set mailto** *<your Internet address>*
> **help**
> **quit**

6. Click the Send icon.

7. Be patient. A response might come back instantly, or it might take anywhere from a few minutes to a few hours to reach your incoming mailbox.

In the above example, the word *help* in the body of the text is, as the name implies, a request for Archie help information.

Archie Writes Back   The response from Archie will be a huge letter (possibly divided into more than one part), looking very much like the one shown in figure 31.4.

FIG. 31.4
Archie's response might be more than you bargained for.

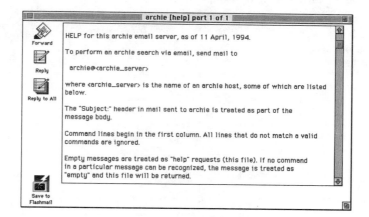

```
                        archie [help] part 1 of 1

  Forward      HELP for this archie email server, as of 11 April, 1994.

  Reply        To perform an archie search via email, send mail to

                 archie@<archie_server>

  Reply to All where <archie_server> is the name of an archie host, some of which are listed
               below.

               The "Subject:" header in mail sent to archie is treated as part of the
               message body.

               Command lines begin in the first column. All lines that do not match a valid
               commands are ignored.

               Empty messages are treated as "help" requests (this file). If no command
  Save to      in a particular message can be recognized, the message is treated as
  Flashmail    "empty" and this file will be returned.
```

The letter you receive will include a large list of Archie servers to seek information from, plus detailed definitions of the UNIX-based commands you can use to enter your search commands. Depending on the complexity of your search routine, you'll want to examine all of these instructions at your leisure and prepare your e-mail carefully.

Cutting to the Chase

I'm sure many of you will want to locate files in the speediest manner possible, so this discussion will avoid the variables and get to the basics. Here's how to locate a file when you know its title or subject:

1. Address an e-mail form to one of the Archie servers mentioned previously.

2. Enter any title you want as the Subject line (one that defines the content of the message would be helpful to you).

3. Use the following commands to make your request:

> **set mailto** *<your Internet address>*
> **set maxhits 10**
> **find** *<title or subject of file>*
> **quit**

The reference to maxhits is made to keep your mailbox from being overwhelmed with choices. It simply states the maximum number of FTP sites that will be included in your search result. If you're willing to take your chances, you can eliminate this line; the default is 100.

In a sample site search, the author requested that the Archie server locate files with the name PowerPC. The result is shown in figure 31.5.

FIG. 31.5
Here's the location of the files searched for.

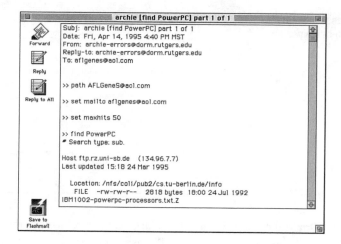

Now, as to actually logging on to that FTP server and accessing the file, that's covered in detail in Chapter 34, "Using File Transfer Protocol."

TROUBLESHOOTING

I'm getting a message that AOL can't retrieve the Gopher information I want. Why? It's important to realize that when you access any of AOL's Internet services, you are calling upon resources that extend beyond the boundaries of the service's computer network. If there's an undue delay in getting the information back to AOL, you'll get a message of this sort (which AOL's host computers will send rather than leaving you hanging for many minutes of billable time). If there's a problem with one of the computers somewhere along the Information Superhighway, that might also prevent you from retrieving the information. But more often than not, if you just make a second attempt—or do your search later—you'll be successful.

Using Jughead to Refine Your Search

Before I get to that listing of some popular databases, I want to cover just one more Internet search tool available on America Online. It's buried somewhat in AOL's Gopher area, however, so getting there takes several steps. The search capability I'm going to describe is called Jughead, which stands for Jonzy's Universal Gopher Hierarchy Excavation And Display.

While AOL's Veronica search tool will scour through all Gopher servers in search of the items you want, Jughead is a tool that allows you to specify a Gopher server by its name, and restrict your search to that one site.

N O T E A Jughead search is not a good idea for an Internet newbie, because you need to know the exact name of the site you want to access to use it most effectively. For most AOL Internet surfers, you'll probably get the best results using the regular Gopher search tool described earlier in this chapter, in the section entitled, "Using AOL's Gopher Database Searching." ■

Here's how to use Jughead to locate a Gopher server:

1. Access the main Gopher area on AOL via the keyword **Gopher** (refer to fig. 31.1).
2. Click the Search icon.
3. Use Jughead as your search word.
4. Scroll through the large list of search results and click any of the items shown.
5. Depending on which item you select, you'll be presented with additional choices, some of which will point to a specific Gopher server.
6. Choose one of the Gopher servers and enter the subjects of your search.

T I P After you've located Gopher databases that provide the information you want, you can easily add them to your list of Favorite Places by clicking the little icon at the right side of the title bar. You'll then be able to quickly revisit those sites whenever you wish.

Expert Access

If you already know the name of a specific Gopher server you'd like to use, click the Quick Go icon at the top left of the main Gopher window, and enter the name of that site (see fig. 31.6). You can also access a Gopher site directly from AOL's WWW window. Just enter the word **gopher://[site name].edu** in the URL field (if you enter the WWW window from AOL's Gopher forum, the word "gopher://" is already typed there). The last part of the address, edu, assumes the site is sponsored by an educational institution (they usually are).

You can use a different Gopher browser if you prefer. Simply click the Gopher Software icon and download the program shown (see fig. 31.7), or click the More button for additional choices.

FIG. 31.6
Enter the location of the Gopher site you want to access at the cursor in the Quick Go window.

FIG. 31.7
AOL makes it easy for you to use a different Gopher browser program, if you prefer.

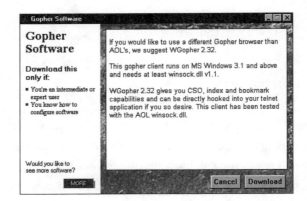

For most users, AOL's own Gopher feature should be enough to get the job done, but that shouldn't deter you from trying out another program, if you want to experiment, or you are happy with the software you've used previously.

You'll also want to check out the Gopher Message Board for helpful advice and the experiences of other AOL members in getting information from particular Gopher sites. As you become more and more experienced in locating specific types of information, you may wish to share your experiences, too.

NOTE Because pointing and clicking is more accurate than entering a long Gopher site's name correctly (and host computers are notoriously picky about precise syntax), just enter the main site name as the URL at the top of the browser window, and navigate through the site's directory to the one you want by clicking the directory names in the body of the browser document. ■

What Do All Those Icons Mean?

Each menu entry in a gopher listing takes you to a different type of resource. AOL's browser identifies the type of resource with an icon, so you know exactly what type of information you're selecting. The following table describes the icons:

Icon	Name	Description
	Text File	When you click this icon, you access a text file that you can read on your computer screen, save, or print.
	File Directory	A list of resources containing information about a particular topic.
	Image file	AOL's software can decode the common image file formats, such as GIF and JPEG.
	Search	This is a file search tool, similar to the ones you find on AOL. Just click this icon and enter the search information in the dialog box that will appear.
	Sound File	Your PC will need appropriate sound drivers to access this file. Most Macs already have the hardware with which to play such files (your AOL software should be able to decode most sound resources).

Part VIII

Ch

31

AOL's Gopher Treasures

As mentioned in earlier chapters, the lists of favorite places that are provided should be considered arbitrary. The Internet's resources are so huge that there's no way to do more than scratch the surface of the databases available to you. Rather than make a faltering attempt to cover everything, this text concentrates on subject matter similar to that dealt with in some of America Online's most popular forums. These examples merely represent the sort of information you find online.

 TIP The fastest way to return to sites you use often is just to add them to your Favorite Sites listing by clicking on the little heart-shaped icon at the upper right of the document window.

The databases shown here are available in AOL's Gopher & WAIS area under Gopher Treasures. These selections are apt to change over time, so don't be surprised if the offerings are different when you look for a specific treasure.

From C-SPAN

AOL's main listing is provided by C-SPAN, and the selection is vast (see fig. 31.8). As you can see from the directory, you can find resources on such diverse subjects as counter-culture and the stock market.

FIG. 31.8
C-SPAN's Gopher site has a huge storehouse of information, from the politically correct to the apolitical.

In the next few pages, I'll cover just a few additional selections in C-SPAN's listing. You'll want to explore the rest during your regular AOL visits.

Monty Python's Flying Circus

If you have access to cable's Comedy Central channel or a local public broadcasting outlet, you'll have the pleasure of revisiting the antics of this British comedy troupe from time to time. Using AOL's Gopher feature, you're now able to access a selection of scripts from your favorite shows (see fig. 31.9).

FIG. 31.9
Monty Python's Flying Circus was a forerunner of the sort of comedy found in such programs as *Saturday Night Live* and a number of popular movies.

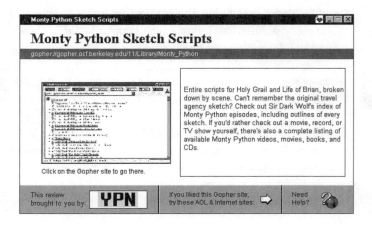

After you find the title of a show that interests you, just click the listing to bring up the script (see fig. 31.10).

FIG. 31.10
The script of a popular Monty Python TV program from the early 1970s.

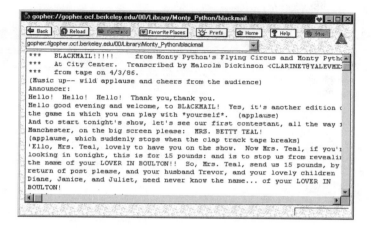

Even if you've never had the chance to watch this program, a quick read of a typical script will give you an idea of the sort of mayhem these world-class comic actors engaged in during these shows. You may just want to rush out to your local video rental store just to see if they have any *Monty Python* tapes in stock.

Glasgow Golf

Just to show you another sample of the wide range of information AOL's Gopher feature makes available, I clicked the item labeled Glasgow Golf. In seconds, I saw a listing of popular golf events (see fig. 31.11).

FIG. 31.11
The Glasgow Golf Gopher site has statistics of popular golfing events.

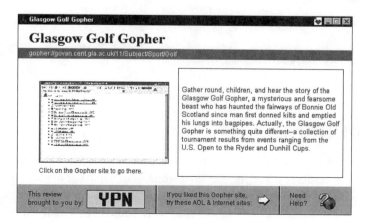

If you're into golfing, or just a trivia lover, you'll want to click on a specific listing to get the statistics about that event. As a sample of what's available, let's choose U.S. Open 1995 (see fig. 31.12).

FIG. 31.12
Just how good is your memory of this event? Compare your recollection to the statistics shown here.

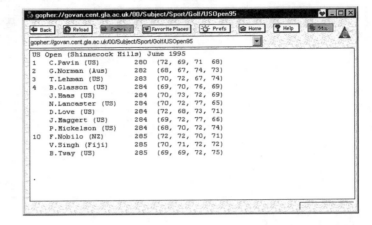

Additional Gopher Resources

When your interests expand beyond the basic listing, you'll want to click the More button, which brings up additional directories of Gopher sites (see fig. 31.13). To find out more about these resources, just double-click the title.

FIG. 31.13
Additional Gopher resources you can tap on AOL with just a few clicks of the mouse.

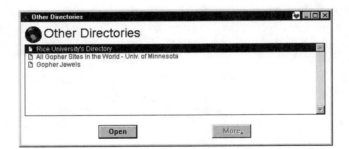

From Here...

Using Gopher & WAIS database resources is similar to seeking out information at your public library, but you can do it while seated in front of your personal computer, all while logged on to America Online. It should come as no surprise that, while writing this book, I often stopped along the way to explore some of this material still further—that is, until my publisher would call and remind me about those deadlines.

- For introductory material on tapping America Online's huge Internet resources, read Chapter 29, "Using AOL's Internet Connection."

- Because the subject of Newsgroups was introduced here, you'll want to move on to Chapter 32, "Joining and Participating in Internet Newsgroups."

- Now that you know the techniques for performing Archie searches of remote FTP sites, you'll want to know how to transfer FTP files to your personal computer, which is explained in Chapter 34, "Using File Transfer Protocol."

- And to keep up-to-date on America Online's fast-growing Internet connection, type the keyword **Internet** and explore the Internet Center.

Part
VIII

Ch
31

Joining and Participating in Internet Newsgroups

What Internet newsgroups are

Learn how to get involved in the wildest message boards around.

What netiquette really means

Discover important hints about proper Internet conduct.

How to find Internet newsgroups

Explore how to find discussions about the topics that interest you.

How to participate in Internet newsgroups

Find step-by-step information on how to write and send messages to a newsgroup.

America Online's own message boards are valuable resources for sharing information and debating topics that interest you. This chapter is devoted to other types of discussion boards. These discussion boards are similar to those you find in message boards through-out AOL, yet quite different, because they are not re-stricted by the boundaries and requirements of a single online service—they're a part of the global Internet network.

Some of the most interesting parts of the wide world of the Internet are newsgroups, also known as *UseNet Newsgroups*. Newsgroups are popular and active ex-changes and are the Internet counterparts of message boards on America Online. Just as with mailing lists, there are newsgroups covering almost any topic you can think of, and then some. ■

Internet Newsgroups—the Ground Rules

Before you begin to examine Internet newsgroups for yourself, it is a good idea to get acquainted with the ground rules. In some respects, newsgroups are quite different from America Online's own message boards. First, they are usually not moderated, which means there is no staff person to examine the structure of the message boards and remove messages that contain inflammatory, irrelevant, or vulgar statements. As a result, participants in newsgroups take a free-wheeling approach to participating in these areas, and sometimes they are a little slow to welcome new visitors, or "newbies," as beginning Internet surfers are called. This doesn't mean, however, that you should abandon considerations of good taste when posting in such areas. Some of the rules of the road, referred to as netiquette, will be explained later in this chapter.

Of course, a smaller number of newsgroups do have moderators. These moderators are somewhat like the forum staff on America Online, but they exercise a greater measure of control over what appears in their message boards. Every message you post is reviewed by the moderators for content, and they will censor messages that they don't consider relevant to the topic at hand. You'll find the decisions of the moderators to be rather arbitrary sometimes; they exert a greater measure of control than you'd find even on one of America Online's own message boards.

America Online's Internet Center provides access to thousands of newsgroups. Using AOL's Newsgroups area, shown in figure 32.1, you will be able to select the newsgroups that interest you and place that list of newsgroups in a customized list. America Online keeps a database of popular newsgroups, but as it is explained later in this chapter, you can seek out others that interest you too. You'll even find a short list of some very popular newsgroups that you might want to add to your list to get started.

FIG. 32.1
One of the most exciting Internet features offered by AOL—newsgroups.

After you've joined, or subscribed to, a list of your favorite newsgroups, you need only click the Read My Newsgroups icon to keep current on your favorite topics. Using this message board, you can discuss your special interests with people from all over the world.

Before you begin to add newsgroups to your lists, take a few moments to review the text files displayed in the main forum directory window (refer to fig. 32.1). You can read these text files while you're online, or you can save and print them for later reference. These files contain some helpful advice on traversing the sometimes wacky world of UseNet Newsgroups.

The next few pages will cover the ground rules of participating in a newsgroup and take you through the steps of configuring AOL's newsreader (the AOL software component you use to view and respond to newsgroup messages), step-by-step. You'll find that the features of the Macintosh and Windows versions of AOL's newsreader are somewhat different from those of other areas of AOL service.

Understanding Netiquette

No doubt when you first visit AOL's Newsgroups area, you'll want to jump right in and get involved in a discussion board yourself. Before you do so, however, you should learn something about newsgroups in general and about how to introduce yourself to a discussion group. Over the years, the Internet, although largely unregulated and unsupervised, has developed some forms and conventions you should know about first.

Here are a few tips based on hard-won experience on the Net:

- You will be tempted to dive right in and participate in a discussion that interests you. My advice: Don't. Spend a little time reading messages or following discussions (which experienced net visitors sometimes call *lurking*). Often you'll find a set of FAQs (Frequently Asked Questions), text files that provide a list of ground rules for a specific discussion group, and responses to typical user questions. After you've developed a feel for the flavor of a particular group, it's time to consider posting a message of your own.

- There are thousands of newsgroups. The number of messages you are likely to encounter will be in the hundreds of thousands. You can quickly become overwhelmed by the sheer volume of information if you don't pick and choose carefully. To begin with, you should restrict yourself to only a small number of discussion groups, take time to digest the messages, and add more newsgroups only when you think you can devote the time necessary to keep up-to-date on all the information you'll receive.

- When you respond to a message, consider that you are posting a response to not just a single person, but an audience that could number in the millions. If you decide you want to restrict your audience to a single person, send that person e-mail instead. The option to reply to just the author rather than the group is available in America Online's Newsgroup reader.

- Before writing your message, carefully choose the appropriate forum. It wouldn't necessarily be a good idea to promote the use of a Macintosh in a discussion group oriented toward users of Microsoft Windows, for example, unless you want to risk generating a lot of ill will. (There are advocacy newsgroups where you can debate the merits of one computer platform over another, of course.)

- Show respect and be polite when you post a message. If you disagree with someone's statement, try to stick to the issues and refrain from personal attack. Such attacks are regarded as *flaming*, and although they might be entertaining on some television talk shows, they are not considered good taste on the Internet.

- When responding to someone else's message, quote the relevant portions of that message at the beginning of your response, or before each part of your message that refers to the other message. The usual convention is to place an angle bracket (>), to signify a quotation mark, at the beginning of each line, as shown here:

```
> I've access to a Mac Centris 610.
> When I try to run Norton Speed Disk,
> I get "System files not supported in System 7"
> Where can I get an update of Norton, or
> is this software now obsolete/upgraded/replaced??????
```

N O T E The Windows version of America Online software can automate the quoting process somewhat, as you'll find out later in this chapter, in the section titled "Quoting Messages on Your PC." If you're quoting material using the Mac version, you'll want to look for a copy of a program such as Signature Quote in the Macintosh computing and software libraries that will help you easily quote selected material and have it converted to the correct format. ▪

- It is customary to use your Internet address (described in Chapter 29, "Using AOL's Internet Connection") as your personal signature, but your name and affiliations can be placed there as well, as shown in figure 32.2. Some users also include their address and phone number, but before you do this, consider how you feel about giving this information out to millions of strangers. Other users add a statement or motto that reflects some aspect of their personality. Before preparing your own signature, you might want to see how others do it.

- Keep your messages short and to the point. You are reaching an audience of millions of people, and you don't want to waste anyone's time because many users pay high prices for Internet access. Also, try not to cross-post, or send your message to more than one newsgroup at a time (unless you think it's really necessary).

N O T E When you create an online signature for yourself, try to keep it short and to the point (such as your name and, if needed, company affiliation or a short motto). Long signatures with elaborate artwork simply waste bandwidth and may upset users who pay large amounts for Internet access. ▪

FIG. 32.2
A typical UseNet Newsgroup signature is shown in the text block at the center of the screen. The information below the signature is the long and twisted path that was taken by that message before it reached its destination.

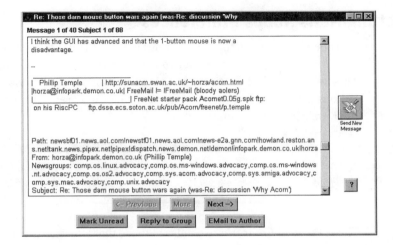

- Choose a subject title that specifically describes the topic of your message. It is better to use "Type 11 Crash in System 7.5.3" than "System Crash" if you are seeking advice on solving a problem in a Macintosh Newsgroup.

- Express emotions and humor with care. When you speak with someone in person, very often body language and the inflection of your voice would reveal whether you are serious, or whether you are angry or happy about something. But in your messages, your words alone must be the mirror of your feelings. Experienced online users express emotions with smileys :). See Chapter 10, "Chatting Online," for a list of common online shorthand characters (known as smileys and emoticons).

- Before you respond to a message, take the time to see whether someone else has already answered it. Time on the busy Internet is at a premium, and reading the same sort of message over and over wastes everyone's time, including your own.

Using AOL's Newsgroup Reader

Keyword: **Newsgroups**

If you've used a newsgroup reader on another online service, you're apt to find some differences in the newsreader offered by AOL, because this is a graphical service, and some of those other Internet services still use text-based software.

In the next few pages, I'll explain how to set up AOL's newsreader for best performance; then you'll begin to seek out and participate in some popular newsgroup discussions.

Setting Newsgroups Preferences

The opening Newsgroup window (refer to fig. 32.1) has two sets of preferences. There is yet a third set of preferences, but you can't access that until you open a list of messages. This third set will be described later in this chapter. For now, look at the two rectangular buttons at the bottom of the Newsgroups window, Parental Controls and Set Preferences. First, we'll look at Parental Controls (see fig. 32.3).

FIG. 32.3

Whoops! Can't set Parental Controls from this account!

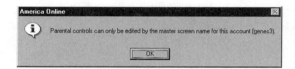

These Parental Controls are similar to those that affect access to AOL's regular service. They are designed to limit access of those who use your account to certain parts of the service. Because the Internet might contain content that is not suitable for young people, you'll want to establish controls on the account your child is using. These controls have to be set while you are logged on under your master account name. For more information on establishing Parental Controls, both on AOL's regular service and in the Newsgroups area, read Chapter 16, "Parental Issues and Internet Access."

The Set Preferences button produces a collection of preferences you can set separately for each screen name on your AOL account (see fig. 32.4). Using these preferences, you can create a signature that automatically appears at the bottom of your newsgroup messages and dictates how those messages appear.

FIG. 32.4

Set your global newsgroup preferences in this dialog box.

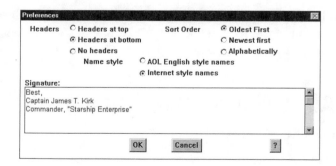

There are three types of preferences; all are described in the sections that follow.

Headers   As you saw in figure 32.2, Internet transactions go through a circuitous route, from computer to computer, on their way to America Online. You can choose whether you want to see any of this header information that displays the long, complex path your message takes (you might want to leave it off, to keep message windows free of unwanted clutter). Here are the header options to choose from:

- *Headers at top.* The path your message travels is included at the top of your message window.

- *Headers at bottom.* The path your message travels is included at the bottom of your message window.

- *No headers.* Ah, that's more like it (this is the default setting). The headers are stripped from the messages you see. The header is limited to the date and time the message was sent, the message ID information, and the Internet address of the message's author.

Sort Order   How would you like your messages displayed? By default, you see the oldest first, and then you move through them, in chronological order, with messages grouped by thread (topic). Here are your choices:

- *Oldest first.* This is the default setting, which enables you to read the messages in their normal sequence.

- *Newest first.* To some, this choice might seem like reading the end of a book before the beginning, but if you have a huge number of messages to read through, you might find it convenient to look at the latest messages first. This option makes following a message thread difficult, however, because the response comes before the question.

- *Alphabetically.* This setting groups messages by topic, in alphabetical order.

Name Style   The names of a newsgroup follow a specific naming convention, which might seem confusing to some who are visiting the Internet for the first time. You have two options as to how the names in your newsgroups list are shown (see fig. 32.5).

FIG. 32.5
A list of newsgroups shown with their standard Internet names.

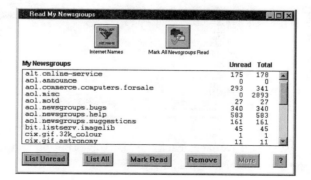

Part
VIII

Ch
32

There are two types of preferences:

- *AOL English style names.* For this setting, which is the default configuration, a newsgroup might be identified as Help with Newsgroups.

- *Internet style names.* When you select this option, Help with Newsgroups is shown as aol.newsgroups.help.

As you can see, the Internet name, despite its odd syntax, is really not difficult to comprehend even for the newbie, but whether to choose this option is up to you. There's nothing wrong with trying both methods. You can change your preferences at any time by opening the Set Preferences window, making your alterations, and then opening your list of newsgroups again. The changes take effect immediately.

 TIP If you are viewing your newsgroups with English style names, you can see the actual Internet name by clicking the Internet Names icon at the top of the Newsgroup message window. This action brings up a window showing the Internet versions.

How to Add Newsgroups

As I explained earlier in this chapter, there are thousands upon thousands of newsgroups, catering to interests of all sorts. Many newsgroups overlap in terms of content, too, so you will probably want to select more than a single newsgroup that caters to topics in which you're interested.

America Online maintains a listing of the most popular newsgroups in its own database. Just click the Add Newsgroups icon. You'll see a directory listing, shown in figure 32.6, that displays many subjects of interest.

FIG. 32.6
The first step in locating a newsgroup to join is to get a list that caters to your favorite subjects.

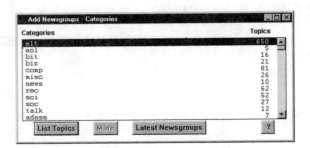

After you've picked a subject, click the List Topics button to bring up a list of newsgroups that fit the description (see fig. 32.7).

FIG. 32.7
Here's a list of newsgroup categories catering to one area of interest.

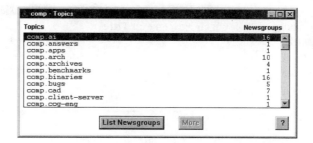

Now you've gotten to the heart of the matter. To see a specific newsgroup, you need only click one of the categories shown to bring up the final listing. To Add a newsgroup, simply click the newsgroup's name once to select it, then click the Add button to include it among your listing.

Of course, you don't have to join that newsgroup yet. If you'd rather sample the flavor of a particular discussion group, just click its name and you'll see a listing of the available messages, shown in figure 32.8. You can read those messages, but because you are just sampling the newsgroup for now, you cannot actually post a response to a message or create a topic of your own. To do that, you must actually add that newsgroup to your list.

Part
VIII

Ch
32

FIG. 32.8
Before you actually join a newsgroup, you might want to look over some of the messages.

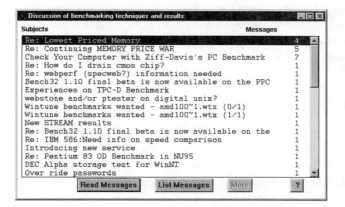

When you've actually added a newsgroup, it appears under the Read My Newsgroups listing, which will be discussed later in this chapter.

How to Search All Newsgroups

If you don't find a newsgroup that interests you, you'll want to perform a more thorough search of the available newsgroups. Click the Search All Newsgroups icon in the Newsgroups area to bring up a search window, as shown in figure 32.9. Enter the subject for which you want to locate a newsgroup in the list field.

FIG. 32.9

You can search from among thousands of newsgroups for one that piques your curiosity.

If there is a newsgroup that meets your search criteria (and sometimes you have to refine the phrases a bit or even try related ones), the newsgroup title appears in a window. From there, you can read a capsule description by double-clicking the newsgroup title. You'll find, however, that many newsgroups do not actually have any description other than the titles themselves, which they consider sufficient to describe what their mission is all about.

Unlike the Add Newsgroups feature, the searching mechanism doesn't give you the ability to sample a newsgroup before adding it to your list. This isn't a major shortcoming, though, because you can remove a newsgroup later, if you choose, with the mere click of a button.

N O T E If you want to search for more than a single item, you should insert **and** between words and phrases to separate subjects. You may expand your search with the word **or** when you want to look for one option or the other, and you can exclude an item with the word **not** to designate a subject or word you don't want to use in the search result listing. ▪

Using Expert Add

As with e-mail addresses, the titles of newsgroups are identified by a special syntax, with words generally separated by a period. An example is comp.sys.mac.advocacy, which as the title suggests, is a discussion group with active debates on the subject of the Apple Macintosh versus other computing platforms. If you know the exact title of a newsgroup, you can bypass the search mechanism or America Online's own listing and join by using the Expert Add feature, shown in figure 32.10.

FIG. 32.10

If you know the name of the newsgroup you want to join, enter it here.

Expert Add	▬ □ ×
If you know the Internet style name of a newsgroup (e.g., news.answers) that you would like to access, type the newsgroup name below.	
Internet Name: alt.cult-movies	
Add Latest Newsgroups ?	

N O T E America Online's Expert Add feature is quite literal-minded. For it to work, you need to enter a newsgroup name using the exact spelling and punctuation. Otherwise, the newsgroup won't be located, or, worse, you'll add the wrong newsgroup. ▨

After you've subscribed to the newsgroups that interest you, it's time to read the messages.

Joining and Participating in a Newsgroup

Click the Read My Newsgroups icon at the main screen of the Newsgroups area, and you'll see a listing of all the newsgroups you've subscribed to, as shown in figure 32.11. When you enter this area for the first time, you'll see a list of popular newsgroups that America Online has automatically included for you, but you can remove them at any time, by highlighting the name of the newsgroup and clicking the Remove button. The Mark Read button enables you to flag the messages in a selected group as read without actually opening the messages themselves (so use this feature with caution if you want to read those messages later).

FIG. 32.11
Here are the newsgroups you've joined.

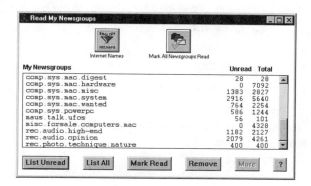

Before you begin to read the messages in your selected newsgroups, you'll want to review the section on netiquette earlier in this chapter. After you've done that, take some time to read the messages themselves. The first time you read the messages, you might find there are thousands in a single newsgroup. But, because the messages are grouped by topic (also known as message threading), as shown in figure 32.12, you'll be able to easily pick the messages you want to read.

Part
VIII

Ch
32

FIG. 32.12
Newsgroup messages are threaded—grouped according to topic.

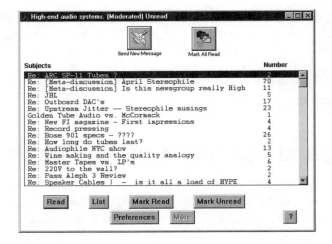

How to Follow a Message Thread

All newsgroup messages are normally sorted by date and then by topic. You can choose to display them in a different order, using the Set Preferences feature described previously. But in this description, the messages will be referred to in their regular order.

The process of organizing the messages into topics is known as *threading*. It enables you to read messages and responses about a single topic, without having to read through messages on other subjects.

After you've read all the messages in a single thread, the next message you bring up, by clicking the Next button, takes you to a new thread. If you want to bypass that subject, just close the message window; you can then look over the directory of unread messages for another topic you want to follow.

> **NOTE** Because messages in a single thread are often posted at widely varying times, you might actually find two or more listings for messages concerning a single topic. ■

Setting Message Preferences

There's another set of newsgroup preferences, that cover the time frame of messages shown when you open a message window. It's very similar to the Find Since feature that you use on a regular AOL message board. By clicking the Preferences button in a Newsgroup message window, you'll have options that will serve you now and in the future (see fig. 32.13).

FIG. 32.13
Choose the time frame under which messages will be displayed.

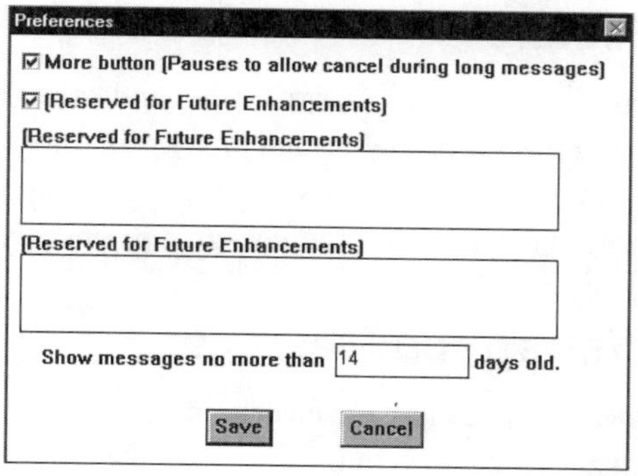

Preferences

☑ More button (Pauses to allow cancel during long messages)
☑ (Reserved for Future Enhancements)
(Reserved for Future Enhancements)

(Reserved for Future Enhancements)

Show messages no more than [14] days old.

[Save] [Cancel]

As you can see, at the time this book was written, some of the message preferences hadn't been activated. The sole option that was available was the one at the bottom, where you can select the time frame in which messages are displayed. This option can save you the drudgery of having to pore over thousands of accumulated messages during your first visit to a newsgroup, or when visiting a newsgroup after a few days' absence from AOL.

The option at the top, the More button, can be ignored, because the choice is now replaced by one that enables you to download a long message to your computer. In the future, you'll be able to ignore messages with certain words or phrases in them, or those sent by certain users you'd rather not read messages from.

N O T E The message board options you choose apply only to the individual newsgroup in which you select them. Preferences must be selected separately for every newsgroup to which you subscribe. ■

TROUBLESHOOTING

Help! I selected the option to show messages for no more than a day or so, yet I'm still seeing thousands of messages displayed after I click the Save button and close the Preferences window. Why? You need to reload the message list on your computer. Here's how:

1. Close the window containing the message list that displays when you select Read.

2. Open the Read My Newsgroups window (if it's not already opened), and then double-click the Newsgroup you just closed.

You'll then see only the unread messages posted within the time frame you set on your message preferences.

Using the List All Feature

When you first open your personal newsgroup list and select a topic, double-clicking the topic name or pressing the Enter key brings up a list of unread messages. If you want to review messages you've read previously, click the List All button instead, which brings up a display of all messages available in that newsgroup, whether you've read them or not.

How to Reply to a Newsgroup Message

After you've read the messages in your favorite newsgroup, no doubt you'll be tempted to respond to a particular message. When you bring up a message window, you can use the Reply button to add your message to the existing thread so that others will see your response, also. There are two ways to respond to a message. First is simply to click the Reply button, which brings up the screen shown in figure 32.14. If you want the author of the original message to receive a reply by e-mail, check the box at the lower left corner of the message window.

FIG. 32.14
Responding to someone who has written a news-group message is easy with AOL's newsreader.

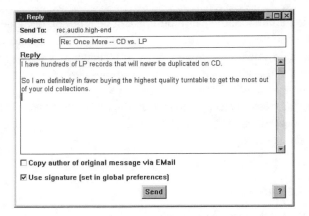

The second option shown in a message window is Reply to Author, which enables you to send your response as e-mail instead. This window (which looks similar to the one shown in 32.14) gives you the choice of having the same message posted in the newsgroup, by clicking the check box.

Before actually writing your response, it's customary to first quote the relevant passages of the original message you are writing about. This technique is described earlier in this chapter, in the section "Understanding Netiquette." It is common for newsgroup subscribers to quote several passages of a previous message and intersperse their own comments between them.

> **CAUTION**
>
> When I say, "the relevant passages of the original message," I mean just that. If you quote the entire message, and intend only to respond to a small part of it, you waste everyone's time with material that has no bearing on the message you're trying to convey. If you just want to say you agree with someone's long message, just quote a short paragraph from that message that seems to summarize it reasonably well, and leave it at that, along with your statement of agreement. Remember, everyone's time is precious, especially when they pay an hourly charge for their Internet access, and you will make a better impression if you keep your messages as short as possible.

The Use Signature (set in global preferences) check box automatically adds the signature you set in the Newsgroup preferences box to your message (you don't have to add it). If you prefer not to use this signature, or to use a different signature, click the check box to disable this option.

TROUBLESHOOTING

Help! I'm getting offensive messages from the Internet. What do I do? America Online's Terms of Service, of course, do not apply to members of other services (although they do govern your conduct on the Internet, so be careful). But if you get objectionable or threatening material, you often do have a way to protect yourself. The easiest way to deal with this situation is to check the sender's return address, especially at the domain of the service that person is using (such as @<service>.com).

If you received the material as e-mail, you can use AOL's forward feature to send the offensive message in e-mail form directly to the folks who administer that service—in this case, it would be postmaster@<service>.com. If the material was contained in a message posted in an Internet newsgroup, select the entire message, choose Copy from the Edit menu, and insert the message into the body of an e-mail form, along with your own request that the problem be dealt with.

Most services have rules and regulations for their users, and they do not consider such conduct any more acceptable than you do. They will act against that member in accordance with the rules covering their service.

It's also true that some Internet-based services may only be concerned with whether the messages get through, not their content. But you should complain anyway if the message you received is especially offensive.

About Cross-Posting

Although cross-posting the same message to different newsgroups isn't always a good idea, some of the messages to which you respond are already posted in more than one place. If you respond to any of these messages, you'll see the message shown in figure

32.15. There is nothing you can do to change the route of the response, so just click the OK button.

FIG. 32.15
The message you're answering will appear in more than one newsgroup.

This message will be posted to:
alt.destroy.microsoft,comp.os.ms-windows.advocac

OK

How to Post a Newsgroup Message

If you are not responding to a message in a particular thread and you want to create a new topic, click the Send New Message icon, at the top of a message window. This action brings up a blank message window, into which you can insert the topic and then the body of your message.

After you've finished reading the messages in your selected newsgroup and responding to the ones that interest you, click the Mark All Read icon, at the top of the directory of available messages. That way, you won't be presented with the same list of messages the next time you visit your newsgroup.

TROUBLESHOOTING

Help! The message I posted still hasn't shown up in the newsgroup I sent it to. What's wrong? The Internet e-mail and messages you send must pass through a number of computer networks before they make their way to your newsgroup, or to the recipient of your message. Your message can sometimes get to the other side of the world in a matter of minutes, yet other times it takes a day or two to arrive. This is to be expected, and you should be patient and give the message some time. In a very few cases, a message does get lost in cyberspace, but because the systems are quite reliable, that doesn't happen very often.

CAUTION

When you are in the Read My Newsgroups window, before you actually select an individual newsgroup to browse through, using the Mark All Newsgroups Read icon marks all messages in all the discussion groups on your list as having been read. So be careful when you choose this option; otherwise, none of the messages in those newsgroups will be available for reading unless you select the List All option. The latter option forces you to plow through thousands of messages (even ones you've read before).

If the Newsgroup Has No Unread Messages

If you've read all the messages in a newsgroup and closed the message window, and then you decide you want to add a message of your own, here's what to do:

1. Double-click the directory listing for that newsgroup, which brings up a sequence of two messages, shown in figure 32.16 and figure 32.17. You must click the OK button of the first message to see the second.

2. If you want to add a new message of your own, click the OK button, which brings up a standard blank Newsgroup message window.

3. If you decide not to prepare that message, click the Cancel button.

FIG. 32.16
You're notified that no unread messages are available.

FIG. 32.17
Decide whether you want to post a new message.

Quoting Messages on Your Macintosh

As described earlier, it's proper netiquette to quote the relevant portions of a message you're replying to in a newsgroup, or via Internet e-mail, for that matter. Here's how:

1. Select the text you want to quote, and then choose Copy from the File menu.

2. Open a blank message window, and then choose Paste from the File menu.

3. Manually break each line in the message window and insert an angle bracket (>) plus a space at the beginning of each line.

If you find this process a little cumbersome, you'll definitely want to search the computing and software libraries on America Online for a program such as Signature Quote, which automates the quoting process for you.

Quoting Messages on Your PC

It's much easier to follow your response to a message if you quote the relevant portions of the message you are replying to. Here's how to do it easily using the Windows version of AOL's software:

1. Select the text you want to quote, and then choose Copy from the File menu.

2. Click the Reply button in your Newsgroup message window.

3. The material you've selected is automatically inserted into the message window, as shown in figure 32.18, correctly formatted and ready for you to add your response.

FIG. 32.18
See quoted material formatted and inserted into a Newsgroup message window.

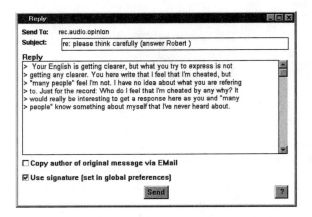

N O T E By the time you read this book, additional quoting features may have been added to AOL's Newsgroups reader, including the automatic quoting feature on the Mac version. ■

Offline Message Reading

You can use the same time-saving techniques you learned in Chapter 8, "Using America Online E-Mail," to stay abreast of your favorite newsgroups. All you have to do is schedule your FlashSessions to include newsgroups, and then use AOL's Offline Reading feature to include the latest messages from your favorite newsgroups as part of that session.

Here's how the process works:

1. Click the Read Offline icon in the opening Newsgroups window, which brings up the screen shown in figure 32.19.

   The listing at the left contains all the newsgroups to which you've subscribed.

FIG. 32.19
Add the newsgroups you
select for offline reading
from the list on the left.

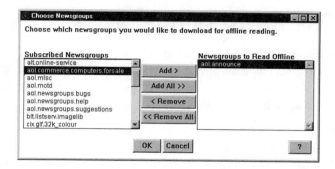

2. Click once on a newsgroup you want to add to highlight that selection.

3. Click the Add button to include it among the newsgroup messages to be down-loaded during your FlashSession.

4. To add all the newsgroups at once, click the Add All button.

> **CAUTION**
>
> Use the Add All option with caution, otherwise you may be inundated with unread messages next time you run your AOL FlashSession.

5. To remove a newsgroup from the roster slated for offline reading, simply click the newsgroup once to select it, then click the Remove button.

6. To remove all newsgroups from the offline reading list, simply click the Removal All button.

The unread messages in your selected newsgroups will be downloaded to your Personal Filing Cabinet during your FlashSessions. To find those messages, choose Mail, Personal Filing Cabinet from the AOL program menu bar. The newsgroup messages you down-loaded during your session will appear in the Newsgroups folder.

The neat thing about this feature is that you can not only read your messages while offline, but respond to them as well. Your new messages will be posted in the appropriate newsgroup during your next FlashSession.

To learn more about scheduling your FlashSessions and selecting the options to transfer mail, files, and newsgroup messages, check out Chapter 8, "Using America Online E-Mail."

Decoding Newsgroup Files

In Chapter 30, "Secrets of Internet E-Mail and Mailing Lists," I explained how AOL's host computer can automatically decode files sent via the Internet. The process is transparent to you, so you don't have to worry about configuring your e-mail in any special way to attach a file to it for Internet delivery.

When it comes to reading encoded newsgroup messages, you can let AOL's software do the work for you, using AOL's File Grabber feature. When you open an encoded message, or one too long for AOL's newsreader to display in one piece, you'll get the message shown in figure 32.20.

This article contains data that has been encoded to allow it to be sent through USENET. America Online can usually automatically decode these files for you.
You can download the original file, download the encoded data, or cancel
If you download this article, you'll need special software to convert it to a usable form. You may also need to download other articles.
Please read the newsgroup aol.newsgroups.help.binaries for more information.
Download File
Download Article
Cancel

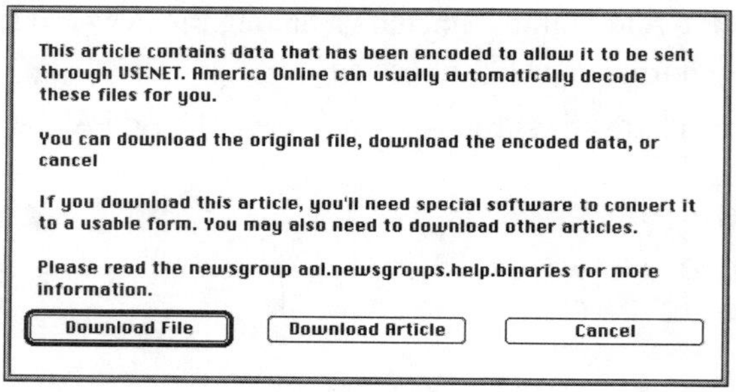

FIG. 32.20
The message is too long, or it's encoded. What action do you want to take?

If you OK the message, AOL's File Grabber will work behind the scenes to locate all portions of the file and then retranslate the file to its original form. Then you'll get a dialog box (see fig. 32.21) asking where you'd like the file to be downloaded to.

Online Downloads
Starship One
AOL Folder
AOL Folder.1
AOL Folder.2
AOL Folder.3
AOL Logo 1
AOL Logs
Eject
Desktop
New
Cancel
Save
Save as:
anlintro.mov

FIG. 32.21
Choose a directory or folder that you want the file transferred to.

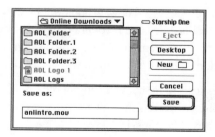

The remainder of the process brings up a display that's identical to the one you receive when you transfer files directly from America Online. You have the same option to Finish Later, if you'd rather not complete the download during your present session.

A Favorite Newsgroup Listing

Thousands of Internet newsgroups are active at any one time. New ones are always being introduced, and others are being discontinued. When you first visit AOL's Newsgroups area, you'll find a list of several newsgroups automatically added to your list. Over time, you can choose to change or add to this listing. The Add Newsgroups icon shown on the main Newsgroups area window lists many of the popular newsgroups you'll want to add.

The following listing includes many of my own favorites, along with other noteworthy newsgroups, just to give you a brief cross-section of the sort of topics discussed. This selection has been limited to one or two items per category, but you'll find many more as you begin to seek out other resources.

Adding Newsgroups to Your List

To subscribe to these newsgroups, follow these steps:

1. Go to the main Newsgroups area, keyword **Newsgroups**.
2. Click the Expert Add button.
3. Enter the exact name of the newsgroup in the Internet Name list field.
4. Click the Go button.
5. The newsgroup is added to your list, and you will see it displayed when you click the Read My Newsgroups icon.

N O T E   If you don't enter the newsgroup name exactly as listed, with proper capitalization, you'll receive a message that the group cannot be added. If this happens, recheck the newsgroup name and enter it again. ■

The Short List

alt.alien.visitors

If you've visited the Antimatter area of AOL's *OMNI* magazine forum, you'll find the subject matter familiar here. It ranges from stories of alien abductions to Bigfoot, the Abominable Snowman, and UFOs.

alt.cd-rom

Just about every new personal computer these days includes a CD-ROM, or offers one as a low-cost option. This newsgroup is designed to answer your questions about using CD-ROMs, coping with common problems, or learning about new products.

Part
VIII

Ch
32

alt.coffee

This discussion group covers the various types of good coffee, coffee cafes, trends in the coffee industry, and so on. If your taste in coffee goes beyond the instant level, you'll have a lot of interest in this newsgroup.

alt.computer.consultants

If you're a Mac or PC computer consultant, you'll want to visit this area to share viewpoints and to offer your services to others.

alt.cyberspace

When you see the designation alt, you know you're in for a special experience, because many of the comments in such a newsgroup can be offbeat and inflammatory (and that can be an understatement). This particular newsgroup covers the entire online world, from America Online to the Internet.

alt.missing.kids

The other newsgroups discussed in this chapter are for discussion and information. This one serves a very important public service; its efforts are devoted to helping locate missing children.

alt.online.service

This newsgroup is devoted to all the major online services: America Online, CompuServe, Prodigy, and others. Again, the content can be quite controversial and sometimes offensive, so keep that in mind before you add it to your list.

alt.rush.limbaugh

This is a very active newsgroup, devoted to the popular and controversial conservative talk show host and the subjects he discusses on his radio and TV shows. Prepare to spend lots of time here, if you choose to subscribe to this newsgroup; there are hundreds of new messages posted each day.

comp.benchmarks

How fast is your personal computer? Just as a lot of us want to know how high a speed our automobiles can reach (even if we'll never dare to go that fast), it's fun to know the speeds our computers are capable of. You'll find many benchmarks posted here, and just watch out for those Pentium versus Power Macintosh comparisons!

comp.fonts

Most of us take fonts for granted. They're just little files we get with our computers that generate characters on-screen. Thousands of fonts are available for your personal computer, and you often have to cope with the question of PostScript versus TrueType, what Adobe Type Manager is all about, and other complex issues. Here's where you can find some answers or share your own experiences.

comp.sys.ibm.pc

Those of you who use an IBM or compatible computer will want to visit this area often for questions, answers, advice on new purchases, and news of the latest developments from IBM, Intel, and other manufacturers.

comp.sys.mac

This is the newsgroup for Mac users who want to learn what is afoot with Apple and the Mac clone builders, the future of the Mac operating system, and how best to cope with the routine problems one encounters in using a computer.

comp.unix.questions

This book is devoted to Macintosh and Windows users, but many of you who work with large networks have no doubt been at least exposed to the UNIX environment as well. Here's a place where you can get information about enhancing your UNIX experience.

misc.forsale

Most newsgroups are noncommercial. That is, you shouldn't use them as a medium to post commercial or private advertising. If you have that sort of message to send, here's the newsgroup you want to check.

misc.jobs.offered

Looking to find a new job? Perhaps you want a higher salary, or you want to gain a foot-hold in a new profession. If that's the case, this is the newsgroup for you. And if you want to hire someone for your business, this is a resource (in addition to AOL's own Classified area) that will be useful.

misc.writing

This is a newsgroup where writers and would-be writers can hang out, trade tips and discuss novels, magazine articles, techniques to get published, and other relevant topics. When I first decided to try my hand at freelance writing, I would have loved to have had access to such a discussion group, but the Internet had barely begun in those days.

news.announce.important

As the title states, this newsgroup is a repository of important announcements regarding newsgroups and similar issues.

Part
VIII

Ch
32

news.announce.newusers

If you're a new user, you'll want to check out this newsgroup first. You'll get handy advice here on how to deal with many of the issues you'll confront during your Internet travels.

news.answers

From time to time, newsgroups post FAQs (Frequently Asked Questions) that contain helpful information for when you visit a newsgroup for the first time. You'll find that many of your initial questions are already answered here.

rec.arts.startrek

It's hard to believe that nearly 30 years have passed since the original *Star Trek* TV series premiered. Well, Gene Roddenberry, the creator of *Star Trek*, has left us, but new movies, TV shows, and books based on his creation continue to get extraordinary interest.

rec.arts.sf.starwars

Here's another newsgroup in which the title says everything. The *Star Wars* movies paved the way for intense and renewed interest in science fiction and the space program. You'll find messages here about the three *Star Wars* movies, possible future projects from George Lucas, those popular novels, and related subjects.

rec.audio.opinion

I've probably made it clear here and there that I'm an audio hobbyist. In a past life, I wrote manuals for one of the audio manufacturers (and still do that occasionally). This newsgroup is one of several devoted to home audio. It's one I frequent regularly, and (although it might seem strange that the subject can generate controversy), the discussions here are spirited and very often inflammatory. You cannot imagine how much debate is generated on the subject of whether there's an audible difference between two audio cables.

rec.games.misc

Just as computer and video games forums are among the most popular visiting spots on America Online, you'll find that this forum is also a busy place to visit. You can visit here for those hard-to-find tips and tricks about specific games, and you can share some of your own ideas, too.

rec.humor

This is another popular newsgroup where you can read and share jokes and funny stories. You won't necessarily find professional humorists represented here, but you'll get a lot of good laughs, anyway.

rec.music

This is a newsgroup for music lovers, covering all forms from classical to rock. Pay a visit and get ready to learn about your favorite artists and recordings and share your own views, too (**rec.travel**).

If you're a regular visitor to America Online's Shopping and Travel departments, you'll want to check out this newsgroup, as well. It's a place to share your travel experiences and to learn about new tour packages, updated airline ticket prices, and the hot tourist spots you'll want to visit.

The Next Step

If you want to keep up-to-date on the latest round of newsgroups, here's what to do:

1. Enter the Newsgroups area.
2. Click the Expert Add icon.
3. Click the Latest Newsgroups button, and you'll see a list of newsgroups added since your last visit.

From Here...

Part
VIII

Ch
32

Internet newsgroups are one of the most popular features of the Information Superhighway for good reason. The messages are informative, angry, intimidating, funny, happy, and sad, but always interesting. You'll want to visit America Online's Newsgroups area often.

■ For more information about working with America Online's own discussion boards, read Chapter 9, "Using America Online Message Boards."

■ For advice on how to prepare your children for an Internet session, and to activate Parental Controls, read Chapter 16, "Parental Issues and Internet Access."

■ For a detailed overview of America Online's huge selection of Internet resources, read Chapter 29, "Using AOL's Internet Connection."

Internet Chats

Chapter 10, "Chatting Online," talked about all the information and excitement you can discover when you visit an online conference. You learned about Instant Messages, AOL's one-on-one method of interactive chatting with your online friends.

In this chapter, you learn about another form of online conference; but, this kind of conference is not confined to one network or one online service. It is a conference that can be shared by computers worldwide—the Internet Relay Chat. ■

AOL's Chat Feature and IRC—What's the Difference?

When you attend a conference on America Online, you know the ground rules, and you know that it is happening within the safe confines of AOL's own network. There are thousands of conferences across the network every single day. They range from informal chats in a forum's meeting room to large gatherings that have thousands in attendance and feature representatives from industry, the government, and some of your favorite show business personalities.

Shortly before I wrote this chapter, I had completed hosting chores on a series of online conferences held not only on America Online, but on the Internet as well. It was quite literally a simulcast, such as you might find when something is broadcast over two or more TV networks, or on both radio and TV. The Internet variation was done via Internet Relay Chat, a way to hold conferences that transcends the borders of any single service.

In the following pages, I'll tell you how to configure your AOL software to run not only an Internet Relay Chat (IRC) program, but how you can use the same setup to run other Internet software as well, such as a different WWW browser. I'll also set up a typical IRC program and we'll join a chat already in progress (as the TV announcers say).

IRC versus AOL Chats: Let's Count the Ways

It's not only the location that makes an Internet conference different; it's also the setup and ground rules. Here are some of the specifics:

- There are thousands of Internet chats in progress at any one time, compared to maybe a few dozen on AOL.

- You can participate in several Internet conferences at the same time, but only attend one conference at a time on AOL. (When you switch to a second conference on AOL, you are automatically moved out of the first one.)

And perhaps the most important:

- America Online's Terms of Service do not apply to an IRC. In an IRC, you will find discussions with content and behavior that you may consider objectionable. As an AOL member, you are expected to behave in accordance with AOL's rules of the road. In addition, those who moderate such chats can kick you out if you violate the rules, or just, frankly, because they want to.

> **CAUTION**
>
> Because AOL's Terms of Service are not enforced outside of the service, and Internet conferences may sometimes contain material that is not suitable for children, you should carefully monitor your child's use of the IRC feature.

A Brief History of IRC

The Internet Relay Chat is the Information Superhighway's variation of a telephone party line. Folks in widely separated parts of the world are able to meet in a single location in virtual space and talk about the state of the world, their favorite show business personality, or just involve themselves in general chit-chat.

As with many Internet communication techniques, IRC started strictly as a local project. Back in the 1980s, a Finnish college student wanted to find a way build upon the usual methods of interacting with fellow students on his bulletin board, such as e-mail and message boards. He developed the forerunner to IRC to let students interact with each other in real time.

Through the years, IRC chatting expanded from basic interaction between users to include many more features, such as the ability to pick out a single person to share conversation with, and the ability to exchange files.

Participating in an IRC requires installing a client program that is able to communicate with the Internet-based IRC servers that exist in various parts of the world. Such client programs range from simple freeware utilities that get you connected and little else, to full-blown programs that provide the ability to search IRC servers for the conferences in which you want to participate, add color and basic formatting to the chat text, and provide a variety of sound effects to enhance the presentation. Some programs will even "speak" the chat text back to you in a variety of computerized voices.

Part
VIII

Ch
33

The Language of IRC

As with other Internet protocols, IRC has a language of its own. The following list briefly describes some of the most common terms; you will be acquainted with other terms during the remainder of this chapter:

- Participating in IRC is sometimes called *IRCing* (pronounced urk-ing).
- An individual IRC conference is called a *channel*. Each channel has its own discussion, its own ground rules (some of which can be quite arbitrary), and its own regular participants.

■ When you join an IRC session, you give yourself a *nickname* to identify yourself to the crowd. You may use your regular AOL screen name, your real name, or another name that you feel uniquely identifies yourself to others. Such names are limited to nine characters.

■ As participation in IRC increased, another server system was built to handle the additional traffic. It's called the *Undernet*.

Setting Up for IRC Chats

Because Internet chats are not a normal feature of AOL's software, you need to install a separate IRC client program and do a few setup tricks to make AOL's program communicate with that IRC program.

Setting Up AOL for Third-Party Internet Software

Getting a third-party Internet program to work while you're hooked up to AOL is easy, because you really don't have to do anything special. Although you used to have to struggle with extra helper files (such as Winsock files for AOL Windows users), that's no longer necessary. Version 3.0 of AOL's Mac and Windows software will automatically load the resources necessary to run your favorite Internet software when you log on. After you are connected to AOL, just launch your Internet program and you're ready to go.

> **CAUTION**
>
> Although AOL's client and WWW browser are easy to use, the same can't be said for some Internet programs. So, before you attempt to install a third-party Internet program, read the installation and setup instructions carefully. AOL's Internet channel (keyword: **Internet**) offers text files and other helpful information on setting up these programs so that they work efficiently as part of your AOL session.

N O T E The ability to run third-party Internet software with your AOL session doesn't apply if you already access AOL via TCP/IP through a dedicated Internet provider (such as AT&T WorldNet or NETCOM). With services of that sort, you already have the ability to run multiple Internet programs at once. ■

Setting Up an IRC Client Program

After you've followed the steps I've just described, you'll be able to run a number of handy Internet programs while connected to AOL. The keyword **Net Software** will produce a list of programs that are known to work reasonably well. You'll probably want to try several and see which ones perform best.

In this chapter, I'll be setting up a popular freeware Internet program for Windows that will let you participate in Internet chats. It's called mIRC, written by Khaled Mardam-Bey. Although it's not the only IRC client available, it is a good way to begin. The program doesn't take long to download, isn't too hard to install, doesn't cost anything, and runs swiftly and reliably. In addition, it can be easily configured to your tastes, and has a handy toolbar for easy navigation through its most used features.

N O T E Mac users shouldn't feel left out. You'll find a good selection of Mac IRC chat client software as well from AOL and Internet-based software libraries. When you get past the differences in program installation, the basic steps to configure the software to recognize AOL's host computer and get started with Internet chatting are pretty much the same. ■

Here are some basic hints on how to get the program installed and running from within your AOL software:

N O T E The instructions that follow apply to both the 16-bit (Windows 3.x) and 32-bit versions (Windows 95 and Windows NT) of mIRC version 4.0. Because mIRC is updated often, you may find some of the features have changed or that new ones have been added, when you check out this program. ■

Windows 3.x Installation:

1. mIRC comes in compressed form. After you've downloaded the latest mIRC software, log off AOL. This will automatically launch AOL's PKZip expansion tool, and will expand the program into its own directory.
2. Open the program group where you want to place the icon.
3. Open Windows Program Manager and click File, New.
4. Select Program Item.
5. Enter the path and name of the exe file in the Command Line. An example would be C:\AOL30\MIRC40\MIRC.EXE.
6. Click OK. This final step should create an icon for your mIRC software.

Windows 95 Installation:

1. mIRC comes in compressed form. After you've downloaded the latest mIRC software, log off AOL. This will automatically launch AOL's PKZip expansion tool, and will expand the program into its own directory.
2. Right-click in the Windows 95 Start menu.

3. Click the folder labeled Start Menu Programs and select Properties.

4. Click Advanced, which brings up the last of Start Program Categories.

5. The next step is to click Programs, and then the program group to which you want to add mIRC. In this case, it's AOL 3.0.

6. With the program group displayed, click File, New.

7. Select Shortcut from the choices available.

8. On the Command Line that appears, enter the path and file name. For example, enter C:\AOL30\MIRC40\MIRC.EXE.

9. After you click the Finish button, the new program icon should appear.

 T I P When you are running your third-party Internet program, you can reduce screen clutter by minimizing your AOL software window.

How to Join an IRC Channel

The first time you open mIRC, you see a Setup screen (see fig. 33.1). You just need to make a few simple settings, and soon you'll be chatting away on your favorite subjects. We'll get to the IRC Servers setup last.

FIG. 33.1
Set up your network and nickname preferences in mIRC's handy Setup window.

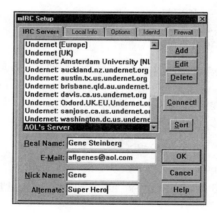

1. Enter your Real Name in the appropriate box.

2. Enter your AOL Internet e-mail address where requested. Remember, that's your AOL screen name to which you add @aol.com.

3. Choose a nickname and enter it where requested. The nickname doesn't have to be your real name or your screen name. You could use a name your friends might have

given you (but keep it clean). As mentioned earlier in this chapter, a nickname is limited to nine characters.

4. If you sometimes want to be known by a second nickname, enter it in the Alternate information field.

Now you want to choose an IRC server to log on to. Your best bet in getting a fast, stable connection is AOL's own server, so you want to add it to the list:

1. Click the Add button.

2. In the first list field, give a name to your new IRC server. I choose, to be totally unoriginal, AOL's Server.

3. Insert **irc02.irc.aol.com** in the next list field.

4. If it's not already included, add **6667** as your Port #.

5. Click Add Server to include your selection in the listing, and return to the main Setup screen.

Now it's time to get your fingers ready to chat. To hook up to AOL's IRC server, select it in the list field, and then click the Connect! button. This will immediately bring up a window with the Message of the Day! from AOL and then the programs' default mIRC Channels Folder (see fig. 33.2).

FIG. 33.2
Here are a few IRC channels AOL has selected to help you get started with Internet chatting.

Entering a chat is simply a matter of clicking the name once, and then clicking the Join button. Within seconds, you see a message window showing the chat in progress (see fig. 33.3).

The IRC chat window has some of the elements of AOL's regular chat windows. At the right is the list of others who are attending the chat, and the larger window contains the dialogue that will scroll onto your screen (usually quite rapidly) as the meeting progresses. If you want to participate, simply enter your comment in the line at the bottom, and press the Return or Enter key to send it out into Cyberspace. As I said, the process is very much like the one you find in AOL's own chat rooms.

FIG. 33.3

The #wasteland channel's chat was already going full tilt as I joined it.

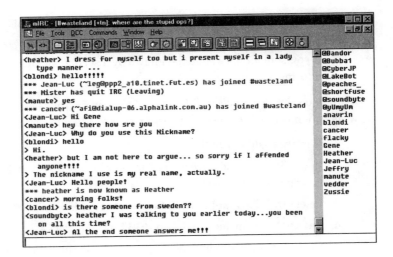

N O T E The quality of Internet traffic is unpredictable. Don't be surprised if there's a long delay between the time a comment is sent via IRC and the time it appears in your document window. Don't expect it to be nearly as fast as AOL's own chat rooms, although most often the happenings in an IRC channel may move along at a reasonably smooth pace. ■

To leave the chat, simply close the window. You can, of course, leave it open and join more chats, each of which will occupy a separate document window. The Windows menu of the mIRC software will list the open windows, so you don't lose your way.

N O T E If you don't contribute to an IRC chat for a long while, the channel operator might bump you from the chat. Don't be offended, they usually just want to keep things active. ■

Finding a Place to Talk

There may be several thousand chats in progress at any one time, and if you don't know the address, you'll want to search the IRC server for discussions about topics that interest you. mIRC offers a List Channels feature (see fig. 33.4) that lets you quickly (well, relatively quickly) search the topics of the chats for those that match your search string.

After you enter your search string, click the List! button and the IRC server will be checked for topics that match your request. Depending on the speed of your modem's connection and how much network traffic is present, it may take several minutes for the list to be consulted.

After the available channels are checked, you'll see the list of likely prospects (see fig. 33.5) along with the number of people already involved in the discussion. All you need do now is select and double-click the chat that interests you.

FIG. 33.4
Use the List Channels window to search for chats you may want to join.

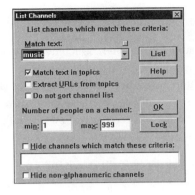

FIG. 33.5
Here's your list of active channels on the subject you selected.

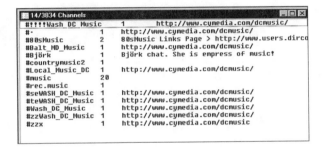

TIP You can add the name of your favorite IRC channels to the mIRC Channels Folder, so you can access them whenever you want.

Additional IRC Features

In addition to sharing conversation in the manner of AOL's own conference rooms, most IRC programs let you send direct messages to a single person, just as you do with AOL's Instant Message feature. You can also exchange files with individuals and, as a measure of self-protection if someone gets out of hand, prevent someone else from communicating with you.

Although I've focused on some of the basic features of one software package in this chapter, your explorations of AOL's software libraries will yield other Internet chatting clients. Some of them will add voice features and other handy variations on the original theme.

From Here...

Chatting on the Internet is rapidly expanding to include voice and video conferencing, just like it is being added to America Online. So, one day you'll be able to dial up someone on your favorite online service, and, no matter where that person is on this world (and maybe some day on another world, too), you'll be able to share a conversation by text, by picture, and by sound. You may never want to use the telephone again, except to log on to AOL, of course.

And, if you want to discover more about online conferences, check out the following:

■ In Chapter 7, "America Online's People Connection," you'll learn how to meet and stay in touch with fellow AOL members.

■ In Chapter 10, "Chatting Online," you'll learn how to participate in chats, conferences, and one-on-one communication with fellow members.

CHAPTER 34

Using File Transfer Protocol

What is FTP?

Learn all about Internet file transfers.

How to get the most out of FTP

Learn how to use AOL's FTP feature.

Get the latest software

This chapter shows you how to download files from some popular FTP sites.

Your own FTP Site

Learn how to set up and maintain your own FTP site on AOL, using AOL's special features.

Throughout this book, I've described AOL's simple, flexible software libraries. These libraries contain tens of thousands of files, ranging from text material to one of the biggest selections of Macintosh and PC software that you can find anywhere. The libraries are easy to access, and downloading can be automated, using AOL's Download Manager, so that you can get the files you want when network traffic is lowest and therefore get the fastest data throughput.

Yet another method of downloading files on America Online exists. The source of these files is not AOL's host computer system, but remote computer systems located throughout the world. The software is accessed on AOL through the global Internet, using a feature called File Transfer Protocol, or FTP for short.

What Is File Transfer Protocol?

The closest equivalent of an FTP site is the server on a regular computer network. You may have such a setup at your office. The *server* is a computer used as the repository of files that are meant to be accessed by other users on the network, who are called *clients*. When you need to access a file or transfer data to the server, you log on to the server, using your networking software, and then send or retrieve the files that you want.

The difference between this setup and an FTP site is the fact that the server you are accessing is not located in the same room or in a nearby office, but perhaps in another city, another state, or even another country. The network transfer protocol may be different, too, but the underlying principle is the same.

America Online's Internet connection brings FTP access online in an easy-to-use format, so you don't have to deal with text-based commands or the other complexities that are often involved in Internet file transfers. This feature allows you to tap a huge source of software libraries containing files that may not yet be available on America Online, such as the latest system software updates from Apple and Microsoft. As you'll soon learn, access to these files is not much more complex than locating and downloading files from AOL's own software libraries.

Anonymous FTP

Experienced network users know the routine: When you access your server, you usually have to establish what is, essentially, an account with the network administrator, using your name and a password. A similar technique is used to access America Online; your screen name is given to AOL's host computer automatically when you log on, then your password (typed or stored) is presented for verification.

The usual method of hooking up to one of these remote file servers is Anonymous FTP, which means that you access these sources as a guest; you don't have to establish an account that has an Internet address and a password. The time-honored technique is to type **anonymous** as the user name and your screen name (such as aflgenes@aol.com) as your password. The beauty of AOL's Anonymous FTP feature is that the logon routine is done for you behind the scenes, giving you easy entry to an FTP file server.

Restricted FTP Access

Not all FTP servers allow anonymous logons, however. Some servers require you to establish an account before you can access the server. After you register your name and a password with the site administrator, you must enter that information whenever you want to access the site.

Access to an FTP site may be restricted for several reasons. A computer manufacturer, for example, may set aside certain directories or folders on its server for public (anonymous) access and establish other areas for restricted access (just as a local area network might be organized). Restricted access may be available to allow employees of a company or beta testers (those testing pre-release versions) of a hardware or software products, to send and retrieve information with a reasonable measure of security.

In addition to accessing FTP servers anonymously on AOL, you can connect by providing your user name and password, using AOL's FTP feature.

Finding FTP Files

Later in this chapter, in the section entitled, "When You Don't Know the Address," I'll tell you how AOL's FTP search function works. This feature allows you to seek out FTP sites across the world by name or subject and then, using that information, log on to those servers to examine and retrieve files.

Although this technique enables you to locate a specific server, you don't know what's actually on those servers except in a general way, based on the information retrieved in your site search. If you need to find a particular file, you'll want to use Archie, the Internet-based mechanism designed to locate files on the Internet. On AOL, you can access Archie by sending an e-mail message to an Archie server, listing the search criteria, and then waiting for an e-mail response. This procedure is explained in Chapter 31, "Searching for Information on the Internet," so I'll refer you to that chapter for the specifics.

When you locate an interesting FTP site, you may prefer to browse through the libraries directly with the assistance of the Archie server. Because the Archie search mechanism may be updated daily or weekly (depending on who administers the site), direct access sometimes is the best way to keep abreast of the latest files posted on the FTP server.

Part
VIII

Ch
34

Although the underlying technology is highly complex, the following section shows you that using AOL's FTP feature is easy and fast—nearly as fast as getting a file from AOL's own libraries, although an extra step is involved (getting a file to AOL's host computer before it's sent on to you).

Transferring Files

Keyword: **FTP**

America Online's Anonymous FTP area (see fig. 34.1), which appears when you click the Go to FTP icon, is a very important part of the Internet Connection, offering easy access to files on remote Internet servers worldwide. You can log on as a guest, using the automatic anonymous feature, or you can use an account name and password. As you'll discover later in this chapter, AOL offers a list of popular FTP sites, as described in the section entitled, "Favorite Mac and Windows FTP Sites." You can connect to any of the sites simply by double-clicking the site's name.

FIG. 34.1

AOL's anonymous FTP area maintains a list of popular FTP sites for your downloading pleasure.

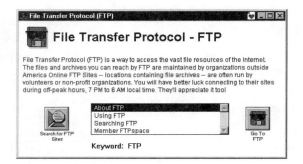

When you first visit the FTP area (unless you want to connect to a specific site directly), you'll want to review the Favorite Sites choices, which appeal to both Mac and PC users. Depending on which platform you're using to connect to AOL, you'll find a slightly different listing, and that listing will change from time to time as new sites are discovered, checked, and added to the roster.

If the FTP site to which you want to connect doesn't appear in the Anonymous FTP window, you can click the Other Site button and then enter the address of the site (see fig. 34.2). As you do with any Internet address, you have to enter the name accurately, or you will not be able to make a connection.

I'll get to the login name and password in the section entitled, "When the Other Site Isn't Anonymous," later in this chapter.

 TIP Under normal use, AOL's FTP transfer process prevents use of the Download Later function (part of the Download Manager feature). There is a way around this; one that I've used often. After the file-transfer process begins, simply click the Finish Later button. The file is included in your Download Manager, and you can complete the download whenever it's convenient for you (perhaps after you select several files this way).

FIG. 34.2
The name of the FTP site you want to access is entered in the Site Address field.

After you connect to an FTP site, the next step is to look through the file directory to locate files that you want to retrieve. You normally do not attach these files to your FlashMail session because the Download Later option isn't available. Files are normally received one at a time, while you are actually logged on to the FTP site. In figure 34.3, I have selected a file to retrieve.

FIG. 34.3
Choose the file that you want to download.

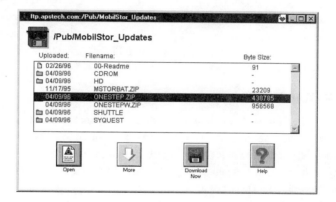

N O T E Files at FTP sites are often stored as encoded text files. As I explain in the section entitled, "How to Translate Files," later in this chapter, you need to translate these files after they are downloaded to make use of them. ▪

When the Other Site Isn't Anonymous

Not all FTP sites are anonymous. Some sites won't grant you access to the entire site or to a special area unless you have established an account with the site administrator. If you work for a firm that has an FTP site, or you're a beta tester or registered user of a software product and need to retrieve files that are not available to the public, you'll want to contact the firm involved for information on gaining access to its site.

After you set up an account, however, the process of logging on is no more difficult than beginning an AOL session. Type the site address in the Other Site text box and then click the Ask For Login Name And Password check box. When you're connected to the remote FTP site, you are asked to enter your name and password in the Remote Sign-On dialog box (see fig. 34.4).

FIG. 34.4
Enter your account name and password in the appropriate text boxes.

The password that you type is displayed as a series of asterisks, so that anyone who happens to look over your shoulder won't see what password you're entering. After you enter the correct information (enter it carefully, because the entry has to be exact), click the Continue button to go to the appropriate FTP-site directory.

TROUBLESHOOTING

I entered my name and password, but I still can't connect to the FTP site. What's wrong?
Sometimes, the inability to access an FTP site is just caused by a network error, but most often, it's because you didn't ase letters accurately; otherwise, the login process fails. Whatever the cause of the problem, you return to the Other Site dialog box. You have to check the Ask For Login Name And Password check box again before you click the Connect button to repeat the login process.

When You Don't Know the Address

If you want to locate an FTP site but don't know the site's exact address, you can use the FTP Search function to get the site address. To access the search feature, click the Search For FTP Sites icon in the main FTP window; AOL's FTP Search dialog box appears (see fig. 34.5). Type the search string in the text box and then click the Search button. If the search is successful, you'll see a list of potential matches in a few seconds.

N O T E If your search doesn't yield a positive result, you may want to enter the information a little differently (maybe with a different spelling of a product or company name, for example). Sometimes that procedure succeeds, because Internet search mechanisms can be rather literal-minded at times. ▪

FIG. 34.5
To search for an FTP site, enter the name or subject of your search here.

 TIP Instead of trying to remember the complex FTP site address when you use the FTP search feature, try this procedure: double-click the title of the site in the search window; then select and copy the site name from the text that appears. Paste that address in the Other Site text box, and click Connect.

When you're confronted by a list of prospects, you may want to learn more about each site before choosing the one to visit. Double-click an entry in the FTP Search dialog box; usually (but not always), you see some information about the software that the site contains (see fig. 34.6).

 TIP If you know the address of a firm's WWW site, many times you can access the FTP site simply by substituting FTP for WWW. A common example is Microsoft's Web site, www.microsoft.com, and its FTP site, ftp.microsoft.com.

FIG. 34.6
Clicking an entry in the FTP Search dialog box gives information about what that FTP site contains.

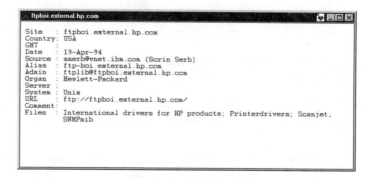

When you determine that you have the right FTP site, enter the FTP area. Click the Other Site button, and type the name of the site. Then click the Connect button to initiate the anonymous login process.

TROUBLESHOOTING

Help! I tried to log on to an FTP site, and I got a message that I couldn't because there were too many users. What do I do? Many FTP sites consist of a single computer that can handle a limited number of networked connections. Even a computer manufacturer's support sites, for example, may support fewer than 100 or 200 users at any one time. When too many folks are trying to hook up simultaneously, you get a message signifying that the server has too many anonymous users. The situation is just like a telephone busy signal; you have to try again from time to time until the server can handle your anonymous login request from AOL.

Downloading the Files

When you select a file to download, double-click the file name. You see a window that allows you to initiate the download process (see fig. 34.7).

FIG. 34.7
This screen gives information about the file that you're about to download.

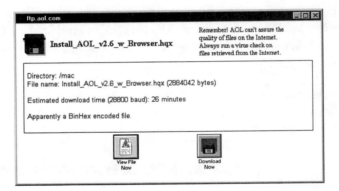

The window identifies the file by name and displays the estimated download time for the modem speed at which you're connected. When you click the Download Now button, the following three-step process begins:

1. AOL's host computer network retrieves the file from its remote source (see fig. 34.8).

2. When the process is complete, a dialog box appears, asking you to specify the directory on your hard drive where you want to receive the file (see fig. 34.9).

3. The file transfer begins in earnest (see fig. 34.10). If you want to stop or delay the transfer, click the Finish Later button.

FIG. 34.8
AOL's computers retrieve your file for you.

Retrieving data .....

Cancel

FIG. 34.9
Choose the location where you want the file to be stored.

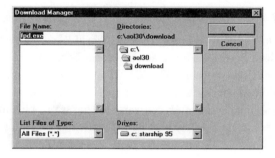

FIG. 34.10
The selected file is being sent to your computer.

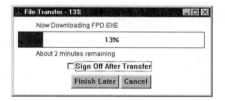

N O T E Small files that have a TXT extension can be displayed on your computer's screen without being transferred to your computer. When you can read a file this way, a View File Now icon is available; double-click this icon to produce a text window that contains the contents of that file. As you can with text windows in other areas of AOL, you can save and print the text for later review.

Part
VIII

Ch
34

CAUTION
AOL displays a virus warning in the information window about a file you're about to download. The files that you get from an FTP site cannot be analyzed by AOL for the presence of computer viruses. Therefore, you should download files only from popular, well-maintained sites; you also should check all files that you download with up-to-date virus-protection software. You can get such software from AOL's libraries or buy a commercial virus-protection product. Examples include Virus Scan from McAfee (you can get evaluation versions online for both Mac and Windows users), Norton Anti-Virus for Windows, and Symantec Anti-Virus Utilities for Macintosh (also known as SAM). The latter two are from Symantec.

A quick way to get to a particular file directory at an FTP site is to use the following commands (which are UNIX-based) after typing the site address in the Other Site window: **:/<name of directory>**. By linking directory names with a slash preceding them, you can easily navigate a complex directory hierarchy.

Another Way to Get Those Files

You can also access an FTP site with AOL's World Wide Web browser (see Chapter 35, "Using the World Wide Web"). In fact, the sheer beauty of AOL's Web access is the fact that you can seamlessly access WWW, FTP, and Gopher sites using the same easy-access interface; clicking a specific underlined hypertext link will move you from one to the other without needing to use any other software. If a password becomes necessary, AOL's browser will put up a dialog box into which you enter that information.

Translating Files

Internet-based servers may be Macs, PCs, or UNIX workstations, and they may use any of several computer operating systems. The format of the files may also vary, depending on the source from which you get the file. By looking at the file extension attached to a file name, you can determine the file's format. Following are some of the common formats that you may encounter during FTP visits:

- PC users commonly find files with EXE extensions. These represent executable files that you run with your Windows File Manager. They are also found with TXT extensions, which represent files that you can open in any word processor or text-editing program (even AOL's own software, if the files aren't too large).

- PC files with a ZIP extension are saved in PKZip format. AOL's Windows software expands most of these files automatically when you log off, or you can simply choose the File, Open command; then select the file that you want to expand.

- Macintosh files consist of two parts: a data fork and a resource fork. So that these files can be transferred on the Internet, they generally are saved in BinHex format, which converts the files to ASCII text. Therefore, these files have the extension HQX.

If you download an HQX file, follow these steps to translate the file into a readable form:

1. Download a BinHex decoder program from AOL's software libraries. You can find such products by using AOL's File Search feature.

2. Download StuffIt Expander or StuffIt Lite from the software libraries. These programs are available from the Aladdin Systems forum on AOL (Keyword: **Aladdin**). StuffIt Expander is free; StuffIt Lite is shareware. Each utility can convert BinHex files to binary form and also expand files saved in StuffIt (SIT) or Compact Pro (CPT) format.

3. Download the shareware program Compact Pro from AOL's software libraries. This program converts BinHex files and expands files saved in Compact Pro (CPT) format.

NOTE America Online's own FTP site, which you can access through Favorite Sites, includes several Macintosh and Windows compression utilities that you can use to expand the files that you download via FTP. ■

Secrets of File Compression

Because your online time costs money, and Internet bandwidth may be an expensive commodity for some network users, programmers have found a technique that makes a file smaller for speedier transfer via modem and then restores that file to its normal size after the file is transferred. This technique is called *compression*. For most AOL members, compression is seldom noticeable, because your AOL software expands files that are compressed in some common Mac and PC formats as soon as you log off the service (it's a preference option you can turn off, if you prefer).

Although the programming schemes used to make files smaller are quite complex, the principle is simple. The compression software looks for redundant data and uses a shortcut of some sort to identify this redundant information. (An example is finding all the occurrences of the letter *e* in a text document.) When you expand the compressed file, the program uses its programming algorithm to identify and restore the redundant information.

Macintosh programs are generally compressed in Compact Pro (CPT), DiskDoubler (DD), and StuffIt (SIT) formats. The extension SEA (self-extracting archive) indicates that the file itself contains the code for extracting its contents; you begin the process by double-clicking the file. An SEA file does not require additional software to extract the contents.

PC programs are generally compressed in PKZip (ZIP) and ARC (ARC) formats. For user convenience, files are often saved in self-extracting form (similar to the way it's done on the Mac). When you use the Run command in your Windows Start menu, these files (which have an EXE extension) are expanded automatically, sometimes in connection with a software-installation process.

Part
VIII

Ch
34

N O T E America Online's Mac and Windows software automatically expands compressed files in such formats as ARC, StuffIt, and PKZip when you log off (unless you turn off that option in your downloading preferences). You also can extract files by choosing File, Open, and then choosing the files that you want to expand. ■

Both the Mac and Windows software libraries have a large selection of compression software (some of it free) that you can use to expand files saved in formats that your regular AOL program doesn't support.

Maintaining Your Own FTP Site on AOL

In addition to being able to access FTP sites across the world, AOL has set aside up to two megabytes of space on its computer network for you to establish and maintain your own FTP site. The feature is called FTPspace. If you have more than one screen name, you'll get up to two megabytes of storage space for each one. You can even upload an HTML (HyperText Markup Language) file there and set up your own World Wide Web page. I'll tell you more about that in the next chapter.

How to Get There from Here

Accessing your personal FTP site is simple. Just double-click members.aol.com from the Favorite Sites box in AOL's FTP area, and your own FTP page appears (see fig. 34.11). How you use your site is up to you. You can place files there for other members to access. If you use your AOL account for business purposes, you can place promotional files and other useful information there, up to the 2M limit imposed by AOL's host computer.

FIG. 34.11
Your FTP site is available not only to other AOL members, but to anyone with Internet access.

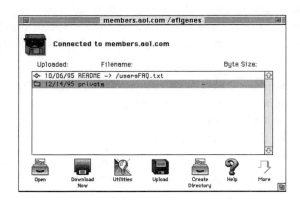

To reach someone else's FTP site, click the Other Site button, and enter the following site address: **members.aol.com:/<*membername*>**.

You can organize your personal FTP site in the way that suits you best. In the example shown in fig. 34.12, I've created a special directory for file uploads. At the bottom of the FTP window is a row of icons that can be used for file transfers and to organize your site.

FIG. 34.12
The icons along the bottom of the screen can be used to organize your FTP site.

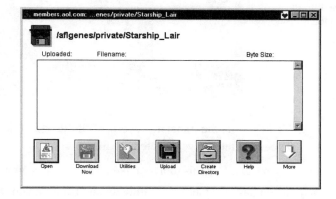

Here's what the FTP icons do:

- *Open.* Opens a file or file directory.
- *Download Now.* Transfers files from your FTP site.
- *Utilities.* Deletes or renames a file or directory.
- *Upload.* Transfers files to your FTP site or to any other FTP site that allows file uploads, using the following process:

  1. First type the name of the file you're sending in the Remote Filename text field. Then you select from two options—ASCII (for text files) or Binary (for programs and graphic files).

     Apple Macintosh users will have a third choice (see fig. 34.13), that of MacBinary, which allows the uploaded file to retain the proper Mac file format.

Part
VIII

Ch
34

FIG. 34.13
First identify the name and the kind of file you're sending.

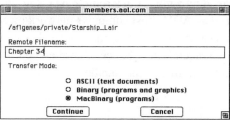

2. Click the Continue button.

3. In the next window, click the Select File button, and then locate the file you want to send (see fig. 34.14) and click OK.

FIG. 34.14

Select the file from your computer's drive that you want to send to the FTP site.

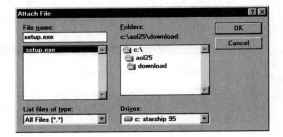

4. To begin the file transfer process, click the Send File button on the screen that appears after you've selected the file.

■ *Create Directory.* Use this tool to make your own directory at your FTP site.

■ *Help.* If you have problems in setting up and running your FTP site, you'll want to consult this handy help text for additional information.

■ *More.* If the site has more items than will fit in a single document window, click the More button to bring up additional selections.

Favorite Mac and Windows FTP Sites

America Online's FTP area includes a list of Favorite Sites, consisting of remote file servers run by major universities and computer firms, such as Apple and Microsoft. Some of these sites are *mirrored* by America Online, which means that the files themselves are duplicated on AOL's host computer network to allow more users to access them at the same time. The procedure is similar to using a backup of your own computer's hard drive. Like many backups, mirroring is done on a daily basis, so you can always keep abreast of the latest software and related information from these sites.

The advantage of providing a mirror of a remote FTP source is speed and convenience. Having the files stored on AOL's host computer network means that the files do not have to be retrieved from a remote site (which may mean slow going when network traffic is high). Also, you have a much lower chance of getting a busy signal when an FTP site has more users trying to log on than it can handle.

The following sections review the list of Favorite Sites, where you'll find a huge array of material that you'll want to explore further during your online visits. To access these sites, simply enter the FTP area via the keyword **FTP**, click the Go to FTP icon, and then choose a site from the list of Favorite Sites.

N O T E The Favorite Sites listings included in this chapter are subject to change. Listings may be added and removed over time in response to member interest. In addition, Mac and Windows users will see a slightly different selection. If a site no longer is available from this list, you still can access it directly. Click the Other Sites button and then type the appropriate site address. (The additional material that begins with a colon is used to take you to the directory where the software is located).

ftp.winsite.com:/pub/pc

This is a very active site that contains huge repositories of DOS, Windows, Windows NT, and Windows 95 files. You'll spend many enjoyable hours locating useful files in these libraries.

ftp.simtel.net:/pub/simtelnet

Simtel.Net collections, is the origin point of Keith Petersen's worldwide distribution network for Shareware, Freeware, and Public Domain programs. You'll find literally thousands of files here, with an emphasis on MS/DOS software.

mirrors.aol.com:/pub/pc_games

This site is run by AOL and contains mirrors of several remote archives:

- PCGA (PC Games Archive) ftp.uwp.edu:/pub/msdos/games as "games"
- PC Games Developers' Archive (x2ftp.oulu.fi:/pub/msdos/programming as "programming")
- MS/DOS Cheats, Cracks, Hints, etc. (ftp.uwp.edu:/pub/msdos/games/romulus as "romulus")
- DOOM (ftp.cdrom.com:/pub/idgames as "doom")
- GAMEHEAD (ftp.pht.com:/pub/gamehead as "gamehead")

PC game lovers will find a huge number of useful and fun-filled treasures among these files.

Part
VIII

Ch
34

sumex-aim.stanford.edu:/info-mac

If you are looking for a source of Macintosh software other than America Online, this site is one of the favorites. The site was established at Stanford University in Menlo Park, California, and has literally thousands of Macintosh files, ranging from freeware and shareware offerings to software updates from major publishers.

rtfm.mit.edu

This site, run by Massachusetts Institute of Technology, is a popular resource for text-based files, ranging from FAQs to discussions, stories, humorous material, and Newsgroup archives.

mac.archive.emich.edu

Located at the University of Michigan in Ann Arbor, this site is an excellent source of Macintosh software, and the files generally are up to date. You'll find games, system extensions, virus software, and other useful files. Files are grouped neatly into folders so that you can easily browse through the file categories that interest you.

ftp.nevada.edu:/pub/guitar

If you're a musician (or thinking about becoming one), you may want to visit this site; it has a strong emphasis on music-oriented files. The site is run by the System Computing Services department of the University of Nevada in Las Vegas.

ftp.aol.com

This site is America Online's own FTP site, which is available not just to AOL members, but also to anyone who has Internet FTP access. The lineup of files isn't extensive. You'll always find the latest versions of AOL's DOS, Mac, and Windows software, along with helpful compression utilities so that you can work with files that can't be expanded through AOL's own software.

members.aol.com

You can use this site to access your personal FTP site.

oak.oakland.edu

This site is a catch-all location, with a nice selection of files covering the DOS, Macintosh, Windows, and UNIX platforms. It is run by the Academic Computing Services department of Oakland University in Rochester, Michigan. You'll find lists of BBSs and ham-radio information in the site's libraries.

ftp.info.apple.com

As the name signifies, this site is Apple Computer's own FTP server, which is used to provide software updates for Apple II, Macintosh, and Windows products. Whenever a new System update or peripheral-software update comes along, that software almost always gets to this site within days (and sometimes within hours) of its release. The server sometimes gets busy when a major file is posted, however, because the site is not mirrored. Many of these files are also available from Apple's support forum on AOL. Keyword: **Apple Computer**.

ftp.borland.com

This site is Borland's support site, providing product updates and support information for the publisher's PC-based product line. You'll find directories of the files that you need by accessing the Pub directory.

ftp.microsoft.com

Microsoft's FTP site contains thousands of files, ranging from text information to product updates for Mac and PC users. The directory that you'll want to access is named Softlib. During a recent visit, I found files containing hints on how to make the Macintosh and Windows versions of Microsoft Word run better, as well as news about the Windows 95 operating system.

Extending Your FTP Site Search

Most of the sites that I've described contain computer-related files. But these files don't represent what you find at all FTP sites. As you begin to explore these wide-ranging libraries, you'll find photos and text documents covering a wide variety of fields.

Welcome to the Information Superhighway!

Part
VIII

Ch
34

From Here...

You can consider AOL's FTP capability as providing access to the largest software library in the entire world, but divided into literally thousands of branches (like a huge chain of software stores). Whatever category of software you're interested in, even if it's not Macintosh- or PC-specific, you're bound to locate a resource somewhere that you can access through AOL's FTP feature. And using the techniques described above, you'll be able to quickly get the files you want.

- For information on locating files on America Online, see Chapter 20, "Tips and Tricks on Finding Software."
- For information on Internet Newsgroups, see Chapter 32, "Joining and Participating in Internet Newsgroups."
- To keep up to date on America Online's fast-growing Internet connection, type the keyword **Internet** and explore the Internet connection.

CHAPTER 35

Using the World Wide Web

I wouldn't be surprised if you agree that the Internet is an exciting, wonderful, and sometimes intimidating place to visit. But until now, except for AOL's fancy graphic display, everything I've described on the global Information Superhighway has been text-based. Even graphic files consist simply of text, unless you download them using AOL's handy decoder feature.

The World Wide Web is something different, which explains why Web access is becoming one of the fastest growing Internet services. It adds full-color pictures, and sometimes sound and video, to the otherwise somewhat drab interface the Internet puts forward. The Web is not only a constant source of information about a huge range of subjects, but also an area where you can observe the creative efforts of a growing number of computer artists who have generated the fancy artwork you see.

To understand how the Web works, I want to describe a Macintosh program that's been provided free on every new Mac that Apple has sold for a number of years. If you are using a Windows-based PC, you'll probably be familiar with Windows variations of this software.

What the World Wide Web is

Discover the history of the World Wide Web and its humble beginnings.

All about AOL's WWW capabilities

Learn how to use AOL's Macintosh and Windows Web browsers.

How to use another browser

Explore using Microsoft Internet Explorer and Netscape with AOL.

What's on the Web

Check out a list of some of the most popular sites you can access.

Where the best sites are

Learn how to search for the information you want on the Web.

The program I'm referring to is HyperCard (see fig. 35.1), an extremely flexible utility that stores document windows, called *cards* (often thought to resemble a computer-based version of a Rolodex card in its basic form), in a file known as a *stack*. To move from one card to another, simply click an icon or text label. This transports you to another card or window that contains the material identified in that label.

FIG. 35.1
Apple Computer's HyperCard program provides a strong indicator of how navigating through the World Wide Web works (notice the Home button, for example).

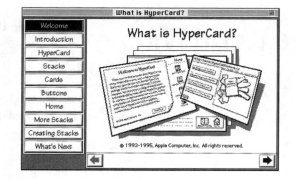

While the technique isn't terribly different, when you access a page on the World Wide Web (the equivalent of that card in your HyperCard stack or even your Windows help menu), you are not necessarily moving to another part of a single file, but often to another file, located on another computer, in another part of the world. But the entire process is transparent to the user; you never see the complex, sometimes convoluted path the data must travel before it reaches your PC. ■

What Is the Web?

As with the origins of the global Internet, the World Wide Web began as a development in a scientific laboratory. It was the outgrowth of experiments conducted in the latter part of the 1980s by CERN (European Laboratory for Particle Physics). The original intention was to develop a communications protocol that would allow scientists and researchers to have fast access to data they wished to share. The traditional Internet-based search tools could be cumbersome at times. You had to do a separate search for each item you wanted. Because there wasn't an integrated Internet access tool, such as AOL's own software, you often had to launch separate programs for each step of your Internet travels.

By 1990, the work of CERN had resulted in a technique that integrated text and graphics into a single, easily accessible document that could be retrieved from anywhere in the world using a single program, known as a *browser*. The browser is an application that can locate documents on what is now known as the *World Wide Web* (it's often referred to as simply the Web or WWW, which is what I'll be doing often through the rest of this chapter). These documents, which are known as *pages*, are retrieved by the browser program, which then interprets them in a form that's readable by your computer.

The first browser programs, released in 1990, came in both text and graphical form, and supported the NeXT computer. By 1993, browser programs were available for most popular computing platforms, including Macs and PCs. Some of these programs were provided in the form of fully integrated Internet access tools. In addition to being able to locate and open Web pages, you could do Gopher database searches or access files through FTP.

The Elements of a Web Page

Because the Internet is text-based, the CERN researchers developed a way to format a text document so that it could be read in fully formatted dress on any computer by using the browser program to translate the format to a readable form.

If you're into desktop publishing, and familiar with such programs as QuarkXPress and Ventura Publisher, no doubt you've seen how a page is *tagged*, or marked with commands that describe the way the document is to be formatted. Such tags may designate a particular type style, or the overall elements of a paragraph or table format. A closer example to the technique used for the World Wide Web is Adobe's PostScript language, which describes all of the elements of the printed page in a text-based command structure.

Web pages use a document creation scheme known as *HTML* (short for HyperText Markup Language), a series of commands that are inserted adjacent to text items in a Web document that identify how the page is formatted and where graphic images are included. Like PostScript, it isn't really necessary to know the nuts and bolts of how the Web page is constructed in order to use it effectively.

It's even possible to make such a page yourself (of course, you need access to a firm that can put your page on the Internet, which is beyond the scope of this book). You can locate a number of HTML translation programs on AOL that will automatically take your word processing or publishing document and insert the correct HTML codes in it. To locate these files, simply use the keyword **File Search** to bring up AOL's software library search screen, and enter **HTML** in the text field.

To make the resemblance between the typical Web page and Apple's HyperCard even stronger, there are actually software files online that will convert HyperCard commands to HTML. You'll find many handy Web-creation utilities in the PC Applications (keyword: **PC Applications**), Mac Telecommunications (keyword: **MCM**), and Mac Utilities (keyword: **MUT**) forums, just to name a few, but AOL's File Search is the best tool to use to see all of the files in your chosen platform in one handy list.

Part
VIII

Ch
35

AOL distributes a free program, GNNPress, from its Global Network Navigator division, that you can use to make your own WWW pages. You can download a copy from the publisher's forum (keyword: **GNNPress**).

Hypertext: The Web Method of Turning Pages

With the page of a regular printed book, you simply turn the page. With your publishing or word processing document, you have a Go To command of some sort that allows you to select the page you wish to see. On America Online, you use a keyword to get to a specific forum or department, double-click an item in a directory, or click an icon to access another area.

The closest match to the Web technique of moving among pages is the Help menu provided on many Mac and Windows programs (see fig. 35.2).

FIG. 35.2
Here's the Help menu from Microsoft Word 6.0.1 for the Macintosh.

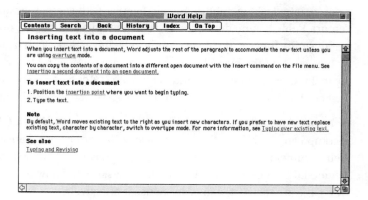

To access another part of your Help document, simply click the underlined text that describes the topic of the item you wish to see. In a Web page, it's called *hypertext*, which is the name for text that has a built-in link to other text. Figure 35.3 shows a typical Web page with hypertext links.

When you click those underlined items, you are telling your Web browser program to find and access the page that's identified by that link. The chosen page appears on your computer in a few moments. The Web page shown in figure 35.4 is the one activated by clicking the first underlined title, Progressive Networks' Real Audio, that you see in figure 35.3.

FIG. 35.3
Notice the underlined text entries, which are links to other Web pages.

FIG. 35.4
Clicking the underlined text in figure 35.3 takes you here.

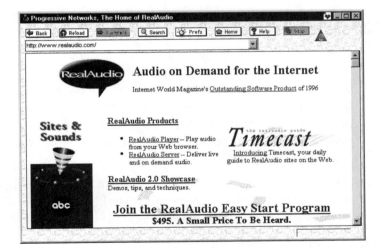

A fancier form of Web page navigation is activated in Web pages that use *hypermedia*, which are documents that include not only text, but also graphics, sound, and sometimes even animation. A typical hypermedia Web page contains not only text-based links to other documents or Web sites, but icon links as well (just like AOL's own forum windows). You just click the icon or photo (see fig. 35.5), rather than the text, to get to the area identified.

N O T E One of the neat things about the World Wide Web is the fact that clicking a hypertext or hypermedia link can either take you to another page at the same Web site, or transport you to another Web site located clear across the world. ▮

Part
VIII

Ch
35

FIG. 35.5
A hypermedia document lets you turn Web pages by clicking underlined text or pictures.

Addressing a Web Site

Everything has to have a beginning, and before you can use the handy links among Web pages and Web sites, you need to get from here to there. As Chapter 29, "Using AOL's Internet Connection," described, before you can visit any Internet site, you need to know its address. The same technique is only partly true for a Web site. Once you access one area, quite often clicking the hypertext or hypermedia link is sufficient to transport you to another site; the route of travel and the locations to which you travel are determined by what links you click.

To get to a particular site from scratch, though, you need to know its address, known as its *URL* (short for Uniform Resource Locator). The URL information you enter contains information that references the location of the site. Here's the format of a typical URL:

http://www.aol.com

The letters *http* stand for HyperText Transfer Protocol, which is the technique developed by the architects of the World Wide Web to locate and access Web sites. The colon (:) and the two slashes (//) inform the software that the information that follows is the actual Internet address of the site being accessed (www stands for World Wide Web). The last extension added to this particular Web site, com, identifies this particular location as a commercial enterprise. If the extension is edu, it refers to an educational institution. You'll find more information about Internet site naming conventions in Chapter 29, "Using AOL's Internet Connection."

CAUTION

Be sure to enter the exact URL information shown to visit one of these sites. Even a single incorrect character will result in failure to access these locations. The author and publisher are not responsible for errors, however, so if you cannot find a particular site using the information provided in this and the next chapter, you can contact that source directly for additional assistance, or use one of the search tools described in this chapter for up-to-date information.

In addition, a URL can get you a lot more than just a WWW site. The prefix ftp:// will take you to an FTP site, the prefix Gopher:// will take you to a Gopher site, and the prefix news:// will allow you to access a UseNet newsgroup.

TIP A really cool feature of a URL is the ability to access a file on your own computer or network. You need the prefix file/// plus the name and path of the file you want to retrieve.

What's a Home Page (and Can You Really Go Home Again?)

When you access a Web site, you normally go to its *home page*, which is Web parlance for the opening window of a particular site. It's similar to a book or magazine's cover page. The home page will usually offer information on how a particular site is set up and briefly list its contents (see fig. 35.6).

FIG. 35.6
A typical Web home page tells you about the site and lets you access other features of that site.

From the home page, you can easily navigate to other pages simply by clicking an icon or underlined text. You need not know the URL for that additional page to get to its precise location. That's the beauty of hypertext and hypermedia links.

 TIP You can navigate directly to a specific Web page if you know its full URL (including the name of the actual page). An example is the URL **http://www.blue.aol.com/preview/welcome.html**, which accesses AOL's own Web site and, by the part of the address following the com/, takes you to a specific page located at that site.

For information on how to create your own home page, see the section, "Using AOL's My Home Page Feature" at the end of this chapter.

Using AOL's Macintosh Web Browsers

Keyword: **WWW**

Depending on the version of AOL's Mac software you're using, you may see a different type of WWW browser. For version 2.6 and 2.7, it comes as a separate application that you can launch in two ways:

■   Enter a URL in your AOL software's keyword field (or just WWW).

AOL is busy integrating WWW content into the service behind the scenes. So simply accessing an online forum might automatically take you to the corresponding WWW page instead. If the WWW browser isn't open, it will open, and then the site will be accessed. ▨

■   Choose Switch to Browser from the Windows menu of your AOL software.

N O T E   The Macintosh Web browser provided for versions 2.6 and 2.7 of your AOL software consists of a separate application that's linked to your AOL software. Before you use this application, it must first be installed. If you did not receive a disk containing the Web browser software, you'll want to use the keyword **Upgrade** to obtain the latest version of the Web browser. ▨

Either action will launch AOL's browser, taking you either to the WWW site you selected, or to AOL's home page (see fig. 35.7) via the keyword **WWW**.

If you are using version 3.0 or later, the browser is fully integrated into your regular AOL software, and will show itself as just another document window (see fig. 35.8), same as any regular AOL forum.

FIG. 35.7
America Online's home page on the World Wide Web guides you to many other interesting Web sites, simply by clicking the appropriate icon.

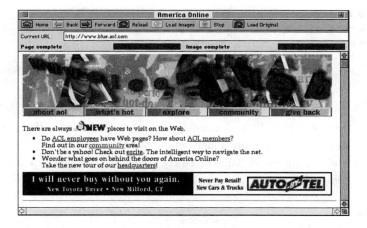

FIG. 35.8
If you look at the bottom of the screen (and are familiar with the original), you'll see that the integrated WWW browser for version 3.0 of AOL's Mac software is based on Microsoft Internet Explorer.

If you want to visit another Web site, simply enter the URL or site address in the Current URL field. If you're using the browser that comes with AOL 2.6 and 2.7, you may also bring up a WWW site by choosing Open URL from the Services menu, which brings up the dialog box shown in figure 35.9.

Part
VIII

Ch
35

FIG. 35.9
Enter the name of your WWW site here in the URL dialog box.

However you type the information, after you press Enter, AOL's Web browser will access the site. If the site is successfully accessed, the image of the new site will begin to appear on your Mac's screen in just a moment or two (see fig. 35.10). It will always take a little while for the entire page to display. How fast it appears depends on the speed of your AOL connection.

FIG. 35.10
A WWW home page begins to display on your Mac's screen. The blurry look will sharpen when the display is complete.

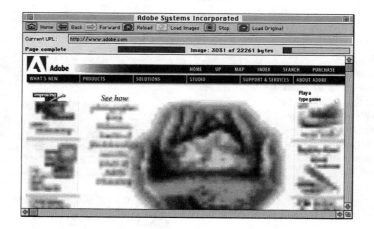

 If you're using AOL 3.0, you can add your favorite sites to your list of Favorite Places for fast retrieval.

TROUBLESHOOTING

I'm using Mac AOL 2.7. Why has my Mac browser's link gone down? To connect to a Web site on your Mac, you need to be not only running your AOL Web browser and your AOL software, but also logged on to AOL. If you log off, you're disconnected, or AOL's Internet access has briefly become interrupted, and you'll receive a message about it. You will also see the flashing icon of the Web browser application in your Mac's menu bar.

To remove the message, just click it, and then check to make sure that your AOL application is running and that you are logged on to AOL. If you are logged on to AOL at the time this message is seen, log off immediately and then log on again. If the problem continues, you might want to try using the World Wide Web at a later time.

CAUTION

To use both the regular AOL Mac software and the WWW browser, you need at least 5M of free RAM on your computer. This is in addition to the amount of RAM your Mac uses for system software (including any system extensions you might be using). If you don't have that amount of free RAM available, you will want to consider a RAM upgrade before visiting the World Wide Web.

Making Hot Links (Mac 2.6 and 2.7 Only)

As you see, moving from Web site to Web site is simple. You just enter the correct URL site address, and press Return or Enter to send AOL's browser on the path to locating and displaying your selected site's page. The Next and Previous buttons will take you directly to pages previously retrieved (the Next button, of course, will only function if another page was retrieved after the one you're presently viewing).

As you begin to visit Web sites, you will quickly find places you want to return to from time to time. AOL's Mac 2.6 and 2.7 Web browser lets you build a default listing of your favorite sites, a Hot List, to enable you to easily revisit the sites of your choice. To add the Web site you've just accessed to that list, simply choose Add to Main Hot List from the Services menu. The Web site shown on your Mac's screen will be added to a list such as one shown in figure 35.11 (where I've already included some of my favorite sites).

FIG. 35.11
You can create a list of your favorite WWW sites using the AOL Hot List feature.

To add a new item to your list, follow these steps:

1. Click the New Item icon in the Main Hot List window. The Hot List Item dialog box appears (see fig. 35.12).

Part
VIII

Ch
35

FIG. 35.12

Enter a site you want to add to your hot list here. The item I've chosen takes you to the site run by Quark Inc., a publisher of desktop publishing software.

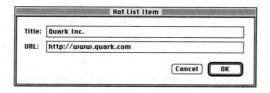

2. Enter the name of the site in the Title field.

3. Enter the URL address in the URL field.

4. Click the OK button to save your listing.

Because Web site addresses can change from time to time, you might want to change a listing in your hot list. To do so, follow these steps:

1. Open the Services menu and choose Add to Main Hot List.

2. Click the entry you want to edit to select that entry.

3. Click the Edit Item icon.

4. Make the changes you want and click the OK button to save those changes.

If you want to remove an item from the hot list, follow these steps:

1. Open the Services menu and choose Add to Main Hot List.

2. Click the entry you want to edit to highlight that entry.

3. Click the Remove Item icon, or open the File menu and choose Cut.

4. When the dialog box appears asking you to confirm that the item is to be deleted, click the OK button to remove that site from the hot list.

5. If you change your mind and want to leave the entry intact, just click the Cancel button.

You aren't restricted just to a single hot list. As your Web browsing becomes more intense, you might choose to create a hot list for different categories of Web sites; perhaps one for computer-based sites, another for entertainment, and another for education. To make a new hot list, simply open the Services menu and choose Hot Lists, and select New Hot List from the submenu. This will bring up a standard Mac Save As dialog box, where you can name your new hot list (see fig. 35.13).

Once you've named your new hot list, you'll see a brand-new hot list with the name you selected. Your new hot list is edited in exactly the same way as your main hot list (described above), with one exception; you can only select your newly created hot list by opening the Services menu and choosing Hot Lists. The Add to Main Hot List command will only access your main hot list listing.

FIG. 35.13
Name your new WWW hot list
in the dialog box shown here.

TROUBLESHOOTING

Why does it take so long for Web images to appear on my computer's screen, especially compared to the images I see on AOL? There are a couple of reasons. One is that the images retrieved by AOL's Web browser are sent from a remote computer and the transmission process is not as efficient as it would be on AOL's host computers. Also, the speed at which you connect to AOL is a major factor in how long it takes for a Web page's image to appear. At the very least, you need a 14,400 bps modem and 14,400 bps AOL connection to get adequate speed on the World Wide Web. The new generation of V.34 (28,800 bps) modems would be something worth considering if there's an AOLNet access number in your city. If you are limited to a 9,600 bps modem or access number or something slower, my suggestion is that you use the World Wide Web feature judiciously, because you will be disappointed with the performance you get.

Additional Mac Web Browser Features (Mac 2.6 and 2.7 Only)

Besides addressing your chosen Web site and building one or more hot lists, AOL's WWW browser provides a set of easy-access control buttons below the title bar window (see fig. 35.14), with matching commands in the Services menu. If the button is grayed out, that function is not available.

FIG. 35.14
Control the way WWW
images are displayed by
using these handy controls.

- *Home.* Click this icon to return to AOL's home page.
- *Back. (when not grayed out).* Click this icon to return to the previous page.
- *Forward. (when not grayed out)* Click this icon to go to the next page.
- *Reload.* Click this icon to reload a Web page in the program's document window.
- *Load Images.* Click this icon to reload graphic images on the selected Web page.
- *Stop. (when not grayed out)* If you want to halt the process of retrieving a Web page, click this icon.

Part
VIII

Ch
35

■ *Load Original.* Click this icon to reload the original selected page from a site (rather than retrieve the cached copy on your hard drive).

The commands described above are probably sufficient to cover most of your WWW needs; they'll allow you to quickly navigate to your favorite sites without delay, and easily switch from page to page.

 Just like any document window you access via AOL, the pages you retrieve by the World Wide Web can be printed, using the File, Print command. And they'll be fully formatted too, very much as you see them on your screen. (They'll look even better if you have a color printer.)

CAUTION

A WWW browser will cache (store) a copy of each graphic it accesses on your hard drive. Unlike the integrated browser provided on AOL's Mac and Windows 3.0 software, the older Mac browser doesn't give you the option to have older cached files automatically deleted when a certain folder size is reached. To ensure maximum performance, you'll want to delete the files every week or so. You'll find those files in a folder labeled Cache, inside the Online Browser's Web Files folder.

 AOL's software libraries contain AppleScript files that can be used to automatically remove the browser's file cache.

In addition to the easy access features of the Mac 2.6 and 2.7 browser, here are some additional menu bar features you'll want to check into.

Windows Menu   The Windows menu lets you access a log of your recent FTP site visits (so long as they were done through the browser program), and displays a list of open WWW page windows (see fig. 35.15). If you've elected to open more than a single page at the same time (one of the items shown in the Configure preferences list described earlier), the final command, Rotate Windows, will let you move from one window to the other.

AOL Menu   The AOL menu provides just two functions (see fig. 35.16). The first, Connect, is used if you are not presently logged on to AOL. It will log you on using the screen name that has previously been selected in the Setup and Sign On window. If the AOL program hasn't been launched, it will also open the application. The other option shown does precisely what it describes; it switches you to the regular AOL program.

FIG. 35.15
Here's the Mac 2.7 Web
browser's Windows menu.

FIG. 35.16
Begin an AOL session or
switch to the AOL program
using this menu.

Mac 3.0 Web Browser Features

To bring your Mac 3.0 WWW browser to the screen, simply enter the URL you want to
access with AOL's Keyword feature (Command-K), choose it from your list of Favorite
Places, or just type the keyword **WWW**. Any of these actions will bring up a WWW
browser screen similar to the one shown in figure 35.17.

FIG. 35.17
The WWW browser that
comes with version 3.0 of
AOL's Mac software looks
very similar to the Windows
version described later in this
chapter.

Once AOL's home page has appeared on your screen, you'll notice eight buttons located
below the title bar at the top of your WWW document window that allow you to control the
display of pages, and choose additional options. If the button is grayed out, that option
isn't available or doesn't apply to the page that's displaying. These are:

- *Back.* This option returns to the previously selected Web page, if applicable.

- *Reload.* This option reloads the WWW page currently being displayed. It's an option you want to use if a transmission problem prevents clear display of the original page.

- *Forward.* This option switches to the next Web page, if one is available.

- *Favorite Places.* Click this icon to see your own custom list of bookmarks of your favorite AOL and Web-based stopping points. To add a WWW site to this list, just click the handy heart-shaped icon if it appears at the right side of the title bar.

- *Prefs.* This option brings up a window where you can set your AOL browser preferences. Unless you have a specific, specialized need (such as changing the cache you've set aside for stored WWW graphics), you can pretty well leave things as they are.

- *Home.* This option returns you to AOL's home page.

- *Help.* This option lets you access WWW pages that contain helpful information to guide you through some of the Web features.

- *Stop.* If you decide you'd rather not load the current Web page, you can use this button to stop the process.

Using AOL's Windows Web Browser

Keyword: **WWW**

Using the World Wide Web from your AOL Windows software is no different from accessing other Internet-based services on AOL. Use the keyword **WWW**, or just click the World Wide Web icon in AOL's Internet Center (keyword: **Internet**). When you enter this area, AOL's home page appears on your screen in a new document window (see fig. 35.18).

N O T E   To access the World Wide Web via AOL's Windows software, you need Windows AOL version 2.5 or later, which contains an integrated Web browser. Previous versions of AOL's Windows software will not access the World Wide Web. The newest versions of the software can usually be downloaded from an area free of online charges that is accessed via keyword. ■

If you want to visit another Web site, simply enter the URL or site address in the list field shown by the text entry beginning with http://. Then press the Enter key to call up the remote site you want to reach.

T I P   You can use AOL's Keyword feature (Ctrl+K) to directly access a WWW site with AOL's Windows software. Simply enter the URL address in the Keyword screen, then click the Go button to access that site.

FIG. 35.18
AOL's home page, as seen in the Windows software.

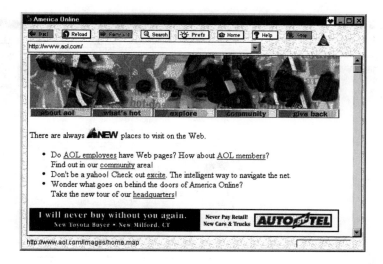

Once AOL's home page has appeared on your screen, you'll notice eight buttons located below the title bar at the top of your WWW document window that allow you to control the display of pages, and choose additional options. If the button is grayed out, that option isn't available or doesn't apply to the page that's displaying.

The buttons at the top of the window give you these options:

- *Back.* This option returns to the previous selected Web page, if applicable.

- *Reload.* This option reloads the WWW page currently being displayed. It's an option you want to use if a transmission problem prevents clear display of the original page.

- *Forward.* This option switches to the next Web page, if one is available.

- *Search.* This choice accesses AOL's own Internet search tools, such as WebCrawler (see fig. 35.19). You can use this option to find precisely the information you need on a particular subject.

- *Prefs.* This option brings up a window where you can set your AOL browser preferences. Unless you have a specific, specialized need, you can pretty well leave things as they are.

- *Home.* This option returns you to AOL's home page.

- *Help.* This option lets you access WWW pages that contain helpful information to guide you through some of the Web features.

- *Stop.* If you decide you'd rather not load the current Web page, you can use this button to stop the process.

Part
VIII

Ch
35

FIG. 35.19
AOL's Internet search engines help you look for the information you want.

Using AOL with Another WWW Browser

Although AOL's regular WWW browser can meet most of your needs, you may have already become accustomed to using another browser on another service. You may be surprised to learn, then, that AOL contracts with other publishers to deliver browser technology to its members. For example, as I explained in my introduction to version 3.0 of the Mac browser (see "Mac 3.0 Web Browser Features," earlier in this chapter), it's based on Microsoft's Internet Explorer.

As this book went to press, AOL was preparing to deliver a Windows version of the same browser with version 3.0 of its Windows software. Again, while the underlying technology will change, the interface that you see as a member will not change significantly.

If you'd rather use another browser anyway, that's no problem. All you have to do is log on to AOL, and then launch the other Internet program. You'll find more information about it in Chapter 33, "Internet Chats."

Using AOL with Netscape

Right now, perhaps the most popular browser on the planet is Netscape (see fig. 35.20). Making it a part of your AOL connection is simple. Just log on to AOL first, then launch Netscape. The version I'm displaying for this book is Macintosh version 3.0, which offers a new interface, support for the Java programming language, and easy access bookmarks.

FIG. 35.20
Netscape's WWW browser has taken the Internet by storm.

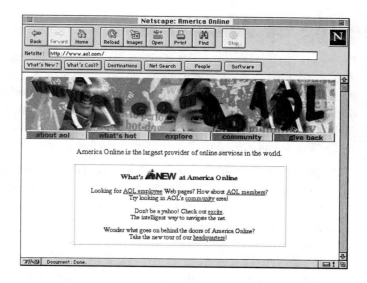

Netscape is quite expandable, and you can add to its functions with plug-in modules (somewhat like the components you'd add to such programs as Adobe Illustrator and Adobe Photoshop to enhance their capabilities).

While Microsoft's Internet Explorer is becoming the standard browser with AOL's regular client software, Netscape replaces the browser used with AOL's GNN Internet service (see Chapters 37 and 38 for more information about GNN).

> **CAUTION**
>
> Although you can access other Internet software as part of your AOL connection, they are not linked to your AOL program. Thus, you won't be able to access another browser with a keyword, or use another browser's e-mail or newsgroup features.

TROUBLESHOOTING

Why does the appearance of a WWW page vary from browser to browser? Which is the correct version? The formatting of a WWW page isn't as precise a standard as Adobe's PostScript description language. Different browsers interpret HTML commands in different fashions, and support some commands but not others. In addition, there are various options for you to adjust fonts and colors. When you combine all these, you may begin to feel you're lucky that a WWW document looks good at all, and you should definitely expect the appearance to change from browser to browser. Even the illustrations I've shown in this book, where I've accessed AOL's home page with several browsers, will give you a little example of how the appearance might vary.

Speeding Up Web Access

Under any circumstances, the World Wide Web can tax the fastest computer's CPU with its roster of photos, sounds, and animation. As convenient and as useful as WWW access is, don't expect speedy performance. Sometimes, heavy network traffic will slow image displays to a crawl, and there's nothing you can do about it, other than trying to log on to AOL at a different time, or using a different access number. But there are ways to make AOL's Web software perform better. Here are a few considerations:

- *Get a faster modem.* Chapter 41, "Secrets of High-Speed Access on AOL," provides information on the modem options available to you, and how to configure your modem for the best possible performance.

- *Find a faster access number.* Chapter 5, "America Online and Mobile Computing," describes the steps to take to locate other access numbers on America Online. Because AOL's new AOLNet network, with 28,800 bps access, is expanding, you'll want to check occasionally for newer phone connection choices.

- *Get a faster computer.* It goes without saying that Macs and PCs are getting faster and cheaper. If you have an older model, it might be time to look at a new modem equipped with an Intel Pentium or PowerPC microprocessor. These new models can out-perform older models by a huge factor.

- **For Mac Users:** *Give a program more RAM.* This is done by selecting AOL's software and the Web browser software (programs must not be running when you perform this operation) with the Finder's Get Info command (see fig. 35.21). You then enter a higher preferred memory setting, usually in increments of 500K or higher.

FIG. 35.21
Enter a higher memory setting in the Get Info window. In this example, using System 7.5, make the setting in the Preferred size field.

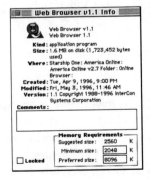

■ **For Windows Users:** *Give your Windows AOL browser a bigger cache.* This is done by choosing your AOL Preferences window, and clicking the WWW, Advanced Preferences options. In the dialog box that appears, increase the size of the image cache (see fig. 35.22). This provides a greater memory space for Web graphic images to be stored. When the number of images loaded requires more memory than you've selected, the older pages will be purged from memory.

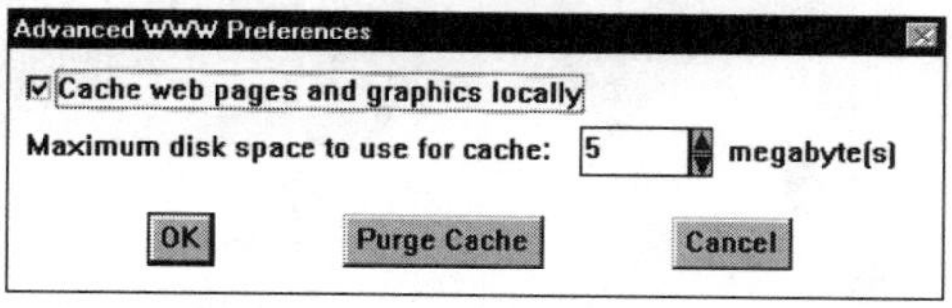

FIG. 35.22
Set aside more RAM to store WWW pages after you've retrieved them.

Advanced WWW Preferences	☒
☑ Cache web pages and graphics locally	
Maximum disk space to use for cache: 5 ▲▼ megabyte(s)	
OK Purge Cache Cancel	

N O T E To give your Mac or Windows AOL WWW browsers a greater dose of RAM, you need to have enough free memory to accomplish this task. If your computer has less than 8M of RAM, it might be time to consider a memory upgrade. ■

Searching for the Information You Want on the WWW

As mentioned so far in this chapter, AOL provides a basic listing of Web sites, and will be incorporating more in the Internet Connection department. To begin this section, let's briefly review some of these sites. You'll read about many more in Chapter 36, "Popular Web Sites."

URL address: http://espnet.sportszone.com/

This site is a quick way to review current sports news, courtesy of the ESPN cable TV sports channel. Besides the top sports headlines, you can also review selected stories on your favorite sporting events and teams.

URL address: http://www.iuma.com/

If your musical tastes are eclectic, you'll want to visit the Internet Underground Music Archive, which, at the very least, has one of the most interesting selections of entertainment you're apt to find on the World Wide Web (see fig. 35.23). This site is designed to represent the interests of hundreds of budding musical acts, and allows you to get in touch with the artists, buy their recordings, and to share comments about them with fellow music lovers.

Part
VIII

Ch
35

FIG. 35.23
The Underground Music
Archive is a popular resource
for music information on the
WWW.

URL address: http://www.npr.org/mosaic.html

When shock jocks and loud music become a little too much to bear, many of you probably URL to National Public Radio for a less frenetic look at the world around you. Their Web page is simply designed, so it loads onto your computer quickly, but it covers a wide range of subject matter. This site offers information about current programming, a listing of stations in your area carrying this network, and includes special areas set up for regular listeners of some of their shows.

URL address: http://www.wines.com/

If you're into gourmet cooking or just having a glass of superior wine with dinner, you'll want to check out the Wines on the Internet site (see fig. 35.24). When you visit this site, you'll take a virtual tour of a winery and consult a list of featured products. You'll find lots of useful information that will help you make a better selection for your home or at a restaurant.

FIG. 35.24
Learn all about fine wines here.

URL address: http://www.movies.com

The Buena Vista MoviePlex is dedicated to movies produced by Walt Disney Pictures and its related companies, Hollywood Pictures and Touchstone (see fig. 35.25). From this screen you can learn about current releases and some that were due for future release when this book went to press. This is a place where you can download movie trailers from these flicks and learn more about the stars of these productions.

FIG. 35.25
Information about the newest flicks released by Buena Vista can be accessed here.

Part
VIII

Ch
35

Locating Other WWW Sites

The above selections, which are part of AOL's standard listing, are but a few of thousands of Web sites that can be found across the world. The question, then, is how do you find a particular site, or find out if a particular business or educational concern has a Web site.

Fortunately, this is becoming easier to do because more and more representatives of such firms include their URL on their business cards and stationery. You also find WWW listings in popular magazines and newspapers. Press releases announcing new products or services will also mention the Web site address somewhere in the text.

I'll cover some of AOL's convenient Web site search tools shortly. But for now, here's a quick technique to find out if a company has a Web site.

Let's say, for example, that you want to look for a site run by Power Computing Corporation, a manufacturer of Apple Macintosh computers. Having read this far, you know that all Web sites have the same prefix, http://www. You also know that a business will have a com suffix on its URL, so now you just need to fill in the blanks.

First, you can try **http://www.powercomputing.com** and see what happens (see fig. 35.26).

FIG. 35.26
The Web site address doesn't work, according to this message.

Because the first attempt didn't work, let's try an abbreviation for that company's name instead: **http://www.powercc.com**. You'll be pleased to discover that this is a valid WWW address and that it works (see fig. 35.27)!

TROUBLESHOOTING

Why am I getting a `Fatal Error` message when I try to access a WWW page? Most of the time, you get that error when the page you are trying to reach isn't available, or you've entered the URL information incorrectly. When you get this message, recheck the URL and make sure that every character is accurately entered. Remember, there are no word spaces, for example, in a URL. If you've confirmed that the URL is correct, you might want to recheck the source from which you got that site location to make sure the address hasn't changed. Or maybe you should just try again. Sometimes network glitches (or simply a system problem on the site's own server) along the Internet will make a site easily available one day, and unavailable the next.

FIG. 35.27
Success! This Web site was quickly accessed through trial and error.

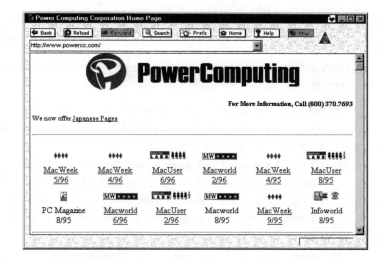

Other Search Tools

The technique described previously will also easily get you to sites run by Adobe, Apple, Compaq, IBM, Intel, Microsoft, and many, many other firms. But, very often, URLs are not so simply labeled, nor is their meaning as obvious. This is especially true for sites that cater to a hobby or special interest, or sites run by an educational institution.

To locate those sites, you want to have access to a site that can do the searches for you. AOL offers a selection of those from its own Web site, which you can access simply by clicking Search on the Mac and Windows 3.0 WWW browsers (see fig. 35.28).

Part
VIII

Ch
35

FIG. 35.28
AOL offers a selection of Web search tools that provide an extensive capability to help you to find the sites that interest you.

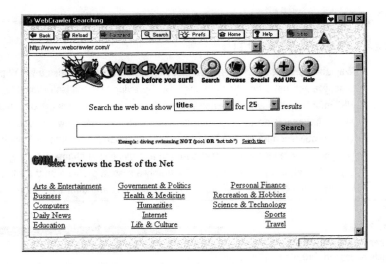

Here's a quick summary of a couple of the tools AOL provides to find information on the Internet:

- **WebCrawler Searching:** This site allows you to locate a specific site by its name and topic. It also provides a Top 25 Sites listing and helpful advice on how to locate sites that may interest you.

- **Global Network Navigator:** This is the online version of *The Whole Internet Catalog,* run by AOL's GNN division, and it lists a large number of sites by subject. By clicking a subject, you get a list of sites meeting that criteria. The next step, clicking the site's name, gets you a one-paragraph description and the option to go right to that site to see it for yourself.

- **JumpStation II Front Page:** Here's another valuable search tool that helps you quickly locate sites that may interest you. Before you give it a try, you'll want to review some of their text documents to learn all about the search procedures.

- **The Lycos Home Page:** Clicking this entry takes you to Carnegie-Mellon University's own Web site, which lets you search a database of more than 500,000 documents.

Another search facility worth trying is **http://www.Yahoo.com**, which provides extremely comprehensive Web search capabilities. That site and other selections, most of which are not part of AOL's standard listing, are covered in Chapter 36, "Popular Web Sites."

Some Quick Tips on Finding the Internet Information You Want

There is a huge amount of information that you can access on the World Wide Web. But first you have to find it, and for that there are a number of handy search tools, some of which are briefly described in this book.

Most of these tools work essentially the same way, and if you follow these short steps you'll quickly find the information you want.

- Be as specific in your request as possible. If you want to know about camcorders, don't just ask about "video" or "consumer electronics" because you'll then get a lot of matches that don't cover the subject you want to know about.

- If you want to search a phrase rather than single words, place the phrase in quotes. For example "upright vacuum cleaners."

- To keep your screen from being cluttered with extra information, limit the number of search results you want. The default setting is usually 25, and the results are listed in descending order, with the items that come closest to your search request at the top of the list.

- If your search request isn't calling up enough information, go the reverse route. Broaden the subject. In this case, if "camcorders" doesn't cut it, you may indeed want to try "video" or "consumer electronics" as well.

- If you want your search to include more than one word, place AND between them. Example: "cars" AND "V-8s."

- If you want your search to include either of the words or both, put the word OR between them. Example: "Buick" OR "cars."

- If you want to exclude the second word in a search request, place the word NOT between the two. Example: "Apple" NOT "fruit."

Using AOL's My Home Page Feature

Keyword: **My Home Page** or **Personal Publisher**

If you want to get involved in making your own Web pages, AOL has a quick solution for you. It's called My Home Page. It's a place where you can easily assemble the text and pictures to make your own WWW page, and then have it made available to other AOL members (or to the entire Internet if you prefer). It will give color and depth to your online profile, so it's definitely worth checking out.

The Basic Ingredients

Your AOL Web page begins with your online profile, but then expands to include some additional elements:

Part
VIII

Ch
35

■ *Web links*. You enter the URL of your favorite Web sites and they'll be added to your home page.

■ *Graphics*. You can transfer photos and drawings (in GIF and JPEG formats). In addition to graphics you may have on hand, you can find some useful clipart by clicking the Home Page Graphics icon in AOL's Personal Publisher area.

■ *Text*. You can add text captions to the photos and provide information about you, your family, your philosophy of life, your business. You can write about anything you think would interest AOL's members or the Internet at large, so long as you keep it in good taste (within the bounds of AOL's Terms of Service).

But It's Only the Beginning

The WWW page you make on AOL is simple and highly structured. The text formatting is already taken care of for you. You cannot, for example, eliminate your profile, or change the style or size of the type. You cannot customize the background color, or position graphics and links any differently if you decide you have a better idea on how it should look.

If you are truly interested in exploring the possibilities of making (authoring) Web pages, you may want to check out software that can create an HTML document. AOL has already set aside an area online where you can get some additional assistance and download some more sophisticated software. Just return to the My Home Page main screen and click the title Advanced Tools in the directory listing and look over the information about NaviPress, a program provided free to you by AOL's NaviSoft division. NaviPress is just one of many Web authoring programs available. You'll find other tools, both shareware and commercial, that will help you assemble your personal WWW page in short order. After you make up your page, you can upload it directly to your personal FTP site on AOL. For information on how to manage your FTP site, see Chapter 34, the section entitled "Maintaining Your Own FTP Site on AOL."

Here are just a few things to consider if you want to take the plunge and get involved in more sophisticated web page creation:

■ *Appearance*. The look is half the battle. You will want to spend a little time seeing how other WWW pages are organized, so you can use them as a guidepost as to what looks good to you.

■ *Easy navigation*. You will be tempted to put lots of graphics and URL links on your page. Best thing to do is keep it simple and label everything clearly.

■ *Keep text short and sweet*. No sense writing your first novel on a WWW page. Be brief and to the point, and consider that visitors to your page will be viewing everything on a computer screen where too much text may strain the eyes.

- *Practice, practice, practice.* WWW authoring is no different from other artistic skills. You want to read as much as you can about the subject, and practice as much as you can to hone your skills. Don't be afraid to be a little daring, and don't expect your first effort to be a finished product.

Finding AOL Member Home Pages

To view the page you've created for yourself, or access one belonging to another member, use this URL: **http://home.aol.com/<screen name>**. If you're not sure whether a member has such a page, use this URL: **http://home. aol.com/**. You'll bring up a document window in which you can enter the screen name of the person whose page you're trying to find.

For Further Reading

This chapter only covered the basics of the World Wide Web, including a history of the Web and a tutorial on how to use AOL's Mac and Windows Web browsers. No doubt you'll want to read more about this very fascinating subject, and perhaps you'll want to learn more about creating your own Web page.

I can highly recommend two resources for this information, *Special Edition Using the Internet, 2nd Edition,* and *Special Edition Using the World Wide Web.* Both are from Que Corporation and available from your favorite bookseller. The first book provides a well-written introduction to the Web, and lists some popular sites you'll want to examine further. If you desire additional information, the second book provides complete background details on every imaginable Web-related subject and easy, step-by-step instructions to help you master just about every nuance of Web techniques and terminology.

From Here...

The World Wide Web is, for now, the most sophisticated and possibly the fastest-growing Internet-based information resource. Combined with AOL's easy-to-use browsers and a fast modem, you'll spend many hours enjoying this service. If you want to learn more about the global Internet and AOL's growing Internet capability, refer to the following chapters:

- For a basic overview of the history of the Internet and AOL's Internet Connection, read Chapter 29, "Using AOL's Internet Connection."

Part
VIII

Ch
35

■ For information on how to send e-mail across the Internet and join mailing lists, read Chapter 30, "Secrets of Internet E-Mail and Mailing Lists."

■ For information on how to join and participate in Internet newsgroups, see Chapter 32, "Joining and Participating in Internet Newsgroups."

■ If you want to discover how to have a one-on-one chat with fellow net surfers, read Chapter 33, "Internet Chats."

■ If you want to download software from Internet FTP sites, see Chapter 34, "Using File Transfer Protocol."

■ A listing of some interesting Web sites that you'll want to visit can be found in Chapter 36, "Popular Web Sites."

■ And to keep up-to-date on America Online's fast-growing Internet connection, simply type the keyword **Internet** and explore the Internet Connection.

Popular Web Sites

In Chapter 35, I demonstrated AOL's Mac and Windows
World Wide Web (WWW) browsers and explained how
you can hook up a different browser if you prefer. I
described some popular WWW sites just to show how
particular features of the browsers are used.

There's little doubt that developing an Internet presence is very important for business and educational
institutions. The growing popularity of the WWW and
the development of easy-to-use software to create Web
pages have resulted in an avalanche of new entries into
this colorful, exciting aspect of the Internet.

You can find literally thousands of sites from which
to choose on the World Wide Web, covering every
conceivable category from your favorite forms of entertainment to areas where you can read merchandise
catalogs and place your order. This chapter is devoted
to listing just a few of the popular Web sites along with
their URLs (locations). You can easily visit these sites
by entering the URL information (precisely as shown)
in AOL's Web browser. Navigation through these sites
involves clicking the underlined titles or descriptions,
which provide quick access to the named areas.

Some of the selections that follow are arbitrary, based strictly on the preferences of the author and some of the sources consulted during the preparation of this book. No doubt you'll find others equally compelling during your online travels. ■

N O T E Some Web sites offer the ability to display material in text or graphic form. If you don't have a 14,400 bps or faster modem (and an AOL connection to match that speed), you'll want to pick the text option where possible, to improve performance and reduce the time it takes for Web site material to appear on your computer. ■

N O T E To visit one of these sites, be sure to enter the exact URL (Web site address) information shown. Even a single incorrect character will result in failure to access these locations. The author and publisher are not responsible for errors, however, so if you cannot find a particular site using the information provided, you can contact that source directly for additional assistance or use the Yahoo search site, described at the end of the chapter, for up-to-date information. ■

> **CAUTION**
> Although visiting the World Wide Web can be fun and often very educational, it is not so much fun if you have a slow modem. Consider a 14,400 bps modem and comparable AOL connection speed as the minimum performance level for regular Web visits. A slower modem makes the artwork displays seem to take forever. You'll also be eager to check out AOL's AOLNet service, which offers access at speeds up to 28,800 bps, and even faster options, such as ISDN and TCP/IP. You'll also want to read Chapter 41, "Secrets of High-Speed Access on AOL," for further insights into getting high-speed performance with America Online.

Commercial Web Sites

The sites in this first section are commercial, ranging from business services to sites run by major retailers. As with other locations described in this chapter, what you find here represents a very brief, somewhat arbitrary, listing. There are many more sites that might prove equally interesting. You'll want to read the end of this chapter to learn about the Yahoo database search tool, to aid further explorations on your part.

CommerceNet

URL address: **http://www.commerce.net**

Think of CommerceNet (see fig. 36.1) not just as a single business resource, but more as a huge shopping mall, containing Web pages from various businesses. You'll find areas devoted to such firms as California's Bank of America, Apple Computer, Dun & Bradstreet, and a number of smaller firms, too. CommerceNet is very much a work in progress. Some firms represented at this site provide product catalogs, and others will even let you place electronic orders for merchandise. And, best of all, if you're looking to gain access to the Internet for your business, this might be one resource you'll want to consider joining so that you can click your way to your own Web site.

FIG. 36.1
CommerceNet is practically a shopping mall in cyberspace.

1st in Flowers

URL address: **http://www.1stinflowers.com/**

1st in Flowers (see fig. 36.2) is a fourth-generation florist now doing business online. You can view photos of its offerings at its WWW site. And if something interests you, you can place your order via its 800 telephone number, or make your purchase through a secured transaction direct from its Internet resource. If you have questions about what flower is appropriate for a particular occasion, you'll want to check its Frequently Asked Questions area. According to the information at this WWW site, 1st in Flowers can arrange for delivery of your selection via local florists throughout the USA and in many parts of the world.

FIG. 36.2
Here's a WWW site where you can definitely say it with flowers.

The NASDAQ *Financial Executive Journal*

URL address: **http://www.law.cornell.edu/nasdaq/nasdtoc.html**

Here's a resource where you can read the current issue of the NASDAQ *Financial Executive Journal*, which is published for NASDAQ customers (see fig. 36.3). If your trip to the business pages online or in your daily newspaper includes a review of NASDAQ stock quotations, you'll find it a useful repository of business-related information. This Web site was put together with the cooperation of Cornell Law School, and it offers not only the current issue of this publication, but a way to search through back issues as well.

Nordstrom Personal Touch America

URL address: **http://www2.pentagoncity.mci.net/marketplace/nordstrom/**

The purpose of this site, run by the popular department store chain, is to provide a personal shopping experience. Nordstrom Personal Touch America (see fig. 36.4) will help assist you in selecting from its line of clothing and accessories. What it does is select a Personal Shopper, someone who will work with you to select the items you want. You can contact this person and get information and even place your order via e-mail or (for customers in the USA) via Nordstrom's 800 number.

FIG. 36.3
Learn about the goings on in NASDAQ at this Web site.

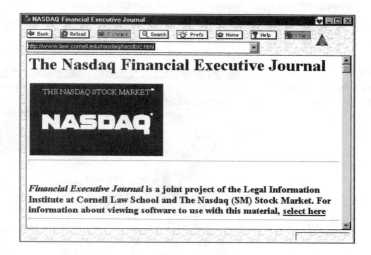

FIG. 36.4
A major department store chain has set up this site to provide custom services to its customers around the world.

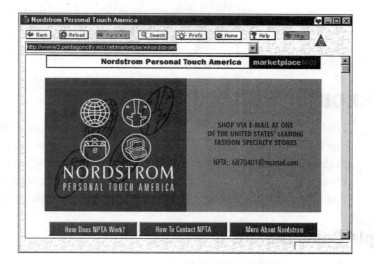

Small and Home-Based Business Links

URL address: **http://www.ro.com/small_business/homebased.html**

An increasing number of people have found comfort and sometimes wealth in working at home. This site (see fig. 36.5) is devoted to providing information about setting up and running such a business. You'll find information about franchises, business opportunities, reference materials, and advice on how to make your business successful. Of course, whenever you read about a potential business opportunity through this resource or anywhere else, you'll want to check it out thoroughly before getting more involved in the enterprise. But this is a good place for you to get started.

FIG. 36.5
Here you'll find information about home-based businesses of all sorts.

Computer-Related Sites

I didn't compile this listing to push one platform over another. We have quite enough of that in the online debates involving Mac versus PC versus UNIX fans. Instead, I just want to show you a sample of the sites set up by major manufacturers and publishers. In fact, it's a rare computer maker who doesn't have an online presence of one sort or another. The question "What's your URL?" is on most every computer user's mind these days.

Apple Computer, Inc.

URL address: **http://www.apple.com/**

Apple Computer has established an attractive visual display (see fig. 36.6) that enables you to learn about its full array of products, ranging from its popular line of personal computers to its operating system and other software products. You'll be able to tap the resources of Apple's huge technical information library, so you can learn first-hand about dealing with common problems and finding quick solutions. In addition, you'll receive up-to-date information about new products, and you'll be able to download updates to system software, plus additional utilities, such as the latest versions of QuickDraw GX and QuickTime. Traveling through this Web site is easy, because all the buttons and hypertext links (underlined text) are clearly labeled. Just choose the area that most interests you, and in a few seconds you'll see the Web page appear on-screen.

FIG. 36.6
Apple Computer's main Web site.

N O T E Remember that visiting a Web site doesn't just involve reading text and looking at pretty pictures. It represents a valuable resource for software, and you might actually find that downloading from a Web site seems easier than rummaging through various folders or directories to locate the files you want. ▪

Compaq Computer

URL address: **http://www.compaq.com**

Compaq Computer's Web site (see fig. 36.7) has complex, colorful artwork, and it's apt to overtax a slower modem or slow connection. But you have a choice here. When you enter this site, you can choose from a graphic or text display. I chose the graphical display shown here. If you want information about a particular product or service, simply choose the appropriately labeled window pane.

The rectangular buttons at the bottom of Compaq's fancy home page can be used to search the contents of this site, view its index, or receive additional help. And if you want to return to a text display, simply click the appropriate text entry right at the bottom of the page.

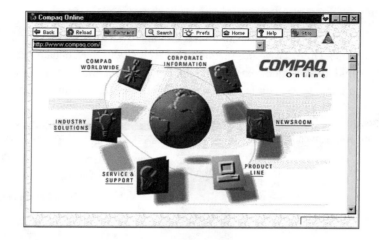

IBM Corporation

URL address: **http://www.ibm.com**

When you first visit IBM's Web site (see fig. 36.8), you realize how literally they've taken the concept of a home page. It looks for all the world like a newspaper or a monthly newsletter. To read a particular story, simply click its headline.

Beneath the IBM window I've shown here are pictures representing different support areas, and clicking the appropriate picture takes you to the area that is labeled beneath it, such as News, Products, Services and support, and so on. And you also have a text display option, if the graphical images take too long to display on your PC.

Intel

URL address: **http://www.intel.com**

Because Apple Computer is listed here, it is only fair that Intel be represented as well (see fig. 36.9). This Web site provides a useful resource for information about Intel's existing line of products, including the latest Pentium chips, along with useful technical information that will interest both manufacturers and users.

In addition to information about CPU technology (which gets most of the attention), you can also look up reports about other Intel technological achievements, such as the PCI bus—the expansion slot protocol that's being embraced by many computer makers, including Apple.

FIG. 36.8
IBM's home page takes the paper metaphor to its logical conclusion.

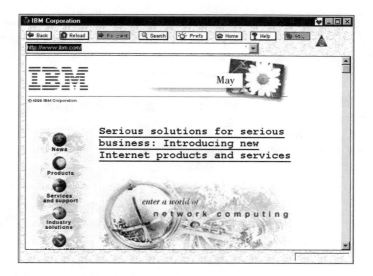

FIG. 36.9
At Intel's Web site, the out-of-focus graphic is deliberate.

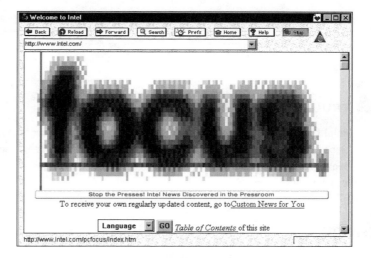

Power Computing Corporation

URL address: **http://www.powercc.com**

The first firm to license the Mac operating system was a young upstart company named Power Computing. The firm recruited a number of former Apple employees plus experienced computer engineers and marketing people from a variety of companies and began producing Mac-compatible computers in 1995. Its WWW site (see fig. 36.10) not only provides a catalog of its product line, but you can actually use it to price out your new computer. Armed with this information, you can place your order direct from its order center, or buy from a local dealer.

FIG. 36.10
Learn about Power Computing's line of Mac OS compatible computers here.

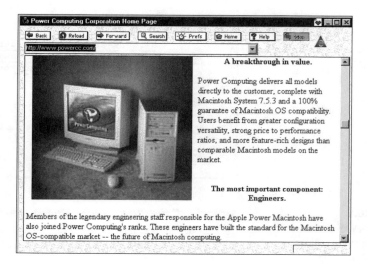

TROUBLESHOOTING

Help! I can't get to the World Wide Web site you described in your book. The Web is a fluid place, and sites are always being added, removed, and changed. If a site address shown in this book is no longer correct, use the Yahoo search site, described at the end of this chapter, to locate a site's correct URL.

Microsoft

URL address: **http://www.microsoft.com**

Microsoft's Web site will be valuable not only to PC users, but also those who own an Apple Macintosh, because Microsoft's software is so popular on both computing platforms. You'll find this site (see fig. 36.11) a helpful resource for further information on both Windows-related issues and matters concerning the publisher's popular productivity software, such as Excel and Word. You'll learn about the newest software versions of your favorite products. You'll also find useful technical information that will help you solve common software-related conflicts, as well as increase your productivity and teach you to use certain features much more effectively than ever before. There are extra results to help guide you if you're converting to Windows 95.

FIG. 36.11
Microsoft's Web site offers support and information about its products.

Novell, Inc.

URL address: **http://www.novell.com**

Novell (see fig. 36.12) is the well-known publisher of networking software for both the Macintosh and the Windows environments. The company's Web site takes full advantage of the terrific graphics you can create on the World Wide Web. When you first reach the home page, you'll see a library in cyberspace that represents support services. If you need support for a particular product, click the title that interests you. There are icons that represent different products in the company's line, and a set of buttons at the bottom of the page that take you to different areas of the Web-based services.

A Visit to Bug Net

URL address: **http://www.bugnet.com/~bugnet**

Bugs are the bane of all personal computer users. So many hardware and system setups, combined with thousands of kinds of software, create many sources of trouble for you. The folks who put together Bug Net have set up a database of bugs and solutions (if any). So, if and when your computer starts acting up and crashing when you least expect it (probably when you're on a deadline), pay a visit to Bug Net (see fig. 36.13).

FIG. 36.12
Pay a visit to Novell, Inc.'s Internet-based support facility.

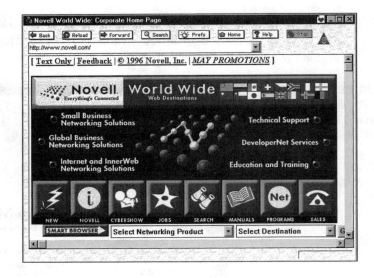

FIG. 36.13
Here's where you can find out whether one software product is compatible with another.

Ziff-Davis

URL address: **http://www.ziff.com**

Many of you are probably regular readers of some of the various Ziff-Davis computer magazines (see fig. 36.14), such as *MacUser*, *PC User*, *MacWeek*, and *PC Week*. The publisher's Web site offers a colorful repository of the latest material from all of these publications. If you want to read more about the newest software from Microsoft, or a hot announcement about a new computer from Apple, or the latest Pentium chip from Intel, you'll find navigating through the Ziff-Davis area to be really simple. You'll also want to take a little time to check out some of the popular benchmarking software products from this source, such as MacBench, which is used by owners of the Apple Macintosh to determine how well their computers perform.

FIG. 36.14
The popular Web site run by Ziff-Davis.

Educational Resources

A huge number of educationally oriented institutions have realized the benefit of providing information and support through the World Wide Web. You'll find that your local college or university might already have a Web server lurking somewhere in a computer lab. And it should come as no surprise that many of the major museums and scientific laboratories are similarly represented. After you whet your Internet surfing appetite by visiting the sites described next, you'll probably be eager to explore additional resources. It's recommended that you read the section "Searching for Additional Sites," near the end of this chapter, about techniques for seeking out other popular Web sites.

The Franklin Institute Science Museum

URL address: **http://sln.fi.edu**

If you've ever wanted to take a trip to Philadelphia to explore some of the educational exhibits, you'll definitely want to visit the Franklin Institute (see fig. 36.15). I remember the first trip I took to this museum, when I lived for several years in the Philadelphia suburbs more years ago than I care to remember. Of course, in those years, there were no personal computers, online services, or a World Wide Web. The museum has definitely stayed abreast of the latest technological developments, and its Web facility enables you to tap the huge range of information resources. You can look up books and publications and learn about upcoming exhibits. You can take a virtual visit to this museum or, using the various visitor services resources, plan an in-person trip. There's also an interactive multimedia file that you can download and use to experience a short, colorful visit to the museum, complete with sound and motion.

FIG. 36.15
Visit one of the major science museums without ever leaving your home or office.

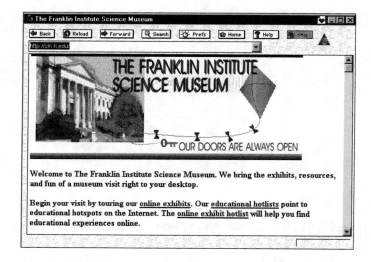

Indiana University

URL address: **http://www.indiana.edu**

Indiana University is just one of a growing number of educational institutions to provide Internet access. By clicking the appropriate hypertext links at this site (see fig. 36.16), you can learn more about the educational programs offered by this institution and visit any or all of its eight campuses. The Internet is widely represented here, and you'll find a wealth of information about a wide variety of subjects, some educational, some just entertaining, such as the news of the day, the weather, plus the various library resources. You also can easily access all the available Internet-based servers, which cover just about every department.

FIG. 36.16
Indiana University's home page is your gateway to learning more about the institution's extensive programs.

National Aeronautics and Space Administration (NASA)

URL address: **http://www.nasa.gov**

If you continue to be amazed at man's efforts to explore the vast reaches of space, you'll want to visit NASA's Web site (see fig. 36.17). By clicking the hypertext links shown, you can get information on a host of subjects. You'll learn the latest about space shuttle exploits and other efforts at space exploration. The increasing cooperative efforts with the former Soviet Union are often covered here. You can also read about NASA's strategies for the future and receive a full directory of additional information resources. If you want to explore further space-related topics, click the NASA Information Sources by Subject listing, which provides additional Web pages you'll want to explore during your travels through the Internet. You'll often find that clicking entries such as this one introduces a huge range of areas to visit.

FIG. 36.17
NASA's Web site offers a wealth of information about the U.S. space program.

Web Sites Devoted to Entertainment

It can be a special-interest club or a site devoted strictly to fans of a particular television network or even a particular show, but the growth in this area of the World Wide Web is proceeding at an extraordinary rate. The following listings represent self-interest in part, though I've tried to include a few sites that I thought others would like too. Even if a particular site doesn't seem to be too interesting to you, sometimes a quick trip to your AOL browser reveals related areas that you want to know more about.

The Internet Movie Database

URL address: **http://www.msstate.edu/Movies**

This popular Web site (see fig. 36.18) can be thought of as a trivia lover's delight. It's a graphical front-end to an active UseNet newsgroup, rec.arts.movies. Here you can read an active discussion about some of your favorite movies, popular actors, plots, sets, and trivia of all sorts. If you want to know the entire cast of the original version of *Dracula* or who the first person was to portray the Shadow in a movie serial, you enter the subject of your search to access a huge library of movie-related information, consisting of literally tens of thousands of entries. No doubt you'll want to read the newsgroup discussions as well. In these discussions, you'll find additional information that has yet to be recorded in a database, plus messages about upcoming flicks and quick reviews of some new movies you'll want to check before you pack up the family and drive to the local cinema.

FIG. 36.18
A Web site devoted
entirely to motion picture
entertainment information.

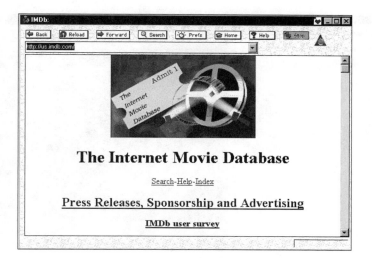

The Howard Stern Show

URL address: **http://www.urshan.com/stern/**

Here's a Web site devoted to the self-proclaimed "King of All Media" (see fig. 36.19). Howard has been praised and vilified (sometimes by the same people) for a radio show that can be irritating, controversial, exciting, funny, or none of the above. The syndicated show is heard in several dozen major cities across the United States, and a television version is shown nightly on the E! Entertainment cable television network. Although this site is not actually run by Stern or those connected with his show, it's a good resource to keep up to date on what he's up to. As I was writing this book, he was hard at work on a movie, in fact.

Lois & Clark

URL address: **http://www.webcom.com/lnc/**

OK, here's the scene. A young and beautiful investigative reporter for a great metropolitan newspaper gets involved with a handsome, bespectacled young man who has a penchant for putting on a red and blue uniform and flying off into the night. Sounds like the stuff dreams are made of, right? ABC's *Lois and Clark* (see fig. 36.20) provides a unique twist to the Superman legend, which keeps fans coming back week after week. This site and the section of AOL's ABC Online forum devoted to the show are quite popular indeed.

FIG. 36.19
Where radio has never gone before (and may never go again): *The Howard Stern Show.*

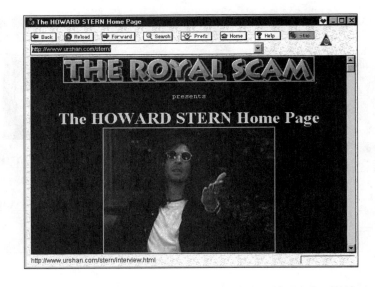

FIG. 36.20
Who is that man who flies in the skies with the greatest of ease?

Star Trek: Voyager

URL address: **http://voyager.paramount.com/VoyagerIntro.html**

There are many WWW sites devoted to *Star Trek*, but I hunted up only one of them, sponsored by producers, Paramount Pictures (see fig. 36.21). Even when these shows finally go off the air, one expects that these resources will still be available as fans continue to exchange information, photos, and other memorabilia. But right now, interest in *Star Trek* shows no sign of abating, and this is one WWW locale you'll want to visit often.

FIG. 36.21
Star Trek Voyager finds a home on the World Wide Web.

The Web site devoted to this program offers information about past episodes, the cast and crew, and the strange and wonderful beings who appeared on the show. It also enables you to experience some of the finest moments of the program, and it offers insights into new developments (such as possible future movie projects) that will interest all Trekkies, and probably anyone interested in exciting family entertainment.

A Trip to The Gate

URL address: **http://www.sfgate.com/**

The Gate is a Web site (see fig. 36.22) that is run by the publishers of the *San Francisco Chronicle* and the *San Francisco Examiner*. It is very much an online daily newspaper, with separate departments devoted to each aspect or section of the daily newspaper. There are also special areas established on this Web site, such as The Gate Conferences, where you can engage in an interactive chat with other online visitors and the staff of these newspapers, and The Internet On The Gate, which is devoted to articles of special interest to users of online services in general, and Internet surfers in particular. Another department you'll want to check out is San Francisco On The Gate, which has information that will appeal to both residents and visitors to that city.

FIG. 36.22
San Francisco's major
newspapers are represented
on The Gate.

At the time this chapter was written, The Gate was very much in a state of construction. One text item found there said that in six months, some parts of the site will change so much that they won't be recognizable. One feature that will be of special interest is a search function, one that you can use to examine specific items of interest in past issues of both the *Chronicle* and the *Examiner*.

The Young and the Restless

URL address: **http://ourworld.compuserve.com/homepages/mgraham/**

The plot of the typical television soap opera is often difficult to describe in a pithy paragraph or two, so I won't even try. *The Young and the Restless* (see fig. 36.23) has been on the air for more than 20 years. It involves the lives of dozens of characters whose activities intermingle in many related (and sometimes unrelated) story lines. If you are a follower of this program, you'll find a complete description of some of the most popular story lines, learn about the doings of your favorite characters, and locate descriptions about what you might expect in future shows.

Besides learning about what the cast and crew are doing on the show, you'll learn something about the private lives of your favorite stars too. And if you aren't a fan of this program, you'll find other daytime dramas represented on the Web, such as *Days of Our*

Lives, *General Hospital*, and the *Bold and the Beautiful*. During my Web travels in preparation for this book, I also located a Web site dedicated to fans of a New Zealand-based soap opera, *Shortland Street* (a program that hadn't spread to the states when this book was being written).

FIG. 36.23
Fans of the *Young and the Restless* will find lots to read about here.

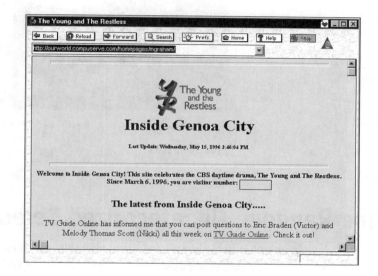

The X-Files

URL address: **http://www.rutgers.edu/x-files.html**

The Fox television program *The X-Files* (see fig. 36.24) is most definitely a cult classic, garnering popularity in the tradition of such shows as *Star Trek* and *Dr. Who*. *The X-Files* details the exploits of two FBI agents who choose to investigate weird or unusual cases that might involve UFO visitation or psychic phenomena—ghosts and things that go bump in the night. This Web page enables you to download sounds from the program, learn about past and future episodes, read summaries about the premise of the show (in case you haven't seen it before), and read enough information (some of it quite obscure) to win almost any trivia contest. During my first visit to this site, I downloaded the theme song of the show, which sounds quite good on any personal computer with a decent sound system.

In addition to exploring the nooks and crannies of this Web site, you'll find links to other sites as well that are dedicated to *X-File*-related material.

FIG. 36.24
Learn about the most
popular episodes of the Fox
TV show *The X-Files.*

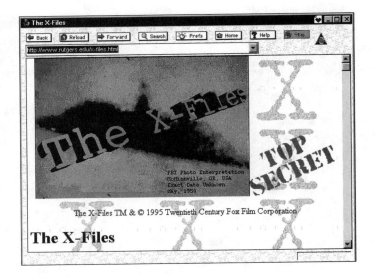

Some Random, Uncategorized Selections

This listing, as with others shown here so far, attempts to provide only a brief overview to whet your curiosity about the possibilities of the World Wide Web. The following entries don't fit into any specific category but are worth visiting because of either the interface or the depth of resources.

The Central Intelligence Agency

URL address: **http://www.odci.gov/cia**

What's this, a Web site devoted to the Central Intelligence Agency (see fig. 36.25)? Nope, you won't find any top-secret information here, but you will find online publications about the agency's mission and place in the world. One useful resource is the *Factbook on Intelligence,* which you can read while visiting the Web site. It tells of the CIA's early history and informs you about the setup of its headquarters, or at least as much as can be described without actually compromising national security. The Factbook is indexed by topic, and just clicking the appropriate item brings up additional information. One topic worth reading about is entitled "Key Events in CIA's History."

FIG. 36.25
Learn about the CIA by
visiting its Web site.

Planet Earth Home Page

URL address: **http://www.nosc.mil/planet_earth/images.html**

Here's an exciting way to travel across the world via artwork, photos, picture postcards, and more. Planet Earth (see fig. 36.26) provides easy access to a vast resource of fascinating information, from major cities to remote corners of the world. That's why it's called a "virtual library," and by accessing its many links, you'll be thrust into an endless journey that will be fun and educational.

FIG. 36.26
The images of the world
are just a click or two
away at this WWW
resource.

One handy way of getting around is a floor plan that was established to get you quickly to the places you want to visit. It looks very much like the floor plan of a new home, with the resources you want to tap clearly labeled.

The Institution of Egyptian Art and Archaeology

URL address: **http://www.memst.edu/egypt/main.html**

When you visit this museum, either by traveling to Memphis, Tennessee, or by traveling through cyberspace (see fig. 36.27), you'll quickly realize that archaeology isn't just the subject matter of Indiana Jones movies. Although the reality might not be quite the thrill-a-minute adventure that the motion pictures depict, learning about past cultures and their achievements can be exciting in itself. Among the features offered is a color tour of Egypt, which presents brilliant color photographs and informative descriptions about this fascinating land and its incredible history. You also can view photographs and read about the museum's exhibits, which cover many aspects of ancient Egyptian culture.

FIG. 36.27
An online tour of ancient Egypt by virtue of the World Wide Web.

Library of Congress

URL address: **http://lcweb.loc.gov/homepage/lchp.html**

As you probably know, the Library of Congress maintains an active forum on America Online. In Chapter 25, "Learning and Reference," this Library and other educational resources are detailed. Because the Library is very much involved with the cutting edge of technology, it should come as no surprise to learn that it also maintains an active presence on the World Wide Web (see fig. 36.28). The Library's home page resembles the card catalog file and voluminous shelves at your local library, except that it's much more comprehensive than many local facilities. You can access information about your favorite books or learn about current exhibits that you might want to check out should you decide to journey to the facilities of the Library of Congress in Washington, D.C.

FIG. 36.28
The Library of Congress home page is just a starting point for what may become a fascinating educational experience.

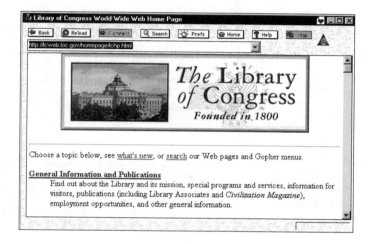

Searching for Additional Sites

URL address: **http://www.Yahoo.com**

Out of so many thousands of available WWW sites, this chapter can only scratch the surface. New sites are being added almost daily, covering all sorts of interests from commercial to lifestyle-related. No doubt you'll want to find a way to look up additional sites that you might want to visit, and the Yahoo Web site (see fig. 36.29) is one handy way to do this.

Having learned how to search for data on America Online, you'll find using Yahoo's Web facility to be similar. If you want to seek out sites dealing with a specific topic, simply click the underlined item representing the category. Or you can click the Search item and look up Web sites devoted strictly to a specific topic (see fig. 36.30). After you have found the area you want to visit, you can click the underlined reference to transport you directly to that site.

FIG. 36.29
Use Yahoo to search through a directory of thousands of Web sites.

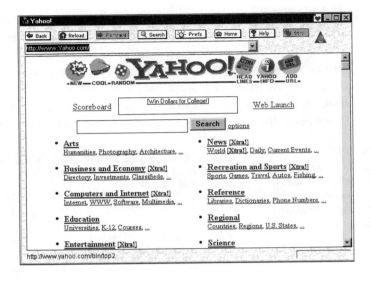

FIG. 36.30
Yahoo provides an efficient way to search for other Web sites that might warrant further exploration.

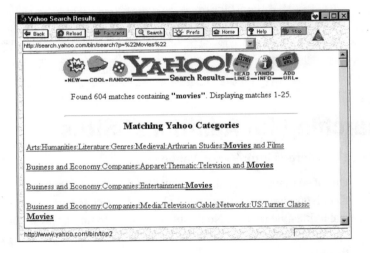

The popularity of the World Wide Web means that the lineup of available sites can change often, so you'll want to examine the Yahoo database regularly to find out about sites that might warrant further visitation.

From Here...

The World Wide Web can be a useful resource where you'll spend many, many enjoyable hours learning more about your favorite subject, locating software updates, or discovering ways to use your computer more effectively. Its bright, colorful interface represents the latest and best and perhaps easiest-to-use Internet resource. As you continue to use AOL's Web browser, you'll locate many additional sites you'll want to add to your list of favorites.

- For more information on using America Online's e-mail features, read Chapters 5, 6, and 10.

- For information on locating files on America Online, see Chapter 20, "Tips and Tricks on Finding Software."

- For information on how to be part of an Internet newsgroup, see Chapter 32, "Joining and Participating in Internet Newsgroups."

- And to keep up to date on America Online's fast-growing Internet connection, simply type the keyword **Internet** and explore the Internet Connection.

Introducing GNN: AOL's Internet-Based Online Service

America Online is a full-featured online service. In addition to offering easy Internet access, it provides 14 channels containing a huge number of forums, files, message boards, and conference areas. Even without checking out the Internet, America Online's range of features is so vast, you could spend literally weeks exploring it all and not be finished.

But what if you want just Internet access, nothing else? Just a World Wide Web browser, and programs to handle e-mail, newsgroup reading, and IRC? Well, America Online has an answer for you there too. It's called Global Network Navigator, or GNN for short. ∎

Learn about GNN
Explore America Online's new Internet-based online service.

What is GNN?
Take a look at GNN's exclusive program features.

How to get started
Learn how to install the software and join GNN.

How to tune up the software
Discover tips and tricks to get the best performance.

Where to find it on GNN
Take a quick look at a few of the services' hot spots.

What Is GNN?

GNN is America Online's dedicated Internet-only online provider. Unlike many of the Internet providers that have sprung up in recent years, GNN doesn't just plug you into the Internet without a safety net. The service offers its own software and a wide range of features that you can tap directly from its own site on the World Wide Web. In the next few pages, I'll let you in on some of the most important features of GNN, then we'll sign you up to the service and take a brief look at its offerings.

When you install your GNN software and set up your account, you'll find that four new programs have been installed on your hard drive in addition to the registration application. Each program has a handy toolbar that will let you easily switch from one component to the other simply by clicking the appropriate icon.

Let's look at the GNN programs and briefly cover what they do. I'll describe this in much more detail in Chapter 38, "A Look at GNN's Internet Software."

- *GNNconnect*. This is the telecommunications program used to select access numbers to the GNN network, adjust your modem settings, and actually make your GNN connection.

- *GNNworks*. This is the service's swift, multitasking World Wide Web browser. It forms the core of GNN's software. You can use it to visit your favorite WWW sites and download files from both WWW and FTP locations.

- *GNNmessenger*. This is GNN's mail and newsgroup client. The program is used to prepare, send, and receive your e-mail, and to handle your newsgroup reading.

- *GNNchat*. This program is used for Internet-based interactive sessions. Using IRC (see also Chapter 33, "Internet Chats"), you can participate in live, one-on-one conversations with fellow Net visitors. IRC is similar and yet not quite the same as AOL's own chats, as you'll see in Chapters 33 and 38.

The GNN software components also include a number of handy features to provide more efficient Internet performance and let you work with your other Windows 95 software. I'll cover just a few of them here:

- *Direct V.34 (28,800 bps) access*. Through the GNNNet and SprintNet access networks (using the same phone numbers you use to reach AOL), GNN lets you quickly reach the service from all over the USA, and many parts of Canada and other worldwide centers.

- *Multitasking and multithreading*. As with other Windows software, GNN's Web browser takes full advantage of multitasking and multithreading capabilities.

You can open multiple document windows (panes) with your GNN software, and work on other Windows programs while downloading files.

- *OLE 2.0 support*. GNNworks is fully OLE compliant, so you can easily link to other Windows programs.

- *Intelligent document caching*. Just as with AOL's own WWW browser, the artwork you download with GNN's software from the Internet is cached on your hard drive, so you can access it more quickly when you want to see it again.

- *Offline mail reading*. Just as you do with your AOL software, you can read and write your messages offline with your GNN software to keep your online bills as low as possible.

- *Card catalogs*. This feature can be used to build a personal collection of your favorite sites.

- *Winsock compliance*. You can use any Winsock-compatible program to run GNN sessions. This allows you to choose another WWW browser, such as Internet Explorer and Netscape, and other mail and newsgroup programs.

Part

VIII

Ch

37

How to Order GNN Software

GNN is using very much the same marketing techniques that made America Online so popular, which explains why it attracted hundreds of thousands of subscribers within just a few months.

Major computing magazines already carry ads for GNN. And the software disks are bundled in those magazines and sent via snail mail (I cannot tell you how many GNN disks I've put next to my AOL disks, and I was a charter subscriber to both services).

In case you don't have a disk handy, just call GNN at (800) 819-6112 and request a disk. If you cannot wait, you can download the latest version of GNN software **ftp.gnn.com**. After you download the software, however, you have to ring up GNN and request a certificate number and password. This information is needed for you to set up your new account (and it's done in very much the same fashion as you set up your AOL account, as you'll see shortly).

N O T E At the time this book was written, GNN had not released a Mac version of its software. The Mac edition of the GNN program suite could be out by the time you read this book, and installation instructions will (aside from the Windows specific information) be very much the same for you, too.

Installing GNN Software on Your PC (Windows Only)

The GNN software packet contains one floppy disk, but as you'll see a bit later on, that's not quite enough to get you all the components that make up the GNN software suite. If you download the file direct from GNN's FTP site, however, you'll get it all in one convenient package, and you won't have to wait a few minutes for a file download when you first join the service.

Installing your GNN software is very easy (you don't even have to use your Windows 95 Add/Remove Programs utility). If you've installed the Window's version of America Online's software on your PC, you'll find the entire process of installing the software and setting up an account is very similar.

Before you begin the installation, you'll want to make a backup of your original software disk. You'll also want to get ready to join the service, so with that in mind, you'll need to have the initial registration information you got in your software package or from GNN at hand. You need that information, which consists of a certificate name and password, to activate your account.

You'll also want to keep your credit card or checking account information handy so that you can provide the right information when you see the appropriate information prompts.

Now you're ready to get your GNN software up and running. Just follow these steps and you'll be online within a few minutes:

1. Insert the GNN floppy disk into your PC's floppy drive.
2. Click the Windows 95 Start button.
3. Choose Run.
4. Type **A:\SETUP.EXE**. (If you've simply downloaded the installer program to your PC, substitute "A:" with the correct drive label.)

Within a few seconds, the GNN installer program will be running (see fig. 37.1), and you'll be taken through several information screens to reflect the progress of the installation.

The installation process will take a few minutes to complete, and you see an ongoing progress bar that shows the files being installed on your computer (see fig. 37.2). Unless you choose to customize settings at the start of the installation to recognize a custom modem setup, you don't have to do anything during the installation but observe the march of the progress bar.

FIG. 37.1
If this screen looks familiar, it's because the installer program for GNN is very similar to the one used for AOL's Windows software.

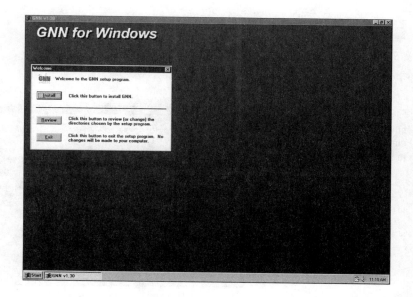

FIG. 37.2
As the installation progresses, you'll see the name of the component being installed above the progress bar.

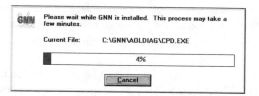

What you see on your Windows 95 desktop depends on whether you install from a floppy disk or a downloaded file. When the software installation process is done, the open GNN software directory window will contain two programs, GNNconnect and GNNregistration. The second program is used to help you create your new account. After you set up your account, you can use either GNNconnect or one of the other GNN programs to initiate your connection to the service.

If you install from a downloaded file, there will be five files in that program directory, the other three being the GNN components I mentioned earlier—for WWW browsing, e-mail and newsgroup reading, and IRC chats.

Don't worry about the whereabouts of those files if you installed from a floppy. I'll show you where they come into the picture later on in this chapter.

Establishing Your GNN Account

Before your new GNN software dials up the service, you'll be asked for your registration information (see fig. 37.3).

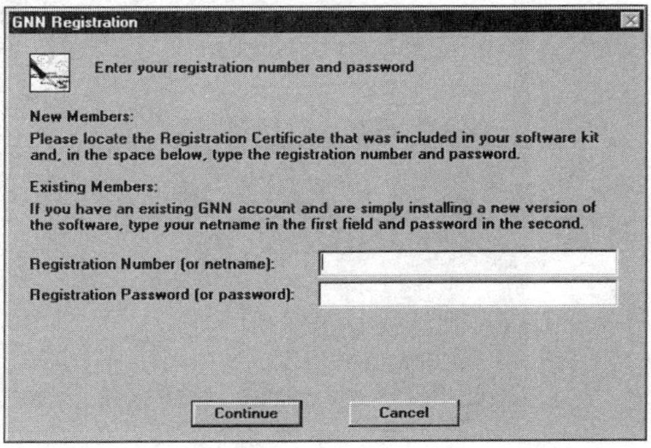

FIG. 37.3
Enter your registration number and password here to begin the sign-up process.

If you ever need to reinstall your GNN software, all you have to do is enter your network name (GNN's equivalent of an AOL screen name) and your password in the GNN registration screen to record your account information on your newly installed software.

If you are signing up as a new member, you'll be connected to GNN's 800 service number, and then you'll be taken through several information screens that will ask you the following:

- Your name and billing address
- Your billing information
- Your Network Name, which is GNN's equivalent of the screen name you have on America Online.

Finding a Connection

After you create your new account, the service will help you select a local access number located in your city. You'll see an information screen requesting your area code (see fig. 37.4) and any custom dialing information you need to include (such as a special dialing prefix).

After the number is dialed, a database will be consulted and within seconds you should see the list of access numbers in your city (see fig. 37.5). If the list looks familiar to you, it's because GNN uses the very same telephone network as America Online.

FIG. 37.4

Type your area code where requested, to get a listing of local GNN connection numbers.

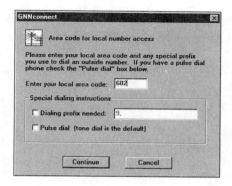

FIG. 37.5

Select your first local access number from this list.

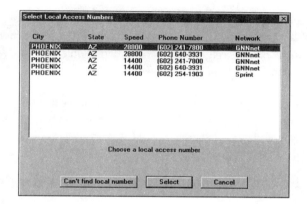

If you cannot locate a local number, click the Can't Find Local Number button to bring up a list of other choices. You'll have the option of picking a number from a nearby city or selecting GNN's extra-cost 800 phone service.

After your first number is selected, you'll be given the chance to select an alternate phone number, if one is available. GNN's software will then offer you a list of the phone numbers you picked, so you can change your mind if you want to make a different choice (see fig. 37.6). For now, if the numbers are the ones you wanted, click the Continue button.

There's one more screen you may see before you connect to that local number. If the COM port of your PC uses older hardware, you'll have the option of running a UART Compatibility Test, which is essentially a warning that older hardware may not be able to keep up with high-speed modems. If your PC is one of the newer models, though, you won't see this screen.

After you enter that information, you see a number of information prompts that ask for your name and address and other billing information. After you fill in the blanks, the final selection is the one where you can exert your creativity. You can select your own network name (also called a *screen name*), which will be used as your Internet mailing address.

FIG. 37.6
Here are the phone numbers GNN will use to provide direct access to the service.

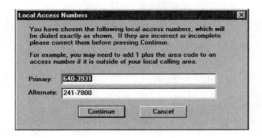

The most common choices in a network name are of course your own name, or your first name and last initial (my GNN net name is GeneS). Your Internet mailing address will thus be: *<networkname>*@gnn.com. The information after the @, or "at" symbol, represents GNN's Internet domain or address.

N O T E You cannot automatically use your AOL screen name for GNN because it's a separate online service. You have to make up a new one. You can try the same name you use on AOL, for simplicity's sake, assuming nobody has taken it yet. ■

Fast Tips on Setting Up Your Modem for Top Grade Performance

Right at the beginning of the software installation, GNN's connection software will take a quick peek at your modem and make a basic profile of its capabilities. The program isn't nearly as sophisticated as Windows 95's Modem Setup Wizard, and it'll usually select a generic setting, such as "Hayes Extended" for a high-speed modem, no matter which modem you have.

To get the best possible performance, you'll want to change this modem setting. Simply click the Modem menu of your GNNconnect software (or type Ctrl+M) to bring up a list of modem drivers (see fig. 37.7). Unless you have a very new or obscure make and model modem, you're likely to find one that matches the one you have. When you choose that modem driver and then click OK, it's stored in the program's settings. From then on, GNN's software will use that information to provide optimum connections to its network servers.

FIG. 37.7
Choose your modem file
from this handy screen.

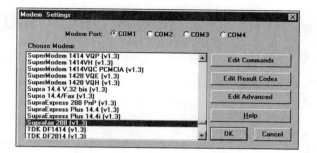

TROUBLESHOOTING

Help! My modem keeps disconnecting each time I try to run a GNN session. What's wrong?
Maybe you just need to set up GNN's software to work better with your modem. Just follow the
steps I have outlined in this section to configure the program for the make and model of the
modem you have. You may also want to check your Windows 95 modem settings to make sure
they are also adjusted to recognize your modem properly.

For more advice on getting the best performance from your modem (and this information
applies to GNN as well as to AOL), read Chapter 41, "Secrets of High-Speed Access on
AOL."

Choosing Access Numbers

When you first joined GNN, you were given a chance to select two local area access numbers.

If you move, or you're traveling, or you want to see if you can get a better connection with
another number, you'll want to obtain a new set of connection numbers. To do that, simply
click the Area Code for Local Number Access icon from the GNNconnect. Within seconds, you will be logged on to GNN's servers through an 800 phone number, and you will
be presented with a listing of available numbers in the area code you select. From that list,
you can make a new Network profile to offer you more access options.

 If you plan to access GNN from different locations (say your home or office or various places to
which you travel regularly), you can create a separate Network file for each to help speed up your
connections.

Part **VIII**

Ch **37**

Your First Visit to GNN—A Quick Tour of the Service

Even if you're an experienced traveler to the Internet via AOL, you'll want to spend your first visit or two to GNN touring the service to see the specific range of features that are offered.

Because the primary purpose of GNN is to get you Internet access, the range of content isn't near as comprehensive as the services you find on America Online. However, there are quite a number of areas of the service that you'll find unique for this sort of service.

 After you establish your GNN account, you can begin the logon process by launching any of the GNN programs, rather than the connection utility itself.

The remainder of this chapter describes some of the most popular GNN services. As you get comfortable with the service, you'll want to take some time to check these areas further. As with any of the major access services, GNN will be signing up many new information centers as the service grows, so you can be assured that what you see here is just the beginning.

 Because GNN's Web site is a public information center, you can also access it via AOL's WWW browser or any other browser.

Your visit to GNN begins with the opening screen (see fig. 37.8). From there, you can access a set of informative features that are exclusive to GNN's own Web site. Each of these services shown can be selected from GNN's home page.

 You can access a WWW site from GNN with a keyboard shortcut. Simply press Ctrl+U and then enter the URL you want to access, press the Enter key, and you'll see it on your computer's screen in seconds.

Because we're in a touring mood, let's take a quick run around the block, virtually speaking. To begin our visit, click the Map button at the lower left of GNN's main artwork, which brings up the screen shown in figure 37.9.

As a new visitor to the service, you'll want to take in a little of each of the sights, so let's begin by clicking the GNN Tour label (shown among Member Services). From there you'll see a full directory of services, and by clicking on the Next Page icon, you can commence your tour. For now, let's look at the What's On At GNN listing to help us select the next stop on our brief tour (see fig. 37.10).

FIG. 37.8
The day's highlights are shown when you access GNN's Home Page.

FIG. 37.9
From this vantage point, you can get an overview of GNN's range of services.

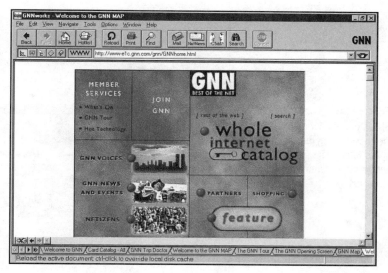

Find it Fast on GNN

One of GNN's most popular features is the Whole Internet Catalog (see fig. 37.11). It's the one resource that has made the company famous worldwide, and the name brings to mind the Whole Earth Catalog of the 1960s. And just like that publication, the Whole Internet Catalog is a vast, sprawling resource that you'll find endlessly valuable as you begin to explore the nooks and crannies of the Internet firsthand.

Having the Internet at your beck and call doesn't mean much, unless you can quickly find the information you want. Another of GNN's most popular search resources is WebCrawler (see fig. 37.12). You can call up a list of WebCrawler's Best of the Net recommendations in various categories, ranging from Arts and Entertainment to Recreation, or you can initiate a search on the topics you select.

FIG. 37.10
It would take a much larger screen than the one on my PC to list all of the features displayed on this screen.

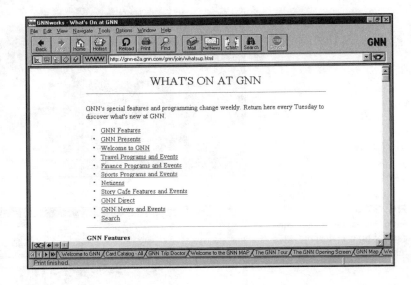

FIG. 37.11
GNN's popular Whole Internet Catalog puts many of the Internet's most important features at your fingertips.

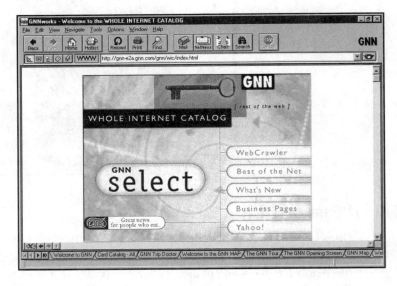

WebCrawler has a fast search engine that uses the very latest technology, a technology that is being used on America Online as well. So when you make a search request, you'll see the result within seconds, and you'll find that the results very accurately reflect the information you wanted.

Shopping and Current Events

Next up on our brief tour is GNN's Internet shopping service, GNNdirect (see fig. 37.13). With the development of comprehensive WWW security tools, the process of ordering merchandise on the Internet has become quite safe. I've even ordered merchandise from some of these online shopping malls myself (it sure beats navigating through the voice mail systems some firms offer). With GNNdirect, you'll be able to establish your own account to place orders directly with the services that have joined with GNN. Or you can quickly navigate to other Web-based shopping sources.

FIG. 37.12
WebCrawler is a sophisti-
cated Internet search engine
that makes fast work of your
search requests.

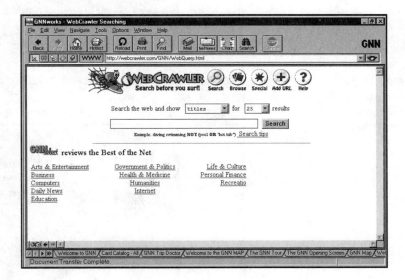

To conclude our brief tour, let's take a look at GNN's information service, News and Events (see fig. 37.14). From this starting point, you can read GNN's online newspaper. You can check the latest headlines courtesy of Reuters, or have a gander at the latest information from the world of sports. You'll also find topic headings for international news, and information from the worlds of politics and entertainment.

 TIP Here's more keyboard power to make your GNN session go faster: Use Ctrl+left arrow to return to a previously opened WWW page, and Ctrl+right arrow to go forward to the next page you've accessed.

FIG. 37.13

Online shopping is fast, safe, and fun on GNN via GNNdirect.

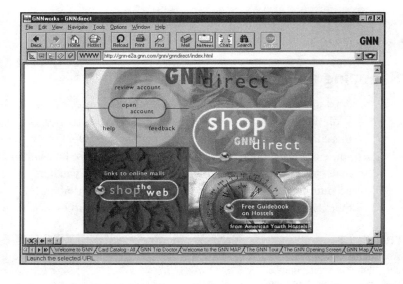

FIG. 37.14

Here's GNN's comprehensive news service, providing the latest news, updated regularly each and every day.

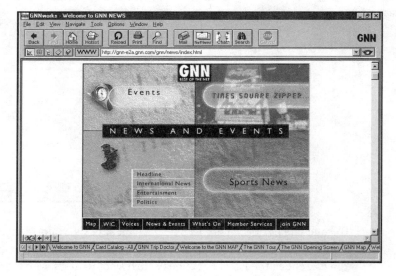

You can look at the Internet as a large, circular chain. Each information site can link you to another information site, or back to where you actually started. In addition to the local content described in this chapter, GNN gets you easy access to the entire worldwide Internet. Simply click a title or icon, and you're instantly transported to the place you've selected.

If you want to print text you see in a GNN document window for later reference, simply click the Print icon in your GNN software (or File, Print). The active document window will be printed. If you haven't set up your printer yet, you'll first see a dialog box prompting you to set up your printer before printing can proceed.

 TROUBLESHOOTING

When I connect to GNN, I notice the images on their WWW site don't match the ones in this book. Why? The World Wide Web is a fluid place, and service providers are always changing their look and feel to attract more people to their sites. This is normal, and you shouldn't be alarmed if things don't look quite the same as pictured in this book.

 You can easily return to a place you've visited with GNN's browser simply by clicking the appropriate folder tab at the bottom of the browser screen. The left and right arrows at the bottom will take you to tabs that have scrolled off your screen.

Part VIII

Ch 37

From Here...

Because GNN, like America Online, offers a trial membership with a decent number of free hours, you may just want to join the service and test it out. As I said earlier in this chapter, GNN represents a different sort of Internet experience from the one provided on America Online. And having more than one online option is very common these days.

In fact, many of us have accounts at both AOL and GNN to experience the best each service has to offer.

In this chapter, we've signed you up to GNN and taken a brief tour of the service. No doubt you'll want to spend more time now learning the ins and outs of their WWW browser, and the software that handles your e-mail, newsgroup reading, and IRC chatting. These software components are abundant with features to simplify your net access. I'll cover all of that and more in Chapter 38, "A Look at GNN's Internet Software."

A Look at GNN's Internet Software

Chapter 37, "Introducing GNN: AOL's Internet-Based Online Service," took you through the process of joining the service and taking your first visit to GNN's WWW site. Now having become accustomed to the special features GNN offers you, it's time to get the most mileage out of the new software you've installed. ■

> **CAUTION**
>
> At the time this book was written, GNN was not available for Macintosh users (unless you have a Mac with a DOS card or Insignia Solutions' SoftWindows software installed). A Mac version, however, may appear by the time you read this book, and you can expect many of the Windows-based features I'm describing in this chapter will apply to the Mac version as well, just as the Mac and Windows versions of AOL's regular software provide a similar look and feel.

Using GNN's World Wide Web Browser

When you first sign on to GNN using the GNNconnect program, you're given three options as to what software you want to use to begin your session (see fig. 38.1). The first option is probably the one you'll use most frequently, GNNworks.

FIG. 38.1
Choose the software you want to open to begin your GNN visit here.

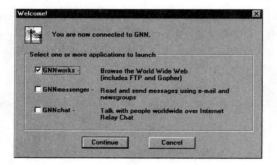

TROUBLESHOOTING

Hey, wait a minute! When I installed my GNN software from a floppy disk, I saw just two icons in the directory created for that program. Where's all this other stuff coming from? Did I do my installation wrong? When you install your GNN software from a floppy disk, there's not enough room on the disk to contain the files for all of GNN's programs. So there's an additional process that must be completed before you can start to experience GNN's services. You'll have to download the rest of the software, which happens right after you've signed on with your brand-new account.

When you connect to GNN, the host computer will receive a message from the connect utility if you don't have all of the software installed (those host computers can be really smart). In that case, you'll see an information prompt that you must select to begin the final file transfer process. Once you've accepted the download, all the remaining GNN software components will be transferred to your computer and placed in the GNN program folder. The process will usually take from 10 to 20 minutes—but, of course, you won't need to go through this download if you downloaded the installer program direct from GNN.

To use all that new software, you need to end your session once again, repeat the log on process, and select the program module you want to use for your initial connection.

GNNworks is a full-featured browser program that offers you speedy access to your favorite WWW sites. Through its convenient toolbar (see fig. 38.2) you're able to quickly access other GNN features without having to launch any of the other programs—they'll be opened when necessary.

FIG. 38.2
The clearly labeled GNNworks toolbar lets you quickly navigate throughout the World Wide Web.

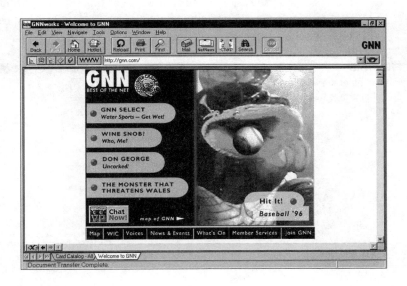

 If you don't have this book handy during your GNN session and you need to know what a particular button in the toolbar does, just place the mouse pointer over the button to see its label. To see a full description of the function in the status bar, press and hold down the left mouse button.

Using GNN's E-Mail Reader

Sending e-mail to your friends and business associates around the world is one of the joys of Internet service, and GNN's e-mail reader is an extremely flexible tool that makes the task truly simple.

If you're experienced with the e-mail functions of Netscape, you'll find the basic layout of the message window looks a bit familiar to you.

If you want to get right down to the business of writing e-mail, just launch the GNNmessenger program directly by double-clicking the program icon. Or, if you are already working in another GNN program, click the Mail button from the toolbar to bring the e-mail program to the front. The first thing you see is your GNNmessenger In Box, which displays a list of the e-mail you've received since your last visit. During your session, your software frequently checks GNN's mail servers for new mail, and you see your display updated if new e-mail has arrived.

If you have a color monitor, you'll see a little red box next to your unread mail. Just double-click the appropriate directory listing to open your e-mail. After you've read your message, you can respond to it simply by clicking the Reply window, which brings up a document window showing the text of the message you've just read, with standard Internet quote marks (see fig. 38.3).

FIG. 38.3
You can enter the text of your e-mail message below the quoted text.

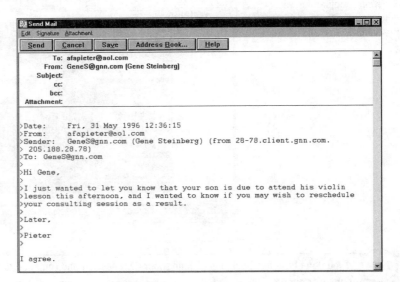

Another important e-mail option is activated by the Forward button. That function lets you send the original e-mail, along with any comments you care to make, to another recipient or group of recipients.

One of the most convenient features of GNN's e-mail reader is the Address Book function, which allows you to keep a handy Rolodex of your regular contacts. Once you've written your e-mail message, click the Address Book button to bring up this list (see fig. 38.4).

FIG. 38.4
GNNmessenger's Address Book is a place where you can make your personal file of frequent Internet contacts.

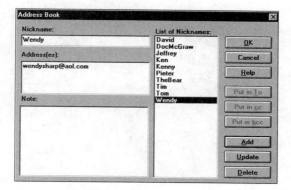

That's just the beginning. You have a full range of useful features in GNNmessenger. Here are some of them:

- As with other e-mail services, your standard GNN e-mail message includes a To line, for the recipient; the From line, where your GNN e-mail address is shown, and a Subject line.

- If you're responding to an existing message, the subject of that message will be listed in the subject line, preceded by "Re."

- You can send a carbon copy of your message to another recipient or group of recipients by entering their e-mail addresses next in the cc: field.

- You may prefer to use the blind carbon copy (bcc) feature, which hides the names of anyone other than the actual recipient in the message.

- You can also attach a file to your GNN e-mail. If the recipient of the message is on another service, you may want to contact them in case they need a special translator program to be able to use the file you send.

- If you want to keep your e-mail on hand, you can Save it, which will store the messages in a File Box for later retrieval.

Getting There Again Is Half the Fun

Over time, you'll begin to build up a list of your favorite sites, ones you want to visit over and over again. Your GNNworks software offers a convenient way to create your own customized list of your favorite sites that you can easily access during your online sessions (see fig. 38.5). It's called a Hotlist, and it's reminiscent of the Favorite Places feature of your AOL software (or the Hotlist in older versions of AOL's Macintosh WWW browser).

FIG. 38.5
Use a Hotlist for fast access
to your favorite Internet-
based areas, whether on
GNN's own site or elsewhere.

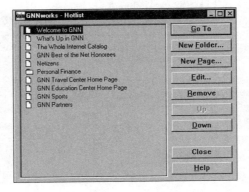

Here's how to make your own Hotlist:

1. Be sure the document representing the site you want to add is active by clicking anywhere in that document window.

2. Click the Navigate menu and choose Add to Hotlist.

3. Choose File, Close.

From now on, whenever you want to access that site, simply click the Hotlist button on the toolbar of your GNNworks program, and you'll see a handy list of your favorite places. You'll also see some other documents listed there, representing areas specially selected by GNN's own staff for you to check out further.

 Need assistance in using your GNN software? Simply press the F1 key to bring up a comprehensive Help menu that offers answers to most of the questions you may have.

TROUBLESHOOTING

Why are some of my favorite WWW sites no longer available? What am I doing wrong?
Sometimes the inability to communicate with a WWW site just indicates a network problem with GNN's host computer network, or a problem with the site's own server computers. But it's a sure thing that many Web sites will disappear or change their URL addresses over time. If you find you cannot locate a particular site you've accessed previously, you can use GNN's search tools (such as Yahoo and WebCrawler) to find the current site address.

Using GNN's UseNet Newsgroups Reader

In Chapter 32, "Joining and Participating in Internet Newsgroups," I described one of the Net's most popular features, newsgroups. Integrated with your GNNmessenger software is a newsgroup reader, which lets you subscribe and participate in those freewheeling message boards with a simple, user-friendly interface.

To access GNN's newsgroup feature, just click the NetNews button that you find on the GNNmessenger or GNNworks software. It brings up the News Box, which allows you to access any newsgroup available from GNN's host computer.

When you first install your software, you'll already have a small list of newsgroups GNN has selected for you, as shown in the Subscribed directory at the left of your GNNmessenger News Box (see fig. 38.6).

FIG. 38.6
Here are some of my favorite newsgroups, selected by way of GNNmessenger.

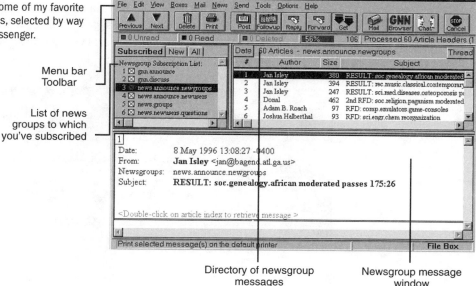

Menu bar
Toolbar

List of news groups to which you've subscribed

Directory of newsgroup messages

Newsgroup message window

When you click the name of your newsgroup, you see the listing of the unread articles on the right. Once the list is displayed on your computer, just double-click the article index to bring up the message on your screen. And once again, if you're familiar with Netscape, you'll find this sort of display has a similar layout.

Your newsgroup messages are grouped by thread (topic), so that you can quickly scroll to the ones that interest you.

If you decide you want to subscribe to another newsgroup, you can click the All tab at the top right of your News Box, which brings up a list of the available newsgroups.

Because there are thousands of available newsgroups, your initial effort to bring up the list will take a few minutes to finish. As you scroll through the list, just click the check box adjacent to a newsgroup's title to subscribe to that newsgroup (or uncheck the ones you no longer want). The next time you open GNN's newsreader, only the newsgroups to which you've subscribed will show in the list, and it'll take only seconds to display.

The New tab brings up a list of newsgroups added since your last visit to GNN.

T I P You can jump quickly from one GNN document to another simply by clicking the appropriately labeled tab at the bottom of the document window.

After you've read one message, you can go right to the next one, which will display on your screen in seconds.

If you are aching to answer that message, you can either reply via e-mail to the message's sender, or directly to the newsgroup itself (see fig. 38.7). Messages can be deleted one at a time, or as a group. To get rid of all the messages at once, choose Purge All Articles from the News menu.

FIG. 38.7
GNN's software displays nearly the same message window format (at the bottom) to send a newsgroup message as to send e-mail.

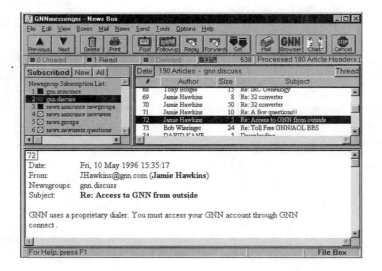

T I P You can also use the GNNworks browser window to access a newsgroup. Just click the URL text field, enter the name of the newsgroup in the exact Internet format (news://[newsgroup name]), and the contents of the unread messages are then transferred to your computer.

Although most newsgroup messages are all text, some are in binary form. You'll know that because the message itself displays a blue triangle next to the title in the message index. If the files are in binary form, your GNNmessenger software can decode it automatically; you don't have to reconfigure the software (unless you want to turn off the feature to automatically translate such files).

Using GNN's IRC Software

In Chapter 33, "Internet Chats," I told you about one of the most exciting features of the Internet—the capability to have a one-to-one conversation in real time. GNN provides fast access to Internet Relay through your GNNchat software.

> **CAUTION**
>
> Although the Internet can sometimes be a free-for-all, you should always be on your best behavior. Show respect to others, refrain from using vulgar language, and resist the temptation to get involved in a "flamefest," which is the Internet equivalent of having a shouting match. And, remember, GNN offers a Terms of Service similar to AOL's.

When you first access GNN's IRC server, you are given a nickname, which is based on the first nine characters of your network name. If that name is already taken, you are asked to choose a different name.

Each available chat group is listed as a channel in the Channels dialog box (see fig. 38.8). The listing is grouped into titles that roughly describe the topics under discussion.

FIG. 38.8
Here's a list of current chats available, along with the number of people actually participating in each one.

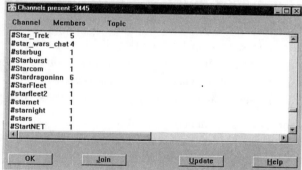

To join a specific chat, simply select a Channel by clicking its name once; then click the Join button. Within seconds, you'll be off to a world of exciting conversations about subjects in which you're interested.

As you see an IRC chat in progress, you'll want to jump in and make some comments yourself. To do that, simply type your message in the Outgoing Messages field, and then press Enter to send it on its way.

In seconds, you'll see your nickname appear in the chat window and your comments will appear to the right of it. From time to time, you'll also see comments from members whose network name has an "@" before it. That member is the Channel operator or host (very much like one of America Online's own forum staff members).

Your GNNchat software also lets you chat and exchange files with another person without having to use the IRC network feature. To send a private message to another user, simply click the Private button on the GNNchat program's toolbar. You then see a message window similar to an e-mail window where you can enter the nickname of the person you want to contact and then the body of the message.

To send files, you need to set up what's called a *Direct Client Connection*. To start that process, choose Options, DCC Send and enter the name of the file you want to transfer in the Send File field. The recipient's nickname should be entered in the To field. If you're not sure of the name and path of the file, use the Browse feature to locate it on your computer's hard drive.

> **CAUTION**
>
> Internet Relay Chats are not governed by the rules of conduct that you find on a regular online service, such as America Online. Discussions can be freewheeling, and even over-the-top in terms of the use of language and discussions about erotica. Expect the unexpected, and be careful about allowing your children to access these features of your GNN software.

Searching Databases and Transferring Files via GNN

A WWW page is quite a flexible document. As I explain in Chapter 35, "Using the World Wide Web," access to other Internet features, such as FTP or Gopher database searching, is almost seamless. Under normal circumstances, you do not have to follow any special steps to use these features; just click the appropriate underlined title or button on a particular WWW page. When you do that, you access the FTP or Gopher sites automatically.

If you want to access a particular site directly, just press Ctrl+U, and enter the correct URL (using a "gopher" or "ftp" prefix as needed). Then press Enter to quickly bring up the service (assuming it's active, of course).

 If you decide that you don't want to download a file being transferred during your GNN session, simply click the Cancel button (in the toolbar) while the file transfer is taking place. In just seconds, the file transfer will stop.

GNN Power User Settings

As with AOL's regular access software, GNN's software components are quite powerful indeed. After a few sessions of getting used to the service, you'll want to look for ways to make your visits more productive. That's the time to begin to fine-tune the software to work best for you. In the following section, I'll cover some of the most important settings you'll want to use with GNNworks, because most of the settings lie with that component. As you continue to work with the software, you'll find additional settings that will make the GNN software more effective.

First, let's customize GNNworks, using the Options, Preferences menu:

- *User Tab*. Here's where you can change your connection information for both the GNNworks and GNNmessenger software components (see fig. 38.9). You can enter such things as your business or personal affiliations as part of this description. You can also specify a directory on your computer's drive in which to store files transferred to your computer from the service.

FIG. 38.9
Your basic user settings can be established here. The e-mail and news host settings are created automatically when you join GNN and shouldn't be changed.

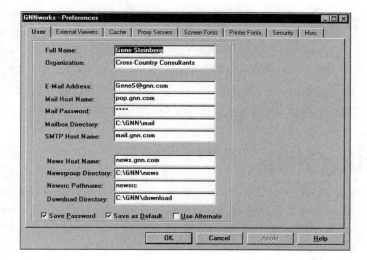

CAUTION
Although the E-Mail and News Host settings shown in fig. 38.9 look similar to those offered by other Internet providers, you cannot access GNN except through the proprietary software offered by the service. The firewall (or security system) established by GNN's host computer network will not allow connection through any other online service.

- *External Viewers*. You can use this feature to associate other programs with files you download during your visits to GNN. For example, you can use a painting program to handle bitmap (BMP) files.
- *Cache*. As explained earlier in this chapter, the WWW pages and other items you download from GNN are saved to your computer's hard drive to speed retrieval next

time you visit a WWW site. You can use this setting to control the amount of hard drive space you specify as a cache for these documents. When that space is filled, the oldest pages are automatically deleted.

- *Proxy Servers*. You can use this setting to select a different home page to access when you first connect to GNN (perhaps one representing a favorite site or a business you're connected with). You can also use these settings to set up the appearance and size of the document windows that display on your computer.

- *Screen Fonts*. You can use these settings to change the fonts in which documents and card catalogs are displayed on your screen. Only the fonts that appear on your screen are changed; the fonts that appear in your printed documents are not changed. For that you need printer fonts (see the next item).

- *Printer Fonts*. You can use this feature to change the fonts used in the documents you print. And remember, the changes you make to your printed documents are not shown on the screen unless you make the same choices in the Screen Fonts option.

In addition to the changes you make in the GNNworks program, you can adjust the settings in your GNNmessenger and GNNchat software to make them run the way you want.

Getting Help

You should expect your GNN sessions to run trouble-free. The software, as you've seen so far, is easy to configure and should perform reliably in most systems. In addition, the toolbar commands and menu bar functions are clearly labeled, and there's a complete Help menu for both novice and power users alike.

If the information in the Help menu doesn't answer your question or solve your problem, you can try one of the following:

- Click the Help listing you'll see near the top of GNN's home page to bring up a list of frequently asked questions and answers.

- Send an e-mail message to **gnnsupport@gnn.com**. Please be sure to provide as much information as you can about your problem, and also describe your PC setup, including the kind of modem you have, and some basic details about your computer, memory, and hard drive capacity.

- If the problem needs a quick solution (perhaps you cannot get connected or the software is crashing), you may reach GNN's technical support department at (800) 819-6112. Before you dial your phone, you may want to write down a brief outline of your PC setup, so you'll have the information ready when the technical support person answers.

The Future of GNN?

As this book went to press, AOL (GNN's parent company) announced that it had inked a deal with Netscape to include that company's browser with GNN's software. This will mean that the GNNworks software will ultimately be phased out and replaced with Netscape (see fig. 38.10).

FIG. 38.10
Here's the future of GNN. This is GNN's home page as shown when accessed via Netscape.

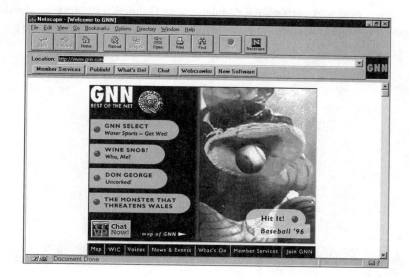

Part
VIII

Ch
38

While the actual graphics don't look altogether different when you compare the GNN browser with Netscape, you'll notice that the toolbar at the top of the document window is designed quite differently. Netscape offers access to its mail and newsreaders from the Windows menu. GNN's existing browser offers you these capabilities as separate programs, and you can switch between the programs by convenient toolbar icons.

A Mac version of GNN is also earmarked for future release. You can expect that the user interface will closely match the Windows version (just as the regular Mac and Windows versions of Netscape have a very similar look). You will also see additional support for features that are specific to the Mac operating system, such as Apple's QuickTime technology.

From Here...

If you just want Internet access without the exclusive content offered by the regular AOL service, GNN might be your cup of tea. In this chapter and in Chapter 37, I've covered the basics of GNN's services and profiled its highly flexible software.

Thus concludes our look at the Information Superhighway, AOL (and GNN) style. In the next part of this book, "Making Your Online Visits More Productive," I'll tell you how to keep your online bills low and how to maximize your modem's performance.

Making Your Online Visits More Productive

CHAPTER 39

How to Save Time and Money

Get more value from your AOL experience

Make your online visits more productive by doing your online work when you're offline.

How much do you owe

Quickly check your online billing summary.

Get better performance

Speed up the time it takes to download files.

Get free online time

Enter online contests and visit AOL's free member support areas.

America Online is, of course, a profit-making business, and you do pay for the time you spend online. Fortunately, the service's hourly charges are among the lowest in the industry, and they generally don't charge extra to access specific services. This means that you can spend more time online and run up a lower online charge.

In earlier chapters, I discussed places on America Online where you can save money when going shopping or planning a trip. In this chapter, I'm going to discuss one more place where you can save money— with America Online itself. ■

Making the Most of Your Online Sessions

The best way to get the most of your online time is to plan the session in advance and pay close attention to the time you've spent online. In the next few pages, I'll detail some convenient money saving tips.

 TIP A quick way to track your online hours is to keep a running log of the time spent online. That way you know in advance approximately how much your account will be charged.

Using Your Online Clock

Whenever you want to see just how long you've spent online, type the keyword **clock**, which brings up a display showing the time that has elapsed since you originally logged on (see fig. 39.1). When you are watching your budget, this is a sure way to keep track of the duration of your online session.

FIG. 39.1
The clock records the time
of your AOL visit.

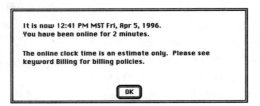

> It is now 12:41 PM MST Fri, Apr 5, 1996.
> You have been online for 2 minutes.
>
> The online clock time is an estimate only. Please see
> keyword Billing for billing policies.
>
> [OK]

N O T E   Older versions of AOL software listed the keyword **time** as the one that activated the online clock. That keyword has since been taken over by *TIME* magazine. ■

Compose E-Mail Offline

I described some of the most efficient ways to use AOL's e-mail capability in Chapter 8, "Using America Online E-Mail," but you don't have to be online to create an e-mail message. Before you log on, just open your AOL software, and then bring up your e-mail compose window (accessible via the Mail menu) and type your message. You can create as many messages as will comfortably fill your computer's screen.

After you've written your e-mail, click the Send Later icon to add the messages to your outgoing mail queue, log on to America Online, and send all your mail. When you use America Online's handy FlashSessions feature (see the following section), you can mail all your letters in a single step.

FlashSessions

FlashSessions are discussed in detail in Chapter 8, "Using America Online E-Mail," so I'll simply restate the benefits here. FlashSessions allow you to automate the process of sending and receiving e-mail (and messages from your selected Internet Newsgroups). You can write your messages offline and then save them to FlashMail. You can activate a FlashSession at any time or simply have the sessions take place at the hours you select.

During your FlashSession, you are logged online automatically for the account name you specify. If you have more than one account, you can designate FlashSessions for, them too. Your prepared e-mail, along with any attached files, are sent, and your incoming e-mail and any attached files (if you select the Files Incoming option) are received—all automatically (see fig. 39.2).

 T I P AOL's computing and software libraries have a number of shareware alarm clock and reminder programs you can use to track your online session. (Also see Chapter 20, "Tips and Tricks on Finding Software.")

FIG. 39.2
You can configure your AOL FlashSessions.

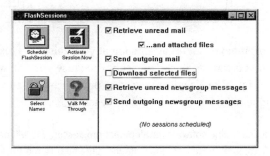

The greatest benefit here is time. You can compose outgoing mail and read new incoming mail offline. This helps reduce online charges.

N O T E Mac users can also run America Online FlashSessions with a neat little program called Claris Emailer, a program that can also be used to access your AppleLink, CompuServe, and various Internet accounts via one simple interface. Windows users will find a similar capability in Global Village's FocalPoint (which also offers faxing and voice mail). ▓

Creating Session Logs

You will often spend a lot of time online simply reading text messages while the online clock is ticking away. If you create a System Log, your America Online software acts like a tape recorder (see fig. 39.3). As you scroll through the text, an information window, or even a message area, AOL creates a file containing all the material that's being sent to your computer. (See Appendix B, "Using Your America Online Macintosh Software," and Appendix C, "Using Your America Online Windows Software," for more information on this topic.)

 TIP System performance may be slower during early evening hours when online traffic is heavy. If you want to download software, choose a non-peak hour, such as early in the morning. This helps reduce the time you spend online (and your bill).

FIG. 39.3
Make a Session Log to record your online visits and read about them when you log off.

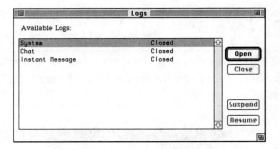

When you are offline, you can read this log at your leisure. This process doesn't work as efficiently when you want to post a message, because you will want to return to the location where the original message appeared to post a response to it, but otherwise, this is another technique to speed up your online session.

N O T E   As America Online software development progresses, you will be able to automate a FlashSession to include your favorite message boards, too (just as you can get your Internet Newsgroup messages now). ■

Other Offline Tasks

The less you do online that isn't related to actually visiting an online area, the lower your online charges. For example, if you want to change the settings in your AOL software, write a memo, or build your address book, you don't have to be online.

You can also review the contents of your FlashSession mailboxes, both incoming and outgoing mail, and read your session logs without actually running a session. If you need further assistance with using your software, you can certainly review this book or consult the Help menu of your AOL software while still offline.

TIP If you are 55 years of age or older, you can get additional savings on your monthly bills. For the specifics, check the SeniorNet forum (keyword **SeniorNet**).

The Cheapest Way to Get Help

Besides this book and AOL's Help menu, there are other ways to get help online without having to increase your online bill. One of these is the free online support area (keyword **Help**), shown in figure 39.4. If you have a problem connecting to America Online, staying connected, downloading or uploading software, or running a FlashSession, you can have a one-to-one chat with an AOL technical representative about it. This support is available seven days a week via the hours posted in the Tech Live forum (keyword: **Tech Live**).

FIG. 39.4
AOL's free support area helps you get assistance online without running up a bill.

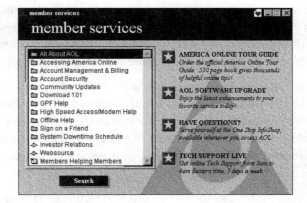

In addition, the support area contains a number of useful help texts that you can read, save, or print for later review. You'll get advice about solving connection problems, dealing with busy host messages, and other sorts of difficulties. There's also a library of modem files that allow many popular modems to communicate more efficiently with AOL software.

The nicest thing about all this is the message you get when you enter the keyword **Help** (see fig. 39.5). That's right, you're entering an area free of online charges. The clock stops on your AOL billing, and the time you spend in that free area isn't computed as part of your online charges.

While in that free area you can do some of the functions that you do offline, such as changing your software preferences, writing memos, fixing your online address book, and opening and closing system logs. You can also consult the Help menu, add or remove a screen name, and change and save passwords.

FIG. 39.5
Yes, the buck truly stops
here.

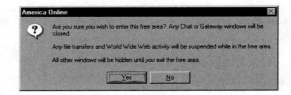

I'll tell you more about AOL's online help in Chapter 40, "How to Use AOL's Free Online Help Forums."

Checking Your Online Bill

Keyword: **Billing**

An important way to keep up-to-date on your accumulated online charges (without having to have a calculator at hand) is simply to review your bill on a regular basis. The keyword **Billing** will take you to AOL's account center, where you can double click the item labeled Current Month's Billing Summary to see the charges you've run up.

According to the billing structure established when this book went to press, each month you receive 300 minutes (5 hours) of online time as part of your minimum monthly charge. You'll be billed at the regular hourly charge for any time you spend online in a chargeable area above that minimum. You're charged by the minute, just like your local phone company, and like most phone companies, even a few seconds used above a full minute counts as a second full minute.

So far in this chapter, I've shown you practical techniques to reduce the amount of time you spend online, which keeps your monthly bill as low as possible. Here are ways in which you can actually receive free time during your online session.

Connect to AOL through Another Online Service

AOL has made agreements with AT&T's WorldNet Internet service and other services that will get you a lower online bill if you log on through their service rather than AOL's own dialup network. You'll want to check with the Internet provider directly for the pricing. It's important to realize, though, that just logging on to an Internet provider and accessing AOL via TCP/IP doesn't get you a lower price (unless the access speed is greater, resulting in being able to do your online work faster). The service provider must have made previous arrangements with AOL.

Signing Up Friends

Keyword: **Friend**

Through the years, I've found America Online to be an enjoyable and rewarding experience, and I spend many hours online throughout the week. If you treasure your online experience, you will want to have your friends share in the experience as well.

What's more, you can become eligible to receive free online time simply by signing up your friends as members. America Online doesn't charge you for the time you spend signing up your friends, because it's done in a free area.

Your first step is to select a software kit that is compatible with your friend's computer and operating system (see fig. 39.6). There are kits available for Macintosh, DOS, and Windows. Be sure to choose the correct floppy disk size when you order the DOS or Windows versions of the software. Macintosh users may receive the software on 1.4M (high density) floppy disks or on the 800K variety (depending on what type of floppy drive your Mac-user friend has).

FIG. 39.6
Choose an AOL membership kit.

This offer changes from time to time, so don't be surprised if it's a bit different when you decide to enroll your friend as a member (see fig. 39.7). The conditions are very simple. At the time this book was published, you are entitled to 15 hours for each new member, was in effect. You are limited to ordering 12 membership kits per month. Also, your friend must register and maintain an online membership for at least 45 days for you to qualify for free time.

FIG. 39.7
Here's a typical sign-up offer from AOL that will get you free hours online.

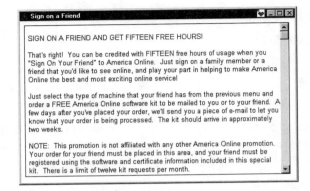

SIGN ON A FRIEND AND GET FIFTEEN FREE HOURS!

That's right! You can be credited with FIFTEEN free hours of usage when you "Sign On Your Friend" to America Online. Just sign on a family member or a friend that you'd like to see online, and play your part in helping to make America Online the best and most exciting online service!

Just select the type of machine that your friend has from the previous menu and order a FREE America Online software kit to be mailed to you or to your friend. A few days after you've placed your order, we'll send you a piece of e-mail to let you know that your order is being processed. The kit should arrive in approximately two weeks.

NOTE: This promotion is not affiliated with any other America Online promotion. Your order for your friend must be placed in this area, and your friend must be registered using the software and certificate information included in this special kit. There is a limit of twelve kit requests per month.

Winning Contests

Here's a method that has no guarantees, but if you are a regular visitor to online chats and conferences, no doubt you've seen the forum staff holding a contest or two from time to time.

These contests may result in the giveaway of free time or even some merchandise (including new books and newly released software), depending on the forum.

As an example, here's the text I logged from a recent chat that explains just how a typical contest is conducted. I've left in some of the humorous asides (and possible spelling oddities) to preserve the flavor of this particular session. So pay attention; you may find yourself winning some free time on America Online some day. (Online Host, by the way, is text that's been generated by AOL host computer with the keystrokes that are described in the following session log.)

```
AFL GeneS: Since we are near the top of the hour I'll turn the mike over to
AFL Bear...

AFL Bear: Thank you, thank you!

AFL Bear: It's that time again for someone to win three free AOL hours! And,
as is our wont, we will be rolling the old AOL dice again to determine the
winner!

JLR63: Hey, I want new dice...these are loaded!

MIKEL617: Yeah!!!

AFL Bear: Does anyone here NOT know how to roll the AOL dice?

AFL GeneS: And Peter loaded them. Blame him!

OnlineHost: AFL Bear rolled 6 12-sided dice: 12 11 7 9 9 5
```

TishTash: Just repeat the command just in case, please.

AFL Bear: I guess everyone knows the rules, then! The command is

    //roll only with no leading space, then hit the Return key.

TishTash: Thanks.

JLR63: Bear, set a good example!

OnlineHost: MIKEL617 rolled 2 6-sided dice: 3 5

OnlineHost: KevinY1 rolled 2 6-sided dice: 5 4

OnlineHost: Kevin W46 rolled 2 6-sided dice: 4 3

OnlineHost: TishTash rolled 2 6-sided dice: 2 3

AFL Bear: OK, you must wait until I say GO! Any ties will be broken by...

AFL GeneS: A sledgehammer.

AFL Bear: a roll-off of the tying folks.

AFL Bear: Ready? Get set...GO!

OnlineHost: KevinY1 rolled 2 6-sided dice: 2 4

OnlineHost: MIKEL617 rolled 2 6-sided dice: 1 2

OnlineHost: Imma rolled 2 6-sided dice: 5 4

OnlineHost: TishTash rolled 2 6-sided dice: 2 2

OnlineHost: StewMiller rolled 2 6-sided dice: 1 3

OnlineHost: Kevin W46 rolled 2 6-sided dice: 2 5

OnlineHost: ChuckS3257 rolled 2 6-sided dice: 5 5

OnlineHost: JLR63 rolled 2 6-sided dice: 6 3

OnlineHost: MIKEL617 rolled 2 6-sided dice: 3 4

OnlineHost: IKEL617 rolled 2 6-sided dice: 1 5

OnlineHost: JLR63 rolled 3 6-sided dice: 6 3 2

OnlineHost: ChuckS!!!!! You win!!!!!

ChuckS3257: Bear, thanks.

AFL Bear: Say a few words, Chuck!

ChuckS3257: This is my first win. Thank you.

Oh yes, one little point. There is truly a secret to rolling more than two virtual dice on America Online. If you catch me online sometime, I'll let you in on how to do it (or you can simply take a peek at this book's glossary, where I've placed the information). My suggestion, though, is that you be careful about imposing this dice game on a chat-only session, unless it's already part of the program.

Get a New Modem

When I first bought a desktop computer, a 2,400 bps modem cost several hundred dollars. Today, modems with 14,400 bps data and fax capability can be purchased for less than $100 and 28,800 modems don't cost all that much more (the difference is just a few chips here and there). America Online has 28,800 bps service in hundreds of U.S. cities through its AOLNet network, and many more access numbers in major cities around the world through its GlobalNet network.

If you have a 2,400 bps modem, switching to 28,800 bps means that your files transfer 12 times faster and that text scrolls in a text window at a much faster rate. Moreover, even if you log on at a higher speed, you pay exactly the same hourly rate you pay now. If you spend a lot of time online, buying a high-speed modem more than pays for itself in just a few months.

High-speed modems are especially valuable when you use America Online's World Wide Web Browser, because Web pages contain many graphics that have to be fed to your computer from points around the world. The faster the data flows to your computer, the faster those terrific graphics appear on your computer's screen.

Now that 28,800 bps modems and access numbers are relatively common, America Online has been exploring even faster ways of delivering the service to its members. In the years to come, America Online will be offering a rich array of multimedia tools (sound and picture) that will make your online visits more rewarding than ever.

From Here...

I had a little innocent fun in this chapter, when I described AOL's dice-roll contests, but I've also given you some solid time-saving information that allows you to get the most from your visits to America Online.

- If you want to make your America Online software work better for you, see Chapter 3, "Getting the Most from AOL's Macintosh Software," and Chapter 4, "Getting the Most from AOL's Windows Software."
- See Chapter 6, "Where Do We Begin?" for advice on how to quickly navigate your way through AOL's online community.
- See Chapter 20, "Tips and Tricks on Finding Software," for quick tips on how to locate software you can download to your computer direct from America Online.

- You'll learn more about getting online support without adding to your online tab in Chapter 40, "How to Use AOL's Free Online Help Forums."

- If you have a high-speed modem in mind for a future purchase, or just want to make your present modem work more efficiently, read Chapter 41, "Secrets of High-Speed Access on AOL."

Part
IX
Ch
39

How to Use AOL's Free Online Help Forums

How to get help on AOL's time

Visit AOL's free online help center.

Where to get help from other members

Visit AOL's Members Helping Members forums (and it's free).

How to talk with AOL online

Learn how to get interactive support direct from AOL's own technical support people.

While it's true that most of your online visits will run smoothly, there is always the chance that something will go wrong, and you'll need some assistance to solve the problem. When trouble arises, you'll want to consult the various troubleshooting sections of this book. But I don't pretend to be able to cover all possible combinations of software and hardware issues, so there will be times you'll want to consult AOL's online help resources directly. ■

The AOL Help Guide (Macintosh Style)

If you need additional information about America Online services or features, make your first stop the extensive information area of AOL's Help guide. Whether you need to know how to use the Download Manager or are connecting to America Online for the first time, this area most likely has the answer you need. For information about AOL's software features, see Appendix B, "Using Your America Online Macintosh Software."

If you are signing on to America Online for the first time, take a moment and open the AOL Guide window from your Mac's Help icon on the right of the menu bar (see fig. 40.1).

FIG. 40.1
AOL uses interactive Apple Guide assistance to show you the way.

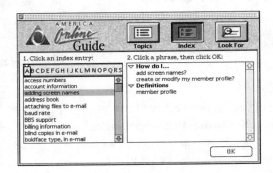

Like Apple Guide in general, America Online's Macintosh Help window is a treat to work with because of its logical organization. Click the Topics, Index, or Look For (for searching) icons at the top, and when a main topic you want to know more about appears in the left side of the screen below, double-click the entry. Double-click the right-hand list to bring up the interactive help information on the subject you select.

The AOL Help Menu (Windows 95 Style)

AOL's Windows Help menu looks pretty much like the ones you find in any other Windows program. If you need basic instructions on doing common AOL tasks, the Help menu will provide a good amount of useful information. For more details about AOL's Windows software features, see Appendix C, "Using Your America Online Windows Software."

If you are signing on to America Online for the first time, take a moment and open the Help menu from your AOL program's menu bar (see fig. 40.2).

FIG. 40.2

Activating Windows AOL's extensive Help features is a snap.

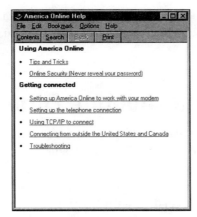

 T I P You can save and print any text item in the Help menu for later reference. Just click the text item you want to print first.

Your first Help option, Contents, brings up the screen shown in figure 40.3 and lists the available topics. You may scroll through the window to display additional topics. Clicking any topic brings up a screen offering easy-to-read advice on that subject. You may also print any topic for later review. The second menu choice, Search for Help On, lets AOL's Help feature locate the information for you. If you need additional assistance on using the Help feature, choose How to Use Help.

FIG. 40.3

The Help menu on America Online's Windows software displays the table of contents.

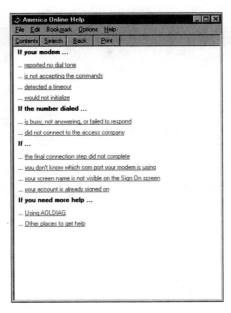

Part
IX

Ch
40

One other help resource is activated by clicking the question mark icon on AOL's Flashbar. This step takes you to AOL's online support area, which is explained in more detail in the next section.

Using Online Troubleshooting Forums

As you wander around the virtual world of AOL and make use of its services, questions may arise that are not covered in the offline Help features. Or you may want to find out more about your own online status. America Online provides a free area online dedicated to providing you with information about its services and your account. You are not charged for the time you spend in this support area.

To go to the free area, follow these steps:

1. Select Members Services from the Members menu, click the question mark icon on the Flashbar or use the keyword **Help** from anywhere online while you are connected to the service (you can also use the keyword **Hotline**).

2. You are asked whether you want to enter the free area. If you okay the message, all of the windows that may have been open when you selected Members Services are temporarily closed (including the sites you've chosen with AOL's World Wide Web browser). They appear again when you leave the free area.

3. You see the comprehensive online help forum, which includes live technical support (see fig. 40.4).

FIG. 40.4
America Online's Member Services area offers a plate of convenient information to answer many of your questions about the service.

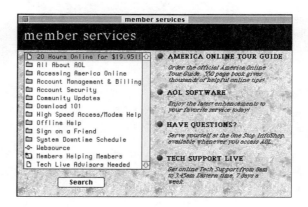

Help with Downloading

America Online's software makes downloading files to your hard drive a simple task; but at one time or another, you might have questions about downloading. Perhaps your downloads are taking longer than their time estimates, or you are being disconnected during file transfers. If so, getting to the right place for assistance is a task involving several steps (though it takes less time to get from here to there than to describe it). First, use the keyword **Help** to reach the Member Services area, then double-click Download 101 from the list box (see fig. 40.5).

FIG. 40.5
AOL will guide you, step-by-step, through the file download process.

You can also find, in the Members Services, help with AOL e-mail, help in working with the Internet gateway, modem and connect help, getting around on AOL, and more. (For more extensive information on the Internet gateway, see the chapters that make up Part VIII, "Entering the Information Superhighway.")

If you are having difficulties with any of these subjects, you'll want to explore AOL's help areas for possible solutions before writing to or calling the AOL staff for answers. A full 95 percent of members' questions to AOL's support staff can be answered by simply reading this section of AOL, without placing a call or waiting for an e-mail answer. (And remember, it's free of connect charges!)

Part
IX

Ch
40

 If a Macintosh file you've downloaded has a "zero" file size, it's probably corrupted. Download it again and request credit for the time lost as a result of the bad download. Just bring up the keyword window, type the keyword **Credit,** and enter your request in the information screen.

Resuming a File Download

After you've been disconnected during a file download, all is not lost. You can usually reconnect to AOL and resume the file download at the point where you were disconnected.

To do this, first check your Download Manager to verify that the file is still listed there. Pull down the File menu and select the Download Manager option (see fig. 40.6).

FIG. 40.6
The AOL Download Manager can be used to resume the download process.

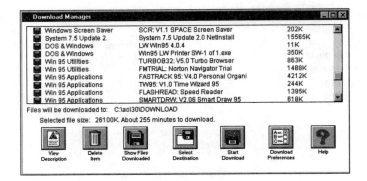

If the partially downloaded file is present, reconnect to America Online, perhaps using a different access number, and click the Start Download icon in the Download Manager window. The file should resume transferring in a few seconds.

In order to resume a download successfully, you must not throw away or move the file that represents your partially completed download. This file is usually located in the c:\waol30\download directory for Windows users, or the Online Downloads folder for Mac users. This partial file has the same name as the file you are downloading, and its icon shows a torn or jagged edge to indicate that it's incomplete.

If you intentionally or inadvertently discarded this file, the partially completed download is still listed in the Download Manager, but you will not be able to resume the download using the Download Manager. Simply select the item in the Download Manager list, and then click the Delete Item icon to remove the entry from the Download Manager's list of files.

Members Helping Members

Keyword: **MHM**

Another handy help resource on AOL is run by your fellow members. It's called Members Helping Members (see fig. 40.7), and it consists of a series of message boards where you can ask your question or state your problem. Whether you're having trouble with your AOL software or navigating through the service, you'll find that a lot of knowledgeable online visitors frequent this message board to answer questions. Best of all, it's free of online charges, and as you become more knowledgeable about handling routine online problems, you might want to help out others who seek advice from this message area. I used to participate in this area often before I began writing books about AOL, and it provided me with much valuable information about the service.

FIG. 40.7
Here's where your fellow AOL members can help you solve a problem with the service.

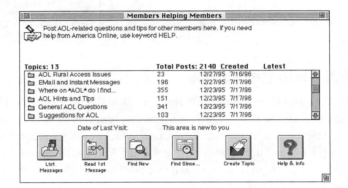

Tech Support Live

Keyword: **Tech Live**

When text files don't give you the assistance you need, interact with a live AOL representative about your problem on Tech Live. The Tech Live Auditorium is open from 8 a.m. to 3:45 a.m. Eastern time, seven days a week (and fortunately no single person needs to staff it for that long a period). Here, you can get live help from AOL's experienced Customer Relations staff in the free Member Services area of America Online.

When you opt to enter the Tech Live area, you will see several information screens describing AOL's live technical service (see fig. 40.8). These information screens offer to take you to the Member Services area and other parts of AOL's member support services, where you may review a large collection of information that may very well offer the answer to your question or problem. The support staff collected some of the most frequently asked questions and answers and compiled them into these text documents. Save yourself some time by looking for a possible solution here, because otherwise you will need to wait your turn when entering the live help auditorium (and it can get a bit crowded in there sometimes).

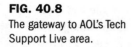

FIG. 40.8

The gateway to AOL's Tech Support Live area.

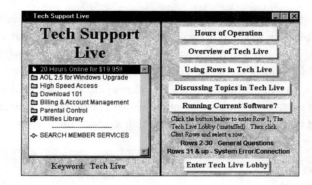

Other AOL Help Resources

Another, and little known, help resource is AOL's own Technical Support BBS, which you can call with any of the numerous terminal program or telecommunications packages available for your computer. The America Online BBS supports modem speeds of up to 28,800 baud and is available 24 hours a day. You can find local access numbers, modem strings, and other connecting and troubleshooting information. The BBS number is toll-free: 1-800-827-5808.

The Technical Support BBS is not a part of the America Online service, so you won't need your screen name(s) or other account information when calling. The information on this BBS is provided to help you only with problems connecting to America Online and using the AOL software.

The communications program you use should be set to use 8 data bits, 1 stop bit, and no parity. If you're using a terminal program that can display ANSI graphics, select Yes when asked if you can display ANSI graphics. If you are unsure, choose No when asked. If you aren't certain how to use these programs, check your instruction manuals very carefully. These programs aren't as intuitive as AOL's graphical software.

If you can get onto the America Online service, you can also get detailed modem assistance from the Members Services area by double-clicking the High Speed Access/Modem Help folder shown in the list box. Much of the information found here is the same as on the AOL BBS—modem setting strings, connecting tips, and some basic troubleshooting tips (see fig. 40.9).

If you have a modem that isn't listed in the Setup box of your America Online software, you may find a driver for your modem available for download in this area. At the very least, you'll find advice on how to customize the existing profiles to work better with your modem.

FIG. 40.9
AOL offers you convenient advice on solving common modem setup and connection problems.

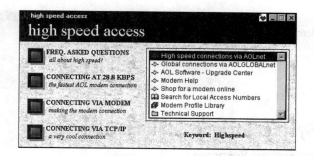

N O T E America Online will usually shut down the service once or twice a week for two to four early morning hours to install system upgrades or to conduct routine maintenance and repair work on the host computer system. Usually when logging on during this period, you'll get a message screen announcing that the service is temporarily shut down, along with the approximate time that the service is expected to be restored. Sometimes you won't. But if you cannot get past the Connecting to America Online screen when logging on, the best thing to do is wait an hour or two and try again. ■

TROUBLESHOOTING

Why am I getting a message that the host is not responding or the system is busy? Your AOL connection to the host computers is a continuing process of communication. You make a request with your software, such as opening a window or accessing another area, and the host computers respond by delivering what you request. If there's a delay of more than a minute or two, users of AOL Mac 2.6 or later will get a message that the system is busy (see fig. 40.10).

When you encounter this symptom, try the following:

1. Log off AOL and immediately log on again. Sometimes that's all it takes to improve system response.

2. Sometimes AOL response is slow during the peak evening hours (equivalent to prime time on network TV), from 8 to 11 p.m. Eastern time. If quickly logging off and on doesn't help, choose an hour when network traffic is lower.

3. Try another access number. Use the keyword **Access** to get the list of the numbers in your city.

4. Check your modem settings. For hints and tips on how to get the best connections, read Chapter 41, "Secrets of High-Speed Access on AOL."

If you still experience host or system response problems, read the next section, "Using the System Response Support Area," for information on how to report the problem to America Online.

FIG. 40.10
AOL's dialog box informs you that the message isn't getting through.

Using the System Response Support Area

Keyword: **System Response**

On most occasions, your connections to AOL should be fast, and your performance good. Sometimes, due to a number of factors, (some related, some not) you'll have problems getting online or maintaining good response during your online visit. You may experience a failure of the host to respond or see a message that the system has too many requests to handle. You may have difficulty getting connected, or experience problems with staying online.

In Chapter 41, "Secrets of High-Speed Access on AOL," I'll outline many of the common connection problems you're apt to encounter and how to configure your modem for the best possible performance.

The troubleshooting item mentioned in the preceding section describes common host-related symptoms.

If none of the steps described in the troubleshooting section of Chapter 41 get you any closer to reliable AOL performance, you'll want to check out the System Response Report Area (see fig. 40.11).

The System Response area has a number of text items for you to read, covering the most common connection problems and their causes. You can save or print these text articles for later review. If none of these articles or the steps I've described in this chapter (or in Chapter 41, which has extensive troubleshooting advice on dealing with modem-related problems) bring you closer to a solution to your problem, you'll want to file a report with AOL's technical staff, by clicking the Report A Problem button.

You'll have a choice of reports you can send, depending on the kind of problem you have. AOL's technicians will investigate your problem and respond to you via e-mail in a day or two.

FIG. 40.11
Report frequent AOL
performance problems here.

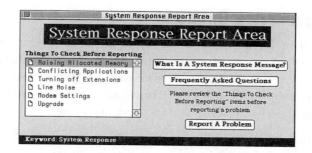

How to Handle a System Crash on Your Mac

No doubt, the most annoying thing to happen to your computer is a system crash. Although they come in a variety of flavors, most system crashes taste pretty bad. If you encounter such a problem, the following are some procedures you can follow to get up and running again:

- If you experience a system error while connected to America Online, turn off your modem. This will disconnect you from America Online before a sizable amount of bad data can be sent to AOL, which can happen during some types of crashes. A data storm, or random data, sent in AOL's direction might confuse the host into not recognizing that you have left and prevent you from signing on again after you have restarted your computer. This does not happen often, but it can be quite annoying to see a message stating that you can't sign on because you are already using AOL. If a simple application error occurred, and if that application was not AOL, you may be able to return to AOL long enough to log off; then restart your Macintosh.

- If the error was with the AOL application or occurred while AOL was the frontmost application, chances are you cannot resume or save any work that may have been in progress. In this case, you should simply select the Restart button in the error message. If you are a System 7 user, look in your Trash for a Rescued Items folder after your machine restarts. If any of your open applications were using temporary files, you may be able to recover some or all of the data you lost from this folder.

- If you cannot get the Restart button in the bomb window to work, try a force quit, holding down the ⌘-Option-Escape keys. If that doesn't free the frozen application, read your Macintosh manual for instructions on activating the reset switch (on some models it's done via keyboard command) to get your Mac to reboot as painlessly as possible.

Part
IX

Ch
40

Reinstalling America Online

What happens if you experience repeated and confusing errors, such as random data in the window where your screen names appear, or the modem lights up like the Fourth of July but never dials or gives an error message? If this is happening to you, it's possible that something in your AOL's files that stores your individual data has become corrupted, especially if you had a recent bout with system crashes.

If you suspect that your America Online software is corrupt, you should reinstall your AOL software. Doing this is a fairly simple task. You can do this in one of two ways—perform a clean installation, where you start your AOL connection from scratch, or perform an update installation, where you upgrade from your previous copy of AOL software. I recommend the clean installation as the best and easiest method of isolating intermittent problems with the AOL software.

To perform a clean installation on your Macintosh, move your existing America Online software to a folder where it can rest undisturbed by the upcoming installation. Then insert your original AOL software diskette (or CD) into your drive and launch the installer found on the disk. Select a folder or directory that will not overwrite your existing AOL software and click the Install button. For complete information on installing your AOL software, read Appendix A, "If You're New to the Online World."

> **CAUTION**
>
> Before reinstalling your AOL software from scratch, save or delete all incoming mail received during a FlashSession (in the Read Incoming Mail list in the Mail menu). Also, move all downloaded files from the Downloads folder to any other available folder outside of the old AOL program folder, so you don't accidentally delete them when you remove your old AOL software.

Signing On After Installation

After your software has been installed, launch the newly installed program and begin the sign-on process as described in Appendix A. When you see the sign-on screen that requests you enter a Certificate Number and Password, type in any one of the screen names you use in the Certificate Number box and your regular password for that screen name in the Password box. Your connection is then established and all of your account information is transferred to the new software.

If the problems that caused you to reinstall your software in the first place do not recur, you can continue setting your preferences and options in your freshly installed software. For all the information about configuring your AOL software to your taste, see Appendix B, "Using Your America Online Macintosh Software."

If, however, the original symptoms persist, the problem probably isn't caused by corrupt AOL software. You can discard the new software and restore the original software to retain your old e-mail and other settings; or to be safe, you may prefer to just continue working with the new copy of your AOL software and discard the older version.

After all this, if you cannot get your AOL software to work, give AOL's customer service people a call at (800) 827-3338 (in Virginia 703-448-8700), or contact the manufacturer of your computer for additional assistance.

How to Handle a System Crash on Your PC

Although the two top computing platforms differ in many ways, both are susceptible to a system crash. In this section, you'll find some advice on how you, as a user of Microsoft Windows, can deal with common system problems. And if you cross computing platforms from time to time, you'll see some of the advice is similar to the section above, where I discussed dealing with problems on a Mac.

The first step if you experience a system error while connected to America Online is to turn off your modem. This disconnects you from America Online before a large amount of bad data is sent to AOL, which can happen during some types of crashes. A data storm, or random data, sent in AOL's direction might confuse the host into not recognizing that you have left and prevent you from signing on again after you have restarted your computer. This does not happen often, but it can be quite annoying to see a message stating that you can't sign on because you are already using AOL. If a simple application error occurred, and if that application was not AOL, you may be able to return to AOL long enough to log off; then reboot your computer.

Part
IX

Ch
40

Getting Out of Trouble

If your America Online Windows software crashes with a General Protection Fault error, try to exit the AOL application, exit any other active applications after saving any documents that are being worked on, and then attempt to restart Windows. If you cannot restart Windows, or if attempts to resume working in Windows after restarting do not succeed, turn off your computer, and then turn it on again.

If you experience a total system lockup, sometimes you can exit a crashing application by pressing Ctrl+Alt+Delete (all at the same time). After you've restarted, you may see a directory alerting you to continue to boot Windows 95 in a Safe Mode, and you should start your computer in this manner to make sure nothing has gone wrong with your operating system software.

Reinstalling America Online

What happens if you experience repeated and confusing problems, such as constant system error messages, or the modem lights up like the Fourth of July but never dials or gives an error message? If this is happening to you, it's possible something in your AOL's files that stores your individual data has become corrupted, especially if you had a recent bout with system crashes.

If you suspect that your America Online software is corrupt, you should reinstall your AOL software. Doing this is a fairly simple task. You can reinstall the software in one of two ways—perform a clean installation, where you start your AOL connection from scratch, or perform an update installation, where your previous settings are copied from your previously installed copy. I recommend the clean installation as the best and easiest method of isolating intermittent problems with the AOL software.

To perform a clean installation on your Windows-equipped PC, delete your existing AOL program folder (after transferring your downloaded files to another directory) and then run the program setup in the normal way, just as I describe in Appendix A, "If You're New to the Online World." By installing your AOL software in this manner, none of the settings or downloaded artwork from the previous version will be copied to your newly installed program, thus reducing the risk of further problems.

Signing On After Installation

Once your AOL software has been reinstalled, launch the program and then start the sign-on process just as I described it in Appendix A. When you see the sign-on screen that requests you enter a Certificate Number and Password, type in any one of the screen names you use in the Certificate Number box and your regular password for that screen name in the Password box. Your connection is then established, and all of your account information is transferred to the new software.

If the problems that caused you to reinstall your software in the first place do not recur, you can continue setting your preferences and options in your freshly installed software. For all the information about configuring your AOL software to your taste, see Appendix C, "Using Your America Online Windows Software."

If the problems continue, it may well be that you have other problems in your operating system or computer to deal with instead. You may want to consider reinstalling Windows 95, or consulting your manuals for further advice on troubleshooting these problems. For some really helpful insights, I suggest you get a copy of my own favorite Windows 95 reference, Que's *Using Windows 95* by Ed Bott.

From Here...

Using the troubleshooting tips throughout this book, you should be able to solve most problems you encounter with your AOL program. And if those tips don't resolve the problem, AOL's free online help services can take you further towards getting you up and running as quickly as possible.

- You'll find a detailed overview of AOL's services throughout this book, but your best launching point is Chapter 6, "Where Do We Begin?"

- And if you want to learn secrets about reducing your online bills, read Chapter 39, "How to Save Time and Money."

- If you're new to America Online, you'll want to read Appendix A, "If You're New to the Online World."

- New Macintosh users of AOL software will want to read Appendix B, "Using Your America Online Macintosh Software."

- New Windows users of AOL software will want to read Appendix C, "Using Your America Online Windows Software."

Part
IX

Ch
40

CHAPTER 41

Secrets of High-Speed Access on AOL

- **Secrets of speedy performance**

  Learn how to get a high-speed connection to America Online.

- **How to select the right modem**

  Hints and tips help you make a choice from the large number of available models.

- **How to set up your modem for best performance**

  Learn how to deal with those hair-pulling modem connection problems with as little fuss as possible.

Unless you have direct Internet access and connect to AOL through TCP/IP (as described in Chapter 29, "Using AOL's Internet Connection"), you will log on to AOL in the same way I do. You'll use your personal computer, a telephone line, and a little box with some flashing lights, known as a modem, to connect to AOL's huge network and to send and receive data. (Sometimes that little box is located inside your computer, but it does the same thing.)

The little box that squawks and squeaks when you connect to another telephone line is a gateway to a vast world. It not only affords you access to America Online but, through that service, opens a direct gateway to that huge, seemingly intangible body known as the Internet. ■

N O T E   If the squawking and squealing sounds your modem makes when it connects disturb you or others, you can turn the noise off by entering an M0 (that's always a zero) in your modem setup string. You'll learn more about doing this later in this chapter. If you just want to make the sounds softer, check your modem manual. Some modems support commands L0 (always a zero) through L3, which regulate modem speaker volume. ■

Increasing Connection Speeds

When America Online first appeared on the scene, the fastest connection speed available was 2,400 bps (you'll read more about what that means later in this chapter). Just as computers have become cheaper and more powerful, the same holds true for modems. Today, modems that support 14,400 bps are commonly available for less than $100, and the newest generation of 28,800 bps and 33,600 bps (V.34) modems can be bought for less than $100.

> **CAUTION**
>
> A high-speed modem sends data at a greater speed through your computer's serial port. Although 14,400 bps modems will work okay on most Macs and PCs, you might want to contact the modem manufacturer about compatibility with the latest generation of V.34 modems. Some older personal computers might require expansion cards to support the higher connection speeds without losing data or disconnecting.

To provide improved service to its members, America Online has established AOLNet, a high-speed, fiber-optic access network that supports modem speeds of up to 28,800 bps in many U.S. cities and, via the GlobalNet network, in major cities around the world. To find out whether your city has such an access number, use the keyword **AOLNet** to examine the latest listing. If an AOLNet number isn't available in your city yet, the keyword **HighSpeed** will enable you to search for other high-speed options, such as 14,400 bps.

 T I P   Even if a high-speed access number is a long-distance call, it might be cheaper to pay the long-distance charges than to log on to America Online for a much longer period and pay a higher online charge.

Here's what you need for a faster connection to AOL:

- A faster modem
- A faster connection number

Use the keyword **HighSpeed** (which takes you to AOL's free support area) to locate a higher speed connection number to AOL while you're online (see fig. 41.1).

FIG. 41.1
AOL's High Speed Access support center, where you can find ways to boost connection speed.

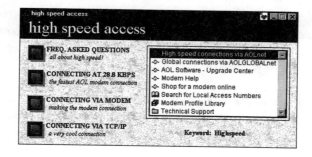

To receive advice on how to get better high-speed connections, click the Frequently Asked Questions button at the left. If you want to locate another access number, just double-click the Search for Local Access Numbers entry in the list box on the right; enter the area code for your city, and you'll see a listing in a few seconds of nearby connection numbers (see fig. 41.2).

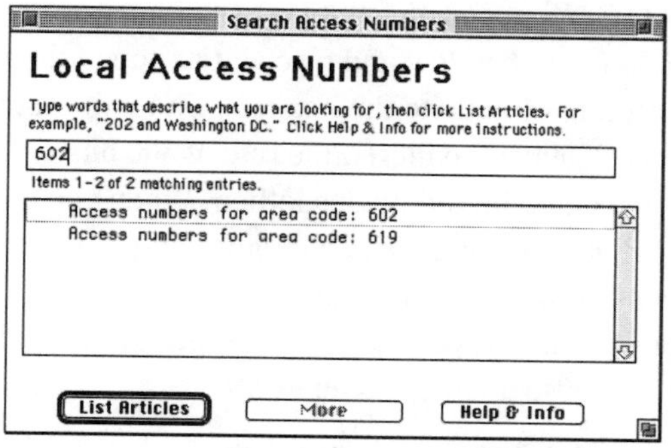

FIG. 41.2
Use AOL's search tool to locate a local phone number that supports higher speed connections.

- An updated modem profile

AOL is always working with modem manufacturers to find ways to make your modem work faster and more efficiently. The Modem Profile Library offered in the high-speed access center shown in the list box enables you to download modem description files that support most popular models.

N O T E If you cannot find an up-to-date modem file for the modem you have, contact the manufacturer's technical support people. They might be able to provide an updated connection file, advise you about using another modem file, or help you tweak the file with new commands that will provide more efficient connections. ▪

Part
IX

Ch
41

A Power User's Modem Guide

The word *modem* stands for modulate/demodulate. Remember that your Mac or PC is a digital device that speaks in little ones and zeros, but your telephone is an analog device that transmits and receives sounds. A modem is a device that converts computer data to sounds that are transmitted across a telephone line and reassembled at the other end into data that can be read by the receiving computer.

 T I P As AOL continues to grow at an incredible rate, you might find performance slow or connections difficult from 9 p.m. until midnight. Schedule long online visits early in the morning or before dinner.

N O T E America Online routinely shuts down the service for system maintenance one or more times a week during the early morning hours, usually from 3:30 a.m. to 7 a.m. eastern time. If you try to connect to AOL during these hours, and you're not successful, try again later. Sometimes you'll get a message window about the maintenance procedure, sometimes you won't. ■

The first modems used an acoustic coupler to connect to your telephone line. You physically took your telephone handset and placed it on top of the modem, or attached a little plastic or rubber fitting directly to the handset. The unit cost hundreds of dollars and managed to transfer data at the incredible rate of 300 bits per second (called bps from here on)—well, it seemed incredible back then. When you consider that there are eight bits to a byte (or characters of data, in computer lingo), plus additional data known as stop bits and sometimes parity bits (which are explained in more detail later in this chapter), you can well imagine that files consisting of several hundred kilobytes of data would take many hours to transfer to another computer.

Later models plugged right into your telephone line. As with all computer-related products, modem performance has increased in huge jumps, and the prices have gone down. High-speed modems are now available for as little as $100, and the more elaborate models provide reliable connection at speeds of up to 28,800 bps (and sometimes 33,600 bps).

External or Internal: What Is Available

If you own a desktop Macintosh, you'll find that the choice is more or less made for you. Internal modems for desktop Macs, with a few exceptions, haven't really caught on. One big reason is that not all Macs have NuBus or PCI expansion slots (some have processor director slots, some have no slots). As a result, few if any of the current crop of high-speed modems are available for installation inside your desktop Mac. Instead, you would normally buy an external modem.

In contrast, modems for an IBM PC or compatible are widely available in the form of a plug-in card installed inside the computer.

N O T E When it comes to an external modem, the nice thing is that most modems that work on a PC will also work on a Mac. You simply need to change the cable and use communications software that's compatible with the specific computing platform. Ask the manufacturer for details. Some users are known to switch modems back and forth regularly between their Macs and PCs. ▪

The options for Mac and PC laptop computers are also similar. The newest Macintosh PowerBooks and PC laptops support PC-card modems, consisting of a modem contained on a small printed circuit board, hardly bigger than a credit card. These modems have the advantage of being easily inserted and removed from a laptop even while the computer is powered on. The downside to PC-card modems is that they can be tricky to configure on the PC side, because most models require that you load specific drivers for that modem. Configuring these drivers properly may be a bit unpredictable, but after it's done, you rarely have to do it again.

The second type of internal modem for laptops are those designed solely to support one specific model line. You'll find this type common on the older Macintosh PowerBooks and Duos, but it is also found on some PC laptops.

One new type of internal modem uses a digital signal processor (DSP) chip to communicate. The IBM Thinkpad 755CE is one of the first laptops to use this type of modem. Because these modems rely entirely on software to control their function, they are supposed to be more configurable and upgradeable than previous models. The downside is that they are also much more subject to software conflicts. The Macintosh GeoPort, available on the AV and Power Macintosh lines, uses the computer itself to emulate a modem, and software to support certain features.

With an internal modem, you don't have to deal with awkward cables, and a separate unit and power supply when you sit in your hotel room trying to dial up an online service or a remote computer. You just plug in a standard telephone cable to the computer's modem jack, launch America Online's software, and get down to the business of connecting to the service. For more information on dealing with modems and laptop computers, read Chapter 5, "America Online and Mobile Computing."

How Fast?

Those 300 bps modems are largely history (I recall them with absolutely no pangs of regret), as are most of the 1,200 bps models that followed it. And it wasn't so long ago that a 2,400 bps modem cost more than $300, and anything faster was out of the question for

Part

IX

Ch

41

most personal computer users. This wasn't only because of the price of admission, but also because very few users, and certainly none of the online services, supported 9,600 bps connections and above.

America Online has been quick to jump on the high-speed bandwagon. Just as you can purchase a new personal computer with workstation performance for less than $2,000, there has been a corresponding performance boost and price drop in high-speed modems. You can buy a V.34 modem, which supports up to 28,800 bps data (sometimes 33,600 bps) and 14,400 bps fax connections, at prices beginning at around $100.

In hundreds of cities around the U.S. and in other parts of the world, you can access AOL at 14,400 bps and also 28,800 bps. To take advantage of these higher access speeds, the service has been adding new graphical features at a breakneck pace. That, coupled with AOL's World Wide Web access, which makes heavy use of graphics and sound, has made it a good idea to get the fastest modem you can to experience the highest possible performance when you use these new features.

> **CAUTION**
>
> Although it's not a bad idea to purchase the fastest modem you can afford, slower computers might not have fast enough serial ports to handle ultra-fast data throughput. When in doubt, ask the modem's manufacturer about which models work best with their products. For some desktop computers, you might have to get an expansion card to support those faster data speeds; a laptop's serial port limitations might not offer a similar solution.

Data Speed versus Fax Speed

Some entry-level products still advertise 2,400 bps data performance and 9,600 bps fax. Other models employ V.42, a hardware compression technique, to gain faster throughput of uncompressed files. The following list discusses some of these strange V-style names and what those names really mean in terms of modem performance:

- *V.22bis.* This designation is just an ordinary 2,400 bps modem.
- *V.32.* This designation is the standard for sending data at up to 9,600 bps.
- *V.32bis.* This designation means the modem is capable of data transmission at speeds of up to 14,400 bps.
- *V.34.* This designation means the modem is capable of data transmission at speeds of up to 28,800 bps (and sometimes 33,600 bps). The next section of this chapter is devoted strictly to the V.34 fast lane.

- *V.42*. This standard involves Microcom Networking Protocol (known as MNP) and relates strictly to various error-correction schemes.

- *V.42bis*. This standard covers hardware compression, in which data is compressed on-the-fly as it is sent by your modem, and decompressed at the other end of the line by the receiving modem. In theory, you are supposed to be able to get 4:1 compression, up to 57,600 bps with a 14,400 bps modem; in practice, figure on something closer to 2:1. The net effect is that file transfers take less time, reducing your connection time, and perhaps your phone bill.

N O T E   Files that are already compressed do not benefit from V.42bis hardware compression. ■

V.Fast and V.34—What's the Difference?

Before the release of the final V.34 standard by the ITU-TSS (an organization that makes these decisions worldwide), some modems came out featuring something called V.Fast (which was the original working title of the V.34 standard), or V.FC for short. This product line used a data pump (data processing engine) from Rockwell based on the preliminary V.34 standard. The final approval of the V.34 standard in 1994 meant that V.Fast modems required new data pump installations to be fully compatible (these were usually extra cost upgrades available strictly from the manufacturer).

N O T E   The new generation of 28,800 bps modems has caught on like wildfire. According to industry sources, more than one million V.Fast modems were sold within nine months before the real V.34 modems came out. ■

How Do They Do It?   Getting modems to talk at 28,800 bps and even faster is no easy achievement. Here's how it's done:

- Manufacturers have built in a lot of DSP (Digital Signal Processing) horsepower. All V.34 modems have several times the computing horsepower of personal computers just a few years ago.

N O T E   Some modems also rely, in part, on the processing power of your computer's CPU to do their work. One common example of this is Apple's GeoPort interface, which lets the computer act as a modem. ■

Part

IX

Ch

41

■ These modems use their DSP capabilities to compensate for some of the inherent problems with phone lines such as echo, attenuation (volume), and delay (think of the wait you hear on some international calls). Techniques such as line probing (looking for sections of a telephone line's bandwidth that might not work as well or might work better than others) and variable transmit levels help to establish the best possible connection on any given phone call.

Pushing the Limits of Technology   Although DSP is a power tool in the modem designer's arsenal, it isn't enough to compensate for all the situations a bad phone line or wiring can present.

It's also true that the current breed of modems is probably taxing the phone system to the limits of its design capability, which is going to limit the top speed at which your modem can operate reliably. As a result, conventional modems are not likely to offer speeds much greater than what is available now. Some modems have already stretched the limits of the V.34 standard to offer 33,600 bps performance, but the vast majority of residential telephone customers may not be able to take advantage of it.

Because modem manufacturers are pushing the frontiers of technology, don't expect 28,800 bps connections all the time. The fact is that many phone systems and phone lines simply do not have the raw quality to hold a full 28,800 bps connection. V.34 is a smart protocol and will negotiate the best possible speed, but even a Ferrari can't go 185 mph on a gravel road.

The Sad Facts of High-Speed Hookups   Even the best V.34 modems will have difficulty getting you consistent 28,800 bps connections. In general, most phone lines in the United States seem capable of supporting at least 21,600 bps. Many more work at 24,000 bps. Many newer systems complete calls at 26,400 or even 28,800 bps. But, if you find connections more consistent at the lower end of the spectrum, you can try the following suggestions, with no guarantee for success:

■ *Modem hardware bugs.* Contact the modem maker and see whether there's a later product update that might make for more efficient connections.

■ *Phone service problems.* Check for bogeymen in your local phone system that can sabotage the prospects for consistent high-speed connections. These include the following problems:

Old wiring. Older phone system wiring in a home or business can make the difference between getting a 28,800 bps connection and not connecting at all. Such phone wiring is solid-core copper. Over time, the copper oxidizes and the solid-core wires wear thin and break when bent. Both of these conditions result in unpredictable signals traveling through the wires that can wreak havoc with high-speed modems. In addition, standard telephone wiring is usually twisted pair (a pair of wires run together beside each other). Signals from one wire often distort signals on the other, causing further difficulties with clear communications.

N O T E Here's one solution for poor or old phone wiring: If you think you have old wiring, have it replaced with data grade twisted pair. Data grade wire has a shield that protects it from crosstalk, and it is generally of higher quality than old solid-core phone wire. Your local telephone company is usually the best resource for information about the condition of your phone wiring.

Old phone equipment. Not every phone company has the latest in all-digital telephone switching equipment. Older telephone companies (particularly in smaller, rural areas) often use analog equipment, sometimes with mechanical relays for switching. The more analog interference between your modem and your destination, the lower your chances of a high-speed connection. Modern phone switches cost millions of dollars, so getting your phone company to upgrade its equipment is a tricky matter, and you might just be stuck with the service you get. Moreover, if and when service is improved, no doubt your phone bill will improve too—to the phone company's benefit.

New phone equipment. Just when you thought technological progress had come to your rescue, virtually all long distance and most local telephone calls are now conducted in a digital environment. Digital transmission provides a nearly loss-free medium for transmitting data, and for the phone company it provides an opportunity. Because the digital data in a telephone call is no different than the digital data on your computer, it can be compressed in the same manner. To the telephone company, compressing the digital voices of telephone calls means they can fit more calls onto those multimillion-dollar pieces of equipment.

■ The technique the telephone company uses to compress the data in a phone call is called ADPCM (which stands for Adaptive Differential Pulse Code Modulation). Although ADPCM can compress the sounds made by a human voice almost undetectably, when the beeps and squeaks a modem makes are compressed, information is lost. When faced with ADPCM phone lines, V.34 modems often will not connect, or will connect at only a fraction of their maximum potential (such as 14,400 bps or 16,800 bps). If your home wiring is good and your phone company uses digital equipment, and you're still having trouble with the connection, check with the phone company to see whether you are connected to an ADPCM compressed line. If you are, have the company move you to a noncompressed line (if it can).

Part
IX
Ch
41

N O T E Take it from the author's personal experience—when you complain about the quality of your phone line, you can bet you'll go through several levels of customer support before someone is ready to listen to you. Most phone repair people are trained to deal with the common problems of lost dial tones and disconnections, and not with the arcane issues of getting a modem to work properly at a higher speed.

- *Other phones in your home or office.* Every telephone connected to a particular number at your home or office is taking a little bit of signal and introducing a little bit more interference onto that phone line. If your modem is using the same phone line as several telephones in your house, the combined effect of the noise and signal loss to the other phones can cause connection and data transfer problems. Luckily, this problem is easy to test for.

  If you're having problems, unplug all the telephones that are on the same line as the modem (even if they're in different rooms).

  If the problem goes away when only the modem is on the line, add the other phones back one at a time (checking that the modem still functions at each step). When the modem stops working, you have found the problem phone. Replace that phone or disconnect it when you're using the modem.

  Be especially suspicious of cordless phones or novelty phones (such as the ones with neon lights in them), because they seem to produce the most interference to other devices on the phone line.

- *Cables.* Check whether the cord that connects your modem to the wall plug for the telephone is in good shape. Also ensure that the modem's power cable and serial cable are in good condition. A worn or frayed cord not only hampers your attempts at high-speed communication, but also poses a safety hazard.

- *Old firmware in your modem.* Firmware is the computer program that runs inside your modem that makes it act like a modem. Typically, this program is stored on a ROM (read-only memory) chip inside your modem. With new standards such as V.34, modem manufacturers often upgrade the firmware inside their modems for better performance over time.

Refer to your modem manual to see how to determine which version of ROM firmware your modem has. You usually need to enter an ATI3 (the letter I) in a telecommunications program, such as HyperTerminal (included with Windows 95) or Microphone, and see what information is displayed (see fig. 41.3).

FIG. 41.3
Here's the ROM version
for a typical Supra 288
modem, as shown in a
communications program's
terminal window.

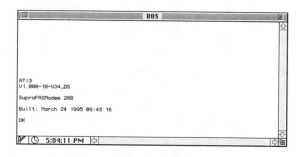

Armed with the knowledge of what firmware version you have, contact your modem manufacturer by e-mail or at its BBS and ask whether there is a newer version you can get. Most modems purchased new off the shelf will be up-to-date, but with new standards such as V.34, changes are often frequent and can make quite a difference in connection speeds and reliability.

N O T E   Many of the newer V.34 modems offer the capability of doing firmware updates via FlashROM. This is accomplished by a software program that you receive from the modem's manufacturer (you might even find it on America Online or at the manufacturer's own BBS). The software program examines the modem and then downloads the new code to its ROM chips, and in a few moments, your modem is up-to-date and ready to use. ■

Remember, even if your best efforts don't get you the highest speed connections, logging on at a somewhat slower speed will still get you much faster performance on America Online than 14,400 bps and slower speeds. This is especially helpful when you are surfing the Internet using America Online's Web browser.

Wireless Modems

If you are among the growing fraternity of cellular telephone users, you might be interested in the new generation of wireless modems designed to cope with the unique conditions presented by this growing technology. One common situation is that transmission quality decreases as you move from one cell to another, or when you pass through an area with tall buildings or tunnels that might inhibit good quality connections.

A standard modem can work, but you would want to purchase a model offering Microcom's MNP Level 10, a special error-correction technique that you need for fast, error-free transfers. A quick check of the modem specification sheets will provide this sort of information.

Part
IX

Ch
41

If you are using a conventional modem, you also need a special interface kit that enables your modem to be attached to the special jacks found on some cellular phones. The other alternative is a dedicated cellular modem, which costs more than a regular modem, but is not so expensive when you factor in the cost of that interface. Higher-cost products incorporate a cellular telephone and a modem in one convenient unit. One such product, from Air Communications Inc., is priced at around $1,500. Motorola, Inc., which makes a line of popular cellular telephones, is also intent on introducing one of these all-in-one products.

 TIP When transferring data by cellular telephone, try not to move your car. When your car is in motion, connections might be inconsistent, resulting in loss of data or an abrupt end to your online connection.

The Future of Modems

With the present-day high-speed modems testing the limits of regular (analog) telephone technology, how does one get higher performance to accommodate the needs of bigger graphics and sound? One possibility is ISDN (Integrated Services Digital Network), which requires an extra-cost digital phone line, a special modem (most priced at $500 or higher), and a serial card for many PCs to support this higher speed. At its best, ISDN can achieve up to 128,000 bps performance, making today's best modems seem awfully slow in comparison.

America Online's new AOLNet access network is promising future support for ISDN. Some dedicated Internet providers offer it now, enabling you to use ISDN to access AOL via TCP/IP at the highest possible speeds. And, as with other emerging technologies, it is not unreasonable to expect that the cost for digital phone lines and ISDN hardware will, in time, be reduced considerably from present levels. That, coupled with increased support from your favorite online service, will create the opportunity for an even more sophisticated degree of multimedia features for your future online visits.

A Brief Guide on Installing Your New Modem

Setting up your new desktop modem is usually easy. Configuring your software to the modem is more difficult, and you'll want to carefully read the instructions the manufacturer provides. This chapter offers some basic configuration information just to get you started. Internal modems on laptop computers that don't use the PC-card protocol might present a different level of installation issues and often require a visit to your dealer.

Attaching Your Modem

This section concentrates instead on how to set up a standard desktop modem. Following are some basic steps you should follow after you unpack your modem:

> **CAUTION**
>
> Even though installing an internal modem into a laptop computer might seem an easy task if you are experienced at probing your computer's innards, remember that you are often dealing with miniaturized circuitry, and there is always a risk if something goes wrong. Many computer and modem manufacturers will not extend product warranties to damage you do to your computer when installing an optional device inside. It might be a good idea to get estimates on installation from your dealer before proceeding.

1. Attach a modular telephone cable, with one end connected to your telephone line, and the other connected to the jack at the rear of your modem, which is usually labeled "line."

2. If you intend to have your regular telephone use the same line, attach its plug to the second jack on the modem, which is usually labeled "phone."

3. Attach the matching connector of the modem cable to the rear of your modem, and plug the other one into the serial port on your personal computer. This is best done with both products off.

> **N O T E** If you intend to attach multiple devices to your computer's serial port, look into a switchbox or a utility that can automatically switch port connections. You can find these devices at computer stores. Because Macs and Windows have different serial port schemes, be sure that the switchbox you buy is compatible with your computer. ■

4. Plug your modem into the wall socket. If it uses an external power supply, as many do, make sure that the other end is attached to the appropriate slot on your modem.

5. Turn on your modem. Check the owner's manual for instructions as to whether certain display lights should be lit when the product is working. Many Supra models, for example, show an OK light in the LED display when they are on and the product is functioning normally.

6. If your modem fails to light, make sure that everything is hooked up correctly. If you cannot get it to work, contact your dealer or the manufacturer's technical support people.

7. If everything works OK, turn on your computer and get ready to run your America Online session.

Part

IX

Ch

41

8. **For Windows 95 users:** After you first install your new modem, you'll want to use the Install New Modem Wizard to optimize your computer to provide the best possible performance with your new modem (see fig. 41.4).

FIG. 41.4
Just double-click the Modems Control Panel in Windows 95, click the Add button, and follow the simple on-screen instructions to adjust your computer to work best with your new modem.

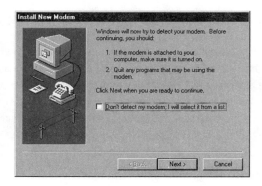

CAUTION

Every time you install a new modem, you might have to configure the modem in a regular communications program with certain commands. So, before jumping in and trying to log on to your favorite online service, be sure to check that your modem is working properly, as described in the next section of this chapter.

Before using your telecommunications software to change any modem settings, first see whether your modem has a built-in profile. This profile will enable a regular telecommunications program to work properly with your modem. But, America Online's software requires special settings for best performance, and the service provides modem files for many of the most popular products.

N O T E When you first install AOL software, the program checks your computer's serial port to verify the type of modem that's installed, but it won't necessarily select the exact make and model; usually a default setting is used. ▦

Adapting AOL's Macintosh Software to Your New Modem

To get the most efficient connections on America Online, you'll want to choose the right modem profile and adjust a few other settings. Here's how:

If the Setup box in your AOL software doesn't display a selection for your modem, download a modem profile from AOL's high-speed access center.

1. Use the keyword **HighSpeed** to enter the free high speed access area.
2. Double-click the Modem Profile Library entry in the list box, and then click the listing for Macintosh modem files, which brings up the selections shown in figure 41.5.

FIG. 41.5

Connection files for many popular modems are free from AOL.

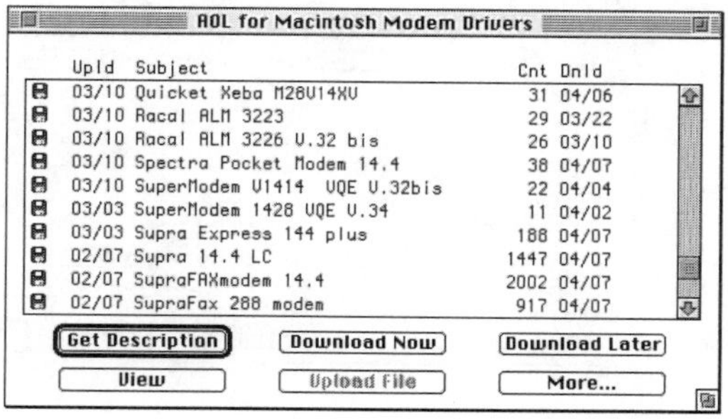

3. When you've selected the correct file, click the Download Now option, and choose the Online Files folder, located inside your AOL application folder, as the location for your file download (see fig. 41.6). The file must be stored there for it to be recognized in the Setup box.

FIG. 41.6

Modem files are stored on the Online Files folder of your AOL software.

4. If you receive a message that a file of the same name is already present, choose another folder for your download, then compare the new file and the old, and use the one with the latest date.
5. Click the OK button when the download is complete.

The next time you choose Modem Type in your AOL software setup box, the modem file you choose will be listed there.

Part
IX

Ch
41

1. Click the Setup button on the main America Online window, which brings up the window shown in figure 41.7.

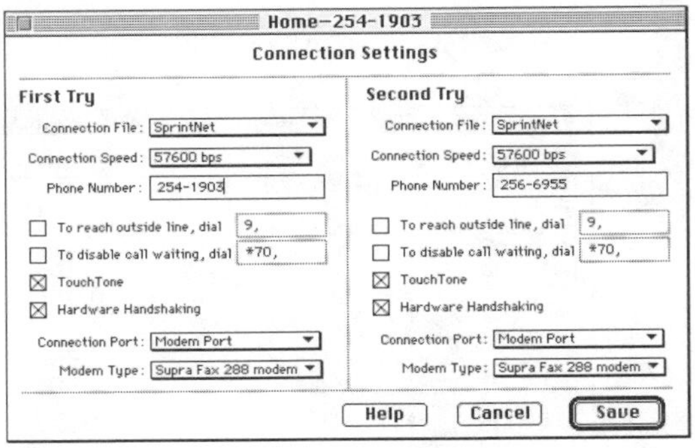

FIG. 41.7
Use the standard Mac AOL modem setup box to change your connection settings.

2. Click the Modem Type pop-up menu, which brings up a listing of the modem files available (see fig. 41.8).

FIG. 41.8
Select the make and model of your modem.

3. Be certain the same Modem Type is selected for both phone numbers shown in the Connection Settings window.

 If a modem file for your modem isn't available, use the keyword **HighSpeed** to view and download a list of up-to-date modem drivers. The modem driver you download installs in the Online Files folder in your AOL application folder.

4. Choose the right Connection File. When you select an access number, you'll see the network provider identified, such as AOLNet, SprintNet, or Tymnet. Be sure the setting is correct for both access numbers.

5. Choose a proper Connection Speed. This setting can be confusing. It refers to the maximum speed supported by your Mac's modem port, but it does not necessarily refer to the maximum speed your modem supports. Normally, you set the baud rate to equal your modem's highest connection speed, or the next highest figure offered by the software.

N O T E AOL's software supports a maximum modem port speed of 57,600 bps. But a slower computer, especially a laptop model, might work more efficiently (with fewer transmission errors) with a lower speed setting (38,400 bps or lower, for example). ▓

6. If you need to dial a special string to access an outside phone number, click the To Reach Outside Line, Dial option. Be sure to confirm the string you need at your office or hotel.

7. If you have call waiting installed on the telephone line to which your modem is connected, you'll want to be sure it's disabled when you visit America Online. The disable string is usually *70 for touch-tone phones, and 1170 for rotary phones. But, you'll want to contact your phone company to be sure this feature is supported.

8. By default, the Touch Tone option is selected. You change it only if you're not using Touch Tone service.

9. Whenever you access America Online at high speed, you need to check the next option, Hardware Handshaking. That and a proper hardware handshake cable are a must for getting a good connection to America Online at 9,600 bps or better.

10. The final setting you need to be concerned about is the Connection Port. Normally, it will be the Modem Port, but that setting will change depending on whether you are using a Macintosh laptop with an internal modem or accessing a networked modem through the Printer Port.

Part
IX

Ch
41

Adapting AOL's Windows Software to Your New Modem

1. If the modems displayed in the Setup Modem list box don't include the make and model of your modem, use the keyword **HighSpeed** to enter the free high-speed access area.

2. Click the Modem Profile Library entry in the directory window, and then click the listing for Windows modem files, which brings up the list shown in figure 41.9.

FIG. 41.9
Connection files for many popular modems are free from AOL.

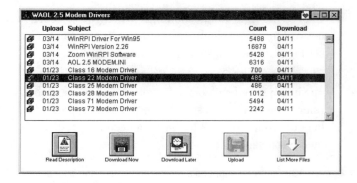

3. When you've selected the correct file, click the Download Now option, which brings up a dialog box showing the download path on top of the Directories scroll box. Double-click the folder that represents your America Online directory (AOL30 is being used for this example).

4. When the list of folders appears beneath the America Online directory, double-click the MPM folder as your destination for the file you're about to download (see fig. 41.10).

FIG. 41.10
AOL Windows modem files are stored in the MPM folder, which is located inside your America Online directory.

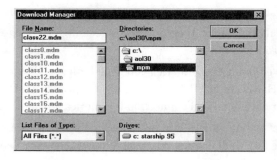

5. Click OK to confirm the destination of your download.

6. When the transfer of the new file is complete, OK that message, too.

The next time you choose Setup Modem in your Network & Modem Setup box, the new modem file you downloaded will be displayed in the directory window.

Now that you have the latest modem file for your modem, it's time to set up your AOL software to work at its best with your new modem.

1. Click the Setup button on the main America Online window, then Edit Location to bring up the Network Setup dialog box (see fig. 41.11).

FIG. 41.11
Choose your setup options from the Network Setup dialog box.

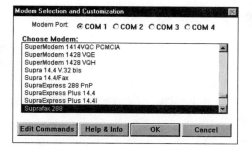

2. To choose the correct modem profile, close the Network Setup dialog box, and click the Setup Modem button at the right of the Network & Modem Setup screen, which brings up the Modem Selection and Customization box, shown in figure 41.12.

FIG. 41.12
Scroll through a listing of popular modem makes and models to find the one you have.

3. Be certain that the COM port you've selected here is the same one you've identified in your Windows 95 Modems Control Panel, under Network & Modem Setup. Later in this chapter, you'll be instructed how to diagnose common Windows modem configuration problems.

 If a modem file for your modem isn't available, use the keyword **HighSpeed** to view and download a list of up-to-date modem drivers. The file is installed in the AOL30/MPM directory.

4. Click the OK button to return to the Network & Modem Setup box.

5. Click the Edit Location option to confirm that your standard connection setup is correct.

6. Choose a proper Modem Speed. This setting can be confusing. It refers to the maximum speed supported by your PC's communication port, but it does not necessarily refer to the maximum speed your modem supports. Normally, you set the baud rate to equal your modem's highest connection speed or the next highest figure offered by the software.

7. If you need to dial a special string to access an outside phone number, click the option Use the Following Prefix to Reach an Outside Line. Be sure to confirm the string you need at your office or hotel.

8. If you have call waiting installed on the telephone line to which your modem is connected, you'll want to be sure it's disabled when you visit America Online. The disable string is usually *70 for touch-tone phones, and 1170 for rotary phones. But, you'll want to contact your phone company to be sure this feature is supported.

9. By default, the Touch Tone option is selected at the top of the Network Setup box. You change it only if you're not using touch-tone service.

What You Need to Know About Modem Setup Strings

Just as with a regular telecommunications program, AOL's software sends special commands, known as initialization and configuration strings, to your modem to communicate properly with it. This action is performed behind the scenes, of course, while you see the initializing command on your main AOL window just before your modem dials AOL's access number.

It's a different story, though, to log on to a BBS, for example, if you work with a regular communications package. If you watch your communications software in action, often you'll see commands displayed, shown as letters and numbers preceded by the letters AT (for attention), that represent the information used by your modem to begin and end a connection (see fig. 41.13).

Literally pages of modem commands can be found in your modem manual. The following list describes a few that apply to a typical Hayes-compatible modem. You will probably use them from time to time during your telecommunicating activities. To activate these commands, you must end your instruction with a return.

FIG. 41.13
The commands at the top of the screen in this Mac program set up the modem to dial a phone number.

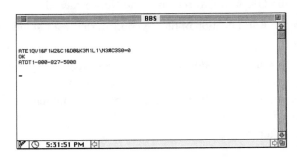

CAUTION

Not every modem supports the exact set of commands described in this chapter. The commands described represent typical models. Check your owner's manual to determine which commands apply to your modem. And, unless you're an expert at manipulating modem setups, don't alter AOL's connection strings until you contact AOL customer service about which ones are needed for the service's software.

- ATA. This command answers the telephone line.

- AT&F. This command reverts your modem to factory settings.

- AT&F1. On some high-speed modem designs, this setting turns on such features as error correction, flow control, and hardware compression. Supra's modems, for example, use this setting as a default when installed on a Macintosh.

- AT&F2. On other high-speed modem designs, this setting turns on such features as error correction, flow control, and hardware compression. Supra's modems, for example, use this setting as a default when installed on a DOS or Windows computer.

- ATLX. This command adjusts the volume of your modem's speaker. If X is 0, the speaker is at its lowest setting, 1 is the next lowest, 2 is the default or medium level, and 3 is the highest volume level.

- ATMX. This command turns your modem's speaker on or off. If X is 0, the speaker is off; if X is 1, the speaker is on.

- ATDT [phone number]. This command tells your modem to connect using the phone number you type. The T at the end of the command represents a typical touch-tone telephone. A pulse phone gets a P instead.

- ATZ. This command resets the modem to its default settings.

Solving Connection Problems: Q & A

It's a sure thing that you usually will be able to connect to America Online without incident or trouble. There are, however, reasons why you sometimes will have difficulty getting and maintaining an online connection. Some of the causes are due to your phone lines, sometimes it's your modem or the way it's set up, and sometimes it's the connection

Part

IX

Ch

41

number you use to access America Online or even the service's own network. In this section, many of the problems you are apt to confront are dealt with. If you have further difficulties, you can contact America Online customer service directly, or the manufacturer of your modem.

TIP Keep a printed list of the access numbers available in your area. That way, if you incorrectly choose the wrong network option with your AOL software, you can refer to the original list to fix it quickly.

I just bought a new V.34 modem, and it still connects at 2,400 bps. Why?

Getting a high-speed modem is half the battle. To log on to AOL at high speed, you need an access number that supports that speed. You can search the full listing of numbers while online via the keyword **HighSpeed**. You might also want to review the rest of this chapter for advice on having AOL's software help you automate the process of getting a new access number.

How do I know I'm connecting at high speed?

Just look at your AOL software window when logging on. Step 3 shows the speed at which you're connecting.

Why am I being disconnected constantly from AOL. What's wrong?

Getting bumped or disconnected from America Online shouldn't happen very often, but it does occur occasionally. Here's some advice on why it happens and what you can do about it:

- *Noise on your phone line.* This could be a problem with your local telephone service; but, before you contact the repair center, try another access number. You can locate AOL access numbers using the tips described in this chapter.

- **For Windows 95 Users:** *Check memory-resident programs.* Such programs as memory managers, device drivers, and terminate-and-stay-resident (TSR) programs can cause your modem to disconnect. You can try to diagnose the cause of this problem by removing these programs, and then restoring them, one at a time, until the problem returns.

- *Hardware problems.* Check your telephone lines, your modem, your connection cables, and your personal computer to see whether they are all working normally.

- *Other telephone equipment.* Additional telephones on your line, an answering machine, a fax machine, or even a cordless telephone can create additional noise that causes your modem connection to fail. You can diagnose this problem by disconnecting those devices and then restoring them, one by one, until the problem returns.

■ *Call waiting.* If you're using call waiting, be sure it's disabled (if that's possible) by using the appropriate check box in your AOL setup box as described in the sections entitled "Adapting AOL's Macintosh Software to Your New Modem" and "Adapting AOL's Windows Software to Your New Modem" in this chapter.

My connection hangs at Step 4, Requesting Network Attention. Why?

This might happen if the network selected in the modem Setup box (or Modem Selection and Customization box for Windows AOL users) is wrong; perhaps you've chosen AOLNet for a SprintNet access number. Because you cannot get online to fix this problem, take the following steps:

1. While offline, choose New Local # from the Screen Name drop-down box of the sign-on screen (see fig. 41.14).

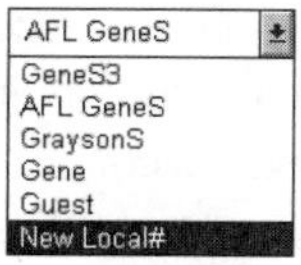

FIG. 41.14

Beginning the process to locate an AOL access number is simple with the Windows AOL software.

2. Click Sign-on. AOL's 800 support number will be automatically dialed.

3. Choose the local access numbers you want. (See Chapter 5, "America Online and Mobile Computing," for more information.)

I'm getting a busy signal. What do I do?

Just as you get a busy signal when you try to call someone who is already using the phone, the number you use to access America Online might be occupied, too. If this happens, log off and try again. If your AOL software is set up with two access numbers, after a few seconds, the second number you selected will be automatically dialed. If you get constant busy signals, use the keyword **Access** while online (see fig. 41.15) or the New Local # option (described earlier) to find another number.

If you get chronic busy signals from a specific number, report the problem. You can do that by using the AOL keyword **Access** and choosing the Report Number Problem option in the list box at the right. Connection numbers get regular updates, but the network carriers don't always know that their lines are clogged unless you tell them.

Part
IX

Ch
41

FIG. 41.15
AOL's modem connection center, known as Accessing America Online, can be used to find a new local connection number.

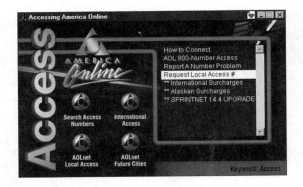

Help. My modem won't dial AOL.

If you've been able to connect to AOL before, something might have changed in your setup. Here are some steps to follow. Because they differ slightly from the Mac to Windows, the differences that apply to one computing platform or the other have been marked throughout this listing:

1. Switch off your modem and turn it back on again. Sometimes the modem's firmware will freeze due to a software defect or a previous connection problem. When you turn the modem on again, it's the equivalent of restarting your computer, and often has the same result.

2. Try another telecommunications program. Windows users can try Windows 95 HyperTerminal. Mac users can use Microphone, White Knight, Zterm, or a similar program. If another telecommunications program can successfully make your modem dial out, the problem is definitely related to the way your AOL software is set up.

3. Make sure the dial prefix or string is correct.

   For Windows users: In your Windows Network & Modem Setup box, click the Setup Modem button. See whether the correct Modem Type is selected (there's one for most makes and models of popular modems). Look at the Edit Commands option, and see whether the Dial Prefix is correct. For many modems, it should be ATV1 S11=55 Q0 E0 D. Note that the 0s are always zeros. If you've selected a special modem option, however, it might be totally different (and still correct). An example is shown in figure 41.16.

   For Macintosh users: Click the Setup box while logged off. Be sure that the correct Modem Type is selected from the pop-up menu.

FIG. 41.16
A typical modem string in
your AOL Windows software.

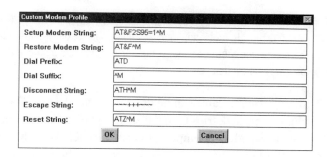

 For a complete list of up-to-date modem files, use the keyword **HighSpeed** to access an area where you can download the latest file for your modem. If a modem file isn't there, contact the manufacturer.

4. Maybe your modem setup string needs to be changed.

   For Windows 95 users: At the AOL welcome screen, click Setup while not logged on to AOL. Choose Setup Modem, and then click the Edit Commands button. Enter the string **ATDT^M** into the modem setup string. When you dial out, you should hear an audible click when the modem tries to dial out. If you don't hear the click, see item number 5 below.

5. **For Windows 95 users:** Check your Windows 95 Modems Control Panel and see if it's properly configured for your new modem. If not, run the Install New Modem Wizard to customize it to your make and model. Most popular modems will be readily recognized during this process.

Solving Typical Modem Connection Problems

Troubleshooting your modem connection on a personal computer is a fairly straightforward process. When trying to figure out where your modem problems lie, you need to look at several factors. The first place you should look is the modem itself. If the modem is OK, you should check to make sure that your PC is configured properly and that your software is set up correctly. By making sure that all three particulars are correct, you should be able to solve more than 90 percent of your modem problems.

Part
IX

Ch

41

■ Whenever you are having problems with your modem, make sure that it is hooked up properly. If you have an external modem, you should make sure that it is plugged in and turned on. Although this might sound simple, the number of people whose sole problem was an unplugged modem is amazing. If your modem is plugged in and turned on, the next thing you should check is the serial and phone cable.

N O T E Use a power strip for your personal computer and peripherals. Not only do some models provide protection against voltage surges, but you also can use the on/off switch on the power strip to turn on your computer's peripherals before starting your computer. That way, you always know that your modem is on. ▨

■ Testing the serial cable can be done a couple of ways. The first way is to watch the modem when AOL tries to initialize it. If you see the modem lights going on and off or hear the modem attempting to dial, the cable is likely good. If the cable seems to be OK but still has problems connecting at high speeds, you might have a non-hardware handshaking modem cable. The simplest way to test cable type is to try to connect to a 2,400 bps access number and see whether it connects properly. If you get a connection at 2,400 bps but not at 9,600 bps, it is possible that you have a non-hardware handshaking modem cable. Unfortunately, the only way to test your cable is to use special equipment that tests the modem directly. Frequently, the best solution in cases like this is to go out and spend a few dollars to buy a brand-new hardware handshaking modem cable from your local computer store.

■ If the serial cable is OK, you should turn your attention to the phone line itself. The first and most obvious test is to plug the modem's phone cable into a phone and see whether there is a dial tone. If there is, the other item you should check is the type of phone system you are connected to. Some office buildings, hotels, and apartment buildings use digital phone systems that are not compatible with high-speed modems. Aside from actually examining the telephone junction box itself, one of the easiest ways to tell whether you have a digital phone system is to try connecting to AOL at 1,200 or 2,400 bps and then at 9,600 bps. If the modem will connect at the lower speed but not at the higher, it is possible that you are using a digital phone system. If this is the case, you will need to contact someone in authority who can arrange for you to get an analog line specifically for your modem.

CAUTION

Many modems, especially PC-card and notebook-based models, can be damaged by connecting to a digital phone system. So, if you are suspicious of the phone system you are connecting to, don't attempt a connection until you have confirmation that the system is compatible with your modem. See Chapter 5, "America Online and Mobile Computing," for more advice on dealing with this situation.

If you have an internal modem, there is not too much you can test easily, aside from listening for the modem's dialing attempt.

I have call waiting, and my online connections are always interrupted when someone tries to call me. What do I do?

Although call waiting is convenient for people (because it allows one phone line to act as two lines), modems don't deal with it very well. Most modems, when confronted with the tone that announces an incoming call, spend several seconds getting back in sync with the connection. In many cases, the call-waiting click or tone causes a connection to drop.

When logging on to America Online from a line with call-waiting service, be sure to disable call waiting within your software dialing string. As described earlier in this chapter, the Setup box in the Mac version of AOL's software and the Network Setup box in the Windows version have a check box to activate a disable-call-waiting command. The default setting, 1170, is for rotary phones. Touch tones generally use *70. This setting varies from phone system to phone system, so if you're in doubt, look inside your phone book. Or, you might have to call your phone company and ask for help, because you might have to activate the capability to disable call waiting with a separate work order (and a modest monthly charge). If you're lucky enough to have a separate line for your modem, don't bother having call waiting installed on it.

AOL's Help Resource

If the solutions described here don't help you get a reliable hookup to AOL, there's one more resource—a one-on-one conference with an AOL support person. To visit that service, use the keyword **Tech Live**, which takes you to an area free of online charges (see fig. 41.17).

FIG. 41.17
Get free help here from
America Online.

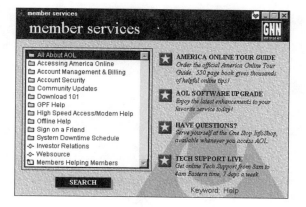

Part

IX

Ch

41

AOL's Member Services area is a full-service support center. To enter the live support section, click the button labeled Tech Support Live, and then two more buttons to reach the actual Tech Live information area. From there, you can check out suggestions on how to deal with your problem before you actually consult an online support person.

From Here...

In this chapter, you've seen the benefits of getting a high-speed modem and the impact it can make on your use of America Online and on your online bill. Although modems sometimes seem a little confusing to deal with, after you get the hang of it, they are relatively easy to set up. After they've been hooked up, modems will give years of trouble-free service without further adjustment.

- In Chapter 5, "America Online and Mobile Computing," you'll learn tips and tricks to stay connected while you're on the road.

- For full details on setting up your AOL software, read Appendix B, "Using Your America Online Macintosh Software," or Appendix C, "Using Your America Online Windows Software."

Appendixes

If You're New to the Online World

This book is a "Special Edition" because it is filled with power-user tips that make your online visits more productive and more fun. I realize some of you haven't joined America Online yet, so I've designed this appendix, and the next two, to serve as a tutorial on joining America Online and using the software. So, I assume that you've followed through on my suggestion in Chapter 1, "Getting Past the Opening Screen," to read this section next.

Whether you are using an Apple Macintosh or a PC equipped with Windows, America Online software is easy to install and use. But, despite the simplicity of these programs, AOL provides an extraordinary set of tools that will make your AOL visits informative and enjoyable.

Before you learn how to install your America Online software, I will give you a couple of quick shortcuts that take you around the online community quickly and enable you to get direct online help if you need it.

The first shortcut is a *keyword*. This is a keyboard command that you can specify *only* while you're connected to America Online. A keyword can take you just about anywhere on America Online, even if you don't know the exact route.

To use keywords, press ⌘-K if you're using a Macintosh or Ctrl+K for Windows; then enter the keyword in the entry field of the Keyword dialog box displayed on your screen. Now press Return or Enter and, in just a few seconds, you'll be transported to the place you want to visit. (Of course, if the keyword is wrong, you'll get a message to that effect; you can then click the Search button to view some suggestions that might match your quest.) You'll learn more about keywords in Appendix B, "Using Your America Online Macintosh Software" and Appendix C, "Using Your America Online Windows Software."

Whenever you're logged on to America Online, you can visit an online support area to get direct assistance with any problem you might have—it's free of charge. To get there, open the Members menu and select Member Services, or use the keyword *Help*. A window appears, asking whether you want to enter this free area.

Okay, now let's get ready to join the online community. ■

Ordering Your America Online Software

America Online disks are often free with your new software or computer purchase. Some of your favorite computing magazines also include the software disks from time to time.

If you don't have a disk on hand, you can order one by calling 1-800-827-6364. Tell the operator the kind of computer you have so that you receive the correct software. You will get your disk in a couple of weeks. In the meantime, you can review this section and the next two about installing your software, establishing your personal online account, and mastering all aspects of the America Online program.

Even if you already have telecommunications software installed on your computer, America Online uses its own proprietary software to provide a unique graphics environment and efficient performance. You need America Online's special software to use the service. It does not work with a general-purpose terminal program. The lone exception is AOL's special support BBS, which you can access from any terminal software.

Installing Your America Online Software

The steps involved in installing the Macintosh and Windows versions of America Online software are similar. Where they differ, I'll explain the differences and provide illustrations to show the process. The basic system requirements are similar, too (in terms of comparable Mac and PC model support).

Knowing What You Need

For a Macintosh, you need at least a 68030 Mac (such as a IIci), running System 7.1.1 or later, with 8MB or more of installed RAM and at least 15MB of free hard drive space.

Any IBM PC or compatible with a 486 CPU or better, a minimum of 8MB RAM, that runs Windows 3.1 or later should be able to use America Online for Windows software efficiently. 256-color capability or better is recommended to view graphics files. You want to have at least 15MB of free space on your hard drive to store your new software.

I wrote this section with the assumption that you are comfortable performing the basic functions of using your computer, such as installing new software from a floppy disk onto your hard drive, performing basic file management chores, opening applications, and using your mouse. If you need a quick refresher course, review the instruction manuals that came with your computer or operating system disks.

Before you install the software, though, make a backup of your original floppy disk. (You should do this with all your software and disks.) Then tuck away the originals in a safe place, in case your copies are damaged. If you have the CD-ROM version of AOL's software, just keep it in a safe place and it should last indefinitely.

You need one more thing, of course, and that is a Hayes-compatible modem with a speed of 2,400 bps (bits per second) or greater. If you don't have a modem, you can buy one at your favorite dealer. If you've never used a modem before, let me just briefly explain that a *modem* is a device that converts the digital information from your computer into analog tones that can be transferred through your telephone lines.

Because America Online has been rolling out its 28,800 bps service throughout the world—and prices for high-speed modems have dropped—buy the fastest modem you can afford. You won't regret it. (If you have Internet-based TCP/IP access, you can access America Online at even higher speeds.)

TIP Before installing AOL software, have your software's registration certificate and your credit card or checkbook handy. Be sure that your modem has been turned on and is hooked up to your computer and to your phone line.

Installing the Macintosh Version

N O T E Depending on whether you receive your Mac AOL software on a floppy disk or a CD, you may see two different versions of the software. Because of the size constraints, floppy disks from AOL include version 2.7 of the program (which is described briefly in Chapters 1 and 2). To get the version of AOL software described in this book, 3.0, you need to download it from AOL's upgrade area—available via keyword Upgrade. ▓

The Macintosh version of America Online's software is compressed—a technique used to make files smaller so that they take up less room. This way, the software can be supplied on a single 1.4MB floppy disk.

N O T E If you are using an older Macintosh that does not have a 1.4MB or super drive installed, please contact America Online customer service for a set of 800K (double-density) software disks. ▓

After you've made a backup of your original software disk, you're ready to get the software up and running. Follow these steps:

1. Insert the floppy disk into your Macintosh's floppy drive.
2. Double-click the America Online icon to bring up the screen shown in fig. A.1.

FIG. A.1
Double-click the AOL icon to begin the installation process and to display this screen.

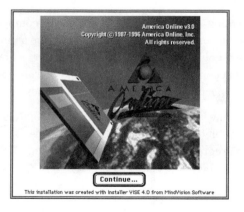

3. The program then asks you to select a destination on your hard drive for installation of your software. Your America Online software gets its own special folder. You can either accept the folder name it suggests or pick one of your own.

After you decide on a location for the new folder, the installation process continues. America Online keeps you informed of its progress, as shown in figure A.2.

FIG. A.2
You can keep track of the installer doing its work.

In a minute or two, you receive a message that the software has been successfully installed. (If you have any problems at this point, call AOL at the phone number shown earlier in this chapter, for personal assistance.)

4. Now you can double-click the AOL application icon to display the screen shown in figure A.3. You then are guided through the steps needed to adjust the computer to your modem.

FIG. A.3
Your first welcome message from America Online appears at this point. Just click Continue to progress through the setup process.

For the next few moments, you see several information windows (see fig. A.4). As America Online software versions are upgraded, the displays might be different from the ones shown here. Just read the instructions carefully before proceeding. If you have any questions or problems, you can choose Cancel to cancel the installation, and resume it at a later time.

FIG. A.4
This screen takes you another step on the way toward your first online connection.

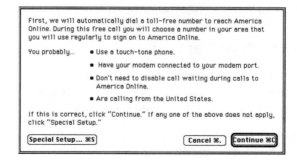

If you've opted for the standard setup routine, your modem will now be checked to get basic information (see fig. A.5).

FIG. A.5
America Online software
checks your modem for
information about its
performance capabilities.

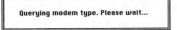

After the modem is probed, AOL software displays its selection for you. If you have a different make and model of modem, you'll want to choose that instead if it's on the list (as I did for fig. A.6). You'll want to make this selection for the best possible hookup to AOL.

FIG. A.6
Select the kind of modem
you have here, and then
click OK.

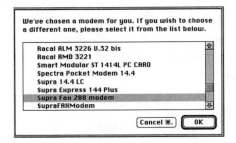

If you chose Special Setup (refer to fig. A.4) at the start of the setup process, you would have been asked whether you want to install the option to disable Call Waiting services when you are online. If you have Call Waiting and someone tries to telephone you while you're online, the tones you hear in your telephone quickly terminate your online connection. You might have to check with your local telephone company, however, before choosing this option. Not all services give you the option of turning off Call Waiting for a single call.

If your online connections are being made from an office, you might have to dial a special number, usually 9, to get an outside line. So, be sure to select this option if you need it under the Special Setup process; otherwise, you can't make your first online connection.

Installing the Windows Version

The Windows version of America Online software, like its Macintosh counterpart, is compressed—a technique used to make files smaller so that they take up less room. That way, the software can be supplied on a single floppy disk.

After you've made a backup of your original software disk, you're ready to get the software up and running by following these steps:

1. Insert the America Online floppy disk into your PC's floppy drive (A or B).

2. Using the Start Menu, choose Run (Windows 3.1 users choose File, Run from the Program Manager).

3. Depending on which floppy drive you inserted the disk in, type either a:\setup or b:\setup. Then press Enter (see figs. A.7 and A.8).

N O T E The version of AOL's Windows software used when this book was prepared is a 16-bit program, which doesn't support the Windows 95 Add/Remove Program utility. By the time you read this book, it is likely that a 32-bit Windows 95 version of AOL's software will be available (with features much the same as the current version). That version will support the Windows 95 Add/Remove utility software.

FIG. A.7
America Online's software installation and setup is easy to follow.

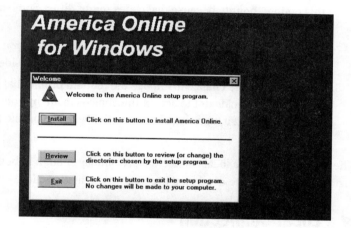

FIG. A.8
A progress bar shows the status of the America Online Windows installation process.

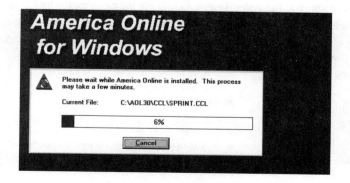

4. When your installation is complete, you return to your Windows 95 desktop. The AOL icon appears in its own application directory. Double-click this icon to open your America Online for Windows software.

5. As soon as the program opens, you're guided step-by-step through the process of setting up your America Online software to work with your modem and telephone. Before making a selection, read the instructions carefully. As America Online software is updated, the information is likely to change.

6. If you decide to opt for a custom installation, you can select Other Options in your first setup window. If you have Call Waiting on the line to which your modem is hooked up, you need to use the option to disable that service so that you aren't knocked offline when a call comes in. Check with your local phone company about this option, though, because dial codes might differ. Some areas might not provide a way to disable Call Waiting.

7. When you are calling America Online from your office, you might need to have your modem dial 9 or another access number to reach an outside line.

8. You also have the chance to choose the modem profile that best fits your needs—that is, if you decide not to accept the choices made by your software. But, if your modem isn't listed, your best bet is to stick with the profile the software chooses for you.

The steps for getting a local connection are similar enough in both the Mac and Windows installation, so they are described together in the next section.

Getting a Local Connection

Now you want to have America Online's host computer find a local connection number (see fig. A.9). As soon as your modem setup has been completed, you are asked to enter your area code so that America Online can hook you up to the closest and fastest (and thus the cheapest) connection in your area.

FIG. A.9
This screen appears when you're making your first connection.

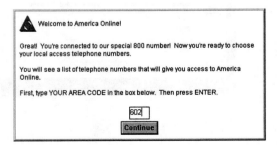

The host computer searches its directory of access numbers for ones that match the area code you entered (see fig. A.10). If you cannot locate a number that's in that area code, you have the option to choose another number from a nearby area code. Because America Online is always adding new connection numbers, you always have the opportunity to change that number later. (See Chapter 6, "America Online and Mobile Computing," for more information about locating and changing your America Online access numbers.)

FIG. A.10
Pick your first local access number here.

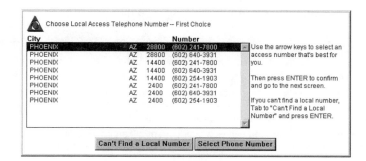

You should select two connection numbers if they are available. That way, if your modem cannot make a connection with the first number—perhaps because it's busy or because of line noise—you have a second chance to connect to America Online.

Establishing Your Online Account

From here on, until you log on to the service for the first time, you are guided through several steps that enable you to establish your own exclusive America Online account and set your billing options. (Now you find out why I suggested that you have the certificate that came with your software disks, and your credit card or checkbook handy.)

The choices you make now are not etched in stone. If you decide to change your password or billing information later, you can easily do so in the free Member Services area.

To establish your online account, follow these steps:

1. First, find the registration numbers on your America Online software package. Enter the certificate number and certificate passwords in the blank Certificate Number and Certificate Password boxes. You can use the Tab key on your computer's keyboard to move from one entry field to the next.

N O T E Because the setup screens change frequently, I am not showing them in this book. But, the instructions are clearly labeled and the steps are easy to follow. ▪

2. Choose the Continue button.

3. Enter your name, mailing address, and telephone number.

4. Choose the Continue button.

5. Indicate how you want to pay for your America Online service. You can choose Modify Billing Information and then choose from American Express, Discover Card, MasterCard, or Visa. Or, if you prefer, you can have your online charges deducted regularly from your checking account.

N O T E   If you decide to pay for your AOL bill by a checking account draft, it may take several days for AOL to verify your account. During that time, you will not be able to log on, so just be patient. ▪

 T I P   To check your usage bill on America Online, use the keyword *Billing*. You are then taken to a free support area where you can view your current bill and make changes to your billing information.

To protect you, America Online verifies all your billing information. If the program encounters a problem in establishing your account, the account is suspended until you are able to update your billing information. This precaution is taken solely for your protection. After all, you wouldn't want to pay for someone else's online charges.

Creating Your Online Mailing Address

Next you need to enter your online mailing address, or screen name. Here's your golden opportunity to be creative. Your online address can contain from three to 10 characters (letters and numbers). You can identify yourself on America Online by your first name, an abbreviation of your name, or even a descriptive word or two that expresses your own unique personality traits, such as "TheBear."

The online name you choose for yourself is used by your master account, and the host computer checks that name (along with the password you select) every time you log on to America Online. You can add as many as four names to your online account, for use by other members of your family, or for yourself. Remember that you can use only one screen name attached to your account at any one time. If you want to log on simultaneously with more than one screen name, you need to establish separate accounts.

If someone already has the name you selected, you are given the option of using that name plus a number—the number reflects how many others are using that same name. You may, for example, be offered the choice of using "GeneS12345" if a number of people online are already using some variation of "GeneS."

CAUTION

Because you cannot change or delete your master account name without deleting your account, take as much time as you need to select an appropriate screen name.

As you try to locate an available online address (or screen name), America Online searches its database to determine whether someone else already has selected that name. Because America Online is a family-oriented service, names that use vulgar language or have a vulgar connotation are not accepted.

After America Online has accepted your screen name, your next step is to select a password. A password is your ounce of protection against someone using your account without your permission, so don't use anything obvious, such as a contraction of your name. Select a unique word or phrase that someone wouldn't stumble on at random. A mix of numbers and letters, or even punctuation marks, is a good option. For additional security, you may want to change your password from time to time.

 TIP

When you select a screen name and password, write it down and place that information in a safe place. That way, if you forget your password, you can find it again quickly when you need it.

After you've chosen your online address, you're ready to make your introduction to the online community.

Before you are welcomed to the America Online family, you are asked whether you accept the Terms of Service. Carefully read the information displayed. You can also check the text of it in the Online Support area, but basically it requests that you be a good citizen during your online visits and avoid using vulgar language. For more about the Terms of Service, see Chapter 16, "Parental Issues and Internet Access."

Exploring America Online in Your First Online Session

The first time you log on to America Online (and assuming that your sound is working), you hear a friendly voice intone, "Welcome," and a few seconds later, you hear, "You've Got Mail." Yes, when you sign onto America Online for the first time, you indeed find a letter in your mailbox. Just click the You Have Mail icon, and you see your first letter listed in the directory. Just double-click that directory listing, and the text appears in a new open document window on your computer's screen. The letter is from Steve Case, the president of America Online. He welcomes you to the service and briefly outlines the special features you may want to examine as you begin your travels through the network.

The first screen you see on your computer, the Welcome screen, is your gateway to all the features offered by America Online (see fig. A.11). Along the right side and bottom of the Welcome screen is a list of special announcements, places to visit, and the Top News headline. Just click the icon to the right of the message you want to investigate (or to the left of the Top News headline), and you are instantly transported to that area of America Online. The list you see here changes several times per day as different services are featured and the top news stories change.

FIG. A.11
Read your first welcome message from America Online.

At the left of the Welcome screen is a shaded rectangular box labeled CHANNELS. When you click this box, you'll be taken to the window that lies beneath the Welcome screen; this is your gateway to all the major services on America Online (see fig. A.12).

FIG. A.12
Consider America Online's Channels menu as its table of contents to all the major features of the service.

The Channels window contains three rows of color icons, each of which takes you to a different AOL department (or channel). They are clearly labeled, and you can click any one of them now to explore the service further. These departments are discussed in detail in Chapter 6, "Where Do We Begin?"

For now, you'll want to just take a brief tour of the service. After you've begun to find your way around, you'll want to learn more about your new software.

And that takes us to the next two appendixes, B and C, where you'll learn how to harness the power of AOL's sophisticated telecommunications software.

 TIP If you're watching your budget, use the keyword *Clock*. You then see an online clock that displays the amount of time you've spent on the service.

Part

X

App

A

Using Your America Online Macintosh Software

Throughout most of this book, I have been talking to folks who are experienced AOL users. In this Appendix, I'm concentrating on those of you who have just joined AOL (and want to know what the fuss is all about) or just want to hone your skills with the latest Macintosh AOL software.

If you're a Windows user, skip to the next appendix, unless you want to learn how the other half lives, or you're working in a mixed-platform environment.

After you have made your introductions on America Online, set up your account, and logged on for the first time, you want to get down to the business of learning your new software. The Macintosh version of the America Online software doesn't come with a manual, although an extensive Help menu, including Apple Guide assistance, is provided. But as long as you know how to do your everyday tasks on your Macintosh, such as moving and clicking your mouse and selecting menus, you shouldn't have any trouble picking up all the ins and outs of using America Online. And with this brief guide in your hands, you can become an expert in a short time. ■

Accessing Your America Online Software

Here's a convenient way to instantly access your America Online software, even at startup:

1. Make an alias of your America Online application icon (highlight the AOL icon, and select Make Alias from the File menu at your Finder desktop).

2. Take the alias and place it inside the Startup Items folder (it's in the System folder).

Next time, and each time, you restart, America Online's software will open seconds after your Mac's desktop appears. An alternative is to place the alias in the Apple Menu Items folder for quick access from the Apple menu.

In the pages that follow, you look at all the features of your new software. The text describes how all the menus work and details the special features that are offered. You also get some helpful hints that can make your online visits more enjoyable.

 If you have a problem using your America Online software and you need an immediate answer, press ⌘-/, or choose one of the handy AOL help guides from the balloon Help menu at the right side of the menu bar.

Changing the Modem Settings

Before you make your first connection to America Online, you'll want to take a moment or two to be sure your modem is set up properly. When you first install your America Online software, the software examines your modem and sets a default modem profile for it. If you buy a new modem, you'll want to change these settings. Or you might want to change your connection numbers to the America Online network.

 A selection of updated modem drivers is available for download from America Online's High Speed Access area (keyword: **highspeed**). To access a list of these files, double-click Modem Profile Library in the list box and then double-click AOL for Macintosh Modem files. You'll see many of the popular modems represented in that list. Sometimes modem makers will even supply an AOL connection file with their own software (so you want to check out the files they give you).

To change your connection settings, follow these steps:

1. Click the Setup button in the main America Online window to display the Locality screen shown in figure B.1. (You can change these settings only when you're not logged on to the America Online network.)

FIG. B.1
You can quickly and easily make changes to your connection setup.

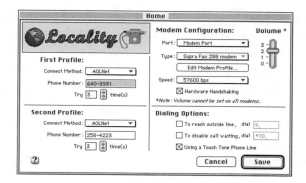

You can set up two connection profiles. Your America Online software uses the one on the top, First Profile, when trying to make your initial connection to the network. If the connection fails for some reason (either because of a busy line or noise on the line), the number will be redialed up to five times, depending on what you select using the up and down arrows below the number.

If repeated attempts to dial the number don't get a response, the number you enter in the Second Profile, at the bottom left, will be used, and the number redialed for as many times as you have chosen.

N O T E   If you're planning to move or you're taking a trip outside your regular calling area, it's simple to find a new connection number to AOL. Just log on as usual, and type the keyword **Access**. You'll be asked whether you want to enter the free AOL support area. Press Return or click Yes. You then see a window with a list of options for finding an access number. For now, just double-click Search. You see a window with a space for you to enter the area code you want to check. When you enter that number, America Online checks its online phone directory and produces a list of phone numbers for the selected area.

2. Changing online numbers is easy. Just type the new number in the Phone Number box. When you change the number, you also might need to change the Connect Method, which represents the service America Online uses to connect you to its network. When you get a list of phone numbers from America Online for your area, you see such names as AOL GlobalNet, AOLNet, SprintNet, or Tymnet attached to the phone numbers. Simply pull down the menu at the right of the Connect Method label and select the correct name of the service provider.

3. Now let's look at the options at the right of the setup box in figure B.1. First there's Modem Configuration.

    The Port option simply enables you to tell the software which jack your modem is hooked up to. The default setting is Modem Port. If you're using the Printer Port instead (perhaps for a network modem), select that option from the pull-down menu.

4. Choose the correct modem type from the Type pop-up menu. If you are an advanced modem user and feel you'd like to try to tweak performance, you can click Edit Modem Profile. Most of you, however, will probably prefer to leave well enough alone (at least without assistance from the modem's manufacturer).

5. When you choose a phone number from America Online's phone directory, the connection speed supported by each phone number is also shown. You need to choose a connection speed from the Speed pop-up menu that's the same or higher than the speed at which you're connecting. In other words, choose at least 28,800 bps if you're going to use a 28,800 bps access number (otherwise the lower speed will limit the rate at which you hook up to AOL).

6. The check box at the bottom of the Modem Configuration box, Hardware Hand-shaking, is needed for a high-speed modem, such as a 9,600 or 14,400 bps (or even faster) model. If you're using one of these models, check this box. If not, you can leave this option off.

7. If you'd rather not put up with the squawking and squealing noise a modem makes when it connects to your favorite online service, you may want to try setting the volume level using the slider switch at the right side of the setup box. Unfortunately, not all modems will take this setting (check the modem's manual to be certain). For example, in some models designed for Apple's PowerBook line you have to use the Sound Control Panel instead.

8. The first of your three Dialing Options is a place to put a special number to reach an outside line. Some businesses (and usually hotels) have special phone lines that require a "dial-out" code. Usually this code is 9, but you can change that number if necessary. Some hotels also use 9 as their dial-out prefix. If you need to dial a special number to reach an outside line, check the To Reach Outside Line box.

9. If you have Call Waiting service, you need to disable it when you make your online connection because the tones that sound in your telephone when someone is trying to reach you can interrupt your connection and end your AOL session prematurely. The number listed in the To Disable Call Waiting check box, *70, is for touch-tone telephones. If you have rotary service, the number is usually 1170. To be certain of which number to use, call your local telephone company. Sometimes the ability to disable Call Waiting for a single phone call is an optional service.

10. If you have a touch-tone phone, check the Using A Touch Tone Phone Line check box (it's checked by default).

TROUBLESHOOTING

Help! I tried to set up AOL to work with my PowerBook modem, but I can't find the right port. I don't see the choices you list in your book. The only ones I see are Internal Modem and Printer/Modem Port. What gives? If you're using a Macintosh PowerBook model, your choice of available ports may be different. If you have an internal modem (a unit installed inside your PowerBook), the Internal Modem choice is the one to make. For an external modem, use the second option (or whatever external modem choice is available in your AOL setup box).

Why does my new V.34 (28,800 bps) modem still hook up at 2,400 bps? Getting a high-speed modem is half the battle. To log on to AOL at high speed, you need an access number that supports that capability. You can search the full listing of numbers via the keyword **Access**.

Setting Preferences

The next thing you want to do is set up your America Online software's preferences so that the software looks and feels the way you want it to. Even if everything looks OK to you, trying out a few settings just to see whether you can adjust things a bit better is worth the effort.

First the Easy Way

Before we look at all the preferences you can choose from with AOL software, let me tell you how you can get AOL to guide you through them all with a few mouse clicks. First choose My AOL from the Member's menu, to bring up the screen shown in figure B.2.

FIG. B.2
My AOL guides you through all the preferences you can select, so you see what they do and why you'd want to change them.

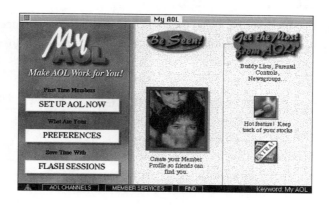

Just click the appropriate icons to be guided through the preference setting process. Let's look over the choices:

- ■ **SET UP AOL NOW.** If you're a new member, this choice will allow AOL to guide you through all the preferences, step-by-step, to show you what you can change and why you would change it.

- ■ **PREFERENCES.** This choice will bring up an attractive graphic display of all of the program settings and what they do.

- ■ **FLASHSESSIONS.** This option will let you set AOL to automatically run sessions (so long as your computer is on) at specified times to get your e-mail, files sent with that mail, and Internet newsgroup messages. I explain more about this one in Chapter 8, "Using America Online E-Mail."

- ■ **BE SEEN!** This choice tells you how to make a member profile, so other members can learn more about you. You do not have to make a profile if you'd prefer not to. Chapter 7, "America Online's People Connection," will take you step-by-step through the process.

- ■ **GET THE MOST FROM AOL!** The choices in this list let you know when your online friends have logged on, and allow you to set Parental Controls and Newsgroup access, so you can regulate what your kids see on AOL. Chapter 16, "Parental Issues and Internet Access," explains this all in more detail.

- ■ **HOT FEATURE!** If you're in the stock market, this option allows you to create your custom stock portfolio so you can track the progress of your favorite companies. Chapter 26, "Online Investment and Tax Information," covers this feature.

- ■ **EXTRA!** This is AOL's News Profiles feature, which lets you receive the latest news on the subjects that interest you in your mailbox each day. Chapter 23, "The News of the Day," covers the details.

Setting Preferences—One by One

If you'd rather set your preferences manually, choose Preferences from the Members menu. The Preferences dialog box appears on the left side with a list of Preference Categories that you can scroll. When you choose one of these categories, the list of appropriate options appears on the right side of the dialog box.

Setting most of your preferences involves the same steps. You click a check box to select it and click again to deselect it, as appropriate.

Setting General Preferences

When you bring up the Preferences dialog box, it'll default to the last preference category you worked in. We'll start from the beginning, with General Preferences (see fig. B.3). Here are your choices:

FIG. B.3
Your most basic AOL program settings are found among General Preferences.

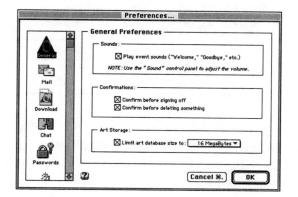

- **Sounds.** AOL's friendly "voice" is one of the most attractive parts of the service. Not only are you greeted with a hearty "welcome" and "goodbye," but you'll find event sounds in other areas as well, such as a brief round of applause when you first enter AOL's Center Stage area. If you'd rather not disturb anyone, though, uncheck the box.

- **Confirmations.** When you click the check boxes (and this is the normal setting), you get confirmation messages before you sign off AOL or you delete something (such as e-mail you've received).

- **Art Storage.** Much of the fancy artwork you see on AOL is stored in a database file. You click the pop-up menu to select the maximum size of your artwork file (be sure you don't fill up your hard drive too much). Once that maximum size is reached, the oldest, least-used artwork will be deleted automatically by AOL's clever software.

Setting Mail Preferences

How do you want to handle your AOL e-mail? You've got a number of choices to make, but the standard ones will usually suit (see fig. B.4). Here are your choices:

FIG. B.4
From quoting style to where to put your received e-mail, AOL gives you a number of choices.

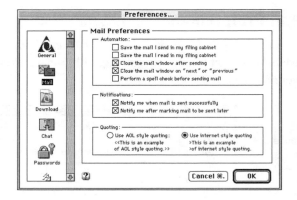

Automation   This is what AOL will do to your e-mail without any further action from you.

- **Save the mail I send in my filing cabinet.** With this option, a copy of your sent mail is stored on your hard drive that you can bring up any time by calling up AOL's convenient Personal Filing Cabinet from the File menu.

- **Save the mail I read in my filing cabinet.** With this option, a copy of your read mail is stored on your hard drive that you can bring up any time by calling up AOL's convenient Personal Filing Cabinet from the File menu.

- **Close the mail window after sending.** This is the default setting. When the mail is sent, gone is the document window too, which keeps your Mac's desktop from being cluttered.

- **Close the mail window on "next" or "previous."** This is another desktop clutter saver (the default). Only the e-mail window you bring up is displayed.

- **Perform a spell check before sending mail.** This feature activates AOL's e-mail spell checker, which examines your e-mail for mistakes before the e-mail is sent. As soon as the checking is done, the mail goes on its way.

Notifications   This is what AOL's software will tell you when you send your e-mail.

- **Notify me when mail is sent successfully.** Just an ounce of assurance to inform you your e-mail is on its way.

- **Notify me after marking mail to be sent later.** If you intend to send your e-mail via AOL's FlashSession (I've explained more about that feature in Chapter 8), this is a useful reminder of the choice you've made.

Quoting   When you select text in an e-mail message you've received and click the Reply or Reply to All icon, that text is "quoted" in the body of your new message. Here's how the quote should be formatted.

- **Use AOL style quoting.** This is the default setting, but you'll notice I didn't use that setting. It places double caret marks at the beginning and end of your quoted passage.

■ **Use Internet style quoting.** Here's where you should go with the flow and follow Internet-style quoting, because it makes your e-mail easier to read by other users, especially those to whom you've written by AOL's Internet e-mail feature. A caret mark is placed at the beginning of each line of quoted text. This is also the standard Internet e-mail convention, and one you will probably want to get used to.

Setting Downloading Preferences

These settings (see fig. B.5) control how the files you download to your computer are handled.

Part
X
App
B

FIG. B.5
Choose where you want your downloaded files placed, as well as various image compression and display options here.

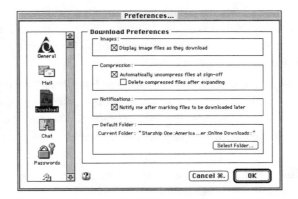

■ **Images.** AOL's software opens more than just text documents or compressed documents. You can also open, view, and print files created in several graphics formats, such as GIF, JPEG, and PICT. If you have Apple's QuickTime software installed (version 2.0 or later), you can also open and play QuickTime movies. This is a great advantage, because there are thousands of graphic-related files for you to download on AOL. You'll find such things as weather maps, pictures of your favorite celebrities, and more. Leave the option shown here checked to see image files actually display during the download process.

N O T E If a graphics file is very large, America Online's software might not have sufficient memory to view it, and you'll receive a message to this effect. You can usually get around this by closing all open document windows and then trying to open the graphics file again. If that technique doesn't work, give America Online's software additional RAM with the Finder's Get Info command (it must be done when the software is not running). An additional 500K or so is often enough. ■

■ **Compression.** Many files you download from America Online are compressed to make them smaller and thus reduce the time needed to get the files to your computer (and reduce your online charges). America Online software includes a tool to automatically decompress files you've just downloaded (most popular formats are supported, except for DiskDoubler and Now QuickFiler). By default, when you end your America Online session, all files you have just downloaded are decompressed automatically (if they were saved in a compression format that's supported, of course).

You should keep this compression option checked, because it results in all compressed files being expanded automatically as soon as you log off (which pretty much mirrors what you'd do with them anyway in many situations). This option makes using your downloaded files much easier. If you don't have enough disk space to store all those files, or you want to decide later whether you want to use the files, just turn this option off.

The second option, Delete Compressed Files After Expanding, will result in only the expanded file staying around after the file expansion process is done. This option is one you should use with caution, as protection against the rare occasion when an expanded file might become damaged somehow and you need to use the source file again.

■ **Default Folder.** Click the Select Folder button to choose the location on your hard drive where downloaded files will be stored.

Setting Chat Preferences

Chats and conferences are often the most enjoyable experiences on America Online. Here's a run-through of the preferences shown in figure B.6:

FIG. B.6
Choose the format in which online conferences are displayed here.

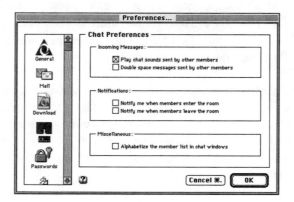

Incoming Messages   These choices govern how AOL will handle text in a conference room window.

■ **Play chat sounds sent by other members.** This option allows you to hear custom sounds generated by other members. However, you do need to have the same sound installed on your Mac. You're apt to find some good sound files in the Mac Music & Sounds Forum, which is described in more detail in Chapter 19.

■ **Double space messages sent by other members.** This option takes up space, and I keep it off (as it is by default).

Notifications   Here's how you adjust AOL software to notify you when new arrivals appear in a conference.

■ **Notify me when members enter the room.** This option also takes up space on your screen if members are constantly leaving and entering the chat room. That's why it's off by default.

■ **Notify me when members leave the room.** This option is also off by default, for the reasons above; it may take up too much screen space.

Miscellaneous   This is one option that you should turn on (though it's not checked by default). It puts the list of those in the conference room in alphabetical order, so you can check the list quickly to see if your online acquaintances are around.

Setting Stored Passwords

The preferences shown in figure B.7 should be set with caution. This setting allows you to store the passwords you use for your AOL screen names when you log on to AOL. You have a second option, to make them valid only for AOL's automated FlashSessions (which I explain in more detail in Chapter 8). When you type the password, it'll appear as a series of bullets (small round circles) on your screen, so someone looking over your shoulder won't see what you've typed.

FIG. B.7
Be cautious about whether to store your password in your AOL program, especially if others use your Mac.

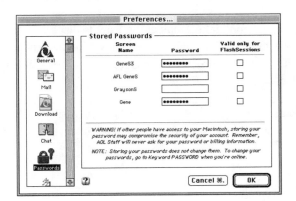

> **CAUTION**
>
> When you store any of your passwords in your AOL software, anyone who has access to your computer can use your account and run up your online bill. If you decide to store your passwords anyway, you may want to consider buying a security program, such as Symantec's Norton Disklock for Macintosh or ASD Software's FileGuard. Remember, as the illustration in B.7 says, no member of AOL's staff will ever ask you for your password or billing information.

Setting Font Preferences

When you choose Font Preferences from the Preferences dialog box (see fig. B.8), you can select fonts for three categories. The pop-up menu adjacent to Font For lets you choose the font for Default Usage (the regular font AOL uses for message boards and other displays), e-mail, and also the text shown in conference rooms. Select your favorite style from the pop-up menu to the right of the Font label. Then choose Size from the pop-up menu, and finally Style and Color.

FIG. B.8

You can choose the fonts AOL uses for display of system messages, e-mail, and online conferences.

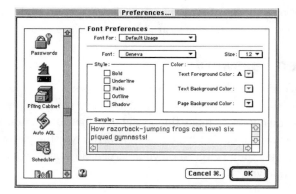

Before choosing a font, take a look at the Sample display at the bottom of the Font Preferences window to get an idea of how the font will look when it's put into regular use. If you don't like the choice, no problem. You can pick another font from any of the fonts installed on your Mac.

 TIP   Choose a monospaced font, such as Monaco or Courier, to display your messages online. That way, material that is formatted with tabs lines up clearly on-screen.

CAUTION

America Online software uses your standard Macintosh system fonts by default, such as Chicago for menu bar titles, Geneva and Monaco for text display, and New York for the sign-off screen and some text windows. In addition, Helvetica and Times are used for various title displays in AOL's forums. All these fonts are automatically installed when you load system software onto your Mac, so don't remove them. If a font is missing, or improperly installed, you may see a bitmapped, blocky screen display in areas where that font is used.

Configuring Your Personal Filing Cabinet

AOL lets you store your e-mail, files, and newsgroup messages on your hard drive in your Personal Filing Cabinet (see fig. B.9 for the preference settings). In order to keep your hard drive from being cluttered with files you don't need, you can have files automatically deleted after a preset period of time. There are four options, depending on the kind of files. The time settings range from Never (the default), and include One Week, Two Weeks, One Month, Two Months, Six Months, and One Year. You can, of course, open the Personal Filing Cabinet from the File menu and manually remove any file you want.

FIG. B.9
By default, all of these options are unchecked, but this is an idea of how you may set up your AOL software to delete older items in your Personal Filing Cabinet.

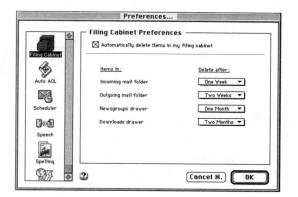

Setting Up AOL for FlashSessions

A very useful feature of your AOL software is a FlashSession, a way for AOL to log on at a scheduled interval and perform the functions you want. Because I cover this subject in more detail in Chapter 8, I'll just touch on the choices briefly here.

You have two sets of FlashSession Options. The First, Auto AOL, is shown in figure B.10. This set of preferences lets you select the actions you want AOL to take during the automated session. All are clearly labeled. The second set, Scheduler Preferences, is shown in figure B.11, and you use it to decide when to run your sessions and which accounts will be used during the scheduled sessions.

FIG. B.10
Use this dialog box to choose what tasks you want AOL to carry out during your automated session.

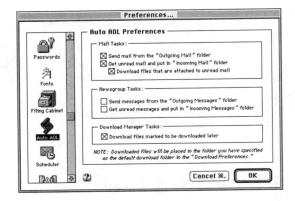

FIG. B.11
After you've decided what you want AOL to do in a FlashSession, you use this dialog box to tell the software when to run those sessions, and which accounts to use.

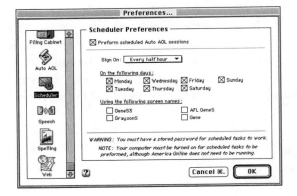

Setting Speech Preferences

Although you will hear sounds playing briefly in various AOL areas (such as Center Stage, where many online conferences originate), this group of settings (see fig. B.12) lets you have online text throughout the service read back to you.

FIG. B.12
A handy group of settings to set up your AOL software to read text back to you.

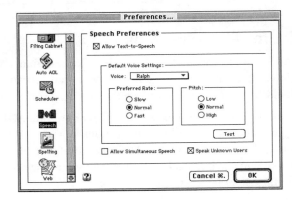

CAUTION

Speech Preferences are only available if you have Apple's PlainTalk or Speech Manager software installed. If you don't have either software running, the options will not be visible in the Preferences box. PlainTalk requires an AV or PowerPC Mac; Speech Manager can be installed on just about any Mac that can run AOL's software. You can find copies of the latest Apple speech software at its AOL forum (keyword: **Apple Computer**).

Part

X

App

B

- **Allow Text-to-Speech.** Before you do anything, you want to turn this feature on.
- **Default Voice Settings.** The choices shown in the pop-up menu are the same ones you placed on your Mac when you installed PlainTalk or Speech Manager software.
- **Preferred Rate.** Talk rapidly, slowly, or at a normal rate. Choose your options by clicking the appropriate box here.
- **Pitch.** Establish the pitch of your default voice here.
- **Allow Simultaneous Speech.** This feature allows more than one voice to be heard at a time, which may be one way to establish an online chorus.
- **Speak Unknown Users.** Checked by default, it allows voices to be heard in conference rooms without having to apply a specific voice to a specific person.

Setting Spelling Preferences

You can spell check your e-mail before it's sent. AOL provides a few simple configuration options for the spell checker:

- **Grammar.** This option covers four basic grammar settings: Whether to capitalize the first word of a sentence, whether to capitalize a proper noun, a warning about a word typed twice, and whether numbers should be allowed in words. By default, the first three choices are checked.
- **Punctuation.** This option determines whether to treat hyphenated words as two words, whether spaces are allowed before punctuation marks, and whether two spaces are allowed after punctuation. Unlike your old-fashioned typewriter, you normally type one space after punctuation on a computer (though some may type two spaces when using a mono- or single-spaced font, such as Courier and Monaco).
- **Dictionary.** This last preference lets you select a dictionary other than the default. It allows for installation of foreign language dictionaries.

World Wide Web Preferences

AOL's Mac software includes an integrated browser for the World Wide Web (it's based on Microsoft's Internet Explorer). There are a few simple settings you'll want to consider (see fig. B.13) when using the browser:

■ **Home Page Address.** This option is set to display AOL's home or introductory page. If you have another page you'd prefer to visit by default, you can enter the site address here.

■ **Display.** The options shown here control whether status bars are shown in the browser window, and whether images are displayed. If you have a slow-speed modem connection to AOL, you can gain lots of speed by turning off the Show Images option.

■ **Warnings and Confirmations.** If you intend to do any Web shopping, you'll want to know if the site you've accessed is secure or not, so you'll probably want to leave the default options in the panel shown in figure B.13 as they are now.

■ **Disk Cache.** Like AOL's own forums, the fancy artwork you retrieve from the World Wide Web is stored on your hard drive for fast retrieval. You can use the pop-up menu at the bottom of the Web Preferences dialog box to set a fixed cache on your hard drive to store these image files. When the size limit is reached, the oldest, least-used artwork files will be deleted. Or you can click the Empty Cache button to clear them all in one step. (No, this has nothing whatever to do with the Disk Cache you set on your Mac's Memory Control Panel, which controls the speed of hard drive access.)

FIG. B.13
You can control the basic functions of AOL's Web browser in this settings panel.

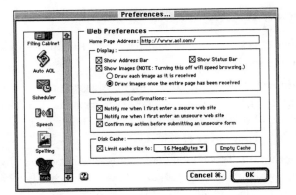

Using the File Menu

The File menu is much like the one you find in any other Macintosh application (see fig. B.14). Most of the commands are familiar to you, but America Online has added a few features to its software that are worth some explanation.

FIG. B.14
Display the File menu to access many file-management options.

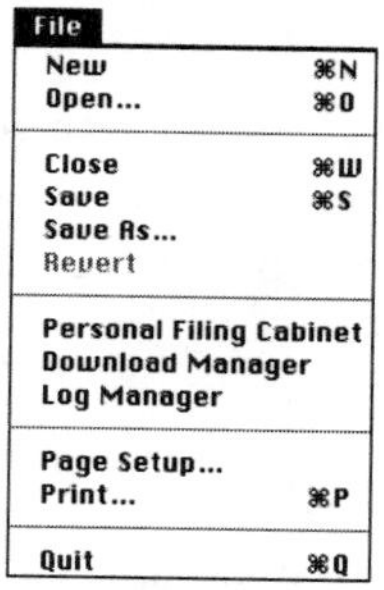

File	
New	⌘N
Open...	⌘O
Close	⌘W
Save	⌘S
Save As...	
Revert	
Personal Filing Cabinet	
Download Manager	
Log Manager	
Page Setup...	
Print...	⌘P
Quit	⌘Q

The following paragraphs take you step-by-step through the options on the File menu.

Using the New Option

When you press ⌘-N, you see a blank document window, much like the one you would find in a text processing program.

America Online comes with a basic text editor, kind of a simple word processor. With the text editor, you can write little memos or a simple letter, or just paste text you have grabbed from other memos or message windows online. You can even format your document by using the Font, Size, Style, and Color commands from the Style menu. These topics are discussed later in this chapter, in the section "Using the Format Menu."

The Memo feature is not as full-featured as your word processing program. It's limited, for example, to 27,000 characters (a little more than 4,000 words)—not quite large enough for your new novel, but enough for a long letter. As in any other America Online text window, you can save and print your memo. These features are discussed later in this chapter.

Using the Open Option

The Open command (⌘-O) brings up your standard Macintosh Open dialog box. It enables you to open documents in formats recognized by America Online.

If you click the pull-down menu next to the Show label at the bottom of the dialog box, you see a list of the formats your software can read. The default is All Available; you should leave it that way, unless you need to find a file saved in a specific format but don't know the file's name. Supported formats include documents required by your AOL software; simple text documents; e-mail; compressed files in several formats; image formats such as GIF, JPEG, and PICT; and QuickTime and MIDI sound files.

Part
X
App
B

Using the Close Option

The Close command (⌘-W) closes the active file window on your screen. If you have made any changes in the contents of the file before you last saved it—or if you've never saved the file—you are asked whether you want to save the changes before the window is closed.

Using the Save Option

The Save command (⌘-S) saves the contents of your window to a file that's written to disk. If you haven't saved the file yet, you see a dialog box, enabling you to give the file a name.

Using the Save As Option

This option enables you to save your document under a new name. You have the choice of saving your document in straight text format or in other formats, depending on the kind of document you have open. For example, if you are reading an e-mail letter, it can be saved in America Online's standard mail format or as a simple text file that can be opened in any text editing or word processing program.

 TIP If you want a paper copy of America Online's Help menu, select the section, use the Copy command on the Edit menu, and paste it into a new document. You can then save and print that document.

Using the Revert Option

Did you make a mistake in updating a saved document, such as a memo? No problem. Choose the Revert option, and America Online restores the document to the last saved version. When you select this option, you are asked whether you want to discard the changes you just made to your document.

Using the Personal Filing Cabinet Option

Your Personal Filing Cabinet is a catch-all feature that includes your Favorite Places, stored e-mail, downloaded newsgroup messages, and other information. You can use the screen shown in figure B.15 to manage your selections. They can be renamed, or selections can be dragged and dropped in a different sequence. The convenient Finder-like interface lets you click at the arrows to the left of the folders to display the contents, and to click again to close or collapse the display.

FIG. B.15
You can configure your Personal Filing Cabinet from this handy screen.

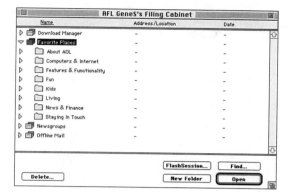

Using the Download Manager Option

Downloading is the process of transferring a file from America Online's huge software libraries to your computer. The Download Manager enables you to choose one or more files to download during your online visit. The files are placed in a download queue or sequence. You can begin the download process at any time during your online session, when you log off, or even during a scheduled FlashSession. You learn how to configure the Download Manager for best performance in Chapter 6, "Where Do We Begin?"

Using the Log Manager Option

During your visits to America Online, you might want to save the contents of a message area or an online conference so that you can view and print it later. You have three logging options in your America Online software:

■ The first is a System Log. This log enables you to record all the text that you read while you're on America Online. It doesn't record the mail you send or the messages you post, but you can save those anyway, using the Save command described previously.

■ The second is the Chat Log. During your online travels, you might attend a chat in America Online's People Connection or an online conference. This feature enables you to record the entire conversation.

■ And finally, you have the Instant Message Log, which enables you to store all the instant messages you get while online. If you're exchanging instant messages with more than one member at a time, however, the log records all those messages in one log, logging the messages in the order in which they are sent and received.

To use your online tape recorder, follow these steps:

1. Open the Logs window by choosing Log Manager from the File menu.

2. Select the kind of log you want (see fig. B.16).

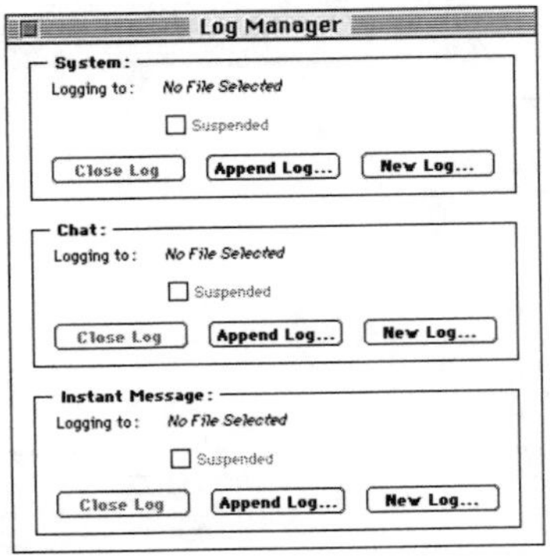

FIG. B.16

Turn on America Online's
virtual tape recorder to log
an online session.

3. Click the Save button. You then see a dialog box much like the Save As prompt, and you are asked to name your file and indicate where it is to be saved (see fig. B.17). The software gives the file a default name based on the kind of log it is, but you can change that if you want.

FIG. B.17

Name your online log in this
dialog box.

If you want to pause the online recording process, return to the File menu, select Log Manager, and select the Suspend check box at the bottom of the Logs window. When you decide to resume the logging process, uncheck the Suspend box button. When you are finished logging, choose the Close Log option.

The logging process is flexible. You can open all three logs simultaneously if you want. What's more, you can suspend and resume and even close each log separately, depending on which one you've highlighted when you make your choice.

Remember that America Online software can capture only about 27,000 characters in a single file. If the log gets bigger than that size, America Online closes the first log and opens a second one automatically. The second log has the same name as the first log file, with a number added to it, such as 2 or 3. This feature helps you view all your logs, just as you can any memo file, from within the America Online software.

N O T E   AOL's logging feature is also a handy tool to capture information from Internet newsgroups or from database text you locate in the Gopher/WAIS areas. For more information about using AOL's Internet features, read the chapters that comprise Part VIII, "Entering the Information Superhighway." ▨

Using the Page Setup Option

Choosing the Page Setup option from the File menu displays the standard Page Setup dialog box. In this dialog box, you can change your page size and orientation (portrait or landscape) and select various printer options. These options vary depending on the kind of printer you have and the version of the printer driver you have installed on your Macintosh.

Using the Print Option

Choosing Print (⌘-P) displays the regular Print dialog box. This option enables you to print from any open text window. You can print a memo, your e-mail, a conference window, a message, or any other displayed text on America Online. If a window has more than one text window, say the opening window of an online department, you should move the cursor to the text file you want to print. You can move the cursor either by clicking with the mouse or by pressing Tab. If the open window contains a directory rather than text, the command changes to Print List.

 TIP Be sure to select your printer in the Chooser *before* you open your America Online software. Otherwise, you might not be able to print a document after the software is open.

Using the Quit Option

If you are still online when you choose Quit (⌘-Q) from the File menu, you see a dialog box asking whether you want to Exit (Quit) or Sign Off, with a few additional options in case you really want to stay online a little longer (see fig. B.18). The Exit option ends your online session and quits the application. The Sign Off option simply logs you off but keeps the application open. The latter feature is useful if you want to continue some of your work in the program offline, such as writing e-mail or memos.

FIG. B.18
Are you sure you really want to log off? Maybe you want to check out a few more online areas first.

Using the Edit Menu

The first six selections on the Edit menu are very much what you would find on any Macintosh application (see fig. B.19). They are Undo (⌘-Z), Cut (⌘-X), Copy (⌘-C), Paste (⌘-V), Clear, and Select All (⌘-A). Because they work the same as in your other Mac software, they aren't discussed further here.

FIG. B.19
The Edit menu contains several familiar Macintosh commands.

Using the Find in Top Window Option

America Online's Mac software enables you to search text in the top document window (the one you've activated on your computer's screen). By choosing this command (see fig. B.20) and entering the text string you want to look for, you can quickly locate a specific item of text. You can make the search case-sensitive, if desired, by selecting the Case Sensitive Search option.

FIG. B.20
AOL's text search tool lets you quickly find text in an open document window.

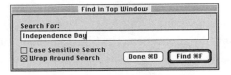

Using the Check Spelling Option

Before you send your e-mail, you'll probably want to check the spelling. AOL includes a built-in spell checking utility, similar to the one found in many word processing programs. When you choose Check Spelling, you see the window shown in figure B.21.

FIG. B.21
AOL's handy spell checker lets you check your e-mail for spelling mistakes.

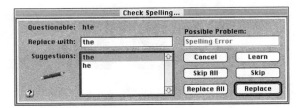

NOTE AOL's spell checker works only for e-mail and will only check the spelling when you invoke the command (unless you've chosen the preference setting to check your e-mail for spelling errors before it's sent). A more flexible way to check spelling is to use Casady & Greene's Spell Catcher or Deneba's Coach Professional. These programs will flag errors as you type them, and will work not only in your AOL e-mail window, but in any message board window (something AOL's speller checking utility didn't support with the initial release of version 3.0). You can also use either of these handy utilities with most word processing and desktop publishing software. ■

Using the Speak Text Option

The Speak Text option (⌘-H) enables you to have any selected text that appears on-screen read to you. But first you have to activate the Use Text-to-Speech preference and have Apple's PlainTalk or Speech Manager software installed (and running).

Using the Stop Speaking Option

The Stop Speaking option (⌘-.) enables you to halt the text-to-speech process (in mid-sentence, if you want).

Using the Format Menu

The various commands in the Format menu (see fig. B.22) will handle the basic text formatting of your e-mail. They are similar to the choices you get in your word processing software. In using these options, you can exercise your online creativity. The options here are similar to the ones you have in your word processing program. You can use any font size (from 1 point to 127 points), but you should restrict your choices to 9 points and larger so that you and the person who receives your message can read the messages easily on-screen.

FIG. B.22

Choose from a standard array of e-mail formatting functions.

Your style choices range from Plain text to Bold and Italic (which can be combined as Bold Italic), as well as Underline.

To provide greater emphasis and flair to your documents, you can also change the color of your text, the background, and the color of the page itself. For example, you may use red or green for text you want to emphasize. This choice, though, won't do much good if the recipient of your e-mail doesn't have a color-capable Mac with a color screen. Text with different color styles will appear in drab shades of gray on a grayscale screen.

To alter the text format, highlight the text in the memo or e-mail document you want to change, and select each command (Size, Style, Color options, Alignment) in turn, or select them from the convenient toolbar in your e-mail form to make your changes. Or you can make your formatting changes with nothing selected, as long as you have opened an active memo or the Compose Mail window. All the text you enter after the insertion point will include those formatting changes.

All these styles work fine and dandy for your memos and e-mail; but the messages that you post online (chats and instant messages too) are limited to your basic 128-character ASCII set. That means, for example, that you cannot use curly quotes, special characters such as ª, ¤, or ¥, or foreign accents for these kinds of messages.

> **CAUTION**
>
> Be careful what font you choose for your preferred e-mail font when you send e-mail to another America Online member. Even though you might love to use some of those fancy fonts, the person who gets the message cannot read the letter in the same typeface unless that person has the font too. If the recipient doesn't have the font, the text defaults to the standard e-mail font. You might be better off using the Size and Style selections to create different point sizes and such fancy effects as outlines and shadows to make your e-mail stand out. Choosing a color for emphasis is useful as long as the recipient of your message has a color monitor.

Using the Insert Hyperlink Option

Find a cool Web site, or online area you want your friends to visit? Just use the Insert Hyperlink command, and enter the URL of the place you want to direct your friends to. They'll be able to access that area just by double-clicking the reference (it'll be underlined in the e-mail message they receive as shown in fig. B.23). You can either show the actual site address of the place you want your friends to visit, or just use a title instead.

Using the Hide/Show Text Format Toolbar

Just like a word processor program, AOL offers you a convenient formatting toolbar, which mirrors the functions described above in a simple icon-like display. The default setting is to hide this toolbar, to keep your screen from being cluttered.

FIG. B.23
Double-click the underlined Hyperlink to be magically transported to the site that's identified.

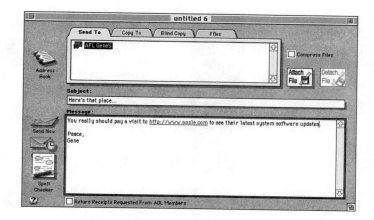

Part
X

App

B

Using the Go To Menu

The Go To menu, shown in figure B.24, is your launching pad in America Online. It's your gateway to loads of undiscovered treasures that you can find during your travels online.

FIG. B.24
Discover the top features on America Online by using the Go To menu.

Set Up and Signing On

The window shown in figure B.25 appears automatically when you open your America Online program. It's the window you use to begin your online session or to change your modem setup.

FIG. B.25
When you launch your America Online software, you see this window.

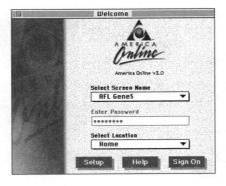

Clicking the Sign On button (or pressing Enter) begins the logon process. You can use the button labeled Setup to change your connection phone numbers or your modem settings. The button at the center, Help, brings up the online Help menu to get you through the rough spots.

Using the Channels Option

America Online divides its service into departments, or channels, each of which represents a specific area of interest (although there is some overlapping of coverage, such as the Learning & Culture and Reference Desk channels). When you log on to AOL, there's a handy display of these channels located just below your Welcome window (see fig. B.26).

FIG. B.26
Choose an online channel or online support option from this screen.

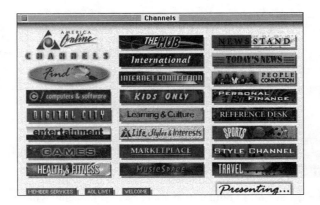

Using the Welcome Menu

When you first log on to America Online, the window shown in figure B.27 serves as your introduction to the service. You can display this window later by choosing the Welcome

Menu option from the Go To menu. At the right and bottom of the window you see information about the latest news, and special features and services you might want to check out further.

Part

X

App

B

FIG. B.27
This Welcome window is your America Online entranceway.

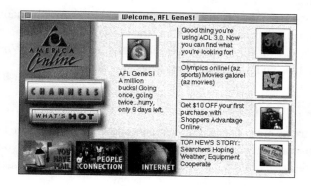

At the bottom left of the Welcome window, you see an icon showing whether you've received e-mail. If you have America Online's default sounds activated, your sign-on is punctuated with a "Welcome" greeting, followed in a few seconds by a "You've got mail" announcement. Clicking the You Have Mail icon brings up a directory of the mail you've received since you last logged on. If no mail is waiting for you, it just says No Mail.

Using the Keyword Option

The Keyword option (see fig. B.28) is the fast and easy way to get anywhere online. Just select this command from the Go To menu or press the keyboard shortcut (⌘-K). Then enter the keyword and click the Go button, and you are transported to that location in just seconds.

FIG. B.28
America Online's Keyword feature enables you to go right to your favorite online spot or seek out points of interest.

Many of the keywords on America Online are intuitive. If you want to learn more about computers, type the keyword **Computing**. If you want to read the latest issue of the *New York Times* online, type the keyword **times**. The Keyword Help button on your Keyword box brings up a list of current America Online keywords. If you want to find sources of information about a particular topic but you don't know the name of the area you want to visit, you also have a search option (the button at the right shown previously in fig. B.28), which brings up a list of probable matches. See Chapter 6, "Where Do We Begin?" for more details on finding information on America Online.

Using the Find Option

There are so many fascinating features on AOL. You just have to find where they are. The Channels menu helps cover the broad categories, but if you want to dig deeper into a specific area, or if you want to find someone online, you'll want to look at AOL's convenient Find tool instead (see fig. B.29).

FIG. B.29
Find places and things, people, and events on AOL with this handy Find screen.

If you want to search for a specific item, click the category, and then enter the search string you wish to look for. If you want a broad category to browse through, just look over the entries in the list box and double-click the one you want.

Using the Online Clock Option

How long have you been online? If you're on a budget, you'll want to check this option, just to be sure.

Using the Favorite Places Option

Many of the areas you visit online have a little heart-shaped icon at the upper right of the screen. When you click that icon, you can add that area (and your favorite Internet sites too) to your Favorite Places list (see fig. B.30). The neat thing about this listing is that you can create custom categories for your favorite online spots, and drag-and-drop entries into different orders for your convenience.

FIG. B.30
Edit your list of Favorite Places on this screen which, like your Personal Filing Cabinet, matches a standard Finder layout.

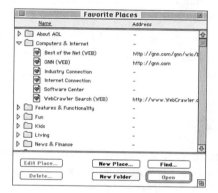

Using the Go To Menu Option

When you install your America Online software, you have a list in your Go To menu of 10 regular spots to which you can travel by pressing two keys (⌘ plus a number from 0 to 9). You can change these destinations by choosing the Edit Go To Menu option to display the Edit Go To Menu dialog box, shown in figure B.31. (A few favorite online areas have been added to the list displayed here; you can add or remove whatever you want.)

FIG. B.31
You can customize your regular stop-off areas on America Online here.

Editing the Go To menu is a simple procedure. You can do it whether or not you're logged on. Follow these steps:

1. Open the Go To menu and choose the Edit Go To Menu option. The Edit Go To Menu dialog box appears.

2. In the left column, type the name of the area you want to visit, and type the online keyword on the right. To move quickly from one entry to the next, press Tab. The field you go to is highlighted automatically so that whatever information you type replaces what's already there.

3. After you've made your changes and additions to the Go To menu, click OK. The changes you've made appear immediately in the Go To menu or through your keyboard shortcuts.

Using the Mail Menu

Perhaps the most rewarding part of your online experience is the ability to send and receive electronic mail. The major features for creating and reading e-mail are found in the Mail menu (see fig. B.32). As mentioned earlier, you can compose your e-mail online or do it offline and send it with a FlashSession.

FIG. B.32
The Mail menu contains options for working with e-mail.

Using the Compose Mail Option

The Compose Mail command (⌘-M) brings up the regular America Online e-mail window. This window consists of a blank mail form that you can fill in and send while online, or send later during a FlashSession.

Read Chapter 8, "Using America Online E-Mail," for the ins and outs of composing your America Online e-mail.

Using the Address Book Option

As you develop a list of regular online friends, you'll want to put their names in your personal Address Book. This list is your own Rolodex that you can use to send mass mailings or merely to look up the name of an individual. To learn more about creating and updating your Address Book, see Chapter 8, "Using America Online E-Mail."

Using the Online Mailbox Option

When you receive an announcement while online that mail is in your mailbox, select the Online Mailbox option, press ⌘-R, or click the You Have Mail icon at the bottom left of your AOL Welcome screen. You'll see a list of the mail you've received, and, by clicking the tabs, you can look at your old mail (the mail you've received) and your sent mail.

Mail you've read is stored in AOL's host computers for several days, and you have up to a month to review the e-mail you've sent to others.

Using the Offline Mail Drawer Option

This feature incorporates two functions that allow you to check mail received. These functions are:

- **Incoming Mail.** This option enables you to view letters that have been saved to your FlashSession mailbox. Letters are stored in your FlashSession mailbox until you delete them. This mail is also available to you offline, because it is stored in your Online Mail folder, part of your AOL program's folder, rather than at AOL's host computer. You can save mail that you've read online to this file by clicking the Save to Flashmail icon in the Open Mail window. Check Chapter 8, "Using America Online E-Mail," for more information on how to run a FlashSession.

- **Outgoing Mail.** E-mail is stored in your FlashSession mailbox before it's sent during a FlashSession or while you're online. You can edit or delete your e-mail before it's sent, or attach a file to your message even while offline (because it is stored, like your Incoming Mail, on your own computer).

A Visit to AOL's Mail Center

Most of your mailing options are available from the Post Office window (keyword: **Mail Center**), as a directory listing at the left of the window, shown in figure B.33, or as a special icon. Each feature will be discussed separately, as it appears on the Mail menu.

FIG. B.33
America Online's virtual post office, your handy e-mail center.

Using the FAX/Paper Mail Option

America Online has a service that enables you to send mail to someone who isn't an online member. You can have your letter sent as a fax or via U.S. mail. When you select the FAX/Paper Mail option while online, you bring up a window that contains full instructions on how to use this service, along with the prices for this extra-cost service. Or just read Chapter 6, "Where Do We Begin?"

Using the FlashSessions Options

You can use these options to automate your America Online sessions. You can compose an e-mail message or Internet newsgroup message offline and then schedule a FlashSession to send those messages. During that FlashSession, any mail or selected newsgroup messages that have been received since your last online visit are saved to your mailbox (choose Incoming Mail from the Offline Mail Drawer to view the mail). In addition, you can opt to download files that have been attached to e-mail during a FlashSession.

See Chapter 8, "Using America Online E-Mail," for the full story on how to schedule your FlashSessions. Briefly, the options available in the Mail menu include Set Up FlashSession, to configure your automated logons to AOL; and Active FlashSession Now, which is used to begin a non-scheduled FlashSession.

Using the Members Menu

You learned about two options in the Members menu earlier in this chapter—the My AOL and Preferences features. The following sections discuss the rest of the options you can select from this menu (see fig. B.34).

FIG. B.34
Use the Members menu to keep in touch with other members.

Using the Member Services Option

If you want to check your America Online bill, solve a problem with your software, or learn more about the features available to you online, here's the option to use: Member Services (or just use the keyword **Help**). What's more, the area you'll go to is free, meaning that you aren't charged for the time you spend in the Online Support section.

Before you enter this area, a window pops up asking whether you're sure you want to enter the free area, because chat areas and gateways are not available there.

Using the Parental Control Option

This choice is available to you only when you log on with your master account (that's the first name shown in the pull-down menu of available accounts on the main screen of your AOL software). The Parental Control option enables you to restrict certain parts of AOL's services to one or more of the screen names on your account. It's described in more detail in Chapter 16, "Parental Issues and Internet Access." This discussion also skips the Preferences option because it was discussed in full detail earlier in this chapter.

Using the Member Directory Option

If you're not sure whether someone is a member of America Online, you can search the member directory and find out. You can look for a member by real name or screen name. You also can examine members' online profiles, if they've posted one, and update your own profile at the same time. Read Chapter 7, "America Online's People Connection," for more information on this subject.

Using the Send an Instant Message Option

An *instant message* is America Online's way of enabling you to hold an interactive, one-on-one "conversation" with another member, in private. Simply select the Send an Instant Message option (⌘-I), type the online address of the person to whom you want to send the message, and then enter your message. Click Send, and your message is sent almost instantly.

Using the Get a Member's Profile Option

If you want to learn more about an online member, using the Get a Member's Profile option (⌘-G) is the way to do it. If the member has created an online profile, you can view it by selecting this option. You can find more information on these and other special features for America Online members in Chapter 7, "America Online's People Connection."

Using the Locate a Member Online Option

Not sure whether your online friend is going to "meet" you at the appointed hour? Here's how to find out if your friend is online. When you select the Locate a Member Online option (⌘-L), enter the screen name of the member for whom you're searching, and press Enter. If the member is attending a chat or an online conference, you receive a message announcing where the person is. Otherwise, you are just notified that the person is online. Either way, if that member is online, you know about it in just a few seconds.

Using the Buddy Lists Option

A Buddy List (see fig. B.35 for the setup screen) is AOL's convenient way of letting you know when your friends or colleagues are online—and to let them know when you're online. You can easily set up a list of your friends or colleagues. When they're online, you'll see the list displayed in a handy AOL window. You have, of course, the option of not allowing your name to be part of this Buddy List (as other members do).

FIG. B.35
Are your friends online?
AOL's handy Buddy List will
tell you.

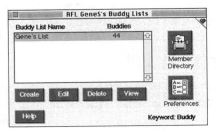

Using the Windows Menu

After you've visited online for a while, you no doubt will have opened up many forum and text windows. The time will come when you want to tidy up your desktop a little. For this clean-up, use the Windows menu (see fig. B.36).

FIG. B.36
Use the Windows menu to
straighten up your screen.

Using the Hide/Show Toolbar Option

AOL's convenient toolbar, defined in detail later in this appendix, provides a handy set of icon shortcuts to get you quickly around the service. But if you'd rather get around via keyboard or menu bar command, and perhaps need to reduce screen clutter, you can use this command to hide the toolbar.

Using the Anchor/Unanchor Toolbar Option

If you decide you'd rather not have the toolbar perched at its customary place just below your AOL software's menu bar, you can unanchor it, and move it around your screen. When you find the right spot, you can use the Anchor feature to keep it there (till you change your mind again, of course).

Using the Clean Up Windows Option

As you travel online, you begin to open window after window, and finally your desktop starts getting awfully cluttered. This little Clean Up Windows feature stacks all your open windows in a neat row, from left to right.

 You also see a list of your open America Online windows when you pull down the Windows menu, and you can activate the one you want by highlighting it in the window. The titles are displayed at the top of each open window so that you can select the one you want quickly and easily.

Using the Close All Except Front Option

Everything has its limits, and your America Online software cannot open an unlimited number of windows. After you've opened a couple of dozen or so windows, you get a warning that the application is running out of memory. At this point, you can choose the Close All Except Front option to close all the windows except the one that's active. This action cleans up your workspace fast.

> **CAUTION**
>
> When you use the Close All Except Front option, all windows except the frontmost window are closed. That includes Instant Message and Chat room windows (which will close with no warning to you about saving the contents of those windows). If you wish to save the contents of those windows, you should open a log, as described in the section entitled "Using the Logs Option," or save the Instant Message or Chat text using the Save As command from the File menu.

Using the Remember Placement Option

You might decide that the default size of an America Online message window is too small or too large for your screen. You can use the Remember Placement option to enable the program to recall the size and position of that type of window (e-mail, message, or whatever) so that America Online always opens that window in the same location and with the same window size.

First, change the size of a window to your taste; then, with that window active, choose Remember Placement from the Windows menu.

The Remember Placement feature doesn't work for all America Online windows. If an active window cannot be resized, this option is replaced with the Forget Placement option.

Using the Forget Placement Option

If you decide to change the window to its default size and location, choose this option.

N O T E If you keep getting messages that your America Online software is running out of memory when you have many windows open, you can allow it to open more windows by giving the software more memory. With the application closed, highlight the AOL application icon, and select Get Info from the File menu at your Finder desktop. All you have to do then is increase the amount of memory the application uses—with a watchful eye to the amount of RAM you've installed on your Mac. It's suggested that you use add RAM in increments of 500K. The next time you log on to America Online, you will be able to open more message windows before you get that annoying message.

Add to Favorite Places

When you find an online area you'd like to visit often, no doubt you'll want to add it to your list of Favorite Places. Here's one option open to you to do just that. This command gives you the choice of adding the selected online document window to your listing.

Using the Toolbar

America Online's Mac software gives you a quick way to go directly to an online depart-ment or take advantage of the most popular features of your software. This feature is called the *toolbar*. The toolbar contains 18 icons, as shown in figure B.37, each of which represents an online area or command.

 TIP If clicking a mouse isn't your favorite way to travel along the America Online Information Super-highway, check Chapter 2 for a complete list of keyboard shortcuts.

FIG. B.37
AOL's toolbar and your mouse are a great combination for act-ivating the most-used features of your America Online software.

When you first open your America Online application, most of these icons are grayed out. But when you log on, the icons become bright and colorful. Clicking the appropriate icon with your mouse takes you directly to the listed online area or activates the listed function.

Table B.1 lists the special functions and destinations attached to each icon. The areas shown correspond, from left to right, to the icons displayed on the toolbar. All of these areas and features are discussed in more detail throughout the rest of this book.

Table B.1   Using the Toolbar

Icon	Destination or Function
	Check Mail
	Compose Mail
	AOL's Channels (by category)
	What's Hot
	People Connection

continues

Part
X

App
B

Table B.1 Continued

Icon	Destination or Function
	File Search
	Stocks and Portfolios
	Today's News
	World Wide Web
	The Marketplace
	My AOL—Personal Choices
	Online Clock
	Print Document
	Personal File Cabinet
	Favorite Places
	Member Services (Help channel)
	Find (Files, Members, Places, More)
	Keywords

From Here...

This appendix covered the basics of using your America Online Macintosh software. In other places in this book, you can find additional information and helpful hints to make your online sessions even more rewarding—and fun too!

■ For advice on logging on to AOL when you're not at your home or office, read Chapter 5, "America Online and Mobile Computing."

■ For a quick tour of AOL, read Chapter 6, "Where Do We Begin?"

■ When you're ready to get in touch with fellow AOL members, read Chapter 7, "America Online's People Connection."

■ Various valuable hints and tips about sending letters online are found in Chapter 8, "Using America Online E-Mail."

■ To learn how to navigate through AOL's huge software libraries, review Chapter 20, "Tips and Tricks on Finding Software."

■ A membership on America Online will also make you a part of the global Internet network. For more information, read the chapters that comprise Part VIII, "Entering the Information Superhighway."

Part

X

App

B

Using Your America Online Windows Software

I've written this section strictly for those who haven't
used America Online's Windows software—or those
who just want a little more information about its special
features. (If you're a Macintosh user, go back to the
preceding appendix, unless you just want to learn how
the other half lives or are working in a mixed platform
environment.)

Before you begin this chapter, you'll want to make sure
you have installed your AOL software, set up your
account, and logged on for the first time. After you've
done that, you want to get down to the business of
learning about your new software.

The Windows version of your America Online software
doesn't come with a manual, although an extensive
Help menu is provided. But as long as you know how
to use Microsoft Windows to do your everyday tasks,
such as moving and clicking your mouse and choosing

commands from menus, you shouldn't have any trouble picking up all the ins and outs of using the America Online software. And with this brief guide in your hands, you can become an expert in no time. ■

N O T E   The illustrations in this chapter show AOL's software running under Windows 95, but the program runs in basically the same fashion under Windows 3.1. So even if you haven't upgraded to Windows 95 yet, there's no need to worry about using AOL. ■

Changing the Network and Modem Settings

When you first install your America Online software, it examines your modem and sets a default modem profile for it. The software doesn't go quite so far as Windows 95 in choosing a profile, though. So for that reason, and if you buy a new modem, you may want to change these settings. Or, you might want to change your connection numbers to the America Online network.

To change your connection settings, follow these steps:

1. Click the Setup button on the main America Online window. The Network & Modem Setup dialog box appears, as shown in figure C.1.

FIG. C.1

Making changes to your network setup is quick and easy.

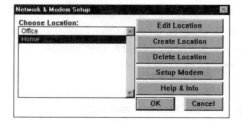

 If you have a problem using your America Online software and you need an immediate answer, press Alt+H or select Help from the AOL application menu bar. You can even print a topic for later review.

2. Click the Edit Location option. (Keep in mind that you can make these settings only when you're not logged onto the America Online network.)

   You can set up two connection profiles in each Location window (see fig. C.2). Your America Online software uses the profile on the left when trying to make your initial connection to the network. If the connection doesn't succeed for any reason—usually due to a busy connection port or noise on the line—the program dials the number on the right.

FIG. C.2
You can change your connection numbers on this screen.

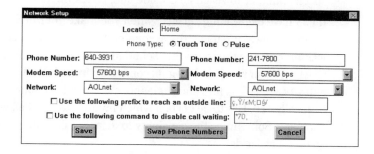

 TIP A quick way to navigate from one data-entry point (field) to another is to press Tab. To return to the preceding field, press Shift+Tab.

3. The first option, Phone Type, enables you to choose between a standard Touch Tone telephone and a Pulse telephone.

   N O T E If you want to change the phone number you are using for any reason—if you've moved to a different location, for example—just log on to America Online. Then type the keyword **Access**. You see a window with a space to enter the area code you want to search. When you enter that number, America Online checks its online phone directory and produces a list of phone numbers for the selected area. For more information on selecting a new connection number, see Chapter 5, "America Online and Mobile Computing." ■

4. Changing online numbers is easy. Just type the new number in the Phone Number box. When you change the number, you also might need to change the Network setting. The Network setting is the service that America Online uses to connect to its host computers. When you get a list of phone numbers from America Online for your area, you see such names as AOLNet, SprintNet, or Tymnet attached to the phone numbers. Pull down the menu at the right of the Network label, and select the correct name of the service provider.

5. America Online's phone directory also lists the maximum baud rate supported by that phone number.

   You need to select the correct speed in the Modem (or Connection) Speed box of the Network Setup dialog box, or you can't connect to the network.

6. The next two check boxes control how the software uses your modem to dial the service. Some businesses have special phone lines that require a dial-out code. Usually it's 9, but you can change that setting if necessary. If you need to dial a special number to reach an outside line, check the first of these two boxes.

7. If you have call-waiting service, when you make your online connection, you should disable call waiting using the second of the two check boxes. You should disable call waiting because the tones that sound in your telephone when someone is trying to reach you can result in being disconnected from AOL. The number listed in this entry box, 1170, is for rotary telephones. If you have touch-tone service, the number is usually *70. But to be certain which number to use, call your local telephone company. Sometimes the capability to disable call waiting for a single phone call is an optional service.

8. The final option you have is to Swap Phone Numbers. Clicking that button transfers the information from the left to the right side of the dialog box, and vice versa. This feature is useful if you find that you are getting better online performance with your second connection number.

T I P   If you get frequent busy signals when trying to connect to AOL (and no other access number is available), use the same phone number on both sides of your setup box. Fast redialing will help you get a connection.

You've just used the Edit Location option to change your modem settings. The following paragraphs explain the rest of the options in the Network & Modem Setup dialog box.

 Create Location. If you want to log on to America Online from different locations, you can create additional location or network setups. The button for Create Location enables you to create separate profiles for each of these locations. The standard Location module is labeled Home, so maybe you want to label a second one Work, Travel, or Mother-in-Law's House.

■ *Delete Location.* If you decide you no longer need a Location profile, use this option to remove it.

■ *Setup Modem.* This option enables you to change the modem setting and the port to which it is connected. When you choose Setup Modem, the dialog box shown in figure C.3 appears.

N O T E   America Online's software does not automatically recognize the modem settings you make in your Modem Control Panel under Windows 95. You must make those settings separately. ■

FIG. C.3

If you've installed a new modem, you can change your modem selection here.

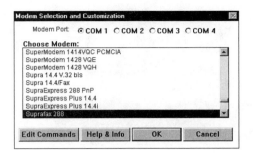

- Under most circumstances, you can pick from one of the standard modem profiles and get satisfactory results. The profile highlighted in figure C.3 supports most high-speed modems. Hayes Compatible (the default) supports a standard 2,400 bps modem. If the exact make and model of your new modem is included in the list, choose that one instead.

N O T E If a modem file that matches the make and model you have isn't offered in AOL's software, you may find one available in AOL's free Members Online Support area (keyword **Help**). I'll explain how to download and install modem files in Chapter 41, "Secrets of High-Speed Access on AOL."

- The option on the bottom of the box, Edit Commands, enables you to tweak a modem profile if you think you can make it perform more efficiently. These options are strictly for advanced users, so proceed with caution. Before you delve into this area, check your modem's manual carefully, or call the manufacturer's technical support people for assistance. For additional help in getting the best possible performance from your AOL connections, read Chapter 41.

Setting Preferences

The next thing you want to do is set up your America Online software's preferences so that the software looks and feels the way you want it to. Even if everything looks okay to you, it's worth the effort to try out a few settings just to see if you can make adjustments. You can always change the settings back the way they were originally.

To set up preferences, choose Preferences from the Members menu. The Preferences dialog box shown in figure C.4 appears.

FIG. C.4

You can choose from eight Preference categories.

Setting most of your preferences involves the same steps. You click the check box next to an item to select it, and you see a check mark appears in that box. You click the box again to turn off the feature, at which time the check mark disappears. Figure C.5 shows an example of several options checked in the General Preferences dialog box.

FIG. C.5

Simply checking a box changes your America Online preferences.

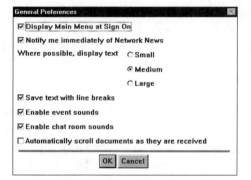

Setting General Preferences

The following paragraphs describe the options you find in the General Preferences dialog box, which appears when you select General Preferences from the Preferences dialog box.

■ *Display Main Menu at Sign On.* When you first log on to America Online, you see two windows. The top window, In The Spotlight, tells you whether e-mail is awaiting you. It also informs you as to the services being highlighted at that time and the top news headline. Beneath that window is the Channels menu, which enables you to jump directly to any one of America Online's channels or other services. To keep your small screen from being cluttered (and speed up screen display), you can opt to keep the Channels menu off at sign on. You can bring it up at any time by choosing Channels from the Go To menu or by pressing Ctrl+D.

■ *Notify me immediately of Network News.* When America Online wants to send you a special announcement, it normally appears in a small window at the top of your screen. Such announcements might alert you to an upcoming service disruption to perform needed maintenance or a similar service-related issue. If you would rather not be disturbed by these notices, turn off this option, and the network announcements are shut off. But it's not something I would recommend because you do want to know if the service will shut down, to avoid suddenly finding yourself knocked offline without knowing why.

■ *Where possible, display text.* This feature gives you three options for displaying your text: Small, Medium, and Large. Choose the option that provides the clearest text display on your computer's screen. The setting takes effect with the window open after you've chosen that setting. The Medium setting gives you the best all-around display of text, but you might prefer something different.

Part
X

App
C

■ *Enable event sounds.* One of the most attractive features of America Online is its voice messages. When you begin your session, you hear a friendly "Welcome" voice. And when you log off, you hear the same voice bid you "Goodbye." But if you work in a busy environment, maybe you just want to turn those sounds off. If so, turn off this option.

■ *Enable chat room sounds.* This feature enables you to hear sounds sent by other America Online members during a chat. For you to be able to hear the sound, though, you have to have the same sound installed on your computer.

■ *Automatically scroll documents as they are received.* Turn on this feature, and you see text items scroll on your computer's screen as they are received. The normal setting (with this feature off) just shows the beginning of the text, as many lines as can fill a single text window. But you can still scroll through this text by using your computer's scroll bars at the right side of the text window.

Setting Password Preferences

The Password Preferences feature (see fig. C.6) is one that you should use with caution. It enables the program to store the passwords you select for each of your screen names. That means you can call up America Online and have the program automatically log on for you without first entering your password. But if others are using your computer and you would prefer not to risk having someone else use your account without your permission, you should not store your passwords in this manner. If no passwords are stored, you are asked to enter your password at the beginning of your online visit.

FIG. C.6

Enter your stored passwords with caution and with no prying eyes around.

If, after reading these warnings, you want to store your online passwords, select this option, which brings up a list of your screen names. Enter the correct password in the text entry field next to the appropriate screen name.

Setting Download Preferences

The ability to download files from America Online's vast software libraries and transfer them through the telephone lines to your computer might become one of your favorite features. You learn some helpful hints on downloading files in Chapter 6, "Where Do We Begin?" In the meantime, you want to set your download preferences for the best performance (or just leave them alone as most members do).

Figure C.7 shows the Download Preferences dialog box that appears when you choose the Download icon from the Preferences dialog box. The following paragraphs describe the options you find in Download Preferences.

FIG. C.7

You can fine-tune the software download process on America Online.

■ *Display image files on Download.* This option enables you to actually see some picture files appear on your screen as they are being transferred to your computer. Depending on how fast your PC is, this choice could slow your computer's performance somewhat. If you don't have at least a 486 (and if you're not connected to AOL at 9,600 bps or faster), you might choose to turn off this option.

■ *Automatically decompress files at sign-off.* Many files you download from America Online are compressed to make them smaller and reduce the time needed to get the files to your computer (and reduce your online charges). America Online software includes a tool to automatically decompress files you've just downloaded. The supported formats include ZIP and ARC. By default, when you end your America Online session, all files you have just downloaded are decompressed automatically (if they're in a format that's supported, of course). You should keep this option checked. It makes using your download files much easier.

If you don't have enough disk space to store all those files, or you want to decide later whether you want to use the files, just turn off this option.

■ *Delete ZIP files after decompression.* This option enables you to automatically delete the original file after it has been expanded. This option is one you should use carefully, as a protection against the rare occasion when an expanded file might become damaged somehow (yes, it's happened to me). But it's useful if space on your hard drive is tight.

■ *Confirm additions to my download list.* This option produces a message that a file you've decided to download has been added to the queue.

■ *Retain information about my last __ downloads.* The Download Manager enables you to review a list of files you've downloaded to your computer. With this option, you can determine how many entries appear in your download log. Unless you need to track a large number of recent downloads, there's little reason to change the default setting.

Setting Chat Preferences

Figure C.8 shows the Chat Preferences dialog box that appears when you choose Chat from the Preferences dialog box. The following paragraphs explain the options you find in Chat Preferences.

FIG. C.8
You can have an online chat organized your way for easier viewing.

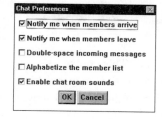

- *Notify me when members arrive.* Chats and conferences are often the most enjoyable experiences on America Online. This first check box is turned off by default. But if you want to be notified when another member arrives at the chat, turn on the option.

- *Notify me when members leave.* When another member leaves the chat, you know about it if you select this option.

- *Double-space incoming messages.* You can have your chat window display text double-spaced so that it's easier to read (the normal mode is single-spaced), at the expense of consuming lots of screen space.

- *Alphabetize the member list.* Normally members who enter a chat room are listed in the order in which they enter, but this option lets you display them alphabetically, and helps you quickly locate a specific person in a crowded chat room.

- *Enable chat room sounds.* You also can decide whether you want to hear sounds that other members might send. This preference is identical to the one provided for General Preferences.

Setting Graphics Preferences

America Online's Windows software enables you to open and print documents created in some graphics formats, such as GIF and JPEG. You can also observe the download of a picture file while it's in progress. You can use the preference box shown in figure C.9 to adjust your graphics viewing options.

FIG. C.9
Choose your online graphics viewing options here.

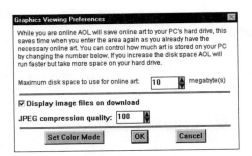

- *Maximum disk space for online art.* This choice let's you set aside a fixed portion of your hard drive for downloaded art (the fancy graphics you see in AOL's forums). When the block you've set aside for downloaded artwork is filled, the oldest, least used artwork is discarded. Setting aside a larger amount of disk space will allow your AOL software to run faster if you visit a lot of areas (because the artwork doesn't have to be downloaded to your PC over and over again).

- *Display image files on download.* This choice is the same as the one you can set as part of your Download Preferences (refer to fig. C.7).

- *JPEG compression quality.* This option enables you to choose the optimum quality versus compression of JPEG images. For most purposes, the default setting is just fine.

N O T E JPEG (pronounced "jay-peg") is a standardized image compression mechanism. JPEG stands for Joint Photographic Experts Group, the original name of the committee that wrote the standard. JPEG is designed for compressing either full-color or grayscale images of natural, real-world scenes. It works well on photographs, naturalistic artwork, and similar material, but not so well on lettering, simple cartoons, or line drawings. Many image files on AOL are provided in JPEG format because of their high quality and small size (making downloads of even large images relatively speedy). ■

- *Set Color Mode.* This button brings up the Color Preference display shown in figure C.10. Normally, Detect Automatically will do fine. But as the text on this screen states, some video drivers might have performance problems with the standard setting. If graphics do not display properly, you might prefer to choose a manual color setting.

FIG. C.10

If graphics opened in your AOL software don't display properly, choose the Set Color Mode option.

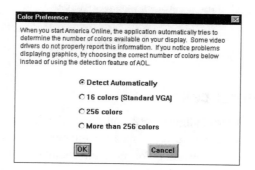

Setting Mail Preferences

The five check box options shown in figure C.11 enable you to decide how to handle your e-mail transactions.

- *Confirm mail after it has been sent.* When you retain this option (which is selected by default), you'll receive a confirmation when your e-mail has been sent on its way.

- *Close mail after it has been sent.* This option, also a default, closes your e-mail window after the message has been sent to its destination. This option helps reduce screen clutter, so it's a choice you'll probably want to keep.

■ *Retain all mail I send in my Personal Filing Cabinet.* The Personal Filing Cabinet is the tool provided in your Windows AOL software to manage your e-mail, file downloads, Favorite Places (which will be explained later in this chapter), and UseNet Newsgroups (see Chapter 32, "Joining and Participating in Internet Newsgroups"). Checking this option automatically archives a copy of the mail you've sent; your sent e-mail is deleted from your regular online mailbox after about a month.

■ *Retain all mail I read in my Personal Filing Cabinet.* Checking this option causes a copy of the mail you've read to be automatically archived. Otherwise, the e-mail you read is automatically deleted from your online mailbox after approximately five days.

■ *Use AOL style quoting in mail.* There are two ways to quote messages in the online world. AOL's method involves placing two marks at the beginning and end of the quote passed. The Internet way involves putting a > mark at the beginning of each line. I usually uncheck this box.

FIG. C.11
Your Mail Preferences are
selected in this dialog box.

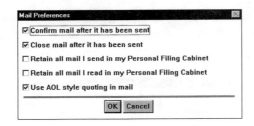

Setting WWW Preferences

Using the choices shown in figure C.12, you can decide how to set up America Online's World Wide Web browser feature. This feature enables you to view multimedia images, called home pages on the Internet. For more information about the World Wide Web, read Chapter 35, "Using the World Wide Web."

■ *No Graphics.* The World Wide Web demands a lot of resources. It takes up disk space, uses your computer's CPU horsepower, and requires a fast modem to transfer data effectively. If you don't have a fast computer and a fast modem, you might choose to turn on this option.

■ *Compressed Graphics.* This option enables you to view graphics on the World Wide Web only if they're compressed, which shortens the amount of time they take to reach your PC.

■ *Uncompressed Graphics.* This is your default option, which allows uncompressed images from the World Wide Web to be viewed on your PC.

■ *Don't show graphics at 2,400 bps.* Checking this option saves you time and money if you do not have a high-speed AOL connection. For effective use of the multimedia features of the World Wide Web, 2,400 bps is just too slow.

■ *Show current location.* This option displays the URL (Uniform Resource Locator) address (its Internet location) of the place you've accessed through the World Wide Web.

■ *Show destination of hyperlinks.* Checking this option simply displays the path used to access a linked Web page.

■ *Advanced.* Clicking this button provides the dialog box shown in figure C.13, which establishes a disk cache (data stored in your computer's hard drive) for graphics transferred from the World Wide Web. This speeds up display of images you've already seen when you want to view them again, because the image file is retrieved from your hard drive rather than downloaded via your computer's modem.

■ *Helper Applications.* This icon brings up a list of programs used to translate material you retrieve from the World Wide Web, such as compressed or graphic files. You may add additional programs, if you want, to translate formats not supported with the ones AOL provides.

■ *Security Alerts.* This setup box is used to select the warnings you see on-screen if you enter a WWW site that is not secured. This is useful if that site is run by a shopping service, and it'll be good reason to think twice about giving that service your credit card number or other personal information.

Part
X
App
C

FIG. C.12

Choose your WWW browser options here.

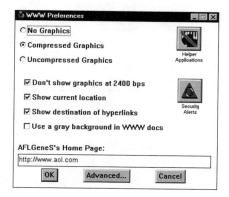

FIG. C.13
Set aside a portion of your
computer's hard drive in
which to store graphics
images transferred through
the Internet.

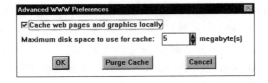

CAUTION

Before setting aside a disk cache for images received from the World Wide Web (or for AOL's own
downloaded artwork), be certain you have enough free storage space on your computer's hard drive.
If you don't have the small amount of space needed to store these files, you may want to finally get
around to the task of archiving all those unneeded files on your computer's drive.

The item labeled AFLGeneS's Home Page (which would show your screen name when
you log on to America Online) simply lists your point of origin in accessing the World
Wide Web, which in this case is America Online's home page.

Setting Personal Filing Cabinet Preferences

The Personal Filing Cabinet feature in your Windows AOL software enables you to customize your ability to archive material from your online visits. You have two options in
using this feature, shown in figure C.14.

FIG. C.14
Choose how confirmation
messages are displayed in
your Personal Filing Cabinet.

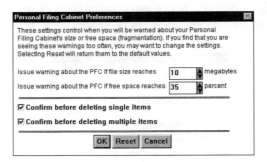

■ *Confirm before deleting single items.* When you check this option, you'll receive
confirmation when you delete a single item from your Personal Filing Cabinet.

■ *Confirm before deleting multiple items.* When you check this option, you'll receive
confirmation when you delete multiple items from your Personal Filing Cabinet.

Using the File Menu

America Online's File menu, shown in figure C.15, is much like the one you find in any other Windows application.

FIG. C.15
America Online's File menu is similar to the File menus found in other Windows applications.

Part
X

App
C

Most of the commands are familiar to you, but America Online has added a few features to its software that are worth some explanation. The following paragraphs explain the File menu's options.

Using the New Option

When you press Ctrl+N, you see a blank document window, much like the one you would find in a text processing program.

America Online comes with a basic text editor, kind of a simple word processor. You can use this text editor to write little memos or a simple letter, or just to paste text you have grabbed from other memos or message windows online.

The Memo feature is not as full-featured as your word processing program. For example, it's limited to 64,000 characters (about 10,000 words), not quite large enough for your new novel, but enough for a long letter. As with any other America Online text window, you can save and print your memo.

Using the Open Option

Choosing the Open command(Ctrl+O) brings up your standard Windows Open dialog box. It enables you to open text documents. You are limited to 64,000 characters in an open file window; if the file is longer, you can view it in separate pieces, each of which can be up to 64,000 characters long. Choose the More button to view the next piece of the file.

Using the Save Option

The Save command (Ctrl+S) saves the contents of your document window to a file that's written to disk. If you haven't saved the file before, you see a dialog box that enables you to give the file a name.

Using the Save As Option

This option enables you to save your document under a new name. When you select this option, you see a standard Windows dialog box in which you can specify the new name of your file.

Using the Print Option

Choosing the Print option (Ctrl+P) produces the regular Print dialog box (see fig. C.16). It enables you to print from any open text window. You can print a memo, your e-mail, a conference window, a message, a fully formatted World Wide Web page, or any other displayed text on America Online. If a window has more than one text window, such as the opening window of an online department, you should move the cursor to the text file you want to print. You can move the cursor either by clicking the mouse or by pressing Tab.

FIG. C.16
Printing a text window from America Online is a snap.

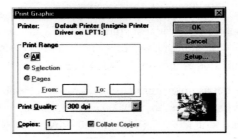

Using the Print Setup Option

Choosing Print Setup displays the standard Print Setup dialog box, in which you can change your page size and orientation (portrait or landscape) and select various printer options. These options vary depending on the kind of printer you have.

Using the Personal Filing Cabinet Option

The Personal Filing Cabinet is a catchall section that includes your Favorite Places, stored e-mail, and other information. You can use the screen shown in figure C.17 to manage your selections. They can be renamed, deleted, compacted to save space, or selections can be dragged and dropped in a different sequence.

FIG. C.17
You can configure your Personal Filing Cabinet from this handy screen.

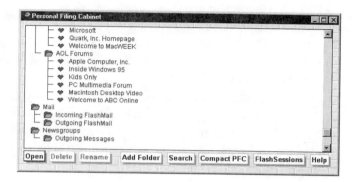

Using the Download Manager Option

Downloading is the process of transferring a file from America Online's huge software libraries to your computer. You use the Download Manager option (Ctrl+T) to choose one or more files to download during your online visit. The files are placed in a download queue or sequence. You can begin the download process at any time during your online session or when you log off.

You learn how to set up the Download Manager to work best for you in Chapter 6, "Where Do We Begin?" Figure C.7, shown earlier in this chapter, shows the Download Preferences available in your America Online software.

Using the Log Manager Option

During your visits to America Online, you sometimes might want to save the contents of a message area or an online conference so that you can view and print them later. You have two main logging options in your America Online software, as shown in figure C.18.

FIG. C.18
Recording your America
Online visit is easy with the
program's Logging feature.

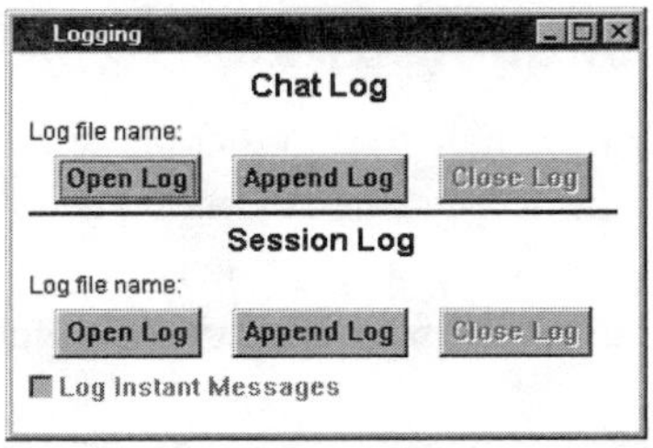

- *Chat Log*. During your online travels, you might attend a chat in America Online's People Connection or an online conference. The Chat Log enables you to record the entire conversation.

- *Session Log*. With this log, you can record all the text you read during your visit to America Online. The log doesn't record the mail you send or the messages you post, but you can save those anyway, using the Save command described previously. (You also can log instant messages if you check that option at the bottom of the Logging dialog box.)

To use your online tape recorder, follow these steps:

1. Choose the Logging option from the File menu, which opens the Logging dialog box.

2. Select the kind of log you want to record by clicking the Open Log button in the appropriate category.

3. Click the Open button. You then see a dialog box much like the Save As dialog box, where you are asked to name your file and indicate where it is to be saved (see fig. C.19). The log is given a default name, such as session.log, but you can give the file any name you want, as long as it contains no more than eight characters (and includes the same file extension); this is true even if you're using Windows 95.

4. If you want to end the online recording process, return to the File menu, select Logging, and choose the Close Log button in the Logging dialog box.

FIG. C.19
Name your open log to begin
the recording process.

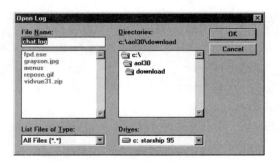

5. When you decide to resume the logging process or add to a previously created log, click the Append Log button in the Logging dialog box.

6. When you finish logging, choose the Close Log button in the Logging dialog box.

The logging process is flexible. You can open both logs at the same time if you want. What's more, you can append or close each log separately, depending on which one you've highlighted when you make your choice.

N O T E Remember, America Online software can read only 64,000 characters in a single text window. When you want to read additional segments of a long file, you need to select the More option in your Open dialog box. ■

Using the Stop Incoming Text Option

When you open a text window, the text begins to display in the window as it is received from America Online. If you want to stop this incoming text, select the Stop Incoming Text option from the File menu, or press the Esc key.

Using the Exit Option

If you are still online when you choose Exit from the File menu, you see a dialog box asking whether you are sure you want to sign off (log off) from America Online (see fig. C.20), with the additional option of staying online if you prefer. You can select Yes to be signed off within a few seconds, but the America Online application remains open for you to continue your work offline. Or you can select No and continue your online session. If you select the Exit Application option at the right side of the dialog box, you are logged off, the America Online application is closed, and you return to Windows.

FIG. C.20
You can log off by using the File menu's Exit option.

Using the Edit Menu

Five of the first six active selections on the Edit menu, as shown in figure C.21, are much like what you'd find in any Windows application. They are Undo (Ctrl+Z), Cut (Ctrl+X), Copy (Ctrl+C), Paste (Ctrl+V), and Select All (Ctrl+A).

FIG. C.21

The Edit menu is typical of what you see in many Windows programs.

The Crop option enables you to crop a portion of an image file you are viewing with the software, and to copy the portion into another document.

Using the Find in Top Window Option

America Online's Windows software enables you to search text in the top window (the one you've activated on your computer's screen). By choosing this command (see fig. C.22) and entering the text string you want to look for, you can quickly locate a specific item of text. You can make the search case-sensitive, if desired, by selecting the Match case option.

FIG. C.22

AOL's text search tool lets you find that word again in the document you just read.

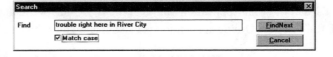

Fit Image to View

Choose Fit Image to View to resize an image file to fit on your screen. This choice works best when the image file is too large for your monitor and you need to shrink it quickly. If you use this feature to enlarge a smaller image, you expand the bitmaps that make up the image too, and you're apt to end up with a poor quality display (depending on how small the image was before you used this command). When the image has been resized, the command changes to Show Image in Original Size.

Using the Show Image Tools Option

The Show Image Tools option (see fig. C.23) works only if you open a picture file (such as a GIF or JPEG file). Then a set of graphics editing tools appears in a movable window. These tools are similar to what you find in an image editing program, although they're not intended to replace one of those programs.

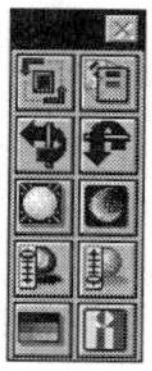

FIG. C.23
AOL's image editing toolbar offers you a set of basic image editing features.

Here's what those tools mean, row by row, from left to right:

- *Rotation.* Rotates a graphics image 90 degrees counterclockwise.
- *Revert.* Reverts the image to the last saved version. It's a quick way to undo multiple changes you've made to an image file.
- *Horizontal Rotation.* Flips the graphics image horizontally.
- *Vertical Rotation.* Flips the graphics image vertically.
- *Brighten Image.* Brightens the graphics image by a preset gradient.
- *Darken Image.* Darkens the graphics image by a preset gradient.
- *Increase Contrast.* Establishes a higher image contrast level.
- *Decrease Contrast.* Establishes a lower image contrast level.
- *Grayscale.* Removes the color bits from a color image and changes it to grayscale.
- *Invert Image.* Makes a positive image negative, and vice versa.

If you need to refresh your skills on these and other standard Windows commands, check the manuals that came with your Microsoft Windows software.

Using the Go To Menu

The Go To menu, as shown in figure C.24, is your launching pad on America Online. It's your gateway to loads of undiscovered treasures that you can find during your travels online.

FIG. C.24
The Go To menu helps you
access some of your favorite
online areas quickly.

Setting Up and Signing On

The window shown in figure C.25 appears automatically when you open your America
Online software. You use this window to begin your online session or to change your
modem setup.

FIG. C.25
This screen is the Sign On
screen for America Online.

Click the Sign On button at the bottom left of the window (or press Enter) to begin the
logon process. You use the Setup button to change your connection phone numbers or
your modem settings; the Help button brings up the online Help menu to get you through
the rough spots.

Welcome to America Online

When you first log on to America Online, the Welcome Menu introduces you to the
service (see fig. C.26).

FIG. C.26

This screen is your introduction to America Online.

At the bottom left of the Welcome window, you see an icon showing whether you've received e-mail. If you have America Online's default sounds activated, your sign-on is punctuated with a "Welcome" greeting, followed in a few seconds by a "You've got mail" announcement. Clicking the You Have Mail icon brings up a directory of the mail you've received since you last logged on. If no mail is waiting for you, you'll just see AOL's Mail Center icon instead.

Below the Welcome Menu when you log on is AOL's Channels menu (which can also be selected, when the window has been closed, from the Go To menu). This window is shown in figure C.27. The large, colorful graphical icons that fill the Channels menu take you directly to AOL's channels. These channels are discussed in full detail throughout this book. After your initial logon to America Online, you'll want to explore them briefly to get a good feel for the service.

FIG. C.27

The Channels menu is your jumping-off point to the far-flung reaches of America Online's virtual city.

Part

X

App

C

If you want to bring up the In The Spotlight screen after closing it, select that command from the Go To menu.

Using the Keyword Option

Using the Keyword option (see fig. C.28) is the fast and easy way to get anywhere online. Just select this command from the Go To menu or press the keyboard shortcut (Ctrl+K). Then enter the keyword and click the Go button, and you are transported to that location in just seconds.

FIG. C.28
America Online's Keyword feature enables you to go right to your favorite online spot or seek out points of interest.

Many of the keywords on America Online are intuitive. If you want to learn more about computers, type the keyword **Computing**. If you want to read the latest edition of the *New York Times* online, type the keyword **Times** (it's not case-sensitive). The Help (?) icon on your Keyword box brings up a list of current America Online keywords. If you want to find sources of information about a particular topic but you don't know the name of the area you want to visit, you also have a Find option (the button at the left shown previously in fig. C.27), which brings up a list of probable matches. See Chapter 6, "Where Do We Begin?" for more details on finding information on America Online.

Using the Find Option

The Find feature on the Go To menu lets you search for members, software, and services, all from a convenient interface. Just enter the member name or the topic you want to learn more about, and AOL's handy search engine will get to work to look up the information you requested.

Using the Online Clock Option

On a budget? Well, that's true for most of us. If you want to bring up a display of how long you've been online, here's a convenient way to do it, but it's just one way. Just click the Clock icon on the FlashBar or type the keyword **clock**.

Using the Favorite Places Option

Many of the areas you visit online have a little heart-shaped icon at the upper right of the screen. When you click that icon, you can add that area (and your favorite Internet sites are part of the bargain) to your Favorite Places list (see fig. C.29). The neat thing about this listing is that you can create custom categories for your favorite online spots, and drag and drop entries into a different order for your convenience.

FIG. C.29
Edit your list of Favorite Places on this screen.

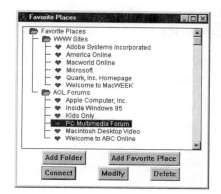

Part
X

App
C

Using the Edit Go To Menu Option

When you install your America Online software, you have a list of 10 regular spots to which you can travel by pressing two keys (Ctrl plus a number from 0 to 9).

Editing the Go To Menu is a simple task. Just proceed with the following steps if you want to change the default destinations shown in figure C.30, which are set by the software.

FIG. C.30
You can list your favorite places on this window for fast access.

Favorite Places		
Key	Menu Entry	Keyword
1	New Services	new
2	Discover America Online	discover
3	Sign on a Friend	friend
4	Top News	top news
5	Stock Quotes	stocks
6	Center Stage	center stage
7	Internet Connection	internet
8		
9		
10		
Save Changes		Cancel

1. In the Favorite Places dialog box, type the name of the area you want to visit on the left, and the online keyword on the right. To move quickly from one entry to the next in the dialog box, press Tab.

2. After you make your changes and additions to the Go To menu, click the Save Changes button. Your changes appear immediately in the Go To menu and are available immediately through the keyboard shortcuts.

Using the Mail Menu

Perhaps the most rewarding part of your online experience is the ability to send and receive electronic mail. The major features for creating and reading e-mail are found in the Mail menu, shown in figure C.31.

FIG. C.31
Use the Mail menu for sending and receiving e-mail.

 To save time and money during your online session, compose your e-mail *before* you sign on.

As mentioned earlier, you can compose your e-mail online, or you can do it offline and send it with a FlashSession. The following paragraphs describe the options you find on the Mail menu.

AOL's Mail Center

AOL's Mail Center (see fig. C.32) is an information center that helps guide you to writing e-mail on AOL and via the Internet. You can also click the handy icons to read and write e-mail.

Using the Compose Mail Option

The Compose Mail command (Ctrl+M) brings up the regular America Online e-mail window. It consists of a blank mail form that you can fill in and send while online.

Read Chapter 8, "Using America Online E-Mail," for the ins and outs of composing your electronic mail on AOL.

FIG. C.32
AOL's convenient Mail Center helps you manage your e-mail tasks.

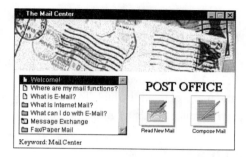

Using the Read New Mail Option

When you receive an announcement online that mail is in your mailbox (or when you see the icon change on your Welcome screen), select this option, press Ctrl+R, or click the You Have Mail icon at the bottom left of your AOL Welcome screen. If you haven't received any new mail, the label No Mail appears under the icon. Read Chapters 6 and 8 for more information about America Online's e-mail feature.

Using the Check Mail You've Read Option

If you want to recheck mail you've previously read, this option is the way to do it while you are online. You can use this feature to find out whether other recipients of this mail have seen it too. Your previously read mail is stored at AOL's host computer and included in this list for four to five days after you've read it.

Using the Check Mail You've Sent Option

If you're not sure whether you've sent a letter to another America Online member or you want to find out when it was received, check this item while you're online. You then see a window listing all the mail you've sent. You can reread the message yourself or click the Status button to find out who read it and when. Unread mail is stored at AOL's host computer and listed here for 30 days; otherwise, it's removed within two weeks.

Using the Fax/Paper Mail Option

America Online has a service that enables you to send mail to someone who isn't an online member. You can have your letter sent as a fax or via U.S. mail. When you select this option while online, you bring up a window that contains full instructions on how to use this service, along with the prices for this extra-cost service. Or just read Chapter 6, "Where Do We Begin?"

Using the Edit Address Book Option

As you develop a list of regular online friends, you'll want to put their names in your personal Address Book. This list is your own Rolodex that you can use to send mass mailings or merely to look up the name of an individual. To learn more about creating and updating your Address Book, see Chapter 8, "Using America Online E-Mail."

Using the FlashSessions Options

You can use the next two options on the Mail menu to automate your America Online sessions. You can compose an e-mail message offline and then schedule a FlashSession to send your message. During that FlashSession, any mail that has been received since your last online visit is saved to your mailbox (choose Read Incoming Mail from the Mail menu to view the mail). In addition, you can opt to download files that have been attached to e-mail during a FlashSession and receive and send files from the Internet newsgroups to which you subscribe.

See Chapter 8 for the full story on how to schedule your FlashSessions.

Using the Read Incoming FlashMail Option

This option enables you to view letters that have been saved to your FlashSession mailbox. Letters are stored in your FlashSession mailbox until you delete them. This mail is also available to you offline, since it is stored on your own computer rather than at AOL's host computer. You can save mail that you've read online to this file by clicking the Save to Flashmail icon in the Open Mail window. Check Chapter 8 for more information on how to run a FlashSession.

Using the Read Outgoing FlashMail Option

E-mail is stored in your FlashSession mailbox before it's sent during a FlashSession or while you're online (it is saved in a file on your own computer rather than at AOL's host computer). You can edit or delete your e-mail before it's sent, or even attach a file to your message.

Using the Members Menu

You learned about one option in the Members menu earlier in this chapter—the option of setting your America Online application preferences. Now you find out about the rest of the options you can select from this menu, shown in figure C.33.

FIG. C.33
The Members menu gives you options for finding out more about other members.

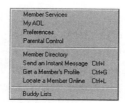

Using the Member Services Option

If you want to check your America Online bill, solve a problem with your software, or just learn more about the features available to you online, this option is the one to use. What's more, this area is free, meaning that you aren't charged for the time you spend in the Member Services section. A dialog box appears, asking you to confirm that you want to go into the free area, because other chat or gateway windows are closed in this area.

Using the My AOL Option

Choosing this brings up the handy window shown in figure C.34. If you're a new user to AOL, you'll find this may be the most convenient way for you to set program preferences. With a few clicks, you'll be taken on a guided tour showing the options you can select to make your software work better for you. Then choose the ones you want to change.

FIG. C.34
Customize the full range of your AOL experience here.

Using the Preferences Option

Choosing this command brings up the window I described in the section entitled "Setting Preferences" (refer to fig. C.4), earlier in this chapter.

Using the Parental Control Option

This choice is available to you only when you log on with your master account (that's the first name shown in the pull-down menu of available accounts on the main screen of your AOL software). The Parental Control option enables you to restrict certain parts of AOL's services to one or more of the screen names on your account. It's described in more detail in Chapter 16, "Parental Issues and Internet Access." This discussion will also skip the Set Preferences option because it was discussed in full detail earlier in this chapter.

Using the Member Directory Option

If you're not sure whether someone is a member of America Online, you can search the member directory and find out. You can look for a member by real name or screen name. You also can examine members' online profiles, if they've posted one, and update your own profile at the same time. Read Chapter 7, "America Online's People Connection," for more information on this subject.

Using the Send an Instant Message Option

An *instant message* is America Online's way of enabling you to hold an interactive, one-on-one "conversation" with another member, in private. Simply select the Send an Instant Message option (Ctrl+I), type the online address of the person to whom you want to send the message, and then enter your message. Click Send, and your message is sent almost instantly.

Using the Get a Member's Profile Option

If you want to learn more about an online member, using the Get a Member's Profile option (Ctrl+G) is the way to do it. If the member has created an online profile, you can view it by selecting this option. You can find more information on these and other special features for America Online members in Chapter 7.

Using the Locate a Member Online Option

Not sure whether your online friend is going to "meet" you at the appointed hour? Here's how to find out whether your friend is online. If the member is attending a chat or an online conference, you receive a message announcing where the person is. Otherwise, you are just notified that the person is online.

When you select the Locate a Member Online option (Ctrl+F), enter the screen name of the member for whom you're searching, and press Enter. If that member is online, you know about it in just a few seconds.

Using the Buddy Lists Option

A Buddy List (see fig. C.35) is AOL's convenient way of letting you know when your friends or colleagues are online—and to let them know when you're online. By setting the convenient preferences, you can build a list of members that AOL will inform you are online. You have, of course, the option of not allowing your name to be part of this Buddy List (as other members do).

FIG. C.35
Are your friends online?
AOL's Buddy List will tell you.

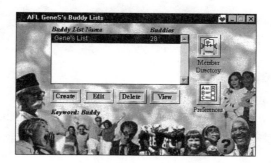

NOTE Because all of your screen names are part of the same master account, you cannot sign on to more than one of these screen names at one time. If you need to have more than one person sign on to AOL at the same time, you would have to establish a separate account for each person. ■

Using the Window Menu

As you continue to travel through the America Online community, your screen will soon become cluttered with many open windows. The Window menu, shown in figure C.36, is your tool for cleaning and clearing your screen.

NOTE At the bottom of the Window menu is a list of all open America Online windows. After you've opened this menu, you can type the listed number to bring that window to the front. ■

Part
X

App
C

FIG. C.36
The Window menu is designed for spring cleaning, so you can clean up a cluttered desktop.

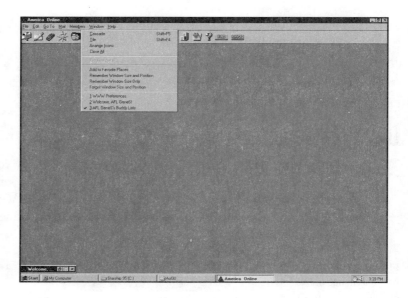

Using the Cascade Option

Cascade is another option you can use to organize your online windows. The Cascade option overlaps windows in neat form, from left to right, with the title of each window clearly displayed.

Using the Tile Option

As you travel online, you begin to open window after window, and finally your desktop starts getting awfully cluttered. Tiling the windows enables you to place them neatly side-by-side.

Using the Arrange Icons Option

The Arrange Icons feature arranges all icons neatly within an active window. This makes it easier for you to locate a specific document title on your computer's screen.

Using the Close All Option

Everything has its limits, and your America Online software cannot open an unlimited number of windows without the chance that the program will run out of memory. Periodically choosing this option to close all the windows is a good idea. It cleans up your workspace quickly.

Reopening the Exit Free Area

If you've entered a free area (to visit the Member Services area or get an AOL program upgrade), here's another way to leave that area.

Using the Add to Favorite Places Option

This option allows the frontmost forum window to be included in your list of Favorite Places. This feature is most convenient when you are visiting multiple sites across the World Wide Web or when you use other Internet features on America Online. You'll find out more about building a list of Favorite Places in Chapter 4, "Getting the Most from AOL's Windows Software."

Using the Remember Window Size and Position Option

You might decide that the default size of an America Online message window is too small or too large for your screen. You can use this option to enable the program to recall the size and position of the type of window (e-mail, message, or whatever) you have just chosen so that the program always opens that window in the same location and with the same window size.

This feature doesn't work for all America Online windows. If it doesn't work in a window you've opened, the option appears grayed in the Window menu.

Using the Remember Window Size Only Option

This option is similar to Remember Window Size and Position, but as you might expect, the position of the window is not saved.

Using the Forget Window Size and Position Option

If you decide to change the window to its default size and location, choose this option.

Using the Help Window

If you hit a sticking point and need a little more assistance in learning a particular function while using America Online's software, you'll find a lot of useful information in the Help menu. The Help menu works precisely the same way as it does in other Windows programs; it uses the Windows-based tools for searching Help information.

The Help menu is divided into three sections, the first of which has three parts. The first part, Contents, displays a listing of the Help topics. Double-clicking the topic that interests you provides a screen filled with the information you need. You can also use the Print Topic command to produce a paper copy of the open Help window.

The second part, Search for Help On, enables you to seek information on a particular topic by typing what you want to look for in the search field.

If you're new to the Microsoft Windows environment, you might want to review the third Help selection, How to Use Help, for information on how to gain the most advantage from this feature.

The next two commands will help assist you while you're online. Online Support takes you to the AOL Member Services forum, located in an area free of online charges. The second, New Member Info, takes you to a forum designed to help new members learn their way around the service.

The final option, About America Online, simply brings up a screen to inform you of the version of AOL software you're using, and that's useful if you're online and need additional support.

Using the FlashBar

America Online's Windows software gives you a quick way to go directly to an online department or take advantage of the most popular features of your software. This feature is called the FlashBar. The FlashBar contains 18 icons, as shown in figure C.37, each of which represents an online area or command.

FIG. C.37
The FlashBar and your mouse are a great combination for activating the most-used features of your America Online software.

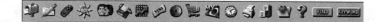

 TIP   If clicking a mouse isn't your favorite way to travel along the America Online road, check the end of this chapter for a complete list of keyboard shortcuts.

When you first open your America Online application, most of these icons are grayed, or inactive. But when you log on, the icons become bright and colorful. Clicking the appropriate icon with your mouse takes you directly to the listed online area or activates the listed function.

 TIP As with many other Windows programs, holding the mouse cursor above a FlashBar icon will bring up a screen message telling you the function of that icon.

Table C.1 lists the special functions and destinations attached to each icon. The areas shown correspond, from left to right, to the icons displayed on the FlashBar. All these areas and features are discussed in more detail throughout the rest of this book.

Part
X

App
C

Table C.1   Using the FlashBar

Icon	Destination or Function
	Check Mail
	Compose Mail
	AOL's Channels, by category
	What's Hot
	People Connection
	File Search
	Stocks and Portfolios
	Today's News
	World Wide Web
	The Marketplace
	My AOL—Personal Choices

continues

Table C.1   Continued

Icon	Destination or Function
	Online Clock
	Print Document
	Personal File Cabinet
	Favorite Places
	Member Services (Help channel)
	Find (Files, Members, Places, More)
	Keywords

Getting There by Keyboard

If you don't have a mouse hooked up to your computer, or you simply prefer using your keyboard, America Online has many keyboard commands that are simple to learn and use. Throughout this chapter, the keyboard shortcuts appear with the matching menu commands, but some of the shortcuts are described in more detail in the following paragraphs.

Using the Tab Key

Suppose that you are composing a letter to another America Online member. You can use the Tab key to move from one field to another, such as from the Subject field to the field where you write your letter. The Tab key works in any area where more than one field is available to choose. Holding down the Shift and Tab keys at the same time reverses the process, so you move back to the preceding field.

Pulling Down a Menu

To use the keyboard to open a menu, follow these steps:

1. Each menu bar item, such as <u>F</u>ile or <u>E</u>dit, has an underlined letter. If you press the Alt key plus that underlined letter, the menu drops down, and a rectangle highlights the first entry in the menu.

2. Use the down-arrow key to move the highlight down to the item you want to use.

3. Use the up-arrow key if you need to move the highlight up to the preceding item.

4. Press Enter to activate the highlighted menu option.

Viewing a List of Keyboard Commands

Table C.2 contains a list of many of the keyboard shortcuts available with your America Online Windows software.

Part
X
App
C

Table C.2 Keyboard Shortcuts for Windows Users

Function	Keyboard Shortcut
Access Download Manager	Ctrl+T
Cancel an action	Esc
Cascade windows	Shift+F5
Close a window	Ctrl+F4
Copy	Ctrl+C
Cut	Ctrl+X
Find a member, file, area	Ctrl+F
Get member profile	Ctrl+G
Locate a member online	Ctrl+L
Move to next button	Tab
Move to next window	Ctrl+F6
Move to previous button	Shift+Tab
Open a new text file	Ctrl+N
Open an existing file	Ctrl+O
Open Channels	Ctrl+D

continues

Table C.2   Continued

Function	Keyboard Shortcut
Open Keyword window	Ctrl+K
Open Mail window	Ctrl+M
Paste	Ctrl+V
Read new mail	Ctrl+R
Save a file	Ctrl+S
Scroll down a page	Page Down
Scroll up a page	Page Up
Send an instant message	Ctrl+I
Tile windows	Shift+F4

From Here ...

In this appendix, you learned the basics of using your America Online Windows software. As you read further through this book, you'll find additional information and helpful hints to make your online sessions even more rewarding—and fun too! You can find additional details on some of the subjects discussed so far in these chapters:

- For advice on logging on to AOL when you're not at your home or office, read Chapter 5, "America Online and Mobile Computing."
- For a quick tour of AOL, read Chapter 6, "Where Do We Begin?"
- To learn how to navigate through AOL's huge software libraries, review Chapter 20, "Tips and Tricks on Finding Software."
- A membership on America Online will also make you a part of the global Internet network. For more information, you'll want to read the chapters that compose Part VIII, "Entering the Information Superhighway."

Glossary

abbreviations   Abbreviations are often used while chatting in the People Connection and other chat rooms and when exchanging instant messages and e-mail. Examples include LOL (laughing out loud) and BRB (be right back). See also *shorthand* and *emoticons*.

access number   Usually a local telephone number that your modem calls to gain access to America Online's main computer. Use the keyword **Access** while online to locate numbers near your current or future calling location. See also *AOLNet*, *SprintNet*, *Tymnet*, and *DataPac*.

Address Book   This is a feature of your AOL software that you can access by double-clicking its Address Book icon when addressing e-mail or by choosing it under your Mail menu. This feature allows you to store screen names for easy access while composing mail. See also *e-mail* and *screen name*.

AFK   Abbreviation for Away From Keyboard. Used in chat/conference rooms and in instant messages to tell people that you are not going to be in front of your computer for a while and that queries may not be answered during that time. Upon return, you use BAK to indicate that you are Back At Keyboard. See also *abbreviations* and *BAK*.

Alt key   The Alt key is a special function key on the PC keyboard. It is the key with the letters Alt on it and is usually located near the space bar. It is used for accessing menu functions and may be used for special-purpose functions within some applications.

America Online, Inc.   Formerly Quantum Computer Services, this parent company runs three online services—America Online, PC-Link, and Q-Link. America Online's stock exchange symbol is AMER on NASDAQ. Compare with *CompuServe Information Service*, *PC-Link*, and *Prodigy*.

AOL   AOL is the most common abbreviation for America Online. See also *America Online, Inc.*

AOLNet   America Online's own high-speed packet network, which offers V.34 (28,800 bps) and ISDN access to the service from many cities. See also *DataPak*, *SprintNet*, and *Tymnet*.

ARC   An older compression utility that was the PC standard prior to ZIP. The ARC utility compresses one or more files into a smaller file—called an archive—that has the extension ARC. The smaller the file, the faster you can download it. See also *archive*, *download file compression*, *PKZip*, and *StuffIt*.

archive   (1) A file or files compressed into a smaller, single file using compression software. (2) A file, usually available in Computing Forum software libraries, consisting of compilations of message board postings that (usually) have been removed from a message board due to inactivity or lack of message board space. See also *file compression*, *ARC*, *PKZip*, and *StuffIt*.

Ask the Staff   This button is available in file libraries while viewing the File Descriptions. Clicking this button brings up a form in which you may compose and send a note to the AOL staff responsible for that library. The message you send using this form is not transmitted to the uploaders of the files. See also *library*, *download*, and *upload*.

AT   The beginning of a modem string, which is the equivalent of an "Attention" command. The letters and numbers that follow this command configure the modem for specific connection setups.

attached file/attachment   A file from your computer, or another's, sent in conjunction with e-mail. The file is separate from the actual message contained within the e-mail item and is downloadable to your computer. An attached file is uploaded or downloaded, but it is a separate entity from files contained within AOL's software libraries. See also *e-mail* and *FlashSession*.

auditorium   Auditoriums are online chat rooms that are designed to allow large groups of AOL members (numbering in the thousands) to meet in a highly organized setting.

Auditoriums are divided into two parts: the stage, where the host and the guests are located, and the chat rows, where the audience is located. Communication between the audience and people onstage is accomplished through the use of special tools. Unless specifically enabled, audience chat is seen only by members in the same chat row. See also *chat rooms*.

BAK   Abbreviation for Back At Keyboard. Used in chat/conference rooms and in instant messages to tell people that you are back in front of your computer after a break and that you are available for queries. When you leave your computer, you use AFK to indicate Away From Keyboard. See also *abbreviations* and *AFK*.

banner   See *Network News*.

baud   A unit for measuring the speed of serial (as opposed to parallel) data transmission. Not the same as bps, but often used as a conceptual equivalent. See also *bits per second*.

BBS   See *bulletin board system*.

BCC   See *blind carbon copy*.

bits per second (bps)   A method of measuring data transmission speed. Currently, 300, 1,200, 2,400, 9,600, 14,400 and 28,800 bps are supported on AOL. See also *baud*.

blind carbon copy (bcc)   A blind carbon copy used in e-mail directs a duplicate of the e-mail to a third party and specifically excludes the recipient's name from the list of people listed in the body of the received e-mail form. The recipient who is bcc'd is said to be blind to other recipients. See also *e-mail* and *carbon copy*.

board   See *message board*.

bps   See *bits per second*.

BRB   Abbreviation for Be Right Back. Used in chats, instant messages, and other areas where live interaction occurs online. See also *abbreviations*, *chat rooms*, and *shorthand*.

browse   Causal examination of messages or file lists, rather than a specific examination of the messages or file descriptions.

Buddy List   A directory window that will show if any of a preselected list of your AOL friends and colleagues are online.

bulletin board system (BBS)   A central system accessed using a computer, a modem, and phone lines or a network connection, where data is placed by users for dissemination to one or more other users. America Online is considered a BBS, but most BBSes are much smaller than AOL and are often run on a single microcomputer with a single phone line in a hobbyist environment. See also *message board* and *message center*.

Part
X

App
D

carbon copy (cc)   The act of sending e-mail to a third party who may only have a secondary or casual interest in the content of said e-mail. A person who is cc'd is also usually not expected to participate or provide a reactive position to the e-mail. See also *e-mail* and *blind carbon copy*.

CC   See *carbon copy*.

Center Stage   Center Stage is the People Connection's primary auditorium, located in the People Connection department or by using the keyword *Center Stage*. See also *auditorium*.

chat protocol   See *protocol*.

chat room   Online "rooms"—that is, special windows—where America Online members congregate and interact by typing messages to one another in real time. See also *auditorium, conference room, guide,* and *host*.

channel   This is the broadest category of information into which America Online divides its material (somewhat similar to the channel you select on your TV). These areas are usually referred to as Departments. See also *Department*.

CIS (CI$)   See *CompuServe Information Service*.

Command key   On the Macintosh keyboard, this is a special function key located near the space bar and contains the Apple symbol (🍎) and the Command symbol (⌘). This key is also called the Open-Apple key. See also *Control key* and *Option key*.

compression   See *file compression*.

CompuServe Information Service (CIS or CI$)   One of the first commercial online services, similar to America Online but with more databases available and less emphasis on community and graphical interface. CompuServe Information Service is owned by H&R Block (they were in the process of selling this division as this book was being prepared). It may be referred to as CIS or CI$ in shorthand during chat. (The latter designation is a humorous reference to the view that CompuServe is a costlier service than America Online). Compare with *America Online, PC-Link,* and *Prodigy*.

conference room   A special meeting room designed to hold 48 people, rather than the 23 of People Connection rooms. While chats are usually spontaneous and ongoing affairs, conferences are usually held periodically and are more structured. Examples of conference rooms can be found in any of the Computing & Software forums, such as the Macintosh Multimedia Forum or the PC Applications Forum. See also *chat room* and *protocol*.

Community Action Team (CAT)   These are AOL staffers who help enforce the rules of the road of the service, which are commonly known as the Terms of Service (or TOS). See also *TOS*.

Control key   The Control key is a special function key on the PC and Macintosh. It is the one with the letters *Ctrl* or *Control* on it. On the PC, the Ctrl key is equivalent to the Macintosh's Command key (⌘) in the America Online environment. See also *Command key*, *Option key*, and *Alt key*.

CS Live   See *Tech Live*.

Customer Relations   You can reach America Online's Customer Relations Hotline by calling 1-800-827-6364 seven days a week. When you call, a voice menu will list current support hours. See also *Tech Live*.

cyberspace   A virtual world created by our computers. No physical entities are present in cyberspace, but intellectual interaction is accomplished through the collective connections of many people. See also *online community*.

database   A database is an organized collection of information, usually maintained by a computer and often searchable. An example of this is the Online Encyclopedia found by using the keyword **Encyclopedia**.

Datapac   A packet-switching network operated by Bell Canada that provides local access numbers for Canadian members at an extra fee. Canadians living near the U.S. border can usually dial a U.S. access number to avoid the extra charge and pay less in toll charges than the Datapac surcharge. See also *access number*, *AOLNet*, *node*, *SprintNet*, and *Tymnet*.

demoware   Software that can be downloaded and used for evaluation, but that is functionally disabled in some areas and/or ceases to operate after a certain length of use. See also *shareware*, *freeware*, and *public domain*.

department   This is the broadest category of information into which America Online divides its material. The Departments window can be brought up from anywhere online by selecting Main Menu from the Go To menu in your menu bar.

Directory of Services   A searchable database that allows AOL members to quickly locate AOL's available services. This database is available at the keyword *Dir. of Services* or by selecting Directory of Services from the Go To menu.

download   The movement of information or files located on a remote host computer to a storage device of your choosing on your computer. Most commonly used to describe the act of transferring files from AOL's libraries to your hard drive for use after disconnecting from AOL. Compare with upload. See also *file compression*.

Part X
App D

download count   The download count is the number of times a file has been downloaded from AOL and is often used to measure a file's popularity. (In other words, 50,000 AOL members can't be wrong!)

Download Manager   A function in the AOL software that allows you to create and manage a list of files for later downloading. See also *download* and *FlashMail*.

e-mail   Short for electronic mail, e-mail is one or more private messages sent from one computer user to another or to a group of users. Using America Online's e-mail, you can send messages to other members or to people who can receive mail through the Internet.

emoticons   A combination of keyboard characters, mostly consisting of punctuation, that convey information about the emotional state of the user. They usually appear sideways; for example, you can type :) to indicate a smile. This emoticon might be the original one and also is probably the source of the term smileys, which refers to all emoticons. A short list of emoticons is available in Chapter 6 and at the keyword **Shorthand**. See also *shorthand* and *chat rooms*.

FAQ   Abbreviation for Frequently Asked Questions, usually in the form of a question-and-answer text file. FAQs are posted to help newcomers find answers to common concerns.

Favorite Places   A custom list you create of the online spots you want to revisit.

file compression   A technique that reduces many computer files to half (or even less) of their original size. Though they must be decompressed to be used, compressed files take up much less storage space than their uncompressed counterparts and require far less time to transfer via the AOL system or any modem. File compression comes in many flavors, the most common of which are StuffIt, DiskDoubler, and Compact Pro for the Macintosh. PC users have PKZip, ARC, and others. See also *download*.

File Transfer Protocol (FTP)   A technique used to transfer binary files over the Internet. See also *Internet*.

FlashSession   This America Online feature allows you to automate the sending and receiving of e-mail and attachments, Internet Newsgroup messages, and retrieve files listed for later download in your Download Manager. See also *attached file/attachment*, *download*, *Download Manager*, and *e-mail*.

forum   AOL's forums are areas where people with similar interests visit to share their ideas, opinions, and comments, and to download or upload software. Most forums offer message boards, articles, chat rooms, and libraries organized in a forum format accessible by an AOL keyword. Forums are overseen by Hosts or Forum Leaders; for example, in the Macintosh Computing department, each forum has a Forum Leader (denoted by

AFL at the beginning of the screen name), who is assisted by Forum Assistants (AFA), Forum Consultants (AFC), and Technical Assistants (AFT). See also *Forum Leader/ Assistant/Consultant/Technical Assistant.*

Forum Leader/Assistant/Consultant/Technical Assistant   These folks are considered staff members of AOL's forums, but are not usually employees of America Online. They moderate the various Computing & Software forums and maintain the file libraries and message boards of each. See also *forum.*

freeware   Software offered for distribution through general channels, including, but not limited to, online services such as AOL. Freeware is specifically copyrighted software for which no monetary charge is made by the author or developer, but to which the author or developer retains rights in accordance with U.S. copyright laws. See also *demoware* and *public domain.*

FTP   See *File Transfer Protocol.*

GA   Abbreviation for Go Ahead, often used during conferences with protocol. See also *protocol.*

gateway   A link to other types of telecommunications services, usually e-mail and other host computing environments. The EAAsy Sabre travel reservations service, for example, is an entirely separate system that is accessed by AOL users through a gateway. See also *Internet.*

Get a Member's Profile   Commonly called Get Info, a feature of America Online that allows you to easily retrieve and view a specific member's online profile, if he or she has provided one, by selecting Get a Member's Info from the Member menu, or by pressing Command-G (Ctrl+G for PC users) and typing a screen name. See also *member, Member Directory,* and *Member Profile.*

Get Info   See *Get a Member's Profile.*

GIF   See *Graphic Interchange Format.*

GNN   An Internet-only online service run by America Online.

Gopher   An Internet-based data search and retrieval tool.

Graphic Interchange Format (GIF)   A type of graphic file that most computer platforms can read—the electronic version of photographic images. The GIF standard was developed by CompuServe as a standard for sharing graphical information across platforms.

guide   Guides are AOL members who specialize in helping other members in the various chat rooms of People Connection.

Part
X
App
D

Guide Pager   An AOL feature allowing you to page a Guide when there is a problem in a chat or conference room. See also *Guide* and *TOS*.

help room   These are virtual rooms where members can go to get interactive assistance on using their AOL software or service, as well as assistance in finding files and areas of special interest online. Help rooms are located in the People Connection area and in the Members' Online Support area. See also *guide, Members Helping Members,* and *Tech Live.*

host   (1) The main computer system of a BBS, such as America Online. AOL's host consists of a high-speed computer network, containing both mini- and microcomputers, as described in this book's Introduction. (2) An AOL member who facilitates discussion in chat rooms.

icon   A pictographic representation of a command or request. When you click an icon with your mouse, the computer usually takes some form of action.

Ignore   (1) The feature that allows a member to stop another member's chat room text from appearing on his or her screen. (2) The ability to designate specific users from whom you want to not receive e-mail.

IM   See *instant message.*

Information Provider (IP)   An individual or company who provides time and effort to, and is responsible for, the content of specific areas on America Online. An AFL, for example, is also referred to as an IP. See also *Remote Staff* and *forum.*

instant message (IM)   Instant messaging is a way to have a private interactive meeting with another AOL member online. By choosing Send Instant Message from the Member menu, you can have a one-on-one mini-chat with another AOL member. IMs may also be thought of as private rooms for two, and only two people at a time, although multiple IM windows can be open on your screen at any given time. See also *e-mail* and *chat room.*

Internet   The Internet can be thought of as a mega-network of computer networks that are interconnected at all times. The Internet began in 1969 as a Defense department computer network and today spans the globe, connecting more than 100,000 machines, many of which serve as hubs for local networks that each serve numerous users. The Internet is maintained by the National Science Foundation. AOL offers File Transfer Protocol, Internet e-mail, UseNet Newsgroup information service, World Wide Web, and other Internet services.

IP   Internet Protocol (as in TCP/IP), referring to the communications technique used for Internet connections. See also *Information Provider.*

keyboard shortcuts   The AOL software provides keyboard command equivalents for menu selections. For example, rather than using your mouse to select Send Instant Message from your menu, you can press Command-I on a Mac or Ctrl+I on a PC.

keyword   (1) Keywords are shortcuts to specific destinations within America Online that allow you to move instantaneously to a different area. You can jump directly to Time Online, for instance, by using the keyword **Time**. To use a keyword, press Command-K (Ctrl+K if you use a PC), type the keyword, and then press Return (or Enter on a PC). (2) A word or words you feel are likely to match one or more entries in a database or file collection. You would use the keyword or combination of keywords in the search form to look for entries matching your needs.

library   An area containing files that you can download or to which you can upload files. The files can be of any type—text, graphics, software, or sounds—and are intended to be transferred to a storage device on your own computer.

line noise   Spurious noise on telephone lines that is often heard as clicks or static and that tends to interfere with computer communications via modem. Line noise on your telephone line can sometimes abruptly terminate an online connection.

Lobby   The Lobby is AOL's primary public chat room. Members can stop by the Lobby at any time to chat with other members or to see a listing of other public rooms. It's also the gateway to America Online's People Connection.

LOL   Abbreviation for Laughing Out Loud, often used in chat rooms and instant message conversations. See also *emoticons* and *shorthand*.

lurk   To sit in a chat or conference room and simply watch what's going on without making any comments of your own.

member   A customer of America Online.

Member Directory   A listing of AOL member screen names that have profiles. To be included in this database, you simply need to create your own Member Profile. You can get to the Member Directory by using the keyword **Members**. See also *member*, *Member Profile*, and *Get a Member's Info*.

Member Profile   An optional online information document that provides a brief description of the AOL member. In addition to your name, such information as your city, birthday, gender, marital status, hobbies, computers you use, occupation, and favorite quotation may be provided by you for others to see. This feature can be explored in the area located at the keyword **Members** or **Profile**. See also *member* and *Member Directory*.

Members Helping Members (MHM)   A message board in the Member's Online Support area where America Online members can assist and get assistance from other members. The keyword is **MHM**. See also *help room*.

Part
X

App
D

menu   A text- or graphics-based window containing a list of options or commands you can use to initiate an action or select an item. A menu can be located anywhere on the computer screen, but most frequently they are in a menu bar at the top of the screen or window.

message board   An area where members can post messages, typically to solicit a reply or to comment on a prior message. See also *bulletin board system*.

message center   A collection of message boards in one convenient area. See also *message board*.

MHM   See *Members Helping Members*.

modem   The word modem is short for modulator/demodulator. It is a peripheral device that allows a computer to transfer data across telephone lines. Your computer interacts with America Online with a modem.

Network News   An announcement that appears intermittently on members' screens promoting one of AOL's services/events, broadcasting AOL maintenance information, and/or providing member feedback. Also known as a banner.

newbie   Affectionate term for a new member (a member for fewer than six months). Newbies are often found in the Beginner's Forum, for which the keyword is **ABF**.

node   The geographical point at which you first connect to the communications network after your modem dials its local access number when connecting to America Online. See also *AOLNet*, *SprintNet*, *Tymnet*, and *Datapac*.

online   Refers to the state of your America Online connection when you are actually connected to the AOL service through your modem.

online community   A group of people bound together by their shared interest or characteristic of interacting with other computer users through online services, BBSs, or networks. See also *cyberspace*.

Online Host   The pseudo-screen name of AOL's host computer. Online Host will, at your choosing, inform you when a member enters or leaves a chat room if you are on a PC platform system. On all platforms except PC-Link, the Online Host will also show you the result of your rolling the AOL dice. See also *chat room*, *conference room*, *auditorium*, and *//roll*.

Online Profile   See *Member Profile*.

Open-Apple key   See *Command key*.

Option key   A special modifier key commonly found on Macintosh keyboards and used for typing special characters. See also *Command key*.

P*   Shorthand for Prodigy Service. See *Prodigy*.

Parental Controls   Parental Control enables the master account holder to restrict access to certain areas and features on AOL, such as blocking instant messages and rooms. It can be set for one or all screen names on the account. Once Parental Control is set for a particular screen name, it is active each time that screen name signs on. Changes can be made by the master account holder at any time. To access controls, use the keyword **Parental Control**.

PC-Link (PCL)   The original name of America Online Inc.'s service for PC users that uses a DeskMate-style interface with special support areas provided by the Tandy Corporation (Tandy Headquarters in PC-Link Basic, for example). Compare with CompuServe and Prodigy. See also *America Online, Inc.*

People Connection (PC)   The AOL department dedicated to real-time chat. Many different rooms can be found here: Lobbies, officially-sanctioned rooms, member-created rooms, private rooms, the Center Stage Auditorium, and PC Studio. You can access this area with the keyword **People**.

PKZip   A compression utility for PCs to compress one or more files into a smaller file (called an archive), which makes for shorter up/downloading. See also *archive, download, file compression, ARC*, and *StuffIt*.

post   (1) The act of putting something online, usually into a message board. (2) A message in a message board.

private room   A chat room created by a member via an option in People Connection where the name is not public knowledge. To enter this room, a member must first know the exact name used to originally create it. This arrangement provides an area where people may converse without fear of interruption by other uninvited members.

Prodigy   The online service founded as a joint venture between IBM and Sears. It is currently one of the larger competitors to America Online. Prodigy's interface differs from that of America Online by its continuous online advertising, screening of messages before they're allowed to be posted, and other quirks. For all its drawbacks, Prodigy still has an enormous subscription base. For those astute members who defected from Prodigy to AOL, check out the Prodigy Refugees Forum, which you can get to by using the keyword **Prodigy**. Compare with America Online, Inc. and CompuServe.

Profile   See *Member Profile*.

Part

X

App

D

protocol The procedure employed in conference rooms to keep order and ensure orderly discussion. When you have a question, you type a question mark (?), when you have a comment, you type an exclamation mark (!), and when you are finished, you type GA. A queue of those waiting with questions and answers is displayed at regular points throughout the conference, and members are invited to speak by the moderator or host. It is considered impolite and a breach of protocol to speak out of turn. See also *conference room*.

public domain Public domain software is completely free software and not copyrighted, so you can use it any way you wish. See also demoware, freeware, and shareware.

punt The process of being knocked offline (disconnected), usually as a result of a problem with telephone line noise, your local access number, or the AOL host computer.

Q-Link America Online's service for Commodore 64 and 128 users. See also *America Online, Inc.*

Remote Staff These are members who staff the various forums and areas but are not employees of AOL; they work from their homes. Usually these are guides, hosts, Forum Leaders, Assistants, or Consultants.

return receipt Somewhat like its counterpart with the mail you send via the post office, it is a message you receive indicating the e-mail you've sent has been read by a particular recipient.

revolving door A chat or conference room has a revolving door when members are quickly moving in and out of the room.

//roll A unique command used in any People Connection or other chat room to roll the AOL Dice. Its default is to produce two random numbers imitating the roll of two six-sided dice; for example, you might see

```
OnlineHost: JLR63 rolled 2 6-sided dice: 6 4
```

You can also roll other combinations of dice by varying the number of dice and the number of sides on each die. The proper use of this command is //roll-dice*nn*-sides*nnn*, where *nn* is 1-15 and *nnn* is 1-999.

It is outside the rules of etiquette to roll dice in public chat rooms without explicit invitation by a host or by previously set ground rules, such as when role-playing in the Red Dragon Inn. Invitations to roll dice are sometimes issued in chats where prizes are offered to the winners by the host. Rolling the AOL Dice is an online form of drawing straws.

Rotunda An auditorium that features conferences with companies or renowned guests in the Computing & Software department. The keyword is **Rotunda**. See also *auditorium*.

screen name   Screen names are the pseudonyms used by America Online members to identify themselves online. See also *member* and *Member Profile*.

scroll   (1) In a chat or conference, the act of repeatedly typing similar words on-screen, spacing out the letters of a word, or sending multiple lines of chat in rapid sequence in such a fashion as to be disruptive. (2) Refers to the movement of incoming text and other information on-screen.

self-extracting archive   Most compressed files must be decompressed using the same software that compressed them originally. A self-extracting file, on the other hand, contains not only the compressed data, but also the program information necessary to decompress itself.

shareware   Shareware is software provided for evaluation by the author or developer for a set period of time before payment is required. Most shareware is distributed through BBSs and online services and almost always contains the necessary disclaimers and conditions that the downloader must legally adhere to, including the payment of fees. See also *demoware, freeware*, and *public domain*.

shorthand   Used to describe emoticons and abbreviations used in message boards and during chats, e-mail, and instant messages. A brief list of these is available at the keyword **Shorthand**. See also *abbreviations* and *emoticons*.

smileys   See *shorthand* and *emoticons*.

snail mail   Mail sent via the U.S. Postal Service, not e-mail. Derogatory in origin, this term refers to the legendary slowness of conventional mail-delivery methods.

SprintNet   Formerly known as Telenet, SprintNet is a data network providing AOL members 1,200, 2,400, 9,600 and 14,400 bps local access numbers to America Online. SprintNet networks are owned and operated by US Sprint. To find SprintNet local access numbers, use the keyword **Access**.

Numbers   See *Tymnet* and *Datapac*.

Stratus   The name applied to the computer system used by America Online to run its service. Actually, the AOL system includes a distributed network that consists not only of Stratus computers, but computers from other manufacturers, as well.

StuffIt   StuffIt is the trade name of a specific type of Macintosh file-compression software published by Aladdin Systems. Various versions of StuffIt are distributed, in both shareware and commercial forms, on almost every online service, including AOL. See also *file compression, download*, and *upload*.

SYSOP   Acronym for system operator, a person who runs a bulletin board system. See *Forum Leader/Assistant/Consultant and Information Provider*.

Part
X
App
D

Tech Live   Also known as CS Live. A free area for members to interactively ask questions and obtain assistance from AOL's Tech Support staff. The Tech Live Auditorium is open from 8 a.m. to 4 a.m. eastern time, seven days a week. This service is available by using the keywords **CS Live** or **Tech Live**.

Telnet   A way of accessing a UNIX server via the Internet through a text-based shell.

TOS   An abbreviation for Terms Of Service—it amounts to your contract with America Online. You agree to abide by these terms when you join the service, and these terms apply to all America Online accounts. The areas covered by AOL's Terms Of Service include General Information, Payment Information, Third-Party Sales and Service, Termination Information, Disclaimer and Liability Notices, Online Conduct, America Online Software License, Copyright Notices, Information Supplied by Members, Electronic Mail, and Other Provisions. You can read these terms at the keyword **TOS**. Also included are avenues of reporting TOS violations to America Online.

Tymnet   A computer data network providing AOL members with 1,200 and 2,400 bps local access numbers to America Online. Tymnet networks are owned and operated by MCI/BT Tymnet. To find Tymnet local access numbers, use the keyword **Numbers** or call 1-800-336-0149. See also *AOLNet*, *Datapac*, *SprintNet*, and *access number*.

Uniform   As used on America Online, a screen name preceded by a prefix of 2-8 letters, and a personal name or initials indicating the title of a Remote Staff person. These special prefixes and their definitions include the following:

Prefix	Definition
Advisor	AOL staffer
AFL	Apple/Mac Forum Leader
AFA	Apple/Mac Forum Assistant
AFC	Apple/Mac Forum Consultant
AFT	Apple/Mac Forum Technical Assistant
CNR	CNN News Room staff
CSS	Company Support Staff
Guide	General system guide
GWRep	GeoWorks Representative
IC	Industry Connection
NPR	National Public Radio Outreach staff
OMNI	OMNI Magazine Online staff

Prefix	Definition
PC	PC Forum Leader
PCA	PC Forum Assistant
PCC	PC Forum Consultant
PCW	PC World Online
PGFA	AOL Portrait Gallery staff
PS1	PS1 Connection staff
Teacher	IES Teacher
TECHLive	Tech Live representative
VGS	Video Game Systems staff
WCC	Chicago Online/Windy City chat staff

See also *guide*, *Forum Leader/Assistant/Consultant*, and *Remote Staff*.

upload The transfer of files from your computer to AOL's host computer. Uploaded files may be attached to e-mail (these files are more frequently referred to as attached files), or they may be uploaded for inclusion in a library. Attached files are typically intended for a single recipient, whereas library files are for all to see and use once the file has been reviewed and released by the library staff. Generally, to make the transfer faster and therefore save money, you should compress any file over 16K (with the exception of text files) before uploading it. Approved compression formats are ZIP, ARC, SIT, and SEAs. Compare with download. See also *file compression* and *library*.

UseNet Also known as Newsgroups, which are discussion groups, similar to the message boards on America Online, devoted to a specific subject, such as cooking, Macintosh computing, Windows computing, and so forth. America Online's Internet Connection provides access to tens of thousands of Newsgroups throughout the world.

Uuencode A way of transferring binaries within an e-mail message or newsgroup posting. This changes the binary file into text, which then must be decoded upon receipt.

virus Computer software that can attach itself to other software or files without the permission or knowledge of the user. Viruses are generally designed with one intent: to propagate themselves. They might be intentionally destructive; however, not all virus damage is intentional. Some benign viruses suffer from having been poorly written and have been known to cause damage, as well. Virus prevention software and information may be found by using the keyword **Virus** on the Mac or **McAfee** on the PC.

WAIS Short for Wide Area Information Servers, an Internet-based set of databases providing text-based information on thousands of topics.

Part

X

App

D

Winsock   Software used to allow Windows-based software to plug into the Internet (it's an abbreviation for *Windows Sockets*). By using AOL's Winsock software, you're able to access non-AOL WWW browsers (such as Netscape) and other Internet-related software during your AOL session. Version 3.0 of Window's AOL software will automatically load Winsock into memory, so you don't need to install the program separately.

World Wide Web (or WWW)   A special Internet service that provides access to text and graphics through a special program, known as a browser. The service is HyperText-based, which provides for sophisticated search capabilities to locate documents on specific subjects. The current version of America Online's client software includes a WWW browser.

zip   See *PKZip*.

America Online Keywords

Keywords are shortcuts that enable you to move quickly from one area of America Online to another area or department. The keywords presented here are current as this book is published, but because services are frequently added and changed on America Online, keywords may change as well.

If you are using America Online for Windows, follow these steps to use keywords:

1. From anywhere on America Online, press Ctrl+K or select Keyword from the Go To menu.

2. When the Keyword window appears, type the keyword of the department or area you want to go to, and choose GO.

If you are using America Online for Macintosh, follow these steps to use keywords:

1. From anywhere on America Online, press ⌘-K or select Keyword from the Go To menu.

2. When the Keyword window appears, type the keyword of the department or area you want to go to, and choose GO.

Although I use upper- and lowercase in this listing, keywords are not case sensitive—so don't worry about whether you're using caps or lowercase.

 TIP If the keyword for the area you want isn't listed in this appendix, just improvise. Enter a keyword for the name or topic of the area you're looking for. More than likely, if that area exists, you can find it this way.

 TIP If improvising a keyword fails to bring a result, click the Search button in the Keyword window, rather than the Go button, to bring up a list of possible matches to the keyword you typed.

AOL General Keywords

Keyword	Area
BESTOFAOL	Best of America Online showcase (25 REASONS, UNIQUE)
AOL GIFT	AOL Gift Certificates (GIFT CERTIFICATE)
AOL LIVE	AOL Live (LIVE, LIVE!)
AOL NET	AOLNET Information
BUDDY	Buddy Lists
CLOCK	Time of day and length of time online (ONLINE CLOCK)
DISCOVER	Discover AOL area (DISCOVER AOL)
GUIDEPAGER	Page a Guide (GUIDEPAGE)
KEYWORDS	Keyword List Area (KEYWORD, KEYWORD LIST)
HIGH SPEED	High-Speed Access area
HOLIDAY	AOL Holiday Central (HOLIDAYS) [Seasonal area; may disappear without warning]
HOT	What's Hot This Month showcase (WHATSHOT)
MAILGATEWAY	Mail Gateway
MEMBER SURVEY	Member Survey
MEMBERS	Member Directory (DIRECTORY, MEMBER DIRECTORY)
MP	Multimedia Preferences (MULTIMEDIA PREFS)
NAME(S)	Add, change or delete screen names (SCREEN NAME(S), HANDLE, USER NAME)
NEW	New Features & Services showcase

Keyword	Area
ORIENTATION	Orientation Express: New Member Area (NEWBIE, NEW MEMBER, ORIENTATION EXPRESS)
PAPERMAIL	Fax/Paper Mail (USMAIL, FAX)
PARENTAL CONTROL	Parental Controls
PHOTOFOCUS	Graphics and Photo Focus area
PRESS AOL	Press Release Library (PRESS RELEASE)
POSTOFFICE	Post Office (MAIL, EMAIL, THE POST OFFICE)
PRODIGY	Prodigy Refugees Forum (PRODIGYREFUGEES)
SERVICES	Directory of Services (DIR OF SVCS, DIR OF SERVICES, DIRECTORY OF SERVICES, SERVICES DIRECTORY, DONT MISS, NOW PLAYING)
SHORTHAND(S)	Online Shorthands
TOP TIPS	Top Tips for AOL
TOUR AOL	Highlights Tour (HIGHLIGHTS)
VIEWER	Viewer Resource Center (PLAYER(S), VIEWERS)

Today's News

Keyword	Area
NEWS	Today's News department (TODAYS NEWS, TOP NEWS, NEWSROOM, HEADLINES, OUR WORLD, NEWSLINK, NEWS TEXT, NEWS & FINANCE, NEWS AND FINANCE, NEWS/SPORTS/MONEY)
1995	1995: The Year in Review
BOSNIA	Balkan Operation Joint Endeavor (BALKAN, UNPROFOR, YUGOSLAVIA)
BURNS	George Burns (GEORGE, GEORGE BURNS)
BUSINESS	Business News area (BUSINESS NEWS)
CQ	Congressional Quarterly (CONGRESSIONAL)
DTSPORTS	DataTimes Sports Reports (DATATIMES, DATATIMES SPORTS)
ENTERTAINMENT NEWS	Entertainment News

Part
X
App
E

continues

Today's News   Continued

Keyword	Area
GENE	Gene Kelly (GENE KELLY, KELLY)
HILLARY	Hillary Rodham Clinton (FIRST LADY)
IOTW	Editor's Choice News (EDITOR'S CHOICE, EDITORS CHOICE)
MARKET NEWS	Market News area (MARKETS)
NEWS BYTES	Newsbytes
NEWSPAPER(S)	Local Newspapers (LOCALNEWS, LOCALNEWSPAPERS)
NEWS PLUS	NewsPlus area
NEWS SEARCH	Search News Articles (SEARCHNEWS, NEWSWATCH)
OLYMPIC NEWS	AOL Olympic News Coverage
PRESIDENT 96	President '96
SKI	Ski Reports (SKIREPORTS, SKICONDITIONS, SKIWEATHER) [seasonal]
SPORTSNEWS	Sport News area
TIME DAILY	TIME Daily News Summary
TROPICAL STORM	Tropical Storm and Hurricane Info (HURRICANE)
TSN	The Sporting News
USNEWS	U.S. & World News (WORLDNEWS)
WEATHER	Weather
WEATHERMAPS	Color Weather Maps (COLORWEATHERMAPS)

Personal Finance

Keyword	Area
FINANCE	Personal Finance department (PF, PERSONAL FINANCE)
20TH	Twentieth-Century (CENTURY, TWENTIETH CENTURY, TWENTIETH-CENTURY)
AAII	AAII Online
ABI	Business Yellow Pages (ABI YELLOW PAGES, YELLOW PAGES)
ADVISOR(S)	Top Advisors' Corner (TOP ADVISOR(S), TAC)

Keyword	Area
BA	Bank of America (BANK AMERICA, BANK OF AMERICA, BOFA, HOME BANKING)
BEATY	Company Research Message Boards (BOB BEATY)
BIZINSIDER	Herb Greenberg's Business Insider
BULLS AND BEARS	Bulls and Bears Game
BUSINESS INSIDER	The Business Insider (HERH GREENBERG)
BUSINESS RANKINGS	Business Rankings (RANKINGS)
CAPITAL	Capital Connection (CAPITAL CONNECTION, CONGRESS, DEBATE, GOVERNMENT, ISSUES, POLITICS, PUBLIC POLICY, WASHINGTON)
CAPMAR	Capital Markets Center (CAPITAL MARKETS, CAPITAL MARKETS CENTER)
CAREERNEWS	USA Today Industry Watch section
CBD	Commerce Business Daily
CCB	Chicago Business Crain's (CRAIN'S, CRAIN'S SMALL BIZ, CRAINS, CSB)
CITIBANK	The Apple Citibank Visa Card
COL NEWS	Chicago Online News, Business & Weather
COMPANY	Hoovers' Handbook of Company Profiles (COMPANY PROFILES, COMPANY RESEARCH, COMPANY UPDATES, CORPORATE PROFILES, HOOVERS UPDATES, UPDATES)
CONSUMER(S)	Consumer Reports (CONSUMERREPORTS)
DISCLOSURE	Disclosure Incorporated
FINANCIALS	Disclosure's Financial Statements (BALANCE SHEET, FINANCIAL STATEMENT, INCOME STATEMENT)
DP	Decision Point Forum (DPA, DECISION, DECISION POINT, STOCKTIMING, STOCK CHARTS)
EDGAR	Disclosure's EdgarPlus
EZONE	The Entrepreneur Zone (BUSINESS CENTER, BUSINESS KNOW HOW, BUSINESS STRATEGIES, ENTREPRENEUR ZONE, EZ, MS BIZ, MSBC, SBC, SMALL BUSINESS, STRATEGIES, ZONE)

Part
X
App
E

continues

Personal Finance Continued	
Keyword	**Area**
FID	Fidelity Online Investments (FIDELITY)
FID AT WORK	Fidelity Online's Working Area
FID FUNDS	Fidelity Online's Funds Area (FID BROKER)
FID GUIDE	Fidelity Online's Guide Area
FID NEWS	Fidelity Online's Newsworthy Area
FID PLAN	Fidelity Online's Planning Area
FIRST CHICAGO ONLINE	First Chicago Online
FOOL	The Motley Fool (COMMONS, COOKIE, COSTARD, FESTE, FOOLISH, LAUNCE, LAVATCH, MFOOL, MOTLEY, MOTLEY FOOL, THE MOTLEY FOOL, TODAY PITCH, TODAYS PITCH, TRINCULO)
FOOL AIR	Motley Fool: Airlines
FOOL CHEM	Motley Fool: Chemicals
FOOL CHIPS	Motley Fool: Semiconductors (FOOL SEM, SEM)
FOOL DTV	Motley Fool: Desktop Video (FOOL VID, DTV)
FOOL HARD	Motley Fool: Hardware
FOOL DOME	Fool Dome (FOOLBALL)
GOLD RUSH	Gold Rush Contest (GOLD RUSH CONTEST)
HOMEOWNER(S)	Homeowner's Forum (HOMEOWNERS FORUM, UHA)
HOOVER(S)	Hoover's Business Resources (BUSINESS RESOURCES, HOOVER'S)
IBD	Investor's Business Daily (INVESTOR'S BUSINESS, INVESTORS BUSINESS, INVESTOR'S DAILY, INVESTORS DAILY)
IE	Investor's Exchange
INVESTOR	Investors Network (INVEST, INVESTING, INVESTOR(S), INVESTMENT(S))
INBIZ	InBusiness (INBUSINESS, INVESTORS NETWORK, INVESTOR'S NETWORK)
INC.	Inc. Magazine (INC, INC MAGAZINE, INC. MAGAZINE, INC ONLINE, INC. ONLINE)

Keyword	Area
INDUSTRY PROFILES	Hoover's Industry Profiles
INTERNET BIZ	InBusiness (IBIZ, INBIZ, IN BUSINESS)
ICF	International Corporate Forum (TICF)
KAUFMANN	The Kaufmann Fund
LIBERTARIAN(S)	Libertarian Party Forum (LIBERTARIANPARTY)
LINGO	Investment Lingo (INVESTMENT LINGO)
MC BUSINESS	Mercury Center Business & Technology area
MER	Merrill Lynch (BULL, LYNCH, MERRILL, MERRILL LYNCH, ML, MLPF&S)
MFC	Mutual Fund Center
MICHIGAN	Michigan Governor's Forum (MICHIGANGOVERNOR)
MIXSTAR	Mixstar Mortgage Information Exchange
MIX CITICORP	Citicorp Mortgage
MIX CMBA	California Mortgage Bankers Association
MIX DATA TRACK	Data Track Systems Inc.
MIX GENESIS	Genesis 2000
MORNINGSTAR	Morningstar Mutual Funds (MUTUALFUND(S), FUND(S))
NBR	The Nightly Business Report (NBR REPORT)
PCFN	PC Financial Network coming soon note (PC FINANCIAL, PC FINANCIAL NETWORK)
PFSOFTWARE	Personal Finance Software Center
PFSS	Personal Finance Software Support (ISS, SOFTWARE SUPPORT)
PLUS	Plus ATM Network
PORTFOLIO	Your Stock Portfolio (STOCKPORTFOLIO)
QUOTES PLUS	Quotes Plus
REAL ESTATE	Real Estate Online (ARM, HOME EQUITY LOAN, HOME REFINANCING, MLS, MORTAGE(S), MORTAGE RATES, NAREE)
REAL LIFE	Real Life Financial Tips (FAMILY FINANCES, INSURANCE, JOB, RETIREMENT, RL)
RSP	RSP Funding Focus

Part

X

App

E

continues

Personal Finance   Continued

Keyword	Area
SOS	Wall Street SOS Forum
STOCK(S)	StockLink: Quotes & Portfolios area (QUOTE(S), STOCKQUOTES, STOCKLINK)
TAX	Tax Forum (TAXES, TAX FORUM)
TAX CHANNEL	NAEA Tax Channel (NAEA)
TAX GUIDE	Ernst & Young Tax Guide
TAXCUT	Kiplinger TaxCut Software Support (KIP, KIPLINGER)
TELESCAN	Telescan Users Group Forum
TRADEPLUS	TradePlus (ETRADE)
TREASURY BILLS	U.S. Treasury Securities (NATIONAL DEBT, PUBLIC DEBT, SAVINGS BONDS, TREASURY BONDS, TREASURY DIRECT, TREASURY NOTES, TREASURY SECURITIES, US SAVINGS BONDS, U.S. SAVINGS BOND, US TREASURY SECURITIES)
UTAH	Utah Forum (UTAHFORUM)
VIRGINIA	Virginia Forum (VIRGINIAFORUM)
WHCSB	White House Conference on Small Business
WHITE HOUSE	White House Forum (CLINTON, THE WHITE HOUSE)
WHITE PAGES	ProCD National Telephone Directory Search (PROCD)
WORTH	Worth Magazine (WORTH MAGAZINE, WORTH ONLINE, WORTHPORTFOLIO)
WSW	Wall Street Words (WALL STREET WORDS)
YOURMONEY	Your Money area

Clubs & Interests

Keyword	Area
CLUBS	Clubs & Interests department (LIFESTYLES, HOBBIES, INTEREST, LIFESTYLES & HOBBIES, LIFESTYLES & INTERESTS, LIFESTYLES & INTEREST, COMMUNITY CENTER, SPECIAL INTERESTS)
CLUBS & INTERNET	Clubs & Interest's Top Internet Sites [WAOL 2.5 only];) Hecklers Online (;-) , HECKLE, HECKLER, HECKLERS, HECKLERS ONLINE, HO, WISE GUYS)

Keyword	Area
1010	A Day in the Life of Cyberspace
AARP	American Association of Retired People
ACCESSPOINT	AccessPoint (ACCESS.POINT, VOLUNTEER)
ACLU	American Civil Liberties Union (CIVIL LIBERTIES)
AFROCENTRIC	Afrocentric Culture (AFRICA, AFRICAN-AMERICAN, BLACK-AMERICAN, BLACK AMERICAN, BLACKS)
AHS	American Hiking Society
AIDS	The Positive Living Forum (HIV, PLF, POSITIVE LIVING)
AIDS DAILY	AIDS Daily Summary
ALA	America Lung Association (AMERICAN LUNG, AMERICAN LUNG ASSOC)
AOL FAMILIES	AOL Families area
ARIZONA	Arizona Central (ARIZONA CENTRAL, AZ CENTRAL, PHOENIX)
AZ ALT	Arizona Central: ALT. (AZ ALT.)
AZ AT EASE	Arizona Central: At Ease (AZ ENTERTAINMENT)
AZ BIZ	Arizona Central: Small Business (AZ SMALL BUSINESS)
AZ CAROUSING	Arizona Central: Carousing (AZ CONCERTS)
AZ COMMUNITY	Arizona Central: Your Community
AZ COMPUTERS	Arizona Central: Computers
AZ DESTINATIONS	Arizona Central: Destinations (AZ TRAVEL, AZ TRIPS)
AZ ENTERTAINMENT	Arizona Central: At Ease (AZ AT EASE)
AZ FUN	Arizona Central: Plan On It (AZ CALENDARS)
AZ GOLF	Arizona Central: Golf
AZ HIGH SCHOOLS	Arizona Central: Preps (AZ PREPS)
AZ HOUSE	Arizona Central: House/Home (AX GARDENING, AZ HOME)
AZ LIFE	Arizona Central: Your Life
AZ MONEY	Arizona Central: Your Money (AZ BUSINESS)
AZ NEWSLINE	Arizona Central: Newsline
AZ SCORES	Arizona Central: Scoreboard (AZ SCOREBOARD)

Part

X

App

E

continues

Clubs & Interests Continued

Keyword	Area
AZ SPORTS	Arizona Central: Sports (AZ ASU, AZ CARDS, AZ DIAMOND BACKS, AZ SUNS, AZ U OF A)
AZ STARDUST	Arizona Central: Stardust (AZ THEATER, AZ THEATRE)
AZ TV	Arizona Central: Couching (AZ COUCHING)
AZ VOLUNTEERS	Arizona Central: Volunteers
ARTISTS	Artists on America Online (ARTIST)
ASK TODD ART	The Image Exchange: Ask Todd Art (ASK TODD, TODD ART)
ASTRONET	ASTRONET (AMERICAN ASTROLOGY, ASTROLOGY, ASTROMATES, CAROLE 2000, CHINESE ASTROLOGY, COSMIC MUFFIN, FINANCIAL ASTROLOGY, GENIE EASY, INTERACTIVE ASTROLOGY, KRAMER, WELCOME TO PLANET EARTH, ZODIAC)
ASTRONOMY	Astronomy Club
AVIATION	Aviation Club (FLY, AIRPLANE, AIRSHOWS, AVFORUM, GENERAL AVIATION, JET, SKYDIVING, ULTRALIGHTS)
AVON	Avon's Breast Cancer Awareness Crusade (CRUSADE)
BABY BOOMERS	Baby Boomers area (BABY BOOMER)
BACKPACKER	Backpacker Magazine (OUTDOOR GEAR, VACATIONS, TRAIL GUIDES, CONSERVATION, ECOTOURISM, HIKER, HIKING, TRAILS, WILDERNESS, CAMPING, BACKCOUNTRY)
BELIEFS	Religion & Beliefs (BELIEF, RELIGION, RELIGION & BELIEFS)
BERNIE	Bernie Siegel Online
BETTER HEALTH	Better Health & Medical Forum (HRS)
BICYCLING	Bicycling Magazine (BICYCLING MAGAZINE, BIC MAG, MOUNTAIN BIKE)
BIKENET	The Bicycle Network (BICYCLE, BFA)
BIRDING	Birding Selections
BLACK VOICES	Orlando Sentinel Online: Black Voices
BOOK NOOK	The Book Nook (BOOK)
BOOKS	Book areas (BOOK BESTSELLERS)
BOSTON	Digital City Boston (BOSTON ONLINE)
CA	Crossword America (XWORDS)

Keyword	Area
CAMPAIGN 96	Decision '96 (DECISION '96)
CANCER	American Cancer Society (ACS)
CAPITAL	Capital Connection (CAPITAL CONNECTION, CONGRESS, DEBATE, GOVERNMENT, ISSUES, POLITICS, PUBLIC POLICY, WASHINGTON)
CATHOLIC	Catholic Community
CE	Consumer Electronics (ALARM, AUTOSOUND, BEEPER, CELLULAR, CELLULAR PHONE, CONSUMER ELECTRONICS, GADGET, HOME AUDIO, PAGER, SECURITY)
CHALLENGER	Challenger Remembered (ASTRONAUTS, KENNEDY SPACE, KENNEDY SPACE CENTER, SHUTTLE, SPACE SHUTTLE)
CHILDREN'S HEALTH	Children's Health Forum
CHRIST	Christianity Online (<><, CHRISTIANITY, XOL)
AGOL	Assemblies of God Online
BC	Christian Books & Culture (BOOKS & CULTURE)
BETHEL	Bethel College and Seminary
BTS	Bethel Theological Seminary
CCDA	Christian Community Development Association
CCG	Christian College Guide (CHRISTIAN COLLEGES)
CCI	Christian Camping International (CHRISTIAN CAMPING)
CEC	Christian Education Center (CHRISTIAN EDUCATION)
CHURCH LEADERS	Christianity Online: Church Leaders Network (CHURCH LEADERS NETWORK, CLN, LEADERS NETWORK)
CLS	Christianity Online Classifieds (CHROL CLASSIFIEDS, CO CLASSIFIEDS)
CM	Christian Ministries Center
CPC	Christian Products Center (CHRISTIAN PRODUCTS)
CR	Christian Resource Center
CN	Christianity Online Newsstand (CNEWS, CO NEWS)
CO ASSOCIATIONS	Christianity Online: Associations & Interests (ASSN, CO INTERESTS)
CO CONTEST	Christianity Online: Contest (CON, XCON)

Part
X

App
E

continues

Clubs & Interests Continued	
Keyword	**Area**
CO FAMILY	Christianity Online: Family (CHRISTIAN FAMILY, CHRISTIAN FAMILIES, CO FAMILIES)
CO INTERESTS	Christianity Online: Associations & Interests (ASSN, CO ASSOCIATIONS)
CO KIDS	Christianity Online: Kids (CHRISTIAN KID, CHRISTIAN KIDS)
CO LIVE	Christianity Online Chats & Live Events (CHRISTIAN CONNECTION, CHROL CHAT, FELLOWSHIP HALL)
CO MEN	Christianity Online: Men (CHRISTIAN MAN, CHRISTIAN MEN, CO MAN)
CO SINGLES	Christianity Online: Singles (CHRISTIAN SINGLE, CHRISTIAN SINGLES, CO SINGLE, CO SINGLES)
CO TEENS	Christianity Online: Teens (CHRISTIAN STUDENT, CHRISTIAN STUDENTS, CO STUDENT, CO STUDENTS, CO TEEN, CO YOUTH)
CO WOMEN	Christianity Online: Women (CHRISTIAN WOMAN, CHRISTIAN WOMEN, CO WOMAN, COW)
GAM	Global Access Music (GLOBAL ACCESS, GLOBAL ACCESS MUSIC)
HUM	Virtual Christian Humor (;-D, VH, VIRTUAL HUMOR)
MES	Messiah College (MESSIAH)
MIN	Minirth Meier New Life Clinics (MINIRTH MEIER, MMNLC, NEW LIFE)
PRAYER NET	The Prayer Network (TPN)
RELIGION NEWS	Religion News Update (RNU)
TAY	Taylor University (TAYLOR UNIVERSITY)
WCN	World Crisis Network (WORLD CRISIS)
WRD	Christianity Online: Word Publishing
ZON	Zondervan Publishing House (ZP, ZONDERVAN)
CITY WEB	City Web (DC WEB, WASHINGTON WEB)
CIVIL WAR	The Civil War Forum
COL	Chicago Online (CHICAGO, CHICAGO ONLINE)
COLUMBIANET	Columbia/HCA Live Physician's Chat (COLUMBIA/HCA, COLUMBIA.NET, HEALTH TODAY, ONE SOURCE, SENIOR FRIENDS)

Keyword	Area
COMIC STRIP	Comic Strip Centennial (POSTAL STAMPS)
COMICS	Wizard World
COOKBOOK	Celebrity Cookbook (CELEBRITY COOKBOOK)
COOKING	Cooking Club (COOKING CLUB, KITCHEN)
CORKSCREWED	Corkscrewed Online
CYBER 24	24 Hours in Cyberspace
CYBERVIEWS	This Week's Best Cyberviews (CYBERVIEW)
DEAD	Grateful Dead Forum (:), GRATEFUL DEAD)
DEAF	Deaf Community
DIABETES	American Diabetes Association (AMERICAN DIABETES)
DIALOGUE	American Dialogue (AMERICAN DIALOGUE, BKG)
DIS	Disabilities Forum (DISABILITY, DISABILITIES, BLIND, PHYSICALLY DISABLED)
DISCOVERY	The Discovery Channel (DSC)
DISCOVERY ED	The Discovery Channel Education Area (DSC-ED, DSC ED)
DISNEY.COM	Disney.com Sneak Preview (DISNEY.COM.LOW)
DL CITY	Digital City London
EARTHLINK	TBS Network Earth/IBM Project (TBIBM)
EFORUM	Environmental Forum (ENVIRONMENT, EARTH)
EGG	Electronic Gourmet Guide (EGG BASKET)
EMERGENCY	Emergency Response Club (ERC, EMERGENCY RESPONSE)
EXCHANGE	The Exchange (BOATS, COINS, COLLECTING, COLLECTOR, GARDENING, MOTORCYCLE, OUTDOORS, RAILROADING, STAMPS, THE EXCHANGE)
COMMUNITIES	The Exchange: Communities Center (AFRICANAMERICAN, AMERICANINDIAN, ASIAN, HISPANIC, MEN, NATIVEAMERICAN)
ANTIQUES	The Exchange: Collector's Corner
GUNS	The Exchange: Interests & Hobbies
FAMILY	Family Areas
FLYING	Flying Magazine (FLYING MAGAZINE, FLYINGMAG, AIR CRAFT, AIRPORTS, PILOTS)

continues

Part

X

App

E

Clubs & Interests Continued	
Keyword	**Area**
FOLKWAYS	Folklife & Folkways
FOOD	Everything Edible! (AOL DINER, BEVERAGES, CHEF, CHEFS, GOURMET)
FOOD & DRINK	Food & Drink Network (BEER, BREW, BREWING, CHEF, CIGAR, CIGARS, COOK, COOKS, DINE, DINING, FDN, HOME BREW, HOME BREWING, PIPE, PIPES, RESTAURANT, RESTAURANTS, SPIRITS, WEDDING, WINE, WINERIES, WINERY)
FOTF	Focus on the Family (DOBSON)
GADGET GURU	Gadget Guru Electronics Forum (ANDY PARGH, ELECTRON-ICS, GADGET, GURU, PARGH, PANASONIC, PRIMESTAR, RCA, RUBBERMAID, TIMEX, TURNER VISION, WAHL)
GARDEN	Good Morning America Gardening Guide
GENEALOGY	Genealogy Club (AFRICAN, AUSTRIAN, BRITISH, DANISH, DUTCH, EASTERN EUROPEAN, GENEALOGY CLUB, GREEK, IMMIGRATION, IRISH, ITALIAN, NEW ENGLAND, NEWSLET-TERS, NORWEGIAN, PORTUGESE, ROOTS, SCANDINAVIAN, SCOT, SCOTCH, SURNAMES, SWEDISH, SWISS, WELSH, WESTERN EUROPEAN)
GENERATIONS	Generations
GLCF	Gay & Lesbian Community Forum (BI, BISEXUAL, GAY, LAMDA, LESBIAN, PINK TRIANGLE, PRIDE, PROUD, QUEER, TRIANGLE)
GAYMES	Gay & Lesbian Community Forum Games (GAYME, GAYMELAND)
GLCF BOARDS	Gay & Lesbian Community Forum Boards (GAY BOARDS, GAY MESSAGE, LESBIAN BOARDS, LESBIAN MESSAGE)
GLCF CHAT	Gay & Lesbian Community Forum Chat (GAY CHAT, GLCF EVENT, GLCF EVENTS, LESBIAN CHAT)
GLCF H2H	Gay & Lesbian Community Forum Heart to Heart (GLCF HEART, GLCF HEART TO HEART, H2H, HEART TO HEART)
GLCF LIBRARY	Gay & Lesbian Community Forum Libraries (GAY SOFTWARE, GLCF SOFTWARE, LESBIAN LIBRARY, LESBIAN SOFTWARE)
GLCF NEWS	Gay & Lesbian Community Forum News (GAY NEWS, GLCF POLITICS, LESBIAN NEWS, LESBIAN POLITICS)

Keyword	Area
GLCF ORGS	Gay & Lesbian Community Forum Organizations (GAY ORG, GAY ORGS, GLCF ORG, GLCF ORGANIZATIONS, LESBIAN ORG, LESBIAN ORGS)
GLCF TRAVEL	Gay & Lesbian Community Forum Travel (GAY TRAVEL, LESBIAN TRAVEL)
GLCF WOMEN GLCF:	Women's Space (GLCF WOMAN, WOMENS SPACE, WS)
GRANDSTAND	The Grandstand (THE GRANDSTAND)
GS ARTS	The Grandstand's Martial Arts (The Dojo)
GS AUTO	The Grandstand's Motor Sports (In The Pits)
ICRS	The Grandstand's Simulation Auto Racing (SIMULATION AUTO)
GS BASEBALL	The Grandstand's Baseball (Dugout)
GBL	The Grandstand's Simulation Baseball (SIMULATION BASEBALL)
FANTASYBASEBALL	The Grandstand's Fantasy Baseball
GSBASKETBALL	The Grandstand's Basketball (Off the Glass)
FANTASY BASKETBALL	The Grandstand's Fantasy Basketball
SIMULATION BASKETBALL	The Grandstand's Simulation Basketball
GSDL	The Grandstand's Simulation Basketball
GS BOXING	The Grandstand's Boxing (Squared Circle)
GS COLLECTING	The Grandstand's Collecting (Sports Cards)
GS FOOTBALL	The Grandstand's Football (50 Yard Line)
FANTASY FOOTBALL	The Grandstand's Fantasy Football
SIMULATION FOOTBALL	The Grandstand's Simulation Football
GSFL	The Grandstand's Simulation Football
GS GOLF	The Grandstand's Golf (On The Green)
GGL	The Grandstand's Simulation Golf (SIMULATION GOLF)
GS HOCKEY	The Grandstand's Hockey (Blue Line)
FANTASY HOCKEY	The Grandstand's Fantasy Hockey

Part
X
App
E

continues

Clubs & Interests   Continued

Keyword	Area
GSHL	The Grandstand's Simulation Hockey (SIMULATION HOCKEY)
GS HORSE	The Grandstand's Horse Sports (Post Time)
GS OTHER	The Grandstand's Other Sports (Whole 9 Yards)
GS SIDELINE	The Grandstand's Sideline
GS SOCCER	The Grandstand's Soccer (The Kop)
GS SOFTWARE	The Grandstand's Sports Software Headquarters
GS SPORTSMART	The Grandstand's Sports Products (Sportsmart)
GS WINTER	The Grandstand's Winter Sports (The Chalet)
GS WRESTLING	The Grandstand's Wrestling (Squared Circle)
GWA	The Grandstand's Simulation Wrestling (SIMULATION WRESTLING)
FANTASY LEAGUE(S)	The Grandstand's Fantasy & Simulation Leagues (SIMULATION LEAGUES)
SPORTS BOARDS	The Grandstand's Sports Boards
SPORTS CHAT	The Grandstand's Chat Rooms (SPORTS ROOMS)
SPORTS LIBRARIES	The Grandstand's Libraries
HAM	Ham Radio Club (HAM RADIO, RADIO, AMATEUR RADIO, SATELLITES)
HATRACK	Hatrack River Town Meeting (ORSON SCOTT CARD, ALVIN, ENDER, HATRACK RIVER TOWN)
HEALTH CARE	League of Women Voters Health Care Summit
HEALTH EXP	Health and Vitamin Express (HEALTH EXPRESS, RX, VITAMIN EXP, VITAMIN EXPRESS)
HEALTH FOCUS	Health Focus
HEALTH LIVE	Health Speakers and Support Groups
HEALTH MAGAZINES	Health Magazines Area
HEALTH NEWS	Health News Area
HEALTH REFERENCE	Health Reference Area
HEALTH RESOURCES	Health Resources
HEALTH WEB	Health Web Sites

Keyword	Area
HEALTH ZONE	The Health Zone (CHOCOLATE, CYBERSLIM, IHRSA, HZ, QUALITY, Z, ZONED, ZONIE)
HERITAGE	Heritage Foundation (HERITAGE FOUNDATION, POLICY REVIEW)
HOBBY	Hobby Central (HOBBY CENTRAL)
HOME	Home Magazine Online (DECORATING, FURNISHINGS, FURNITURE, HOMEDESIGN, HOUSE, INTERIOR DESIGN, LANDSCAPING, REMODELING)
HOMEOWNER(S)	Homeowner's Forum (HOMEOWNERSFORUM, UHA)
HOUSENET	HouseNet (BUILDING, CARPENTRY)
IMAGE	Image Exchange (IMAGE EXCHANGE)
IMH	Issues in Mental Health (MH)
JEWISH	Jewish Community (JCOL, JEWISH COMMUNITY)
JOKES	Jokes! Etc.
KODAK WEB	Kodak Web Site [WAOL 2.5 only]
LAMBDA RISING	Lambda Rising Online (GAY BOOKS, LAMBDA)
LEGAL	Legal Information Network (LEGAL SIG, LIN)
LEGAL PAD	The Legal Pad
LONGEVITY	Longevity Magazine Online (ALTERNATIVE MEDICINE, ANTI-AGING, ANTI AGING, HERB, MEDICINE, PLASTIC SURGERY, SPAS)
MARS	Men Are From Mars (MEN ARE FROM MARS, JOHN GRAY)
MASS	Massachusetts Governor's Forum (MASS., MASSACHUSETTS)
MC	Military City Online (DEFENSE, MCO, MILITARY CITY, MILITARY CITY ONLINE)
MCO BASES	Military City Online Bases
MCO COMM	Military City Online Comm
MCO HQ	Military City Online Headquarters
MCO SHOP	Military City Online Shop
MCO TOUR	Military City Online Tour
MEDLINE	Medline
MEN'S HEALTH	Men's Health Forum
MENTAL HEALTH	Mental Health Forum

Part

X

App

E

continues

Clubs & Interests   Continued

Keyword	Area
MICHIGAN	Michigan Governor's Forum (MICHIGAN GOVERNOR)
MMC	Music Message Center
MOM	Moms Online (MOMS, MOMS ONLINE, MOTHER)
MULTIPLE SCLEROSIS	Multiple Sclerosis Forum
MUSIC	Music menu
NAMI	National Alliance of Mentally Ill
NATURE	The Nature Conservancy (TNC, THE NATURE CONSERVANCY)
NECN	New England Cable News (CABLE NEWS, NEW ENGLAND CABLE, NEW ENGLAND CABLE NEWS, NEW ENGLAND NEWS)
NEIGHBORHOODS	Neighborhoods, USA (NEIGHBORHOODS, USA)
NETGIRL	NetGirl
NETNOIR	NetNoir (NOIR-NET, NET_NOIR, NET_NOIRE, NOIRE_NET, NETNOIR, NETNOIRE, NOIRENET, NOIRENET)
NETWORKEARTH	Network Earth (EARTH)
NEW PRODUCTS	New Product Information (NEW PRODUCT)
NGLTF	Nation Gay & Lesbian Task Force
NONPROFIT	Access.Point: Nonprofit Professionals Network (NPN, NON PROFIT NETWORK)
NMSS	National Multiple Sclerosis Society
NSS	National Space Society (SPACE)
NUL	National Urban League (URBAN LEAGUE)
OGF	Online Gaming Forums
OHIO	Online Ohio
OMNI OMNI	Magazine Online (OMNI MAGAZINE)
PAGAN	Pagan & Magickal Groups (MAGICK, MAGICKAL, WICCA)
PARENT SOUP	Parent Soup
PARENT SOUP LOCAL INFO	Parent Soup: Local Information
PARENTS	AOL Families area (AOL FAMILIES, PARENT, PARENTING, PIN)

Keyword	Area
PEN	Personal Empowerment Network (EMPOWERMENT)
PET(S)	Pet Care Club (ANIMAL, ANIMALS, PET CARE)
PHOTO	Kodak Photography Forum (PHOTOGRAPHY, KODAK, CAMERA)
PNO	PlanetOut (PLANETOUT)
PR	Princeton Review/Student Access Online (PRINCETON RE-VIEW, STUDENT, STUDENT ACCESS)
PSC	Public Safety Center (PUBLIC SAFETY, SAFETY)
PSYCH ONLINE	Psych Online (ONLINE PSYCH)
QUILTING	Quilting Forum (QUILT, QUILTERS)
RBO	Ringling Online (RBO, RINGING, RINGLING BROS, RINGLING ONLINE)
REALESTATE	Real Estate Online (ARM, HOME EQUITY LOAN, HOME REFINANCING, MLS, MORTAGE(S), MORTAGE RATES, NAREE)
RELIGIONS	Religion & Ethics Forum (BUDDHISM, CHRISTIAN(S), ETHICS, ISLAM, JUDAISM, NEW AGE)
R&T	Road & Track (AUTOS, AUTOMOTIVE, ROAD, ROAD & TRACK, TRACK)
ROCK	Rocklink (ROCKLINK, MUSIC)
ROSH HASHANA	Jewish New Year area
SCUBA	Scuba Club (GOSCUBA)
SELF HELP	Self Help area
SENIOR	SeniorNet (SENIOR)
SERVENET	SERVEnet (SERVENET, YOUTH SERVICE AMERICA, YSA)
SF	Science Fiction & Fantasy Forum (ANALOG, ASIMOV, HOR-ROR, MYSTERY, SCIFI, SCI-FI, SCIENCE FICTION)
SHUTTLE	Challenger Remembered (ASTRONAUTS, CHALLENGER, KENNEDY SPACE, KENNEDY SPACE CENTER, SPACE SHUTTLE)
SIMI WINERY	Simi Winery
SPINNING	Needlecrafts/Sewing Center (KNITTING, SEW, WEAVING)
SPORTS	Sport News area (SPORTS NEWS, SPORTS LINK)

continues

Part
X

App
E

Clubs & Interests	Continued
Keyword	**Area**
SRO	Saturday Review Online (SAT REVIEW, SATURDAY REVIEW, LITERATURE, READING, SOCIETY, THEATER, THEATRE)
SPIRITUAL	Spiritual Mosaic
STD	Sexually Transmitted Diseases Forum
STYLE CHANNEL	Style Channel
TCF	Transgender Community Forum (CROSSDRESSER, CROSSDRESSING, F2M, GENDER, GLCF TCF, M2F, SRS, TG, TRANSGENDER, TRANSSEXUAL, TRANSVESTITE)
THE WALL	The Vietnam Veterans Memorial Wall (VIETNAM, WALL)
TICKET	Ticketmaster (TICKETMASTER)
TIMES	@times/The New York Times Online (@TIMES, AT TIMES, NYT, NY TIMES, NEWYORKTIMES, NYC, NEWYORK, NEW YORK CITY, TIMES NEWS)
TIMES ART	@times: Art & Photography
TIMES ARTS	@times: The Arts
TIMES BOOKS	@times: Books of The Times
TIMES DINING	@times: Dining Out & Nightlife
TIMES LEISURE	@times: Leisure Guide
TIMES MOVIES	@times: Movies & Video (VIDEO)
TIMES MUSIC	@times: Music & Dance
TIMES REGION	@times: In The Region
TIMES SPORTS	@times: Sports & Fitness
TIMES STORIES	@times: Top Stories
TIMES THEATER	@times: Theater
TREK	Star Trek Club (STARTREK)
TRIVIA	Trivia Forum
UCPA	United Cerebral Palsy Association, Inc. (CEREBRAL PALSY)
UTAH	Utah Forum (UTAHFORUM)
VETS	Military and Vets Club (MILITARY, VETERANS, VETS CLUB)
VIRGINIA	Virginia Forum (VIRGINIA FORUM)

Keyword	Area
VAA	Virtual Airlines (LYNX, LYNX AIRWAYS, SKYLINE, SKYLINE AIRWAYS, SUNAIR, SUNAIR EXPRESS, VIRTUAL AIRLINES, VAS)
WHCSB	White House Conference on Small Business
WHEELS EXCHANGE	Wheels Exchange
WHITE HOUSE	White House Forum (CLINTON, THE WHITE HOUSE)
WOMANS DAY	Woman's Day (WOMAN, WOMAN'S DAY, RECIPES, SEWING, CRAFTS, TIES)
WOMEN'S HEALTH	Women's Health Forum
WOMENS	Women's Interests
WORLD BELIEFS	World Beliefs
WRITERS	Writer's Club (WRITER'S)
WC CHAT	Writer's Club Chat Rooms (WRITERS CLUB CHAT, WRITE)
YMB	Your Mind & Body Online (MIND & BODY, MIND AND BODY, YOUR MIND & BODY, YOUR MIND AND BODY)
YOUNG CHEFS	Young Chefs
YOUTHNET	National Network for Youth (NNFY, NNY)

Part
X
App
E

Computing

Keyword	Area
C&S	Computing department (COMPUTER, COMPUTERFORUM, COMPUTING, COMPUTINGANDSOFTWARE, COMPUTINGFORUMS, FORUM(S), PCFORUMS, PCSECURITY, SIGS, SIFS, TECHNOLOGY)
CONFERENCE	Weekly calendar of forum activity (CONFERENCECENTER)
CRC	Computing Resource Center (MACRESOURCE(S), MRC, RESOURCE(S), UNIX, VAX, VMS)
FILESEARCH	Search database of files (QUICKFIND, QUICKFINDER)
HALLOFFAME	Downloading Hall of Fame (HOF)
MAC	Mac Computing & Software department (APPLE, MACCOMPUTING, MACINTOSH)
MACSOFTWARE	Mac Software Center (MACDOWNLOADING, MACLIBRARIES, MACSOFTWARECENTER)

continues

Computing   Continued

Keyword	Area
PCSOFTWARE	PC Software Center (PCSW, PCLIBRARIES, PCSOFTWARE)
SOFTWARE	Software Center (DOWNLOAD, DOWNLOADING, FILE, FILES, LIBRARIES, LIBS, SEARCH, SOFT, SOFTWARE, SOFTWARE CENTER, SOFTWARE DIRECTORY, SOFTWARE LIBRARY, SOFTWARE LIBRARIES, SOFTWARE HELP)
TITF	Daily calendar of forum activity
VIEWER	Viewer Resource Center (PLAYER(S), VIEWERS)

Mutual Interest Forums

Keyword	Area
BUNTING	Bunting's Window to the World of Computers (BUNTINGS WINDOW, BUNTING'S WINDOW)
CHIPNET	ChipNet Online (CHIP)
COBB	The Cobb Group Online (COBBGROUP)
COMP SITES	Computing Internet Sites [WAOL 2.5 and MAOL 2.6 only] (COMPUTING SITES)
COMPUTER BOWL	Computer Bowl
COMPUTING NEWS	Computing News [MAOL and GAOL only]
CPB	Computing Print & Broadcast (CP&B)
HELPDESK	Help Desk [platform dependent] (ABF, AOLBEGINNERS, GETTINGSTARTED, GETTINGSTARTEDFORUM, GTSF, BEGINNER(S), NEWLINK, NLF, PCBEGINNERS, PCBG, PCHELP, STARTER)
BBS	BBS Corner (BBSCORNER)
CALENDAR	Forum Calendar (SCHEDULE)
DESIGN SIG	Design SIG (DESIGNER, GRAPHIC DESIGN)
DOL	Designs Online (DESIGNSONLINE, SPEEDY)
FC	Family Computing Forum (FCF)
COMPUTING LIFESTYLES	FCF's Lifestyles & Computing
CONTEST CENTRAL	Family Computing Forum: Contest Central
NEWS & REVIEWS	FCF's News & Reviews (FAMILY NEWS)

Keyword	Area
FAMILY ROOM FCFs	Family Room (FAMILY ALBUM)
FAMILY GAMES	FCF's Rec Room
FAMILY SHOWCASE	Family Product Showcase
SCRAPBOOK	Member Scrapbook
WORKSHOP	FCF's Life's Workshop
FIRST	First Look at How New Products (FIRST LOOK)
FSRC	Flight Sim Resource Center (CRASH, FIREBALL, FLIGHT, FLIGHTCENTER, FLIGHTSIMULATIONS, FLIGHTSIM(S))
MULTIMEDIA	Multimedia menu
NEWTON	Newton Resource Center (MESSAGEPAD)
PDA	PDA/Palmtop Forum (ETEXT, EXPERTPAD, EZINE, NEWTONBOOK, PALMTOP, PDAFORUM, SHARP)
REDGATE	Redgate/IIN Online (IIN, NETWORKS EXPO, NEW PRODUCT SHOWCASE, NPS)
ROTUNDA	Rotunda Forum Auditorium (FORUMAUD, FORUMAUDITORIUM, FORUMROT, STUMP)
@ROTUNDA	Rotunda Auditorium
UGF	User Group Forum (AUG, UGC, USERGROUP(S))
UNIVERSE	UniverseCentral.Com (RALPH Z, RALPH ZERBONIA, UNIVERSE CENTRAL)
VR	Virtual Reality Resource Center (VIRTUALREALITY)

Part
X
App
E

PC Forums

Keyword	Area
HOT PC	What's Hot in Mac Computing (PC HOT)
DOS	DOS Forum (5.0, DOS5.0, DOSFORUM, DRDOS, MS-DOS, MS-DOSFORUM, PCUTILITIES)
OS2	OS/2 Forum (IBMOS2, OSTWO)
PAP	Applications Forum (PCAPS, PCAPPLICATIONS, PCAPPLICATIONSFORUM, APPLICATIONS, APPLICATIONSFORUM, APPS, BUSINESSFORUM, PRODUCTIVITY, PRODUCTIVITYFORUM)

continues

PC Forums   Continued

Keyword	Area
COMPUKIDS	PC Applications: Kids on Computers
PDV	Development Forum (PCDEV, PCDEVELOPMENT, PCDEVELOPMENTFORUM, PROGRAMMING, ASSEMBLY, BASIC, C, COBOL, DEV, DEVELOPER, DEVELOPMENT, DEVELOPMENTFORUM, PASCAL)
PGM	Games Forum (PCGAMES, GAMESFORUM, PCGAMESFORUM, ADVENTURE, ARCADE, SIMULATOR)
PGR	Graphics Forum (PCGRAPHICS, ANIMATION, PCANIMATION, ART, CAD, GRAPHICS, GRAPHICARTS, GRAPHICSFORUM, PCGRAPHICSFORUM)
PHW	Hardware Forum (PCHARDWARE, HARDWARE, HARDWAREFORUM, PCHARDWAREFORUM)
PMM	Multimedia Forum (MM)
PMU	Music and Sound Forum (PCMU, PCMUSIC, MIDI, MUSIC&SOUND, MUSICANDSOUNDFORUM, MUSICFORUM, PCMUSICANDSOUNDFORUM, PCMUSICFORUM, PCSOUND, PCSOUNDFORUM)
PTC	Telecom/Networking Forum (PCM, PCTELECOM, PCTELECOMFORUM, COMMUNICATIONS, NETWORKING, NETWORKINGFORUM, TELECOM, TELECOMFORUM, TELECOMMUNICATIONS)
WIN	Windows Forum (WIN 95, WINDOWS, WINDOWS 95, WINDOWS FORUM, WIN FORUM)
WIN NT	Windows NT Resource Center (WINDOWS NT)

Macintosh Forums

Keyword	Area
MAC	Mac Computing Department (MACINTOSH, MAC COMPUT-ING, APPLE, COMPUTING DEPT)
HOT MAC	What's Hot in Mac Computing (MAC HOT)
MAC HELP	Help Desk (ABF, AOL BEGINNERS, BEGINNER, BEGINNERS, GETTING STARTED, GETTING STARTED FORUM, GTSF, HELP DESK, NEW LINK, NLF, STARTER)

MBS	Business Forum (MACBUSINESS, APPLICATIONS, APPLICATIONS FORUM, APPS, BUSINESS FORUM, PRODUCTIVITY, PRODUCTIVITY FORUM)
MCM	Communications Forum (MTC, MACCOMMUNICATION(S), COMMUNICATIONS, MACTELECOM(M), NETWORKING, NETWORKINGFORUM, TELECOM, TELECOM FORUM, TELECOMMUNICATIONS)
MDP	Desktop Publishing/WP Forum (MAC DESKTOP, MAC DTP, MAC WORLD PROCESSING, DTP, DESKTOP PUBLISHING, WORD PROCESSING)
MDV	Development Forum (MACDEVELOPMENT, PROGRAMMING, MACPROGRAMMING, ASSEMBLY, BASIC, C, COBOL, DEV, DEVELOPER, DEVELOPMENT, DEVELOPMENTFORUM, PASCAL)
MED	Education (MACEDUCATION)
MGM	Games & Entertainment (MACGAME(S), GAMESFORUM, ADVENTURE, ARCADE, SIMULATOR)
MGR	Graphics Art & CAD Forum (MACART, MACGRAPHICS, ANIMATION, ART, CAD, GRAPHICS, GRAPHICARTS, GRAPHICSFORUM)
MHC	HyperCard Forum (MACHYPERCARD, HYPERCARD)
MHW	Hardware (MACHARDWARE, HARDWARE, HARDWAREFORUM, SILICON, SUPERCARD)
MMM	Multimedia Forum (MACMULTIMEDIA, QUICKTIME)
MMS	Music & Sound Forum (MACMUSIC, MACSOUND, MUSIC&SOUND, MUSICANDSOUNDFORUM, MUSICFORUM, MIDI, QMMS)
MOS	Operating Systems Forum (SYSTEM7, MACO/S, MACOS, MACOPERATINGSYSTEMS, SYSTEM7.0, SYSTEM7.1, SYSTEM71)
MUT	Utilities Forum (MVT, MACUTILITIES)

Part
X

App
E

Other Areas of Interest in Computing & Software

Keyword	Area
CROSSMAN	Craig Crossman's Computer America (COMPUTER AMERICA, CRAIG CROSSMAN)
CYBERLAW	CyberLaw, Cyberlex (COMPUTER LAW, CYBERLEX)

continues

Other Areas of Interest in Computing & Software   Continued

Keyword	Area
DES	DeskMate (DESKMATE, PC DESKMATE, PCDM)
DOS6	MS-DOS 6.0 Resource Center (DOS60, MSDOS6, MSDOS60)
IBM	IBM Forum
INCIDER	inCider
KOMANDO	Kim Komando Komputer Tutor (COMMANDO, KOMPUTER TUTOR, KOMPUTER CLINIC)
MACTIVITY	Mactivity '96 Forum
MACWORLD	MacWorld Magazine
MAGICLINK	Sony Magic Link area (SONY, SML)
PCTODAY	PC Today (PC CATALOG)
PCWORLD	PCWorld Online (PCWONLINE, PCWORLD ONLINE)
PERFORMA	Apple Club Performa (PRC, CLUB PERFORMA, PERFORMA CENTER, PERFORMARESOURCE) [Mac only]
PHOTODEX	Photodex
POWERBOOK	PowerBook Resource Center (LAPTOP, NOTEBOOK)
POWERMAC	Power Mac Resource Center (POWERPC)
PRODIGY	Prodigy Refugees' Forum
PU	Programmer University (PROGRAMMERU)
TUNEUP	Tune Up Your PC (TUNEUPYOURPC, AUTOEXEC, CONFIG)
VT	Virtual Tradeshow (VIRTUAL TRADESHOW)
WEB PUB	Web Publishing SIG (WEB PUBLISH, WEB PUBLISHING)
WIN 500	Windows Shareware 500 (WINDOWS 500)
WINNEWS	Windows News area
WPMAG	WordPerfect Magazine

Special Interest Groups

Keyword	Area
3D	3D Resource Center (3-D, 3DRENDERING, 3-DRENDERING, RENDERING, POV, RAYTRACE)
3DSIG	3D Interest Group
ADSIG	Advertising Special Interest Group (ADVERTISING, ADVERTISING SIG)
AECSIG	Architects, Engineers and Construction SIG
APPLESCRIPT	AppleScript SIG
ARTISTS SPOTLIGHT	Artists' Spotlight (ARTIST'S SPOTLIGHT)
AUTOCAD	Cad Resource Center
AUTODESK	Autodesk Resource Center
BCS	Boston Computer Society
BMUG	Berkeley Macintosh Users Group
BOARDWATCH	Boardwatch Magazine
BRAINSTORM	Brainstorm Products
CHARTER	Charter Schools Forum (CHARTER SCHOOL(S))
CMC	Creative Musician's Coalition
COMPOSER(S)	Composer's Coffeehouse (COMPOSER'S)
COREL	CorelDRAW Resource Center (COREL DRAW)
CWUG	ClarisWorks Users Group
DATABASE	Database Support SIG (DATABASES)
DIGITAL IMAGING	Digital Imaging Resource Center (SCANNERS)
DVORAK	Software Hardtalk with John C. Dvorak (SOFTWARE HARDTALK)
DTP	Desktop Publishing Resource Center (DESKTOP PUBLISHING)
EFF	Electronic Frontier Foundation
EPUB(S)	EPub Resource Center (ELECTRONIC PUBLISHING)
FREELANCE	Freelance Artists SIG
GROUPWARE	GroupWare SIG
GSMAG	GS+ Magazine

Part
X
App
E

continues

Special Interest Groups   Continued

Keyword	Area
IA	Instant Artist Resource Center (INSTANT ARTIST, INSTANT ARTIST1, PRINT ARTIST)
ILLUSTRATOR	Mac Graphics Illustrator SIG
IPA	Advanced Color Imaging (IMAGING, COLOR IMAGING)
KARROS	Eric Karros Kronikles
LEGAL	Legal SIG (LEGALSIG)
MACHACK	MacHack (HACK, HACKER(S))
MADA	MacApp Developers Association
MCAFEE	McAfee Associates
NAQP	National Association of Quick Printers (QUICK PRINTERS)
NOMADIC	Nomadic Computing Discussion SIG
PHOTOSHOP	Photoshop SIG (PHOTOSHOP SIG)
PLACES	P.L.A.C.E.S. Interest Group
SSS	Craig Anderton's Sound Studio & Stage (ANDERTON)
VIDEOSIG	Video SIG
VIRUS	Virus Information Center SIG
VB	Visual Basic Area (VISUAL BASIC)
WIRELESS	Wireless Communication

Computing Company Connection

Keyword	Area
CCC	Computing Company Connection (COMPANIES, HARDWARE COMPANIES, IC, INDUSTRY, INDUSTRY CONNECTION, SOFTWARE COMPANIES, SOFTWARE PUBLISHERS, PUBLISHERS)
IC HILITES	IC Hilites
3D FAX	3D Fax Software
3DO	The 3DO Company

Keyword	Area
AATRIX	Aatrix Software, Inc.
ABBATE VIDEO	Abbate Video (VIDEO TOOLKIT)
ACCOLADE	Accolade, Inc.
ACER	Acer America Corporation
ACTIVISION	Activision
ADS	auto*des*sys, Inc. (FORMZ)
ADVANCED	Advanced Software, Inc.
ADVSOFT	Advisor Software
AFFINITY	Affinity Microsystems (AFFINIFILE, AUTOMATION, AUTOMATE, MACRO, MACROS, SCRIPT(S), SCRIPTING, TEMPO, TEMPO II, TEMPO II PLUS)
ALADDIN	Aladdin Systems, Inc. (STUFFIT)
ALDUS	Adobe Systems
ALPHATECH	Alpha Software Corporation (ASCTECH, ASCTS)
ALR	Advanced Logic Research (ADVANCED LOGIC)
ALTSYS	Altsys Corporation
ALYSIS	Alysis Software (SUPERDISK)
AMBROSIA	Ambrosia Software
ANIMATED SOFTWARE	Animated Software
ANOTHERCO	Another Company
APDA	Apple Professional Developer's Association
APPLE COMPUTER	Apple Computer
APOGEE	Apogee Software (3D REALMS)
ARGOSY	Argosy
ARIEL	Ariel Publishing
ARSENAL	Arsenal Communications
ARTEMIS	Artemis Software (EPSCONVERTER)
ARTIFICE	Artifice, Inc.
ARTIST GRAPHICS	Artist Graphics
ASI	Articulate Systems (ARTICULATE)

Part

X

App

E

continues

Computing Company Connection Continued	
Keyword	**Area**
AST	AST Online
ASYMETRIX	Asymetrix Corporation
AT&T	AT&T (ATT, ATT WIRELESS)
ATLUS	Atlus Software
ATONCE	atOnce Software
ATTICUS	Atticus Software
AVID	Avid DTV Group (AVIDDTV)
AVOCAT	Avocat Systems (AVOCAT SYSTEMS)
BASELINE	Baseline Publishing
BASEVIEW	Baseview Products, Inc.
BEE	BeeSoft (BEESOFT)
BERKELEY	Berkeley Systems (BERKSYS, BERKSYSWIN)
BETHESDA	Bethesda Softworks (BETHESDASOFTWORKS, BETHESDA)
BEYOND	Beyond, Inc.
BITJUGGLERS	Bit Jugglers
BLIZZARD ENT	Blizzard Entertainment
BLUE RIBBON	Blue Ribbon Soundworks
BOWERS	Bowers Development (APPMAKER)
BRODERBUND	Broderbund
BUNGIE	Bungie Software
BUSINESS SENSE	Business Sense
BYTE	ByteWorks (BYTEWORKS)
BYTEBYBYTE	Byte By Byte Corporation
CAERE	Caere Corporation (CAERE CORPORATION)
CALIGARI	Caligari Corporation
CALLISTO	Callisto Corporation
CAPSTONE	Capstone Software
CARDINAL	Cardinal Technologies, Inc.
CASABLANCA	Casa Blanca

Keyword	Area
CASADY	Casady & Greene
CE SOFTWARE	CE Software
CHPRODUCTS	CH Products
CLARIS	Claris
CODA	Coda Music Tech (CMT, CODAMUSIC)
COMPAQ	Compaq
COMPUADD	CompuAdd
CONNECTIX	Connectix (RAM DOUBLER)
COOPER	JLCooper Electronics (JLCOOPER)
COSA	Company of Science and Art
COSTAR	CoStar
CPI	Computer Peripherals, Inc. (COMPUTER PERIPHERALS)
CRYSTAL	Crystal Dynamics
DACEASY	DacEasy, Inc.
DANCING RABBIT	Dancing Rabbit Creations (DANCING)
DATAPAK	DataPak Software (DATAPACK)
DATAWATCH	Datawatch (VIREX)
DAVIDSON	Davidson & Associates
DAYNA	Dayna Communications
DAYSTAR	Daystar Digital
DAYTIMER	DayTimer Technologies
DEADLY	Deadly Games
DEC	Digital Equipment Corporation
DELL	Dell Computer Corporation
DELRINA	Delrina Corporation
DELTAPOINT	Delta Point
DELTATAO	Delta Tao (DELTA)
DENEBA	Deneba Software (CANVAS)
DI	Disney Interactive (DISNEY INTERACTIVE, DISNEY SOFT, DISNEY SOFTWARE)

Part
X

App
E

continues

Computing Company Connection   Continued

Keyword	Area
DIAMOND	Diamond Computer Systems (DIAMOND COMPUTERS)
DIGITAL	Digital Vision
DIGITALECLIPSE	Digital Eclipse
DIGITALTECH	Digital Technologies
DIRECT	Direct Software
DJ	Don Johnston, Inc. (DON JOHNSTON)
DOMARK	Domark Software Inc.
DUBLCLICK	Dubl-Click Software
DYNAWARE	Dynaware USA (DYNAWAREUSA)
ECS	Electronic Courseware (COURSEWARE)
EDMARK	Edmark Technologies (KIDDESK, PENPAL)
ELECTRIC	Electric Image (ELECTRIC IMAGE)
EMIGRE	Emigre Fonts
EXPERT	Expert Software, Inc (EXPERTSOFT, SOFTSYNC)
FARALLON	Farallon
FOCUS	Focus Enhancements (FOCUS ENHANCEMENTS, LAPIS)
FORTE	Forte Technologies
FORTNER	Fortner Research (FORTRAN, LANGUAGE SYS)
FRACTAL	Fractal Design (FRACTALDESIGN)
FRANCE & ASSOCIATES	France & Associates
FRANKLIN	Franklin Quest
FREEMAIL	FreeMail, Inc.
FULLWRITE	FullWrite
FUTURELABS	Future Labs, Inc. (TALKSHOW)
GALACTICOMM	Galacticomm
GAMETEK	Gametek
GATEWAY	Gateway 2000, Inc (GATEWAY2000, MOO)
GCC	GCC Technologies

Keyword	Area
GDT	GDT Softworks, Inc. (GDT SOFTWORKS)
GENERALMAGIC	General Magic
GEOWORKS	GeoWorks
GEOSDK	Geoworks SDK Beta area
GIF CONVERTER	GIF Converter
GLOBAL	Global Village Communication (GLOBALVILLAGE, TELEPORT)
GRAPHICSIMULATIONS	Graphic Simulations (GRAPHIC, GRAPHSIM, GSC, SIMULATIONS)
GRAPHISOFT	Graphisoft
GRAPHSOFT	Graphsoft, Inc. (BLUEPRINT, MINICAD)
GRAVIS	Advanced Gravis (ADVANCED GRAVIS)
GRYPHON	Gryphon Software (GRYPHON SOFTWARE, MORPH)
GSS	Global Software Suport
HASH	Hash, Inc. (PLAYMATION)
HDC	hdc Corporation (HDC CORPORATION)
HELIOS	Helios USA (HELIOSUSA)
HSC	HSC Software (BRYCE, HSC SOFTWARE, KPT, KPT BRYCE, LIVEPICTURE)
HP	Hewlett-Packard
HP FILES	Hewlett-Packard: Support Information Files
HP HOME	Hewlett-Packard: Home Products Information
IBVA	IBVA Technologies (IBVATECH, PSYCHIC LAB, PSYCHIC LABS)
INFOCOM	Infocom
INLINE	Inline Design (INLINESOFTWARE)
INNOSYS	InnoSys Inc. [MAOL and GAOL only]
INSIGNIA	Insignia Solutions (INSIGNIASOLUTION)
INTEL	Intel Corporation (CONNECTION, INTEL INSIDE, P6, PENTIUM)
INTELLIMATION	Intellimation

Part
X

App
E

continues

Computing Company Connection   Continued

Keyword	Area
INTERCON	InterCon Systems Corporation
INTERPLAY	Interplay
INTREK	InTrek
INTUIT	Intuit, Inc.
IOMEGA	Iomega Corporation
ISIS	ISIS International (ISISINTERNATIONAL)
ISLAND GRAPHICS	Island Graphics Corporation (ISLAND)
IYM	IYM Software Review (IYM SOFTWARE REVIEW)
JPEGVIEW	JPEGView
KASAN	Kasanjim Research (KASANJIAN, KR)
KENSINGTON	Kensington Microware, Ltd.
KENTMARSH	Kent*Marsh
KNOWLEDGEBASE	Microsoft Knowledge Base (MSKB)
KOALA	Koala/MacVision (MACVISION)
KURZWEIL	Kurzweil Music Systems
LANGUAGESYS	Language Systems
LAWRENCE	Lawrence Productions
LEADER	Leader Technologies (LEADERTECH, LEADER TECHNOLOGIES)
LEADINGEDGE	Leading Edge
LIND	Lind Portable Power
LINKS	Access Software (ACCESSSOFTWARE)
LINKSWARE	LinksWare, Inc.
LINNSOFT	LinnSoftware (LINNSOFTWARE)]
LOGICODE	Logicode Technology, Inc.
LUCAS	LucasArts Games (LUCASARTS)
MACBIBLE	The Macintosh Bible/Peachpit Forum (PEACHPIT, MACINTOSHBIBLE)
MACROMEDIA	MacroMedia, Inc. (MACROMIND)

Keyword	Area
MAINSTAY	Mainstay
MANHATTANGRAPHICS	Manhattan Graphics (RSG)
MARKET	Market Master (MARKETMASTER)
MARKETFIELD	Marketfield Software
MARTINSEN	Martinsen's Software
MAXIS	Maxis
MAXTECH	MaxTech Corporation (GVC)
MECC	MECC
MEDIA VISION	Media Vision (MV)
METRICOM	Metricom, Inc. (RICOCHET)
METROWERKS	Metrowerks
METZ	Metz
MGX	Micrografx, Inc. (MICROGRAFX)
MICRODYNAMICS	Micro Dynamics, Ltd.
MICROFRONTIER	MicroFrontier, Ltd.
MICROJ	Micro J Systems, Inc.
MICROMAT	MicroMat Computer Systems
MICROPROSE	MicroProse
MICROSEEDS	Microseeds Publishing, Inc.
MICROSOFT	Microsoft Resource Center (MS SUPPORT)
MINDSCAPE	Mindscape (STW, SOFTWARE TOOLS WORKS)
MIRROR	Mirror Technologies
MOBILEMEDIA	MobileMedia (PCS)
SEND PAGE	Mobile Media's Page Sender
MORAFFWARE	MoraffWare
MORGANDAVIS	Morgan Davis Group
MOTOROLA	Motorola (ENVOY, MARCO)
MOTU	Mark of the Unicorn
MSA	Management Science Associates

Part

X

App

E

continues

Computing Company Connection   Continued

Keyword	Area
MSTATION	Bentley Systems, Inc.
MUSTANG	Mustang Software (MUSTANG SOFTWARE, QMODEM, WILDCAT, WILDCATBBS)
MYOB	Best! Ware
NCT	Next Century Technologies
NEC	NEC Technologies (NECTECH)
NEOLOGIC	NeoLogic
NETSCAPE	Netscape (TO NETSCAPE)
NEWWORLD	New World Computing
NIKON	Nikon Electronic Imaging
NILES	Niles and Associates (ENDNOTE)
NISUS	Nisus Software
NO HANDS	No Hands Software (NO HANDS SOFTWARE, COMMON GROUND)
NOVELL	Novell Desktop Systems (DIGITAL RESEARCH, DIGITAL RESEARCH INC, DRI)
NOW	Now Software
OBJECTFACTORY	Object Factory
OLDUVAI	Olduvai Software, Inc.
ON	ON Technology
ONYX	Onyx Technology
OPCODE	Opcode Systems, Inc. (OPCODE SYSTEMS)
OPTIMAGE	OptImage Interactive Services
OPTIMAS	OPTIMAS Corporation (BIOSCAN)
ORIGIN	Origin Systems (ORIGIN SYSTEMS)
PACEMARK	PaceMark Technologies, Inc.
PACKER	Packer Software
PALM	Palm Computing (PALMCOMPUTING)
PAPERPORT	Visioneer (VISIONEER)
PAPYRUS	Papyrus

Keyword	Area
PARSONS	Parsons Technology
PASSPORT	Passport Designs
PC CATALOG	PC Catalog
PC DATA	PC Data
PC PC	Personal Computer Peripherals
PEACHTREE	Peachtree Software
PICTORIUS	Pictorius (PEREGRINE, TGS)
PIERIAN	Piereian Spring Software (PIERIAN SP)
PIXAR	Pixar (RENDERMAN)
PIXEL	Pixel Resources (PIXELRESOURCES)
PKWARE	PKWare Inc.
PPI	Practical Peripherals, Inc. (PRACTICAL PERIPHERALS)
PRAIRIE	Prairie Group
PRAIRIESOFT	PrairieSoft, Inc.
PROGRAPH	Prograph International, Inc. (TGS)
PROVUE	ProVUE Development
PSION	Psion
QUALITAS	Qualitas
QUARK	Quark, Inc.
RADIUS	Radius-SuperMac (SUPERMAC)
RASTEROPS	RasterOps
RAY	Ray Dream (RAYDREAM)
REACTOR	Reactor
RESNOVA	ResNova Software (RESNOVASOFTWARE)
ROCKLAND	Rockland Software (ROCKLANDSOFTWARE)
ROLAND	Roland Corporation U.S.
ROGER WAGNER	Roger Wagner Publishing (HYPERSTUDIO, STUDIOWARE)
RYOBI	Ryobi
SERIUS	Serius

Part

X

App

E

continues

Computing Company Connection   Continued

Keyword	Area
SEVENTH	Seventh Level Software (7TH)
SHAREWARE-SOLUTIONS	Shareware Solutions
SIERRA	Sierra On-Line (DYNAMIX)
SOFTARC	SoftArc
SOFTDISK	Softdisk Superstore (SUPERSTORE) [PC platform only]
SOPHCIR	Sophisticated Circuits
SPC	Software Publishing Corporation
SPECTRUM	Spectrum HoloByte
SPECULAR	Specular International
SPIDER	Spider Island Software (SPIDER ISLAND)
SPIRIT	Spirit Technologies
SPRINT	Sprint Annual Report/Old
SRS LABS	SRS Labs (3D AUDIO, 3D SOUND)
SSI	Strategic Simulations (STRATEGIC)
SSSI	SSSi
STAC	STAC Electronics
STARFISH	Starfish Software
STARPLAY	Starplay Productions
STF	STF Technologies (STFTECHNOLOGIES)
STRATA	Strata, Inc.
SUNBURST	Sunburst Communications
SURVIVOR	Survivor Software (SURVIVOR SOFTWARE)
SYMANTEC	Symantec (5TH GENERATION, CENTRAL, CENTRAL POINT, CPS, FIFTH, NORTON, PETERNORTON)
SYNEX	Synex
TACTIC	Tactic Software (NEWERA)
TACTIC	Tactic Software Corporation (NEWERA)
TAKE 2	Take 2 Interactive Software (TAKE 2 INC)
TEAM	Team Concepts (TEAM CONCEPTS)

Keyword	Area
TECHWORKS	Technology Works (TECHNOLOGY WORKS)
TEKNOSYS	Teknosys Works
TEKTRONIX	Tektronix
THREESIXTY	Three-Sixty Software
TRIMBLE	Trimble Navigation, Ltd.
THRUSTMASTER	Thrustmaster
THUNDERWARE	Thunderware
TI	Texas Instruments (TEXAS INSTRUMENTS)
TIA	True Image Audio (TRUE IMAGEAUDIO, MAC SPEAKERZ)
TIGERDIRECT	TIGERDirect, Inc. (TIGER, BLOCDEVELOPMENT)
TIMESLIPS	Timeslips Corporation
TIMEWORKS	Timeworks
TMAKER	T/Maker
TOOLWORKS	Software Toolworks (SOFTWARE TOOLWORKS)
TS	Trendsetter Software (TRENDSETTER)
TSENG	Tseng
TSP	Tom Snyder Productions (TOM SNYDER)
TWI	Time Warner Interactive
UA	Unlimited Adventures (UNLIMITEDADVENTURES)
USERLAND	Userland
USROBOTICS	U.S. Robotics
VANGUARD	Vanguard Online (VANGUARD ONLINE)
VCOMMS	Vanguard Online: Communications
VFUNDS	Vanguard Online: Mutual Funds Campus
VNEWS	Vanguard Online: Vanguard News
VSTRATEGY	Vanguard Online: Planning & Strategy
VDISC	Videodiscovery (VIDEODISC, VIDEODISCOVERY)
VERTISOFT	Vertisoft
VIACOM	Viacom New Media (ICOM, ICOM SIMULATIONS)

Part
X

App
E

continues

Computing Company Connection   Continued

Keyword	Area
VIDI	VIDI
VIEWPOINT	Viewpoint DataLabs
VILLAGE	Village Software (VILLAGE SOFTWARE)
VIRTUS	Virtus Walkthrough (WALKTHROUGH)
VISIONEER	Visioneer
VISIONARY	Visionary Software
VOYAGER	The Voyager Company
VOYETRA	Voyetra Technologies
VRLI	Virtual Reality Labs, Inc.
VV	Vision Video (VISION VIDEO)
WDC	Western Digital Company
WEIGAND	Weigand Report
WESTERN DIGITAL	Western Digital (WDC)
WESTWOOD	Westwood Studios (WESTWOOD STUDIOS)
WILSON	Wilson Windowware (WINDOWWARE)
WORDPERFECT	WordPerfect Support Center
WORKING	Working Software
XAOS	Xoas Tools (XAOS TOOLS)
ZEDCOR	Zedcor, Inc.
ZELOS	Zelos
ZEOS	Zeos International Ltd.
ZOOM TELEPHONICS	Zoom Telephonics

Travel

Keyword	Area
TRAVEL	Travel department (SHOPPING & TRAVEL, SHOPPING AND TRAVEL)
ARTHUR FROMMER	Arthur Frommer's Secret Bargains (SECRET BARGAINS)
B&B	Bed & Breakfast U.S.A. (BED, BED & BREAKFAST, BREAKFAST)

Keyword	Area
BACKPACKER	Backpacker Magazine (OUTDOOR GEAR, VACATIONS, TRAILGUIDES, CONSERVATION, ECOTOURISM, HIKER, HIKING, TRAILS, WILDERNESS, CAMPING, BACKCOUNTRY)
CRUISE	Cruise Critic (CRUISE CRITIC)
BICYCLING	Bicycling Magazine (BICYCLING MAGAZINE, BIC MAG, MOUNTAIN BIKE)
EMERALD COAST	Emerald Coast
FTN	Family Travel Network (FAMILY TRAVEL, FAMILY TRAVEL NETWORK, KID TRAVEL)
FLORIDA	Destination Florida
DF FOOD	Destination Florida: Restaurants and Nightlife
DF OUT	Destination Florida: Outdoors
DF PARKS	Destination Florida: Attractions
DF ROOMS	Destination Florida: Places To Stay
DF SHOP	Destination Florida: Shopping
DF SPACE	Destination Florida: Kennedy Space Center
DF SPORTS	Destination Florida: Sports
DF TICKET	Destination Florida: Ticketmaster
FLORIDA KEYS	The Florida Keys (THE FLORIDA KEYS, THE KEYS)
FLYING	Flying Magazine (FLYING MAGAZINE, FLYING MAG, AIRCRAFT, AIRPORTS, PILOTS)
GOLFIS	Golf Courses & Resort Information (GOLF AMERICA, GOLF COURSES, GOLF INFORMATION, GOLF RESORTS)
GUIDE	Frommer's City Guides (FROMMER, FROMMER'S, FROMMER'S CITY GUIDES, FROMMERS, FROMMERS CITY GUIDES)
INSIDE FLYER	Inside Flyer (FREQUENT FLYER)
KEYWORD	Preview Vacation Keyword Game
OAO	Outdoor Adventures Online (ADVENTURE, OUTDOOR, OUTDOOR ADVENTURE)
PICTURES	Pictures of the World

Part

X

App

E

continues

Travel Continued	
Keyword	**Area**
PREVIEW	Preview Vacations (PREVIEW VACATIONS, VACATION, VACATIONS)
R&T	Road & Track (AUTOS, AUTOMOTIVE, ROAD, ROAD & TRACK, TRACK)
RPM	RPM Worldwide Entertainment & Travel (RPM TRAVEL)
SKI	Ski Reports (SKI REPORTS, SKI CONDITIONS, SKI WEATHER) [seasonal]
SKI ZONE	The Ski Zone
SABRE	EAASY SABRE (EASY, EASY SABRE, AMERICAN AIRLINES)
TRAILSIDE	Trailside Online
TA	Traveler's Advantage (TRAVELERS ADVANTAGE)
TL	Travel & Leisure Magazine (TRAVEL & LEISURE)
TRAVEL ADVISORIES	US State Department Travel Advisories
TRAVELERS CORNER	Traveler's Corner (WEISSMANN)
TRAVEL FORUM	Travel Forum (TRAVELER)
TRAVEL HOLIDAY	Travel Holiday Magazine
TROPICAL STORM	Tropical Storm and Hurricane Info (HURRICANE)
WEATHER	Weather
WEATHER MAPS	Color Weather Maps (COLOR WEATHER MAPS)
ZAGAT	Zagat Restaurant/Hotel/Resort/Spa Surveys (ZAGATS)

Marketplace	
Keyword	**Area**
MARKETPLACE	Marketplace department (MALL, THE MALL, STORE, SHOPPING, STORES)
ABC SPORTS STORE	ABC Sports Store
2MARKET	(CD, TO MARKET, TWO MARKET)
AMEX	ExpressNet/American Express (AMERICAN EXPRESS, EXPRESS NET)

Keyword	Area
AOL PRODUCTS	AOL Products Center (TOUR GUIDE, MUG, TSHIRT, AOLSTORE, AMERICA ONLINE STORE)
AUTO	AutoVantage (AUTOVANTAGE, AV)
BARGAINS	Checkbook Bargains
BLOCKBUSTER	Blockbuster Music's Online Store
BOOKSTORE	Online Bookstore (ONLINE BOOKSTORE, READ USA)
BRAINSTORMS	Brainstorms Store
CADILLAC	Cadillac WWW Home Page
CHATELAINE	Chatelaine Jewelry (JEWELRY)
CHEF'S CATALOG	Chef's Catalog (CHEFS CATALOG)
CITIBANK	The Apple Citibank Visa Card
CLASSIFIED(S)	Classifieds Online (CLASSIFIEDS ONLINE)
CARDS	Hallmark Connections (HALLMARK, HALLMARK CONNECTIONS)
CHEESECAKES	Eli's Cheesecakes (CHEESECAKE, ELI, ELI'S, ELI'S CHEESECAKES, ELIS CHEESECAKES)
COLLECTIBLES	Collectibles Online (COLLECT, COLLECTIBLES ONLINE)
COMPUTER EXPRESS	Computer Express
CONSUMER(S)	Consumer Reports (CONSUMER REPORTS)
DOWNTOWN	Downtown AOL (DOWNTOWN AOL, DT, DT AOL)
DOWNTOWN MSG	Downtown AOL Message Boards
EDDIE BAUER	Eddie Bauer
FAO	F.A.O. Schwarz (FAO SCHWARZ)
FEDEX	FedEx/Federal Express
FLOWERS	800-Flowers (800-FLOWERS, 800 FLOWERS, BALLOON, BALLOONS, GIFTS, PLANTS, ROSES)
FREESHOP	The FreeShop Online (FREE OFFERS, FREESHOP ONLINE)
FOSSIL	Fossil Watches and More (FOSSIL WATCHES)
GLOBAL PLAZA	Global Plaza
GODIVA	Godiva Chocolatiers
GREET ST	Greet Street Greeting Cards (GREET STREET)

Part

X

App

E

continues

Marketplace Continued

Keyword	Area
GWALTNEY	Gwaltney Hams & Turkeys (SMITHFIELD, HAMS)
HAMMACHER	Hammacher Schlemmer (HAMMACHER SCHLEMMER)
HANES	One Hanes Place (BALI, CHAMPION, L'EGGS, PLAYTEX)
HOLIDAY VILLAGE	Marketplace Holiday Village Sales
INFINITI	Infiniti Online (INFINITI ONLINE)
JCPENNEY	JCPenney
KIDSOFT	KidSoft Superstore (CLUB KIDSOFT, KIDSOFT STORE)
KOMANDO	Kim Komando's Komputer Clinic (COMMANDO, KOMPUTER TUTOR, KOMPUTER CLINIC, MR SCIENCE)
LENS	Lens Express (LENS EXPRESS)
LILLIAN	Lillian Vernon (LILLIAN VERNON)
MAMA	Mama's Cucina by Ragu (ITALIAN FOOD, MAMA'S CUCINA, PASTA, RAGU, SAUCE)
MCFAMILY	McFamily Community (MCDONALD'S)
OFFICEMAX	OfficeMax Online (OFFICE)
OLDS	Oldsmobile/Celebrity Circle (CELEBRITY CIRCLE, OLDSMOBILE)
OMAHA	Omaha Steaks (OMAHA STEAKS, STEAKS)
PCCATALOG	PC Catalog
PCCLASSIFIEDS	Browse the PC Catalog
PEAPOD	Peapod Online
PICTUREPLACE	Picture Place Digital Images
PREMIER	Premier Dining (EAT, EAT OUT, DINE OUT, PD, PREMIER DINING)
PRICE	Price Online (PRICE ONLINE)
SA	Shopper's Advantage (COMPUSTORE, SHOPPERS ADVANTAGE)
SHARPER IMAGE	The Sharper Image
SHOPPERS EXPRESS	Shoppers' Express (SE)
STARBUCKS	Caffe Starbucks (CAFFE STARBUCKS)
SWEETHEART	Omaha Steaks Offer

Keyword	Area
TICKET	TicketMaster
TOWER RECORDS	Tower Records (RECORD(S), TOWER)
TOY NET	Pangea Toy Net (BEANIE, BEANIE BOY, CRISPY, PANGEA, PANGEA TOYNET, THE TOY NET, TOY, VIRTUAL TOYS, VTOYS)
USPS	United States Postal Service
WB STORE	Warner Bros. Studio Store (WARNER BROS. STORE, WARNER BROS. STUSTO, WARNER BROS STORE, WARNER STORE)
WEATHER MALL	WSC Weather Mall
WINDHAM	Windham Hill (WINDHAM HILL)
ZIMA	Zima
ZIMA TALK	Zima Events

The Newsstand

Keyword	Area
NEWSSTAND	Newsstand department (MAGAZINES)
ODEON	Center Stage (AUDITORIUM, SHOWS, PCAUD, COLISEUM, CENTERSTAGE, GLOBE)
ABCNEWS	ABC News-On-Demand (20/20, AMERICAN AGENDA, BRINKLEY, DAYONE, NIGHTLINE, PERSON OF THE WEEK, PETER JENNINGS, YOUR CHOICE)
AHS	American Hiking Society
ATLANTIC	The Atlantic Monthly Online (ATLANTIC MONTHLY, ATLANTIC ONLINE, IDEAS)
ASTROGRAPH	Astrograph
BACKPACKER	Backpacker Magazine (OUTDOOR GEAR, VACATIONS, TRAIL GUIDES, CONSERVATION, ECOTOURISM, HIKER, HIKING, TRAILS, WILDERNESS, CAMPING, BACKCOUNTRY)
BP MARKETPLACE	Backpacker Online's Marketplace
BETTER LIVING	Ideas for Better Living (IDEAS FOR BETTER LIVING)
BICYCLING	Bicycling Magazine (BICYCLING MAGAZINE, BICMAG, MOUNTAINBIKE)

Part
X

App
E

continues

The Newsstand	Continued
Keyword	**Area**
BOAT	Boating Online (FISH, FISHING, INBOARD, MARINE, OUT BOARD, POWERBOATS, SPEEDBOATS, WATER, YACHTS)
BW	Business Week Online (BW ONLINE, BUSINESS WEEK)
BW SEARCH	Business Week: Search
CAMPUS LIFE	Campus Life (CL)
CAR(S)	Car & Driver/Road & Track (AUTOMOBILE)
CARANDDRIVER	Car & Driver (DRIVING, RACING)
CC MAG	Christian Computing Magazine (CHRISTIAN COMPUTING)
CH	Christian History Magazine (CHRISTIAN HISTORY)
CHRIST	Christianity Online (<><, CHRISTIANITY, XOL)
CHRISTIAN-COMPUTING	Christian Computing
CHRISTIANHISTORY	Christian History
CNS	Catholic News Service (CATHOLIC NEWS, CATHOLIC NEWS SERVICE)
COL	Chicago Online (CHICAGO, CHICAGO ONLINE)
TRIBUNE	Chicago Tribune (TRIB, CHICAGO TRIBUNE)
COL CALENDAR	Chicago Online Calendar
COL CHAT	Chicago Online Chat
COL EDUCATION	Chicago Online Education (COL EDUCATE)
COL ENTERTAINMENT	Chicago Online Entertainment
COL FILES	Chicago Online Libraries
COL GOVT	Chicago Online Government Guide (COL GOVERNMENT)
COL LIFESTYLES	Chicago Online Lifestyles
COL MALL	Chicago Online Mall
COL MARKETPLACE	Chicago Online Marketplace
COL MEDIA	Chicago Online Media Guide
COL NEWS	Chicago Online News, Business & Weather
COL PLANNER	Chicago Online Planner
COL SPORTS	Chicago Online Sports

Keyword	Area
COL TICKET	Chicago Online Ticketmaster
COL TECH	Chicago Online Technology Guide
COL VISITOR	Chicago Online Visitor Guide
COL WEATHER	Chicago Online Calendar
TRIB ADS	Chicago Online Classifieds (TRIB CLASSIFIED)
TRIB COLUMNISTS	Chicago Online Columnists
TRIB SPORTS	Chicago Tribune: Sports Area
COLUMNISTS	Columnists & Features Online (FEATURES, COLUMNS)
COMPUTE	Compute
COMPUTER LIFE	Computer Life Magazine (CLIFE, LIFE)
CONNECT	Connect Magazine
CONSUMER(S)	Consumer Reports (CONSUMER REPORTS)
DRUG REFERENCE	Consumer Reports Complete Drug Reference Search
COWLES	Cowles/SIMBA Media Information Network (SIMBA, COWLES SIMBA, MEDIA, MEDIA INFORMATION, INSIDE MEDIA)
CR	Christian Reader (CHRISTIAN READER)
CT	Christianity Today (CHRISTIANITY TODAY)
CYCLE	Cycle World Online (BIGTWIN, CYCLING, CYCLE WORLD, HARLEY, HARLEY DAVIDSON, HELMETS, MOTORCYCLING)
DC	DC Comics Online (BATMAN, DCCOMICS, DC COMICS ONLINE, MAD, MAD MAGAZINE, MILESTONE, PARADOX, SUPERMAN, VERTIGO)
DIGIZINES	Digizine Sites on the Web (CYBERZINES, EZINES)
DISNEY ADVENTURES	Disney Adventures Magazine (DISNEY MAGAZINE)
DR WHO	Doctor Who Online (DOCTOR WHO)
ELLE	Elle Magazine Online (BEAUTY, CLOTHES, CLOTHING, DESIGN, DESIGNERS, FASHION, FITNESS, MODELS, STYLE, TRENDS)
FAMILYPC	FamilyPC Online (FAMILYCOMPUTING, GAMESTER, GIGABRAIN, MEGANEWS, MEGAZINE, MEGAZONE)
FLYING	Flying Magazine (AIRCRAFT, AIRCRAFTS, AIRPORTS, FLYING, FLYING MAG, FLYING MAGAZINE, IFR, PILOTS, VFR)

Part
X
App
E

continues

The Newsstand   Continued

Keyword	Area
HACHETTE	Hachette Filipacchi Magazines (HFM MAGNET WORK, MAGNET, MAGNETO)
HEALTH MAGAZINE	Health Magazine
HMCURRENT	Health Magazine's Current area
HMFITNESS	Health Magazine's Fitness area
HMFOOD	Health Magazine's Food area
HMRELATIONSHIPS	Health Magazine's Relationships area
HMREMEDIES	Health Magazine's Remedies area
HOME	Home Magazine Online (ARCHITECTURE, DECORATING, FURNISHINGS, FURNITURE, HOMEDESIGN, HOUSE, INTERIOR DESIGN, LANDSCAPING, REMODELING)
HOME OFFICE	Home Office Computing (HOC, SOHO)
HOMEPC	HomePC Magazine
INSIDER	Industry Insider (INSIDE)
IWIRE	I-Wire Online (COMPUTE, I-WIRE)
LJ	Leadership Journal (LEADERSHIP, LEADERSHIP JOURNAL)
LONGEVITY	Longevity Magazine Online (ANTI-AGING, ANTI AGING, ANTI-OXIDANTS, EXERCISE, HERBS, HOMEOPATHIC REMEDIES, LONGEVITY, MASSAGE, PLASTIC SURGERY, SPA, SPAS, WELLNESS, VITAMINS, WORKOUTS, YOUNGNESS, YOUTHFUL)
MAC HOME	MacHome Journal (MAC HOME JOURNAL, MHJ)
MACTECH	MacTech Magazine (MACTECH MAG, MACTECH MAGAZINE)
MAC TODAY	Mac Today Magazine
MACWORLD	MacWorld Magazine
MARRIAGE PARTNERSHIP	Marriage Partnership (MARRIAGE)
MERCURY	Mercury Center (MERCURY CENTER, SAN JOSE)
MC BUSINESS	Mercury Center Business & Technology area
MC CLASSIFIEDS	Mercury Center Advertising (MCADS, MCMARKET)
MC ENTERTAINMENT	Mercury Center Entertainment area
MC LIBRARY	Mercury Center Newspaper Library

Keyword	Area
MC LIVING	Mercury Center Bay Area Living area
MC NEW	San Jose Mercury News [GAOL only]
MC NEW(S)	Mercury Center In the News area (IN THE NEWS)
MC PR	Mercury Center Newshound (NEWSHOUND, MERC PR, PERSONAL REPORTER)
MC SPORTS	Mercury Center Sports area
MC TALK	Mercury Center Conference area (MCCOMMUNICATION)
NEWS LIBRARY	Mercury Center Newspaper Library (NEWSPAPER LIBRARY)
MET HOME	Metropolitan Home (METROPOLITAN HOME)
MIRABELLA	Mirabella Magazine (MIRABELLA ONLINE)
MMW	Multimedia World Online (MM ONLINE, MMW WORLD, MMW CAFE, MWW CLINIC, MMW GOLDMINE, MMW LIBRARY, MMW NEWS, MMW OFFICE, MMW PAVILION, MMW TESTTRACK, MMW WAREHOUSE, MMW WELCOME, MULTIMEDIA WORLD, X)
MOBILE	Mobile Office Online (PORTABLE, PORTABLE COMPUTING)
MSCOPE	Standard & Poor's Marketscope
NAA	Newspaper Association of America (ASNE, NVN)
NCR	National Catholic Reporter (CATHOLIC REPORTER)
NEXT	Generation Next (GEN NEXT, GENERATION NEXT)
NGS	National Geographic Online (GEOGRAPHIC, NATIONAL GEOGRAPHIC)
NGS WORLD	National Geographic World
NOLO	Nolo Press (NOLO PRESS)
OMNI	OMNI Magazine Online (OMNIMAGAZINE)
OSKAR'S	Oskar's Magazine (OSKARS)
OSO	Orlando Sentinel Online (ORLANDO, ORLANDO SENTINEL)
OSO BUSINESS	Orlando Sentinel's Business
OSO CLASSIFIEDS	Orlando Sentinel Online: Classified Ads (OSO CLASSIFIED)
OSO COLLEGE FB	Orlando Sentinel Online: College Football (OSO COLLEGE FOOTBALL)
OSO ENTERTAIN	Orlando Sentinel's Entertainment

Part

X

App

E

continues

The Newsstand Continued	
Keyword	**Area**
OSO LIVING	Orlando Sentinel's Living
OSO MAGIC	Orlando Sentinel's Magic
OSO PHOTOS	Orlando Sentinel's Photos
OSO REAL ESTATE	Orlando Sentinel Online: Real Estate
OSO RELIGION	Orlando Sentinel Online: Religion NewsOSO SERVICES Orlando Sentinel's Services
OSO SOUND OFF	Orlando Sentinel's Sound Off
OSO SPORTS	Orlando Sentinel's Sports
OSO TO DO	Orlando Sentinel Online: Things To Do
PC TODAY	PC Novice/PC Today (PCNOVICE)
PCWORLD	PCWorld Online (PCWONLINE, PCWORLD ONLINE)
PHOTOS	Popular Photography (CAMERAS, PHOTOGRAPHY, POPULAR PHOTOGRAPHY, POPPHOTO)
R&T	Road & Track (AUTOS, AUTOMOTIVE, ROAD, ROAD & TRACK, TRACK)
SCIAM	Scientific American (SCIENCE, SCIENTIFIC, SCIENTIFICAMERICAN)
SA MED	Scientific American Medical Publications (CANCER JOURNAL, CANCER J SCIAM)
FRONTIERS	Scientific American Frontiers (SAF)
SCI & MED	Scientific American Science & Medicine
SEVENTEEN	Seventeen Magazine Online (17)
SM	Smithsonian Magazine (SMITHSONIAN MAGAZINE)
SPIN	Spin Online (SPINONLINE)
SRO	Saturday Review Online (SATREVIEW, SATURDAY REVIEW, LITERATURE, READING, SOCIETY, THEATER, THEATRE)
SALON	Saturday Review Online: Conference Room (SRO SALON)
STEREO	Stereo Review Online magazine (AMPLIFIERS, AUDIO, CDS, HOMETHEATER, SOUND, SPEAKERS, STEREOEQUIPMENT, STEREOREVIEW)
SUNSET	Sunset Magazine (SUNSET MAGAZINE)

Keyword	Area
SUPERLIBRARY	The Information SuperLibrary (MACMILLAN)
TCW	Today's Christian Woman
TIME	Time Magazine Online
TIMES	@times/The New York Times Online (@TIMES, AT TIMES, NYT, NY TIMES, NEWYORKTIMES, NYC, NEWYORK, NEW YORK CITY, NYNEX, TECHNOTORIUM, TIMES NEWS)
TIMES ART	@times: Art & Photography
TIMES ARTS	@times: The Arts
TIMES BOOKS	@times: Books of The Times
TIMES DINING	@times: Dining Out & Nightlife (DINING)
TIMES LEISURE	@times: Leisure Guide (DANCE, LEISURE)
TIMES MOVIES	@times: Movies & Video (TIMES FILM, VIDEO)
TIMES MUSIC	@times: Music & Dance
TIMES REGION	@times: In The Region
TIMES SPORTS	@times: Sports & Fitness
TIMES STORIES	@times: Top Stories
TIMES THEATER	@times: Theater
TNR	The New Republic Magazine (NEWREPUBLIC, THE NEW REPUBLIC)
USA	USA Weekend (USA WEEKEND)
WINDOWS MAG	Windows Magazine (WINMAG, WINDOWS MAGAZINE)
WIRED	Wired Magazine (WIRED MAGAZINE)
WOMANS DAY	Woman's Day (WD, WOMAN, WOMAN'S DAY, RECIPES, SEWING, CRAFTS, TIES)
WD KITCHEN	Woman's Day Kitchen
WOOD	American Woodworker (WOODWORKER, AMERICAN WOOD WORKER, WOODWORKING)
WORTH	Worth Magazine (WORTH MAGAZINE, WORTH ONLINE, WORTH PORTFOLIO)
WWIR	Washington Week In Review
WWN	Weekly World News (BATBOY, ELVIS, WEEKLY WORLD NEWS)
YC	Your Church Magazine (YOUR CHURCH)

Part
X

App
E

People Connection

Keyword	Area
PEOPLE	People Connection department (CHAT, TALK, PC, PEOPLE CONNECTION)
@AOL LIVE	AOL Live auditorium
@GLOBE	The Globe auditorium
@BOWL	The Bowl auditorium
@COLISEUM	The Coliseum auditorium
@CYBER RAP	Cyber Rap auditorium
@HOLLYWOOD LIVE	Hollywood Live auditorium
@MAINSTAGE	Main Stage auditorium
@ODEON	The Odeon auditorium
@ROTUNDA	The Rotunda auditorium
ADVICE	Advice & Tips (TIPS, ASK THE DOCTOR, ASK THE DR, ASK THE LAWYER, CRYSTAL BALL, TAROT, ASK ANITA, ASK ANDY)
DALAI LAMA	Dalai Lama Conference (DL)
CARTOONS	Cartoon collection (YOURTOONS)
CS	Center Stage (AUDITORIUM, CENTER STAGE, COLISEUM, GLOBE, ODEON, PCAUD, SHOWS)
COMIC STRIP	Comic Strip Centennial (POSTAL STAMPS)
COMPUTOON	CompuToon area
DILBERT	Dilbert Cartoon area (DILBERT COMICS, DILBOARD)
EVENTS	Today's Events in the Center Stage (EVENT, YUBBA)
GALLERY	Portrait Gallery
GUIDEPAGER	Guide Pager (GUIDEPAGE)
KEEFE	Mike Keefe Cartoons (EDITORIAL CARTOONS)
LAPUB	LaPub
OLT	OnLine Tonight (ONLINE TONIGHT)
PARLOR	Games Parlor (GAMES PARLOR, GAMEROOMS)
PCSTUDIO	PC Studio
QUE	The Quantum Que and Graffiti community message boards

Keyword	Area
ROMANCE	Romance Connection message boards (DATING)
SPOTLIGHT	Center Stage Spotlight
TEEN(S)	Teen Scene message boards (TEEN SCENE)
TRANSCRIPTS	Center Stage Transcripts (TRANSCRIPT)
TRIVIA	Trivia Forum

Entertainment

Keyword	Area
ENTERTAINMENT	Entertainment department (GAMES, GOSSIP, LOVE, PLAY, REC CENTER, RECREATION, RECREATION CENTER)
60	60-Second Novelist (60 SECONDS, 60 SECOND NOVELIST, DAN HURLEY, HURLEY, NOVEL, NOVELIST, SIXTY)
777-FILM	MovieLink (MOVIELINK, SHOW TIMES)
90210	90210 Wednesdays (90210 WEDNESDAYS, BEVERLY HILLS, BEVERLY HILLS 90210, WEDNESDAYS)
99.1	WHFS 99.1 FM (HFS, MODERN ROCK, WHFS)
ABC	ABC Online
ABC BETA	ABC Online: Beta area
ABC CLASS	ABC Classroom (ABC CLASSROOM, SMART WATCHING)
ABC DAYTIME	ABC Daytime/Soapline (ABC SOAPS, SOAPLINE, AMC, ONE LIFE TO LIVE, LOVING, LOV, GH, OLTL, ALL MY CHILDREN, GENERAL HOSPITAL)
ABC GMA	ABC Good Morning America (GMA, GOOD MORNING AMERICA, JOEL SIEGEL)
ABC KIDZINE	ABC KIDZINE
ABC NEWS	ABC News-On-Demand (20/20, AMERICAN AGENDA, BRINKLEY, DAYONE, NIGHTLINE, PERSON OF THE WEEK, PETER JENNINGS, YOUR CHOICE)
ABC PRIMETIME	ABC Prime Time (ABC ENTERTAINMENT)
ABC RADIO	ABC Radio (PAULHARVEY)
ABC SPORTS	ABC Sports

Part

X

App

E

continues

Entertainment Continued	
Keyword	**Area**
ABC STATIONS	ABC Stations
ABC VIDEO	ABC Online: Video Store
ABM	Adventures by Mail (ADVENTURES BY MAIL, QUEST, MONSTERISLAND)
ACADEMY AWARDS	Academy Awards (OSCAR, OSCARS)
ADD	AD&D Neverwinter Nights (AD&D, NWN, NEVERWINTER, OADD, UPDATE ADD)
AEN	American Entertainment Network
AOOL	America Out Of Line (AMERICA OUT OF LINE)
AT	Antagonistic Trivia (ANTAG, ANTAGONIST, ANTAGONISTS, ANTAGONIST TRIVIA, ANTAGONISTIC TRIVIA)
ATLANTIC	The Atlantic Monthly Online (ATLANTIC MONTHLY, ATLANTIC ONLINE, IDEAS)
BABYLON	Babylon 5 (BABYLON 5)
BEATLES	The ABC Rock & Road Beatles Anthology
BMG	BMG Distribution
BOXER	Boxer*Jam Gameshows (BOXER JAM, BOXER*JAM, STRIKE-A-MATCH)
BROKEN ARROW	Broken Arrow
BULLS AND BEARS	Bulls and Bears Game
CARTOONNETWORK	Cartoon Network (TOONS)
CARTOONS	Cartoon collection (YOUR TOONS)
CASINO	RabbitJack's Casino (RABBITJACKS CASINO, RABBITJACK'S CASINO)
CASTING	The Casting Forum (CASTING FORUM)
CC	Comedy Central (COMEDY, COMEDY CENTRAL, HUMOR)
COMEDY PUB	The Comedy Pub (LOL, PUB)
DINO	Comedy Pub's Dino Tripodis
COMPUTOON	CompuToon area
CONTESTS	AOL Contest area (CONTEST, CONTEST AREA, WINNER)
COURT TV	Court TV's Law Center (COURTROOM TELEVISION, LAW, LAW CENTER, OJ)

Keyword	Area
CPOV	CinemaPOV (CINEMAPOV)
CRITIC(S)	Critic's Choice (CRITICS CHOICE)
CSPAN	C-SPAN
CYBERJUSTICE	CyberJustice
COURTS	CyberJustice's Courts of Karmic Justice
DOROTHY	CyberJustice's Oasis of Xaiz
GAZETTE	CyberJustice's Letters to The Gazette's Editor
JUDGMENT	CyberJustice's Record Your Judgment
KENNEHORA	CyberJustice's Kennehora Junction (JUNCTION, KENNEHORA JUNCTION)
KIVETCH	CyberJustice's Bridge Over The River Kivetch
LOCALS	CyberJustice's Meet The Locals
MU	CyberJustice: Misst-U & The 7 Pillars of Wisdom (MISST-U)
POLLS	CyberJustice's Arch of Public Opinion Polls
QUIKJUSTICE	CyberJustice's Select Your Just Desserts
TIMECAPSULE	CyberJustice's Istorian's Time Capsule
WORRY	CyberJustice's Worry Free Zone
DEAD	Grateful Dead Forum (THE DEAD, GRATEFUL DEAD)
DILBERT	Dilbert Cartoon area (DILBERT COMICS, DILBOARD)
DISNEYADVENTURES	Disney Adventures Magazine (DISNEY MAGAZINE)
E!	E! Entertainment Television
EW	Entertainment Weekly (ENTERTAINMENT WEEKLY)
EXTRA EXTRA:	Television's Entertainment Show (ACE VENTURA)
FAVE FLICKS	Favorite Flicks! (FAVORITE FLICKS)
FED	Federation (FEDERATION)
FERNDALE	Ferndale
FFGF	Free-Form Gaming Forum (RDI)
FILM STUDIOS	MovieVisions (MOVIEVISIONS)
FILMBALL	Follywood Games (FOLLYWOOD GAMES, MOVIESMASH)
FOG	Fellowship of Online Gamers/RPGA Network (RPGA, RPGA NETWORK, FELLOWSHIP)

Part

X

App

E

continues

Entertainment Continued	
Keyword	**Area**
FOLLYWOOD	Follywood
FRASIER	Fraiser Tuesdays (FRAISER TUESDAYS)
FRIDAY	ABC Online: Friday@4ET (FRIDAY @ 4, FRIDAY @ 4ET, FRIDAY AT 4)
GAME	The Games Channel (GAMES & ENTERTAINMENT, GAMES CHANNEL)
GAME BASE	Game Base
GAME DESIGN	Game Designers Forum (GAMEDESIGNER, GAMEDESIGNERS)
GAMEPRO	GamePro Online
GAME SITES	WWW Game Sites (GS)
GAMEWIZ	Dr. Gamewiz Online (DR GAMEWIZ, GAMEWIZ INC)
GAYMES	Gay & Lesbian Community Forum Games (GAYME, GAYMELAND)
GCS	Gaming Company Support
GEMSTONE	GemStone III (GEM BETA, GEMSTONE III)
GERALDO	The Geraldo Show (GERALDO SHOW)
GIX	Gaming Information Exchange
GRANDSTAND	The Grandstand (THEGRANDSTAND)
GSARTS	The Grandstand's Martial Arts (The Dojo)
GSAUTO	The Grandstand's Motor Sports (In The Pits)
ICRS	The Grandstand's Simulation Auto Racing (SIMULATIONAUTO)
GSBASEBALL	The Grandstand's Baseball (Dugout)
GBL	The Grandstand's Simulation Baseball (SIMULATIONBASEBALL)
FANTASYBASEBALL	The Grandstand's Fantasy Baseball
GSBASKETBALL	The Grandstand's Basketball (Off the Glass)
FANTASYBASKETBALL	The Grandstand's Fantasy Basketball
SIMULATION BASKETBALL	The Grandstand's Simulation Basketball
GSDL	The Grandstand's Simulation Basketball

Keyword	Area
GSBOXING	The Grandstand's Boxing (Squared Circle)
GSCOLLECTING	The Grandstand's Collecting (Sports Cards)
GSFOOTBALL	The Grandstand's Football (50 Yard Line)
FANTASYFOOTBALL	The Grandstand's Fantasy Football
SIMULATION-FOOTBALL	The Grandstand's Simulation Football
GSFL	The Grandstand's Simulation Football
GSGOLF	The Grandstand's Golf (On The Green)
GGL	The Grandstand's Simulation Golf (SIMULATIONGOLF)
GSHOCKEY	The Grandstand's Hockey (Blue Line)
FANTASYHOCKEY	The Grandstand's Fantasy Hockey
GSHL	The Grandstand's Simulation Hockey (SIMULATIONHOCKEY)
GSHORSE	The Grandstand's Horse Sports (Post Time) (HORCE RACING, HORSE SPORTS)
GSOTHER	The Grandstand's Other Sports (Whole 9 Yards) (BOWLING, ROLLERSKATING, SWIMMING)
GSSIDELINE	The Grandstand's Sideline
GSSOCCER	The Grandstand's Soccer (The Kop)
GSSOFTWARE	The Grandstand's Sports Software Headquarters
GSSPORTSMART	The Grandstand's Sports Products (Sportsmart)
GSWINTER	The Grandstand's Winter Sports (The Chalet)
GSWRESTLING	The Grandstand's Wrestling (Squared Circle)
GWA	The Grandstand's Simulation Wrestling (SIMULATIONWRESTLING)
FANTASYLEAGUE(S)	The Grandstand's Fantasy & Simulation Leagues (SIMULATIONLEAGUES)
SPORTSBOARDS	The Grandstand's Sports Boards
SPORTSCHAT	The Grandstand's Chat Rooms (SPORTSROOMS)
SPORTSLIBRARIES	The Grandstand's Libraries
HOL PRO	Hollywood Pro (HOLLYWOOD PRO)
HOLLYWOOD	Hollywood Online (HOLLYWOOD ONLINE)
HOROSCOPE(S)	Horoscopes

Part

X

App

E

continues

Entertainment Continued	
Keyword	**Area**
HOT ENTER-TAINMENT	What's Hot in Entertainment
IG	Intelligent Gamer Online (IG ONLINE, INTELLIGENT GAMER)
IMPROV	The IMPROVisation Online (IMPROVISATION)
JAZZFEST	House of Blues Live from Jazzfest (BLUES, HOB, HOUSE OF BLUES)
KEEFE	Mike Keefe Cartoons (EDITORIAL CARTOONS)
KIDSNET	KIDSNET Forum (EDTV)
KRANK	MTV Online: Krank
LAPUB	LaPub
LAST CALL	Last Call Talk Show (BRANDON TARTIKOFF, MCA, TARTIKOFF)
LIA	Lost in America (LOST, LOST IN AMERICA)
MASTERWORD	MasterWord (MW, MWORD, WORD LIBRARY)
MCLAUGHLIN	The McLaughlin Group (GROUP, MCL, MCLAUGHLIN GROUP)
MELROSE	Melrose Mondays (MELROSE MONDAYS, MELROSE PLACE)
MODUS	Modus Operandi (MODUS OPERANDI)
MOVIE(S)	Movies menu (CINEMA, MOVIEREVIEWS)
MOVIE FORUMS	Movie Forums area
MUSIC MEDIA	Music Media
MUSIC NEWS	MTV Online: News
MUSIC PROMO	MusicSpace Events (SCREAM)
MUSIC TALK	MusicSpace Communications
MUSIC WEB	MusicSpace WEB TopStops
MUSICSPACE	MusicSpace
MTV	MTV Online
MTV NEWS	MTV News
MURDER	Murder Mysteries Online (CYBERSLEUTH, IFORSOOTH, MMO, MURDER MYSTERY, MURDER MYSTERIES)

Keyword	Area
MYSTERIES	Mysteries from the Yard (HOLMES, MYSTERIES FROM THE YARD, SHERLOCK, SHERLOCK HOLMES)
NBC	NBC... NOT! (NOT NBC)
NEW MOVIES	New Release/Movies area (NEW RELEASES)
NEWSGRIEF	NewsGrief
NEWSLETTER	Games & Entertainment Newsletter
NICK AT NITE	Nick at Nite (NAN, NICK @ NITE)
NINTENDO	Nintendo Power Source (NOA, NINTENDO POWER SOURCE)
NTN	NTN Trivia (COUNTDOWN, NTN TRIVIA)
NTN PLAYBOOK	NTN Playbook
OGF	Online Gaming Forums (GAMING, ONLINE GAMING)
OLD FAVES	Old Favorite Movies
OMNI	OMNI Magazine Online (OMNI MAGAZINE)
ON COMPUTERS	On Computers Radio
OPRAH	Get Movin' with Oprah
PBM	Play-By-Mail Gaming Forum (PLAY-BY-MAIL)
PBM CLUBS	Play-By-Mail Clubs & Messaging
PLAYBILL	Playbill Online (BROADWAY)
REVIEW DB	Movie Review Database (CINEMAN, CINEMAN SYNDICATE, FILM REVIEW DATABASE, FILM REVIEW DB, FILM REVIEWS DATABASE, MOVIE REVIEW DATABASE, MOVIE REVIEW DB, MOVIE REVIEWS DATABASE, MRD)
RICKI LAKE	The Ricki Lake Show
ROCKNET	RockNet (ROCKLINK)
ROCK & ROAD	ABC Online: Rock & Road (R&R, RR)
ROCK & ROLL	Rock and Roll Hall of Fame (ROCK AND ROLL, ROCK N ROLL)
ROCKLINE	Rockline Online (CRAZY HORSE, HITS)
ROGUE	Motley Fool's Rogue
RPG	Role-Playing Forum (ROLEPLAYING)
SCIFICHANNEL	The Sci-Fi Channel

Part

X

App

E

continues

Entertainment Continued	
Keyword	**Area**
SCORPIA	Scorpia's Lair (SCORPIA'S LAIR, SCORPIAS LAIR)
SEX	Entertainment (just try it)
SHOWBIZ INFO	Showbiz News & Info (SHOWBIZ NEWS)
SIGHTINGS	Sightings Online
SIM(S)	Simming Forum (SIMMING)
SOD	Soap Opera Digest (DIVA, DIVA LA DISH, SOAP OPERA, SOAP DIGEST)
SOLIII	Sol III Play-by-Email Game
SOUNDBITES	Soundbites Online (SATIRE)
SPACE A&B	Space: Above & Beyond (SPACE ABOVE & BEYOND)
SPIN	Spin Online (SPIN ONLINE)
STARFLEET	Starfleet Online (ACADEMY)
STAR WARS	Star Wars Sim Forum (STAR WARS SIM)
STRATEGY	Strategy & Wargaming Forum (CHESS)
STUDIO	MusicSpace Studio
TAXI TAXI	Independent Artist & Repertoire Co.
TELEVISION	Soap Opera Summaries
THE MOVIES	@the.movies (@ THE MOVIES)
TRIVIA	Trivia Forum
TSR	TSR Online
TV	Television
TV GOSSIP	TV Gossip
TV NETWORKS	TV Networks area
TV VIEWERS	TV Viewers Forum
TV SHOWS	TV Shows
TMS	TMS TV Source (TV SOURCE, TV GUIDE, TV LISTINGS, LISTINGS)
VGAP	VGA Planets (VGA PLANETS)
VH1	VH1 Online

Keyword	Area
VIDEOS	Home Video (HOME VIDEO)
VIDEO GAME(S)	Video Games area (GENESIS, NINTENDO, SEGA, VGS)
VIRGIN	Virgin's Virtual Valley (VALLEY, VIRTUAL VALLEY)
WARNER	Warner/Reprise Records Online (WARNER MUSIC, REPRISE)
WB	The WB Network (THE WB NETWORK, FROG, MICHIGAN J FROG, WBNET)
WEB ENTERTAINMENT	WEBentertainment
WIZARD	Wizard World (IQ, COMICS, WIZARD WORLD)
WWN	Weekly World News (WEEKLY WORLD NEWS)
XFILES	X Files Fan Club Forum (XFILES CLUB)
XFILES SIM	X Files Simming Forum
YOYO	Yoyodyne Entertainment (YOYODYNE)

Education

Keyword	Area
EDUCATION	Education department (LEARN, LEARNING & REFERENCE, LEARNING AND REFERENCE, LEARNING CENTER, LEARNING)
AAC	Academic Assistance Center (HOMEWORK, RESEARCH, TUTORING)
ACCESS EXCELLENCE	Access Excellence (EXCELLENCE)
ACOT	Apple Classrooms of Tomorrow
ACT	Kaplan Online/SAT, ACT, College (SAT)
ADOPTION	Adoption Forum
AFT	American Federation of Teachers
ARTS	Afterwards Coffeehouse (AFTERWARDS, ARTS, OPERA, POETRY)
ASCD	Assoc. for Supervisor & Curriculum Development (CURRICULUM, EDTECH)
BIOLOGY	Simon & Schuster Online: Biology Dept.
BOOKNOTES	Barrons Booknotes (BARRONS)

continues

Education Continued	
Keyword	**Area**
BULL MOOSE	Bull Moose Tavern
BUSINESS SCHOOL	Kaplan Online/GMAT, Business School (GMAT)
CAMPUS	Online Campus (CLASSES, COURSES, IES, INTERACTIVE ED, INTERACTIVE EDUCATION)
CAREER	Career Center (CAREERS)
CB	College Board (COLLEGE, COLLEGE BOARD)
CCE	Columbia Encyclopedia (COLUMBIA)
CERTIFICATION	Teach For America
CHARTER	Charter Schools Forum (CHARTER SCHOOL(S))
CHICO	California State University (CSUC)
CNN	CNN Newsroom Online (CNN NEWSROOM, CNN GUIDES, CHANNEL C, DEMOCRACY, N GUIDES)
CHILD SAFETY	Child Safety Brochure
COMPUTER TERMS	Dictionary of Computer Terms
CONTACTS	Employer Contacts
CORCORAN	Corcoran School of Art
CRIMINAL JUSTICE	Simon & Schuster Online: Criminal Justice Dept.
CSPAN	C-SPAN Online (CSPANONLINE)
CSPAN CLASS	C-SPAN Educational Services (CSPAN BUS, CSPANS CLASSROOM, CSPAN SCHOOLS)
DISCOVERY	The Discovery Channel (DSC)
DISCOVERY ED	The Discovery Channel Education Area (DSC-ED, DSCED)
DISNEY ADVENTURES	Disney Adventures Magazine (DISNEY MAGAZINE)
EDA	Education Advisory Council Online (ED ADVISORY)
ENCYCLOPEDIA	Encyclopedia (COMPTONS)
COMPTONS CUSTOMER SUPPORT	Compton's Customer Support
COMPTONS ENCYCLOPEDIA	Compton's Living Encyclopedia
COMPTONS SOFTWARE	Compton's Software Library

Keyword	Area
EDUCATION CONNECTION	Compton's Education Connection
STUDY BREAK	Compton's Study Break
ENGLISH	Simon & Schuster Online: English Dept.
ERIC	AskERIC (ASKERIC, ACCESSERIC)
ESH	Electronic Schoolhouse (SCHOOLHOUSE)
EUN	Electronic University Network (UNIVERSITY, UNIVERSITIES)
EXAM PREP	Exam Prep Center
GD	Facts on File: Great Dates in History (GREAT DATES)
GEOGRAPHY	Simon & Schuster Online: Geography Dept.
GIFTED	Giftedness Forum (MENSA)
GRADUATE SCHOOL	Kaplan Online/GRE, Graduate School (GRE)
GWU	George Washington University
HBSPUB	Harvard Business School Publishing
HELP WANTED	Search Help Wanted USA
HEM	Home Education Magazine
HH KIDS	Homework Help
HOMER	Homer's Page at The Odyssey Project (HOMER'S PAGE)
HOMESCHOOL	Home Schooling (HOMESCHOOLING)
HUMAN SEXUALITY	Simon & Schuster Online: Human Sexuality Dept.
ICS	International Correspondence Schools
IMPACTII	IMPACT II: The Teachers Network
INFORMED PARENT	Princeton Review Informed Parent (PARENT ADVICE, PARENTAL GUIDANCE)
INTERNATIONAL CAFE	International Cafe (LANGUAGE, LANGUAGES)
JOBS	Job Listings Database
KAPLAN	Kaplan Online (GREENBERG, TEST PREP)
KIDSNET	KIDSNET
L&C STORE	Learning & Culture Store
LABNET	TERC LabNetwork

Part

X

App

E

continues

Education   Continued

Keyword	Area
LAWSCHOOL	Kaplan Online/LSAT, Law School (LSAT)
LOC	Library of Congress Online (LIBRARY, SOVIET, SOVIET ARCHIVES, SOV ARC, VATICAN, DEAD SEA)
MATHEMATICS	Simon & Schuster Online: Mathematics Dept.
MEDICAL SCHOOL	Kaplan Online/MCAT, Medical School (MCAT)
MONTESSORI	Montessori Schools (MONTESSORI SCHOOLS)
MULTIMEDIA	The Multimedia Exchange
NAPC	Employment Agency Database
NCTE	Nat'l Council of Teachers of English (ENGLISH, NCTENET)
NEA	NEA Online (NEAONLINE)
NEA PUBLIC	Public NEA Online
NGS	National Geographic Online (GEOGRAPHIC, NATIONAL GEOGRAPHIC)
NMAA	National Museum of American Art (AMERICAN ART)
NMAH	National Museum of American History (AMERICAN HISTORY)
NOLO	Nolo Press' Self-Help Law Center (NOLO PRESS, LAWYER, SELF-HELP)
NPR	National Public Radio Outreach (TOTN, PUBLIC RADIO)
NSDC	National Staff Development Council
NURSING	Kaplan Online/NCLEX, Nursing School (NCLEX)
ODYSSEY	The Odyssey Project (ODYSSEY PROJECT)
PHYS ED	Simon & Schuster Online: Health, Phys. Ed. & Rec. Dept.
PHS	Practical Homeschooling
PIN	Parents' Information Network (PARENT)
POLITICAL SCIENCE	Simon & Schuster Online: Political Science Dept.
PR	Princeton Review/Student Access Online (PRINCETON REVIEW, STUDENT, STUDENT ACCESS)
PSYCHOLOGY	Simon & Schuster Online: Psychology Dept.
READ	Adult Literacy Forum (LITERACY)
READING ROOM	The Reading Room

Keyword	Area
REFERENCE	Reference Desk department (REFERENCE DESK)
REGISTER	Online Campus Registration Center (REGISTRATION, SIGNUP)
SCHOLARS	Scholars' Hall (SCHOLAR'S HALL, SCHOLARS' HALL, SCHOLARS HALL)
SCHOLASTIC	Scholastic Network/Scholastic Forum
SCOUTS	Scouting Forum (SCOUTING)
SIMON	Simon & Schuster College Online (A&B, ALLYN & BACON, COLLEGE ONLINE, KIRSHNER, PH, PRENTICE HALL, S&S, SIMON & SCHUSTER)
SMITHSONIAN	Smithsonian Online (MUSEUM(S), SI)
SN LIBRARIES	Scholastic Libraries
SN SPACE	Exploring the Star System (SN EXPERIMENTS, SN SCIENCE, SN WEATHER)
SOCIAL WORK	Simon & Schuster Online: Social Work Dept.
SOCIOLOGY	Simon & Schuster Online: Sociology Dept.
SRO	Saturday Review Online (SAT REVIEW, SATURDAY REVIEW, LITERATURE, READING, SOCIETY, THEATER, THEATRE)
STUDY	Study Skills Service (STUDYSKILLS)
TAL	Turner Adventure Learning
TALENT	Talent Bank
TEACHER PAGER	Teacher Pager
TEACHERS' LOUNGE	Teachers' Lounge (TEACHER'S LOUNGE, TEACHERS LOUNGE)
THE LAB	The Lab
TIN	Teachers' Information Network (TEACHER(S))
TLC	The Learning Channel
TNEWS	Teachers' Newsstand
TNPC	The National Parenting Center (NPC, NATIONAL PARENTING)
TOMORROW	Tomorrow's Morning (TOMORROWS MORNING, MORNING)
TRAINING	Career Development Training
TTALK	Teachers' Forum

Part
X
App
E

continues

Education   Continued

Keyword	Area
UCAL	University of California Extension (CMIL, UCX)
WPA	Facts on File: World Political Almanac (WORLD POL ALMANAC)

Reference Desk

Keyword	Area
REFERENCE	Reference Desk department (REFERENCE DESK)
BARTLETTS	Bartlett's Familiar Quotations (BARTLETT)
COMPUTER TERMS	Dictionary of Computer Terms
DICTIONARY	Merriam-Webster Dictionary Search
ENCYCLOPEDIA	Encyclopedia (COMPTONS)
ERIC	AskERIC (ASKERIC, ACCESSERIC)
FILESEARCH	Search database of files (QUICKFIND, QUICKFINDER)
GOPHER	Internet Gopher & WAIS (WAIS, VERONICA)
GROLIER'S	Grolier's Encyclopedia (GROLIER, GROLIERS, MME, GMME)
MEMBERS	Member Directory (DIRECTORY, MEMBER DIRECTORY)
MERRIAM	Merriam-Webster Dictionary (MERRIAM-WEBSTER, WEBSTER)
NEWSSEARCH	Search News Articles (SEARCHNEWS, NEWSWATCH)
PHONE DIRECTORY	Phone Directories (PHONE BOOK, TELEPHONE, TELEPHONE NUMBERS)
QUES DICTIONARY	Computer and Internet Dictionary
REFERENCE HELP	Reference Desk Help area
SERVICES	Directory of Services (DIROFSVCS, DIROFSERVICES, DIRECTORY OF SERVICES, SERVICESDIRECTORY, DONTMISS, NOWPLAYING)
TEACHER PAGER	Teacher Pager
ZIP CODE	Zip Code Directory (ZIP CODES, ZIP CODE DIRECTORY)

Internet Connection

Keyword	Area
INTERNET	Internet Connection department (INTERNET CONNECTION, INTERNET CENTER)
7 WONDERS	Seven Wonders of the Web (SEVEN WONDERS)
ANSWERMAN	Answer Man
AM GLOSSARY	AnswerMan Glossary
COMP SITES	Computing Internet Sites [WAOL 2.5 and MAOL 2.6 only] (COMPUTING SITES)
CORNER	Pro's Corner (EARL'S GARAGE, EARLS GARAGE, GARAGE, NET EXPERT, PRO'S CORNER, PROS CORNER, PRO'S, PROS)
CYBERSMITH	CyberSmith (CSMITH, CYBERCAFE, NET HEAD JED, NET HEAD RED, YBERSMITH)
EFF	Electronic Frontier Foundation
FTP	Internet FTP
GNN	GNN Best of the Net
GOPHER	Internet Gopher & WAIS (WAIS, VERONICA)
HOME PAGE	Personal WWW Publishing area (PP) [WAOL 2.5 only]
INTERNET CHAT	Internet Chat [WAOL 2.5 only]
INTERNET GRAPHICS	Internet Graphic Sites [WAOL 2.5 and MAOL 2.6 only]
INTERNET MAGAZINES	Magazines on the Internet [WAOL 2.5 and MAOL 2.6 only]
INTERNET MAGS	Magazines on the Internet [WAOL 2.5 and MAOL 2.6 only]
INTERNET NEWS	Internet News [WAOL 2.5 only]
MAIL GATEWAY	Mail Gateway
MAILING LISTS	Internet Mailing Lists (LISTSERV)
MCM	Mac Communications Forum (MTC, MAC COMMUNICATION(S), COMMUNICATIONS, MACTELECOM(M), NETWORKING, NETWORKING FORUM, TELECOM, TELECOMFORUM, TELECOMMUNICATIONS)
MY PLACE	My Place (for FTP sites)
NEWSGROUP(S)	Internet Usenet Newsgroup area (KEEPER, USENET)
NET CHAT	Internet Chat [WAOL 2.5 only]

continues

Internet Connection Continued

Keyword	Area
NET NEWS	Internet News [WAOL 2.5 only]
NET SOFTWARE	Internet Software
NET SUGGESTIONS	Internet Suggestions
PTC	PC Telecom/Networking Forum (PCM, PCTELECOM, PC TELECOM FORUM, COMMUNICATIONS, NETWORKING, NETWORKING FORUM, TELECOM, TELECOM FORUM, TELECOMMUNICATIONS)
ROAD TRIP	Road Trip Area (ROAD TRIPS, RT) News [WAOL 2.5 only]
SCOOP	Newsgroup Scoop
TOP COMP SITES	Top Computing Internet Sites [WAOL 2.5 and MAOL 2.6 only] (TOP COMPUTING SITES)
TOP COMPANY SITES	Companies on the Internet [WAOL 2.5 and MAOL 2.6 only]
WINSOCK	Winsock Central (TELNET) News [WAOL 2.5 only]
WIRED	Wired Magazine (WIREDMAGAZINE)
WEB	World Wide Web (WEBCRAWLER, WORLD WIDE WEB, WWW)
WEB DINER	The Web Diner (DINER, DINER CREW, HTML HELP, WEB BIZ, WEBD, WEB HELP, WEBSITE)
WEB MAKEOVER	Web Makeover
WEB PAGE	Web Page Toolkit (HTML, TOOLKIT, WEB PAGE TOOLKIT)
WEB REVIEW	Web Review [WAOL only]
WEBSOURCE	Websource

Sports

Keyword	Area
SPORTS	Sports department (SPORTSLINK, BASEBALL, BASKETBALL, BOXING, GOLF, HOCKEY, TENNIS)
ABC FOOTBALL	ABC Sports College Football
ABC SPORTS	ABC Sports
ABC SPORTS STORE	ABC Sports Store

Area	Keyword
ABC TRACK	ABC Track (EQUIBASE, WINNER'S CIRCLE)
ABC TRIPLECROWN	ABC Triple Crown (TRIPLE CROWN)
ALL STAR	MLB All-Star Ballot
AMERICA'S CUP	The America's Cup (AMERICAS CUP)
AOL SPORTS LIVE	AOL Sports Live (LIVE SPORTS, SPORTS EVENTS, SPORTS LIVE)
AUTO RACING	AOL Auto Racing (NASCAR)
BK	Burger King College Football (BURGER KING)
BOWL GAMES	NCAA Football Bowl Info (BOWLS)
CAPS	Washington Capitals (CAPITALS)
DTSPORTS	DataTimes Sports Reports (DATATIMS, DATATIMES, DATATIMESSPORTS)
DATATIMESBASEBALL	DataTimes: Baseball (DTBASEBALL, DTMLB)
DATATIMESFOOTBALL	DataTimes: Football (DATATIMESNFL, DTFOOBALL, DTNFL)
DATATIMESHOCKEY	DataTimes: Hockey (DATATIMESNHL, DTHOCKEY, DTNHL)
DATATIMESNBA	DataTimes: Basketball (DTBASKETBALL, DTNBA)
DTCOLLEGE	DataTimes: College Sports
DTGOLF	DataTimes: Golf
DTRACING	DataTimes: Racing
EDELSTEIN	Fred Edelstein's Pro Football Insider
EXTREME FANS	Extreme Fans (FANS)
HOOPS BOARDS	Extreme Fans: Message Boards
FOOTBALL	AOL Football (COLLEGE FOOTBALL)
FRENCH OPEN	French Open [May disappear without notice]
GOLF DATA	GolfCentral
GRANDSTAND	The Grandstand (THE GRANDSTAND)
GS ARTS	The Grandstand's Martial Arts (The Dojo) (KARATE, MARTIAL ARTS)
GS AUTO	The Grandstand's Motor Sports (In The Pits)
ICRS	The Grandstand's Simulation Auto Racing (SIMULATION AUTO)

continues

Sports Continued	
Keyword	**Area**
GS BASEBALL	The Grandstand's Baseball (Dugout)
GBL	The Grandstand's Simulation Baseball (SIMULATION BASEBALL)
FANTASY BASEBALL	The Grandstand's Fantasy Baseball
GS BASKETBALL	The Grandstand's Basketball (Off the Glass)
FANTASY BASKETBALL	The Grandstand's Fantasy Basketball
SIMULATION BASKETBALL	The Grandstand's Simulation Basketball
GS DL	The Grandstand's Simulation Basketball
GS BOXING	The Grandstand's Boxing (Squared Circle)
GS COLLECTING	The Grandstand's Collecting (Sports Cards)
GS FOOTBALL	The Grandstand's Football (50 Yard Line)
FANTASY FOOTBALL	The Grandstand's Fantasy Football
SIMULATION FOOTBALL	The Grandstand's Simulation Football (ASFL, CNFA, GCFL, GPFL, GMFL, GSFL, GUFL, NWFL, OFL, RSFL)
GSFL	The Grandstand's Simulation Football
GS GOLF	The Grandstand's Golf (On The Green)
GGL	The Grandstand's Simulation Golf (ALPT, GGL, MAC ALPT)
GS HOCKEY	The Grandstand's Hockey (Blue Line)
FANTASY HOCKEY	The Grandstand's Fantasy Hockey
GSHL	The Grandstand's Simulation Hockey (SIMULATION HOCKEY)
GS HORSE	The Grandstand's Horse Sports (Post Time) (HORCE RACING, HORSE SPORTS)
GS OTHER	The Grandstand's Other Sports (Whole 9 Yards) (BOWLING, ROLLERSKATING, SWIMMING)
GS SIDELINE	The Grandstand's Sideline
GS SOCCER	The Grandstand's Soccer (The Kop)
GS SOFTWARE	The Grandstand's Sports Software Headquarters
GS SPORTSMART	The Grandstand's Sports Products (Sportsmart)

Keyword	Area
GS TRIVIA	The Grandstand's Sports Trivia (GS SPORTS TRIVIA, GRANDSTAND TRIVIA)
GS WINTER	The Grandstand's Winter Sports (The Chalet)
GS WRESTLING	The Grandstand's Wrestling (Squared Circle)
GWA	The Grandstand's Simulation Wrestling (SIMULATION WRESTLING)
FANTASYLEAGUE(S)	The Grandstand's Fantasy & Simulation Leagues (SIMULATIONLEAGUES)
SPORTS BOARDS	The Grandstand's Sports Boards
SPORTS CHAT	The Grandstand's Chat Rooms (SPORTS ROOMS)
SPORTS LIBRARIES	The Grandstand's Libraries
HOCKEY TRIVIA	NTN Hockey Trivia (NTN HOCKEY TRIVIA)
HOOPS	NCAA Hoops (NCAA)
HOOPS TRIVIA NTN	Basketball Trivia (BASKETBALL TRIVIA, NTN BASKETBALL TRIVIA, NTN HOOPS TRIVIA)
HORSE	The Horse Forum (HORSES)
IDITAROD	Iditarod Trail Sled Dog Race
IGOLF	iGolf
IGOLF HISTORY	iGolf History
INDY	The 80th Indianapolis 500 (INDY 500)
ISKI	iSKI
JORDAN	Air Jordan Area (AIRJORDAN, MJ)
KOB	King of the Beach Invitational (KING OF THE BEACH, VOLLEYBALL)
LAX	The Lacrosse Forum (LACROSSE)
MATT	Matt Williams' Hot Corner (MATT WILLIAMS)
MOTORSPORT	Motorsport '96 Online (MOTORSPORTS)
NBA DRAFT	1996 NBA Draft
NCAA	NCAA Hoops
NABER	John Naber (JOHN NABER)
NFL DRAFT	NFL Draft

Part

X

App

E

continues

Sports Continued	
Keyword	**Area**
NHL	The Stanley Cup Online (STANLEY CUP)
PAT O	The Pat O'Brien Report (PAT O'BRIEN, PAT OBRIEN)
PLAYWELL	U.S. Golf Society Online
PRO BOWL	1996 Pro Bowl
REV	ABC Sports' REV Speedway (REV SPEEDWAY, SPEEDWAY)
ROGER CLEMENS	Roger Clemens' Playoff Baseball Journal
OLYMPICS	Olympic Festival Online (CoffeeMug)
OLYMPIC	Olympic Festival Online
OLYMPIC FESTIVAL	Olympic Festival Online
OLYMPIC SHOP	The Olympic Shop
OLYMPIC STORE	The Olympic Shop
QB1	Super Bowl Interactive
SAILING	Sailing Forum
SEA-DOO	Sea-Doo Online
SOCCER	AOL Soccer (FUTBOL)
SPORTSARCHIVE	AOL Sports Archive
SPORTSNEWS	Sport News area
STATS	Pro Sports Center (STATS INC, STATS, INC, STATS, INC., STATS INC.)
STATS HOOPS	Pro Basketball Center (STATS BASKETBALL)
SUPER BOWL	Super Bowl XXX Online
SURFLINK	SurfLink (SURF, SURFBOARD, SURFER, SURFERS, SURFING)
SURF SHACK	The Surf Shack
TA FOOTRACE	Trans America Footrace
TYSON	Tyson vs. McNeely
USFSA	United States Figure Skating Association
WIMBLEDON	Wimbledon [may disappear without notice]
WSF	Women's Sports World (WOMENS SPORTS)

Keyword	Area
WWF	World Wrestling Federation (SUMMER SLAM, SUPERSTARS, WRESTLING)
WWOS ABC	Online: Wide World of Sports (WIDE WORLD OF SPORTS)

Kids Only

Keyword	Area
KIDS	Kids Only department (KIDS ONLY)
BLACKBERRY	Blackberry Creek (BLACKBERRY CREEK)
CARTOONNETWORK	Cartoon Network (TOONS)
COMPUKIDS	PC Applications: Kids on Computers
DC	DC Comics Online (BATMAN, DCCOMICS, DC COMICS ONLINE, MAD, MAD MAGAZINE, MILESTONE, PARADOX, SUPERMAN, VERTIGO)
DISNEY ADVENTURES	Disney Adventures Magazine (DISNEY MAGAZINE)
ENCYCLOPEDIA	Encyclopedia (COMPTONS)
COMPTONS CUSTOMER SUPPORT	Compton's Customer Support
COMPTONS ENCYCLOPEDIA	Compton's Living Encyclopedia
COMPTONS SOFTWARE	Compton's Software Library
EDUCATION CONNECTION	Compton's Education Connection
STUDY BREAK	Compton's Study Break
HATRACK	Hatrack River Town Meeting (ORSON SCOTT CARD, ALVIN, ENDER, HATRACK RIVER TOWN)
KIDSBIZ	KidsBiz
KIDSNET	KIDSNET Forum (EDTV)
KIDS' WB	Kids' WB Online
KIDSOFT	KidSoft Superstore (CLUB KIDSOFT)
KIDS WEB	Kid's Top Internet Sites

Part
X

App
E

continues

Kids Only Continued

Keyword	Area
KOOL	Kids Only Online
KO HELP	Kids' Guide Pager
NGS	National Geographic Online (GEOGRAPHIC, NATIONAL GEOGRAPHIC)
NICK	Nickelodeon Online (NICK KIDS, NICKELODEON, ORANGE, SLIME)
POGS	KidzBiz' POG Area (POG)
SCHOLASTIC	Scholastic Network/Scholastic Forum
TEACHER PAGER	Teacher Pager
TIME	Time Magazine Online
TMS	TMS TV Source (TV SOURCE, TV GUIDE, TV LISTINGS, LISTINGS)
TOMORROW	Tomorrow's Morning (TOMORROWS MORNING, MORNING)
WEATHER	Weather
WEATHER MAPS	Color Weather Maps (COLOR WEATHER MAPS)

Member Services

Keyword	Area
HELP	Member Services (SUPPORT, SERVICE, INFORMATION, CUSTOMER SERVICE, FREE, ASK AOL, ASK AMERICA ONLINE, ASKCS, FEEDBACK, HOTLINE, MANUAL, MEMBERS GUIDE, ONLINE GUIDE, MEMBERS ONLINE GUIDE, MOG, SYSOP)
9600	9600 Baud Access Center (9600 CENTER, 9600 ACCESS)
ACCESS	Local access numbers (NUMBERS, ACCESS NUMBERS, PETITIONS)
AMEX ART	ExpressNet artwork updates (EXPRESSNET ART)
AOL PREVIEW	WAOL 2.5 Preview (WWW)
BILLING	Account and Billing (BILL, CHANGES)
BROWSER FIX	Web Browser Fix
CANCEL	Cancel Account

Keyword	Area
CREDIT	Credit for connect problems (CREDIT REQUEST, DOWNLOAD CREDIT, PC-LINK HOTLINE)
DESKTOP CINEMA	Desktop Cinema [WAOL 2.5 and MAOL 2.6 only]
DOWNLOAD GAMES	Download Online Games (GAMES DOWNLOAD)
DOWNLOAD 101	Download Help
FRIEND	Sign on a friend to AOL
LETTER	A Letter From Steve Case
MARKETING PREFS	Marketing Preferences (MARKETING PREFERENCES, MP)
MODEM HELP	Modem Help area
MHM	Members Helping Members message board
MM SHOWCASE	Multimedia Showcase
NEWAOL	New AOL Information area
PASSWORD	Change your password (CHANGE PASSWORD)
PROFILE	Edit your member profile (EDIT PROFILE, CHANGE PROFILE, MEMBER PROFILE)
QUESTION	One Stop Infoshop* (QUESTIONS)
SOUND ROOM	Sound Room
STEVE CASE	Community Updates from Steve Case
SYSTEM RESPONSE	System Response Report Area [MAOL and WAOL only]
SUGGESTION(S)	Suggestion boxes (SUGGEST)
TECHLIVE	Tech Help Live (TECHHELPLIVE, CSLIVE)
TOS	Terms of Service (TERMS, TERMS OF SERVICE, TOSADVISOR)
UPGRADE	Upgrade to the latest version of AOL
WRITE TO STAFF	Questions (ASK STAFF, WRITE TO THE STAFF)

Miscellaneous

Keyword	Area
95APPLY	AOL for Windows 95 Beta Test Application [WAOL only]
AAPMR	American Academy of Physical Medicine and Rehabilitation

Part **X**

App **E**

continues

Miscellaneous Continued	
Keyword	**Area**
AOL CRUISE	AOL Member Cruise (AOL MEMBER CRUISE)
AOL WORLD	AOL World
AUSTRALIA	Australia
AUSTRIA	Austria
BELGIUM	Belgium
BULGARIA	Bulgaria
CAMEROON	Cameroon
CANADA	Canada Launch Centre
COUNTRIES	AOL Around the World
CROATIA	Croatia
CZECH REPUBLIC	Czech Republic
DENMARK	Denmark
EGYPT	Egypt
FINLAND	Finland
FRANCE	France
GERMANY	Germany
GREECE	Greece
GUAM	Guam
HONG KONG	Hong Kong
HUNGARY	Hungary
ICELAND	Iceland
IRELAND	Ireland
ISRAEL	Israel
ITALY	Italy
JAPAN	Japan
KAZAKHSTAN	Kazakhstan
KOREA	Korea
LATVIA	Latvia

Keyword	Area
LUXEMBOURG	Luxembourg
MALAWI	Malawi
MEXICO	Mexico
N MARIANA ISLANDS	Northern Mariana Islands
NETHERLANDS	Netherlands
NEW ZEALAND	New Zealand
NIGERIA	Nigeria
NORWAY	Norway
PHILIPPINES	Philippines
POLAND	Poland
PORTUGAL	Portugal
PUERTO RICO	Puerto Rico
RUSSIA	Russia
SINGAPORE	Singapore
SOUTH AFRICA	South Africa
SPAIN	Spain
SWEDEN	Sweden
SWITZERLAND	Switzerland
TAIWAN	Taiwan
TURKEY	Turkey
UKRAINE	Ukraine
UNITED KINGDOM	United Kingdom
UZBEKISTAN	Uzbekistan
AOLSEWHERE	AOLsewhere
ALF	American Leadership Forum
BETA APPLY	Beta Test Application Area [may disappear without notice]
BLACK HISTORY	Black History Month (BLACK HERITAGE)
BLIZZARD	Blizzard '96
BURP	AOL Plays With Sounds (BELCH)

Part

X

App

E

continues

Miscellaneous Continued	
Keyword	**Area**
CLUBCALL	ClubCall
CYBERSALON	Cybersalon
DO SOMETHING	Do Something! (DS)
DD	Dial/Data (DIAL)
EMINDER	Bill e-Minder (E-MINDER)
EQUIS	Equis International [MAOL and WAOL only]
GAIN	Global Action and Information Network
GREENHOUSE	AOL Greenhouse
INFORMATIQUE	AOL in France (MICRO)
ISCNI	Institute for the Study of Contact with Non-human Intelligence (UFO(S))
LATINONET	LatinoNet Registration
LTUR	German Travel Area
MANAGER(S)	Manager's Network (MANAGER'SNETWORK, MANAGING)
MCINTIRE	University of Virginia Alumni/McIntire School of Commerce
MLK	Martin Luther King (MARTIN, MARTIN LUTHER, MARTIN LUTHER KING, KING)
NAS	NAS Online (AGRICULTURE, ENGINEERING, MATH, SOCIAL SCIENCE, TRANSPORTATION)
NACHRICHTEN	German News
NISSAN	Nissan Online
PAGE	Page Sender (SEND PAGE)
PRODIGY	Prodigy Refugees' Forum
UKBETA	AOL in United Kingdom Beta
WOODSTOCK	Woodstock Online

Index

Symbols

A

I

X-Z

Licensing Agreement

By opening this package, you are agreeing to be bound by the following:

Go Online With America's Most Popular Online Service...FREE!

Explore the benefits of being online for 15 hours—free! Everything you need to try America Online is on the enclosed disk.

1. Insert the above disk into your floppy disk drive (A or B).

2. Click on the **File** menu of your **Windows Program Manager**, then select **Run**.

3. Type **A:\SETUP** (or B:\SETUP) and press **Enter**. Follow the easy instructions on your computer screen and you'll be online in minutes!

Use this special registration number & password to begin your free trial

3Y-0379-8352
CRESTS-COTS

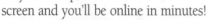

AMERICA
Online

If you need a Mac disk, or have questions about connecting, call us toll-free at
1-800-827-6364